LOEB CLA

FOUNDED

JEFFRE

P

L

PLATO

EUTHYPHRO · APOLOGY
CRITO · PHAEDO · PHAEDRUS

WITH AN ENGLISH TRANSLATION BY

HAROLD NORTH FOWLER

INTRODUCTION BY W. R. M. LAMB

HARVARD UNIVERSITY PRESS
CAMBRIDGE, MASSACHUSETTS
LONDON, ENGLAND

First published 1914

LOEB CLASSICAL LIBRARY® is a registered trademark
of the President and Fellows of Harvard College

ISBN 978-0-674-99040-1

*Printed on acid-free paper and bound by
The Maple-Vail Book Manufacturing Group*

CONTENTS

PREFACE

THE Greek text in this volume is based upon that of Schanz, and all variations from his readings are noted in the margin at the foot of the page. In some cases deviations from the reading of the manuscripts have been noted, even when adopted by Schanz. In the introductions to the separate dialogues no attempt has been made to discuss the philosophy of Plato or to do anything more than to supply such information as is needed for the intelligent reading of these particular dialogues. For further discussion and information the reader is referred to the General Introduction by Mr. W. R. M. Lamb, of Trinity College, Cambridge.

HAROLD N. FOWLER.

GENERAL INTRODUCTION

PLATO was born in 427 B.C. of Athenian parents who
could provide him with the best education of the
day, and ample means and leisure throughout his life.
He came to manhood in the dismal close of the
Peloponnesian War, when Aristophanes was at the
height of his success, and Sophocles and Euripides
had produced their last plays. As a boy he doubtless
heard the lectures of Gorgias, Protagoras, and other
sophists, and his early bent seems to have been towards
poetry. But his intelligence was too progressive to
rest in the agnostic position on which the sophistic
culture was based. A century before, Heracleitus
had declared knowledge to be impossible, because
the objects of sense are continually changing; yet
now a certain Cratylus was trying to build a theory
of knowledge over the assertion of flux, by developing
some hints let fall by its oracular author about the
truth contained in names. From this influence Plato
passed into contact with Socrates, whose character
and gifts have left a singular impress on the thought
of mankind. This effect is almost wholly due to
Plato's applications and extensions of his master's

thought; since, fortunately for us, the pupil not only became a teacher in his turn, but brought his artistic genius into play, and composed the memorials of philosophic talk which we know as the Dialogues. Xenophon, Antisthenes, and Aeschines were other disciples of Socrates who drew similar sketches of his teaching: the suggestion came from the "mimes" of the Syracusan Sophron,—realistic studies of conversation between ordinary types of character. As Plato became more engrossed in the Socratic speculations, this artistic impulse was strengthened by the desire of recording each definite stage of thought as a basis for new discussion and advance.

When Plato was twenty years old, Socrates was over sixty, and had long been notorious in Athens for his peculiar kind of sophistry. In the *Phaedo* he tells how he tried, in his youth, the current scientific explanations of the universe, and found them full of puzzles. He then met with the theory of Anaxagoras,—that the cause of everything is "mind." This was more promising: but it led nowhere after all, since it failed to rise above the conception of physical energy; this "mind" showed no intelligent aim. Disappointed of an assurance that the universe works for the best, Socrates betook himself to the plan of making *definitions* of "beautiful," "good," "large" and so on, as qualities observed in the several classes of beautiful, good and large material things, and then employing these propositions, if they appeared to be sound, for the erection of higher

hypotheses. The point is that he made a new science out of a recognised theory of "ideas" or "forms," which had come of reflecting on the quality predicated when we say "this man is good," and which postulates some sure reality behind the fleeting objects of sense. His "hypothetical" method, familiar to mathematicians, attains its full reach and significance in the *Republic*.

The Pythagoreans who appear in the intimate scene of the *Phaedo* were accustomed to the theory of ideas, and were a fit audience for the highest reasonings of Socrates on the true nature of life and the soul. For some years before the master's death (399 B.C.) Plato, if not a member of their circle, was often a spell-bound hearer of the "satyr." But ordinary Athenians had other views of Socrates, which varied according to their age and the extent of their acquaintance with him. Aristophanes' burlesque in the *Clouds* (423 B.C.) had left a common impression not unlike what we have of the King of Laputa. Yet the young men who had any frequent speech with him in his later years, while they felt there was something uncanny about him, found an irresistible attraction in his simple manner, his humorous insight into their ways and thoughts, and his fervent eloquence on the principles of their actions and careers. He kept no school, and took no fees; he distrusted the pretensions of the regular sophists, with whom he was carelessly confounded; moreover, he professed to have no knowledge himself, except so far as to

know that he was ignorant. The earliest Dialogues, such as the *Apology, Crito, Euthyphro, Charmides, Laches* and *Lysis*, show the manner in which he performed his ministry. In rousing men, especially those whose minds were fresh, to the need of knowing themselves, he promoted the authority of the intellect, the law of definite individual knowledge, above all reason of state or tie of party; and it is not surprising that his city, in the effort of recovering her political strength, decided to hush such an inconvenient voice. He must have foreseen his fate, but he continued his work undeterred.

Though he seems, in his usual talk, to have professed no positive doctrine, there were one or two beliefs which he frequently declared. Virtue, he said, is knowledge; for each man's good is his happiness, and once he knows it clearly, he needs must choose to ensue it. Further, this knowledge is innate in our minds, and we only need to have it awakened and exercised by " dialectic," or a systematic course of question and answer. He also believed his mission to be divinely ordained, and asserted that his own actions were guided at times by the prohibitions of a "spiritual sign." He was capable, as we find in the *Symposium,* of standing in rapt meditation at any moment for some time, and once for as long as twenty-four hours.

It is clear that, if he claimed no comprehensive theory of existence, and although his ethical reliance on knowledge, if he never analysed it, leaves him in

a very crude stage of psychology, his logical and mystical suggestions must have led his favourite pupils a good way towards a new system of metaphysics. These intimates learnt, as they steeped their minds in his, and felt the growth of a unique affection amid the glow of enlightenment, that happiness may be elsewhere than in our dealings with the material world, and that the mind has prerogatives and duties far above the sphere of civic life.

After the death of Socrates in 399, Plato spent some twelve years in study and travel. For the first part of this time he was perhaps at Megara, where Eucleides, his fellow-student and friend, was forming a school of dialectic. Here he may have composed some of the six Dialogues already mentioned as recording Socrates' activity in Athens. Towards and probably beyond the end of this period, in order to present the Socratic method in bolder conflict with sophistic education, he wrote the *Protagoras, Meno, Euthydemus,* and *Gorgias.* These works show a much greater command of dramatic and literary art, and a deeper interest in logic. The last of them may well be later than 387, the year in which, after an all but disastrous attempt to better the mind of Dionysius of Syracuse, he returned to Athens, and, now forty years of age, founded the Academy; where the memory of his master was to be perpetuated by continuing and expanding the Socratic discussions among the elect of the new

generation. The rivalry of this private college with the professional school of Isocrates is discernible in the subject and tone of the *Gorgias*. Plato carried on the direction of the Academy till his death, at eighty-one, in 346; save that half-way through this period (367) he accepted the invitation of his friend Dion to undertake the instruction of the younger Dionysius at Syracuse. The elder tyrant had been annoyed by the Socratic freedom of Plato's talk: now it was a wayward youth who refused the yoke of a systematic training. What that training was like we see in the *Republic*, where true political wisdom is approached by an arduous ascent through mathematics, logic, and metaphysics. Plato returned, with less hopes of obtaining the ideal ruler, to make wonderful conquests in the realm of thought.

The *Meno* and *Gorgias* set forth the doctrine that knowledge of right is latent in our minds: dialectic, not the rhetoric of the schools, is the means of eliciting it. The method, as Plato soon perceived, must be long and difficult: but he felt a mystical rapture over its certainty, which led him to picture the immutable "forms" as existing in a world of their own. This feeling, and the conviction whence it springs—that knowledge is somehow possible, had come to the front of his mind when he began to know Socrates. Two brilliant compositions, the *Cratylus* and *Symposium*, display the strength of the conviction, and then, the noble fervour of the feeling. In the latter of these works, the highest

xiv

powers of imaginative sympathy and eloquence are summoned to unveil the sacred vision of absolute beauty. The *Phaedo* turns the logical theory upon the soul, which is seen to enjoy, when freed from the body, familiar cognition of the eternal types of being. Here Orphic dogma lends its aid to the Socratic search for knowledge, while we behold an inspiring picture of the philosopher in his hour of death.

With increasing confidence in himself as the successor of Socrates, Plato next undertook, in the *Republic*, to show the master meeting his own unsatisfied queries on education and politics. We read now of a " form " of good to which all thought and action aspire, and which, contemplated in itself, will explain not merely why justice is better than injustice, but the meaning and aim of everything. In order that man may be fully understood, we are to view him " writ large " in the organisation of an ideal state. The scheme of description opens out into many subsidiary topics, including three great proposals already known to Greece,—the abolition of private property, the community of women and children, and the civic equality of the sexes. But the central subject is the preparation of the philosopher, through a series of ancillary sciences, for dialectic ; so that, once possessed of the supreme truth, he may have light for directing his fellow-men. As in the *Phaedo*, the spell of mythical revelation is brought to enhance the discourse of reason. The

Phaedrus takes up the subject of rhetoric, to lead us allegorically into the realm of " ideas," and thence to point out a new rhetoric, worthy of the well-trained dialectician. We get also a glimpse of the philosopher's duty of investigating the mutual relations of the " forms " to which his study of particular things has led him.

A closer interest in logical method, appearing through his delight in imaginative construction, is one distinctive mark of this middle stage in Plato's teaching. As he passes to the next two Dialogues, the *Theaetetus* and *Parmenides,* he puts off the aesthetic rapture, and considers the ideas as categories of thought which require co-ordination. The discussion of knowledge in the former makes it evident that the Academy was now the meeting-place of vigorous minds, some of which were eager to urge or hear refuted the doctrines they had learnt from other schools of thought; while the arguments are conducted with a critical caution very different from the brilliant and often hasty zeal of Socrates. The *Parmenides* corrects an actual or possible misconception of the theory of ideas in the domain of logic, showing perhaps how Aristotle, now a youthful disciple of Plato, found fault with the theory as he understood it. The forms are viewed in the light of the necessities of thought : knowledge is to be attained by a careful practice which will raise our minds to the vision of all particulars in their rightly distinguished and connected classes.

Plato is here at work on his own great problem :—
If what we know is a single permanent law under
which a multitude of things are ranged, what is the
link between the one and the many? The *Sophist*
contains some of his ripest thought on this increas-
ingly urgent question : his confident advance beyond
Socratic teaching is indicated by the literary form,
which hardly disguises the continuous exposition of a
lecture. We observe an attention to physical science,
the association of soul, motion, and existence, and
the comparative study of being and not-being. The
Politicus returns to the topic of state-government,
and carries on the process of acquiring perfect
notions of reality by the classification of things.
Perhaps we should see in the absolute "mean"
which is posited as the standard of all arts, business,
and conduct, a contribution from Aristotle. The
Philebus, in dealing with pleasure and knowledge,
dwells further on the correct division and classification required if our reason, as it surely must, is to
apprehend truth. The method is becoming more
thorough and more complex, and Plato's hope of
bringing it to completion is more remote. But he is
gaining a clearer insight into the problem of unity
and plurality.

The magnificent myth of the *Timaeus*, related
by a Pythagorean, describes the structure of the
universe, so as to show how the One manifests
itself as the Many. We have here the latest
reflections of Plato on space, time, soul, and many

physical matters. In the lengthy treatise of the *Laws*, he addresses himself to the final duty of the philosopher as announced in the *Republic* : a long habituation to abstract thought will qualify rather than disqualify him for the practical regulation of public and private affairs. Attention is fixed once more on soul, as the energy of the world and the vehicle of our sovereign reason.

Thus Plato maintains the fixity of the objects of knowledge in a great variety of studies, which enlarge the compass of Socrates' teaching till it embraces enough material for complete systems of logic and metaphysics. How far these systems were actually worked out in the discussions of the Academy we can only surmise from the Dialogues themselves and a careful comparison of Aristotle ; whose writings, however, have come down to us in a much less perfect state. But it seems probable that, to the end, Plato was too fertile in thought to rest content with one authoritative body of doctrine. We may be able to detect in the *Timaeus* a tendency to view numbers as the real principles of things ; and we may conjecture a late-found interest in the physical complexion of the world. As a true artist, with a keen sense of the beauty and stir of life, Plato had this interest, in a notable degree, throughout : but in speaking of his enthusiasm for science we must regard him rather as a great inventor of sciences than as what we should now call a scientist. This is giving him a splendid name, which few men

have earned. Some of his inventions may be unrealisable, but it is hard to find one that is certainly futile. There are flaws in his arguments: to state them clearly and fairly is to win the privilege of taking part in a discussion at the Academy.

W. R. M. Lamb.

BIBLIOGRAPHICAL NOTE (1990)

For comprehensive bibliographies the reader is referred
to W. K. C. Guthrie, *A History of Greek Philosophy*,
Volume Four: Plato, The Man and His Dialogues, Earlier
Period, Cambridge, 1975, pages 562–581, and Volume
Five: The Later Plato and the Academy, Cambridge,
1978, pages 493–514. The following is a selection of
recent work on the dialogues included in this volume.

Euthyphro
Reginald E. Allen: *Plato's 'Euthyphro' and Earlier Theory of Forms*, London, 1970.
Laszlo Versenyi: *Holiness and Justice: An Interpretation
of Plato's Euthyphro*, Washington, D.C., 1982.

Apology
Reginald E. Allen: *Socrates and Legal Obligation* (includ-
ing trs. of *Apology* and *Crito*), Minneapolis, 1980.
T. C. Brickhouse and N. D. Smith: *Socrates on Trial*,
Oxford, 1988.
C. D. C. Reeve: *Socrates in the Apology*, Indianapolis,
1989.
I. F. Stone: *The Trial of Socrates*, New York, 1988.
Thomas G. West: *Plato's Apology of Socrates: An Inter-
pretation with a New Translation*, Ithaca, 1979.

Crito

Anthony Douglas Woozley: *Law and Obedience: The Arguments of Plato's Crito*, Chapel Hill, 1979.

Phaedo

David Bostock: *Plato's Phaedo*, Oxford, 1986.

Kenneth Dorter: *Plato's Phaedo, An Interpretation*, Toronto, 1982.

David Gallop: *Plato's Phaedo, Translation and Notes*, Oxford, 1975.

Phaedrus

Giovanni Ferrari: *Listening to the Cicadas: A Study of Plato's Phaedrus*, Cambridge, 1987.

Charles L. Griswold: *Self-knowledge in Plato's Phaedrus*, New Haven, 1986.

General

Terence Irwin: *Plato's Moral Theory: The Early and Middle Dialogues*, Oxford, 1977.

Surveys

L. Brisson: "Platon 1958–1975," *Lustrum* xx (1977) 5–304.

L. Brisson (with H. Ioannidi): "Platon 1975–1980," *Lustrum* xxv (1983) 31–320.

EUTHYPHRO

INTRODUCTION TO THE *EUTHYPHRO*

THE *Euthyphro* probably owes its place at the head of the list of dialogues to the fact that it is the first of four dialogues dealing with the trial and death of Socrates. It is probably one of the earliest in date of composition, though that fact is not likely to have affected its position in the series.

Socrates comes to the court of the king archon to attend to some preliminaries of his trial on the charge of impiety and corrupting the youth. Here he meets Euthyphro, who is bringing a charge of manslaughter against his father, on account of the death from exposure of a servant who is himself a murderer. Euthyphro says that he is bringing the charge in the interest of piety, and claims to know more than other men about the nature of piety, proper religious observances, and the will of the gods.[1] It is this claim which leads to the discussion of the nature of piety, or holiness, the chief theme of the dialogue.

The purpose of the dialogue is in part to inculcate correct methods of thinking, more especially the dialectic method. Euthyphro, when requested to give a definition of piety or holiness says (5 D) " I say that holiness is doing what I am doing now, prosecuting the wrongdoer who commits murder or

[1] Of Euthyphro nothing further is known. He may be identical with the Euthyphro who appears in the Cratylus as a philologian addicted to fanciful etymologies.

3

steals from the temples or does any such thing, whether he be your father or your mother or anyone else; and not prosecuting him is unholy." This reply leads at once to the proof that a particular example does not constitute a definition of a general concept. The second definition offered by Euthyphro is emended until it takes the form (9 E) " What all the gods love is holy, and on the other hand, what they all hate is unholy." The question then arises whether a thing is holy because the gods love it, or the gods love it because it is holy. Cause and effect are discussed. In an attempt to arrive at a third definition, Euthyphro flounders hopelessly, whereupon Socrates shows how terms may be defined by referring a species to a genus.[1] Finally Euthyphro states (12 E) that "the part of the right which has to do with attention to the gods constitutes piety and holiness." Hereupon Socrates tries to get him to tell what attention the gods require, what end human service to the gods has in view. In this he does not succeed, and the dialogue ends with this question unanswered.

Instruction in methods of thinking may perhaps seem needless to modern readers; even they, however, may find it interesting, and in Plato's times it was undoubtedly necessary. Such instruction occupies an important place in most of the Platonic dialogues. In the *Euthyphro* the correct method of thinking is illustrated and inculcated in the course of an attempt to define piety or holiness. The two definitions offered by Euthyphro are rejected; the third is left unchallenged, though a further limitation is demanded. It may therefore be regarded as

[1] See 11 c note.

a definition accepted by Plato, but not considered complete until the purpose of our service to the gods is determined. How Plato would determine it may be seen in the *Apology* (30 A), where Socrates says his life has been spent in the endeavour to persuade men to care chiefly for the perfection of their souls. The *Euthyphro* may perhaps be regarded as a sort of scientific justification of the position taken in the *Apology*.

Special editions of the *Euthyphro* are numerous. Among them those of Schanz (1887), Christ (1890), Adam (1890), and Heidel (1902) may be chosen for especial mention. The last named contains an exhaustive bibliography.

ΕΥΘΥΦΡΩΝ

[Η ΠΕΡΙ ΟΣΙΟΥ, ΠΕΙΡΑΣΤΙΚΟΣ]

ΤΑ ΤΟΥ ΔΙΑΛΟΓΟΥ ΠΡΟΣΩΠΑ

ΕΥΘΥΦΡΩΝ, ΣΩΚΡΑΤΗΣ

A 1. ΕΥΘΥΦΡΩΝ. Τί νεώτερον, ὦ Σώκρατες, γέγονεν, ὅτι σὺ τὰς ἐν Λυκείῳ καταλιπὼν διατριβὰς ἐνθάδε νῦν διατρίβεις περὶ τὴν τοῦ βασιλέως στοάν; οὐ γάρ που καὶ σοί γε δίκη τις οὖσα τυγχάνει πρὸς τὸν βασιλέα ὥσπερ ἐμοί.

ΣΩΚΡΑΤΗΣ. Οὔτοι δὴ Ἀθηναῖοί γε, ὦ Εὐθύφρον, δίκην αὐτὴν καλοῦσιν, ἀλλὰ γραφήν.

ΕΥΘΥΦΡΩΝ. Τί φῄς; γραφήν σέ τις, ὡς ἔοικε, B γέγραπται; οὐ γὰρ ἐκεῖνό γε καταγνώσομαι, ὡς σὺ ἕτερον.

ΣΩΚΡΑΤΗΣ. Οὐ γὰρ οὖν.

ΕΥΘΥΦΡΩΝ. Ἀλλὰ σὲ ἄλλος;

ΣΩΚΡΑΤΗΣ. Πάνυ γε.

ΕΥΘΥΦΡΩΝ. Τίς οὗτος;

ΣΩΚΡΑΤΗΣ. Οὐδ' αὐτὸς πάνυ τι γιγνώσκω, ὦ Εὐθύφρον, τὸν ἄνδρα· νέος γάρ τίς μοι φαίνεται καὶ ἀγνώς· ὀνομάζουσι μέντοι αὐτόν, ὡς ἐγῷμαι, Μέλητον. ἔστι δὲ τῶν δήμων Πιτθεύς, εἴ τινα νῷ ἔχεις Πιτθέα Μέλητον οἷον τετανότριχα καὶ οὐ πάνυ εὐγένειον, ἐπίγρυπον δέ.

6

EUTHYPHRO

[or ON HOLINESS, a tentative dialogue]

CHARACTERS

Euthyphro, Socrates

EUTHYPHRO. What strange thing has happened, Socrates, that you have left your accustomed haunts in the Lyceum and are now haunting the portico where the king archon sits ? For it cannot be that you have an action before the king, as I have.

SOCRATES. Our Athenians, Euthyphro, do not call it an action, but an indictment.

EUTHYPHRO. What ? Somebody has, it seems, brought an indictment against you ; for I don't accuse you of having brought one against anyone else.

SOCRATES. Certainly not.

EUTHYPHRO. But someone else against you ?

SOCRATES. Quite so.

EUTHYPHRO. Who is he?

SOCRATES. I don't know the man very well myself, Euthyphro, for he seems to be a young and unknown person. His name, however, is Meletus, I believe. And he is of the deme of Pitthus, if you remember any Pitthian Meletus, with long hair and only a little beard, but with a hooked nose.

ΕΥΘΥΦΡΩΝ. Οὐκ ἐννοῶ, ὦ Σώκρατες· ἀλλὰ δὴ

C τίνα γραφήν σε γέγραπται;

ΣΩΚΡΑΤΗΣ. Ἥντινα; οὐκ ἀγεννῆ, ἔμοιγε δοκεῖ·
τὸ γὰρ νέον ὄντα τοσοῦτον πρᾶγμα ἐγνωκέναι οὐ
φαῦλόν ἐστιν· ἐκεῖνος γάρ, ὥς φησιν, οἶδε, τίνα
τρόπον οἱ νέοι διαφθείρονται καὶ τίνες οἱ διαφθεί-
ροντες αὐτούς· καὶ κινδυνεύει σοφός τις εἶναι· καὶ
τὴν ἐμὴν ἀμαθίαν κατιδὼν ὡς διαφθείροντος τοὺς
ἡλικιώτας αὐτοῦ, ἔρχεται κατηγορήσων μου ὡς
πρὸς μητέρα πρὸς τὴν πόλιν. καὶ φαίνεταί μοι
τῶν πολιτικῶν μόνος ἄρχεσθαι ὀρθῶς· ὀρθῶς γάρ

D ἐστι τῶν νέων πρῶτον ἐπιμεληθῆναι, ὅπως ἔσονται
ὅ τι ἄριστοι, ὥσπερ γεωργὸν ἀγαθὸν τῶν νέων
φυτῶν εἰκὸς πρῶτον ἐπιμεληθῆναι, μετὰ δὲ τοῦτο
καὶ τῶν ἄλλων· καὶ δὴ καὶ Μέλητος ἴσως πρῶ-

3 τον μὲν ἡμᾶς ἐκκαθαίρει τοὺς τῶν νέων τὰς
βλάστας διαφθείροντας, ὥς φησιν· ἔπειτα μετὰ
τοῦτο δῆλον ὅτι τῶν πρεσβυτέρων ἐπιμεληθεὶς
πλείστων καὶ μεγίστων ἀγαθῶν αἴτιος τῇ πόλει
γενήσεται, ὥς γε τὸ εἰκὸς ξυμβῆναι ἐκ τοιαύτης
ἀρχῆς ἀρξαμένῳ.

2. ΕΥΘΥΦΡΩΝ. Βουλοίμην ἄν, ὦ Σώκρατες, ἀλλ᾽
ὀρρωδῶ, μὴ τοὐναντίον γένηται. ἀτεχνῶς γάρ μοι
δοκεῖ ἀφ᾽ ἑστίας ἄρχεσθαι κακουργεῖν τὴν πόλιν,
ἐπιχειρῶν ἀδικεῖν σέ. καί μοι λέγε, τί καὶ
ποιοῦντά σέ φησι διαφθείρειν τοὺς νέους;

B ΣΩΚΡΑΤΗΣ. Ἄτοπα, ὦ θαυμάσιε, ὡς οὕτω γ᾽
ἀκοῦσαι. φησὶ γάρ με ποιητὴν εἶναι θεῶν, καὶ
ὡς καινοὺς ποιοῦντα θεούς, τοὺς δ᾽ ἀρχαίους οὐ
νομίζοντα, ἐγράψατο τούτων αὐτῶν ἕνεκα, ὥς
φησιν.

ΕΥΘΥΦΡΩΝ. Μανθάνω, ὦ Σώκρατες· ὅτι δὴ σὺ

8

EUTHYPHRO. I don't remember him, Socrates. But what sort of an indictment has he brought against you?

SOCRATES. What sort? No mean one, it seems to me; for the fact that, young as he is, he has apprehended so important a matter reflects no small credit upon him. For he says he knows how the youth are corrupted and who those are who corrupt them. He must be a wise man; who, seeing my lack of wisdom and that I am corrupting his fellows, comes to the State, as a boy runs to his mother, to accuse me. And he seems to me to be the only one of the public men who begins in the right way; for the right way is to take care of the young men first, to make them as good as possible, just as a good husbandman will naturally take care of the young plants first and afterwards of the rest. And so Meletus, perhaps, is first clearing away us who corrupt the young plants, as he says; then after this, when he has turned his attention to the older men, he will bring countless most precious blessings upon the State,—at least, that is the natural outcome of the beginning he has made.

EUTHYPHRO. I hope it may be so, Socrates; but I fear the opposite may result. For it seems to me that he begins by injuring the State at its very heart, when he undertakes to harm you. Now tell me, what does he say you do that corrupts the young?

SOCRATES. Absurd things, my friend, at first hearing. For he says I am a maker of gods; and because I make new gods and do not believe in the old ones, he indicted me for the sake of these old ones, as he says.

EUTHYPHRO. I understand, Socrates; it is because

τὸ δαιμόνιον φῂς σαυτῷ ἑκάστοτε γίγνεσθαι. ὡς
οὖν καινοτομοῦντός σου περὶ τὰ θεῖα γέγραπται
ταύτην τὴν γραφήν, καὶ ὡς διαβαλῶν δὴ ἔρχεται
εἰς τὸ δικαστήριον, εἰδὼς ὅτι εὐδιάβολα τὰ
τοιαῦτα πρὸς τοὺς πολλούς. καὶ ἐμοῦ γάρ τοι,
C ὅταν τι λέγω ἐν τῇ ἐκκλησίᾳ περὶ τῶν θείων,
προλέγων αὐτοῖς τὰ μέλλοντα, καταγελῶσιν ὡς
μαινομένου. καίτοι οὐδὲν ὅ τι οὐκ ἀληθὲς εἴρηκα
ὧν προεῖπον, ἀλλ᾽ ὅμως φθονοῦσιν ἡμῖν πᾶσι τοῖς
τοιούτοις. ἀλλ᾽ οὐδὲν αὐτῶν χρὴ φροντίζειν, ἀλλ᾽
ὁμόσε ἰέναι.

3. ΣΩΚΡΑΤΗΣ. Ὦ φίλε Εὐθύφρον, ἀλλὰ τὸ
μὲν καταγελασθῆναι ἴσως οὐδὲν πρᾶγμα. Ἀθηναίοις γάρ τοι, ὡς ἐμοὶ δοκεῖ, οὐ σφόδρα μέλει, ἄν
τινα δεινὸν οἴωνται εἶναι, μὴ μέντοι διδασκαλικὸν
τῆς αὑτοῦ σοφίας· ὃν δ᾽ ἂν καὶ ἄλλους οἴωνται
D ποιεῖν τοιούτους, θυμοῦνται, εἴτ᾽ οὖν φθόνῳ, ὡς
σὺ λέγεις, εἴτε δι᾽ ἄλλο τι.

ΕΥΘΥΦΡΩΝ. Τούτου οὖν πέρι ὅπως ποτὲ πρὸς
ἐμὲ ἔχουσιν, οὐ πάνυ ἐπιθυμῶ πειραθῆναι.

ΣΩΚΡΑΤΗΣ. Ἴσως γὰρ σὺ μὲν δοκεῖς σπάνιον
σεαυτὸν παρέχειν καὶ διδάσκειν οὐκ ἐθέλειν τὴν
σεαυτοῦ σοφίαν· ἐγὼ δὲ φοβοῦμαι, μὴ ὑπὸ φιλαν-
θρωπίας δοκῶ αὐτοῖς ὅ τί περ ἔχω ἐκκεχυμένως
παντὶ ἀνδρὶ λέγειν, οὐ μόνον ἄνευ μισθοῦ, ἀλλὰ
καὶ προστιθεὶς ἂν ἡδέως, εἴ τίς μου ἐθέλοι ἀκούειν.
εἰ μὲν οὖν, ὃ νῦν δὴ ἔλεγον, μέλλοιέν μου καταγελᾶν, ὥσπερ σὺ φῂς σαυτοῦ, οὐδὲν ἂν εἴη ἀηδὲς
E παίζοντας καὶ γελῶντας ἐν τῷ δικαστηρίῳ διαγα-
γεῖν, εἰ δὲ σπουδάσονται, τοῦτ᾽ ἤδη ὅπῃ ἀποβήσεται ἄδηλον πλὴν ὑμῖν τοῖς μάντεσιν.

you say the divine monitor keeps coming to you. So he has brought the indictment against you for making innovations in religion, and he is going into court to slander you, knowing that slanders on such subjects are readily accepted by the people. Why, they even laugh at me and say I am crazy when I say anything in the assembly about divine things and foretell the future to them. And yet there is not one of the things I have foretold that is not true; but they are jealous of all such men as you and I are. However, we must not be disturbed, but must come to close quarters with them.

SOCRATES. My dear Euthyphro, their ridicule is perhaps of no consequence. For the Athenians, I fancy, are not much concerned, if they think a man is clever, provided he does not impart his clever notions to others; but when they think he makes others to be like himself, they are angry with him, either through jealousy, as you say, or for some other reason.

EUTHYPHRO. I don't much desire to test their sentiments toward me in this matter.

SOCRATES. No, for perhaps they think that you are reserved and unwilling to impart your wisdom. But I fear that because of my love of men they think that I not only pour myself out copiously to anyone and everyone without payment, but that I would even pay something myself, if anyone would listen to me. Now if, as I was saying just now, they were to laugh at me, as you say they do at you, it would not be at all unpleasant to pass the time in the court with jests and laughter; but if they are in earnest, then only soothsayers like you can tell how this will end.

ΕΤΘΥΦΡΩΝ. Ἀλλ' ἴσως οὐδὲν ἔσται, ὦ Σώκρατες, πρᾶγμα, ἀλλὰ σύ τε κατὰ νοῦν ἀγωνιεῖ τὴν δίκην, οἶμαι δὲ καὶ ἐμὲ τὴν ἐμήν.

4. ΣΩΚΡΑΤΗΣ. Ἔστιν δὲ δή σοι, ὦ Εὐθύφρον, τίς ἡ δίκη; φεύγεις αὐτὴν ἢ διώκεις;

ΕΤΘΥΦΡΩΝ. Διώκω.

ΣΩΚΡΑΤΗΣ. Τίνα;

4   ΕΤΘΥΦΡΩΝ. Ὃν διώκων αὖ δοκῶ μαίνεσθαι.

ΣΩΚΡΑΤΗΣ. Τί δέ; πετόμενόν τινα διώκεις;

ΕΤΘΥΦΡΩΝ. Πολλοῦ γε δεῖ πέτεσθαι, ὅς γε τυγχάνει ὢν εὖ μάλα πρεσβύτης.

ΣΩΚΡΑΤΗΣ. Τίς οὗτος;

ΕΤΘΥΦΡΩΝ. Ὁ ἐμὸς πατήρ.

ΣΩΚΡΑΤΗΣ. Ὁ σός, ὦ βέλτιστε;

ΕΤΘΥΦΡΩΝ. Πάνυ μὲν οὖν.

ΣΩΚΡΑΤΗΣ. Ἔστιν δὲ τί τὸ ἔγκλημα καὶ τίνος ἡ δίκη;

ΕΤΘΥΦΡΩΝ. Φόνου, ὦ Σώκρατες.

ΣΩΚΡΑΤΗΣ. Ἡράκλεις! ἦ που, ὦ Εὐθύφρον, ἀγνοεῖται ὑπὸ τῶν πολλῶν, ὅπῃ ποτὲ ὀρθῶς ἔχει.[1] οὐ γὰρ οἶμαί γε τοῦ ἐπιτυχόντος ὀρθῶς αὐτὸ
B πρᾶξαι, ἀλλὰ πόρρω που ἤδη σοφίας ἐλαύνοντος.

ΕΤΘΥΦΡΩΝ. Πόρρω μέντοι νὴ Δία, ὦ Σώκρατες.

ΣΩΚΡΑΤΗΣ. Ἔστιν δὲ δὴ τῶν οἰκείων τις ὁ τεθνεὼς ὑπὸ τοῦ σοῦ πατρός; ἢ δῆλα δή· οὐ γὰρ ἄν πού γε ὑπὲρ ἀλλοτρίου ἐπεξῇεισθα φόνου αὐτῷ.

ΕΤΘΥΦΡΩΝ. Γελοῖον, ὦ Σώκρατες, ὅτι οἴει τι διαφέρειν, εἴτε ἀλλότριος εἴτε οἰκεῖος ὁ τεθνεώς,

---

[1] Schanz, following Madvig, marks a lacuna here. For the meaning of the missing word or words he refers to 9 A and 15 D.

EUTHYPHRO. Well, Socrates, perhaps it won't amount to much, and you will bring your case to a satisfactory ending, as I think I shall mine.

SOCRATES. What is your case, Euthyphro? Are you defending or prosecuting?

EUTHYPHRO. Prosecuting.

SOCRATES. Whom?

EUTHYPHRO. Such a man that they think I am insane because I am prosecuting [1] him.

SOCRATES. Why? Are you prosecuting one who has wings to fly away with?

EUTHYPHRO. No flying for him at his ripe old age.

SOCRATES. Who is he?

EUTHYPHRO. My father.

SOCRATES. Your father, my dear man?

EUTHYPHRO. Certainly.

SOCRATES. But what is the charge, and what is the suit about?

EUTHYPHRO. Murder, Socrates.

SOCRATES. Heracles! Surely, Euthyphro, most people do not know where the right lies; for I fancy it is not everyone who can rightly do what you are doing, but only one who is already very far advanced in wisdom.

EUTHYPHRO. Very far, indeed, Socrates, by Zeus.

SOCRATES. Is the one who was killed by your father a relative? But of course he was; for you would not bring a charge of murder against him on a stranger's account.

EUTHYPHRO. It is ridiculous, Socrates, that you think it matters whether the man who was killed

---

[1] The Greek word has much the same meaning as the Latin *prosequor*, from which the English 'prosecute' is derived, 'follow,' 'pursue,' and is at the same time the technical term for 'prosecute.'

ἀλλ' οὐ τοῦτο μόνον δεῖν φυλάττειν, εἴτε ἐν δίκῃ
ἔκτεινεν ὁ κτείνας εἴτε μή, καὶ εἰ μὲν ἐν δίκῃ, ἐᾶν,
εἰ δὲ μή, ἐπεξιέναι, ἐάν περ ὁ κτείνας συνέστιός σοι
C καὶ ὁμοτράπεζος ᾖ. ἴσον γὰρ τὸ μίασμα γίγνεται,
ἐὰν ξυνῇς τῷ τοιούτῳ ξυνειδὼς καὶ μὴ ἀφοσιοῖς
σεαυτόν τε καὶ ἐκεῖνον τῇ δίκῃ ἐπεξιών, ἐπεὶ ὅ γε
ἀποθανὼν πελάτης τις ἦν ἐμός, καὶ ὡς ἐγεωργοῦ-
μεν ἐν τῇ Νάξῳ, ἐθήτευεν ἐκεῖ παρ' ἡμῖν. παρ-
οινήσας οὖν καὶ ὀργισθεὶς τῶν οἰκετῶν τινι τῶν
ἡμετέρων ἀποσφάττει αὐτόν· ὁ οὖν πατὴρ συνδή-
σας τοὺς πόδας καὶ τὰς χεῖρας αὐτοῦ, καταβαλὼν
εἰς τάφρον τινά, πέμπει δεῦρο ἄνδρα πευσόμενον
τοῦ ἐξηγητοῦ, ὅ τι χρείη ποιεῖν. ἐν δὲ τούτῳ τῷ
D χρόνῳ τοῦ δεδεμένου ὠλιγώρει τε καὶ ἠμέλει ὡς
ἀνδροφόνου καὶ οὐδὲν ὂν πρᾶγμα, εἰ καὶ ἀποθάνοι·
ὅπερ οὖν καὶ ἔπαθεν. ὑπὸ γὰρ λιμοῦ καὶ ῥίγους
καὶ τῶν δεσμῶν ἀποθνῄσκει πρὶν τὸν ἄγγελον
παρὰ τοῦ ἐξηγητοῦ ἀφικέσθαι. ταῦτα δὴ οὖν
καὶ ἀγανακτεῖ ὅ τε πατὴρ καὶ οἱ ἄλλοι οἰκεῖοι,
ὅτι ἐγὼ ὑπὲρ τοῦ ἀνδροφόνου τῷ πατρὶ φόνου
ἐπεξέρχομαι, οὔτε ἀποκτείναντι, ὥς φασιν ἐκεῖνοι,
οὔτ' εἰ ὅ τι μάλιστα ἀπέκτεινεν, ἀνδροφόνου γε
ὄντος τοῦ ἀποθανόντος, οὐ δεῖν φροντίζειν ὑπὲρ
E τοῦ τοιούτου· ἀνόσιον γὰρ εἶναι τὸ υἰὸν πατρὶ
φόνου ἐπεξιέναι· κακῶς εἰδότες, ὦ Σώκρατες,
τὸ θεῖον ὡς ἔχει τοῦ ὁσίου τε πέρι καὶ τοῦ
ἀνοσίου.

ΣΩΚΡΑΤΗΣ. Σὺ δὲ δὴ πρὸς Διός, ὦ Εὐθύφρον,
οὑτωσὶ ἀκριβῶς οἴει ἐπίστασθαι περὶ τῶν θείων,

was a stranger or a relative, and do not see that the only thing to consider is whether the action of the slayer was justified or not, and that if it was justified one ought to let him alone, and if not, one ought to proceed against him, even if he share one's hearth and eat at one's table. For the pollution is the same if you associate knowingly with such a man and do not purify yourself and him by proceeding against him. In this case, the man who was killed was a hired workman of mine, and when we were farming at Naxos, he was working there on our land. Now he got drunk, got angry with one of our house slaves, and butchered him. So my father bound him hand and foot, threw him into a ditch, and sent a man here to Athens to ask the religious adviser what he ought to do. In the meantime he paid no attention to the man as he lay there bound, and neglected him, thinking that he was a murderer and it did not matter if he were to die. And that is just what happened to him. For he died of hunger and cold and his bonds before the messenger came back from the adviser. Now my father and the rest of my relatives are angry with me, because for the sake of this murderer I am prosecuting my father for murder. For they say he did not kill him, and if he had killed him never so much, yet since the dead man was a murderer, I ought not to trouble myself about such a fellow, because it is unholy for a son to prosecute his father for murder. Which shows how little they know what the divine law is in regard to holiness and unholiness.

SOCRATES. But, in the name of Zeus, Euthyphro, do you think your knowledge about divine laws and

ὅπῃ ἔχει, καὶ τῶν ὁσίων τε καὶ ἀνοσίων, ὥστε
τούτων οὕτω πραχθέντων, ὡς σὺ λέγεις, οὐ φοβεῖ
δικαζόμενος τῷ πατρί, ὅπως μὴ αὖ σὺ ἀνόσιον
πρᾶγμα τυγχάνῃς πράττων;

ΕΥΘΥΦΡΩΝ. Οὐδὲν γὰρ ἄν μου ὄφελος εἴη, ὦ
5 Σώκρατες, οὐδέ τῳ ἂν διαφέροι Εὐθύφρων τῶν
πολλῶν ἀνθρώπων, εἰ μὴ τὰ τοιαῦτα πάντα
ἀκριβῶς εἰδείην.

5. ΣΩΚΡΑΤΗΣ. Ἆρ' οὖν μοι, ὦ θαυμάσιε Εὐθύφρων, κράτιστόν ἐστι μαθητῇ σῷ γενέσθαι καὶ
πρὸ τῆς γραφῆς τῆς πρὸς Μέλητον αὐτὰ ταῦτα
προκαλεῖσθαι αὐτὸν λέγοντα, ὅτι ἔγωγε καὶ ἐν τῷ
ἔμπροσθεν χρόνῳ τὰ θεῖα περὶ πολλοῦ ἐποιούμην
εἰδέναι, καὶ νῦν ἐπειδή με ἐκεῖνος αὐτοσχεδιάζοντά
φησι καὶ καινοτομοῦντα περὶ τῶν θείων ἐξαμαρτάνειν, μαθητὴς δὴ γέγονα σός· καὶ εἰ μέν, ὦ
B Μέλητε, φαίην ἄν, Εὐθύφρονα ὁμολογεῖς σοφὸν
εἶναι τὰ τοιαῦτα, καὶ ὀρθῶς νομίζειν ἐμὲ ἡγοῦ
καὶ μὴ δικάζου· εἰ δὲ μή, ἐκείνῳ τῷ διδασκάλῳ
λάχε δίκην πρότερον ἢ ἐμοί, ὡς τοὺς πρεσβυτέρους
διαφθείροντι, ἐμέ τε καὶ τὸν αὐτοῦ πατέρα, ἐμὲ
μὲν διδάσκοντι, ἐκεῖνον δὲ νουθετοῦντί τε καὶ
κολάζοντι· καὶ ἂν μή μοι πείθηται μηδ' ἀφίῃ τῆς
δίκης ἢ ἀντ' ἐμοῦ γράφηται σέ, αὐτὰ ταῦτα λέγειν
ἐν τῷ δικαστηρίῳ, ἃ προυκαλούμην αὐτόν.

ΕΥΘΥΦΡΩΝ. Ναὶ μὰ Δία, ὦ Σώκρατες, εἰ ἄρα με
C ἐπιχειρήσειε γράφεσθαι, εὕροιμ' ἄν, ὡς οἶμαι,
ὅπῃ σαθρός ἐστιν, καὶ πολὺ ἂν ἡμῖν πρότερον
περὶ ἐκείνου λόγος ἐγένετο ἐν τῷ δικαστηρίῳ ἢ
περὶ ἐμοῦ.

ΣΩΚΡΑΤΗΣ. Καὶ ἐγώ τοι, ὦ φίλε ἑταῖρε, ταῦτα
γιγνώσκων μαθητὴς ἐπιθυμῶ γενέσθαι σός, εἰδώς,

holiness and unholiness is so exact that, when the facts are as you say, you are not afraid of doing something unholy yourself in prosecuting your father for murder?

EUTHYPHRO. I should be of no use, Socrates, and Euthyphro would be in no way different from other men, if I did not have exact knowledge about all such things.

SOCRATES. Then the best thing for me, my admirable Euthyphro, is to become your pupil and, before the suit with Meletus comes on, to challenge him and say that I always thought it very important before to know about divine matters and that now, since he says I am doing wrong by acting carelessly and making innovations in matters of religion, I have become your pupil. And "Meletus," I should say, "if you acknowledge that Euthyphro is wise in such matters, then believe that I also hold correct opinions, and do not bring me to trial; and if you do not acknowledge that, then bring a suit against him, my teacher, rather than against me, and charge him with corrupting the old, namely, his father and me, which he does by teaching me and by correcting and punishing his father." And if he does not do as I ask and does not release me from the indictment or bring it against you in my stead, I could say in the court the same things I said in my challenge to him, could I not?

EUTHYPHRO. By Zeus, Socrates, if he should undertake to indict me, I fancy I should find his weak spot, and it would be much more a question about him in court than about me.

SOCRATES. And I, my dear friend, perceiving this, wish to become your pupil; for I know that neither

ὅτι καὶ ἄλλος πού τις καὶ ὁ Μέλητος οὗτος σὲ μὲ·
οὐδὲ δοκεῖ ὁρᾶν, ἐμὲ δὲ οὕτως ὀξέως καὶ ῥαδίως·
κατεῖδεν, ὥστε ἀσεβείας ἐγράψατο. νῦν οὖν πρὸς
Διὸς λέγε μοι, ὃ νῦν δὴ σαφῶς εἰδέναι διισχυρίζου
ποῖόν τι τὸ εὐσεβὲς φῂς εἶναι καὶ τὸ ἀσεβὲς καὶ
D περὶ φόνου καὶ περὶ τῶν ἄλλων; ἢ οὐ ταὐτόν
ἐστιν ἐν πάσῃ πράξει τὸ ὅσιον αὐτὸ αὑτῷ, καὶ
τὸ ἀνόσιον αὖ τοῦ μὲν ὁσίου παντὸς ἐναντίον, αὐτὸ
δὲ αὑτῷ ὅμοιον καὶ ἔχον μίαν τινὰ ἰδέαν[1] πᾶν, ὃ
τί περ ἂν μέλλῃ ἀνόσιον εἶναι;

ΕΥΘΥΦΡΩΝ. Πάντως δήπου, ὦ Σώκρατες.

6. ΣΩΚΡΑΤΗΣ. Λέγε δή, τί φῂς εἶναι τὸ ὅσιον
καὶ τὸ ἀνόσιον;

ΕΥΘΥΦΡΩΝ. Λέγω τοίνυν, ὅτι τὸ μὲν ὅσιόν ἐστιν
ὅπερ ἐγὼ νῦν ποιῶ, τῷ ἀδικοῦντι ἢ περὶ φόνους
ἢ περὶ ἱερῶν κλοπὰς ἤ τι ἄλλο τῶν τοιούτων
ἐξαμαρτάνοντι ἐπεξιέναι, ἐάν τε πατὴρ ὢν τυγχάνῃ
E ἐάν τε μήτηρ ἐάν τε ἄλλος ὁστισοῦν, τὸ δὲ μὴ
ἐπεξιέναι ἀνόσιον· ἐπεί, ὦ Σώκρατες, θέασαι, ὡς
μέγα σοι ἐρῶ τεκμήριον τοῦ νόμου ὅτι οὕτως ἔχει,
ὃ καὶ ἄλλοις ἤδη εἶπον, ὅτι ταῦτα ὀρθῶς ἂν εἴη
οὕτω γιγνόμενα, μὴ ἐπιτρέπειν τῷ ἀσεβοῦντι μηδ'
ἂν ὁστισοῦν τυγχάνῃ ὤν· αὐτοὶ γὰρ οἱ ἄνθρωποι
6 τυγχάνουσι νομίζοντες τὸν Δία τῶν θεῶν ἄριστον
καὶ δικαιότατον, καὶ τοῦτον ὁμολογοῦσι τὸν αὑτοῦ
πατέρα δῆσαι, ὅτι τοὺς υἱεῖς κατέπινεν οὐκ ἐν
δίκῃ, κἀκεῖνόν γε αὖ τὸν αὑτοῦ πατέρα ἐκτεμεῖν
δι' ἕτερα τοιαῦτα· ἐμοὶ δὲ χαλεπαίνουσιν, ὅτι τῷ
πατρὶ ἐπεξέρχομαι ἀδικοῦντι, καὶ οὕτως αὐτοὶ

---

[1] After ἰδέαν BD read κατὰ τὴν ἀνοσιότητα, which Schanz
brackets.

this fellow Meletus, nor anyone else, seems to notice you at all, but he has seen through me so sharply and so easily that he has indicted me for impiety. Now in the name of Zeus, tell me what you just now asserted that you knew so well. What do you say is the nature of piety and impiety, both in relation to murder and to other things? Is not holiness always the same with itself in every action, and, on the other hand, is not unholiness the opposite of all holiness, always the same with itself and whatever is to be unholy possessing some one characteristic quality?

EUTHYPHRO. Certainly, Socrates.

SOCRATES. Tell me then, what do you say holiness is, and what unholiness?

EUTHYPHRO. Well then, I say that holiness is doing what I am doing now, prosecuting the wrong-doer who commits murder or steals from the temples or does any such thing, whether he be your father or your mother or anyone else, and not prosecuting him is unholy. And, Socrates, see what a sure proof I offer you,—a proof I have already given to others,— that this is established and right and that we ought not to let him who acts impiously go unpunished, no matter who he may be. Men believe that Zeus is the best and most just of the gods, and they acknow- ledge that he put his father in bonds because he wickedly devoured his children, and he in turn had mutilated his father for similar reasons; but they are incensed against me because I proceed against my father when he has done wrong, and so they are

αὐτοῖς τὰ ἐναντία λέγουσι περί τε τῶν θεῶν καὶ περὶ ἐμοῦ.

ΣΩΚΡΑΤΗΣ. Ἀρά γε, ὦ Εὐθύφρον, τοῦτ' ἔστιν, οὗ ἔνεκα τὴν γραφὴν φεύγω, ὅτι τὰ τοιαῦτα ἐπειδάν τις περὶ τῶν θεῶν λέγῃ, δυσχερῶς πως ἀποδέχομαι; δι' ἃ δή, ὡς ἔοικε, φήσει τίς με ἐξαμαρτάνειν. νῦν οὖν εἰ καὶ σοὶ ταῦτα ξυνδοκεῖ
B τῷ εὖ εἰδότι περὶ τῶν τοιούτων, ἀνάγκη δή, ὡς ἔοικε, καὶ ἡμῖν ξυγχωρεῖν. τί γὰρ καὶ φήσομεν, οἵ γε αὐτοὶ ὁμολογοῦμεν περὶ αὐτῶν μηδὲν εἰδέναι; ἀλλά μοι εἰπὲ πρὸς Φιλίου, σὺ ὡς ἀληθῶς ἡγεῖ ταῦτα οὕτως γεγονέναι;

ΕΥΘΥΦΡΩΝ. Καὶ ἔτι γε τούτων θαυμασιώτερα, ὦ Σώκρατες, ἃ οἱ πολλοὶ οὐκ ἴσασιν.

ΣΩΚΡΑΤΗΣ. Καὶ πόλεμον ἄρα ἡγεῖ σὺ εἶναι τῷ ὄντι ἐν τοῖς θεοῖς πρὸς ἀλλήλους, καὶ ἔχθρας γε δεινὰς καὶ μάχας καὶ ἄλλα τοιαῦτα πολλά, οἷα λέγεταί τε ὑπὸ τῶν ποιητῶν, καὶ ὑπὸ τῶν
C ἀγαθῶν γραφέων τά τε ἄλλα ἱερὰ ἡμῖν καταπεποίκιλται, καὶ δὴ καὶ τοῖς μεγάλοις Παναθηναίοις ὁ πέπλος μεστὸς τῶν τοιούτων ποικιλμάτων ἀνάγεται εἰς τὴν ἀκρόπολιν; ταῦτα ἀληθῆ φῶμεν εἶναι, ὦ Εὐθύφρον;

ΕΥΘΥΦΡΩΝ. Μὴ μόνον γε, ὦ Σώκρατες· ἀλλ' ὅπερ ἄρτι εἶπον, καὶ ἄλλα σοι ἐγὼ πολλά, ἐάνπερ βούλῃ, περὶ τῶν θείων διηγήσομαι, ἃ σὺ ἀκούων εὖ οἶδ' ὅτι ἐκπλαγήσει.

7. ΣΩΚΡΑΤΗΣ. Οὐκ ἂν θαυμάζοιμι. ἀλλὰ ταῦτα μέν μοι εἰς αὖθις ἐπὶ σχολῆς διηγήσει· νυνὶ δέ, ὅπερ ἄρτι σε ἠρόμην, πειρῶ σαφέστερον εἰπεῖν.
D οὐ γάρ με, ὦ ἑταῖρε, τὸ πρότερον ἱκανῶς ἐδίδαξας ἐρωτήσαντα τὸ ὅσιον, ὅ τι ποτ' εἴη, ἀλλά μοι

inconsistent in what they say about the gods and about me.

SOCRATES. Is not this, Euthyphro, the reason why I am being prosecuted, because when people tell such stories about the gods I find it hard to accept them? And therefore, probably, people will say I am wrong. Now if you, who know so much about such things, accept these tales, I suppose I too must give way. For what am I to say, who confess frankly that I know nothing about them? But tell me, in the name of Zeus, the god of friendship, do you really believe these things happened?

EUTHYPHRO. Yes, and still more wonderful things than these, Socrates, which most people do not know.

SOCRATES. And so you believe that there was really war between the gods, and fearful enmities and battles and other things of the sort, such as are told of by the poets and represented in varied designs by the great artists in our sacred places and especially on the robe which is carried up to the Acropolis at the great Panathenaea? for this is covered with such representations. Shall we agree that these things are true, Euthyphro?

EUTHYPHRO. Not only these things, Socrates; but, as I said just now, I will, if you like, tell you many other things about the gods, which I am sure will amaze you when you hear them.

SOCRATES. I dare say. But you can tell me those things at your leisure some other time. At present try to tell more clearly what I asked you just now. For, my friend, you did not give me sufficient information before, when I asked what holiness was, but you told me that this was holy

εἶπες, ὅτι τοῦτο τυγχάνει ὅσιον ὄν, ὃ σὺ νῦν ποιεῖς, φόνου ἐπεξιὼν τῷ πατρί.

ΕΥΘΥΦΡΩΝ. Καὶ ἀληθῆ γε ἔλεγον, ὦ Σώκρατες.

ΣΩΚΡΑΤΗΣ. Ἴσως. ἀλλὰ γάρ, ὦ Εὐθύφρον, καὶ ἄλλα πολλὰ φῂς εἶναι ὅσια.

ΕΥΘΥΦΡΩΝ. Καὶ γὰρ ἔστιν.

ΣΩΚΡΑΤΗΣ. Μέμνησαι οὖν, ὅτι οὐ τοῦτό σοι διεκελευόμην, ἕν τι ἢ δύο με διδάξαι τῶν πολλῶν ὁσίων, ἀλλ᾽ ἐκεῖνο αὐτὸ τὸ εἶδος, ᾧ πάντα τὰ ὅσια ὅσιά ἐστιν; ἔφησθα γάρ που μιᾷ ἰδέᾳ τά τε ἀνόσια ἀνόσια εἶναι καὶ τὰ ὅσια ὅσια· ἢ οὐ μνημονεύεις;

ΕΥΘΥΦΡΩΝ. Ἔγωγε.

ΣΩΚΡΑΤΗΣ. Ταύτην τοίνυν με αὐτὴν δίδαξον τὴν ἰδέαν, τίς ποτέ ἐστιν, ἵνα εἰς ἐκείνην ἀποβλέπων καὶ χρώμενος αὐτῇ παραδείγματι, ὃ μὲν ἂν τοιοῦτον ᾖ, ὧν ἂν ἢ σὺ ἢ ἄλλος τις πράττῃ, φῶ ὅσιον εἶναι, ὃ δ᾽ ἂν μὴ τοιοῦτον, μὴ φῶ.

ΕΥΘΥΦΡΩΝ. Ἀλλ᾽ εἰ οὕτω βούλει, ὦ Σώκρατες, καὶ οὕτω σοι φράσω.

ΣΩΚΡΑΤΗΣ. Ἀλλὰ μὴν βούλομαί γε.

ΕΥΘΥΦΡΩΝ. Ἔστι τοίνυν τὸ μὲν τοῖς θεοῖς προσ-
7 φιλὲς ὅσιον, τὸ δὲ μὴ προσφιλὲς ἀνόσιον.

ΣΩΚΡΑΤΗΣ. Παγκάλως, ὦ Εὐθύφρον, καὶ ὡς ἐγὼ ἐζήτουν ἀποκρίνασθαί σε, οὕτω νῦν ἀπεκρίνω. εἰ μέντοι ἀληθές, τοῦτο οὔπω οἶδα, ἀλλὰ σὺ δῆλον ὅτι ἐπεκδιδάξεις, ὡς ἔστιν ἀληθῆ ἃ λέγεις.

ΕΥΘΥΦΡΩΝ. Πάνυ μὲν οὖν.

8. ΣΩΚΡΑΤΗΣ. Φέρε δή, ἐπισκεψώμεθα, τί λέγομεν. τὸ μὲν θεοφιλές τε καὶ ὁ θεοφιλὴς ἄνθρωπος ὅσιος, τὸ δὲ θεομισὲς καὶ ὁ θεομισὴς

which you are now doing, prosecuting your father
for murder.

EUTHYPHRO. Well, what I said was true, Socrates.

SOCRATES. Perhaps. But, Euthyphro, you say that
many other things are holy, do you not?

EUTHYPHRO. Why, so they are.

SOCRATES. Now call to mind that this is not what
I asked you, to tell me one or two of the many
holy acts, but to tell the essential aspect, by which
all holy acts are holy; for you said that all unholy
acts were unholy and all holy ones holy by one
aspect. Or don't you remember?

EUTHYPHRO. I remember.

SOCRATES. Tell me then what this aspect is, that I
may keep my eye fixed upon it and employ it as a
model and, if anything you or anyone else does agrees
with it, may say that the act is holy, and if not, that
it is unholy.

EUTHYPHRO. If you wish me to explain in that
way, I will do so.

SOCRATES. I do wish it.

EUTHYPHRO. Well then, what is dear to the gods
is holy, and what is not dear to them is unholy.

SOCRATES. Excellent, Euthyphro; now you have
answered as I asked you to answer. However,
whether it is true, I am not yet sure; but you will,
of course, show that what you say is true.

EUTHYPHRO. Certainly.

SOCRATES. Come then, let us examine our words.
The thing and the person that are dear to the gods
are holy, and the thing and the person that are
hateful to the gods are unholy; and the two are
not the same, but the holy and the unholy are the

ἀνόσιος· οὐ ταὐτὸν δ᾽ ἐστίν, ἀλλὰ τὸ ἐναντιώ-
τατον τὸ ὅσιον τῷ ἀνοσίῳ· οὐχ οὕτως;

ΕΥΘΥΦΡΩΝ. Οὕτω μὲν οὖν.

ΣΩΚΡΑΤΗΣ. Καὶ εὖ γε φαίνεται εἰρῆσθαι;

B   ΕΥΘΥΦΡΩΝ. Δοκῶ, ὦ Σώκρατες.[1]

ΣΩΚΡΑΤΗΣ. Οὐκοῦν καὶ ὅτι στασιάζουσιν οἱ
θεοί, ὦ Εὐθύφρον, καὶ διαφέρονται ἀλλήλοις καὶ
ἔχθρα ἐστὶν ἐν αὐτοῖς πρὸς ἀλλήλους, καὶ τοῦτο
εἴρηται;

ΕΥΘΥΦΡΩΝ. Εἴρηται γάρ.

ΣΩΚΡΑΤΗΣ. Ἔχθραν δὲ καὶ ὀργάς, ὦ ἄριστε, ἡ
περὶ τίνων διαφορὰ ποιεῖ; ὧδε δὲ σκοπῶμεν. ἆρ᾽
ἂν εἰ διαφεροίμεθα ἐγώ τε καὶ σὺ περὶ ἀριθμοῦ,
ὁπότερα πλείω, ἡ περὶ τούτων διαφορὰ ἐχθροὺς
ἂν ἡμᾶς ποιοῖ καὶ ὀργίζεσθαι ἀλλήλοις, ἢ ἐπὶ
λογισμὸν ἐλθόντες περί γε τῶν τοιούτων ταχὺ ἂν
C   ἀπαλλαγεῖμεν;

ΕΥΘΥΦΡΩΝ. Πάνυ γε.

ΣΩΚΡΑΤΗΣ. Οὐκοῦν καὶ περὶ τοῦ μείζονος καὶ
ἐλάττονος εἰ διαφεροίμεθα, ἐπὶ τὸ μέτρον ἐλθόντες ταχὺ παυσαίμεθ᾽ ἂν τῆς διαφορᾶς;

ΕΥΘΥΦΡΩΝ. Ἔστι ταῦτα.

ΣΩΚΡΑΤΗΣ. Καὶ ἐπί γε τὸ ἱστάναι ἐλθόντες,
ὡς ἐγῷμαι, περὶ τοῦ βαρυτέρου τε καὶ κουφοτέρου
διακριθεῖμεν ἄν;

ΕΥΘΥΦΡΩΝ. Πῶς γὰρ οὔ;

ΣΩΚΡΑΤΗΣ. Περὶ τίνος δὲ δὴ διενεχθέντες καὶ
ἐπὶ τίνα κρίσιν οὐ δυνάμενοι ἀφικέσθαι ἐχθροί γε
ἂν ἀλλήλοις εἶμεν καὶ ὀργιζοίμεθα; ἴσως οὐ πρό-
D   χειρόν σοί ἐστιν. ἀλλ᾽ ἐμοῦ λέγοντος σκόπει, εἰ

[1] The manuscripts read Δοκῶ, ὦ Σώκρατες· εἴρηται γάρ.
Schanz brackets this and the preceding line. I follow

24

exact opposites of each other. Is not this what we have said ?

EUTHYPHRO. Yes, just this.

SOCRATES. And it seems to be correct ?

EUTHYPHRO. I think so, Socrates.

SOCRATES. Well then, have we said this also, that the gods, Euthyphro, quarrel and disagree with each other, and that there is enmity between them ?

EUTHYPHRO. Yes, we have said that.

SOCRATES. But what things is the disagreement about, which causes enmity and anger ? Let us look at it in this way. If you and I were to disagree about number, for instance, which of two numbers were the greater, would the disagreement about these matters make us enemies and make us angry with each other, or should we not quickly settle it by resorting to arithmetic ?

EUTHYPHRO. Of course we should.

SOCRATES. Then, too, if we were to disagree about the relative size of things, we should quickly put an end to the disagreement by measuring ?

EUTHYPHRO. Yes.

SOCRATES. And we should, I suppose, come to terms about relative weights by weighing ?

EUTHYPHRO. Of course.

SOCRATES. But about what would a disagreement be, which we could not settle and which would cause us to be enemies and be angry with each other ? Perhaps you cannot give an answer offhand ; but let

Hermann in omitting εἴρηται γάρ, which may have been once a marginal note or may have been copied by mistake from the next words of Euthyphro.

PLATO

τάδε ἐστὶ τό τε δίκαιον καὶ τὸ ἄδικον καὶ καλὸν
καὶ αἰσχρὸν καὶ ἀγαθὸν καὶ κακόν. ἆρα οὐ ταῦτά
ἐστιν, ὧν διενεχθέντες καὶ οὐ δυνάμενοι ἐπὶ ἱκανὴν
κρίσιν αὐτῶν ἐλθεῖν ἐχθροὶ ἀλλήλοις γιγνόμεθα,
ὅταν γιγνώμεθα, καὶ ἐγὼ καὶ σὺ καὶ οἱ ἄλλοι
ἄνθρωποι πάντες;

ΕΥΘΥΦΡΩΝ. Ἀλλ' ἔστιν αὕτη ἡ διαφορά, ὦ Σώκρατες, καὶ περὶ τούτων.

ΣΩΚΡΑΤΗΣ. Τί δέ; οἱ θεοί, ὦ Εὐθύφρον, οὐκ
εἴπερ τι διαφέρονται, διὰ ταῦτα διαφέροιντ' ἄν;

ΕΥΘΥΦΡΩΝ. Πολλὴ ἀνάγκη.

E   ΣΩΚΡΑΤΗΣ. Καὶ τῶν θεῶν ἄρα, ὦ γενναῖε Εὐθύφρον, ἄλλοι ἄλλα δίκαια καὶ ἄδικα[1] ἡγοῦνται
κατὰ τὸν σὸν λόγον, καὶ καλὰ καὶ αἰσχρὰ καὶ
ἀγαθὰ καὶ κακά· οὐ γὰρ ἄν που ἐστασίαζον
ἀλλήλοις, εἰ μὴ περὶ τούτων διεφέροντο· ἢ γάρ;

ΕΥΘΥΦΡΩΝ. Ὀρθῶς λέγεις.

ΣΩΚΡΑΤΗΣ. Οὐκοῦν ἅπερ καλὰ ἡγοῦνται ἕκαστοι καὶ ἀγαθὰ καὶ δίκαια, ταῦτα καὶ φιλοῦσιν,
τὰ δὲ ἐναντία τούτων μισοῦσιν;

ΕΥΘΥΦΡΩΝ. Πάνυ γε.

ΣΩΚΡΑΤΗΣ. Ταὐτὰ δέ γε, ὡς σὺ φῄς, οἱ μὲν
δίκαια ἡγοῦνται, οἱ δὲ ἄδικα· περὶ ἃ καὶ
8 ἀμφισβητοῦντες στασιάζουσί τε καὶ πολεμοῦσιν
ἀλλήλοις. ἆρα οὐχ οὕτω;

ΕΥΘΥΦΡΩΝ. Οὕτω.

ΣΩΚΡΑΤΗΣ. Ταῦτ' ἄρα, ὡς ἔοικεν, μισεῖται ὑπὸ
τῶν θεῶν καὶ φιλεῖται, καὶ θεομισῆ τε καὶ
θεοφιλῆ ταῦτ' ἂν εἴη.

ΕΥΘΥΦΡΩΝ. Ἔοικεν.

[1] καὶ ἄδικα inserted by Hirchig, followed by Schanz.

me suggest it. Is it not about right and wrong, and noble and disgraceful, and good and bad? Are not these the questions about which you and I and other people become enemies, when we do become enemies, because we differ about them and cannot reach any satisfactory agreement?

EUTHYPHRO. Yes, Socrates, these are the questions about which we should become enemies.

SOCRATES. And how about the gods, Euthyphro? If they disagree, would they not disagree about these questions?

EUTHYPHRO. Necessarily.

SOCRATES. Then, my noble Euthyphro, according to what you say, some of the gods too think some things are right or wrong and noble or disgraceful, and good or bad, and others disagree; for they would not quarrel with each other if they did not disagree about these matters. Is that the case?

EUTHYPHRO. You are right.

SOCRATES. Then the gods in each group love the things which they consider good and right and hate the opposites of these things?

EUTHYPHRO. Certainly.

SOCRATES. But you say that the same things are considered right by some of them and wrong by others; and it is because they disagree about these things that they quarrel and wage war with each other. Is not this what you said?

EUTHYPHRO. It is.

SOCRATES. Then, as it seems, the same things are hated and loved by the gods, and the same things would be dear and hateful to the gods.

EUTHYPHRO. So it seems.

ΣΩΚΡΑΤΗΣ. Καὶ ὅσια ἄρα καὶ ἀνόσια τὰ αὐτὰ ἂν εἴη, ὦ Εὐθύφρον, τούτῳ τῷ λόγῳ.

ΕΥΘΥΦΡΩΝ. Κινδυνεύει.

9. ΣΩΚΡΑΤΗΣ. Οὐκ ἄρα ὃ ἠρόμην ἀπεκρίνω, ὦ θαυμάσιε. οὐ γὰρ τοῦτό γε ἠρώτων, ὃ[1] τυγχάνει ταὐτὸν ὂν ὅσιόν τε καὶ ἀνόσιον· ὃ δ᾽ ἂν θεοφιλὲς ᾖ, καὶ θεομισές ἐστιν, ὡς ἔοικεν. ὥστε, ὦ
B Εὐθύφρον, ὃ σὺ νῦν ποιεῖς τὸν πατέρα κολάζων, οὐδὲν θαυμαστόν, εἰ τοῦτο δρῶν τῷ μὲν Διὶ προσφιλὲς ποιεῖς, τῷ δὲ Κρόνῳ καὶ τῷ Οὐρανῷ ἐχθρόν, καὶ τῷ μὲν Ἡφαίστῳ φίλον, τῇ δὲ Ἥρᾳ ἐχθρόν· καὶ εἴ τις ἄλλος τῶν θεῶν ἕτερος ἑτέρῳ διαφέρεται περὶ αὐτοῦ, καὶ ἐκείνοις κατὰ τὰ αὐτά.

ΕΥΘΥΦΡΩΝ. Ἀλλ᾽ οἶμαι, ὦ Σώκρατες, περί γε τούτου τῶν θεῶν οὐδένα ἕτερον ἑτέρῳ διαφέρεσθαι, ὡς οὐ δεῖ δίκην διδόναι ἐκεῖνον, ὃς ἂν ἀδίκως τινὰ ἀποκτείνῃ.

ΣΩΚΡΑΤΗΣ. Τί δέ; ἀνθρώπων, ὦ Εὐθύφρον, ἤδη τινὸς ἤκουσας ἀμφισβητοῦντος, ὡς τὸν ἀδίκως
C ἀποκτείναντα ἢ ἄλλο ἀδίκως ποιοῦντα ὁτιοῦν οὐ δεῖ δίκην διδόναι;

ΕΥΘΥΦΡΩΝ. Οὐδὲν μὲν οὖν παύονται ταῦτα ἀμφισβητοῦντες καὶ ἄλλοθι καὶ ἐν τοῖς δικαστηρίοις. ἀδικοῦντες γὰρ πάμπολλα, πάντα ποιοῦσι καὶ λέγουσι φεύγοντες τὴν δίκην.

ΣΩΚΡΑΤΗΣ. Ἦ καὶ ὁμολογοῦσιν, ὦ Εὐθύφρον, ἀδικεῖν, καὶ ὁμολογοῦντες ὅμως οὐ δεῖν φασι σφᾶς διδόναι δίκην;

ΕΥΘΥΦΡΩΝ. Οὐδαμῶς τοῦτό γε.

[1] Schanz reads ᾧ for ὅ.

EUTHYPHRO

SOCRATES. And then the same things would be both holy and unholy, Euthyphro, according to this statement.

EUTHYPHRO. I suppose so.

SOCRATES. Then you did not answer my question, my friend. For I did not ask you what is at once holy and unholy; but, judging from your reply, what is dear to the gods is also hateful to the gods. And so, Euthyphro, it would not be surprising if, in punishing your father as you are doing, you were performing an act that is pleasing to Zeus, but hateful to Cronus and Uranus, and pleasing to Hephaestus, but hateful to Hera, and so forth in respect to the other gods, if any disagree with any other about it.

EUTHYPHRO. But I think, Socrates, that none of the gods disagrees with any other about this, or holds that he who kills anyone wrongfully ought not to pay the penalty.

SOCRATES. Well, Euthyphro, to return to men, did you ever hear anybody arguing that he who had killed anyone wrongfully, or had done anything else whatever wrongfully, ought not to pay the penalty?

EUTHYPHRO. Why, they are always arguing these points, especially in the law courts. For they do very many wrong things; and then there is nothing they will not do or say, in defending themselves, to avoid the penalty.

SOCRATES. Yes, but do they acknowledge, Euthyphro, that they have done wrong and, although they acknowledge it, nevertheless say that they ought not to pay the penalty?

EUTHYPHRO. Oh, no, they don't do that.

ΣΩΚΡΑΤΗΣ. Οὐκ ἄρα πᾶν γε ποιοῦσι καὶ λέγουσι. τοῦτο γάρ, οἶμαι, οὐ τολμῶσι λέγειν οὐδ'
D ἀμφισβητεῖν, ὡς οὐχί, εἴπερ ἀδικοῦσί γε, δοτέον
δίκην· ἀλλ', οἶμαι, οὔ φασιν ἀδικεῖν. ἢ γάρ;

ΕΥΘΥΦΡΩΝ. Ἀληθῆ λέγεις.

ΣΩΚΡΑΤΗΣ. Οὐκ ἄρα ἐκεῖνό γε ἀμφισβητοῦσιν,
ὡς οὐ τὸν ἀδικοῦντα δεῖ διδόναι δίκην· ἀλλ'
ἐκεῖνο ἴσως ἀμφισβητοῦσι, τὸ τίς ἐστιν ὁ ἀδικῶν
καὶ τί δρῶν καὶ πότε.

ΕΥΘΥΦΡΩΝ. Ἀληθῆ λέγεις.[1]

ΣΩΚΡΑΤΗΣ. Οὐκοῦν αὐτά γε ταῦτα καὶ οἱ θεοὶ
πεπόνθασιν, εἴπερ στασιάζουσι περὶ τῶν δικαίων
καὶ ἀδίκων, ὡς ὁ σὸς λόγος, καὶ οἱ μέν φασιν
ἀλλήλους ἀδικεῖν, οἱ δὲ οὔ φασιν; ἐπεὶ ἐκεῖνό
γε δήπου, ὦ θαυμάσιε, οὐδεὶς οὔτε θεῶν οὔτε
E ἀνθρώπων τολμᾷ λέγειν, ὡς οὐ τῷ γε ἀδικοῦντι
δοτέον δίκην.

ΕΥΘΥΦΡΩΝ. Ναί, τοῦτο μὲν ἀληθὲς λέγεις, ὦ
Σώκρατες, τὸ κεφάλαιον.

ΣΩΚΡΑΤΗΣ. Ἀλλ' ἕκαστόν γε οἶμαι, ὦ Εὐθύφρον, τῶν πραχθέντων ἀμφισβητοῦσιν οἱ ἀμφισβητοῦντες, καὶ ἄνθρωποι καὶ θεοί, εἴπερ ἀμφισβητοῦσιν θεοί· πράξεώς τινος πέρι διαφερόμενοι
οἱ μὲν δικαίως φασὶν αὐτὴν πεπρᾶχθαι, οἱ δὲ
ἀδίκως· ἆρ' οὐχ οὕτω;

ΕΥΘΥΦΡΩΝ. Πάνυ γε.

10. ΣΩΚΡΑΤΗΣ. Ἴθι νῦν, ὦ φίλε Εὐθύφρον,
9 δίδαξον καὶ ἐμέ, ἵνα σοφώτερος γένωμαι, τί
σοι τεκμήριόν ἐστιν, ὡς πάντες θεοὶ ἡγοῦνται
ἐκεῖνον ἀδίκως τεθνάναι, ὃς ἂν θητεύων ἀνδρο-

---

[1] οὐκ ἄρα ... Ἀληθῆ λέγεις bracketed by Schanz following
Schenkl.

30

SOCRATES. Then there is something they do not do and say. For they do not, I fancy, dare to say and argue that, if they have really done wrong, they ought not to pay the penalty; but, I think, they say they have not done wrong; do they not?

EUTHYPHRO. You are right.

SOCRATES. Then they do not argue this point, that the wrongdoer must not pay the penalty; but perhaps they argue about this, who is a wrongdoer, and what he did, and when.

EUTHYPHRO. That is true.

SOCRATES. Then is not the same thing true of the gods, if they quarrel about right and wrong, as you say, and some say others have done wrong, and some say they have not? For surely, my friend, no one, either of gods or men, has the face to say that he who does wrong ought not to pay the penalty.

EUTHYPHRO. Yes, you are right about this, Socrates, in the main.

SOCRATES. But I think, Euthyphro, those who dispute, both men and gods, if the gods do dispute, dispute about each separate act. When they differ with one another about any act, some say it was right and others that it was wrong. Is it not so?

EUTHYPHRO. Certainly.

SOCRATES. Come now, my dear Euthyphro, inform me, that I may be made wiser, what proof you have that all the gods think that the man lost his life wrongfully, who, when he was a servant, committed

φόνος γενόμενος, ξυνδεθεὶς ὑπὸ τοῦ δεσπότου
τοῦ ἀποθανόντος, φθάσῃ τελευτήσας διὰ τὰ
δεσμά, πρὶν τὸν ξυνδήσαντα παρὰ τῶν ἐξηγητῶν
περὶ αὐτοῦ πυθέσθαι, τί χρὴ ποιεῖν, καὶ ὑπὲρ
τοῦ τοιούτου δὴ ὀρθῶς ἔχει ἐπεξιέναι καὶ ἐπι-
σκήπτεσθαι φόνου τὸν υἱὸν τῷ πατρί· ἴθι, περὶ
τούτων πειρῶ τί μοι σαφὲς ἐνδείξασθαι, ὡς
B παντὸς μᾶλλον πάντες θεοὶ ἡγοῦνται ὀρθῶς
ἔχειν ταύτην τὴν πρᾶξιν· κἄν μοι ἱκανῶς ἐνδείξῃ,
ἐγκωμιάζων σε ἐπὶ σοφίᾳ οὐδέποτε παύσομαι.

ΕΥΘΥΦΡΩΝ. Ἀλλ᾽ ἴσως οὐκ ὀλίγον ἔργον ἐστίν,
ὦ Σώκρατες· ἐπεὶ πάνυ γε σαφῶς ἔχοιμι ἂν
ἐπιδεῖξαί σοι.

ΣΩΚΡΑΤΗΣ. Μανθάνω· ὅτι σοι δοκῶ τῶν δικαστῶν δυσμαθέστερος εἶναι· ἐπεὶ ἐκείνοις γε
ἐνδείξει δῆλον ὅτι, ὡς ἄδικά τέ ἐστιν καὶ οἱ θεοὶ
ἅπαντες τὰ τοιαῦτα μισοῦσιν.

ΕΥΘΥΦΡΩΝ. Πάνυ γε σαφῶς, ὦ Σώκρατες, ἐάν
περ ἀκούσωσί γέ μου λέγοντος.

11. ΣΩΚΡΑΤΗΣ. Ἀλλ᾽ ἀκούσονται, ἐάν περ εὖ
C δοκῇς λέγειν. τόδε δέ σου ἐνενόησα ἅμα λέγοντος,
καὶ πρὸς ἐμαυτὸν σκοπῶ· εἰ ὅ τι μάλιστά με
Εὐθύφρων διδάξειεν, ὡς οἱ θεοὶ ἅπαντες τὸν
τοιοῦτον θάνατον ἡγοῦνται ἄδικον εἶναι, τί μᾶλλον
ἐγὼ μεμάθηκα παρ᾽ Εὐθύφρονος, τί ποτ᾽ ἐστὶν τὸ
ὅσιόν τε καὶ τὸ ἀνόσιον; θεομισὲς μὲν γὰρ τοῦτο
τὸ ἔργον, ὡς ἔοικεν, εἴη ἄν· ἀλλὰ γὰρ οὐ τούτῳ
ἐφάνη ἄρτι ὡρισμένα τὸ ὅσιον καὶ μή· τὸ γὰρ
θεομισὲς ὂν καὶ θεοφιλὲς ἐφάνη· ὥστε τούτου
ἀφίημί σε, ὦ Εὐθύφρον· εἰ βούλει, πάντες αὐτὸ
D ἡγείσθων θεοὶ ἄδικον καὶ πάντες μισούντων.
ἀλλ᾽ ἆρα τοῦτο νῦν ἐπανορθώμεθα ἐν τῷ λόγῳ,

a murder, was bound by the master of the man he killed, and died as a result of his bonds before the master who had bound him found out from the advisers what he ought to do with him, and that it is right on account of such a man for a son to proceed against his father and accuse him of murder. Come, try to show me clearly about this, that the gods surely believe that this conduct is right ; and if you show it to my satisfaction, I will glorify your wisdom as long as I live.

EUTHYPHRO. But perhaps this is no small task, Socrates ; though I could show you quite clearly.

SOCRATES. I understand ; it is because you think I am slower to understand than the judges ; since it is plain that you will show them that such acts are wrong and that all the gods hate them.

EUTHYPHRO. Quite clearly, Socrates ; that is, if they listen to me.

SOCRATES. They will listen, if they find that you are a good speaker. But this occurred to me while you were talking, and I said to myself : " If Euthyphro should prove to me no matter how clearly that all the gods think such a death is wrongful, what have I learned from Euthyphro about the question, what is holiness and what is unholiness ? For this act would, as it seems, be hateful to the gods ; but we saw just now that holiness and its opposite are not defined in this way ; for we saw that what is hateful to the gods is also dear to them ; and so I let you off any discussion of this point, Euthyphro. If you like, all the gods may think it wrong and may hate it. But shall we now emend our definition and

33

ὡς ὃ μὲν ἂν πάντες οἱ θεοὶ μισῶσιν, ἀνόσιόν ἐστιν,
ὃ δ' ἂν φιλῶσιν, ὅσιον· ὃ δ' ἂν οἱ μὲν φιλῶσιν,
οἱ δὲ μισῶσιν, οὐδέτερα ἢ ἀμφότερα; ἆρ' οὕτω
βούλει ἡμῖν ὡρίσθαι νῦν περὶ τοῦ ὁσίου καὶ τοῦ
ἀνοσίου;

ΕΥΘΥΦΡΩΝ. Τί γὰρ κωλύει, ὦ Σώκρατες;

ΣΩΚΡΑΤΗΣ. Οὐδὲν ἐμέ γε, ὦ Εὐθύφρον, ἀλλὰ
σὺ δὴ τὸ σὸν σκόπει, εἰ τοῦτο ὑποθέμενος οὕτω
ῥᾷστά με διδάξεις ὃ ὑπέσχου.

E ΕΥΘΥΦΡΩΝ. 'Αλλ' ἔγωγε φαίην ἂν τοῦτο εἶναι
τὸ ὅσιον, ὃ ἂν πάντες οἱ θεοὶ φιλῶσιν, καὶ τὸ
ἐναντίον, ὃ ἂν πάντες θεοὶ μισῶσιν, ἀνόσιον.

ΣΩΚΡΑΤΗΣ. Οὐκοῦν ἐπισκοπῶμεν αὖ τοῦτο, ὦ
Εὐθύφρον, εἰ καλῶς λέγεται, ἢ ἐῶμεν καὶ οὕτω
ἡμῶν τε αὐτῶν ἀποδεχώμεθα καὶ τῶν ἄλλων, ἐὰν
μόνον φῇ τίς τι ἔχειν οὕτω, ξυγχωροῦντες ἔχειν;
ἢ σκεπτέον, τί λέγει ὁ λέγων;

ΕΥΘΥΦΡΩΝ. Σκεπτέον· οἶμαι μέντοι ἔγωγε τοῦτο
νυνὶ καλῶς λέγεσθαι.

12. ΣΩΚΡΑΤΗΣ. Τάχ', ὦγαθέ, βέλτιον εἰσό-
10 μεθα, ἐννόησον γὰρ τὸ τοιόνδε. ἆρα τὸ ὅσιον,
ὅτι ὅσιόν ἐστιν, φιλεῖται ὑπὸ τῶν θεῶν, ἢ ὅτι
φιλεῖται, ὅσιόν ἐστιν;

ΕΥΘΥΦΡΩΝ. Οὐκ οἶδ' ὅ τι λέγεις, ὦ Σώκρατες.

ΣΩΚΡΑΤΗΣ. 'Αλλ' ἐγὼ πειράσομαι σαφέστερον
φράσαι. λέγομέν τι φερόμενον καὶ φέρον καὶ
ἀγόμενον καὶ ἄγον καὶ ὁρώμενον καὶ ὁρῶν. καὶ
πάντα τὰ τοιαῦτα μανθάνεις ὅτι ἕτερα ἀλλήλων
ἐστὶ καὶ ᾗ ἕτερα;

ΕΥΘΥΦΡΩΝ. Ἔγωγέ μοι δοκῶ μανθάνειν.

34

say that whatever all the gods hate is unholy and whatever they all love is holy, and what some love and others hate is neither or both? Do you wish this now to be our definition of holiness and unholiness?

EUTHYPHRO. What is to hinder, Socrates?

SOCRATES. Nothing, so far as I am concerned, Euthyphro, but consider your own position, whether by adopting this definition you will most easily teach me what you promised.

EUTHYPHRO. Well, I should say that what all the gods love is holy and, on the other hand, what they all hate is unholy.

SOCRATES. Then shall we examine this again, Euthyphro, to see if it is correct, or shall we let it go and accept our own statement, and those of others, agreeing that it is so, if anyone merely says that it is? Or ought we to inquire into the correctness of the statement?

EUTHYPHRO. We ought to inquire. However, I think this is now correct.

SOCRATES. We shall soon know more about this, my friend. Just consider this question:—Is that which is holy loved by the gods because it is holy, or is it holy because it is loved by the gods?

EUTHYPHRO. I don't know what you mean, Socrates.

SOCRATES. Then I will try to speak more clearly. We speak of being carried and of carrying, of being led and of leading, of being seen and of seeing; and you understand—do you not?—that in all such expressions the two parts differ one from the other in meaning, and how they differ.

EUTHYPHRO. I think I understand.

ΣΩΚΡΑΤΗΣ.   Οὐκοῦν καὶ φιλούμενόν τί ἐστιν καὶ τούτου ἕτερον τὸ φιλοῦν;

ΕΥΘΥΦΡΩΝ.   Πῶς γὰρ οὔ;

B   ΣΩΚΡΑΤΗΣ.   Λέγε δή μοι, πότερον τὸ φερόμενον, διότι φέρεται, φερόμενόν ἐστιν, ἢ δι᾽ ἄλλο τι;

ΕΥΘΥΦΡΩΝ.   Οὔκ, ἀλλὰ διὰ τοῦτο.

ΣΩΚΡΑΤΗΣ.   Καὶ τὸ ἀγόμενον δή, διότι ἄγεται, καὶ τὸ ὁρώμενον, διότι ὁρᾶται;

ΕΥΘΥΦΡΩΝ.   Πάνυ γε.

ΣΩΚΡΑΤΗΣ.   Οὐκ ἄρα διότι ὁρώμενόν γέ ἐστιν, διὰ τοῦτο ὁρᾶται, ἀλλὰ τὸ ἐναντίον διότι ὁρᾶται, διὰ τοῦτο ὁρώμενον· οὐδὲ διότι ἀγόμενόν ἐστιν, διὰ τοῦτο ἄγεται, ἀλλὰ διότι ἄγεται, διὰ τοῦτο ἀγόμενον· οὐδὲ διότι φερόμενον, φέρεται, ἀλλὰ διότι φέρεται, φερόμενον. ἆρα κατάδηλον, ὦ

C Εὐθύφρον, ὃ βούλομαι λέγειν; βούλομαι δὲ τόδε, ὅτι, εἴ τι γίγνεται ἤ τι πάσχει, οὐχ ὅτι γιγνόμενόν ἐστι, γίγνεται, ἀλλ᾽ ὅτι γίγνεται, γιγνόμενόν ἐστιν· οὐδ᾽ ὅτι πάσχον ἐστί, πάσχει, ἀλλ᾽ ὅτι πάσχει, πάσχον ἐστίν· ἢ οὐ ξυγχωρεῖς οὕτω;

ΕΥΘΥΦΡΩΝ.   Ἔγωγε.

ΣΩΚΡΑΤΗΣ.   Οὐκοῦν καὶ τὸ φιλούμενον ἢ γιγνόμενόν τί ἐστιν ἢ πάσχον τι ὑπό του;

ΕΥΘΥΦΡΩΝ.   Πάνυ γε.

ΣΩΚΡΑΤΗΣ.   Καὶ τοῦτο ἄρα οὕτως ἔχει, ὥσπερ τὰ πρότερα· οὐχ ὅτι φιλούμενόν ἐστιν, φιλεῖται ὑπὸ ὧν φιλεῖται, ἀλλ᾽ ὅτι φιλεῖται, φιλούμενον;

ΕΥΘΥΦΡΩΝ.   Ἀνάγκη.

SOCRATES. Then, too, we conceive of a thing being loved and of a thing loving, and the two are different?

EUTHYPHRO. Of course.

SOCRATES. Now tell me, is a thing which is carried a carried thing because one carries it, or for some other reason?

EUTHYPHRO. No, for that reason.

SOCRATES. And a thing which is led is led because one leads it, and a thing which is seen is so because one sees it?

EUTHYPHRO. Certainly.

SOCRATES. Then one does not see it because it is a seen thing, but, on the contrary, it is a seen thing because one sees it; and one does not lead it because it is a led thing, but it is a led thing because one leads it; and one does not carry it because it is a carried thing, but it is a carried thing because one carries it. Is it clear, Euthyphro, what I am trying to say? I am trying to say this, that if anything becomes or undergoes, it does not become because it is in a state of becoming, but it is in a state of becoming because it becomes, and it does not undergo because it is a thing which undergoes, but because it undergoes it is a thing which undergoes; or do you not agree to this?

EUTHYPHRO. I agree.

SOCRATES. Is not that which is beloved a thing which is either becoming or undergoing something?

EUTHYPHRO Certainly.

SOCRATES. And is this case like the former ones: those who love it do not love it because it is a beloved thing, but it is a beloved thing because they love it?

EUTHYPHRO. Obviously.

ΣΩΚΡΑΤΗΣ. Τί δὴ οὖν λέγομεν περὶ τοῦ ὁσίου,
D ὦ Εὐθύφρον; ἄλλο τι φιλεῖται ὑπὸ θεῶν πάντων,
ὡς ὁ σὸς λόγος;

ΕΥΘΥΦΡΩΝ. Ναί.

ΣΩΚΡΑΤΗΣ. Ἆρα διὰ τοῦτο, ὅτι ὅσιόν ἐστιν, ἢ
δι' ἄλλο τι;

ΕΥΘΥΦΡΩΝ. Οὔκ, ἀλλὰ διὰ τοῦτο.

ΣΩΚΡΑΤΗΣ. Διότι ἄρα ὅσιόν ἐστιν, φιλεῖται,
ἀλλ' οὐχ ὅτι φιλεῖται, διὰ τοῦτο ὅσιόν ἐστιν;

ΕΥΘΥΦΡΩΝ. Ἔοικεν.

ΣΩΚΡΑΤΗΣ. Ἀλλὰ μὲν δὴ διότι γε φιλεῖται ὑπὸ
θεῶν, φιλούμενόν ἐστι καὶ θεοφιλὲς τὸ θεοφιλές.[1]

E   ΕΥΘΥΦΡΩΝ. Πῶς γὰρ οὔ;

ΣΩΚΡΑΤΗΣ. Οὐκ ἄρα τὸ θεοφιλὲς ὅσιόν ἐστιν, ὦ
Εὐθύφρον, οὐδὲ τὸ ὅσιον θεοφιλές, ὡς σὺ λέγεις,
ἀλλ' ἕτερον τοῦτο τούτου.

ΕΥΘΥΦΡΩΝ. Πῶς δή, ὦ Σώκρατες;

ΣΩΚΡΑΤΗΣ. Ὅτι ὁμολογοῦμεν τὸ μὲν ὅσιον διὰ
τοῦτο φιλεῖσθαι, ὅτι ὅσιόν ἐστιν, ἀλλ' οὐ διότι
φιλεῖται, ὅσιον εἶναι· ἦ γάρ;

ΕΥΘΥΦΡΩΝ. Ναί.

13. ΣΩΚΡΑΤΗΣ. Τὸ δέ γε θεοφιλὲς ὅτι φιλεῖται
ὑπὸ θεῶν, αὐτῷ τούτῳ τῷ φιλεῖσθαι θεοφιλὲς
εἶναι, ἀλλ' οὐχ ὅτι θεοφιλές, διὰ τοῦτο φιλεῖσθαι.

ΕΥΘΥΦΡΩΝ. Ἀληθῆ λέγεις.

ΣΩΚΡΑΤΗΣ. Ἀλλ' εἴ γε ταὐτὸν ἦν, ὦ φίλε
Εὐθύφρον, τὸ θεοφιλὲς καὶ τὸ ὅσιον, εἰ μὲν διὰ τὸ
11 ὅσιον εἶναι ἐφιλεῖτο τὸ ὅσιον, καὶ διὰ τὸ θεοφιλὲς
εἶναι ἐφιλεῖτο ἂν τὸ θεοφιλές, εἰ δὲ διὰ τὸ φιλεῖσθαι ὑπὸ θεῶν τὸ θεοφιλὲς θεοφιλὲς ἦν, καὶ τὸ

[1] τὸ θεοφιλές added by Schanz following Bast.

38

socrates. Now what do you say about that which is holy, Euthyphro? It is loved by all the gods, is it not, according to what you said?

euthyphro. Yes.

socrates. For this reason, because it is holy, or for some other reason?

euthyphro. No, for this reason.

socrates. It is loved because it is holy, not holy because it is loved?

euthyphro. I think so.

socrates. But that which is dear to the gods is dear to them and beloved by them because they love it.

euthyphro. Of course.

socrates. Then that which is dear to the gods and that which is holy are not identical, but differ one from the other.

euthyphro. How so, Socrates?

socrates. Because we are agreed that the holy is loved because it is holy and that it is not holy because it is loved; are we not?

euthyphro. Yes.

socrates. But we are agreed that what is dear to the gods is dear to them because they love it, that is, by reason of this love, not that they love it because it is dear.

euthyphro. Very true.

socrates. But if that which is dear to the gods and that which is holy were identical, my dear Euthyphro, then if the holy were loved because it is holy, that which is dear to the gods would be loved because it is dear, and if that which is dear to the gods is dear because it is loved, then that which is holy would be holy because

ὅσιον ἂν διὰ τὸ φιλεῖσθαι ὅσιον ἦν· νῦν δὲ ὁρᾷς,
ὅτι ἐναντίως ἔχετον, ὡς παντάπασιν ἑτέρω ὄντε
ἀλλήλων. τὸ μὲν γάρ, ὅτι φιλεῖται, ἐστὶν οἷον
φιλεῖσθαι· τὸ δ' ὅτι ἐστὶν οἷον φιλεῖσθαι, διὰ
τοῦτο φιλεῖται. καὶ κινδυνεύεις, ὦ Εὐθύφρον,
ἐρωτώμενος τὸ ὅσιον, ὅ τί ποτ' ἔστιν, τὴν μὲν
οὐσίαν μοι αὐτοῦ οὐ βούλεσθαι δηλῶσαι, πάθος
δέ τι περὶ αὐτοῦ λέγειν, ὅ τι πέπονθε τοῦτο τὸ
B ὅσιον, φιλεῖσθαι ὑπὸ πάντων θεῶν· ὅ τι δὲ ὄν,
οὔπω εἶπες. εἰ οὖν σοι φίλον, μή με ἀποκρύψῃ,
ἀλλὰ πάλιν εἰπὲ ἐξ ἀρχῆς, τί ποτε ὂν τὸ ὅσιον
εἴτε φιλεῖται ὑπὸ θεῶν εἴτε ὁτιδὴ πάσχει· οὐ γὰρ
περὶ τούτου διοισόμεθα· ἀλλ' εἰπὲ προθύμως, τί
ἔστιν τό τε ὅσιον καὶ τὸ ἀνόσιον;

ΕΥΘΥΦΡΩΝ. Ἀλλ', ὦ Σώκρατες, οὐκ ἔχω ἔγωγε,
ὅπως σοι εἴπω ὃ νοῶ. περιέρχεται γάρ πως ἡμῖν
ἀεὶ ὃ ἂν προθώμεθα, καὶ οὐκ ἐθέλει μένειν ὅπου
ἂν ἱδρυσώμεθα αὐτό.

ΣΩΚΡΑΤΗΣ. Τοῦ ἡμετέρου προγόνου, ὦ Εὐθύ-
C φρον, ἔοικεν εἶναι Δαιδάλου τὰ ὑπὸ σοῦ λεγόμενα.
καὶ εἰ μὲν αὐτὰ ἐγὼ ἔλεγον καὶ ἐτιθέμην, ἴσως
ἄν με ἐπέσκωπτες, ὡς ἄρα καὶ ἐμοὶ κατὰ τὴν
ἐκείνου ξυγγένειαν τὰ ἐν τοῖς λόγοις ἔργα ἀποδι-
δράσκει καὶ οὐκ ἐθέλει μένειν ὅπου ἄν τις αὐτὰ
θῇ· νῦν δέ—σαὶ γὰρ αἱ ὑποθέσεις εἰσίν· ἄλλου δή
τινος δεῖ σκώμματος. οὐ γὰρ ἐθέλουσι σοὶ μένειν,
ὡς καὶ αὐτῷ σοι δοκεῖ.

ΕΥΘΥΦΡΩΝ. Ἐμοὶ δὲ δοκεῖ σχεδόν τι τοῦ αὐτοῦ

it is loved; but now you see that the opposite is the case, showing that the two are entirely different from each other. For the one becomes lovable from the fact that it is loved, whereas the other is loved because it is in itself lovable. And, Euthyphro, it seems that when you were asked what holiness is you were unwilling to make plain its essence, but you mentioned something that has happened to this holiness, namely, that it is loved by the gods. But you did not tell as yet what it really is. So, if you please, do not hide it from me, but begin over again and tell me what holiness is, no matter whether it is loved by the gods or anything else happens to it; for we shall not quarrel about that. But tell me frankly, What is holiness, and what is unholiness?

EUTHYPHRO. But, Socrates, I do not know how to say what I mean. For whatever statement we advance, somehow or other it moves about and won't stay where we put it.

SOCRATES. Your statements, Euthyphro, are like works of my [1] ancestor Daedalus, and if I were the one who made or advanced them, you might laugh at me and say that on account of my relationship to him my works in words run away and won't stay where they are put. But now—well, the statements are yours; so some other jest is demanded; for they won't stay fixed, as you yourself see.

EUTHYPHRO. I think the jest does very well as it

[1] Socrates was the son of a sculptor and was himself educated to be a sculptor. This is doubtless the reason for his reference to Daedalus as an ancestor. Daedalus was a half mythical personage whose statues were said to have been so lifelike that they moved their eyes and walked about.

σκώμματος, ὦ Σώκρατες, δεῖσθαι τὰ λεγόμενα·
D τὸ γὰρ περιιέναι τούτοις[1] τοῦτο καὶ μὴ μένειν ἐν
τῷ αὐτῷ οὐκ ἐγώ εἰμι ὁ ἐντιθείς, ἀλλὰ σύ μοι
δοκεῖς ὁ Δαίδαλος· ἐπεὶ ἐμοῦ γε ἕνεκα ἔμενεν ἂν
ταῦτα οὕτως.

ΣΩΚΡΑΤΗΣ. Κινδυνεύω ἄρα, ὦ ἑταῖρε, ἐκείνου
τοῦ ἀνδρὸς δεινότερος γεγονέναι τὴν τέχνην τοσούτῳ, ὅσῳ ὁ μὲν τὰ αὑτοῦ μόνα ἐποίει οὐ
μένοντα, ἐγὼ δὲ πρὸς τοῖς ἐμαυτοῦ, ὡς ἔοικε, καὶ
E τὰ ἀλλότρια. καὶ δῆτα τοῦτό μοι τῆς τέχνης
ἐστὶ κομψότατον, ὅτι ἄκων εἰμὶ σοφός. ἐβουλόμην γὰρ ἄν μοι τοὺς λόγους μένειν καὶ ἀκινήτως
ἱδρῦσθαι μᾶλλον ἢ πρὸς τῇ Δαιδάλου σοφίᾳ
τὰ Ταντάλου χρήματα γενέσθαι. καὶ τούτων
μὲν ἅδην· ἐπειδὴ δέ μοι δοκεῖς σὺ τρυφᾶν, αὐτός
σοι ξυμπροθυμήσομαι,[2] ὅπως ἄν με διδάξῃς περὶ
τοῦ ὁσίου. καὶ μὴ προαποκάμῃς. ἰδὲ γάρ, εἰ
οὐκ ἀναγκαῖόν σοι δοκεῖ δίκαιον εἶναι πᾶν τὸ
ὅσιον.

ΕΥΘΥΦΡΩΝ. Ἔμοιγε.

ΣΩΚΡΑΤΗΣ. Ἆρ' οὖν καὶ πᾶν τὸ δίκαιον ὅσιον,
12 ἢ τὸ μὲν ὅσιον πᾶν δίκαιον, τὸ δὲ δίκαιον οὐ πᾶν
ὅσιον, ἀλλὰ τὸ μὲν αὐτοῦ ὅσιον, τὸ δέ τι καὶ
ἄλλο;

ΕΥΘΥΦΡΩΝ. Οὐχ ἕπομαι, ὦ Σώκρατες, τοῖς
λεγομένοις.

ΣΩΚΡΑΤΗΣ. Καὶ μὴν νεώτερός γέ μου εἶ οὐκ
ἐλάττονι ἢ ὅσῳ σοφώτερος· ἀλλ', ὃ λέγω, τρυφᾷς
ὑπὸ πλούτου τῆς σοφίας. ἀλλ', ὦ μακάριε,

---

[1] τούτοις is bracketed by Schanz following Stallbaum.
[2] ξυμπροθυμήσομαι δεῖξαι the manuscripts. Schanz follows
Hermann in omitting δεῖξαι.

is ; for I am not the one who makes these statements move about and not stay in the same place, but you are the Daedalus ; for they would have stayed, so far as I am concerned.

socrates. Apparently then, my friend, I am a more clever artist than Daedalus, inasmuch as he made only his own works move, whereas I, as it seems, give motion to the works of others as well as to my own. And the most exquisite thing about my art is that I am clever against my will ; for I would rather have my words stay fixed and stable than possess the wisdom of Daedalus and the wealth of Tantalus besides. But enough of this. Since you seem to be indolent, I will aid you myself, so that you may instruct me about holiness. And do not give it up beforehand. Just see whether you do not think that everything that is holy is right.

euthyphro. I do.

socrates. But is everything that is right also holy ? Or is all which is holy right, and not all which is right holy, but part of it holy and part something else ?

euthyphro. I can't follow you, Socrates.

socrates. And yet you are as much younger than I as you are wiser ; but, as I said, you are indolent on account of your wealth of wisdom. But exert

ξύντεινε σαυτόν· καὶ γὰρ οὐδὲ χαλεπὸν κατανοῆσαι ὃ λέγω. λέγω γὰρ δὴ τὸ ἐναντίον ἢ ὁ
ποιητὴς ἐποίησεν ὁ ποιήσας·

   Ζῆνα δὲ τόν θ' ἔρξαντα, καὶ ὃς τάδε πάντ'
      ἐφύτευσεν,
B οὐκ ἐθέλεις εἰπεῖν· ἵνα γὰρ δέος, ἔνθα καὶ αἰδώς.

ἐγὼ οὖν τούτῳ διαφέρομαι τῷ ποιητῇ. εἴπω σοι
ὅπῃ;

ΕΥΘΥΦΡΩΝ. Πάνυ γε.

ΣΩΚΡΑΤΗΣ. Οὐ δοκεῖ μοι εἶναι, ἵνα δέος, ἔνθα
καὶ αἰδώς. πολλοὶ γάρ μοι δοκοῦσι καὶ νόσους
καὶ πενίας καὶ ἄλλα πολλὰ τοιαῦτα δεδιότες
δεδιέναι μέν, αἰδεῖσθαι δὲ μηδὲν ταῦτα ἃ δεδίασιν.
οὐ καὶ σοὶ δοκεῖ;

ΕΥΘΥΦΡΩΝ. Πάνυ γε.

ΣΩΚΡΑΤΗΣ. 'Αλλ' ἵνα γε αἰδώς, ἔνθα καὶ δέος
εἶναι· ἐπεὶ ἔστιν ὅστις αἰδούμενός τι πρᾶγμα καὶ
C αἰσχυνόμενος οὐ πεφόβηταί τε καὶ δέδοικεν ἅμα
δόξαν πονηρίας;

ΕΥΘΥΦΡΩΝ. Δέδοικε μὲν οὖν.

ΣΩΚΡΑΤΗΣ. Οὐκ ἄρ' ὀρθῶς ἔχει λέγειν· ἵνα γὰρ
δέος, ἔνθα καὶ αἰδώς· ἀλλ' ἵνα μὲν αἰδώς, ἔνθα καὶ
δέος, οὐ μέντοι ἵνα γε δέος, πανταχοῦ αἰδώς. ἐπὶ
πλέον γάρ, οἶμαι, δέος αἰδοῦς· μόριον γὰρ αἰδὼς
δέους, ὥσπερ ἀριθμοῦ περιττόν, ὥστε οὐχ ἵνα περ
ἀριθμός, ἔνθα καὶ περιττόν, ἵνα δὲ περιττόν, ἔνθα
καὶ ἀριθμός. ἔπει γάρ που νῦν γε;

ΕΥΘΥΦΡΩΝ. Πάνυ γε.

ΣΩΚΡΑΤΗΣ. Τὸ τοιοῦτον τοίνυν καὶ ἐκεῖ λέγων
ἠρώτων, ἆρα ἵνα δίκαιον, ἔνθα καὶ ὅσιον, ἢ ἵνα
D μὲν ὅσιον, ἔνθα καὶ δίκαιον, ἵνα δὲ δίκαιον, οὐ

44

yourself, my friend; for it is not hard to understand
what I mean. What I mean is the opposite of what
the poet[1] said, who wrote: "Zeus the creator, him
who made all things, thou wilt not name; for where
fear is, there also is reverence." Now I disagree
with the poet. Shall I tell you how?

EUTHYPHRO. By all means.

SOCRATES. It does not seem to me true that
where fear is, there also is reverence; for many
who fear diseases and poverty and other such things
seem to me to fear, but not to reverence at all these
things which they fear. Don't you think so, too?

EUTHYPHRO. Certainly.

SOCRATES. But I think that where reverence is,
there also is fear; for does not everyone who has a
feeling of reverence and shame about any act also
dread and fear the reputation for wickedness?

EUTHYPHRO. Yes, he does fear.

SOCRATES. Then it is not correct to say "where
fear is, there also is reverence." On the contrary,
where reverence is, there also is fear; but reverence
is not everywhere where fear is, since, as I think,
fear is more comprehensive than reverence; for
reverence is a part of fear, just as the odd is a
part of number, so that it is not true that where
number is, there also is the odd, but that where the
odd is, there also is number. Perhaps you follow
me now?

EUTHYPHRO. Perfectly.

SOCRATES. It was something of this sort that I
meant before, when I asked whether where the
right is, there also is holiness, or where holiness is,

[1] Stasinus, author of the "Cypria" (Fragm. 20, ed.
Kinkel).

PLATO

πανταχοῦ ὅσιον· μόριον γὰρ τοῦ δικαίου τὸ ὅσιον.
οὕτω φῶμεν ἢ ἄλλως σοι δοκεῖ;

ΕΥΘΥΦΡΩΝ. Οὔκ, ἀλλ᾽ οὕτω. φαίνει γάρ μοι
ὀρθῶς λέγειν.

14. ΣΩΚΡΑΤΗΣ. Ὅρα δὴ τὸ μετὰ τοῦτο. εἰ γὰρ
μέρος τὸ ὅσιον τοῦ δικαίου, δεῖ δὴ ἡμᾶς, ὡς ἔοικεν,
ἐξευρεῖν τὸ ποῖον μέρος ἂν εἴη τοῦ δικαίου τὸ
ὅσιον. εἰ μὲν οὖν σύ με ἠρώτας τι τῶν νῦν δή,
οἷον ποῖον μέρος ἐστὶν ἀριθμοῦ τὸ ἄρτιον καὶ τίς
ὢν τυγχάνει οὗτος ὁ ἀριθμός, εἶπον ἄν, ὅτι ὃς ἂν
μὴ σκαληνὸς ᾖ, ἀλλ᾽ ἰσοσκελής· ἢ οὐ δοκεῖ σοι;

ΕΥΘΥΦΡΩΝ. Ἔμοιγε.

Ε   ΣΩΚΡΑΤΗΣ. Πειρῶ δὴ καὶ σὺ ἐμὲ οὕτω διδάξαι,
τὸ ποῖον μέρος τοῦ δικαίου ὅσιόν ἐστιν, ἵνα καὶ
Μελήτῳ λέγωμεν μηκέθ᾽ ἡμᾶς ἀδικεῖν μηδὲ ἀσεβείας γράφεσθαι, ὡς ἱκανῶς ἤδη παρὰ σοῦ μεμα-
θηκότας τά τε εὐσεβῆ καὶ ὅσια καὶ τὰ μή.

ΕΥΘΥΦΡΩΝ. Τοῦτο τοίνυν ἔμοιγε δοκεῖ, ὦ Σώκρατες, τὸ μέρος τοῦ δικαίου εἶναι εὐσεβές τε καὶ
ὅσιον, τὸ περὶ τὴν τῶν θεῶν θεραπείαν· τὸ δὲ
περὶ τὴν τῶν ἀνθρώπων τὸ λοιπὸν εἶναι τοῦ
δικαίου μέρος.

15. ΣΩΚΡΑΤΗΣ. Καὶ καλῶς γέ μοι, ὦ Εὐθύ-
13 φρον, φαίνει λέγειν· ἀλλὰ σμικροῦ τινος ἔτι
ἐνδεής εἰμι. τὴν γὰρ θεραπείαν οὔπω ξυνίημι
ἥντινα ὀνομάζεις. οὐ γάρ που λέγεις γε, οἷαί περ
καὶ αἱ περὶ τὰ ἄλλα θεραπεῖαί εἰσιν, τοιαύτην
καὶ περὶ θεούς. λέγομεν γάρ που—οἷον φαμέν,
ἵππους οὐ πᾶς ἐπίσταται θεραπεύειν, ἀλλὰ ὁ
ἱππικός· ἢ γάρ;

there also is the right; but holiness is not everywhere where the right is, for holiness is a part of the right. Do we agree to this, or do you dissent?

EUTHYPHRO. No, I agree; for I think the statement is correct.

SOCRATES. Now observe the next point. If holiness is a part of the right, we must, apparently, find out what part of the right holiness is. Now if you asked me about one of the things I just mentioned, as, for example, what part of number the even was, and what kind of a number it was I should say, "that which is not indivisible by two, but divisible by two"; or don't you agree?

EUTHYPHRO. I agree.

SOCRATES. Now try in your turn to teach me what part of the right holiness is, that I may tell Meletus not to wrong me any more or bring suits against me for impiety, since I have now been duly instructed by you about what is, and what is not, pious and holy.

EUTHYPHRO. This then is my opinion, Socrates, that the part of the right which has to do with attention to the gods constitutes piety and holiness, and that the remaining part of the right is that which has to do with the service of men.

SOCRATES. I think you are correct, Euthyphro; but there is one little point about which I still want information, for I do not yet understand what you mean by "attention." I don't suppose you mean the same kind of attention to the gods which is paid to other things. We say, for example, that not everyone knows how to attend to horses, but only he who is skilled in horsemanship, do we not?

ΕΥΘΥΦΡΩΝ. Πάνυ γε.

ΣΩΚΡΑΤΗΣ. Ἡ γάρ που ἱππικὴ ἵππων θεραπεία.

ΕΥΘΥΦΡΩΝ. Ναί.

ΣΩΚΡΑΤΗΣ. Οὐδέ γε κύνας πᾶς ἐπίσταται θεραπεύειν, ἀλλὰ ὁ κυνηγετικός.

ΕΥΘΥΦΡΩΝ. Οὕτω.

ΣΩΚΡΑΤΗΣ. Ἡ γάρ που κυνηγετικὴ κυνῶν
θεραπεία.

B ΕΥΘΥΦΡΩΝ. Ναί.

ΣΩΚΡΑΤΗΣ. Ἡ δὲ βοηλατικὴ βοῶν.

ΕΥΘΥΦΡΩΝ. Πάνυ γε.

ΣΩΚΡΑΤΗΣ. Ἡ δὲ δὴ ὁσιότης τε καὶ εὐσέβεια
θεῶν, ὦ Εὐθύφρον; οὕτω λέγεις;

ΕΥΘΥΦΡΩΝ. Ἔγωγε.

ΣΩΚΡΑΤΗΣ. Οὐκοῦν θεραπεία γε πᾶσα ταὐτὸν
διαπράττεται; οἷον τοιόνδε· ἐπ᾽ ἀγαθῷ τινί ἐστι
καὶ ὠφελείᾳ τοῦ θεραπευομένου, ὥσπερ ὁρᾷς δή,
ὅτι οἱ ἵπποι ὑπὸ τῆς ἱππικῆς θεραπευόμενοι
ὠφελοῦνται καὶ βελτίους γίγνονται· ἢ οὐ δοκοῦσί σοι;

ΕΥΘΥΦΡΩΝ. Ἔμοιγε.

ΣΩΚΡΑΤΗΣ. Καὶ οἱ κύνες γέ που ὑπὸ τῆς κυνη-
C γετικῆς, καὶ οἱ βόες ὑπὸ τῆς βοηλατικῆς, καὶ
τἆλλα πάντα ὡσαύτως· ἢ ἐπὶ βλάβῃ οἴει τοῦ
θεραπευομένου τὴν θεραπείαν εἶναι;

ΕΥΘΥΦΡΩΝ. Μὰ Δί᾽ οὐκ ἔγωγε.

ΣΩΚΡΑΤΗΣ. Ἀλλ᾽ ἐπ᾽ ὠφελείᾳ;

ΕΥΘΥΦΡΩΝ. Πῶς δ᾽ οὔ;

ΣΩΚΡΑΤΗΣ. Ἡ οὖν καὶ ἡ ὁσιότης θεραπεία οὖσα
θεῶν ὠφελειά τέ ἐστι θεῶν καὶ βελτίους τοὺς θεοὺς

EUTHYPHRO

EUTHYPHRO. Certainly.

SOCRATES. Then horsemanship is the art of attending to horses?

EUTHYPHRO. Yes.

SOCRATES. And not everyone knows how to attend to dogs, but only the huntsman?

EUTHYPHRO. That is so.

SOCRATES. Then the huntsman's art is the art of attending to dogs?

EUTHYPHRO. Yes.

SOCRATES. And the oxherd's art is that of attending to oxen?

EUTHYPHRO. Certainly.

SOCRATES. And holiness and piety is the art of attending to the gods? Is that what you mean, Euthyphro?

EUTHYPHRO. Yes.

SOCRATES. Now does attention always aim to accomplish the same end? I mean something like this: It aims at some good or benefit to the one to whom it is given, as you see that horses, when attended to by the horseman's art are benefited and made better; or don't you think so?

EUTHYPHRO. Yes, I do.

SOCRATES. And dogs are benefited by the huntsman's art and oxen by the oxherd's and everything else in the same way? Or do you think care and attention are ever meant for the injury of that which is cared for?

EUTHYPHRO. No, by Zeus, I do not.

SOCRATES. But for its benefit?

EUTHYPHRO. Of course.

SOCRATES. Then holiness, since it is the art of attending to the gods, is a benefit to the gods, and

49

ποιεῖ; καὶ σὺ τοῦτο ξυγχωρήσαις ἄν, ὡς ἐπειδάν τι ὅσιον ποιῇς, βελτίω τινὰ τῶν θεῶν ἀπεργάζει;

ΕΥΘΥΦΡΩΝ.   Μὰ Δί᾽ οὐκ ἔγωγε.

ΣΩΚΡΑΤΗΣ.   Οὐδὲ γὰρ ἐγώ, ὦ Εὐθύφρον, οἶμαί σε τοῦτο λέγειν· πολλοῦ καὶ δέω· ἀλλὰ τούτου δὴ
D ἕνεκα καὶ ἀνηρόμην, τίνα ποτὲ λέγοις τὴν θεραπείαν τῶν θεῶν, οὐχ ἡγούμενός σε τοιαύτην λέγειν.

ΕΥΘΥΦΡΩΝ.   Καὶ ὀρθῶς γε, ὦ Σώκρατες· οὐ γὰρ τοιαύτην λέγω.

ΣΩΚΡΑΤΗΣ.   Εἶεν· ἀλλὰ τίς δὴ θεῶν θεραπεία εἴη ἂν ἡ ὁσιότης;

ΕΥΘΥΦΡΩΝ.   Ἥπερ, ὦ Σώκρατες, οἱ δοῦλοι τοὺς δεσπότας θεραπεύουσιν.

ΣΩΚΡΑΤΗΣ.   Μανθάνω· ὑπηρετική τις ἄν, ὡς ἔοικεν, εἴη θεοῖς.

ΕΥΘΥΦΡΩΝ.   Πάνυ μὲν οὖν.

16.   ΣΩΚΡΑΤΗΣ.   Ἔχεις οὖν εἰπεῖν, ἡ ἰατροῖς ὑπηρετικὴ εἰς τίνος ἔργου ἀπεργασίαν τυγχάνει οὖσα ὑπηρετική; οὐκ εἰς ὑγιείας οἴει;

ΕΥΘΥΦΡΩΝ.   Ἔγωγε.

ΣΩΚΡΑΤΗΣ.   Τί δέ; ἡ ναυπηγοῖς ὑπηρετικὴ εἰς
E τίνος ἔργου ἀπεργασίαν ὑπηρετική ἐστιν;

ΕΥΘΥΦΡΩΝ.   Δῆλον ὅτι, ὦ Σώκρατες, εἰς πλοίου.

ΣΩΚΡΑΤΗΣ.   Καὶ ἡ οἰκοδόμοις γέ που εἰς οἰκίας;

ΕΥΘΥΦΡΩΝ.   Ναί.

ΣΩΚΡΑΤΗΣ.   Εἰπὲ δή, ὦ ἄριστε· ἡ δὲ θεοῖς ὑπηρετικὴ εἰς τίνος ἔργου ἀπεργασίαν ὑπηρετικὴ ἂν εἴη; δῆλον γὰρ ὅτι σὺ οἶσθα, ἐπειδήπερ τά γε θεῖα κάλλιστά γε φὴς εἰδέναι ἀνθρώπων.

ΕΥΘΥΦΡΩΝ.   Καὶ ἀληθῆ γε λέγω, ὦ Σώκρατες.

ΣΩΚΡΑΤΗΣ.   Εἰπὲ δὴ πρὸς Διός, τί ποτέ ἐστιν

makes them better? And you would agree that when you do a holy or pious act you are making one of the gods better?

EUTHYPHRO. No, by Zeus, not I.

SOCRATES. Nor do I, Euthyphro, think that is what you meant. Far from it. But I asked what you meant by "attention to the gods" just because I did not think you meant anything like that.

EUTHYPHRO. You are right, Socrates; that is not what I mean.

SOCRATES. Well, what kind of attention to the gods is holiness?

EUTHYPHRO. The kind, Socrates, that servants pay to their masters.

SOCRATES. I understand. It is, you mean, a kind of service to the gods?

EUTHYPHRO. Exactly.

SOCRATES. Now can you tell me what result the art that serves the physician serves to produce? Is it not health?

EUTHYPHRO. Yes.

SOCRATES. Well then; what is it which the art that serves shipbuilders serves to produce?

EUTHYPHRO. Evidently, Socrates, a ship.

SOCRATES. And that which serves housebuilders serves to build a house?

EUTHYPHRO. Yes.

SOCRATES. Then tell me, my friend; what would the art which serves the gods serve to accomplish? For it is evident that you know, since you say you know more than any other man about matters which have to do with the gods.

EUTHYPHRO. And what I say is true, Socrates.

SOCRATES. Then, in the name of Zeus, tell me,

ἐκεῖνο τὸ πάγκαλον ἔργον, ὃ οἱ θεοὶ ἀπεργάζονται
ἡμῖν ὑπηρέταις χρώμενοι;

ΕΥΘΥΦΡΩΝ.   Πολλὰ καὶ καλά, ὦ Σώκρατες.

14   ΣΩΚΡΑΤΗΣ.   Καὶ γὰρ οἱ στρατηγοί, ὦ φίλε· ἀλλ᾽
ὅμως τὸ κεφάλαιον αὐτῶν ῥᾳδίως ἂν εἴποις, ὅτι
νίκην ἐν τῷ πολέμῳ ἀπεργάζονται· ἢ οὔ;

ΕΥΘΥΦΡΩΝ.   Πῶς δ᾽ οὔ;

ΣΩΚΡΑΤΗΣ.   Πολλὰ δέ γ᾽, οἶμαι, καὶ καλὰ καὶ οἱ
γεωργοί· ἀλλ᾽ ὅμως τὸ κεφάλαιον αὐτῶν ἐστιν
τῆς ἀπεργασίας ἡ ἐκ τῆς γῆς τροφή.

ΕΥΘΥΦΡΩΝ.   Πάνυ γε.

ΣΩΚΡΑΤΗΣ.   Τί δὲ δή; τῶν πολλῶν καὶ καλῶν, ἃ
οἱ θεοὶ ἀπεργάζονται, τί τὸ κεφάλαιόν ἐστι τῆς
ἐργασίας;

ΕΥΘΥΦΡΩΝ.   Καὶ ὀλίγον σοι πρότερον εἶπον, ὦ
B Σώκρατες, ὅτι πλείονος ἔργου ἐστὶν ἀκριβῶς πάντα
ταῦτα ὡς ἔχει μαθεῖν· τόδε μέντοι σοι ἁπλῶς λέγω,
ὅτι ἐὰν μὲν κεχαρισμένα τις ἐπίστηται τοῖς θεοῖς
λέγειν τε καὶ πράττειν εὐχόμενός τε καὶ θύων,
ταῦτ᾽ ἔστι τὰ ὅσια, καὶ σῴζει τὰ τοιαῦτα τούς
τε ἰδίους οἴκους καὶ τὰ κοινὰ τῶν πόλεων· τὰ δ᾽
ἐναντία τῶν κεχαρισμένων ἀσεβῆ, ἃ δὴ καὶ
ἀνατρέπει ἅπαντα καὶ ἀπόλλυσιν.

17. ΣΩΚΡΑΤΗΣ.   Ἦ πολύ μοι διὰ βραχυτέρων, ὦ
Εὐθύφρον, εἰ ἐβούλου, εἶπες ἂν τὸ κεφάλαιον ὧν
ἠρώτων.   ἀλλὰ γὰρ οὐ πρόθυμός με εἶ διδάξαι·
C δῆλος εἶ.   καὶ γὰρ νῦν ἐπειδὴ ἐπ᾽ αὐτῷ ἦσθα,
ἀπετράπου· ὃ εἰ ἀπεκρίνω, ἱκανῶς ἂν ἤδη παρὰ
σοῦ τὴν ὁσιότητα ἐμεμαθήκη.   νῦν δέ—ἀνάγκη
γὰρ τὸν ἐρῶντα τῷ ἐρωμένῳ ἀκολουθεῖν, ὅπῃ ἂν
ἐκεῖνος ὑπάγῃ· τί δὴ αὖ λέγεις τὸ ὅσιον εἶναι καὶ

what is that glorious result which the gods accomplish by using us as servants?

EUTHYPHRO. They accomplish many fine results, Socrates.

SOCRATES. Yes, and so do generals, my friend; but nevertheless, you could easily tell the chief of them, namely, that they bring about victory in war. Is that not the case?

EUTHYPHRO. Of course.

SOCRATES. And farmers also, I think, accomplish many fine results; but still the chief result of their work is food from the land?

EUTHYPHRO. Certainly.

SOCRATES. But how about the many fine results the gods accomplish? What is the chief result of their work?

EUTHYPHRO. I told you a while ago, Socrates, that it is a long task to learn accurately all about these things. However, I say simply that when one knows how to say and do what is gratifying to the gods, in praying and sacrificing, that is holiness, and such things bring salvation to individual families and to states; and the opposite of what is gratifying to the gods is impious, and that overturns and destroys everything.

SOCRATES. You might, if you wished, Euthyphro have answered much more briefly the chief part of my question. But it is plain that you do not care to instruct me. For now, when you were close upon it you turned aside; and if you had answered it, I should already have obtained from you all the instruction I need about holiness. But, as things are, the questioner must follow the one questioned wherever he leads. What do you say the holy, or

τὴν ὁσιότητα; οὐχὶ ἐπιστήμην τινὰ τοῦ θύειν τε
καὶ εὔχεσθαι;

ΕΥΘΥΦΡΩΝ. Ἔγωγε.

ΣΩΚΡΑΤΗΣ. Οὐκοῦν τὸ θύειν δωρεῖσθαί ἐστι τοῖς
D θεοῖς, τὸ δ᾽ εὔχεσθαι αἰτεῖν τοὺς θεούς;

ΕΥΘΥΦΡΩΝ. Καὶ μάλα, ὦ Σώκρατες.

ΣΩΚΡΑΤΗΣ. Ἐπιστήμη ἄρα αἰτήσεως καὶ δόσεως
θεοῖς ὁσιότης ἂν εἴη ἐκ τούτου τοῦ λόγου.

ΕΥΘΥΦΡΩΝ. Πάνυ καλῶς, ὦ Σώκρατες, ξυνῆκας ὃ
εἶπον.

ΣΩΚΡΑΤΗΣ. Ἐπιθυμητὴς γάρ εἰμι, ὦ φίλε, τῆς
σῆς σοφίας καὶ προσέχω τὸν νοῦν αὐτῇ, ὥστε οὐ
χαμαὶ πεσεῖται ὅ τι ἂν εἴπῃς. ἀλλά μοι λέξον, τίς
αὕτη ἡ ὑπηρεσία ἐστὶ τοῖς θεοῖς; αἰτεῖν τε φῂς
αὐτοὺς καὶ διδόναι ἐκείνοις;

ΕΥΘΥΦΡΩΝ. Ἔγωγε.

18. ΣΩΚΡΑΤΗΣ. Ἆρ᾽ οὖν οὐ τὸ ὀρθῶς αἰτεῖν ἂν
εἴη, ὧν δεόμεθα παρ᾽ ἐκείνων, ταῦτα αὐτοὺς αἰτεῖν;

ΕΥΘΥΦΡΩΝ. Ἀλλὰ τί;

ΣΩΚΡΑΤΗΣ. Καὶ αὖ τὸ διδόναι ὀρθῶς, ὧν ἐκεῖνοι
E τυγχάνουσιν δεόμενοι παρ᾽ ἡμῶν, ταῦτα ἐκείνοις
αὖ ἀντιδωρεῖσθαι; οὐ γάρ που τεχνικόν γ᾽ ἂν
εἴη δωροφορεῖν διδόντα τῳ ταῦτα ὧν οὐδὲν δεῖται.

ΕΥΘΥΦΡΩΝ. Ἀληθῆ λέγεις, ὦ Σώκρατες.

ΣΩΚΡΑΤΗΣ. Ἐμπορικὴ ἄρα τις ἂν εἴη, ὦ Εὐθύφρον, τέχνη ἡ ὁσιότης θεοῖς καὶ ἀνθρώποις παρ᾽
ἀλλήλων.

ΕΥΘΥΦΡΩΝ. Ἐμπορική, εἰ οὕτως ἥδιόν σοι ὀνομάζειν.

ΣΩΚΡΑΤΗΣ. Ἀλλ᾽ οὐδὲν ἥδιον ἔμοιγε, εἰ μὴ τυγχάνει ἀληθὲς ὄν. φράσον δέ μοι, τίς ἡ ὠφέλεια
τοῖς θεοῖς τυγχάνει οὖσα ἀπὸ τῶν δώρων ὧν παρ᾽

holiness, is? Do you not say that it is a kind of science of sacrificing and praying?

EUTHYPHRO. Yes.

SOCRATES. And sacrificing is making gifts to the gods and praying is asking from them?

EUTHYPHRO. Exactly, Socrates.

SOCRATES. Then holiness, according to this definition, would be a science of giving and asking.

EUTHYPHRO. You understand perfectly what I said, Socrates.

SOCRATES. Yes, my friend, for I am eager for your wisdom, and give my mind to it, so that nothing you say shall fall to the ground. But tell me, what is this service of the gods? Do you say that it consists in asking from them and giving to them?

EUTHYPHRO. Yes.

SOCRATES. Would not the right way of asking be to ask of them what we need from them?

EUTHYPHRO. What else?

SOCRATES. And the right way of giving, to present them with what they need from us? For it would not be scientific giving to give anyone what he does not need.

EUTHYPHRO. You are right, Socrates.

SOCRATES. Then holiness would be an art of barter between gods and men?

EUTHYPHRO. Yes, of barter, if you like to call it so.

SOCRATES. I don't like to call it so, if it is not true. But tell me, what advantage accrues to the gods from

ἡμῶν λαμβάνουσιν; ἃ μὲν γὰρ διδόασι, παντὶ
15 δῆλον· οὐδὲν γὰρ ἡμῖν ἐστιν ἀγαθόν, ὅ τι ἂν μὴ
ἐκεῖνοι δῶσιν· ἃ δὲ παρ᾽ ἡμῶν λαμβάνουσιν, τί
ὠφελοῦνται; ἢ τοσοῦτον αὐτῶν πλεονεκτοῦμεν
κατὰ τὴν ἐμπορίαν, ὥστε πάντα τἀγαθὰ παρ᾽
αὐτῶν λαμβάνομεν, ἐκεῖνοι δὲ παρ᾽ ἡμῶν οὐδέν;

ΕΥΘΥΦΡΩΝ. Ἀλλ᾽ οἴει, ὦ Σώκρατες, τοὺς θεοὺς
ὠφελεῖσθαι ἀπὸ τούτων, ἃ παρ᾽ ἡμῶν λαμβάνουσιν;

ΣΩΚΡΑΤΗΣ. Ἀλλὰ τί δήποτ᾽ ἂν εἴη ταῦτα, ὦ
Εὐθύφρον, τὰ παρ᾽ ἡμῶν δῶρα τοῖς θεοῖς;

ΕΥΘΥΦΡΩΝ. Τί δ᾽ οἴει ἄλλο ἢ τιμή τε καὶ γέρα
καί, ὅπερ ἐγὼ ἄρτι ἔλεγον, χάρις;

B ΣΩΚΡΑΤΗΣ. Κεχαρισμένον ἄρα ἐστίν, ὦ Εὐθύφρον, τὸ ὅσιον, ἀλλ᾽ οὐχὶ ὠφέλιμον οὐδὲ φίλον
τοῖς θεοῖς;

ΕΥΘΥΦΡΩΝ. Οἶμαι ἔγωγε πάντων γε μάλιστα
φίλον.

ΣΩΚΡΑΤΗΣ. Τοῦτο ἄρ᾽ ἐστὶν αὖ, ὡς ἔοικε, τὸ
ὅσιον, τὸ τοῖς θεοῖς φίλον.

ΕΥΘΥΦΡΩΝ. Μάλιστά γε.

19. ΣΩΚΡΑΤΗΣ. Θαυμάσει οὖν ταῦτα λέγων, ἐάν
σοι οἱ λόγοι φαίνωνται μὴ μένοντες ἀλλὰ βαδίζοντες,
καὶ ἐμὲ αἰτιάσει τὸν Δαίδαλον βαδίζοντας αὐτοὺς
ποιεῖν, αὐτὸς ὢν πολύ γε τεχνικώτερος τοῦ Δαιδάλου καὶ κύκλῳ περιιόντα ποιῶν; ἢ οὐκ αἰ-
C σθάνει, ὅτι ὁ λόγος ἡμῖν περιελθὼν πάλιν εἰς
ταὐτὸν ἥκει; μέμνησαι γάρ που, ὅτι ἐν τῷ ἔμπροσθεν τό τε ὅσιον καὶ τὸ θεοφιλὲς οὐ ταὐτὸν
ἡμῖν ἐφάνη, ἀλλ᾽ ἕτερα ἀλλήλων· ἢ οὐ μέμνησαι;

ΕΥΘΥΦΡΩΝ. Ἔγωγε.

ΣΩΚΡΑΤΗΣ. Νῦν οὖν οὐκ ἐννοεῖς, ὅτι τὸ τοῖς

the gifts they get from us? For everybody knows what they give, since we have nothing good which they do not give. But what advantage do they derive from what they get from us? Or have we so much the better of them in our bartering that we get all good things from them and they nothing from us?

EUTHYPHRO. Why you don't suppose, Socrates, that the gods gain any advantage from what they get from us, do you?

SOCRATES. Well then, what would those gifts of ours to the gods be?

EUTHYPHRO. What else than honour and praise, and, as I said before, gratitude?

SOCRATES. Then, Euthyphro, holiness is grateful to the gods, but not advantageous or precious to the gods?

EUTHYPHRO. I think it is precious, above all things.

SOCRATES. Then again, it seems, holiness is that which is precious to the gods.

EUTHYPHRO. Certainly.

SOCRATES. Then will you be surprised, since you say this, if your words do not remain fixed but walk about, and will you accuse me of being the Daedalus who makes them walk, when you are yourself much more skilful than Daedalus and make them go round in a circle? Or do you not see that our definition has come round to the point from which it started? For you remember, I suppose, that a while ago we found that holiness and what is dear to the gods were not the same, but different from each other; or do you not remember?

EUTHYPHRO. Yes, I remember.

SOCRATES. Then don't you see that now you say

θεοῖς φίλον φῂς ὅσιον εἶναι; τοῦτο δ᾽ ἄλλο τι ἢ θεοφιλὲς γίγνεται ἢ οὔ;

ΕΥΘΥΦΡΩΝ. ˙ Πάνυ γε.

ΣΩΚΡΑΤΗΣ. Οὐκοῦν ἢ ἄρτι οὐ καλῶς ὡμολογοῦμεν, ἢ εἰ τότε καλῶς, νῦν οὐκ ὀρθῶς τιθέμεθα.

ΕΥΘΥΦΡΩΝ. Ἔοικεν.

20. ΣΩΚΡΑΤΗΣ. Ἐξ ἀρχῆς ἄρα ἡμῖν πάλιν σκεπτέον, τί ἐστι τὸ ὅσιον· ὡς ἐγώ, πρὶν ἂν μάθω, ἑκὼν
D εἶναι οὐκ ἀποδειλιάσω. ἀλλὰ μή με ἀτιμάσῃς, ἀλλὰ παντὶ τρόπῳ προσέχων τὸν νοῦν ὅ τι μάλιστα νῦν εἰπὲ τὴν ἀλήθειαν. οἶσθα γάρ, εἴπερ τις ἄλλος ἀνθρώπων, καὶ οὐκ ἀφετέος εἶ, ὥσπερ ὁ Πρωτεύς, πρὶν ἂν εἴπῃς. εἰ γὰρ μὴ ᾔδησθα σαφῶς τό τε ὅσιον καὶ τὸ ἀνόσιον, οὐκ ἔστιν ὅπως ἄν ποτε ἐπεχείρησας ὑπὲρ ἀνδρὸς θητὸς ἄνδρα πρεσβύτην πατέρα διωκάθειν φόνου, ἀλλὰ καὶ τοὺς θεοὺς ἂν ἔδεισας παρακινδυνεύειν, μὴ οὐκ ὀρθῶς αὐτὸ ποιήσοις, καὶ τοὺς ἀνθρώπους ᾐσχύνθης. νῦν δὲ
E εὖ οἶδα ὅτι σαφῶς οἴει εἰδέναι τό τε ὅσιον καὶ μή· εἰπὲ οὖν, ὦ βέλτιστε Εὐθύφρον, καὶ μὴ ἀποκρύψῃ ὅ τι αὐτὸ ἡγεῖ.

ΕΥΘΥΦΡΩΝ. Εἰς αὖθις τοίνυν, ὦ Σώκρατες· νῦν γὰρ σπεύδω ποι, καί μοι ὥρα ἀπιέναι.

ΣΩΚΡΑΤΗΣ. Οἷα ποιεῖς, ὦ ἑταῖρε! ἀπ᾽ ἐλπίδος με καταβαλὼν μεγάλης ἀπέρχει, ἣν εἶχον, ὡς παρὰ σοῦ μαθὼν τά τε ὅσια καὶ μὴ καὶ τῆς πρὸς Μέλητον γραφῆς ἀπαλλάξομαι, ἐνδειξάμενος
16 ἐκείνῳ ὅτι σοφὸς ἤδη παρ᾽ Εὐθύφρονος τὰ θεῖα γέγονα καὶ ὅτι οὐκέτι ὑπ᾽ ἀγνοίας αὐτοσχεδιάζω οὐδὲ καινοτομῶ περὶ αὐτά, καὶ δὴ καὶ τὸν ἄλλον βίον ἄμεινον βιωσοίμην.

that what is precious to the gods is holy? And is not this what is dear to the gods?

EUTHYPHRO. Certainly.

SOCRATES. Then either our agreement a while ago was wrong, or if that was right, we are wrong now.

EUTHYPHRO. So it seems.

SOCRATES. Then we must begin again at the beginning and ask what holiness is. Since I shall not willingly give up until I learn. And do not scorn me, but by all means apply your mind now to the utmost and tell me the truth; for you know, if any one does, and like Proteus, you must be held until you speak. For if you had not clear knowledge of holiness and unholiness, you would surely not have undertaken to prosecute your aged father for murder for the sake of a servant. You would have been afraid to risk the anger of the gods, in case your conduct should be wrong, and would have been ashamed in the sight of men. But now I am sure you think you know what is holy and what is not. So tell me, most excellent Euthyphro, and do not conceal your thought.

EUTHYPHRO. Some other time, Socrates. Now I am in a hurry and it is time for me to go.

SOCRATES. Oh my friend, what are you doing? You go away and leave me cast down from the high hope I had that I should learn from you what is holy, and what is not, and should get rid of Meletus's indictment by showing him that I have been made wise by Euthyphro about divine matters and am no longer through ignorance acting carelessly and making innovations in respect to them, and that I shall live a better life henceforth.

THE APOLOGY

INTRODUCTION TO THE *APOLOGY*

In the spring of 399 B.C., when Socrates was seventy years old, he was accused of impiety and of corrupting the youth. The chief accuser was Meletus, who was seconded by Anytus and Lyco. In the *Euthyphro* Meletus is spoken of as an insignificant youth, and in the *Apology* he is said to have been incensed by Socrates' criticism of the poets. Nothing further is known of him, though he may be identical with the Meletus mentioned in the *Frogs* (1302) of Aristophanes as a poet of *Skolia*. The statement of Diodorus Siculus (XIV, 37), that the Athenians, overcome by repentance for their injustice to Socrates, put Meletus and Anytus to death, deserves no credence. Anytus, who is one of the characters in the *Meno*, was a man of substance, who had served as general of the Athenian armies and had recently been active in expelling the Thirty Tyrants. He was a bitter enemy of all the sophists, and, according to the author of the *Apology* attributed to Xenophon, he had been irritated by Socrates' criticism of his conduct in employing his son in his tannery, when the young man was fitted for higher things. Lyco was charged by the comic poet Eupolis with being of foreign descent, and the comic poet Cratinus refers to his poverty and effeminacy, though Aristophanes (*Wasps*, 1301) mentions him among

aristocrats. He seems to have been a person of no great importance.

Cases involving religion came under the jurisdiction of the King Archon, to whom Meletus submitted his indictment of Socrates (see the beginning of the *Euthyphro*), and such cases, like others, were tried before the heliastic court, which consisted altogether of six thousand citizens chosen by lot, six hundred from each of the ten tribes. The court did not however, usually sit as a whole, but was divided, so that cases were tried before smaller bodies, consisting generally of five hundred jurymen or judges, though sometimes the number was less, as four hundred or two hundred, and sometimes more, as one thousand. One additional judge was added to these even numbers to avoid a tie. Socrates was tried before a court of 501 (*Apology*, 36 A). If the accuser did not receive a fifth part of the votes cast in a case of this kind, he was subject to a fine of 1000 drachmae (about £35 or $175). No penalty was prescribed by law for the offence with which Socrates was charged. After Socrates was found guilty the penalty still remained to be determined. The rule was that the accused, after conviction, should propose a counter penalty, the court being obliged to choose one of the two penalties proposed (*Apology*, 36 B–38 B); no compromise was permitted.

The question has frequently been asked, whether the *Apology* is substantially the speech made by Socrates before the court or a product of Plato's imagination. In all probability it is essentially the speech delivered by Socrates, though it may well be that the actual speech was less finished and less charming than that which Plato has reported. The

legal procedure is strictly followed, and the manner
of speech is that which was, as we know from Plato
and also from Xenophon, usual with Socrates. There
is nothing inconsistent with what we know of Socrates,
and no peculiarly Platonic doctrine is suggested.
The purpose of the dialogue, or rather, of the speech,
for it is hardly a dialogue, is to present Socrates in a
true and favourable light to posterity, and that end
could hardly be gained by publishing a fiction as the
speech which many Athenians must have remembered
at the time of publication, which was, in all probability, not long after the trial.

In form the *Apology*, if we disregard the two
short addresses after the conviction and the condemnation, follows the rules in vogue for public speeches.
A brief introduction is followed by the narrative and
argument, after which the speech closes with a
brief appeal to the judges and to God (36 D). It
conforms to Plato's own rule (*Phaedrus* 264 c), that
every discourse should, like a living being, have its
middle parts and its members, all in proper agreement with each other and with the whole, which is,
after all, the rule of common sense, followed for the
most part even by those teachers of rhetoric whose
elaborate subdivisions and high-sounding nomenclature Plato ridicules in the *Phaedrus* (266 E–267 D).
The two shorter addresses after the case had been
decided against Socrates cannot be expected to stand
as independent and complete speeches; they are,
and must be, treated as supplementary and subordinate to the speech delivered before the first
adverse vote. Yet they are symmetrically arranged
and their topics are skilfully presented. A perora-
tion would hardly be appropriate before the last of

these and the last itself needs no formal introduction; it serves as a fitting conclusion for the entire discourse. As such it is a brilliant example of oratorical composition.

The high moral character and genuine religious faith of Socrates are made abundantly clear throughout this whole discourse. It would seem almost incredible that the Athenian court voted for his condemnation, if we did not know the fact. His condemnation is to be explained by the general hostility to the sophists. Socrates was, to be sure, not a sophist, though Aristophanes in the *Clouds* selects him as the representative of that profession to be ridiculed. He did not teach for pay and did not promise any definite result from his instruction. He did not investigate natural phenomena or claim to ensure the political or financial success of his hearers; his aim was to show the way to righteousness, to the perfection of the individual soul. This seems harmless enough, but Socrates endeavoured to lead men to righteousness by making them think, and thinking, especially on matters of religion, is not welcomed by the slothful or the conservative. The mere fact that he was a leader of thought caused Socrates to be confounded with the sophists who were also leaders of thought, and were, chiefly, perhaps, for that reason, regarded with suspicion and hostility. Moreover, Socrates claimed to possess a *daimonion*, or spiritual monitor, which guided his actions. He did not, so far as we know, attribute a distinct personality to this inner voice, but his belief in it caused him to be accused of introducing " new spiritual beings " or divinities and of disbelieving in the gods of the state, although he was apparently punctilious in religious observances.

His method had also, without doubt, aroused many personal antagonisms (*Apology* 21 c–23 A). Probably Meletus and the judges who voted for the condemnation of Socrates believed that they were acting in the interest of religion and piety, though their verdict has not been approved by later generations.

Editions of the *Apology* are very numerous. One of the best is that of Cron (*Apology* and *Crito*), upon which the excellent edition of Dyer is based (revised, 1908, by Seymour). Another good edition is that of J. Adam.

ΑΠΟΛΟΓΙΑ ΣΩΚΡΑΤΟΥΣ

[ΗΘΙΚΟΣ]

A 1. Ὅ τι μὲν ὑμεῖς, ὦ ἄνδρες Ἀθηναῖοι, πεπόν-
θατε ὑπὸ τῶν ἐμῶν κατηγόρων, οὐκ οἶδα· ἐγὼ δ᾽
οὖν καὶ αὐτὸς ὑπ᾽ αὐτῶν ὀλίγου ἐμαυτοῦ ἐπελαθό-
μην· οὕτω πιθανῶς ἔλεγον. καίτοι ἀληθές γε, ὡς
ἔπος εἰπεῖν, οὐδὲν εἰρήκασιν. μάλιστα δὲ αὐτῶν
ἓν ἐθαύμασα τῶν πολλῶν ὧν ἐψεύσαντο, τοῦτο, ἐν
ᾧ ἔλεγον ὡς χρὴ ὑμᾶς εὐλαβεῖσθαι, μὴ ὑπ᾽ ἐμοῦ
B ἐξαπατηθῆτε, ὡς δεινοῦ ὄντος λέγειν. τὸ γὰρ μὴ
αἰσχυνθῆναι, ὅτι αὐτίκα ὑπ᾽ ἐμοῦ ἐξελεγχθήσονται
ἔργῳ, ἐπειδὰν μηδ᾽ ὁπωστιοῦν φαίνωμαι δεινὸς
λέγειν, τοῦτό μοι ἔδοξεν αὐτῶν ἀναισχυντότατον
εἶναι, εἰ μὴ ἄρα δεινὸν καλοῦσιν οὗτοι λέγειν τὸν
τἀληθῆ λέγοντα· εἰ μὲν γὰρ τοῦτο λέγουσιν,
ὁμολογοίην ἂν ἔγωγε οὐ κατὰ τούτους εἶναι ῥήτωρ.
οὗτοι μὲν οὖν, ὥσπερ ἐγὼ λέγω, ἤ τι ἢ οὐδὲν
ἀληθὲς εἰρήκασιν· ὑμεῖς δ᾽ ἐμοῦ ἀκούσεσθε πᾶσαν
τὴν ἀλήθειαν. οὐ μέντοι μὰ Δία, ὦ ἄνδρες Ἀθηναῖοι, κεκαλλιεπημένους γε λόγους, ὥσπερ οἱ
C τούτων, ῥήμασί τε καὶ ὀνόμασιν, οὐδὲ κεκοσμη-
μένους, ἀλλὰ ἀκούσεσθε εἰκῇ λεγόμενα τοῖς
ἐπιτυχοῦσιν ὀνόμασιν· πιστεύω γὰρ δίκαια εἶναι
ἃ λέγω, καὶ μηδεὶς ὑμῶν προσδοκησάτω ἄλλως·

68

THE DEFENCE OF SOCRATES
AT HIS TRIAL

[ETHICAL]

How you, men of Athens, have been affected by my accusers, I do not know; but I, for my part, almost forgot my own identity, so persuasively did they talk; and yet there is hardly a word of truth in what they have said. But I was most amazed by one of the many lies that they told—when they said that you must be on your guard not to be deceived by me, because I was a clever speaker. For I thought it the most shameless part of their conduct that they are not ashamed because they will immediately be convicted by me of falsehood by the evidence of fact, when I show myself to be not in the least a clever speaker, unless indeed they call him a clever speaker who speaks the truth; for if this is what they mean, I would agree that I am an orator—not after their fashion. Now they, as I say, have said little or nothing true; but you shall hear from me nothing but the truth. Not, however, men of Athens, speeches finely tricked out with words and phrases, as theirs are, nor carefully arranged, but you will hear things said at random with the words that happen to occur to me. For I trust that what I say is just; and let none of you expect anything else.

οὐδὲ γὰρ ἂν δήπου πρέποι, ὦ ἄνδρες, τῇδε τῇ
ἡλικίᾳ ὥσπερ μειρακίῳ πλάττοντι λόγους εἰς
ὑμᾶς εἰσιέναι. καὶ μέντοι καὶ πάνυ, ὦ ἄνδρες
Ἀθηναῖοι, τοῦτο ὑμῶν δέομαι καὶ παρίεμαι· ἐὰν
διὰ τῶν αὐτῶν λόγων ἀκούητέ μου ἀπολογουμένου,
δι᾽ ὧνπερ εἴωθα λέγειν καὶ ἐν ἀγορᾷ ἐπὶ τῶν
τραπεζῶν, ἵνα ὑμῶν πολλοὶ ἀκηκόασι, καὶ ἄλλοθι,
D μήτε θαυμάζειν μήτε θορυβεῖν τούτου ἕνεκα. ἔχει
γὰρ οὑτωσί. νῦν ἐγὼ πρῶτον ἐπὶ δικαστήριον
ἀναβέβηκα, ἔτη γεγονὼς ἑβδομήκοντα· ἀτεχνῶς
οὖν ξένως ἔχω τῆς ἐνθάδε λέξεως. ὥσπερ οὖν ἄν,
εἰ τῷ ὄντι ξένος ἐτύγχανον ὤν, ξυνεγιγνώσκετε
δήπου ἄν μοι, εἰ ἐν ἐκείνῃ τῇ φωνῇ τε καὶ τῷ
18 τρόπῳ ἔλεγον, ἐν οἷσπερ ἐτεθράμμην, καὶ δὴ καὶ
νῦν τοῦτο ὑμῶν δέομαι δίκαιον, ὥς γέ μοι δοκῶ,
τὸν μὲν τρόπον τῆς λέξεως ἐᾶν· ἴσως μὲν γὰρ
χείρων, ἴσως δὲ βελτίων ἂν εἴη· αὐτὸ δὲ τοῦτο
σκοπεῖν καὶ τούτῳ τὸν νοῦν προσέχειν, εἰ δίκαια
λέγω ἢ μή· δικαστοῦ μὲν γὰρ αὕτη ἀρετή, ῥήτορος
δὲ τἀληθῆ λέγειν.

2. Πρῶτον μὲν οὖν δίκαιός εἰμι ἀπολογήσασθαι, ὦ ἄνδρες Ἀθηναῖοι, πρὸς τὰ πρῶτά μου
ψευδῆ[1] κατηγορημένα καὶ τοὺς πρώτους κατηγόρους, ἔπειτα δὲ πρὸς τὰ ὕστερα καὶ τοὺς
B ὑστέρους. ἐμοῦ γὰρ πολλοὶ κατήγοροι γεγόνασι
πρὸς ὑμᾶς καὶ πάλαι πολλὰ ἤδη ἔτη καὶ οὐδὲν
ἀληθὲς λέγοντες, οὓς ἐγὼ μᾶλλον φοβοῦμαι ἢ τοὺς
ἀμφὶ Ἄνυτον, καίπερ ὄντας καὶ τούτους δεινούς·
ἀλλ᾽ ἐκεῖνοι δεινότεροι, ὦ ἄνδρες, οἳ ὑμῶν τοὺς
πολλοὺς ἐκ παίδων παραλαμβάνοντες ἔπειθόν τε

[1] Schanz brackets ψευδῆ, following Hirschig.

For surely it would not be fitting for one of my age to come before you like a youngster making up speeches. And, men of Athens, I urgently beg and beseech you if you hear me making my defence with the same words with which I have been accustomed to speak both in the market place at the bankers' tables, where many of you have heard me, and elsewhere, not to be surprised or to make a disturbance on this account. For the fact is that this is the first time I have come before the court, although I am seventy years old; I am therefore an utter foreigner to the manner of speech here. Hence, just as you would, of course, if I were really a foreigner, pardon me if I spoke in that dialect and that manner in which I had been brought up, so now I make this request of you, a fair one, as it seems to me, that you disregard the manner of my speech—for perhaps it might be worse and perhaps better—and observe and pay attention merely to this, whether what I say is just or not; for that is the virtue of a judge, and an orator's virtue is to speak the truth.

First then it is right for me to defend myself against the first false accusations brought against me, and the first accusers, and then against the later accusations and the later accusers. For many accusers have risen up against me before you, who have been speaking for a long time, many years already, and saying nothing true; and I fear them more than Anytus and the rest, though these also are dangerous; but those others are more dangerous, gentlemen, who gained your belief, since they got

καὶ κατηγόρουν ἐμοῦ[1] οὐδὲν ἀληθές, ὡς ἔστι τις
Σωκράτης σοφὸς ἀνήρ, τά τε μετέωρα φροντιστὴς
καὶ τὰ ὑπὸ γῆς ἅπαντα ἀνεζητηκὼς καὶ τὸν ἥττω
λόγον κρείττω ποιῶν. οὗτοι, ὦ ἄνδρες Ἀθηναῖοι,

C οἱ ταύτην τὴν φήμην κατασκεδάσαντες, οἱ δεινοί
εἰσίν μου κατήγοροι· οἱ γὰρ ἀκούοντες ἡγοῦνται
τοὺς ταῦτα ζητοῦντας οὐδὲ θεοὺς νομίζειν. ἔπειτά
εἰσιν οὗτοι οἱ κατήγοροι πολλοὶ καὶ πολὺν χρόνον
ἤδη κατηγορηκότες, ἔτι δὲ καὶ ἐν ταύτῃ τῇ ἡλικίᾳ
λέγοντες πρὸς ὑμᾶς, ἐν ᾗ ἂν μάλιστα ἐπιστεύσατε,
παῖδες ὄντες, ἔνιοι δ᾽ ὑμῶν καὶ μειράκια, ἀτεχνῶς
ἐρήμην κατηγοροῦντες ἀπολογουμένου οὐδενός. ὃ
δὲ πάντων ἀλογώτατον, ὅτι οὐδὲ τὰ ὀνόματα οἷόν

D τε αὐτῶν εἰδέναι καὶ εἰπεῖν, πλὴν εἴ τις κωμῳ-
διοποιὸς τυγχάνει ὤν· ὅσοι δὲ φθόνῳ καὶ διαβολῇ
χρώμενοι ὑμᾶς ἀνέπειθον, οἱ δὲ καὶ αὐτοὶ πεπεισ-
μένοι ἄλλους πείθοντες, οὗτοι πάντων ἀπορώτατοί
εἰσιν· οὐδὲ γὰρ ἀναβιβάσασθαι οἷόν τ᾽ ἐστὶν αὐτῶν
ἐνταυθοῖ οὐδ᾽ ἐλέγξαι οὐδένα, ἀλλ᾽ ἀνάγκη
ἀτεχνῶς ὥσπερ σκιαμαχεῖν ἀπολογούμενόν τε
καὶ ἐλέγχειν μηδενὸς ἀποκρινομένου. ἀξιώσατε
οὖν καὶ ὑμεῖς, ὥσπερ ἐγὼ λέγω, διττούς μου τοὺς

E κατηγόρους γεγονέναι, ἑτέρους μὲν τοὺς ἄρτι
κατηγορήσαντας, ἑτέρους δὲ τοὺς πάλαι, οὓς ἐγὼ
λέγω, καὶ οἰήθητε δεῖν πρὸς ἐκείνους πρῶτόν με
ἀπολογήσασθαι· καὶ γὰρ ὑμεῖς ἐκείνων πρότερον
ἠκούσατε κατηγορούντων καὶ πολὺ μᾶλλον ἢ

---

[1] After ἐμοῦ the MSS. read μᾶλλον "more" or "rather."
Schanz reads μὰ τόν—, "by—," Hermann brackets μᾶλλον
and also οὐδὲν ἀληθές, Wohlrab omits μᾶλλον.

hold of most of you in childhood, and accused me without any truth, saying, "There is a certain Socrates, a wise man, a ponderer over the things in the air and one who has investigated the things beneath the earth and who makes the weaker argument the stronger." These, men of Athens, who have spread abroad this report, are my dangerous enemies. For those who hear them think that men who investigate these matters do not even believe in gods. Besides, these accusers are many and have been making their accusations already for a long time, and moreover they spoke to you at an age at which you would believe them most readily (some of you in youth, most of you in childhood), and the case they prosecuted went utterly by default, since nobody appeared in defence. But the most unreasonable thing of all is this, that it is not even possible to know and speak their names, except when one of them happens to be a writer of comedies. And all those who persuaded you by means of envy and slander—and some also persuaded others because they had been themselves persuaded—all these are most difficult to cope with ; for it is not even possible to call any of them up here and cross-question him, but I am compelled in making my defence to fight, as it were, absolutely with shadows and to cross-question when nobody answers. Be kind enough, then, to bear in mind, as I say, that there are two classes of my accusers—one those who have just brought their accusation, the other those who, as I was just saying, brought it long ago, and consider that I must defend myself first against the latter ; for you heard them making their charges first and with

τῶνδε τῶν ὕστερον. εἶεν· ἀπολογητέον δή, ὦ
19 ἄνδρες Ἀθηναῖοι, καὶ ἐπιχειρητέον ὑμῶν ἐξελέσθαι τὴν διαβολήν, ἣν ὑμεῖς ἐν πολλῷ χρόνῳ
ἔσχετε, ταύτην ἐν οὕτως ὀλίγῳ χρόνῳ. βουλοίμην
μὲν οὖν ἂν τοῦτο οὕτως γενέσθαι, εἴ τι ἄμεινον
καὶ ὑμῖν καὶ ἐμοί, καὶ πλέον τί με ποιῆσαι ἀπο-
λογούμενον· οἶμαι δὲ αὐτὸ χαλεπὸν εἶναι, καὶ οὐ
πάνυ με λανθάνει οἷόν ἐστιν. ὅμως τοῦτο μὲν
ἴτω ὅπῃ τῷ θεῷ φίλον, τῷ δὲ νόμῳ πειστέον καὶ
ἀπολογητέον.

3. Ἀναλάβωμεν οὖν ἐξ ἀρχῆς, τίς ἡ κατηγορία
ἐστίν, ἐξ ἧς ἡ ἐμὴ διαβολὴ γέγονεν, ᾗ δὴ καὶ
B πιστεύων Μέλητός με ἐγράψατο τὴν γραφὴν
ταύτην. εἶεν· τί δὴ λέγοντες διέβαλλον οἱ διαβάλλοντες; ὥσπερ οὖν κατηγόρων τὴν ἀντωμοσίαν δεῖ ἀναγνῶναι αὐτῶν· Σωκράτης ἀδικεῖ
καὶ περιεργάζεται, ζητῶν τά τε ὑπὸ γῆς καὶ
οὐράνια καὶ τὸν ἥττω λόγον κρείττω ποιῶν καὶ
C ἄλλους τὰ αὐτὰ ταῦτα διδάσκων. τοιαύτη τίς
ἐστιν· ταῦτα γὰρ ἑωρᾶτε καὶ αὐτοὶ ἐν τῇ Ἀρι-
στοφάνους κωμῳδίᾳ, Σωκράτη τινὰ ἐκεῖ περι-
φερόμενον, φάσκοντά τε ἀεροβατεῖν καὶ ἄλλην
πολλὴν φλυαρίαν φλυαροῦντα, ὧν ἐγὼ οὐδὲν
οὔτε μέγα οὔτε μικρὸν πέρι ἐπαΐω. καὶ οὐχ ὡς
ἀτιμάζων λέγω τὴν τοιαύτην ἐπιστήμην, εἴ τις
περὶ τῶν τοιούτων σοφός ἐστιν. μή πως ἐγὼ ὑπὸ
Μελήτου τοσαύτας δίκας φύγοιμι![1] ἀλλὰ γὰρ
ἐμοὶ τούτων, ὦ ἄνδρες Ἀθηναῖοι, οὐδὲν μέτεστιν.
D μάρτυρας δὲ αὐτοὺς ὑμῶν τοὺς πολλοὺς παρέχομαι, καὶ ἀξιῶ ὑμᾶς ἀλλήλους διδάσκειν τε καὶ

---

[1] Schanz brackets μή πως . . . φύγοιμι.

much greater force than these who made them later.
Well, then, I must make a defence, men of Athens,
and must try in so short a time to remove from you
this prejudice which you have been for so long a
time acquiring.   Now I wish that this might turn
out so, if it is better for you and for me, and that
I might succeed with my defence ; but I think it is
difficult, and I am not at all deceived about its
nature.   But nevertheless, let this be as is pleasing
to God, the law must be obeyed and I must make
a defence.

Now let us take up from the beginning the
question, what the accusation is from which the false
prejudice against me has arisen, in which Meletus
trusted when he brought this suit against me.   What
did those who aroused the prejudice say to arouse
it ?   I must, as it were, read their sworn statement
as if they were plaintiffs : " Socrates is a criminal
and a busybody, investigating the things beneath
the earth and in the heavens and making the
weaker argument stronger and teaching others these
same things."   Something of that sort it is.   For you
yourselves saw these things in Aristophanes' comedy,
a Socrates being carried about there, proclaiming
that he was treading on air and uttering a vast
deal of other nonsense, about which I know nothing,
either much or little.   And I say this, not to cast
dishonour upon such knowledge, if anyone is wise
about such matters (may I never have to defend
myself against Meletus on so great a charge as
that !),—but I, men of Athens, have nothing to do
with these things.   And I offer as witnesses most
of yourselves, and I ask you to inform one another

φράζειν, ὅσοι ἐμοῦ πώποτε ἀκηκόατε διαλεγο-
μένου· πολλοὶ δὲ ὑμῶν οἱ τοιοῦτοί εἰσιν· φράζετε
οὖν ἀλλήλοις, εἰ πώποτε ἢ μικρὸν ἢ μέγα ἤκουσέ
τις ὑμῶν ἐμοῦ περὶ τῶν τοιούτων διαλεγομένου·
καὶ ἐκ τούτων γνώσεσθε, ὅτι τοιαῦτ' ἐστὶν καὶ
τἄλλα περὶ ἐμοῦ, ἃ οἱ πολλοὶ λέγουσιν.

4. Ἀλλὰ γὰρ οὔτε τούτων οὐδέν ἐστιν,[1] οὐδέ γ'
εἴ τινος ἀκηκόατε ὡς ἐγὼ παιδεύειν ἐπιχειρῶ
E ἀνθρώπους καὶ χρήματα πράττομαι, οὐδὲ τοῦτο
ἀληθές. ἐπεὶ καὶ τοῦτό γέ μοι δοκεῖ καλὸν εἶναι,
εἴ τις οἷός τ' εἴη παιδεύειν ἀνθρώπους ὥσπερ
Γοργίας τε ὁ Λεοντῖνος καὶ Πρόδικος ὁ Κεῖος
καὶ Ἱππίας ὁ Ἠλεῖος. τούτων γὰρ ἕκαστος, ὦ
ἄνδρες, οἷός τ' ἐστὶν[2] ἰὼν εἰς ἑκάστην τῶν πόλεων
τοὺς νέους, οἷς ἔξεστι τῶν ἑαυτῶν πολιτῶν προῖκα
ξυνεῖναι ᾧ ἂν βούλωνται, τούτους πείθουσιν τὰς
20 ἐκείνων ξυνουσίας ἀπολιπόντας σφίσιν ξυνεῖναι
χρήματα διδόντας καὶ χάριν προσειδέναι. ἐπεὶ
καὶ ἄλλος ἀνήρ ἐστι Πάριος ἐνθάδε σοφός, ὃν ἐγὼ
ᾐσθόμην ἐπιδημοῦντα· ἔτυχον γὰρ προσελθὼν
ἀνδρὶ ὃς τετέλεκε χρήματα σοφισταῖς πλείω ἢ
ξύμπαντες οἱ ἄλλοι, Καλλίᾳ τῷ Ἱππονίκου·
τοῦτον οὖν ἀνηρόμην—ἐστὸν γὰρ αὐτῷ δύο υἱέε—
Ὦ Καλλία, ἦν δ' ἐγώ, εἰ μέν σου τὼ υἱέε πώλω ἢ
μόσχω ἐγενέσθην, εἴχομεν ἂν αὐτοῖν ἐπιστάτην
λαβεῖν καὶ μισθώσασθαι, ὃς ἔμελλεν αὐτὼ καλώ
B τε καὶ ἀγαθὼ ποιήσειν τὴν προσήκουσαν ἀρετήν·
ἦν δ' ἂν οὗτος ἢ τῶν ἱππικῶν τις ἢ τῶν γεωρ-
γικῶν· νῦν δ' ἐπειδὴ ἀνθρώπω ἐστόν, τίνα αὐτοῖν
ἐν νῷ ἔχεις ἐπιστάτην λαβεῖν; τίς τῆς τοιαύτης

---

[1] Schanz brackets ἐστιν. [2] Schanz brackets οἷός τ' ἐστίν.

and to tell, all those of you who ever heard me conversing—and there are many such among you—now tell, if anyone ever heard me talking much or little about such matters. And from this you will perceive that such are also the other things that the multitude say about me.

But in fact none of these things are true, and if you have heard from anyone that I undertake to teach people and that I make money by it, that is not true either. Although this also seems to me to be a fine thing, if one might be able to teach people, as Gorgias of Leontini and Prodicus of Ceos and Hippias of Elis are. For each of these men, gentlemen, is able to go into any one of the cities and persuade the young men, who can associate for nothing with whomsoever they wish among their own fellow citizens, to give up the association with those men and to associate with them and pay them money and be grateful besides.

And there is also another wise man here, a Parian, who I learned was in town; for I happened to meet a man who has spent more on sophists than all the rest, Callias, the son of Hipponicus; so I asked him—for he has two sons—"Callias," said I, "if your two sons had happened to be two colts or two calves, we should be able to get and hire for them an overseer who would make them excellent in the kind of excellence proper to them; and he would be a horse-trainer or a husbandman; but now, since they are two human beings, whom have you in mind to get as overseer? Who has knowledge of that kind

ἀρετῆς, τῆς ἀνθρωπίνης τε καὶ πολιτικῆς, ἐπιστήμων ἐστίν; οἶμαι γάρ σε ἐσκέφθαι διὰ τὴν
τῶν υἱέων κτῆσιν. ἔστιν τις, ἔφην ἐγώ, ἢ οὔ;
Πάνυ γε, ἢ δ' ὅς. Τίς, ἦν δ' ἐγώ, καὶ ποδαπός,
καὶ πόσου διδάσκει; Εὔηνος, ἔφη, ὦ Σώκρατες,
Πάριος, πέντε μνῶν. καὶ ἐγὼ τὸν Εὔηνον ἐμα-
C κάρισα, εἰ ὡς ἀληθῶς ἔχει ταύτην τὴν τέχνην καὶ
οὕτως ἐμμελῶς διδάσκει. ἐγὼ οὖν καὶ αὐτὸς
ἐκαλλυνόμην τε καὶ ἡβρυνόμην ἄν, εἰ ἠπιστάμην
ταῦτα· ἀλλ' οὐ γὰρ ἐπίσταμαι, ὦ ἄνδρες
Ἀθηναῖοι.

5. Ὑπολάβοι ἂν οὖν τις ὑμῶν ἴσως· Ἀλλ', ὦ
Σώκρατες, τὸ σὸν τί ἐστι πρᾶγμα; πόθεν αἱ δια-
βολαί σοι αὗται γεγόνασιν; οὐ γὰρ δήπου σοῦ γε
οὐδὲν τῶν ἄλλων περιττότερον πραγματευομένου
ἔπειτα τοσαύτη φήμη τε καὶ λόγος γέγονεν, εἰ μή
τι ἔπραττες ἀλλοῖον ἢ οἱ πολλοί·[1] λέγε οὖν
D ἡμῖν, τί ἐστιν, ἵνα μὴ ἡμεῖς περὶ σοῦ αὐτοσχε-
διάζωμεν. ταυτί μοι δοκεῖ δίκαια λέγειν ὁ λέγων,
κἀγὼ ὑμῖν πειράσομαι ἀποδεῖξαι, τί ποτ' ἔστιν
τοῦτο ὃ ἐμοὶ πεποίηκεν τό τε ὄνομα καὶ τὴν
διαβολήν. ἀκούετε δή. καὶ ἴσως μὲν δόξω τισὶν
ὑμῶν παίζειν, εὖ μέντοι ἴστε, πᾶσαν ὑμῖν τὴν
ἀλήθειαν ἐρῶ. ἐγὼ γάρ, ὦ ἄνδρες Ἀθηναῖοι, δι'
οὐδὲν ἀλλ' ἢ διὰ σοφίαν τινὰ τοῦτο τὸ ὄνομα
ἔσχηκα. ποίαν δὴ σοφίαν ταύτην; ἥπερ
ἐστὶν ἴσως ἀνθρωπίνη σοφία. τῷ ὄντι γὰρ
κινδυνεύω ταύτην εἶναι σοφός· οὗτοι δὲ τάχ' ἄν,
E οὓς ἄρτι ἔλεγον, μείζω τινὰ ἢ κατ' ἄνθρωπον
σοφίαν σοφοὶ εἶεν, ἢ οὐκ ἔχω, τί λέγω. οὐ γὰρ
δὴ ἔγωγε αὐτὴν ἐπίσταμαι, ἀλλ' ὅστις φησὶ

[1] Schanz brackets εἰ μή τι . . . πολλοί.

of excellence, that of a man and a citizen? For I think you have looked into the matter, because you have the sons. Is there anyone," said I, " or not? " " Certainly," said he. " Who," said I, " and where from, and what is his price for his teaching?" "Evenus," he said, " Socrates, from Paros, five minae." And I called Evenus blessed, if he really had this art and taught so reasonably. I myself should be vain and put on airs, if I understood these things; but I do not understand them, men of Athens.

Now perhaps someone might rejoin: " But, Socrates, what is the trouble about you? Whence have these prejudices against you arisen? For certainly this great report and talk has not arisen while you were doing nothing more out of the way than the rest, unless you were doing something other than most people; so tell us what it is, that we may not act unadvisedly in your case." The man who says this seems to me to be right, and I will try to show you what it is that has brought about my reputation and aroused the prejudice against me. So listen. And perhaps I shall seem to some of you to be joking; be assured, however, I shall speak perfect truth to you.

The fact is, men of Athens, that I have acquired this reputation on account of nothing else than a sort of wisdom. What kind of wisdom is this? Just that which is perhaps human wisdom. For perhaps I really am wise in this wisdom; and these men, perhaps, of whom I was just speaking, might be wise in some wisdom greater than human, or I don't know what to say; for I do not understand it, and whoever says I do, is lying and speaking to

ψεύδεταί τε καὶ ἐπὶ διαβολῇ τῇ ἐμῇ λέγει. καί μοι, ὦ ἄνδρες Ἀθηναῖοι, μὴ θορυβήσητε, μηδὲ ἂν δόξω τι ὑμῖν μέγα λέγειν· οὐ γὰρ ἐμὸν ἐρῶ τὸν λόγον, ὃν ἂν λέγω, ἀλλ' εἰς ἀξιόχρεων ὑμῖν τὸν λέγοντα ἀνοίσω. τῆς γὰρ ἐμῆς, εἰ δή τίς ἐστιν σοφία καὶ οἵα, μάρτυρα ὑμῖν παρέξομαι τὸν θεὸν τὸν ἐν Δελφοῖς. Χαιρεφῶντα γὰρ ἴστε που.

21 οὗτος ἐμός τε ἑταῖρος ἦν ἐκ νέου καὶ ὑμῶν τῷ πλήθει ἑταῖρός τε καὶ[1] ξυνέφυγε τὴν φυγὴν ταύτην καὶ μεθ' ὑμῶν κατῆλθε. καὶ ἴστε δή, οἷος ἦν Χαιρεφῶν, ὡς σφοδρὸς ἐφ' ὅ τι ὁρμήσειεν. καὶ δή ποτε καὶ εἰς Δελφοὺς ἐλθὼν ἐτόλμησε τοῦτο μαντεύσασθαι· καί, ὅπερ λέγω, μὴ θορυ- βεῖτε, ὦ ἄνδρες· ἤρετο γὰρ δή, εἴ τις ἐμοῦ εἴη σοφώτερος. ἀνεῖλεν οὖν ἡ Πυθία μηδένα σοφώ- τερον εἶναι. καὶ τούτων πέρι ὁ ἀδελφὸς ὑμῖν αὐτοῦ οὑτοσὶ μαρτυρήσει, ἐπειδὴ ἐκεῖνος τε- τελεύτηκεν.

B 6. Σκέψασθε δέ, ὧν ἔνεκα ταῦτα λέγω· μέλλω γὰρ ὑμᾶς διδάξειν, ὅθεν μοι ἡ διαβολὴ γέγονεν. ταῦτα γὰρ ἐγὼ ἀκούσας ἐνεθυμούμην οὑτωσί· τί ποτε λέγει ὁ θεός, καὶ τί ποτε αἰνίττεται; ἐγὼ γὰρ δὴ οὔτε μέγα οὔτε σμικρὸν ξύνοιδα ἐμαυτῷ σοφὸς ὤν· τί οὖν ποτε λέγει φάσκων ἐμὲ σοφώτατον εἶναι; οὐ γὰρ δήπου ψεύδεταί γε· οὐ γὰρ θέμις αὐτῷ. καὶ πολὺν μὲν χρόνον ἠπόρουν, τί ποτε λέγει. ἔπειτα μόγις πάνυ ἐπὶ ζήτησιν αὐτοῦ τοιαύτην τινὰ ἐτραπόμην.

Ἦλθον ἐπί τινα τῶν δοκούντων σοφῶν εἶναι, C ὡς ἐνταῦθα, εἴ περπου, ἐλέγξων τὸ μαντεῖον καὶ ἀποφανῶν τῷ χρησμῷ, ὅτι οὑτοσὶ ἐμοῦ

[1] Schanz brackets ἑταῖρός τε καί.

arouse prejudice against me. And, men of Athens, do not interrupt me with noise, even if I seem to you to be boasting; for the word which I speak is not mine, but the speaker to whom I shall refer it is a person of weight. For of my wisdom—if it is wisdom at all—and of its nature, I will offer you the god of Delphi as a witness. You know Chaerephon, I fancy. He was my comrade from a youth and the comrade of your democratic party, and shared in the recent exile and came back with you. And you know the kind of man Chaerephon was, how impetuous in whatever he undertook. Well, once he went to Delphi and made so bold as to ask the oracle this question; and, gentlemen, don't make a disturbance at what I say; for he asked if there were anyone wiser than I. Now the Pythia replied that there was no one wiser. And about these things his brother here will bear you witness, since Chaerephon is dead.

But see why I say these things; for I am going to tell you whence the prejudice against me has arisen. For when I heard this, I thought to my-self: "What in the world does the god mean, and what riddle is he propounding? For I am conscious that I am not wise either much or little. What then does he mean by declaring that I am the wisest? He certainly cannot be lying, for that is not possible for him." And for a long time I was at a loss as to what he meant; then with great reluctance I proceeded to investigate him somewhat as follows.

I went to one of those who had a reputation for wisdom, thinking that there, if anywhere, I should prove the utterance wrong and should show the

PLATO

σοφώτερός ἐστι, σὺ δ' ἐμὲ ἔφησθα. διασκοπῶν
οὖν τοῦτον—ὀνόματι γὰρ οὐδὲν δέομαι λέγειν,
ἦν δέ τις τῶν πολιτικῶν, πρὸς ὃν ἐγὼ σκοπῶν
τοιοῦτόν τι ἔπαθον, ὦ ἄνδρες Ἀθηναῖοι,—καὶ
διαλεγόμενος αὐτῷ,[1] ἔδοξέ μοι οὗτος ὁ ἀνὴρ
δοκεῖν μὲν εἶναι σοφὸς ἄλλοις τε πολλοῖς
ἀνθρώποις καὶ μάλιστα ἑαυτῷ, εἶναι δ' οὔ·
κἄπειτα ἐπειρώμην αὐτῷ δεικνύναι, ὅτι οἴοιτο
D μὲν εἶναι σοφός, εἴη δ' οὔ. ἐντεῦθεν οὖν τούτῳ
τε ἀπηχθόμην καὶ πολλοῖς τῶν παρόντων, πρὸς
ἐμαυτὸν δ' οὖν ἀπιὼν ἐλογιζόμην, ὅτι τούτου
μὲν τοῦ ἀνθρώπου ἐγὼ σοφώτερός εἰμι· κινδυνεύει
μὲν γὰρ ἡμῶν οὐδέτερος οὐδὲν καλὸν κἀγαθὸν
εἰδέναι, ἀλλ' οὗτος μὲν οἴεταί τι εἰδέναι οὐκ
εἰδώς, ἐγὼ δέ, ὥσπερ οὖν οὐκ οἶδα, οὐδὲ οἴομαι·
ἔοικα γοῦν τούτου γε σμικρῷ τινι αὐτῷ τούτῳ
σοφώτερος εἶναι, ὅτι ἃ μὴ οἶδα οὐδὲ οἴομαι
εἰδέναι. ἐντεῦθεν ἐπ' ἄλλον ᾖα τῶν ἐκείνου
E δοκούντων σοφωτέρων εἶναι, καί μοι ταὐτὰ ταῦτα
ἔδοξε· καὶ ἐνταῦθα κἀκείνῳ καὶ ἄλλοις πολλοῖς
ἀπηχθόμην.

7. Μετὰ ταῦτ' οὖν ἤδη ἐφεξῆς ᾖα, αἰσθανόμενος μὲν καὶ[2] λυπούμενος καὶ δεδιὼς ὅτι ἀπηχθα-
νόμην, ὅμως δὲ ἀναγκαῖον ἐδόκει εἶναι τὸ τοῦ
θεοῦ περὶ πλείστου ποιεῖσθαι· ἰτέον οὖν σκο-
ποῦντι τὸν χρησμόν, τί λέγει, ἐπὶ ἅπαντας τούς
τι δοκοῦντας εἰδέναι. καὶ νὴ τὸν κύνα, ὦ ἄνδρες
22 Ἀθηναῖοι· δεῖ γὰρ πρὸς ὑμᾶς τἀληθῆ λέγειν·
ἦ μὴν ἐγὼ ἔπαθόν τι τοιοῦτον· οἱ μὲν μάλιστα
εὐδοκιμοῦντες ἔδοξάν μοι ὀλίγου δεῖν τοῦ πλείστου

---

[1] Schanz brackets καὶ διαλεγόμενος αὐτῷ.
[2] Schanz brackets καί.

oracle "This man is wiser than I, but you said I was wisest." So examining this man—for I need not call him by name, but it was one of the public men with regard to whom I had this kind of experience, men of Athens—and conversing with him, this man seemed to me to seem to be wise to many other people and especially to himself, but not to be so; and then I tried to show him that he thought he was wise, but was not. As a result, I became hateful to him and to many of those present; and so, as I went away, I thought to myself, "I am wiser than this man; for neither of us really knows anything fine and good, but this man thinks he knows something when he does not, whereas I, as I do not know anything, do not think I do either. I seem, then, in just this little thing to be wiser than this man at any rate, that what I do not know I do not think I know either." From him I went to another of those who were reputed to be wiser than he, and these same things seemed to me to be true; and there I became hateful both to him and to many others.

After this then I went on from one to another, perceiving that I was hated, and grieving and fearing, but nevertheless I thought I must consider the god's business of the highest importance. So I had to go, investigating the meaning of the oracle, to all those who were reputed to know anything. And by the Dog, men of Athens—for I must speak the truth to you—this, I do declare, was my experience: those who had the most reputation seemed to me to be almost the most deficient,

ἐνδεεῖς εἶναι ζητοῦντι κατὰ τὸν θεόν, ἄλλοι δὲ
δοκοῦντες φαυλότεροι ἐπιεικέστεροι εἶναι ἄνδρες
πρὸς τὸ φρονίμως ἔχειν. δεῖ δὴ ὑμῖν τὴν ἐμὴν
πλάνην ἐπιδεῖξαι ὥσπερ πόνους τινὰς πονοῦντος,
ἵνα[1] μοι καὶ ἀνέλεγκτος ἡ μαντεία γένοιτο. μετὰ
γὰρ τοὺς πολιτικοὺς ᾖα ἐπὶ τοὺς ποιητὰς τούς
τε τῶν τραγῳδιῶν καὶ τοὺς τῶν διθυράμβων
B καὶ τοὺς ἄλλους, ὡς ἐνταῦθα ἐπ' αὐτοφώρῳ
καταληψόμενος ἐμαυτὸν ἀμαθέστερον ἐκείνων
ὄντα. ἀναλαμβάνων οὖν αὐτῶν τὰ ποιήματα,
ἅ μοι ἐδόκει μάλιστα πεπραγματεῦσθαι αὐτοῖς,
διηρώτων ἂν αὐτούς, τί λέγοιεν, ἵν' ἅμα τι καὶ
μανθάνοιμι παρ' αὐτῶν. αἰσχύνομαι οὖν ὑμῖν
εἰπεῖν, ὦ ἄνδρες, τἀληθῆ· ὅμως δὲ ῥητέον. ὡς
ἔπος γὰρ εἰπεῖν ὀλίγου αὐτῶν ἅπαντες οἱ παρόντες ἂν βέλτιον ἔλεγον περὶ ὧν αὐτοὶ ἐπεποιή-
κεσαν. ἔγνων οὖν καὶ περὶ τῶν ποιητῶν ἐν
C ὀλίγῳ τοῦτο, ὅτι οὐ σοφίᾳ ποιοῖεν ἃ ποιοῖεν,
ἀλλὰ φύσει τινὶ καὶ ἐνθουσιάζοντες, ὥσπερ οἱ
θεομάντεις καὶ οἱ χρησμῳδοί· καὶ γὰρ οὗτοι
λέγουσι μὲν πολλὰ καὶ καλά, ἴσασιν δὲ οὐδὲν
ὧν λέγουσι. τοιοῦτόν τί μοι ἐφάνησαν πάθος
καὶ οἱ ποιηταὶ πεπονθότες· καὶ ἅμα ᾐσθόμην
αὐτῶν διὰ τὴν ποίησιν οἰομένων καὶ τἆλλα
σοφωτάτων εἶναι ἀνθρώπων, ἃ οὐκ ἦσαν. ἀπῇα
οὖν καὶ ἐντεῦθεν τῷ αὐτῷ[2] οἰόμενος περιγεγονέναι
ᾧπερ καὶ τῶν πολιτικῶν.

8. Τελευτῶν οὖν ἐπὶ τοὺς χειροτέχνας ᾖα·
D ἐμαυτῷ γὰρ ξυνῄδη οὐδὲν ἐπισταμένῳ, ὡς ἔπος
εἰπεῖν, τούτους δέ γ' ἤδη ὅτι εὑρήσοιμι πολλὰ

---

[1] Schanz, following Stephanus, inserts μὴ after ἵνα.
[2] Schanz inserts αὐτῶν after τῷ αὐτῷ.

as I investigated at the god's behest, and others who
were of less repute seemed to be superior men in
the matter of being sensible. So I must relate to
you my wandering as I performed my Herculean
labours, so to speak, in order that the oracle might
be proved to be irrefutable. For after the public
men I went to the poets, those of tragedies, and
those of dithyrambs, and the rest, thinking that
there I should prove by actual test that I was less
learned than they. So, taking up the poems of
theirs that seemed to me to have been most carefully
elaborated by them, I asked them what they meant,
that I might at the same time learn something from
them. Now I am ashamed to tell you the truth, gentlemen; but still it must be told. For there was hardly a
man present, one might say, who would not speak
better than they about the poems they themselves had
composed. So again in the case of the poets also I
presently recognised this, that what they composed
they composed not by wisdom, but by nature and
because they were inspired, like the prophets and
givers of oracles; for these also say many fine things,
but know none of the things they say; it was evident
to me that the poets too had experienced something
of this same sort. And at the same time I perceived
that they, on account of their poetry, thought that
they were the wisest of men in other things as well,
in which they were not. So I went away from them
also thinking that I was superior to them in the
same thing in which I excelled the public men.

Finally then I went to the hand-workers. For I
was conscious that I knew practically nothing, but
I knew I should find that they knew many fine

καὶ καλὰ ἐπισταμένους. καὶ τούτου μὲν οὐκ
ἐψεύσθην, ἀλλ᾽ ἠπίσταντο ἃ ἐγὼ οὐκ ἠπιστάμην
καί μου ταύτῃ σοφώτεροι ἦσαν. ἀλλ᾽, ὦ ἄνδρες
Ἀθηναῖοι, ταὐτόν μοι ἔδοξαν ἔχειν ἁμάρτημα, ὅπερ
καὶ οἱ ποιηταί, καὶ οἱ ἀγαθοὶ δημιουργοί·[1] διὰ
τὸ τὴν τέχνην καλῶς ἐξεργάζεσθαι ἕκαστος
ἠξίου καὶ τἆλλα τὰ μέγιστα σοφώτατος εἶναι,
καὶ αὐτῶν αὕτη ἡ πλημμέλεια ἐκείνην τὴν
σοφίαν ἀπέκρυπτεν· ὥστ᾽ ἐμὲ ἐμαυτὸν ἀνερωτᾶν
E ὑπὲρ τοῦ χρησμοῦ, πότερα δεξαίμην ἂν οὕτω
ὥσπερ ἔχω ἔχειν, μήτε τι σοφὸς ὢν τὴν ἐκείνων
σοφίαν μήτε ἀμαθὴς τὴν ἀμαθίαν, ἢ ἀμφότερα
ἃ ἐκεῖνοι ἔχουσιν ἔχειν. ἀπεκρινάμην οὖν ἐμαυτῷ
καὶ τῷ χρησμῷ, ὅτι μοι λυσιτελοῖ ὥσπερ ἔχω
ἔχειν.

9. Ἐκ ταυτησὶ δὴ τῆς ἐξετάσεως, ὦ ἄνδρες
23 Ἀθηναῖοι, πολλαὶ μὲν ἀπέχθειαί μοι γεγόνασι
καὶ οἷαι χαλεπώταται καὶ βαρύταται, ὥστε
πολλὰς διαβολὰς ἀπ᾽ αὐτῶν γεγονέναι, ὄνομα
δὲ τοῦτο λέγεσθαι, σοφὸς εἶναι. οἴονται γάρ με
ἑκάστοτε οἱ παρόντες ταῦτα αὐτὸν εἶναι σοφόν,
ἃ ἂν ἄλλον ἐξελέγξω· τὸ δὲ κινδυνεύει, ὦ ἄνδρες,
τῷ ὄντι ὁ θεὸς σοφὸς εἶναι, καὶ ἐν τῷ χρησμῷ
τούτῳ τοῦτο λέγειν, ὅτι ἡ ἀνθρωπίνη σοφία
ὀλίγου τινὸς ἀξία ἐστὶν καὶ οὐδενός· καὶ φαίνεται
τοῦτ᾽ οὐ λέγειν τὸν Σωκράτη, προσκεχρῆσθαι
B δὲ τῷ ἐμῷ ὀνόματι, ἐμὲ παράδειγμα ποιούμενος,
ὥσπερ ἂν εἰ εἴποι, ὅτι οὗτος ὑμῶν, ὦ ἄνθρωποι,
σοφώτατός ἐστιν, ὅστις ὥσπερ Σωκράτης ἔγνωκεν
ὅτι οὐδενὸς ἄξιός ἐστι τῇ ἀληθείᾳ πρὸς σοφίαν.
Ταῦτ᾽ οὖν ἐγὼ μὲν ἔτι καὶ νῦν περιιὼν ζητῶ

[1] Schanz brackets καὶ οἱ ἀγαθοὶ δημιουργοί.

things. And in this I was not deceived; they did know what I did not, and in this way they were wiser than I. But, men of Athens, the good artisans also seemed to me to have the same failing as the poets; because of practising his art well, each one thought he was very wise in the other most important matters, and this folly of theirs obscured that wisdom, so that I asked myself in behalf of the oracle whether I should prefer to be as I am, neither wise in their wisdom nor foolish in their folly, or to be in both respects as they are. I replied then to myself and to the oracle that it was better for me to be as I am.

Now from this investigation, men of Athens, many enmities have arisen against me, and such as are most harsh and grievous, so that many prejudices have resulted from them and I am called a wise man. For on each occasion those who are present think I am wise in the matters in which I confute someone else; but the fact is, gentlemen, it is likely that the god is really wise and by his oracle means this: "Human wisdom is of little or no value." And it appears that he does not really say this of Socrates, but merely uses my name, and makes me an example, as if he were to say: "This one of you, O human beings, is wisest, who, like Socrates, recognises that he is in truth of no account in respect to wisdom."

Therefore I am still even now going about and

καὶ ἐρευνῶ κατὰ τὸν θεόν, καὶ τῶν ἀστῶν καὶ
ξένων ἄν τινα οἴωμαι σοφὸν εἶναι· καὶ ἐπειδάν
μοι μὴ δοκῇ, τῷ θεῷ βοηθῶν ἐνδείκνυμαι ὅτι
οὐκ ἔστι σοφός. καὶ ὑπὸ ταύτης τῆς ἀσχολίας
οὔτε τι τῶν τῆς πόλεως πρᾶξαί μοι σχολὴ
γέγονεν ἄξιον λόγου οὔτε τῶν οἰκείων, ἀλλ' ἐν
C πενίᾳ μυρίᾳ εἰμὶ διὰ τὴν τοῦ θεοῦ λατρείαν.

10. Πρὸς δὲ τούτοις οἱ νέοι μοι ἐπακολου-
θοῦντες, οἷς μάλιστα σχολή ἐστιν, οἱ τῶν πλου-
σιωτάτων, αὐτόματοι χαίρουσιν ἀκούοντες ἐξε-
ταζομένων τῶν ἀνθρώπων, καὶ αὐτοὶ πολλάκις
ἐμὲ μιμοῦνται, εἶτα ἐπιχειροῦσιν ἄλλους ἐξετά-
ζειν· κἄπειτα, οἶμαι, εὑρίσκουσι πολλὴν ἀφθονίαν
οἰομένων μὲν εἰδέναι τι ἀνθρώπων, εἰδότων δὲ
ὀλίγα ἢ οὐδέν. ἐντεῦθεν οὖν οἱ ὑπ' αὐτῶν
ἐξεταζόμενοι ἐμοὶ ὀργίζονται, ἀλλ' οὐχ αὑτοῖς,
καὶ λέγουσιν ὡς Σωκράτης τίς ἐστι μιαρώτατος
D καὶ διαφθείρει τοὺς νέους· καὶ ἐπειδάν τις αὐτοὺς
ἐρωτᾷ, ὅ τι ποιῶν καὶ ὅ τι διδάσκων, ἔχουσι μὲν
οὐδὲν εἰπεῖν, ἀλλ' ἀγνοοῦσιν,[1] ἵνα δὲ μὴ δοκῶσιν
ἀπορεῖν, τὰ κατὰ πάντων τῶν φιλοσοφούντων
πρόχειρα ταῦτα λέγουσιν, ὅτι τὰ μετέωρα καὶ
τὰ ὑπὸ γῆς, καὶ θεοὺς μὴ νομίζειν, καὶ τὸν ἥττω
λόγον κρείττω ποιεῖν. τὰ γὰρ ἀληθῆ, οἶμαι,
οὐκ ἂν ἐθέλοιεν λέγειν, ὅτι κατάδηλοι γίγνονται
προσποιούμενοι μὲν εἰδέναι, εἰδότες δὲ οὐδέν.
E ἅτε οὖν, οἶμαι, φιλότιμοι ὄντες καὶ σφοδροὶ καὶ
πολλοί, καὶ ξυντεταγμένως[2] καὶ πιθανῶς λέγοντες
περὶ ἐμοῦ, ἐμπεπλήκασιν ὑμῶν τὰ ὦτα καὶ πάλαι
καὶ σφοδρῶς διαβάλλοντες. ἐκ τούτων καὶ

---

[1] Schanz reads ἀμφιγνοοῦσιν, " they are in doubt."
[2] Schanz reads ξυντεταμένως, " earnestly."

searching and investigating at the god's behest anyone, whether citizen or foreigner, who I think is wise; and when he does not seem so to me, I give aid to the god and show that he is not wise. And by reason of this occupation I have no leisure to attend to any of the affairs of the state worth mentioning, or of my own, but am in vast poverty on account of my service to the god.

And in addition to these things, the young men who have the most leisure, the sons of the richest men, accompany me of their own accord, find pleasure in hearing people being examined, and often imitate me themselves, and then they undertake to examine others; and then, I fancy, they find a great plenty of people who think they know something, but know little or nothing. As a result, therefore, those who are examined by them are angry with me, instead of being angry with themselves, and say that "Socrates is a most abominable person and is corrupting the youth."

And when anyone asks them "by doing or teaching what?" they have nothing to say, but they do not know, and that they may not seem to be at a loss, they say these things that are handy to say against all the philosophers, "the things in the air and the things beneath the earth" and "not to believe in the gods" and "to make the weaker argument the stronger." For they would not, I fancy, care to say the truth, that it is being made very clear that they pretend to know, but know nothing. Since, then, they are jealous of their honour and energetic and numerous and speak concertedly and persuasively about me, they have filled your ears both long ago and now with vehement slanders.

Μέλητός μοι ἐπέθετο καὶ Ἄνυτος καὶ Λύκων,
Μέλητος μὲν ὑπὲρ τῶν ποιητῶν ἀχθόμενος,
Ἄνυτος δὲ ὑπὲρ τῶν δημιουργῶν καὶ τῶν πολι-
24 τικῶν,[1] Λύκων δὲ ὑπὲρ τῶν ῥητόρων· ὥστε, ὅπερ
ἀρχόμενος ἐγὼ ἔλεγον, θαυμάζοιμ᾽ ἄν, εἰ οἷός τ᾽
εἴην ἐγὼ ὑμῶν ταύτην τὴν διαβολὴν ἐξελέσθαι ἐν
οὕτως ὀλίγῳ χρόνῳ οὕτω πολλὴν γεγονυῖαν. ταῦτ᾽
ἔστιν ὑμῖν, ὦ ἄνδρες Ἀθηναῖοι, τἀληθῆ, καὶ ὑμᾶς
οὔτε μέγα οὔτε μικρὸν ἀποκρυψάμενος ἐγὼ λέγω
οὐδ᾽ ὑποστειλάμενος. καίτοι οἶδα σχεδόν, ὅτι
τοῖς αὐτοῖς ἀπεχθάνομαι· ὃ καὶ τεκμήριον, ὅτι
ἀληθῆ λέγω καὶ ὅτι αὕτη ἐστὶν ἡ διαβολὴ ἡ
ἐμὴ καὶ τὰ αἴτια ταῦτά ἐστιν. καὶ ἐάν τε νῦν
B ἐάν τε αὖθις ζητήσητε ταῦτα, οὕτως εὑρήσετε.

11. Περὶ μὲν οὖν ὧν οἱ πρῶτοί μου κατήγοροι
κατηγόρουν αὕτη ἐστὶν ἱκανὴ ἀπολογία πρὸς
ὑμᾶς. πρὸς δὲ Μέλητον τὸν ἀγαθόν τε καὶ
φιλόπολιν, ὥς φησι, καὶ τοὺς ὑστέρους μετὰ
ταῦτα πειράσομαι ἀπολογεῖσθαι. αὖθις γὰρ δή,
ὥσπερ ἑτέρων τούτων ὄντων κατηγόρων, λάβωμεν
αὖ τὴν τούτων ἀντωμοσίαν. ἔχει δέ πως ὧδε·
Σωκράτη φησὶν ἀδικεῖν τούς τε νέους διαφθείροντα
καὶ θεοὺς οὓς ἡ πόλις νομίζει οὐ νομίζοντα, ἕτερα
C δὲ δαιμόνια καινά. τὸ μὲν δὴ ἔγκλημα τοιοῦτόν
ἐστιν· τούτου δὲ τοῦ ἐγκλήματος ἓν ἕκαστον
ἐξετάσωμεν. φησὶ γὰρ δὴ τοὺς νέους ἀδικεῖν με
διαφθείροντα. ἐγὼ δέ γε, ὦ ἄνδρες Ἀθηναῖοι,
ἀδικεῖν φημι Μέλητον, ὅτι σπουδῇ χαριεντίζεται,
ῥᾳδίως εἰς ἀγῶνα καθιστὰς ἀνθρώπους, περὶ πραγμάτων προσποιούμενος σπουδάζειν καὶ κήδεσθαι,

[1] Schanz follows Cobet in bracketing καὶ τῶν πολιτικῶν.

From among them Meletus attacked me, and Anytus and Lycon, Meletus angered on account of the poets, and Anytus on account of the artisans and the public men, and Lycon on account of the orators; so that, as I said in the beginning, I should be surprised if I were able to remove this prejudice from you in so short a time when it has grown so great. There you have the truth, men of Athens, and I speak without hiding anything from you, great or small or prevaricating. And yet I know pretty well that I am making myself hated by just that conduct; which is also a proof that I am speaking the truth and that this is the prejudice against me and these are its causes. And whether you investigate this now or hereafter, you will find that it is so.

Now so far as the accusations are concerned which my first accusers made against me, this is a sufficient defence before you; but against Meletus, the good and patriotic, as he says, and the later ones, I will try to defend myself next. So once more, as if these were another set of accusers, let us take up in turn their sworn statement. It is about as follows: it states that Socrates is a wrongdoer because he corrupts the youth and does not believe in the gods the state believes in, but in other new spiritual beings.

Such is the accusation. But let us examine each point of this accusation. He says I am a wrongdoer because I corrupt the youth. But I, men of Athens, say Meletus is a wrongdoer, because he jokes in earnest, lightly involving people in a lawsuit, pretending to be zealous and concerned about things

ὧν οὐδὲν τούτῳ πώποτε ἐμέλησεν. ὡς δὲ τοῦτο
οὕτως ἔχει, πειράσομαι καὶ ὑμῖν ἐπιδεῖξαι.

12. Καί μοι δεῦρο, ὦ Μέλητε, εἰπέ· ἄλλο τι ἢ
D περὶ πολλοῦ ποιεῖ, ὅπως ὡς βέλτιστοι οἱ νεώτεροι
ἔσονται; Ἔγωγε. Ἴθι δή νυν εἰπὲ τούτοις, τίς
αὐτοὺς βελτίους ποιεῖ. δῆλον γὰρ ὅτι οἶσθα,
μέλον γέ σοι. τὸν μὲν γὰρ διαφθείροντα ἐξευρών,
ὡς φής, ἐμὲ εἰσάγεις τουτοισὶ[1] καὶ κατηγορεῖς· τὸν
δὲ δὴ βελτίους ποιοῦντα ἴθι εἰπὲ καὶ μήνυσον
αὐτοῖς, τίς ἐστιν. ὁρᾷς, ὦ Μέλητε, ὅτι σιγᾷς καὶ
οὐκ ἔχεις εἰπεῖν; καίτοι οὐκ αἰσχρόν σοι δοκεῖ
εἶναι καὶ ἱκανὸν τεκμήριον οὗ δὴ ἐγὼ λέγω, ὅτι
σοι οὐδὲν μεμέληκεν; ἀλλ᾿ εἰπέ, ὦ ᾿γαθέ, τίς
E αὐτοὺς ἀμείνους ποιεῖ; Οἱ νόμοι. Ἀλλ᾿ οὐ τοῦτο
ἐρωτῶ, ὦ βέλτιστε, ἀλλὰ τίς ἄνθρωπος, ὅστις
πρῶτον καὶ αὐτὸ τοῦτο οἶδε, τοὺς νόμους. Οὗτοι
ὦ Σώκρατες, οἱ δικασταί. Πῶς λέγεις, ὦ Μέλητε;
οἵδε τοὺς νέους παιδεύειν οἷοί τέ εἰσι καὶ βελτίους
ποιοῦσιν; Μάλιστα. Πότερον ἅπαντες, ἢ οἱ μὲν
αὐτῶν, οἱ δ᾿ οὔ; Ἅπαντες. Εὖ γε νὴ τὴν Ἥραν
λέγεις, καὶ πολλὴν ἀφθονίαν τῶν ὠφελούντων. τί
25 δὲ δή; οἵδε οἱ ἀκροαταὶ βελτίους ποιοῦσιν ἢ οὔ;
Καὶ οὗτοι. Τί δὲ οἱ βουλευταί; Καὶ οἱ βουλευταί.
Ἀλλ᾿ ἄρα, ὦ Μέλητε, μὴ οἱ ἐν τῇ ἐκκλησίᾳ, οἱ
ἐκκλησιασταί,[2] διαφθείρουσι τοὺς νεωτέρους; ἢ
κἀκεῖνοι βελτίους ποιοῦσιν ἅπαντες; Κἀκεῖνοι.
Πάντες ἄρα, ὡς ἔοικεν, Ἀθηναῖοι καλοὺς κἀγαθοὺς
ποιοῦσι πλὴν ἐμοῦ, ἐγὼ δὲ μόνος διαφθείρω. οὕτω
λέγεις; Πάνυ σφόδρα ταῦτα λέγω. Πολλήν γ᾿

---

[1] Cobet's suggestion of εἰς τουτουσὶ for τουτοισὶ is adopted
by Schanz.
[2] Schanz follows Hirschig in bracketing οἱ ἐκκλησιασταί.

for which he never cared at all. And that this is so I will try to make plain to you also.

Come here, Meletus, tell me : don't you consider it of great importance that the youth be as good as possible ? "I do." Come now, tell these gentlemen who makes them better ? For it is evident that you know, since you care about it. For you have found the one who corrupts them, as you say, and you bring me before these gentlemen and accuse me; and now, come, tell who makes them better and inform them who he is. Do you see, Meletus, that you are silent and cannot tell ? And yet does it not seem to you disgraceful and a sufficient proof of what I say, that you have never cared about it ? But tell, my good man, who makes them better ? "The laws." But that is not what I ask, most excellent one, but what man, who knows in the first place just this very thing, the laws. "These men, Socrates, the judges." What are you saying, Meletus ? Are these gentlemen able to instruct the youth, and do they make them better ? "Certainly." All, or some of them and others not ? "All." Well said, by Hera, and this is a great plenty of helpers you speak of. But how about this ? Do these listeners make them better, or not ? "These also." And how about the senators ? "The senators also." But, Meletus, those in the assembly, the assembly-men, don't corrupt the youth, do they ? or do they also all make them better ? "They also." All the Athenians, then, as it seems, make them excellent, except myself, and I alone corrupt them. Is this what you mean ? "Very decidedly, that is

ἐμοῦ κατέγνωκας δυστυχίαν. καί μοι ἀπόκριναι·
ἦ καὶ περὶ ἵππους οὕτω σοι δοκεῖ ἔχειν; οἱ μὲν

B βελτίους ποιοῦντες αὐτοὺς πάντες ἄνθρωποι εἶναι,
εἷς δέ τις ὁ διαφθείρων; ἢ τοὐναντίον τούτου πᾶν
εἷς μέν τις ὁ βελτίους οἷός τ᾽ ὢν ποιεῖν ἢ πάνυ
ὀλίγοι, οἱ ἱππικοί· οἱ δὲ πολλοὶ ἐάνπερ ξυνῶσι καὶ
χρῶνται ἵπποις, διαφθείρουσιν; οὐχ οὕτως ἔχει,
ὦ Μέλητε, καὶ περὶ ἵππων καὶ τῶν ἄλλων ἁπάντων ζῴων; πάντως δήπου, ἐάν τε σὺ καὶ Ἄνυτος
οὐ φῆτε ἐάν τε φῆτε· πολλὴ γὰρ ἄν τις εὐδαιμονία
εἴη περὶ τοὺς νέους, εἰ εἷς μὲν μόνος αὐτοὺς
διαφθείρει, οἱ δ᾽ ἄλλοι ὠφελοῦσιν. ἀλλὰ γάρ,

C ὦ Μέλητε, ἱκανῶς ἐπιδείκνυσαι, ὅτι οὐδεπώ-
ποτε ἐφρόντισας τῶν νέων, καὶ σαφῶς ἀποφαίνεις
τὴν σαυτοῦ ἀμέλειαν, ὅτι οὐδέν σοι μεμέληκεν
περὶ ὧν ἐμὲ εἰσάγεις.

13. Ἔτι δὲ ἡμῖν εἰπέ, ὦ πρὸς Διὸς Μέλητε,
πότερον ἔστιν οἰκεῖν ἄμεινον ἐν πολίταις χρηστοῖς
ἢ πονηροῖς; ὦ τᾶν, ἀπόκριναι· οὐδὲν γάρ τοι
χαλεπὸν ἐρωτῶ. οὐχ οἱ μὲν πονηροὶ κακόν τι
ἐργάζονται τοὺς ἀεὶ ἐγγυτάτω ἑαυτῶν ὄντας, οἱ δ᾽
ἀγαθοὶ ἀγαθόν τι; Πάνυ γε. Ἔστιν οὖν ὅστις

D βούλεται ὑπὸ τῶν ξυνόντων βλάπτεσθαι μᾶλλον
ἢ ὠφελεῖσθαι; ἀπόκριναι, ὦ ἀγαθέ· καὶ γὰρ ὁ
νόμος κελεύει ἀποκρίνεσθαι. ἔσθ᾽ ὅστις βούλεται
βλάπτεσθαι; Οὐ δῆτα. Φέρε δή, πότερον ἐμὲ
εἰσάγεις δεῦρο ὡς διαφθείροντα τοὺς νεωτέρους
καὶ πονηροτέρους ποιοῦντα ἑκόντα ἢ ἄκοντα;
Ἑκόντα ἔγωγε. Τί δῆτα, ὦ Μέλητε; τοσοῦτον σὺ
ἐμοῦ σοφώτερος εἶ τηλικούτου ὄντος τηλικόσδε
ὤν, ὥστε σὺ μὲν ἔγνωκας ὅτι οἱ μὲν κακοὶ κακόν

E τι ἐργάζονται ἀεὶ τοὺς μάλιστα πλησίον ἑαυτῶν,

94

what I mean." You have condemned me to great unhappiness! But answer me; does it seem to you to be so in the case of horses, that those who make them better are all mankind, and he who injures them some one person? Or, quite the opposite of this, that he who is able to make them better is some one person, or very few, the horse-trainers, whereas most people, if they have to do with and use horses, injure them? Is it not so, Meletus, both in the case of horses and in that of all other animals? Certainly it is, whether you and Anytus deny it or agree; for it would be a great state of blessedness in the case of the youth if one alone corrupts them, and the others do them good. But, Meletus, you show clearly enough that you never thought about the youth, and you exhibit plainly your own carelessness, that you have not cared at all for the things about which you hale me into court.

But besides, tell us, for heaven's sake, Meletus, is it better to live among good citizens, or bad? My friend, answer; for I am not asking anything hard. Do not the bad do some evil to those who are with them at any time and the good some good? "Certainly." Is there then anyone who prefers to be injured by his associates rather than benefited? Answer, my good man; for the law orders you to answer. Is there anyone who prefers to be injured? "Of course not." Come then, do you hale me in here on the ground that I am corrupting the youth and making them worse voluntarily or involuntarily? "Voluntarily I say." What then, Meletus? Are you at your age so much wiser than I at my age, that you have recognized that the evil always do some evil to those nearest them, and the good some

οἱ δὲ ἀγαθοὶ ἀγαθόν· ἐγὼ δὲ δὴ εἰς τοσοῦτον
ἀμαθίας ἥκω, ὥστε καὶ τοῦτ' ἀγνοῶ, ὅτι, ἐάν τινα
μοχθηρὸν ποιήσω τῶν ξυνόντων, κινδυνεύσω κακόν
τι λαβεῖν ἀπ' αὐτοῦ, ὥστε τοῦτο τὸ τοσοῦτον
κακὸν ἑκὼν ποιῶ, ὡς φῂς σύ; ταῦτα ἐγώ σοι οὐ
πείθομαι, ὦ Μέλητε, οἶμαι δὲ οὐδὲ ἄλλον ἀνθρώ-
26 πων οὐδένα· ἀλλ' ἢ οὐ διαφθείρω, ἢ εἰ διαφθείρω,
ἄκων, ὥστε σύ γε κατ' ἀμφότερα ψεύδει. εἰ δὲ
ἄκων διαφθείρω, τῶν τοιούτων καὶ ἀκουσίων [1]
ἁμαρτημάτων οὐ δεῦρο νόμος εἰσάγειν ἐστίν, ἀλλὰ
ἰδίᾳ λαβόντα διδάσκειν καὶ νουθετεῖν· δῆλον γὰρ
ὅτι, ἐὰν μάθω, παύσομαι ὅ γε ἄκων ποιῶ. σὺ δὲ
ξυγγενέσθαι μέν μοι καὶ διδάξαι ἔφυγες καὶ οὐκ
ἠθέλησας, δεῦρο δὲ εἰσάγεις, οἷ νόμος ἐστὶν
εἰσάγειν τοὺς κολάσεως δεομένους, ἀλλ' οὐ μαθήσεως.

14. Ἀλλὰ γάρ, ὦ ἄνδρες Ἀθηναῖοι, τοῦτο μὲν
δῆλον ἤδη ἐστίν, ὃ ἐγὼ ἔλεγον, ὅτι Μελήτῳ τού-
B των οὔτε μέγα οὔτε μικρὸν πώποτε ἐμέλησεν.
ὅμως δὲ δὴ λέγε ἡμῖν, πῶς με φῂς διαφθείρειν, ὦ
Μέλητε, τοὺς νεωτέρους; ἢ δῆλον δὴ ὅτι κατὰ τὴν
γραφήν, ἣν ἐγράψω, θεοὺς διδάσκοντα μὴ νομίζειν
οὓς ἡ πόλις νομίζει, ἕτερα δὲ δαιμόνια καινά; οὐ
ταῦτα λέγεις, ὅτι διδάσκων διαφθείρω; Πάνυ μὲν
οὖν σφόδρα ταῦτα λέγω. Πρὸς αὐτῶν τοίνυν, ὦ
C Μέλητε, τούτων τῶν θεῶν, ὧν νῦν ὁ λόγος ἐστίν,
εἰπὲ ἔτι σαφέστερον καὶ ἐμοὶ καὶ τοῖς ἀνδράσιν
τούτοις. ἐγὼ γὰρ οὐ δύναμαι μαθεῖν, πότερον
λέγεις διδάσκειν με νομίζειν εἶναί τινας θεούς, καὶ
αὐτὸς ἄρα νομίζω εἶναι θεούς, καὶ οὐκ εἰμὶ τὸ
παράπαν ἄθεος οὐδὲ ταύτῃ ἀδικῶ, οὐ μέντοι

[1] Schanz brackets καὶ ἀκουσίων.

good ; whereas I have reached such a depth of ignorance that I do not even know this, that if I make anyone of my associates bad I am in danger of getting some harm from him, so that I do this great evil voluntarily, as you say ? I don't believe this, Meletus, nor do I think anyone else in the world does ! but either I do not corrupt them, or if I corrupt them, I do it involuntarily, so that you are lying in both events. But if I corrupt them involuntarily, for such involuntary errors the law is not to hale people into court, but to take them and instruct and admonish them in private. For it is clear that if I am told about it, I shall stop doing that which I do involuntarily. But you avoided associating with me and instructing me, and were unwilling to do so, but you hale me in here, where it is the law to hale in those who need punishment, not instruction.

But enough of this, for, men of Athens, this is clear, as I said, that Meletus never cared much or little for these things. But nevertheless, tell us, how do you say, Meletus, that I corrupt the youth ? Or is it evident, according to the indictment you brought, that it is by teaching them not to believe in the gods the state believes in, but in other new spiritual beings ? Do you not say that it is by teaching this that I corrupt them ? " Very decidedly that is what I say." Then, Meletus, for the sake of these very gods about whom our speech now is, speak still more clearly both to me and to these gentlemen. For I am unable to understand whether you say that I teach that there are some gods, and myself then believe that there are some gods, and am not altogether godless and am not a wrongdoer in that way, that these, however, are not the gods whom the

PLATO

οὔσπερ γε ἡ πόλις, ἀλλὰ ἑτέρους, καὶ τοῦτ' ἔστιν
ὅ μοι ἐγκαλεῖς, ὅτι ἑτέρους· ἢ παντάπασί με φῂς
οὔτε αὐτὸν νομίζειν θεοὺς τούς τε ἄλλους ταῦτα
διδάσκειν. Ταῦτα λέγω, ὡς τὸ παράπαν οὐ νομίζεις
θεούς. Ὦ θαυμάσιε Μέλητε, ἵνα τί ταῦτα λέγεις;

D οὐδὲ ἥλιον οὐδὲ σελήνην ἄρα νομίζω θεοὺς εἶναι,
ὥσπερ οἱ ἄλλοι ἄνθρωποι; Μὰ Δί', ὦ ἄνδρες δικασταί, ἐπεὶ τὸν μὲν ἥλιον λίθον φησὶν εἶναι, τὴν δὲ
σελήνην γῆν. Ἀναξαγόρου¹ οἴει κατηγορεῖν, ὦ
φίλε Μέλητε, καὶ οὕτω καταφρονεῖς τῶνδε καὶ
οἴει αὐτοὺς ἀπείρους γραμμάτων εἶναι, ὥστε οὐκ
εἰδέναι, ὅτι τὰ Ἀναξαγόρου βιβλία τοῦ Κλαζο-
μενίου γέμει τούτων τῶν λόγων; καὶ δὴ καὶ οἱ
νέοι ταῦτα παρ' ἐμοῦ μανθάνουσιν, ἃ ἔξεστιν

E ἐνίοτε, εἰ πάνυ πολλοῦ, δραχμῆς ἐκ τῆς ὀρχήστρας
πριαμένοις Σωκράτους καταγελᾶν, ἐὰν προσποιῆ-
ται ἑαυτοῦ εἶναι, ἄλλως τε καὶ οὕτως ἄτοπα ὄντα.
ἀλλ', ὦ πρὸς Διός, οὑτωσί σοι δοκῶ² οὐδένα νομίζειν θεὸν εἶναι; Οὐ μέντοι μὰ Δία οὐδ' ὁπωστιοῦν.
Ἄπιστός γ' εἶ, ὦ Μέλητε, καὶ ταῦτα μέντοι, ὡς
ἐμοὶ δοκεῖς, σαυτῷ. ἐμοὶ γὰρ δοκεῖ οὑτοσί, ὦ
ἄνδρες Ἀθηναῖοι, πάνυ εἶναι ὑβριστὴς καὶ ἀκόλαστος, καὶ ἀτεχνῶς τὴν γραφὴν ταύτην ὕβρει
τινὶ καὶ ἀκολασίᾳ καὶ νεότητι γράψασθαι. ἔοικεν

27 γὰρ ὥσπερ αἴνιγμα ξυντιθέντι διαπειρωμένῳ, ἆρα
γνώσεται Σωκράτης ὁ σοφὸς δὴ ἐμοῦ χαριεντιζο-
μένου καὶ ἐναντί' ἐμαυτῷ λέγοντος, ἢ ἐξαπατήσω
αὐτὸν καὶ τοὺς ἄλλους τοὺς ἀκούοντας; οὗτος γὰρ
ἐμοὶ φαίνεται τὰ ἐναντία λέγειν αὐτὸς ἑαυτῷ ἐν
τῇ γραφῇ, ὥσπερ ἂν εἰ εἴποι· ἀδικεῖ Σωκράτης

¹ Schanz brackets Ἀναξαγόρου. ² Schanz brackets δοκῶ.

state believes in, but others, and this is what you accuse me for, that I believe in others; or you say that I do not myself believe in gods at all and that I teach this unbelief to other people. "That is what I say, that you do not believe in gods at all." You amaze me, Meletus! Why do you say this? Do I not even believe that the sun or yet the moon are gods, as the rest of mankind do? "No, by Zeus, judges, since he says that the sun is a stone and the moon earth." Do you think you are accusing Anaxagoras, my dear Meletus, and do you so despise these gentlemen and think they are so unversed in letters as not to know, that the books of Anaxagoras the Clazomenian are full of such utterances? And forsooth the youth learn these doctrines from me, which they can buy sometimes (if the price is high) for a drachma in the orchestra and laugh at Socrates, if he pretends they are his own, especially when they are so absurd! But for heaven's sake, do you think this of me, that I do not believe there is any god? "No, by Zeus, you don't, not in the least." You cannot be believed, Meletus, not even, as it seems to me, by yourself. For this man appears to me, men of Athens, to be very violent and unrestrained, and actually to have brought this indictment in a spirit of violence and unrestraint and rashness. For he seems, as it were, by composing a puzzle to be making a test: "Will Socrates, the wise man, recognize that I am joking and contradicting myself, or shall I deceive him and the others who hear me?" For he appears to me to contradict himself in his speech, as if he were to say, "Socrates is a wrongdoer, because he does

99

PLATO

θεοὺς οὐ νομίζων, ἀλλὰ θεοὺς νομίζων. καίτοι
τοῦτό ἐστι παίζοντος.

15. Ξυνεπισκέψασθε δή, ὦ ἄνδρες, ᾗ μοι φαίνεται ταῦτα λέγειν· σὺ δὲ ἡμῖν ἀπόκριναι, ὦ
B Μέλητε· ὑμεῖς δέ, ὅπερ κατ᾽ ἀρχὰς ὑμᾶς παρῃτη-
σάμην, μέμνησθέ μοι μὴ θορυβεῖν, ἐὰν ἐν τῷ
εἰωθότι τρόπῳ τοὺς λόγους ποιῶμαι. Ἔστιν ὅστις
ἀνθρώπων, ὦ Μέλητε, ἀνθρώπεια μὲν νομίζει
πράγματ᾽ εἶναι, ἀνθρώπους δὲ οὐ νομίζει; ἀποκρινέσθω, ὦ ἄνδρες, καὶ μὴ ἄλλα καὶ ἄλλα θορυβείτω. ἔσθ᾽ ὅστις ἵππους μὲν οὐ νομίζει, ἱππικὰ
δὲ πράγματα; ἢ αὐλητὰς μὲν οὐ νομίζει εἶναι,
αὐλητικὰ δὲ πράγματα; οὐκ ἔστιν, ὦ ἄριστε
ἀνδρῶν· εἰ μὴ σὺ βούλει ἀποκρίνασθαι, ἐγὼ σοὶ
λέγω καὶ τοῖς ἄλλοις τουτοισί. ἀλλὰ τὸ ἐπὶ
C τούτῳ γε ἀπόκριναι· ἔσθ᾽ ὅστις δαιμόνια μὲν
νομίζει πράγματ᾽ εἶναι, δαίμονας δὲ οὐ νομίζει;
Οὐκ ἔστιν. Ὡς ὤνησας, ὅτι μόγις ἀπεκρίνω ὑπὸ
τουτωνὶ ἀναγκαζόμενος. οὐκοῦν δαιμόνια μὲν φῄς
με καὶ νομίζειν καὶ διδάσκειν, εἴτ᾽ οὖν καινὰ εἴτε
παλαιά· ἀλλ᾽ οὖν δαιμόνιά γε νομίζω κατὰ τὸν
σὸν λόγον, καὶ ταῦτα καὶ διωμόσω ἐν τῇ ἀντι-
γραφῇ. εἰ δὲ δαιμόνια νομίζω, καὶ δαίμονας δήπου πολλὴ ἀνάγκη νομίζειν μέ ἐστιν· οὐχ οὕτως
ἔχει; ἔχει δή· τίθημι γάρ σε ὁμολογοῦντα,
ἐπειδὴ οὐκ ἀποκρίνει. τοὺς δὲ δαίμονας οὐχὶ ἤτοι
D θεούς γε ἡγούμεθα ἢ θεῶν παῖδας; φῂς ἢ οὔ;
Πάνυ γε. Οὐκοῦν εἴπερ δαίμονας ἡγοῦμαι, ὡς σὺ
φῄς, εἰ μὲν θεοί τινές εἰσιν οἱ δαίμονες, τοῦτ᾽ ἂν
εἴη ὃ ἐγώ φημί σε αἰνίττεσθαι καὶ χαριεντίζεσθαι,
θεοὺς οὐχ ἡγούμενον φάναι ἐμὲ θεοὺς αὖ ἡγεῖσθαι

not believe in gods, but does believe in gods."
And yet this is the conduct of a jester.

Join me, then, gentlemen, in examining how
he appears to me to say this; and do you, Meletus,
answer; and you, gentlemen, as I asked you in the
beginning, please bear in mind not to make a disturbance if I conduct my argument in my accustomed
manner.

Is there any human being who believes that there
are things pertaining to human beings, but no human
beings? Let him answer, gentlemen, and not make
a disturbance in one way or another. Is there anyone
who does not believe in horses, but does believe in
things pertaining to horses? or who does not believe
that flute-players exist, but that things pertaining to
flute-players do? There is not, best of men; if you do
not wish to answer, I say it to you and these others
here. But answer at least the next question. Is there
anyone who believes spiritual things exist, but does
not believe in spirits? "There is not." Thank you
for replying reluctantly when forced by these gentlemen. Then you say that I believe in spiritual beings,
whether new or old, and teach that belief; but then
I believe in spiritual beings at any rate, according to
your statement, and you swore to that in your indictment. But if I believe in spiritual beings, it is quite
inevitable that I believe also in spirits; is it not so?
It is; for I assume that you agree, since you do not
answer. But do we not think the spirits are gods or
children of gods? Yes, or no? "Certainly." Then
if I believe in spirits, as you say, if spirits are a kind
of gods, that would be the puzzle and joke which I
say you are uttering in saying that I, while I do not
believe in gods, do believe in gods again, since I

πάλιν, ἐπειδήπερ γε δαίμονας ἡγοῦμαι· εἰ δ' αὖ
οἱ δαίμονες θεῶν παῖδές εἰσιν νόθοι τινὲς ἢ ἐκ
νυμφῶν ἢ ἔκ τινων ἄλλων, ὧν δὴ καὶ λέγονται,
τίς ἂν ἀνθρώπων θεῶν μὲν παῖδας ἡγοῖτο
εἶναι, θεοὺς δὲ μή; ὁμοίως γὰρ ἂν ἄτοπον εἴη,
E ὥσπερ ἂν εἴ τις ἵππων μὲν παῖδας ἡγοῖτο καὶ
ὄνων, τοὺς ἡμιόνους, ἵππους δὲ καὶ ὄνους μὴ
ἡγοῖτο εἶναι. ἀλλ', ὦ Μέλητε, οὐκ ἔστιν
ὅπως σὺ[1] οὐχὶ ἀποπειρώμενος ἡμῶν ἐγράψω
τὴν γραφὴν ταύτην ἢ ἀπορῶν ὅτι ἐγκαλοῖς
ἐμοὶ ἀληθὲς ἀδίκημα· ὅπως δὲ σύ τινα πείθοις
ἂν καὶ σμικρὸν νοῦν ἔχοντα ἀνθρώπων, ὡς[2]
τοῦ αὐτοῦ ἐστιν καὶ δαιμόνια καὶ θεῖα ἡγεῖσθαι,
καὶ αὖ τοῦ αὐτοῦ[3] μήτε δαίμονας μήτε θεοὺς μήτε
28 ἥρωας,[4] οὐδεμία μηχανή ἐστιν.

16. Ἀλλὰ γάρ, ὦ ἄνδρες Ἀθηναῖοι, ὡς μὲν ἐγὼ
οὐκ ἀδικῶ κατὰ τὴν Μελήτου γραφήν, οὐ πολλῆς
μοι δοκεῖ εἶναι ἀπολογίας, ἀλλὰ ἱκανὰ καὶ ταῦτα·
ὃ δὲ καὶ ἐν τοῖς ἔμπροσθεν ἔλεγον, ὅτι πολλή μοι
ἀπέχθεια γέγονεν καὶ πρὸς πολλούς, εὖ ἴστε ὅτι
ἀληθές ἐστιν. καὶ τοῦτ' ἔστιν ὃ ἐμὲ αἱρήσει,
ἐάνπερ αἱρῇ, οὐ Μέλητος οὐδὲ Ἄνυτος, ἀλλ' ἡ τῶν
πολλῶν διαβολή τε καὶ φθόνος. ἃ δὴ πολλοὺς
καὶ ἄλλους καὶ ἀγαθοὺς ἄνδρας ᾕρηκεν, οἶμαι δὲ
B καὶ αἱρήσειν· οὐ. ὲ δὲ δεινόν, μὴ ἐν ἐμοὶ στῇ. ἴσως
δ' ἂν οὖν εἴποι τις· εἶτ' οὐκ αἰσχύνει, ὦ Σώκρατες,
τοιοῦτον ἐπιτήδευμα ἐπιτηδεύσας, ἐξ οὗ κινδυνεύεις
νυνὶ ἀποθανεῖν; ἐγὼ δὲ τούτῳ ἂν δίκαιον λόγον

[1] Schanz brackets ταῦτα, which the MSS. give after σύ.
[2] After ὡς the MSS., and Schanz, read οὐ. It was omitted
by Stephanus.
[3] Schanz, following Hirschig, brackets τοῦ αὐτοῦ.
[4] Schanz, following Prammer, brackets μήτε ἥρωας.

believe in spirits; but if, on the other hand, spirits are a kind of bastard children of gods, by nymphs or by any others, whoever their mothers are said to be, what man would believe that there are children of gods, but no gods? It would be just as absurd as if one were to believe that there are children of horses and asses, namely mules, but no horses and asses. But, Meletus, you certainly must have brought this suit either to make a test of us or because you were at a loss as to what true wrongdoing you could accuse me of; but there is no way for you to persuade any man who has even a little sense that it is possible for the same person to believe in spiritual and divine existences and again for the same person not to believe in spirits or gods or heroes.

Well then, men of Athens, that I am not a wrong-doer according to Meletus's indictment, seems to me not to need much of a defence, but what has been said is enough. But you may be assured that what I said before is true, that great hatred has arisen against me and in the minds of many persons. And this it is which will cause my condemnation, if it is to cause it, not Meletus or Anytus, but the prejudice and dislike of the many. This has condemned many other good men, and I think will do so; and there is no danger that it will stop with me. But perhaps someone might say: "Are you then not ashamed, Socrates, of having followed such a pursuit, that you are now in danger of being put to death as a result?" But I should make to him a

ἀντείποιμι, ὅτι οὐ καλῶς λέγεις, ὦ ἄνθρωπε, εἰ
οἴει δεῖν κίνδυνον ὑπολογίζεσθαι τοῦ ζῆν ἢ
τεθνάναι ἄνδρα, ὅτου τι καὶ σμικρὸν ὄφελός ἐστιν,
ἀλλ' οὐκ ἐκεῖνο μόνον σκοπεῖν, ὅταν πράττῃ,
πότερα δίκαια ἢ ἄδικα πράττει, καὶ ἀνδρὸς
ἀγαθοῦ ἔργα ἢ κακοῦ. φαῦλοι γὰρ ἂν τῷ γε σῷ
C λόγῳ εἶεν τῶν ἡμιθέων ὅσοι ἐν Τροίᾳ τετελευτή-
κασιν οἵ τε ἄλλοι καὶ ὁ τῆς Θέτιδος υἱός, ὃς
τοσοῦτον τοῦ κινδύνου κατεφρόνησεν παρὰ τὸ
αἰσχρόν τι ὑπομεῖναι, ὥστε ἐπειδὴ εἶπεν ἡ μήτηρ
αὐτῷ προθυμουμένῳ Ἕκτορα ἀποκτεῖναι, θεὸς
οὖσα, οὑτωσί πως, ὡς ἐγὼ οἶμαι· ὦ παῖ, εἰ τιμωρή-
σεις Πατρόκλῳ τῷ ἑταίρῳ τὸν φόνον καὶ Ἕκτορα
ἀποκτενεῖς, αὐτὸς ἀποθανεῖ· αὐτίκα γάρ τοι,
φησί, μεθ' Ἕκτορα πότμος ἑτοῖμος· ὁ δὲ ταῦτα
ἀκούσας τοῦ μὲν θανάτου καὶ τοῦ κινδύνου ὠλιγώ-
D ρησε, πολὺ δὲ μᾶλλον δείσας τὸ ζῆν κακὸς ὢν καὶ
τοῖς φίλοις μὴ τιμωρεῖν, αὐτίκα, φησί, τεθναίην
δίκην ἐπιθεὶς τῷ ἀδικοῦντι, ἵνα μὴ ἐνθάδε μένω
καταγέλαστος παρὰ νηυσὶ κορωνίσιν ἄχθος ἀρού-
ρης. μὴ αὐτὸν οἴει φροντίσαι θανάτου καὶ κινδύνου; οὕτω γὰρ ἔχει, ὦ ἄνδρες Ἀθηναῖοι, τῇ
ἀληθείᾳ· οὗ ἄν τις ἑαυτὸν τάξῃ ἡγησάμενος
βέλτιστον εἶναι ἢ ὑπ' ἄρχοντος ταχθῇ, ἐνταῦθα
δεῖ, ὡς ἐμοὶ δοκεῖ, μένοντα κινδυνεύειν, μηδὲν ὑπο-
λογιζόμενον μήτε θάνατον μήτε ἄλλο μηδὲν πρὸ
τοῦ αἰσχροῦ.

17. Ἐγὼ οὖν δεινὰ ἂν εἴην εἰργασμένος, ὦ
E ἄνδρες Ἀθηναῖοι, εἰ, ὅτε μέν με οἱ ἄρχοντες ἔταττον, οὓς ὑμεῖς εἵλεσθε ἄρχειν μου, καὶ ἐν Ποτιδαίᾳ
καὶ ἐν Ἀμφιπόλει καὶ ἐπὶ Δηλίῳ, τότε μὲν οὗ

just reply : " You do not speak well, Sir, if you think a man in whom there is even a little merit ought to consider danger of life or death, and not rather regard this only, when he does things, whether the things he does are right or wrong and the acts of a good or a bad man. For according to your argument all the demigods would be bad who died at Troy, including the son of Thetis, who so despised danger, in comparison with enduring any disgrace, that when his mother (and she was a goddess) said to him, as he was eager to slay Hector, something like this, I believe, 'My son, if you avenge the death of your friend Patroclus and kill Hector, you yourself shall die ; "for straightway," ' she says, ' " after Hector, is death appointed unto thee " ' ;[1] he, when he heard this, made light of death and danger, and feared much more to live as a coward and not to avenge his friends, and 'Straightway,' said he, 'may I die,[2] after doing vengeance upon the wrongdoer, that I may not stay here, jeered at beside the curved ships, a burden of the earth.'[3] Do you think he considered death and danger ? "

For thus it is, men of Athens, in truth ; wherever a man stations himself, thinking it is best to be there, or is stationed by his commander, there he must, as it seems to me, remain and run his risks, considering neither death nor any other thing more than disgrace.

So I should have done a terrible thing, if, when the commanders whom you chose to command me stationed me, both at Potidaea and at Amphipolis and at Delium, I remained where they stationed me,

---

[1] Homer, *Iliad*, xviii, 96. [2] Homer, *Iliad*, xviii, 98.
[3] Homer, *Iliad*, xviii, 104.

ἐκεῖνοι ἔταττον ἔμενον ὥσπερ καὶ ἄλλος τις καὶ
ἐκινδύνευον ἀποθανεῖν, τοῦ δὲ θεοῦ τάττοντος, ὡς
ἐγὼ ᾠήθην τε καὶ ὑπέλαβον, φιλοσοφοῦντά με
δεῖν ζῆν καὶ ἐξετάζοντα ἐμαυτὸν καὶ τοὺς ἄλλους,
29 ἐνταῦθα δὲ φοβηθεὶς ἢ θάνατον ἢ ἄλλο ὁτιοῦν
πρᾶγμα λίποιμι τὴν τάξιν. δεινὸν τἂν εἴη, καὶ ὡς
ἀληθῶς τότ' ἄν με δικαίως εἰσάγοι τις εἰς δικαστήριον, ὅτι οὐ νομίζω θεοὺς εἶναι ἀπειθῶν τῇ
μαντείᾳ καὶ δεδιὼς θάνατον καὶ οἰόμενος σοφὸς
εἶναι οὐκ ὤν. τὸ γάρ τοι θάνατον δεδιέναι, ὦ
ἄνδρες, οὐδὲν ἄλλο ἐστὶν ἢ δοκεῖν σοφὸν εἶναι
μὴ ὄντα· δοκεῖν γὰρ εἰδέναι ἐστὶν ἃ οὐκ οἶδεν.
οἶδε μὲν γὰρ οὐδεὶς τὸν θάνατον οὐδ' εἰ
τυγχάνει τῷ ἀνθρώπῳ πάντων μέγιστον ὂν τῶν
ἀγαθῶν, δεδίασι δ' ὡς εὖ εἰδότες ὅτι μέγιστον τῶν
B κακῶν ἐστι. καὶ τοῦτο πῶς οὐκ ἀμαθία ἐστὶν
αὕτη ἡ ἐπονείδιστος, ἡ τοῦ οἴεσθαι εἰδέναι ἃ οὐκ
οἶδεν; ἐγὼ δ', ὦ ἄνδρες, τούτῳ καὶ ἐνταῦθα ἴσως
διαφέρω τῶν πολλῶν ἀνθρώπων, καὶ εἰ δή τῳ
σοφώτερός του φαίην εἶναι, τούτῳ ἄν, ὅτι οὐκ
εἰδὼς ἱκανῶς περὶ τῶν ἐν Ἅιδου οὕτω καὶ οἴομαι
οὐκ εἰδέναι· τὸ δὲ ἀδικεῖν καὶ ἀπειθεῖν τῷ βελτίονι, καὶ θεῷ καὶ ἀνθρώπῳ, ὅτι κακὸν καὶ αἰσχρόν
ἐστιν οἶδα. πρὸ οὖν τῶν κακῶν, ὧν οἶδα ὅτι
κακά ἐστιν, ἃ μὴ οἶδα εἰ ἀγαθὰ ὄντα τυγχάνει
οὐδέποτε φοβήσομαι οὐδὲ φεύξομαι· ὥστε οὐδ' εἴ
C με νῦν ὑμεῖς ἀφίετε Ἀνύτῳ ἀπιστήσαντες, ὃς ἔφη
ἢ τὴν ἀρχὴν οὐ δεῖν ἐμὲ δεῦρο εἰσελθεῖν ἤ, ἐπειδὴ
εἰσῆλθον, οὐχ οἷόν τ' εἶναι τὸ μὴ ἀποκτεῖναί με,
λέγων πρὸς ὑμᾶς ὡς, εἰ διαφευξοίμην, ἤδη ἂν
ὑμῶν οἱ υἱεῖς ἐπιτηδεύοντες ἃ Σωκράτης διδάσκει
πάντες παντάπασι διαφθαρήσονται,—εἰ μοι πρὸς

like anybody else, and ran the risk of death, but when the god gave me a station, as I believed and understood, with orders to spend my life in philosophy and in examining myself and others, then I were to desert my post through fear of death or anything else whatsoever. It would be a terrible thing, and truly one might then justly hale me into court, on the charge that I do not believe that there are gods, since I disobey the oracle and fear death and think I am wise when I am not. For to fear death, gentlemen, is nothing else than to think one is wise when one is not; for it is thinking one knows what one does not know. For no one knows whether death be not even the greatest of all blessings to man, but they fear it as if they knew that it is the greatest of evils. And is not this the most reprehensible form of ignorance, that of thinking one knows what one does not know? Perhaps, gentlemen, in this matter also I differ from other men in this way, and if I were to say that I am wiser in anything, it would be in this, that not knowing very much about the other world, I do not think I know. But I do know that it is evil and disgraceful to do wrong and to disobey him who is better than I, whether he be god or man. So I shall never fear or avoid those things concerning which I do not know whether they are good or bad rather than those which I know are bad. And therefore, even if you acquit me now and are not convinced by Anytus, who said that either I ought not to have been brought to trial at all, or since I was brought to trial, I must certainly be put to death, adding that if I were acquitted your sons would all be utterly ruined by practising what I teach—if you should say

ταῦτα εἴποιτε· ὦ Σώκρατες, νῦν μὲν Ἀνύτῳ οὐ
πεισόμεθα, ἀλλ' ἀφίεμέν σε, ἐπὶ τούτῳ μέντοι,
ἐφ' ᾧτε μηκέτι ἐν ταύτῃ τῇ ζητήσει διατρίβειν
μηδὲ φιλοσοφεῖν· ἐὰν δὲ ἁλῷς ἔτι τοῦτο πράττων,
D ἀποθανεῖ· εἰ οὖν με, ὅπερ εἶπον, ἐπὶ τούτοις
ἀφίοιτε, εἴποιμ' ἂν ὑμῖν ὅτι ἐγὼ ὑμᾶς, ἄνδρες
Ἀθηναῖοι, ἀσπάζομαι μὲν καὶ φιλῶ, πείσομαι δὲ
μᾶλλον τῷ θεῷ ἢ ὑμῖν, καὶ ἕωσπερ ἂν ἐμπνέω καὶ
οἷός τε ὦ, οὐ μὴ παύσωμαι φιλοσοφῶν καὶ ὑμῖν
παρακελευόμενός τε καὶ ἐνδεικνύμενος ὅτῳ ἂν ἀεὶ
ἐντυγχάνω ὑμῶν, λέγων οἷάπερ εἴωθα, ὅτι, ὦ
ἄριστε ἀνδρῶν, Ἀθηναῖος ὤν, πόλεως τῆς μεγίστης
καὶ εὐδοκιμωτάτης εἰς σοφίαν καὶ ἰσχύν, χρημάτων μὲν οὐκ αἰσχύνει ἐπιμελούμενος, ὅπως σοι
E ἔσται ὡς πλεῖστα, καὶ δόξης καὶ τιμῆς, φρονήσεως
δὲ καὶ ἀληθείας καὶ τῆς ψυχῆς, ὅπως ὡς βελτίστη
ἔσται, οὐκ ἐπιμελεῖ οὐδὲ φροντίζεις; καὶ ἐάν τις
ὑμῶν ἀμφισβητῇ καὶ φῇ ἐπιμελεῖσθαι, οὐκ εὐθὺς
ἀφήσω αὐτὸν οὐδ' ἄπειμι, ἀλλ' ἐρήσομαι αὐτὸν
καὶ ἐξετάσω καὶ ἐλέγξω, καὶ ἐάν μοι μὴ δοκῇ
κεκτῆσθαι ἀρετήν, φάναι δέ, ὀνειδιῶ, ὅτι τὰ
30 πλείστου ἄξια περὶ ἐλαχίστου ποιεῖται, τὰ δὲ
φαυλότερα περὶ πλείονος. ταῦτα καὶ νεωτέρῳ καὶ
πρεσβυτέρῳ, ὅτῳ ἂν ἐντυγχάνω, ποιήσω, καὶ ξένῳ
καὶ ἀστῷ, μᾶλλον δὲ τοῖς ἀστοῖς, ὅσῳ μου ἐγγυ-
τέρω ἐστὲ γένει. ταῦτα γὰρ κελεύει ὁ θεός, εὖ
ἴστε, καὶ ἐγὼ οἴομαι οὐδέν πω ὑμῖν μεῖζον ἀγαθὸν
γενέσθαι ἐν τῇ πόλει ἢ τὴν ἐμὴν τῷ θεῷ ὑπηρεσίαν.
οὐδὲν γὰρ ἄλλο πράττων ἐγὼ περιέρχομαι ἢ
πείθων ὑμῶν καὶ νεωτέρους καὶ πρεσβυτέρους
μήτε σωμάτων ἐπιμελεῖσθαι μήτε χρημάτων
B πρότερον μηδὲ οὕτω σφόδρα ὡς τῆς ψυχῆς,

to me in reply to this : " Socrates, this time we will
not do as Anytus says, but we will let you go, on this
condition, however, that you no longer spend your
time in this investigation or in philosophy, and if you
are caught doing so again you shall die " ; if you
should let me go on this condition which I have
mentioned, I should say to you, " Men of Athens, I
respect and love you, but I shall obey the god rather
than you, and while I live and am able to continue,
I shall never give up philosophy or stop exhorting
you and pointing out the truth to any one of you
whom I may meet, saying in my accustomed way :
" Most excellent man, are you who are a citizen of
Athens, the greatest of cities and the most famous
for wisdom and power, not ashamed to care for the
acquisition of wealth and for reputation and honour,
when you neither care nor take thought for wisdom
and truth and the perfection of your soul ? "   And if
any of you argues the point, and says he does care, I
shall not let him go at once, nor shall I go away, but
I shall question and examine and cross-examine him,
and if I find that he does not possess virtue, but says
he does, I shall rebuke him for scorning the things
that are of most importance and caring more for
what is of less worth.   This I shall do to whomever
I meet, young and old, foreigner and citizen, but
most to the citizens, inasmuch as you are more
nearly related to me.   For know that the god
commands me to do this, and I believe that no
greater good ever came to pass in the city than my
service to the god.   For I go about doing nothing
else than urging you, young and old, not to care for
your persons or your property more than for the
perfection of your souls, or even so much ; and I tell

PLATO

ὅπως ὡς ἀρίστη ἔσται, λέγων, ὅτι οὐκ ἐκ
χρημάτων ἀρετὴ γίγνεται, ἀλλ' ἐξ ἀρετῆς
χρήματα καὶ τὰ ἄλλα ἀγαθὰ τοῖς ἀνθρώποις
ἅπαντα καὶ ἰδίᾳ καὶ δημοσίᾳ. εἰ μὲν οὖν ταῦτα
λέγων διαφθείρω τοὺς νέους, ταῦτ' ἂν εἴη βλαβερά·
εἰ δέ τίς μέ φησιν ἄλλα λέγειν ἢ ταῦτα, οὐδὲν
λέγει. πρὸς ταῦτα, φαίην ἄν, ὦ Ἀθηναῖοι, ἢ
πείθεσθε Ἀνύτῳ ἢ μή, καὶ ἢ ἀφίετε ἢ μὴ ἀφίετε,
ὡς ἐμοῦ οὐκ ἂν ποιήσοντος ἄλλα, οὐδ' εἰ μέλλω
C πολλάκις τεθνάναι.

18. Μὴ θορυβεῖτε, ἄνδρες Ἀθηναῖοι, ἀλλ'
ἐμμείνατέ μοι οἷς ἐδεήθην ὑμῶν, μὴ θορυβεῖν ἐφ'
οἷς ἂν λέγω, ἀλλ' ἀκούειν· καὶ γάρ, ὡς ἐγὼ οἶμαι,
ὀνήσεσθε ἀκούοντες. μέλλω γὰρ οὖν ἄττα ὑμῖν
ἐρεῖν καὶ ἄλλα, ἐφ' οἷς ἴσως βοήσεσθε· ἀλλὰ
μηδαμῶς ποιεῖτε τοῦτο. εὖ γὰρ ἴστε, ἐὰν ἐμὲ
ἀποκτείνητε τοιοῦτον ὄντα, οἷον ἐγὼ λέγω, οὐκ
ἐμὲ μείζω βλάψετε ἢ ὑμᾶς αὐτούς· ἐμὲ μὲν γὰρ
οὐδὲν ἂν βλάψειεν οὔτε Μέλητος οὔτε Ἄνυτος·
D οὐδὲ γὰρ ἂν δύναιτο· οὐ γὰρ οἶμαι θεμιτὸν εἶναι
ἀμείνονι ἀνδρὶ ὑπὸ χείρονος βλάπτεσθαι. ἀπο-
κτείνειε μέντ' ἂν ἴσως ἢ ἐξελάσειεν ἢ ἀτιμώσειεν·
ἀλλὰ ταῦτα οὗτος μὲν ἴσως οἴεται καὶ ἄλλος τίς
που μεγάλα κακά, ἐγὼ δ' οὐκ οἶμαι, ἀλλὰ πολὺ
μᾶλλον ποιεῖν ἃ οὗτος νυνὶ ποιεῖ, ἄνδρα ἀδίκως
ἐπιχειρεῖν ἀποκτιννύναι. νῦν οὖν, ὦ ἄνδρες Ἀθηναῖοι, πολλοῦ δέω ἐγὼ ὑπὲρ ἐμαυτοῦ ἀπολογεῖσθαι,
ὥς τις ἂν οἴοιτο, ἀλλὰ ὑπὲρ ὑμῶν, μή τι ἐξαμάρ-
τητε περὶ τὴν τοῦ θεοῦ δόσιν ὑμῖν ἐμοῦ καταψη-
E φισάμενοι. ἐὰν γὰρ ἐμὲ ἀποκτείνητε, οὐ ῥᾳδίως
ἄλλον τοιοῦτον εὑρήσετε, ἀτεχνῶς, εἰ καὶ γελοιό-

you that virtue does not come from money, but from
virtue comes money and all other good things to
man, both to the individual and to the state. If by
saying these things I corrupt the youth, these things
must be injurious; but if anyone asserts that I say
other things than these, he says what is untrue.
Therefore I say to you, men of Athens, either do
as Anytus tells you, or not, and either acquit me, or
not, knowing that I shall not change my conduct
even if I am to die many times over.

Do not make a disturbance, men of Athens;
continue to do what I asked of you, not to interrupt
my speech by disturbances, but to hear me; and I
believe you will profit by hearing. Now I am going
to say some things to you at which you will perhaps
cry out; but do not do so by any means. For know
that if you kill me, I being such a man as I say I am,
you will not injure me so much as yourselves; for
neither Meletus nor Anytus could injure me; that
would be impossible, for I believe it is not God's will
that a better man be injured by a worse. He might,
however, perhaps kill me or banish me or disfranchise
me; and perhaps he thinks he would thus inflict
great injuries upon me, and others may think so, but
I do not; I think he does himself a much greater
injury by doing what he is doing now—killing a man
unjustly. And so, men of Athens, I am now making
my defence not for my own sake, as one might
imagine, but far more for yours, that you may not by
condemning me err in your treatment of the gift the
God gave you. For if you put me to death, you will
not easily find another, who, to use a rather absurd

τερον εἰπεῖν, προσκείμενον τῇ πόλει,[1] ὥσπερ
ἵππῳ μεγάλῳ μὲν καὶ γενναίῳ, ὑπὸ μεγέθους δὲ
νωθεστέρῳ καὶ δεομένῳ ἐγείρεσθαι ὑπὸ μύωπός
τινος· οἶον δή μοι δοκεῖ ὁ θεὸς ἐμὲ τῇ πόλει
προστεθεικέναι τοιοῦτόν τινα, ὃς ὑμᾶς ἐγείρων
31 καὶ πείθων καὶ ὀνειδίζων ἕνα ἕκαστον οὐδὲν
παύομαι τὴν ἡμέραν ὅλην πανταχοῦ προσκαθίζων.
τοιοῦτος οὖν ἄλλος οὐ ῥᾳδίως ὑμῖν γενήσεται, ὦ
ἄνδρες, ἀλλ' ἐὰν ἐμοὶ πείθησθε, φείσεσθέ μου·
ὑμεῖς δ' ἴσως τάχ' ἂν ἀχθόμενοι, ὥσπερ οἱ νυστά-
ζοντες ἐγειρόμενοι, κρούσαντες ἄν με, πειθόμενοι
Ἀνύτῳ, ῥᾳδίως ἂν ἀποκτείναιτε, εἶτα τὸν λοιπὸν
βίον καθεύδοντες διατελοῖτε ἄν, εἰ μή τινα ἄλλον
ὁ θεὸς ὑμῖν ἐπιπέμψειεν κηδόμενος ὑμῶν. ὅτι δ'
ἐγὼ τυγχάνω ὢν τοιοῦτος, οἶος ὑπὸ τοῦ θεοῦ τῇ
B πόλει δεδόσθαι, ἐνθένδε ἂν κατανοήσαιτε· οὐ γὰρ
ἀνθρωπίνῳ ἔοικε τὸ ἐμὲ τῶν μὲν ἐμαυτοῦ ἁπάντων
ἠμεληκέναι καὶ ἀνέχεσθαι τῶν οἰκείων ἀμελου-
μένων τοσαῦτα ἤδη ἔτη, τὸ δὲ ὑμέτερον πράττειν
ἀεί, ἰδίᾳ ἑκάστῳ προσιόντα ὥσπερ πατέρα ἢ
ἀδελφὸν πρεσβύτερον, πείθοντα ἐπιμελεῖσθαι
ἀρετῆς. καὶ εἰ μέν τι ἀπὸ τούτων ἀπέλαυον καὶ
μισθὸν λαμβάνων ταῦτα παρεκελευόμην, εἶχεν[2]
ἄν τινα λόγον· νῦν δὲ ὁρᾶτε δὴ καὶ αὐτοί, ὅτι οἱ
κατήγοροι τἆλλα πάντα ἀναισχύντως οὕτω κατηγοροῦντες τοῦτό γε οὐχ οἷοί τε ἐγένοντο ἀπ-
C αναισχυντῆσαι παρασχόμενοι μάρτυρα, ὡς ἐγώ
ποτέ τινα ἢ ἐπραξάμην μισθὸν ἢ ᾔτησα. ἱκανὸν

---

[1] The MSS. give ὑπὸ τοῦ θεοῦ, "by the god," after πόλει.
Schanz, following Hirschig, brackets it.
[2] Schanz, with some inferior MS. authority, reads εἶχεν for
εἶχον of the best MSS.

figure, attaches himself to the city as a gadfly to a horse, which, though large and well bred, is sluggish on account of his size and needs to be aroused by stinging. I think the god fastened me upon the city in some such capacity, and I go about arousing, and urging and reproaching each one of you, constantly alighting upon you everywhere the whole day long. Such another is not likely to come to you, gentlemen; but if you take my advice, you will spare me. But you, perhaps, might be angry, like people awakened from a nap, and might slap me, as Anytus advises, and easily kill me; then you would pass the rest of your lives in slumber, unless God, in his care for you, should send someone else to sting you. And that I am, as I say, a kind of gift from the god, you might understand from this; for I have neglected all my own affairs and have been enduring the neglect of my concerns all these years, but I am always busy in your interest, coming to each one of you individually like a father or an elder brother and urging you to care for virtue; now that is not like human conduct. If I derived any profit from this and received pay for these exhortations, there would be some sense in it; but now you yourselves see that my accusers, though they accuse me of everything else in such a shameless way, have not been able to work themselves up to such a pitch of shamelessness as to produce a witness to testify that I ever exacted or asked pay of anyone. For I think

γάρ, οἶμαι, ἐγὼ παρέχομαι τὸν μάρτυρα, ὡς ἀληθῆ λέγω, τὴν πενίαν.

19. Ἴσως ἂν οὖν δόξειεν ἄτοπον εἶναι, ὅτι δὴ ἐγὼ ἰδίᾳ μὲν ταῦτα ξυμβουλεύω περιιὼν καὶ πολυπραγμονῶ, δημοσίᾳ δὲ οὐ τολμῶ ἀναβαίνων εἰς τὸ πλῆθος τὸ ὑμέτερον ξυμβουλεύειν τῇ πόλει. τούτου δὲ αἴτιόν ἐστιν ὃ ὑμεῖς ἐμοῦ πολλάκις D ἀκηκόατε πολλαχοῦ λέγοντος, ὅτι μοι θεῖόν τι καὶ δαιμόνιον γίγνεται,[1] ὃ δὴ καὶ ἐν τῇ γραφῇ ἐπικωμῳδῶν Μέλητος ἐγράψατο· ἐμοὶ δὲ τοῦτ' ἔστιν ἐκ παιδὸς ἀρξάμενον φωνή τις γιγνομένη, ἣ ὅταν γένηται, ἀεὶ ἀποτρέπει με τοῦτο ὃ ἂν μέλλω πράττειν, προτρέπει δὲ οὔποτε· τοῦτ' ἔστιν ὅ μοι ἐναντιοῦται τὰ πολιτικὰ πράττειν. καὶ παγκάλως γέ μοι δοκεῖ ἐναντιοῦσθαι· εὖ γὰρ ἴστε, ὦ ἄνδρες Ἀθηναῖοι, εἰ ἐγὼ ἐπεχείρησα πράττειν τὰ πολιτικὰ πράγματα, πάλαι ἂν ἀπολώλη καὶ οὔτ' E ἂν ὑμᾶς ὠφελήκη οὐδὲν οὔτ' ἂν ἐμαυτόν. καί μοι μὴ ἄχθεσθε λέγοντι τἀληθῆ· οὐ γὰρ ἔστιν ὅστις ἀνθρώπων σωθήσεται οὔτε ὑμῖν οὔτε ἄλλῳ πλήθει οὐδενὶ γνησίως ἐναντιούμενος καὶ διακωλύων πολλὰ ἄδικα καὶ παράνομα ἐν τῇ πόλει γίγνεσθαι, 32 ἀλλ' ἀναγκαῖόν ἐστι τὸν τῷ ὄντι μαχούμενον ὑπὲρ τοῦ δικαίου, καὶ εἰ μέλλει ὀλίγον χρόνον σωθήσεσθαι, ἰδιωτεύειν ἀλλὰ μὴ δημοσιεύειν.

20. Μεγάλα δ' ἔγωγε ὑμῖν τεκμήρια παρέξομαι τούτων, οὐ λόγους, ἀλλ' ὃ ὑμεῖς τιμᾶτε, ἔργα. ἀκούσατε δή μου τὰ ἐμοὶ ξυμβεβηκότα, ἵνα εἰδῆτε, ὅτι οὐδ' ἂν ἑνὶ ὑπεικάθοιμι παρὰ τὸ δίκαιον δείσας θάνατον, μὴ ὑπείκων δὲ ἅμ' ἂν καὶ ἀπολοίμην.

---

[1] The MSS. read φωνή, "voice," after γίγνεται. Schanz, following others, omits it.

I have a sufficient witness that I speak the truth, namely, my poverty.

Perhaps it may seem strange that I go about and interfere in other people's affairs to give this advice in private, but do not venture to come before your assembly and advise the state. But the reason for this, as you have heard me say at many times and places, is that something divine and spiritual comes to me, the very thing which Meletus ridiculed in his indictment. I have had this from my childhood; it is a sort of voice that comes to me, and when it comes it always holds me back from what I am thinking of doing, but never urges me forward. This it is which opposes my engaging in politics. And I think this opposition is a very good thing; for you may be quite sure, men of Athens, that if I had undertaken to go into politics, I should have been put to death long ago and should have done no good to you or to myself. And do not be angry with me for speaking the truth; the fact is that no man will save his life who nobly opposes you or any other populace and prevents many unjust and illegal things from happening in the state. A man who really fights for the right, if he is to preserve his life for even a little while, must be a private citizen, not a public man.

I will give you powerful proofs of this, not mere words, but what you honour more,—actions. And listen to what happened to me, that you may be convinced that I would never yield to any one, if that was wrong, through fear of death, but would die rather than yield. The tale I am going to tell

ἐρῶ δὲ ὑμῖν φορτικὰ μὲν καὶ δικανικά, ἀληθῆ δέ.
B ἐγὼ γάρ, ὦ Ἀθηναῖοι, ἄλλην μὲν ἀρχὴν οὐδεμίαν
πώποτε ἦρξα ἐν τῇ πόλει, ἐβούλευσα δέ· καὶ
ἔτυχεν ἡμῶν ἡ φυλὴ πρυτανεύουσα, ὅτε ὑμεῖς
τοὺς δέκα στρατηγοὺς τοὺς οὐκ ἀνελομένους τοὺς
ἐκ τῆς ναυμαχίας ἐβούλεσθε ἀθρόους κρίνειν,
παρανόμως ὡς ἐν τῷ ὑστέρῳ χρόνῳ πᾶσιν ὑμῖν
ἔδοξε. τότ᾿ ἐγὼ μόνος τῶν πρυτάνεων ἠναντιώθην
ὑμῖν μηδὲν ποιεῖν παρὰ τοὺς νόμους¹ καὶ ἑτοί-
μων ὄντων ἐνδεικνύναι με καὶ ἀπάγειν τῶν ῥη-
τόρων, καὶ ὑμῶν κελευόντων καὶ βοώντων, μετὰ
C τοῦ νόμου καὶ τοῦ δικαίου ᾤμην μᾶλλόν με δεῖν
διακινδυνεύειν ἢ μεθ᾿ ὑμῶν γενέσθαι μὴ δίκαια
βουλευομένων, φοβηθέντα δεσμὸν ἢ θάνατον. καὶ
ταῦτα μὲν ἦν ἔτι δημοκρατουμένης τῆς πόλεως·
ἐπειδὴ δὲ ὀλιγαρχία ἐγένετο, οἱ τριάκοντα αὖ
μεταπεμψάμενοί με πέμπτον αὐτὸν εἰς τὴν θόλον
προσέταξαν ἀγαγεῖν ἐκ Σαλαμῖνος Λέοντα τὸν
Σαλαμίνιον, ἵνα ἀποθάνοι· οἷα δὴ καὶ ἄλλοις
ἐκεῖνοι πολλοῖς πολλὰ προσέταττον, βουλόμενοι
ὡς πλείστους ἀναπλῆσαι αἰτιῶν· τότε μέντοι
D ἐγὼ οὐ λόγῳ ἀλλ᾿ ἔργῳ αὖ ἐνεδειξάμην, ὅτι ἐμοὶ
θανάτου μὲν μέλει, εἰ μὴ ἀγροικότερον ἦν εἰπεῖν,
οὐδ᾿ ὁτιοῦν, τοῦ δὲ μηδὲν ἄδικον μηδ᾿ ἀνόσιον ἐργάζεσθαι, τούτου δὲ τὸ πᾶν μέλει. ἐμὲ γὰρ ἐκείνη ἡ
ἀρχὴ οὐκ ἐξέπληξεν οὕτως ἰσχυρὰ οὖσα, ὥστε
ἄδικόν τι ἐργάσασθαι, ἀλλ᾿ ἐπειδὴ ἐκ τῆς θόλου
ἐξήλθομεν, οἱ μὲν τέτταρες ᾤχοντο εἰς Σαλαμῖνα
καὶ ἤγαγον Λέοντα, ἐγὼ δὲ ᾠχόμην ἀπιὼν οἴκαδε.
καὶ ἴσως ἂν διὰ ταῦτα ἀπέθανον, εἰ μὴ ἡ ἀρχὴ

¹ Schanz, following Hermann, brackets καὶ ἐναντία ἐψη-
φισάμην, "and I voted against it," which the MSS. give after

you is ordinary and commonplace, but true. I, men of Athens, never held any other office in the state, but I was a senator; and it happened that my tribe held the presidency when you wished to judge collectively, not severally, the ten generals who had failed to gather up the slain after the naval battle; this was illegal, as you all agreed afterwards. At that time I was the only one of the prytanes who opposed doing anything contrary to the laws, and although the orators were ready to impeach and arrest me, and though you urged them with shouts to do so, I thought I must run the risk to the end with law and justice on my side, rather than join with you when your wishes were unjust, through fear of imprisonment or death. That was when the democracy still existed; and after the oligarchy was established, the Thirty sent for me with four others to come to the rotunda and ordered us to bring Leon the Salaminian from Salamis to be put to death. They gave many such orders to others also, because they wished to implicate as many in their crimes as they could. Then I, however, showed again, by action, not in word only, that I did not care a whit for death if that be not too rude an expression, but that I did care with all my might not to do anything unjust or unholy. For that government, with all its power, did not frighten me into doing anything unjust, but when we came out of the rotunda, the other four went to Salamis and arrested Leon, but I simply went home; and perhaps I should have been put to death for it, if the government had not quickly been

νόμους. Xenophon, *Mem.* iv. 4. 2, states that Socrates, as presiding officer, refused to put the question to vote.

Ε δι ὰ ταχέων κατελύθη· καὶ τούτων ὑμῖν ἔσονται
πολλοὶ μάρτυρες.

21. Ἀρ' οὖν ἄν με οἴεσθε τοσάδε ἔτη διαγε-
νέσθαι, εἰ ἔπραττον τὰ δημόσια, καὶ πράττων
ἀξίως ἀνδρὸς ἀγαθοῦ ἐβοήθουν τοῖς δικαίοις καί,
ὥσπερ χρή, τοῦτο περὶ πλείστου ἐποιούμην;
πολλοῦ γε δεῖ, ὦ ἄνδρες Ἀθηναῖοι. οὐδὲ γὰρ ἂν
33 ἄλλος ἀνθρώπων οὐδείς. ἀλλ' ἐγὼ διὰ παντὸς
τοῦ βίου δημοσίᾳ τε, εἴ πού τι ἔπραξα, τοιοῦτος
φανοῦμαι, καὶ ἰδίᾳ ὁ αὐτὸς οὗτος, οὐδενὶ πώποτε
ξυγχωρήσας οὐδὲν παρὰ τὸ δίκαιον οὔτε ἄλλῳ
οὔτε τούτων οὐδενί, οὓς οἱ διαβάλλοντες ἐμέ φασιν
ἐμοὺς μαθητὰς εἶναι. ἐγὼ δὲ διδάσκαλος μὲν
οὐδενὸς πώποτ' ἐγενόμην· εἰ δέ τίς μου λέγοντος
καὶ τὰ ἐμαυτοῦ πράττοντος ἐπιθυμεῖ ἀκούειν, εἴτε
νεώτερος εἴτε πρεσβύτερος, οὐδενὶ πώποτε ἐφθό-
Β νησα, οὐδὲ χρήματα μὲν λαμβάνων διαλέγομαι
μὴ λαμβάνων δὲ οὔ, ἀλλ' ὁμοίως καὶ πλουσίῳ
καὶ πένητι παρέχω ἐμαυτὸν ἐρωτᾶν, καὶ ἐάν τις
βούληται ἀποκρινόμενος ἀκούειν ὧν ἂν λέγω.
καὶ τούτων ἐγὼ εἴτε τις χρηστὸς γίγνεται εἴτε
μή, οὐκ ἂν δικαίως τὴν αἰτίαν ὑπέχοιμι, ὧν μήτε
ὑπεσχόμην μηδενὶ μηδὲν πώποτε μάθημα μήτε
ἐδίδαξα· εἰ δέ τίς φησι παρ' ἐμοῦ πώποτέ τι
μαθεῖν ἢ ἀκοῦσαι ἰδίᾳ ὅ τι μὴ καὶ οἱ ἄλλοι πάντες,
εὖ ἴστε, ὅτι οὐκ ἀληθῆ λέγει.

22. Ἀλλὰ διὰ τί δή ποτε μετ' ἐμοῦ χαίρουσί
C τινες πολὺν χρόνον διατρίβοντες; ἀκηκόατε, ὦ
ἄνδρες Ἀθηναῖοι· πᾶσαν ὑμῖν τὴν ἀλήθειαν ἐγὼ
εἶπον· ὅτι ἀκούοντες χαίρουσιν ἐξεταζομένοις τοῖς
οἰομένοις μὲν εἶναι σοφοῖς, οὖσι δ' οὔ· ἔστι γὰρ οὐκ
ἀηδές. ἐμοὶ δὲ τοῦτο, ὡς ἐγώ φημι, προστέτακται

put down. Of these facts you can have many witnesses.

Do you believe that I could have lived so many years if I had been in public life and had acted as a good man should act, lending my aid to what is just and considering that of the highest importance? Far from it, men of Athens; nor could any other man. But you will find that through all my life, both in public, if I engaged in any public activity, and in private, I have always been the same as now, and have never yielded to any one wrongly, whether it were any other person or any of those who are said by my traducers to be my pupils. But I was never any one's teacher. If any one, whether young or old, wishes to hear me speaking and pursuing my mission, I have never objected, nor do I converse only when I am paid and not otherwise, but I offer myself alike to rich and poor; I ask questions, and whoever wishes may answer and hear what I say. And whether any of them turns out well or ill, I should not justly be held responsible, since I never promised or gave any instruction to any of them; but if any man says that he ever learned or heard anything privately from me, which all the others did not, be assured that he is lying.

But why then do some people love to spend much of their time with me? You have heard the reason, men of Athens; for I told you the whole truth; it is because they like to listen when those are examined who think they are wise and are not so; for it is amusing. But, as I believe, I

ὑπὸ τοῦ θεοῦ πράττειν καὶ ἐκ μαντείων καὶ ἐξ
ἐνυπνίων καὶ παντὶ τρόπῳ, ᾧπέρ τίς ποτε καὶ
ἄλλη θεία μοῖρα ἀνθρώπῳ καὶ ὁτιοῦν προσέταξε
πράττειν. ταῦτα, ὦ Ἀθηναῖοι, καὶ ἀληθῆ ἐστιν
καὶ εὐέλεγκτα. εἰ γὰρ δὴ ἔγωγε τῶν νέων τοὺς
D μὲν διαφθείρω, τοὺς δὲ διέφθαρκα, χρῆν δήπου,
εἴτε τινὲς αὐτῶν πρεσβύτεροι γενόμενοι ἔγνωσαν
ὅτι νέοις οὖσιν αὐτοῖς ἐγὼ κακὸν πώποτέ τι
ξυνεβούλευσα, νυνὶ αὐτοὺς ἀναβαίνοντας ἐμοῦ
κατηγορεῖν καὶ τιμωρεῖσθαι· εἰ δὲ μὴ αὐτοὶ ἤθελον,
τῶν οἰκείων τινὰς τῶν ἐκείνων, πατέρας καὶ ἀδελ-
φοὺς καὶ ἄλλους τοὺς προσήκοντας, εἴπερ ὑπ᾽
ἐμοῦ τι κακὸν ἐπεπόνθεσαν αὐτῶν οἱ οἰκεῖοι, νῦν
μεμνῆσθαι.¹ πάντως δὲ πάρεισιν αὐτῶν πολλοὶ
ἐνταυθοῖ, οὓς ἐγὼ ὁρῶ, πρῶτον μὲν Κρίτων
E οὑτοσί, ἐμὸς ἡλικιώτης καὶ δημότης, Κριτοβούλου
τοῦδε πατήρ, ἔπειτα Λυσανίας ὁ Σφήττιος, Αἰ-
σχίνου τοῦδε πατήρ, ἔτι Ἀντιφῶν ὁ Κηφισιεὺς
οὑτοσί, Ἐπιγένους πατήρ· ἄλλοι τοίνυν οὗτοι,
ὧν οἱ ἀδελφοὶ ἐν ταύτῃ τῇ διατριβῇ γεγόνασιν,
Νικόστρατος ὁ Θεοζοτίδου, ἀδελφὸς Θεοδότου—
καὶ ὁ μὲν Θεόδοτος τετελεύτηκεν, ὥστε οὐκ ἂν
ἐκεῖνός γε αὐτοῦ καταδεηθείη—,καὶ Πάραλος
ὅδε ὁ Δημοδόκου, οὗ ἦν Θεάγης ἀδελφός. ὅδε δὲ
34 Ἀδείμαντος ὁ Ἀρίστωνος, οὗ ἀδελφὸς οὑτοσὶ
Πλάτων, καὶ Αἰαντόδωρος, οὗ Ἀπολλόδωρος ὅδε
ἀδελφός. καὶ ἄλλους πολλοὺς ἐγὼ ἔχω ὑμῖν
εἰπεῖν, ὧν τινα ἐχρῆν μάλιστα μὲν ἐν τῷ
ἑαυτοῦ λόγῳ παρασχέσθαι Μέλητον μάρτυρα· εἰ

¹ After μεμνῆσθαι the best MSS. give καὶ τιμωρεῖσθαι, "and
punish." Schanz follows Bekker and some MSS. in omitting
these words.

have been commanded to do this by the God through oracles and dreams and in every way in which any man was ever commanded by divine power to do anything whatsoever. This, Athenians, is true and easily tested. For if I am corrupting some of the young men and have corrupted others, surely some of them who have grown older, if they recognise that I ever gave them any bad advice when they were young, ought now to have come forward to accuse me. Or if they did not wish to do it themselves, some of their relatives—fathers or brothers or other kinsfolk— ought now to tell the facts. And there are many of them present, whom I see; first Crito here, who is of my own age and my own deme and father of Critobulus, who is also present; then there is Lysanias the Sphettian, father of Aeschines, who is here; and also Antiphon of Cephisus, father of Epigenes. Then here are others whose brothers joined in my conversations, Nicostratus, son of Theozotides and brother of Theodotus (now Theodotus is dead, so he could not stop him by entreaties), and Paralus, son of Demodocus; Theages was his brother; and Adimantus, son of Aristo, whose brother is Plato here; and Aeantodorus, whose brother Apollodorus is present. And I can mention to you many others, some one of whom Meletus ought certainly to have produced as a witness in his speech; but if he forgot it then, let

PLATO

δὲ τότε ἐπελάθετο, νῦν παρασχέσθω, ἐγὼ παρα-
χωρῶ, καὶ λεγέτω, εἴ τι ἔχει τοιοῦτον. ἀλλὰ
τούτου πᾶν τοὐναντίον εὑρήσετε, ὦ ἄνδρες, πάντας
ἐμοὶ βοηθεῖν ἑτοίμους τῷ διαφθείροντι, τῷ κακὰ
ἐργαζομένῳ τοὺς οἰκείους αὐτῶν, ὥς φασι Μέ-
B λητος καὶ Ἄνυτος. αὐτοὶ μὲν γὰρ οἱ διεφθαρμένοι τάχ᾽ ἂν λόγον ἔχοιεν βοηθοῦντες· οἱ δὲ
ἀδιάφθαρτοι, πρεσβύτεροι ἤδη ἄνδρες, οἱ τούτων
προσήκοντες, τίνα ἄλλον ἔχουσι λόγον βοηθοῦντες
ἐμοὶ ἀλλ᾽ ἢ τὸν ὀρθόν τε καὶ δίκαιον, ὅτι ξυνίσασι
Μελήτῳ μὲν ψευδομένῳ, ἐμοὶ δὲ ἀληθεύοντι;
23. Εἶεν δή, ὦ ἄνδρες· ἃ μὲν ἐγὼ ἔχοιμ᾽ ἂν
ἀπολογεῖσθαι, σχεδόν ἐστι ταῦτα καὶ ἄλλα ἴσως
τοιαῦτα. τάχα δ᾽ ἄν τις ὑμῶν ἀγανακτήσειεν
C ἀναμνησθεὶς ἑαυτοῦ, εἰ ὁ μὲν καὶ ἐλάττω τουτουὶ
τοῦ ἀγῶνος ἀγῶνα ἀγωνιζόμενος ἐδεήθη τε καὶ
ἱκέτευσε τοὺς δικαστὰς μετὰ πολλῶν δακρύων,
παιδία τε αὑτοῦ ἀναβιβασάμενος, ἵνα ὅ τι μάλιστα
ἐλεηθείη, καὶ ἄλλους τῶν οἰκείων καὶ φίλων πολλούς, ἐγὼ δὲ οὐδὲν ἄρα τούτων ποιήσω, καὶ ταῦτα
κινδυνεύων, ὡς ἂν δόξαιμι, τὸν ἔσχατον κίνδυνον.
τάχ᾽ οὖν τις ταῦτα ἐννοήσας αὐθαδέστερον ἂν
πρός με σχοίη, καὶ ὀργισθεὶς αὐτοῖς τούτοις θεῖτο
ἂν μετ᾽ ὀργῆς τὴν ψῆφον. εἰ δή τις ὑμῶν οὕτως
D ἔχει,—οὐκ ἀξιῶ μὲν γὰρ ἔγωγε· εἰ δ᾽ οὖν, ἐπιεικῆ
ἄν μοι δοκῶ πρὸς τοῦτον λέγειν λέγων ὅτι
ἐμοί, ὦ ἄριστε, εἰσὶν μέν πού τινες καὶ οἰκεῖοι·
καὶ γὰρ τοῦτο αὐτὸ τὸ τοῦ Ὁμήρου, οὐδ᾽ ἐγὼ ἀπὸ
δρυὸς οὐδ᾽ ἀπὸ πέτρης πέφυκα, ἀλλ᾽ ἐξ ἀνθρώπων,
ὥστε καὶ οἰκεῖοί μοί εἰσι καὶ υἱεῖς, ὦ ἄνδρες Ἀθηναῖοι, τρεῖς, εἷς μὲν μειράκιον ἤδη, δύο δὲ παιδία·

him do so now; I yield the floor to him, and let him
say, if he has any such testimony. But you will
find that the exact opposite is the case, gentlemen,
and that they are all ready to aid me, the man who
corrupts and injures their relatives, as Meletus and
Anytus say. Now those who are themselves corrupted might have some motive in aiding me; but
what reason could their relatives have, who are not
corrupted and are already older men, unless it be
the right and true reason, that they know that
Meletus is lying and I am speaking the truth?

Well, gentlemen, this, and perhaps more like
this, is about all I have to say in my defence.
Perhaps some one among you may be offended when
he remembers his own conduct, if he, even in a
case of less importance than this, begged and besought
the judges with many tears, and brought forward
his children to arouse compassion, and many other
friends and relatives; whereas I will do none of
these things, though I am, apparently, in the very
greatest danger. Perhaps some one with these
thoughts in mind may be harshly disposed toward
me and may cast his vote in anger. Now if any one
of you is so disposed—I do not believe there is such
a person—but if there should be, I think I should
be speaking fairly if I said to him, My friend, I too
have relatives, for I am, as Homer has it, "not born
of an oak or a rock," [1] but of human parents, so
that I have relatives and, men of Athens, I have
three sons, one nearly grown up, and two still

[1] Homer, *Odyssey*, xix, 163.

ἀλλ' ὅμως οὐδένα αὐτῶν δεῦρο ἀναβιβασάμενος
δεήσομαι ὑμῶν ἀποψηφίσασθαι. τί δὴ οὖν οὐδὲν
τούτων ποιήσω; οὐκ αὐθαδιζόμενος, ὦ Ἀθηναῖοι,
E οὐδ' ὑμᾶς ἀτιμάζων, ἀλλ' εἰ μὲν θαρραλέως ἐγὼ
ἔχω πρὸς θάνατον ἢ μή, ἄλλος λόγος, πρὸς δ'
οὖν δόξαν καὶ ἐμοὶ καὶ ὑμῖν καὶ ὅλῃ τῇ πόλει οὔ
μοι δοκεῖ καλὸν εἶναι ἐμὲ τούτων οὐδὲν ποιεῖν καὶ
τηλικόνδε ὄντα καὶ τοῦτο τοὔνομα ἔχοντα, εἴτ' οὖν
ἀληθὲς εἴτ' οὖν ψεῦδος· ἀλλ' οὖν δεδογμένον γέ ἐστι
35 τῷ Σωκράτει διαφέρειν τινὶ τῶν πολλῶν ἀνθρώπων.
εἰ οὖν ὑμῶν οἱ δοκοῦντες διαφέρειν εἴτε σοφίᾳ εἴτε
ἀνδρείᾳ εἴτε ἄλλῃ ᾑτινιοῦν ἀρετῇ τοιοῦτοι ἔσονται,
αἰσχρὸν ἂν εἴη· οἵουσπερ ἐγὼ πολλάκις ἑώρακά
τινας, ὅταν κρίνωνται, δοκοῦντας μέν τι εἶναι,
θαυμάσια δὲ ἐργαζομένους, ὡς δεινόν τι οἰομένους
πείσεσθαι, εἰ ἀποθανοῦνται, ὥσπερ ἀθανάτων
ἐσομένων, ἂν ὑμεῖς αὐτοὺς μὴ ἀποκτείνητε· οἳ ἐμοὶ
δοκοῦσιν αἰσχύνην τῇ πόλει περιάπτειν, ὥστ' ἄν
τινα καὶ τῶν ξένων ὑπολαβεῖν ὅτι οἱ διαφέροντες
B Ἀθηναίων εἰς ἀρετήν, οὓς αὐτοὶ ἑαυτῶν ἔν τε ταῖς
ἀρχαῖς καὶ ταῖς ἄλλαις τιμαῖς προκρίνουσιν,
οὗτοι γυναικῶν οὐδὲν διαφέρουσι. ταῦτα γάρ, ὦ
ἄνδρες Ἀθηναῖοι, οὔτε ἡμᾶς χρὴ ποιεῖν τοὺς
δοκοῦντας καὶ ὁπηοῦν τι εἶναι, οὔτ', ἂν ἡμεῖς
ποιῶμεν, ὑμᾶς ἐπιτρέπειν, ἀλλὰ τοῦτο αὐτὸ ἐνδείκνυσθαι, ὅτι πολὺ μᾶλλον καταψηφιεῖσθε τοῦ τὰ
ἐλεεινὰ ταῦτα δράματα εἰσάγοντος καὶ καταγέ-
λαστον τὴν πόλιν ποιοῦντος ἢ τοῦ ἡσυχίαν
ἄγοντος.

24. Χωρὶς δὲ τῆς δόξης, ὦ ἄνδρες, οὐδὲ δί-
C καιόν μοι δοκεῖ εἶναι δεῖσθαι τοῦ δικαστοῦ οὐδὲ
δεόμενον ἀποφεύγειν, ἀλλὰ διδάσκειν καὶ πείθειν.

children; but nevertheless I shall not bring any of them here and beg you to acquit me. And why shall I not do so? Not because I am stubborn, Athenians, or lack respect for you. Whether I fear death or not is another matter, but for the sake of my good name and yours and that of the whole state, I think it is not right for me to do any of these things in view of my age and my reputation, whether deserved or not; for at any rate the opinion prevails that Socrates is in some way superior to most men. If then those of you who are supposed to be superior either in wisdom or in courage or in any other virtue whatsoever are to behave in such a way, it would be disgraceful. Why, I have often seen men who have some reputation behaving in the strangest manner, when they were on trial, as if they thought they were going to suffer something terrible if they were put to death, just as if they would be immortal if you did not kill them. It seems to me that they are a disgrace to the state and that any stranger might say that those of the Athenians who excel in virtue, men whom they themselves honour with offices and other marks of esteem, are no better than women. Such acts, men of Athens, we who have any reputation at all ought not to commit, and if we commit them you ought not to allow it, but you should make it clear that you will be much more ready to condemn a man who puts before you such pitiable scenes and makes the city ridiculous than one who keeps quiet.

But apart from the question of reputation, gentlemen, I think it is not right to implore the judge or to get acquitted by begging; we ought to inform

PLATO

οὐ γὰρ ἐπὶ τούτῳ κάθηται ὁ δικαστής, ἐπὶ τῷ
καταχαρίζεσθαι τὰ δίκαια, ἀλλ' ἐπὶ τῷ κρίνειν ταῦτα· καὶ ὀμώμοκεν οὐ χαριεῖσθαι οἷς ἂν
δοκῇ αὐτῷ, ἀλλὰ δικάσειν κατὰ τοὺς νόμους.
οὔκουν χρὴ οὔτε ἡμᾶς ἐθίζειν ὑμᾶς ἐπιορκεῖν
οὔθ' ὑμᾶς ἐθίζεσθαι· οὐδέτεροι γὰρ ἂν ἡμῶν
εὐσεβοῖεν. μὴ οὖν ἀξιοῦτέ με, ὦ ἄνδρες
Ἀθηναῖοι, τοιαῦτα δεῖν πρὸς ὑμᾶς πράττειν, ἃ
μήτε ἡγοῦμαι καλὰ εἶναι μήτε δίκαια μήτε ὅσια,
D ἄλλως τε μέντοι νὴ Δία καὶ ἀσεβείας φεύγοντα
ὑπὸ Μελήτου τουτουί. σαφῶς γὰρ ἄν, εἰ πείθοιμι
ὑμᾶς καὶ τῷ δεῖσθαι βιαζοίμην ὀμωμοκότας,
θεοὺς ἂν διδάσκοιμι μὴ ἡγεῖσθαι ὑμᾶς εἶναι, καὶ
ἀτεχνῶς ἀπολογούμενος κατηγοροίην ἂν ἐμαυτοῦ,
ὡς θεοὺς οὐ νομίζω. ἀλλὰ πολλοῦ δεῖ οὕτως
ἔχειν· νομίζω τε γάρ, ὦ ἄνδρες Ἀθηναῖοι, ὡς
οὐδεὶς τῶν ἐμῶν κατηγόρων, καὶ ὑμῖν ἐπιτρέπω
καὶ τῷ θεῷ κρῖναι περὶ ἐμοῦ ὅπῃ μέλλει ἐμοί τε
ἄριστα εἶναι καὶ ὑμῖν.

E 25. Τὸ μὲν μὴ ἀγανακτεῖν, ὦ ἄνδρες Ἀθηναῖοι,
36 ἐπὶ τούτῳ τῷ γεγονότι, ὅτι μου κατεψηφίσασθε,
ἄλλα τέ μοι πολλὰ ξυμβάλλεται, καὶ οὐκ ἀνέλ-
πιστόν μοι γέγονεν τὸ γεγονὸς [1] τοῦτο, ἀλλὰ πολὺ
μᾶλλον θαυμάζω ἑκατέρων τῶν ψήφων τὸν γεγο-
νότα ἀριθμόν. οὐ γὰρ ᾠόμην ἔγωγε οὕτω παρ'
ὀλίγον ἔσεσθαι, ἀλλὰ παρὰ πολύ· νῦν δέ, ὡς
ἔοικεν, εἰ τριάκοντα μόναι μετέπεσον τῶν ψήφων,
ἀποπεφεύγη ἄν. Μέλητον μὲν οὖν, ὡς ἐμοὶ δοκῶ,
καὶ νῦν ἀποπέφευγα, καὶ οὐ μόνον ἀποπέφευγα,
ἀλλὰ παντὶ δῆλον τοῦτό γε, ὅτι, εἰ μὴ ἀνέβη
_____
[1] Schanz brackets τὸ γεγονὸς.

and convince him. For the judge is not here to grant favours in matters of justice, but to give judgment; and his oath binds him not to do favours according to his pleasure, but to judge according to the laws; therefore, we ought not to get you into the habit of breaking your oaths, nor ought you to fall into that habit; for neither of us would be acting piously. Do not, therefore, men of Athens, demand of me that I act before you in a way which I consider neither honourable nor right nor pious, especially when impiety is the very thing for which Meletus here has brought me to trial. For it is plain that if by persuasion and supplication I forced you to break your oaths I should teach you to disbelieve in the existence of the gods and in making my defence should accuse myself of not believing in them. But that is far from the truth; for I do believe in them, men of Athens, more than any of my accusers, and I entrust my case to you and to God to decide it as shall be best for me and for you.

I am not grieved, men of Athens, at this vote of condemnation you have cast against me, and that for many reasons, among them the fact that your decision was not a surprise to me. I am much more surprised by the number of votes for and against it; for I did not expect so small a majority, but a large one. Now, it seems, if only thirty votes had been cast the other way, I should have been acquitted. And so, I think, so far as Meletus is concerned, I have even now been acquitted, and not merely acquitted, but anyone can see that, if Anytus and Lycon had

PLATO

Ἄνυτος καὶ Λύκων κατηγορήσοντες ἐμοῦ, κἂν
B ὦφλε χιλίας δραχμάς, οὐ μεταλαβὼν τὸ πέμπτον
μέρος τῶν ψήφων.

26. Τιμᾶται δ᾽ οὖν μοι ὁ ἀνὴρ θανάτου. εἶεν·
ἐγὼ δὲ δὴ τίνος ὑμῖν ἀντιτιμήσομαι, ὦ ἄνδρες
Ἀθηναῖοι; ἢ δῆλον ὅτι τῆς ἀξίας; τί οὖν; τί
ἄξιός εἰμι παθεῖν ἢ ἀποτῖσαι, ὅ τι μαθὼν ἐν τῷ
βίῳ οὐχ ἡσυχίαν ἦγον, ἀλλ᾽ ἀμελήσας ὧνπερ
οἱ πολλοί, χρηματισμοῦ τε καὶ οἰκονομίας καὶ
στρατηγιῶν καὶ δημηγοριῶν καὶ τῶν ἄλλων ἀρχῶν
καὶ ξυνωμοσιῶν καὶ στάσεων τῶν ἐν τῇ πόλει
γιγνομένων, ἡγησάμενος ἐμαυτὸν τῷ ὄντι ἐπιει-
C κέστερον εἶναι ἢ ὥστε εἰς ταῦτ᾽ ἰόντα σῴζεσθαι,
ἐνταῦθα μὲν οὐκ ᾖα, οἷ ἐλθὼν μήτε ὑμῖν μήτε
ἐμαυτῷ ἔμελλον μηδὲν ὄφελος εἶναι, ἐπὶ δὲ τὸ
ἰδίᾳ ἕκαστον ἰὼν[1] εὐεργετεῖν τὴν μεγίστην εὐερ-
γεσίαν, ὡς ἐγώ φημι, ἐνταῦθα ᾖα, ἐπιχειρῶν
ἕκαστον ὑμῶν πείθειν μὴ πρότερον μήτε τῶν
ἑαυτοῦ μηδενὸς ἐπιμελεῖσθαι, πρὶν ἑαυτοῦ ἐπιμε-
ληθείη, ὅπως ὡς βέλτιστος καὶ φρονιμώτατος
ἔσοιτο, μήτε τῶν τῆς πόλεως, πρὶν αὐτῆς τῆς
πόλεως, τῶν τε ἄλλων οὕτω κατὰ τὸν αὐτὸν
τρόπον ἐπιμελεῖσθαι· τί οὖν εἰμι ἄξιος παθεῖν
D τοιοῦτος ὤν; ἀγαθόν τι, ὦ ἄνδρες Ἀθηναῖοι,
εἰ δεῖ γε κατὰ τὴν ἀξίαν τῇ ἀληθείᾳ τιμᾶσθαι·
καὶ ταῦτά γε ἀγαθὸν τοιοῦτον, ὅ τι ἂν πρέποι
ἐμοί. τί οὖν πρέπει ἀνδρὶ πένητι εὐεργέτῃ,
δεομένῳ ἄγειν σχολὴν ἐπὶ τῇ ὑμετέρᾳ παρακε-
λεύσει; οὐκ ἔσθ᾽ ὅ τι μᾶλλον, ὦ ἄνδρες Ἀθηναῖοι,
πρέπει οὕτως, ὡς τὸν τοιοῦτον ἄνδρα ἐν πρυτανείῳ
σιτεῖσθαι, πολύ γε μᾶλλον ἢ εἴ τις ὑμῶν ἵππῳ ἢ

[1] Schanz brackets, ἰών.

128

not come forward to accuse me, he would have been fined a thousand drachmas for not receiving a fifth part of the votes.

And so the man proposes the penalty of death. Well, then, what shall I propose as an alternative? Clearly that which I deserve, shall I not? And what do I deserve to suffer or to pay, because in my life I did not keep quiet, but neglecting what most men care for—money-making and property, and military offices, and public speaking, and the various offices and plots and parties that come up in the state—and thinking that I was really too honourable to engage in those activities and live, refrained from those things by which I should have been of no use to you or to myself, and devoted myself to conferring upon each citizen individually what I regard as the greatest benefit? For I tried to persuade each of you to care for himself and his own perfection in goodness and wisdom rather than for any of his belongings, and for the state itself rather than for its interests, and to follow the same method in his care for other things. What, then, does such a man as I deserve? Some good thing, men of Athens, if I must propose something truly in accordance with my deserts; and the good thing should be such as is fitting for me. Now what is fitting for a poor man who is your benefactor, and who needs leisure to exhort you? There is nothing, men of Athens, so fitting as that such a man be given his meals in the prytaneum. That is much more appropriate for me than for any of you who has won a race at the

ξυνωρίδι ἢ ζεύγει νενίκηκεν Ὀλυμπίασιν. ὁ μὲν γὰρ
ὑμᾶς ποιεῖ εὐδαίμονας δοκεῖν εἶναι,[1] ἐγὼ δὲ εἶναι·
E καὶ ὁ μὲν τροφῆς οὐδὲν δεῖται, ἐγὼ δὲ δέομαι.
εἰ οὖν δεῖ με κατὰ τὸ δίκαιον τῆς ἀξίας τιμᾶσθαι,
37 τούτου τιμῶμαι, ἐν πρυτανείῳ σιτήσεως.

27. Ἴσως οὖν ὑμῖν καὶ ταυτὶ λέγων παραπλησίως δοκῶ λέγειν ὥσπερ περὶ τοῦ οἴκτου
καὶ τῆς ἀντιβολήσεως, ἀπαυθαδιζόμενος· τὸ δὲ
οὐκ ἔστιν, ὦ Ἀθηναῖοι, τοιοῦτον, ἀλλὰ τοιόνδε
μᾶλλον. πέπεισμαι ἐγὼ ἑκὼν εἶναι μηδένα ἀδικεῖν ἀνθρώπων, ἀλλὰ ὑμᾶς τοῦτο οὐ πείθω·
ὀλίγον γὰρ χρόνον ἀλλήλοις διειλέγμεθα· ἐπεί,
ὡς ἐγῷμαι, εἰ ἦν ὑμῖν νόμος, ὥσπερ καὶ ἄλλοις
B ἀνθρώποις, περὶ θανάτου μὴ μίαν ἡμέραν μόνον
κρίνειν, ἀλλὰ πολλάς, ἐπείσθητε ἄν· νῦν δ᾽ οὐ
ῥᾴδιον ἐν χρόνῳ ὀλίγῳ μεγάλας διαβολὰς ἀπο-
λύεσθαι. πεπεισμένος δὴ ἐγὼ μηδένα ἀδικεῖν
πολλοῦ δέω ἐμαυτόν γε ἀδικήσειν καὶ κατ᾽
ἐμαυτοῦ ἐρεῖν αὐτός, ὡς ἄξιός εἰμί του κακοῦ
καὶ τιμήσεσθαι τοιούτου τινὸς ἐμαυτῷ. τί δείσας;
ἢ μὴ πάθω τοῦτο, οὗ Μέλητός μοι τιμᾶται,
ὅ φημι οὐκ εἰδέναι οὔτ᾽ εἰ ἀγαθὸν οὔτ᾽ εἰ κακόν
ἐστιν; ἀντὶ τούτου δὴ ἕλωμαι ὧν εὖ οἶδ᾽ ὅτι
κακῶν ὄντων, τοῦ τιμησάμενος; πότερον δεσμοῦ;
C καὶ τί με δεῖ ζῆν ἐν δεσμωτηρίῳ, δουλεύοντα τῇ
ἀεὶ καθισταμένῃ ἀρχῇ; ἀλλὰ χρημάτων, καὶ
δεδέσθαι, ἕως ἂν ἐκτίσω; ἀλλὰ ταὐτόν μοί
ἐστιν, ὅπερ νῦν δὴ ἔλεγον· οὐ γὰρ ἔστι μοι
χρήματα, ὁπόθεν ἐκτίσω. ἀλλὰ δὴ φυγῆς τιμή-
σωμαι; ἴσως γὰρ ἄν μοι τούτου τιμήσαιτε.
πολλὴ μέντ᾽ ἄν με φιλοψυχία ἔχοι, εἰ οὕτως

[1] Schanz brackets εἶναι, following Hermann.

Olympic games with a pair of horses or a four-in-hand. For he makes you seem to be happy, whereas I make you happy in reality; and he is not at all in need of sustenance, but I am needy. So if I must propose a penalty in accordance with my deserts, I propose maintenance in the prytaneum.

Perhaps some of you think that in saying this, as in what I said about lamenting and imploring, I am speaking in a spirit of bravado; but that is not the case. The truth is rather that I am convinced that I never intentionally wronged any one; but I cannot convince you of this, for we have conversed with each other only a little while. I believe if you had a law, as some other people have, that capital cases should not be decided in one day, but only after several days, you would be convinced; but now it is not easy to rid you of great prejudices in a short time. Since, then, I am convinced that I never wronged any one, I am certainly not going to wrong myself, and to say of myself that I deserve anything bad, and to propose any penalty of that sort for myself. Why should I? Through fear of the penalty that Meletus proposes, about which I say that I do not know whether it is a good thing or an evil? Shall I choose instead of that something which I know to be an evil? What penalty shall I propose? Imprisonment? And why should I live in prison a slave to those who may be in authority? Or shall I propose a fine, with imprisonment until it is paid? But that is the same as what I said just now, for I have no money to pay with. Shall I then propose exile as my penalty? Perhaps you would accept that. I must indeed be

ἀλόγιστός εἰμι, ὥστε μὴ δύνασθαι λογίζεσθαι,
ὅτι ὑμεῖς μὲν ὄντες πολῖταί μου οὐχ οἷοί τε
D ἐγένεσθε ἐνεγκεῖν τὰς ἐμὰς διατριβὰς καὶ τοὺς
λόγους, ἀλλ' ὑμῖν βαρύτεραι γεγόνασιν καὶ
ἐπιφθονώτεραι, ὥστε ζητεῖτε αὐτῶν νυνὶ ἀπαλ-
λαγῆναι, ἄλλοι δὲ ἄρα αὐτὰς οἴσουσι ῥᾳδίως;
πολλοῦ γε δεῖ, ὦ Ἀθηναῖοι. καλὸς οὖν ἄν
μοι ὁ βίος εἴη ἐξελθόντι τηλικῷδε ἀνθρώπῳ
ἄλλην ἐξ ἄλλης πόλεως ἀμειβομένῳ καὶ ἐξελαυ-
νομένῳ ζῆν. εὖ γὰρ οἶδ' ὅτι, ὅποι ἂν ἔλθω,
λέγοντος ἐμοῦ ἀκροάσονται οἱ νέοι ὥσπερ ἐνθάδε·
κἂν μὲν τούτους ἀπελαύνω, οὗτοι ἐμὲ αὐτοὶ
ἐξελῶσι, πείθοντες τοὺς πρεσβυτέρους· ἐὰν δὲ
E μὴ ἀπελαύνω, οἱ τούτων πατέρες τε καὶ οἰκεῖοι
δι' αὐτοὺς τούτους.

28. Ἴσως οὖν ἄν τις εἴποι· σιγῶν δὲ καὶ
ἡσυχίαν ἄγων, ὦ Σώκρατες, οὐχ οἷός τ' ἔσει ἡμῖν
ἐξελθὼν ζῆν; τουτὶ δή ἐστι πάντων χαλεπώτατον
πεῖσαί τινας ὑμῶν. ἐάν τε γὰρ λέγω, ὅτι τῷ
θεῷ ἀπειθεῖν τοῦτ' ἐστὶν καὶ διὰ τοῦτο ἀδύνατον
ἡσυχίαν ἄγειν, οὐ πείσεσθέ μοι ὡς εἰρωνευομένῳ·
38 ἐάν τ' αὖ λέγω, ὅτι καὶ τυγχάνει μέγιστον
ἀγαθὸν ὂν ἀνθρώπῳ τοῦτο, ἑκάστης ἡμέρας περὶ
ἀρετῆς τοὺς λόγους ποιεῖσθαι καὶ τῶν ἄλλων,
περὶ ὧν ὑμεῖς ἐμοῦ ἀκούετε διαλεγομένου καὶ
ἐμαυτὸν καὶ ἄλλους ἐξετάζοντος, ὁ δὲ ἀνεξέταστος
βίος οὐ βιωτὸς ἀνθρώπῳ, ταῦτα δ' ἔτι ἧττον
πείσεσθέ μοι λέγοντι. τὰ δὲ ἔχει μὲν οὕτως,
ὡς ἐγώ φημι, ὦ ἄνδρες, πείθειν δὲ οὐ ῥᾴδιον.
καὶ ἐγὼ ἅμα οὐκ εἴθισμαι ἐμαυτὸν ἀξιοῦν κακοῦ
οὐδενός. εἰ μὲν γὰρ ἦν μοι χρήματα, ἐτιμησάμην
B ἂν χρημάτων ὅσα ἔμελλον ἐκτίσειν· οὐδὲν γὰρ

possessed by a great love of life if I am so irrational as not to know that if you, who are my fellow citizens, could not endure my conversation and my words, but found them too irksome and disagreeable, so that you are now seeking to be rid of them, others will not be willing to endure them. No, men of Athens, they certainly will not. A fine life I should lead if I went away at my time of life, wandering from city to city and always being driven out! For well I know that wherever I go, the young men will listen to my talk, as they do here; and if I drive them away, they will themselves persuade their elders to drive me out, and if I do not drive them away, their fathers and relatives will drive me out for their sakes.

Perhaps someone might say, "Socrates, can you not go away from us and live quietly, without talking?" Now this is the hardest thing to make some of you believe. For if I say that such conduct would be disobedience to the god and that therefore I cannot keep quiet, you will think I am jesting and will not believe me; and if again I say that to talk every day about virtue and the other things about which you hear me talking and examining myself and others is the greatest good to man, and that the unexamined life is not worth living, you will believe me still less. This is as I say, gentlemen, but it is not easy to convince you. Besides, I am not accustomed to think that I deserve anything bad. If I had money, I would have proposed a fine, as large as I could pay; for that would have done me no harm.

ἂν ἐβλάβην· νῦν δὲ οὐ γὰρ ἔστιν, εἰ μὴ ἄρα
ὅσον ἂν ἐγὼ δυναίμην ἐκτῖσαι, τοσούτου βού-
λεσθέ μοι τιμῆσαι. ἴσως δ᾽ ἂν δυναίμην ἐκτῖσαι
ὑμῖν μνᾶν ἀργυρίου· τοσούτου οὖν τιμῶμαι.
Πλάτων δὲ ὅδε, ὦ ἄνδρες Ἀθηναῖοι, καὶ Κρίτων
καὶ Κριτόβουλος καὶ Ἀπολλόδωρος κελεύουσί
με τριάκοντα μνῶν τιμήσασθαι, αὐτοὶ δ᾽ ἐγ-
γυᾶσθαι· τιμῶμαι οὖν τοσούτου, ἐγγυηταὶ δὲ
C ὑμῖν ἔσονται τοῦ ἀργυρίου οὗτοι ἀξιόχρεῳ.

29. Οὐ πολλοῦ γ᾽ ἔνεκα χρόνου, ὦ ἄνδρες
Ἀθηναῖοι, ὄνομα ἕξετε καὶ αἰτίαν ὑπὸ τῶν
βουλομένων τὴν πόλιν λοιδορεῖν, ὡς Σωκράτη
ἀπεκτόνατε, ἄνδρα σοφόν· φήσουσι γὰρ δή με
σοφὸν εἶναι, εἰ καὶ μή εἰμι, οἱ βουλόμενοι ὑμῖν
ὀνειδίζειν. εἰ οὖν περιεμείνατε ὀλίγον χρόνον,
ἀπὸ τοῦ αὐτομάτου ἂν ὑμῖν τοῦτο ἐγένετο· ὁρᾶτε
γὰρ δὴ τὴν ἡλικίαν, ὅτι πόρρω ἤδη ἐστὶ τοῦ
βίου, θανάτου δὲ ἐγγύς. λέγω δὲ τοῦτο οὐ πρὸς
D πάντας ὑμᾶς, ἀλλὰ πρὸς τοὺς ἐμοῦ καταψη-
φισαμένους θάνατον. λέγω δὲ καὶ τόδε πρὸς
τοὺς αὐτοὺς τούτους. ἴσως με οἴεσθε, ὦ ἄνδρες,
ἀπορίᾳ λόγων ἑαλωκέναι τοιούτων, οἷς ἂν ὑμᾶς
ἔπεισα, εἰ ᾤμην δεῖν ἅπαντα ποιεῖν καὶ λέγειν,
ὥστε ἀποφυγεῖν τὴν δίκην. πολλοῦ γε δεῖ. ἀλλ᾽
ἀπορίᾳ μὲν ἑάλωκα, οὐ μέντοι λόγων, ἀλλὰ
τόλμης καὶ ἀναισχυντίας καὶ τοῦ ἐθέλειν λέγειν
πρὸς ὑμᾶς τοιαῦτα, οἷ᾽ ἂν ὑμῖν ἥδιστα ἦν ἀκούειν,
θρηνοῦντός τέ μου καὶ ὀδυρομένου καὶ ἄλλα
E ποιοῦντος καὶ λέγοντος πολλὰ καὶ ἀνάξια ἐμοῦ,
ὡς ἐγώ φημι· οἷα δὴ καὶ εἴθισθε ὑμεῖς τῶν ἄλλων
ἀκούειν. ἀλλ᾽ οὔτε τότε ᾤθην δεῖν ἕνεκα τοῦ

But as it is—I have no money, unless you are willing to impose a fine which I could pay. I might perhaps pay a mina of silver. So I propose that penalty; but Plato here, men of Athens, and Crito and Critobulus, and Apollodorus tell me to propose a fine of thirty minas, saying that they are sureties for it. So I propose a fine of that amount, and these men, who are amply sufficient, will be my sureties.

It is no long time, men of Athens, which you gain, and for that those who wish to cast a slur upon the state will give you the name and blame of having killed Socrates, a wise man; for, you know, those who wish to revile you will say I am wise, even though I am not. Now if you had waited a little while, what you desire would have come to you of its own accord; for you see how old I am, how far advanced in life and how near death. I say this not to all of you, but to those who voted for my death. And to them also I have something else to say. Perhaps you think, gentlemen, that I have been convicted through lack of such words as would have moved you to acquit me, if I had thought it right to do and say everything to gain an acquittal. Far from it. And yet it is through a lack that I have been convicted, not however a lack of words, but of impudence and shamelessness, and of willingness to say to you such things as you would have liked best to hear. You would have liked to hear me wailing and lamenting and doing and saying many things which are, as I maintain, unworthy of me—such things as you are accustomed to hear from others. But I did not think at the time

κινδύνου πρᾶξαι οὐδὲν ἀνελεύθερον, οὔτε νῦν
μοι μεταμέλει οὕτως ἀπολογησαμένῳ, ἀλλὰ πολὺ
μᾶλλον αἱροῦμαι ὧδε ἀπολογησάμενος τεθνάναι ἢ
ἐκείνως ζῆν. οὔτε γὰρ ἐν δίκῃ οὔτ' ἐν πολέμῳ οὔτ'
39 ἐμὲ οὔτ' ἄλλον οὐδένα δεῖ τοῦτο μηχανᾶσθαι, ὅπως
ἀποφεύξεται πᾶν ποιῶν θάνατον. καὶ γὰρ ἐν
ταῖς μάχαις πολλάκις δῆλον γίγνεται, ὅτι τό
γε ἀποθανεῖν ἄν τις ἐκφύγοι καὶ ὅπλα ἀφεὶς
καὶ ἐφ' ἱκετείαν τραπόμενος τῶν διωκόντων· καὶ
ἄλλαι μηχαναὶ πολλαί εἰσιν ἐν ἑκάστοις τοῖς
κινδύνοις, ὥστε διαφεύγειν θάνατον, ἐάν τις τολμᾷ
πᾶν ποιεῖν καὶ λέγειν. ἀλλὰ μὴ οὐ τοῦτ' ᾖ
χαλεπόν, ὦ ἄνδρες, θάνατον ἐκφυγεῖν, ἀλλὰ πολὺ
χαλεπώτερον πονηρίαν· θᾶττον γὰρ θανάτου θεῖ.
B καὶ νῦν ἐγὼ μὲν ἅτε βραδὺς ὢν καὶ πρεσβύτης
ὑπὸ τοῦ βραδυτέρου ἑάλων, οἱ δ' ἐμοὶ κατήγοροι
ἅτε δεινοὶ καὶ ὀξεῖς ὄντες ὑπὸ τοῦ θάττονος,
τῆς κακίας. καὶ νῦν ἐγὼ μὲν ἄπειμι ὑφ' ὑμῶν
θανάτου δίκην ὄφλων, οὗτοι δ' ὑπὸ τῆς ἀληθείας
ὠφληκότες μοχθηρίαν καὶ ἀδικίαν. καὶ ἔγωγε
τῷ τιμήματι ἐμμένω καὶ οὗτοι. ταῦτα μέν που
ἴσως οὕτως καὶ ἔδει σχεῖν, καὶ οἶμαι αὐτὰ μετρίως
ἔχειν.
C   30. Τὸ δὲ δὴ μετὰ τοῦτο ἐπιθυμῶ ὑμῖν χρησ-
μῳδῆσαι, ὦ καταψηφισάμενοί μου· καὶ γὰρ
εἰμι ἤδη ἐνταῦθα, ἐν ᾧ μάλιστα ἄνθρωποι χρησ-
μῳδοῦσιν, ὅταν μέλλωσιν ἀποθανεῖσθαι. φημὶ
γάρ, ὦ ἄνδρες, οἳ ἐμὲ ἀπεκτόνατε, τιμωρίαν ὑμῖν
ἥξειν εὐθὺς μετὰ τὸν ἐμὸν θάνατον πολὺ χαλε-
πωτέραν νὴ Δία ἢ οἵαν ἐμὲ ἀπεκτόνατε· νῦν
γὰρ τοῦτο εἴργασθε οἰόμενοι ἀπαλλάξεσθαι τοῦ
διδόναι ἔλεγχον τοῦ βίου, τὸ δὲ ὑμῖν πολὺ ἐναντίον

that I ought, on account of the danger I was in, to do anything unworthy of a free man, nor do I now repent of having made my defence as I did, but I much prefer to die after such a defence than to live after a defence of the other sort. For neither in the court nor in war ought I or any other man to plan to escape death by every possible means. In battles it is often plain that a man might avoid death by throwing down his arms and begging mercy of his pursuers; and there are many other means of escaping death in dangers of various kinds if one is willing to do and say anything. But, gentlemen, it is not hard to escape death; it is much harder to escape wickedness, for that runs faster than death. And now I, since I am slow and old, am caught by the slower runner, and my accusers, who are clever and quick, by the faster, wickedness. And now I shall go away convicted by you and sentenced to death, and they go convicted by truth of villainy and wrong. And I abide by my penalty, and they by theirs. Perhaps these things had to be so, and I think they are well.

And now I wish to prophesy to you, O ye who have condemned me; for I am now at the time when men most do prophesy, the time just before death. And I say to you, ye men who have slain me, that punishment will come upon you straightway after my death, far more grievous in sooth than the punishment of death which you have meted out to me. For now you have done this to me because you hoped that you would be relieved from rendering an account of your lives, but I say that you will find

ἀποβήσεται, ὡς ἐγώ φημι. πλείους ἔσονται ὑμᾶς
D οἱ ἐλέγχοντες, οὓς νῦν ἐγὼ κατεῖχον, ὑμεῖς δὲ
οὐκ ᾐσθάνεσθε· καὶ χαλεπώτεροι ἔσονται ὅσῳ
νεώτεροί εἰσιν, καὶ ὑμεῖς μᾶλλον ἀγανακτήσετε.
εἰ γὰρ οἴεσθε ἀποκτείνοντες ἀνθρώπους ἐπισχήσειν
τοῦ ὀνειδίζειν τινὰ ὑμῖν ὅτι οὐκ ὀρθῶς ζῆτε, οὐκ
ὀρθῶς διανοεῖσθε· οὐ γὰρ ἔσθ' αὕτη ἡ ἀπαλλαγὴ
οὔτε πάνυ δυνατὴ οὔτε καλή, ἀλλ' ἐκείνη καὶ
καλλίστη καὶ ῥᾴστη, μὴ τοὺς ἄλλους κολούειν,
ἀλλ' ἑαυτὸν παρασκευάζειν ὅπως ἔσται ὡς
βέλτιστος. ταῦτα μὲν οὖν ὑμῖν τοῖς καταψηφι-
E σαμένοις μαντευσάμενος ἀπαλλάττομαι.

31. Τοῖς δὲ ἀποψηφισαμένοις ἡδέως ἂν διαλε-
χθείην ὑπὲρ τοῦ γεγονότος τουτουὶ πράγματος,
ἐν ᾧ οἱ ἄρχοντες ἀσχολίαν ἄγουσι καὶ οὔπω
ἔρχομαι οἷ ἐλθόντα με δεῖ τεθνάναι. ἀλλά μοι,
ὦ ἄνδρες, παραμείνατε τοσοῦτον χρόνον· οὐδὲν
γὰρ κωλύει διαμυθολογῆσαι πρὸς ἀλλήλους,
40 ἕως ἔξεστιν. ὑμῖν γὰρ ὡς φίλοις οὖσιν ἐπιδεῖξαι
ἐθέλω τὸ νυνί μοι ξυμβεβηκὸς τί ποτε νοεῖ. ἐμοὶ
γάρ, ὦ ἄνδρες δικασταί—ὑμᾶς γὰρ δικαστὰς
καλῶν ὀρθῶς ἂν καλοίην—θαυμάσιόν τι γέγονεν.
ἡ γὰρ εἰωθυῖά μοι μαντικὴ ἡ τοῦ δαιμονίου [1] ἐν
μὲν τῷ πρόσθεν χρόνῳ παντὶ πάνυ πυκνὴ ἀεὶ
ἦν καὶ πάνυ ἐπὶ σμικροῖς ἐναντιουμένη, εἴ τι
μέλλοιμι μὴ ὀρθῶς πράξειν· νυνὶ δὲ ξυμβέβηκέ
μοι, ἅπερ ὁρᾶτε καὶ αὐτοί, ταυτὶ ἅ γε δὴ οἰηθείη
ἄν τις καὶ νομίζεται ἔσχατα κακῶν εἶναι. ἐμοὶ δὲ
B οὔτε ἐξιόντι ἕωθεν οἴκοθεν ἠναντιώθη τὸ τοῦ
θεοῦ σημεῖον, οὔτε ἡνίκα ἀνέβαινον ἐνταυθοῖ

---

[1] Schanz follows Schleiermacher in bracketing ἡ τοῦ δαιμονίου.

the result far different. Those who will force you to give an account will be more numerous than heretofore; men whom I restrained, though you knew it not; and they will be harsher, inasmuch as they are younger, and you will be more annoyed. For if you think that by putting men to death you will prevent anyone from reproaching you because you do not act as you should, you are mistaken. That mode of escape is neither possible at all nor honourable, but the easiest and most honourable escape is not by suppressing others, but by making yourselves as good as possible. So with this prophecy to you who condemned me I take my leave.

But with those who voted for my acquittal I should like to converse about this which has happened, while the authorities are busy and before I go to the place where I must die. Wait with me so long, my friends; for nothing prevents our chatting with each other while there is time. I feel that you are my friends, and I wish to show you the meaning of this which has now happened to me. For, judges—and in calling you judges I give you your right name—a wonderful thing has happened to me. For hitherto the customary prophetic monitor always spoke to me very frequently and opposed me even in very small matters, if I was going to do anything I should not; but now, as you yourselves see, this thing which might be thought, and is generally considered, the greatest of evils has come upon me; but the divine sign did not oppose me either when I left my home in the morning, or when I came here to the court, or at any point of my speech,

ἐπὶ τὸ δικαστήριον, οὔτε ἐν τῷ λόγῳ οὐδαμοῦ
μέλλοντί τι ἐρεῖν· καίτοι ἐν ἄλλοις λόγοις
πολλαχοῦ δή με ἐπέσχε λέγοντα μεταξύ· νῦν
δὲ οὐδαμοῦ περὶ ταύτην τὴν πρᾶξιν οὔτ' ἐν ἔργῳ
οὐδενὶ οὔτ' ἐν λόγῳ ἠναντίωταί μοι. τί οὖν αἴτιον
εἶναι ὑπολαμβάνω; ἐγὼ ὑμῖν ἐρῶ· κινδυνεύει γάρ
μοι τὸ ξυμβεβηκὸς τοῦτο ἀγαθὸν γεγονέναι, καὶ
οὐκ ἔσθ' ὅπως ἡμεῖς ὀρθῶς ὑπολαμβάνομεν,
C ὅσοι οἰόμεθα κακὸν εἶναι τὸ τεθνάναι. μέγα μοι
τεκμήριον τούτου γέγονεν· οὐ γὰρ ἔσθ' ὅπως
οὐκ ἠναντιώθη ἄν μοι τὸ εἰωθὸς σημεῖον, εἰ μή
τι ἔμελλον ἐγὼ ἀγαθὸν πράξειν.

32. Ἐννοήσωμεν δὲ καὶ τῇδε, ὡς πολλὴ ἐλπίς
ἐστιν ἀγαθὸν αὐτὸ εἶναι· δυοῖν γὰρ θάτερόν ἐστιν
τὸ τεθνάναι· ἢ γὰρ οἷον μηδὲν εἶναι μηδὲ αἴσθησιν μηδεμίαν μηδενὸς ἔχειν τὸν τεθνεῶτα, ἢ
κατὰ τὰ λεγόμενα μεταβολή τις τυγχάνει οὖσα
καὶ μετοίκησις τῇ ψυχῇ τοῦ τόπου τοῦ [1] ἐνθένδε
εἰς ἄλλον τόπον. καὶ εἴτε μηδεμία αἴσθησίς
D ἐστιν, ἀλλ' οἷον ὕπνος, ἐπειδάν τις καθεύδων μηδ'
ὄναρ μηδὲν ὁρᾷ, θαυμάσιον κέρδος ἂν εἴη ὁ
θάνατος. ἐγὼ γὰρ ἂν οἶμαι, εἴ τινα ἐκλεξάμενον
δέοι ταύτην τὴν νύκτα, ἐν ᾗ οὕτω κατέδαρθεν,
ὥστε μηδὲ ὄναρ ἰδεῖν, καὶ τὰς ἄλλας νύκτας τε
καὶ ἡμέρας τὰς τοῦ βίου τὰς τοῦ ἑαυτοῦ ἀντιπαρα-
θέντα ταύτῃ τῇ νυκτὶ δέοι σκεψάμενον εἰπεῖν,
πόσας ἄμεινον καὶ ἥδιον ἡμέρας καὶ νύκτας
ταύτης τῆς νυκτὸς βεβίωκεν ἐν τῷ ἑαυτοῦ βίῳ,
οἶμαι ἂν μὴ ὅτι ἰδιώτην τινά, ἀλλὰ τὸν μέγαν
E βασιλέα εὐαριθμήτους ἂν εὑρεῖν αὐτὸν ταύτας
πρὸς τὰς ἄλλας ἡμέρας καὶ νύκτας. εἰ οὖν

---

[1] Schanz, following C and Hirschig, brackets τοῦ τόπου τοῦ

when I was going to say anything; and yet on other occasions it stopped me at many points in the midst of a speech; but now, in this affair, it has not opposed me in anything I was doing or saying. What then do I suppose is the reason? I will tell you. This which has happened to me is doubtless a good thing, and those of us who think death is an evil must be mistaken. A convincing proof of this has been given me; for the accustomed sign would surely have opposed me if I had not been going to meet with something good.

Let us consider in another way also how good reason there is to hope that it is a good thing. For the state of death is one of two things: either it is virtually nothingness, so that the dead has no consciousness of anything, or it is, as people say, a change and migration of the soul from this to another place. And if it is unconsciousness, like a sleep in which the sleeper does not even dream, death would be a wonderful gain. For I think if any one were to pick out that night in which he slept a dreamless sleep and, comparing with it the other nights and days of his life, were to say, after due consideration, how many days and nights in his life had passed more pleasantly than that night,—I believe that not only any private person, but even the great King of Persia himself would find that they were few in comparison with the other days and nights. So if such is the nature of death, I

τοιοῦτον ὁ θάνατός ἐστιν, κέρδος ἔγωγε λέγω·
καὶ γὰρ οὐδὲν πλείων ὁ πᾶς χρόνος φαίνεται
οὕτω δὴ εἶναι ἢ μία νύξ. εἰ δ' αὖ οἷον ἀποδη-
μῆσαί ἐστιν ὁ θάνατος ἐνθένδε εἰς ἄλλον τόπον,
καὶ ἀληθῆ ἐστιν τὰ λεγόμενα, ὡς ἄρα ἐκεῖ εἰσιν
ἅπαντες οἱ τεθνεῶτες, τί μεῖζον ἀγαθὸν τούτου
εἴη ἄν, ὦ ἄνδρες δικασταί; εἰ γάρ τις ἀφικόμενος
41 εἰς Ἅιδου, ἀπαλλαγεὶς τούτων τῶν φασκόντων
δικαστῶν εἶναι, εὑρήσει τοὺς ἀληθῶς δικαστάς,
οἵπερ καὶ λέγονται ἐκεῖ δικάζειν, Μίνως τε καὶ
Ῥαδάμανθυς καὶ Αἰακὸς καὶ Τριπτόλεμος καὶ
ἄλλοι ὅσοι τῶν ἡμιθέων δίκαιοι ἐγένοντο ἐν τῷ
ἑαυτῶν βίῳ, ἆρα φαύλη ἂν εἴη ἡ ἀποδημία; ἢ αὖ
Ὀρφεῖ ξυγγενέσθαι καὶ Μουσαίῳ καὶ Ἡσιόδῳ
καὶ Ὁμήρῳ ἐπὶ πόσῳ ἄν τις δέξαιτ' ἂν ὑμῶν;
ἐγὼ μὲν γὰρ πολλάκις θέλω τεθνάναι, εἰ ταῦτ'
ἔστιν ἀληθῆ· ἐπεὶ ἔμοιγε καὶ αὐτῷ θαυμαστὴ ἂν
B εἴη ἡ διατριβὴ αὐτόθι, ὁπότε ἐντύχοιμι Παλα-
μήδει καὶ Αἴαντι τῷ Τελαμῶνος καὶ εἴ τις ἄλλος
τῶν παλαιῶν διὰ κρίσιν ἄδικον τέθνηκεν, ἀντι-
παραβάλλοντι τὰ ἐμαυτοῦ πάθη πρὸς τὰ ἐκείνων,
ὡς ἐγὼ οἶμαι, οὐκ ἂν ἀηδὴς εἴη. καὶ δὴ τὸ
μέγιστον, τοὺς ἐκεῖ ἐξετάζοντα καὶ ἐρευνῶντα
ὥσπερ τοὺς ἐνταῦθα διάγειν, τίς αὐτῶν σοφός
ἐστιν καὶ τίς οἴεται μέν, ἔστιν δ' οὔ. ἐπὶ πόσῳ
δ' ἄν τις, ὦ ἄνδρες δικασταί, δέξαιτο ἐξετάσαι
τὸν ἐπὶ Τροίαν ἀγαγόντα τὴν πολλὴν στρατιὰν
C ἢ Ὀδυσσέα ἢ Σίσυφον, ἢ ἄλλους μυρίους ἄν τις
εἴποι καὶ ἄνδρας καὶ γυναῖκας; οἷς ἐκεῖ διαλέγεσθαι καὶ ξυνεῖναι καί ἐξετάζειν ἀμήχανον ἂν
εἴη εὐδαιμονίας. πάντως οὐ δήπου τούτου γε
ἕνεκα οἱ ἐκεῖ ἀποκτείνουσι· τά τε γὰρ ἄλλα

count it a gain; for in that case, all time seems to be no longer than one night. But on the other hand, if death is, as it were, a change of habitation from here to some other place, and if what we are told is true, that all the dead are there, what greater blessing could there be, judges? For if a man when he reaches the other world, after leaving behind these who claim to be judges, shall find those who are really judges who are said to sit in judgment there, Minos and Rhadamanthus, and Aeacus and Triptolemus, and all the other demigods who were just men in their lives, would the change of habitation be undesirable? Or again, what would any of you give to meet with Orpheus and Musaeus and Hesiod and Homer? I am willing to die many times over, if these things are true; for I personally should find the life there wonderful, when I met Palamedes or Ajax, the son of Telamon, or any other men of old who lost their lives through an unjust judgment, and compared my experience with theirs. I think that would not be unpleasant. And the greatest pleasure would be to pass my time in examining and investigating the people there, as I do those here, to find out who among them is wise and who thinks he is when he is not. What price would any of you pay, judges, to examine him who led the great army against Troy, or Odysseus, or Sisyphus, or countless others, both men and women, whom I might mention? To converse and associate with them and examine them would be immeasurable happiness. At any rate, the folk there do not kill people for it; since, if what we are told is true,

εὐδαιμονέστεροί εἰσιν οἱ ἐκεῖ τῶν ἐνθάδε, καὶ ἤδη τὸν λοιπὸν χρόνον ἀθάνατοί εἰσιν, εἴπερ γε τὰ λεγόμενα ἀληθῆ ἐστιν.

33. Ἀλλὰ καὶ ὑμᾶς χρή, ὦ ἄνδρες δικασταί, εὐέλπιδας εἶναι πρὸς τὸν θάνατον, καὶ ἕν τι τοῦτο D διανοεῖσθαι ἀληθές, ὅτι οὐκ ἔστιν ἀνδρὶ ἀγαθῷ κακὸν οὐδὲν οὔτε ζῶντι οὔτε τελευτήσαντι, οὐδὲ ἀμελεῖται ὑπὸ θεῶν τὰ τούτου πράγματα. οὐδὲ τὰ ἐμὰ νῦν ἀπὸ τοῦ αὐτομάτου γέγονεν, ἀλλά μοι δῆλόν ἐστι τοῦτο, ὅτι ἤδη τεθνάναι καὶ ἀπηλλάχθαι πραγμάτων βέλτιον ἦν μοι. διὰ τοῦτο καὶ ἐμὲ οὐδαμοῦ ἀπέτρεψεν τὸ σημεῖον, καὶ ἔγωγε τοῖς καταψηφισαμένοις μου καὶ τοῖς κατηγόροις οὐ πάνυ χαλεπαίνω. καίτοι οὐ ταύτῃ τῇ διανοίᾳ κατεψηφίζοντό μου καὶ κατηγόρουν, ἀλλ᾽ οἰό- E μενοι βλάπτειν· τοῦτο αὐτοῖς ἄξιον μέμφεσθαι. τοσόνδε μέντοι αὐτῶν δέομαι· τοὺς υἱεῖς μου, ἐπειδὰν ἡβήσωσι, τιμωρήσασθε, ὦ ἄνδρες, ταὐτὰ ταῦτα λυποῦντες, ἅπερ ἐγὼ ὑμᾶς ἐλύπουν, ἐὰν ὑμῖν δοκῶσιν ἢ χρημάτων ἢ ἄλλου του πρότερον ἐπιμελεῖσθαι ἢ ἀρετῆς, καὶ ἐὰν δοκῶσί τι εἶναι μηδὲν ὄντες, ὀνειδίζετε αὐτοῖς, ὥσπερ ἐγὼ ὑμῖν, ὅτι οὐκ ἐπιμελοῦνται ὧν δεῖ, καὶ οἴονταί τι εἶναι ὄντες οὐδενὸς ἄξιοι. καὶ ἐὰν ταῦτα ποιῆτε, δίκαια 42 πεπονθὼς ἐγὼ ἔσομαι ὑφ᾽ ὑμῶν αὐτός τε καὶ οἱ υἱεῖς. ἀλλὰ γὰρ ἤδη ὥρα ἀπιέναι, ἐμοὶ μὲν ἀποθανουμένῳ, ὑμῖν δὲ βιωσομένοις· ὁπότεροι δὲ ἡμῶν ἔρχονται ἐπὶ ἄμεινον πρᾶγμα, ἄδηλον παντὶ πλὴν ἢ τῷ θεῷ.

they are immortal for all future time, besides being happier in other respects than men are here.

But you also, judges, must regard death hopefully and must bear in mind this one truth, that no evil can come to a good man either in life or after death, and God does not neglect him. So, too, this which has come to me has not come by chance, but I see plainly that it was better for me to die now and be freed from troubles. That is the reason why the sign never interfered with me, and I am not at all angry with those who condemned me or with my accusers. And yet it was not with that in view that they condemned and accused me, but because they thought to injure me. They deserve blame for that. However, I make this request of them: when my sons grow up, gentlemen, punish them by troubling them as I have troubled you; if they seem to you to care for money or anything else more than for virtue, and if they think they amount to something when they do not, rebuke them as I have rebuked you because they do not care for what they ought, and think they amount to something when they are worth nothing. If you do this, both I and my sons shall have received just treatment from you.

But now the time has come to go away. I go to die, and you to live; but which of us goes to the better lot, is known to none but God.

CRITO

INTRODUCTION TO THE *CRITO*

THIS dialogue is a conversation between Socrates and his lifelong friend Crito, which takes place in the prison where Socrates is confined after his trial to await the day of his execution. Crito was a man of wealth and position, devotedly attached to Socrates, and greatly interested in philosophical speculation. Diogenes Laertius (II. 121) gives a list of seventeen dialogues on philosophical subjects attributed to him, but Plato represents him throughout as a man of kindly disposition and practical common sense, quite lacking in originality and with no gift for philosophical investigation.

There can be little doubt that Crito tried more than once to induce Socrates to escape from prison, but this dialogue can hardly be considered a mere report of a conversation which actually took place; it is planned and carried out with the exquisite skill peculiar to Plato, and must be recognised as his work. It is difficult, often impossible, to distinguish between the doctrines and beliefs of the real Socrates and those which are put into his mouth by Plato; but in view of the fact that Socrates did not escape from prison, his conduct must have been determined by some consideration of right. We may therefore believe that the doctrine that injustice is always

wrong and that we must not requite injustice with injustice is really Socratic, and that the exalted patriotism and sublime serenity of mind portrayed by Plato in this dialogue were really exhibited in the last days, as in the previous life, of the master whom he delighted to honour.

For editions of the *Crito*, see the Introduction to the *Apology*.

ΚΡΙΤΩΝ

Η ΠΕΡΙ ΠΡΑΚΤΕΟΥ, ΗΘΙΚΟΣ

ΤΑ ΤΟΥ ΔΙΑΛΟΓΟΥ ΠΡΟΣΩΠΑ
ΣΩΚΡΑΤΗΣ, ΚΡΙΤΩΝ

A 1. ΣΩΚΡΑΤΗΣ. Τί τηνικάδε ἀφῖξαι, ὦ Κρίτων; ἦ οὐ πρῴ ἔτι ἐστίν;

ΚΡΙΤΩΝ. Πάνυ μὲν οὖν.

ΣΩΚΡΑΤΗΣ. Πηνίκα μάλιστα;

ΚΡΙΤΩΝ. Ὄρθρος βαθύς.

ΣΩΚΡΑΤΗΣ. Θαυμάζω, ὅπως ἠθέλησέ σοι ὁ τοῦ δεσμωτηρίου φύλαξ ὑπακοῦσαι.

ΚΡΙΤΩΝ. Ξυνήθης ἤδη μοί ἐστιν, ὦ Σώκρατες, διὰ τὸ πολλάκις δεῦρο φοιτᾶν, καί τι καὶ εὐεργέτηταί ὑπ᾽ ἐμοῦ.

ΣΩΚΡΑΤΗΣ. Ἄρτι δὲ ἥκεις ἢ πάλαι;

ΚΡΙΤΩΝ. Ἐπιεικῶς πάλαι.

B ΣΩΚΡΑΤΗΣ. Εἶτα πῶς οὐκ εὐθὺς ἐπήγειράς με, ἀλλὰ σιγῇ παρακάθησαι;

ΚΡΙΤΩΝ. Οὐ μὰ τὸν Δία, ὦ Σώκρατες, οὐδ᾽ ἂν αὐτὸς ἤθελον ἐν τοσαύτῃ τε ἀγρυπνίᾳ καὶ λύπῃ εἶναι. ἀλλὰ καὶ σοῦ πάλαι θαυμάζω αἰσθανόμενος, ὡς ἡδέως καθεύδεις· καὶ ἐπίτηδές σε οὐκ ἤγειρον, ἵνα ὡς ἥδιστα διάγῃς. καὶ πολλάκις μὲν δή σε καὶ πρότερον ἐν παντὶ τῷ βίῳ εὐδαιμόνισα

150

CRITO

[or ON DUTY; ethical]

CHARACTERS
Socrates, Crito

socrates. Why have you come at this time, Crito?
Or isn't it still early?

crito. Yes, very early.

socrates. About what time?

crito. Just before dawn.

socrates. I am surprised that the watchman of
the prison was willing to let you in.

crito. He is used to me by this time, Socrates,
because I come here so often, and besides I have
done something for him.

socrates. Have you just come, or some time
ago?

crito. Some little time ago.

socrates. Then why did you not wake me at
once, instead of sitting by me in silence?

crito. No, no, by Zeus, Socrates, I only wish I
myself were not so sleepless and sorrowful. But I
have been wondering at you for some time, seeing
how sweetly you sleep; and I purposely refrained
from waking you, that you might pass the time as
pleasantly as possible. I have often thought through-

τοῦ τρόπου, πολὺ δὲ μάλιστα ἐν τῇ νυνὶ παρεστώσῃ ξυμφορᾷ, ὡς ῥᾳδίως αὐτὴν καὶ πρᾴως φέρεις.

ΣΩΚΡΑΤΗΣ. Καὶ γὰρ ἄν, ὦ Κρίτων, πλημμελὲς
C εἴη ἀγανακτεῖν τηλικοῦτον ὄντα, εἰ δεῖ ἤδη τελευτᾶν.

ΚΡΙΤΩΝ. Καὶ ἄλλοι, ὦ Σώκρατες, τηλικοῦτοι ἐν τοιαύταις ξυμφοραῖς ἁλίσκονται, ἀλλ' οὐδὲν αὐτοὺς ἐπιλύεται ἡ ἡλικία τὸ μὴ οὐχὶ ἀγανακτεῖν τῇ παρούσῃ τύχῃ.

ΣΩΚΡΑΤΗΣ. Ἔστι ταῦτα. ἀλλὰ τί δὴ οὕτω πρῷ ἀφῖξαι;

ΚΡΙΤΩΝ. Ἀγγελίαν, ὦ Σώκρατες, φέρων χαλεπήν, οὐ σοί, ὡς ἐμοὶ φαίνεται, ἀλλ' ἐμοὶ καὶ τοῖς σοῖς ἐπιτηδείοις πᾶσιν καὶ χαλεπὴν καὶ βαρεῖαν, ἣν ἐγώ, ὡς ἐμοὶ δοκῶ, ἐν τοῖς βαρύτατ' ἂν ἐνέγκαιμι.

ΣΩΚΡΑΤΗΣ. Τίνα ταύτην; ἢ τὸ πλοῖον ἀφῖκται
D ἐκ Δήλου, οὗ δεῖ ἀφικομένου τεθνάναι με;

ΚΡΙΤΩΝ. Οὔτοι δὴ ἀφῖκται, ἀλλὰ δοκεῖ μέν μοι ἥξειν τήμερον ἐξ ὧν ἀπαγγέλλουσιν ἥκοντές τινες ἀπὸ Σουνίου καὶ καταλιπόντες ἐκεῖ αὐτό. δῆλον οὖν ἐκ τούτων τῶν ἀγγέλων[1] ὅτι ἥξει τήμερον, καὶ ἀνάγκη δὲ εἰς αὔριον ἔσται, ὦ Σώκρατες, τὸν βίον σε τελευτᾶν.

2. ΣΩΚΡΑΤΗΣ. Ἀλλ', ὦ Κρίτων, τύχῃ ἀγαθῇ. εἰ ταύτῃ τοῖς θεοῖς φίλον, ταύτῃ ἔστω. οὐ μέντοι
44 οἶμαι ἥξειν αὐτὸ τήμερον.

ΚΡΙΤΩΝ. Πόθεν τοῦτο τεκμαίρει;

ΣΩΚΡΑΤΗΣ. Ἐγώ σοι ἐρῶ. τῇ γάρ που ὑστεραίᾳ δεῖ με ἀποθνῄσκειν ἢ ᾗ ἂν ἔλθῃ τὸ πλοῖον.

---

[1] Schanz brackets ἀγγέλων.

out your life hitherto that you were of a happy disposition, and I think so more than ever in this present misfortune, since you bear it so easily and calmly.

SOCRATES. Well, Crito, it would be absurd if at my age I were disturbed because I must die now.

CRITO. Other men as old, Socrates, become involved in similar misfortunes, but their age does not in the least prevent them from being disturbed by their fate.

SOCRATES. That is true. But why have you come so early?

CRITO. To bring news, Socrates, sad news, though apparently not sad to you, but sad and grievous to me and all your friends, and to few of them, I think, so grievous as to me.

SOCRATES. What is this news? Has the ship come from Delos, at the arrival of which I am to die?

CRITO. It has not exactly come, but I think it will come to-day from the reports of some men who have come from Sunium and left it there. Now it is clear from what they say that it will come to-day, and so to-morrow, Socrates, your life must end.

SOCRATES. Well, Crito, good luck be with us! If this is the will of the gods, so be it. However, I do not think it will come to-day.

CRITO. What is your reason for not thinking so?

SOCRATES. I will tell you. I must die on the day after the ship comes in, must I not?

ΚΡΙΤΩΝ. Φασί γέ τοι δὴ οἱ τούτων κύριοι.

ΣΩΚΡΑΤΗΣ. Οὐ τοίνυν τῆς ἐπιούσης ἡμέρας οἶμαι αὐτὸ ἥξειν, ἀλλὰ τῆς ἑτέρας. τεκμαίρομαι δὲ ἔκ τινος ἐνυπνίου, ὃ ἑώρακα ὀλίγον πρότερον ταύτης τῆς νυκτός· καὶ κινδυνεύεις ἐν καιρῷ τινι οὐκ ἐγεῖραί με.

ΚΡΙΤΩΝ. Ἦν δὲ δὴ τί τὸ ἐνύπνιον;

ΣΩΚΡΑΤΗΣ. Ἐδόκει τίς μοι γυνὴ προσελθοῦσα καλὴ καὶ εὐειδής, λευκὰ ἱμάτια ἔχουσα, καλέσαι
B με καὶ εἰπεῖν· ὦ Σώκρατες,

ἤματί κεν τριτάτῳ Φθίην ἐρίβωλον ἵκοιο.

ΚΡΙΤΩΝ. Ἄτοπον τὸ ἐνύπνιον, ὦ Σώκρατες.

ΣΩΚΡΑΤΗΣ. Ἐναργὲς μὲν οὖν, ὥς γέ μοι δοκεῖ, ὦ Κρίτων.

3. ΚΡΙΤΩΝ. Λίαν γε, ὡς ἔοικεν. ἀλλ᾽, ὦ δαιμόνιε Σώκρατες, ἔτι καὶ νῦν ἐμοὶ πιθοῦ¹ καὶ σώθητι· ὡς ἐμοί, ἐὰν σὺ ἀποθάνῃς, οὐ μία ξυμφορά ἐστιν, ἀλλὰ χωρὶς μὲν τοῦ ἐστερῆσθαι τοιούτου ἐπιτηδείου, οἷον ἐγὼ οὐδένα μή ποτε εὑρήσω, ἔτι δὲ καὶ πολλοῖς δόξω, οἳ ἐμὲ καὶ σὲ
C μὴ σαφῶς ἴσασιν, ὡς οἷός τ᾽ ὢν σε σῴζειν, εἰ ἤθελον ἀναλίσκειν χρήματα, ἀμελῆσαι. καίτοι τίς ἂν αἰσχίων εἴη ταύτης δόξα ἢ δοκεῖν χρήματα περὶ πλείονος ποιεῖσθαι ἢ φίλους; οὐ γὰρ πείσονται οἱ πολλοί, ὡς σὺ αὐτὸς οὐκ ἠθέλησας ἀπιέναι ἐνθένδε ἡμῶν προθυμουμένων.

ΣΩΚΡΑΤΗΣ. Ἀλλὰ τί ἡμῖν, ὦ μακάριε Κρίτων, οὕτω τῆς τῶν πολλῶν δόξης μέλει; οἱ γὰρ ἐπιεικέστατοι, ὧν μᾶλλον ἄξιον φροντίζειν, ἡγήσονται αὐτὰ οὕτω πεπρᾶχθαι, ὥσπερ ἂν πραχθῇ.

D ΚΡΙΤΩΝ. Ἀλλ᾽ ὁρᾷς δή, ὅτι ἀνάγκη, ὦ Σώκρατες,

¹ πιθοῦ Schanz, following Burges, πείθου BCDE.

CRITO. So those say who have charge of these matters.

SOCRATES. Well, I think it will not come in to-day, but to-morrow. And my reason for this is a dream which I had a little while ago in the course of this night. And perhaps you let me sleep just at the right time.

CRITO. What was the dream?

SOCRATES. I dreamed that a beautiful, fair woman, clothed in white raiment, came to me and called me and said, "Socrates, on the third day thou wouldst come to fertile Phthia." [1]

CRITO. A strange dream, Socrates.

SOCRATES. No, a clear one, at any rate, I think, Crito.

CRITO. Too clear, apparently. But, my dear Socrates, even now listen to me and save yourself. Since, if you die, it will be no mere single misfortune to me, but I shall lose a friend such as I can never find again, and besides, many persons who do not know you and me well will think I could have saved you if I had been willing to spend money, but that I would not take the trouble. And yet what reputation could be more disgraceful than that of considering one's money of more importance than one's friends? For most people will not believe that we were eager to help you to go away from here, but you refused.

SOCRATES. But, my dear Crito, why do we care so much for what most people think? For the most reasonable men, whose opinion is more worth considering, will think that things were done as they really will be done.

CRITO. But you see it is necessary, Socrates, to

[1] Homer, *Iliad* ix, 363.

καὶ τῆς τῶν πολλῶν δόξης μέλειν. αὐτὰ δὲ δῆλα
τὰ παρόντα νυνί, ὅτι οἷοί τ᾽ εἰσὶν οἱ πολλοὶ οὐ τὰ
σμικρότατα τῶν κακῶν ἐξεργάζεσθαι, ἀλλὰ τὰ
μέγιστα σχεδόν, ἐάν τις ἐν αὐτοῖς διαβεβλημένος ᾖ.

ΣΩΚΡΑΤΗΣ. Εἰ γὰρ ὤφελον, ὦ Κρίτων, οἷοί τ᾽
εἶναι οἱ πολλοὶ τὰ μέγιστα κακὰ ἐργάζεσθαι, ἵνα
οἷοί τ᾽ ἦσαν καὶ τὰ μέγιστα ἀγαθά, καὶ καλῶς
ἂν εἶχεν· νῦν δὲ οὐδέτερα οἷοί τε· οὔτε γὰρ φρόνιμον οὔτε ἄφρονα δυνατοὶ ποιῆσαι, ποιοῦσι δὲ
τοῦτο ὅ τι ἂν τύχωσι.

E   4. ΚΡΙΤΩΝ. Ταῦτα μὲν δὴ οὕτως ἐχέτω· τάδε
δέ, ὦ Σώκρατες, εἰπέ μοι. ἆρά γε μὴ ἐμοῦ προ-
μηθεῖ καὶ τῶν ἄλλων ἐπιτηδείων, μή, ἐὰν σὺ
ἐνθένδε ἐξέλθῃς, οἱ συκοφάνται ἡμῖν πράγματα
παρέχωσιν ὡς σὲ ἐνθένδε ἐκκλέψασιν, καὶ ἀναγκα-
σθῶμεν ἢ καὶ πᾶσαν τὴν οὐσίαν ἀποβαλεῖν ἢ
συχνὰ χρήματα, ἢ καὶ ἄλλο τι πρὸς τούτοις
45 παθεῖν; εἰ γάρ τι τοιοῦτον φοβεῖ, ἔασον αὐτὸ
χαίρειν· ἡμεῖς γάρ που δίκαιοί ἐσμεν σώσαντές
σε κινδυνεύειν τοῦτον τὸν κίνδυνον καί, ἐὰν δέῃ,
ἔτι τούτου μείζω. ἀλλ᾽ ἐμοὶ πείθου καὶ μὴ ἄλλως
ποίει.

ΣΩΚΡΑΤΗΣ. Καὶ ταῦτα προμηθοῦμαι, ὦ Κρίτων,
καὶ ἄλλα πολλά.

ΚΡΙΤΩΝ. Μήτε τοίνυν ταῦτα φοβοῦ· καὶ γὰρ
οὐδὲ πολὺ τἀργύριόν ἐστιν, ὃ θέλουσι λαβόντες
τινὲς σῶσαί σε καὶ ἐξαγαγεῖν ἐνθένδε. ἔπειτα
οὐχ ὁρᾷς τούτους τοὺς συκοφάντας ὡς εὐτελεῖς,
καὶ οὐδὲν ἂν δέοι ἐπ᾽ αὐτοὺς πολλοῦ ἀργυρίου; σοὶ
B δὲ ὑπάρχει μὲν τὰ ἐμὰ χρήματα, ὡς ἐγὼ οἶμαι,
ἱκανά· ἔπειτα καὶ εἴ τι ἐμοῦ κηδόμενος οὐκ οἴει

care for the opinion of the public, for this very trouble we are in now shows that the public is able to accomplish not by any means the least, but almost the greatest of evils, if one has a bad reputation with it.

SOCRATES. I only wish, Crito, the people could accomplish the greatest evils, that they might be able to accomplish also the greatest good things. Then all would be well. But now they can do neither of the two; for they are not able to make a man wise or foolish, but they do whatever occurs to them.

CRITO. That may well be. But, Socrates, tell me this: you are not considering me and your other friends, are you, fearing that, if you escape, the informers will make trouble for us by saying that we stole you away, and we shall be forced to lose either all our property or a good deal of money, or be punished in some other way besides? For if you are afraid of anything of that kind, let it go; since it is right for us to run this risk, and even greater risk than this, if necessary, provided we save you. Now please do as I ask.

SOCRATES. I am considering this, Crito, and many other things.

CRITO. Well, do not fear this! for it is not even a large sum of money which we should pay to some men who are willing to save you and get you away from here. Besides, don't you see how cheap these informers are, and that not much money would be needed to silence them? And you have my money at your command, which is enough, I fancy; and moreover, if because you care for me you think you

δεῖν ἀναλίσκειν τἀμά, ξένοι[1] ἐνθάδε ἕτοιμοι ἀναλί-
σκειν· εἷς δὲ καὶ κεκόμικεν ἐπ᾽ αὐτὸ τοῦτο ἀρ-
γύριον ἱκανόν, Σιμμίας ὁ Θηβαῖος· ἕτοιμος δὲ καὶ
Κέβης καὶ ἄλλοι πολλοὶ πάνυ. ὥστε, ὅπερ λέγω,
μήτε ταῦτα φοβούμενος ἀποκάμῃς σαυτὸν σῶσαι,
μήτε ὃ ἔλεγες ἐν τῷ δικαστηρίῳ, δυσχερές σοι
γενέσθω, ὅτι οὐκ ἂν ἔχοις ἐξελθὼν ὅ τι χρῷο
σαυτῷ· πολλαχοῦ μὲν γὰρ καὶ ἄλλοσε ὅποι ἂν
C ἀφίκῃ ἀγαπήσουσί σε· ἐὰν δὲ βούλῃ εἰς Θετταλίαν ἰέναι, εἰσὶν ἐμοὶ ἐκεῖ ξένοι, οἵ σε περὶ
πολλοῦ ποιήσονται καὶ ἀσφάλειάν σοι παρέξονται,
ὥστε σε μηδένα λυπεῖν τῶν κατὰ Θετταλίαν.

5. Ἔτι δέ, ὦ Σώκρατες, οὐδὲ δίκαιόν μοι δοκεῖς
ἐπιχειρεῖν πρᾶγμα, σαυτὸν προδοῦναι, ἐξὸν σω-
θῆναι· καὶ τοιαῦτα σπεύδεις περὶ σαυτὸν γενέσθαι, ἅπερ ἂν καὶ οἱ ἐχθροί σου σπεύσαιέν τε καὶ
ἔσπευσάν σε διαφθεῖραι βουλόμενοι. πρὸς δὲ
τούτοις καὶ τοὺς υἱεῖς τοὺς σαυτοῦ ἔμοιγε δοκεῖς
D προδιδόναι, οὓς σοι ἐξὸν καὶ ἐκθρέψαι καὶ ἐκπαι-
δεῦσαι οἰχήσει καταλιπών, καὶ τὸ σὸν μέρος, ὅ τι
ἂν τύχωσι, τοῦτο πράξουσιν· τεύξονται δέ, ὡς τὸ
εἰκός, τοιούτων οἷάπερ εἴωθεν γίγνεσθαι ἐν ταῖς
ὀρφανίαις περὶ τοὺς ὀρφανούς. ἢ γὰρ οὐ χρὴ
ποιεῖσθαι παῖδας ἢ ξυνδιαταλαιπωρεῖν καὶ τρέ-
φοντα καὶ παιδεύοντα· σὺ δέ μοι δοκεῖς τὰ
ῥᾳθυμότατα αἱρεῖσθαι· χρὴ δέ, ἅπερ ἂν ἀνὴρ
ἀγαθὸς καὶ ἀνδρεῖος ἕλοιτο, ταῦτα αἱρεῖσθαι,
φάσκοντά γε δὴ ἀρετῆς διὰ παντὸς τοῦ βίου
ἐπιμελεῖσθαι· ὡς ἔγωγε καὶ ὑπὲρ σοῦ καὶ ὑπὲρ
E ἡμῶν τῶν σῶν ἐπιτηδείων αἰσχύνομαι, μὴ δόξῃ
ἅπαν τὸ πρᾶγμα τὸ περὶ σὲ ἀνανδρίᾳ τινὶ τῇ

[1] After ξένοι the MSS. read οὗτοι, which Schanz brackets.

ought not to spend my money, there are foreigners here willing to spend theirs; and one of them, Simmias of Thebes, has brought for this especial purpose sufficient funds; and Cebes also and very many others are ready. So, as I say, do not give up saving yourself through fear of this. And do not be troubled by what you said in the court, that if you went away you would not know what to do with yourself. For in many other places, wherever you go, they will welcome you; and if you wish to go to Thessaly, I have friends there who will make much of you and will protect you, so that no one in Thessaly shall annoy you.

And besides, Socrates, it seems to me the thing you are undertaking to do is not even right—betraying yourself when you might save yourself. And you are eager to bring upon yourself just what your enemies would wish and just what those were eager for who wished to destroy you. And moreover, I think you are abandoning your children, too, for when you might bring them up and educate them, you are going to desert them and go away, and, so far as you are concerned, their fortunes in life will be whatever they happen to meet with, and they will probably meet with such treatment as generally comes to orphans in their destitution. No. Either one ought not to beget children, or one ought to stay by them and bring them up and educate them. But you seem to me to be choosing the laziest way; and you ought to choose as a good and brave man would choose, you who have been saying all your life that you cared for virtue. So I am ashamed both for you and for us, your friends, and I am afraid people will think that this whole affair of yours has

ἡμετέρᾳ πεπρᾶχθαι, καὶ ἡ εἴσοδος τῆς δίκης εἰς τὸ δικαστήριον ὡς εἰσῆλθεν ἐξὸν μὴ εἰσελθεῖν, καὶ αὐτὸς ὁ ἀγὼν τῆς δίκης ὡς ἐγένετο, καὶ τὸ τελευταῖον δὴ τουτί, ὥσπερ κατάγελως τῆς πράξεως, κακίᾳ τινὶ καὶ ἀνανδρίᾳ τῇ ἡμετέρᾳ

46 διαπεφευγέναι ἡμᾶς δοκεῖν, οἵτινές σε οὐχὶ ἐσώσαμεν οὐδὲ σὺ σαυτόν, οἷόν τε ὂν καὶ δυνατόν, εἴ τι καὶ μικρὸν ἡμῶν ὄφελος ἦν. ταῦτα οὖν, ὦ Σώκρατες, ὅρα μὴ ἅμα τῷ κακῷ καὶ αἰσχρὰ ᾖ σοί τε καὶ ἡμῖν. ἀλλὰ βουλεύου, μᾶλλον δὲ οὐδὲ βουλεύεσθαι ἔτι ὥρα, ἀλλὰ βεβουλεῦσθαι. μία δὲ βουλή· τῆς γὰρ ἐπιούσης νυκτὸς πάντα ταῦτα δεῖ πεπρᾶχθαι. εἰ δέ τι περιμενοῦμεν, ἀδύνατον καὶ οὐκέτι οἷόν τε. ἀλλὰ παντὶ τρόπῳ, ὦ Σώκρατες, πείθου μοι καὶ μηδαμῶς ἄλλως ποίει.

B   6. ΣΩΚΡΑΤΗΣ. Ὦ φίλε Κρίτων, ἡ προθυμία σου πολλοῦ ἀξία, εἰ μετά τινος ὀρθότητος εἴη· εἰ δὲ μή, ὅσῳ μείζων, τοσούτῳ χαλεπωτέρα. σκοπεῖσθαι οὖν χρὴ ἡμᾶς, εἴτε ταῦτα πρακτέον εἴτε μή· ὡς ἐγὼ οὐ μόνον νῦν ἀλλὰ καὶ ἀεὶ τοιοῦτος, οἷος τῶν ἐμῶν μηδενὶ ἄλλῳ πείθεσθαι ἢ τῷ λόγῳ, ὃς ἄν μοι λογιζομένῳ βέλτιστος φαίνηται. τοὺς δὲ λόγους, οὓς ἐν τῷ ἔμπροσθεν ἔλεγον, οὐ δύναμαι νῦν ἐκβαλεῖν, ἐπειδή μοι ἥδε ἡ τύχη γέγονεν, ἀλλὰ σχεδόν τι ὅμοιοι φαίνονταί μοι,

C καὶ τοὺς αὐτοὺς πρεσβεύω καὶ τιμῶ οὕσπερ καὶ πρότερον· ὧν ἐὰν μὴ βελτίω ἔχωμεν λέγειν ἐν τῷ παρόντι, εὖ ἴσθι ὅτι οὐ μή σοι ξυγχωρήσω, οὐδ᾽ ἂν πλείω τῶν νῦν παρόντων ἢ τῶν πολλῶν δύναμις ὥσπερ παῖδας ἡμᾶς μορμολύττηται, δεσμοὺς καὶ θανάτους ἐπιπέμπουσα καὶ χρημάτων ἀφαιρέσεις. πῶς οὖν ἂν μετριώτατα σκοποίμεθα

been conducted with a sort of cowardice on our part
—both the fact that the case came before the court,
when it might have been avoided, and the way in
which the trial itself was carried on, and finally they
will think, as the crowning absurdity of the whole
affair, that this opportunity has escaped us through
some base cowardice on our part, since we did
not save you, and you did not save yourself, though
it was quite possible if we had been of any use whatever. Take care, Socrates, that these things be
not disgraceful, as well as evil, both to you and to us.
Just consider, or rather it is time not to consider any
longer, but to have finished considering. And there
is just one possible plan; for all this must be done in
the coming night. And if we delay it can no longer
be done. But I beg you, Socrates, do as I say and
don't refuse.

socrates. My dear Crito, your eagerness is worth
a great deal, if it should prove to be rightly directed ;
but otherwise, the greater ·it is, the more hard to
bear. So we must examine the question whether we
ought to do this or not; for I am not only now but
always a man who follows nothing but the reasoning
which on consideration seems to me best. And
I cannot, now that this has happened to us, discard
the arguments I used to advance, but they seem to
me much the same as ever, and I revere and honour
the same ones as before. And unless we can bring
forward better ones in our present situation, be
assured that I shall not give way to you, not even if
the power of the multitude frighten us with even
more terrors than at present, as children are frightened with goblins, threatening us with imprison-
ments and deaths and confiscations of property. Now

αὐτά; εἰ πρῶτον μὲν τοῦτον τὸν λόγον ἀναλά-
βοιμεν, ὃν σὺ λέγεις περὶ τῶν δοξῶν, πότερον
καλῶς ἐλέγετο ἑκάστοτε ἢ οὔ, ὅτι ταῖς μὲν δεῖ τῶν
D δοξῶν προσέχειν τὸν νοῦν, ταῖς δὲ οὔ· ἢ πρὶν μὲν
ἐμὲ δεῖν ἀποθνήσκειν καλῶς ἐλέγετο, νῦν δὲ
κατάδηλος ἄρα ἐγένετο, ὅτι ἄλλως ἕνεκα λόγου
ἐλέγετο, ἦν δὲ παιδιὰ καὶ φλυαρία ὡς ἀληθῶς;
ἐπιθυμῶ δ' ἔγωγ' ἐπισκέψασθαι, ὦ Κρίτων, κοινῇ
μετὰ σοῦ, εἴ τί μοι ἀλλοιότερος φανεῖται, ἐπειδὴ
ᾧδε ἔχω, ἢ ὁ αὐτός, καὶ ἐάσομεν χαίρειν ἢ πεισόμεθα αὐτῷ. ἐλέγετο δέ πως, ὡς ἐγῷμαι, ἑκάστοτε ᾧδε ὑπὸ τῶν οἰομένων τι λέγειν, ὥσπερ νῦν
δὴ ἐγὼ ἔλεγον, ὅτι τῶν δοξῶν, ἃς οἱ ἄνθρωποι
E δοξάζουσιν, δέοι τὰς μὲν περὶ πολλοῦ ποιεῖσθαι,
τὰς δὲ μή. τοῦτο πρὸς θεῶν, ὦ Κρίτων, οὐ δοκεῖ
καλῶς σοι λέγεσθαι; σὺ γάρ, ὅσα γε τἀνθρώπεια,
47 ἐκτὸς εἶ τοῦ μέλλειν ἀποθνήσκειν αὔριον, καὶ οὐκ
ἄν σε παρακρούοι ἡ παροῦσα ξυμφορά· σκόπει δή·
οὐχ ἱκανῶς δοκεῖ σοι λέγεσθαι, ὅτι οὐ πάσας χρὴ
τὰς δόξας τῶν ἀνθρώπων τιμᾶν, ἀλλὰ τὰς μέν, τὰς
δ' οὔ; οὐδὲ πάντων, ἀλλὰ τῶν μέν, τῶν δ' οὔ; τί
φῄς; ταῦτα οὐχὶ καλῶς λέγεται;

ΚΡΙΤΩΝ. Καλῶς.

ΣΩΚΡΑΤΗΣ. Οὐκοῦν τὰς μὲν χρηστὰς τιμᾶν, τὰς
δὲ πονηρὰς μή;

ΚΡΙΤΩΝ. Ναί.

ΣΩΚΡΑΤΗΣ. Χρησταὶ δὲ οὐχ αἱ τῶν φρονίμων,
πονηραὶ δὲ αἱ τῶν ἀφρόνων;

ΚΡΙΤΩΝ. Πῶς δ' οὔ;

7. ΣΩΚΡΑΤΗΣ. Φέρε δή, πῶς αὖ τὰ τοιαῦτα
B ἐλέγετο; γυμναζόμενος ἀνὴρ καὶ τοῦτο πράττων

how could we examine the matter most reasonably?
By taking up first what you say about opinions and
asking whether we were right when we always used
to say that we ought to pay attention to some
opinions and not to others? Or were we right
before I was condemned to death, whereas it has
now been made clear that we were talking merely
for the sake of argument and it was really mere play
and nonsense? And I wish to investigate, Crito, in
common with you, and see whether our former
argument seems different to me under our present
conditions, or the same, and whether we shall give it
up or be guided by it. But it used to be said, I
think, by those who thought they were speaking
sensibly, just as I was saying now, that of the
opinions held by men some ought to be highly
esteemed and others not. In God's name, Crito, do
you not think this is correct? For you, humanly
speaking, are not involved in the necessity of dying
to-morrow, and therefore present conditions would
not lead your judgment astray. Now say, do you
not think we were correct in saying that we ought
not to esteem all the opinions of men, but some
and not others, and not those of all men, but only of
some? What do you think? Is not this true?

CRITO. It is.

SOCRATES. Then we ought to esteem the good
opinions and not the bad ones?

CRITO. Yes.

SOCRATES. And the good ones are those of the
wise and the bad ones those of the foolish?

CRITO. Of course.

SOCRATES. Come then, what used we to say about
this? If a man is an athlete and makes that his

PLATO

πότερον παντὸς ἀνδρὸς ἐπαίνῳ καὶ ψόγῳ καὶ δόξῃ
τὸν νοῦν προσέχει, ἢ ἑνὸς μόνου ἐκείνου, ὃς ἂν
τυγχάνῃ ἰατρὸς ἢ παιδοτρίβης ὤν;

ΚΡΙΤΩΝ. Ἑνὸς μόνου.

ΣΩΚΡΑΤΗΣ. Οὐκοῦν φοβεῖσθαι χρὴ τοὺς ψόγους
καὶ ἀσπάζεσθαι τοὺς ἐπαίνους τοὺς τοῦ ἑνὸς
ἐκείνου, ἀλλὰ μὴ τοὺς τῶν πολλῶν.

ΚΡΙΤΩΝ. Δῆλα δή.

ΣΩΚΡΑΤΗΣ. Ταύτῃ ἄρα αὐτῷ πρακτέον καὶ
γυμναστέον καὶ ἐδεστέον γε καὶ ποτέον, ᾗ ἂν τῷ
ἑνὶ δοκῇ τῷ ἐπιστάτῃ καὶ ἐπαΐοντι, μᾶλλον ἢ ᾗ
ξύμπασι τοῖς ἄλλοις.

ΚΡΙΤΩΝ. Ἔστι ταῦτα.

C ΣΩΚΡΑΤΗΣ. Εἶεν. ἀπειθήσας δὲ τῷ ἑνὶ καὶ
ἀτιμάσας αὐτοῦ τὴν δόξαν καὶ τοὺς ἐπαίνους,[1]
τιμήσας δὲ τοὺς τῶν πολλῶν λόγους καὶ μηδὲν
ἐπαΐόντων, ἆρα οὐδὲν κακὸν πείσεται;

ΚΡΙΤΩΝ. Πῶς γὰρ οὔ;

ΣΩΚΡΑΤΗΣ. Τί δ' ἔστι τὸ κακὸν τοῦτο; καὶ ποῖ
τείνει, καὶ εἰς τί τῶν τοῦ ἀπειθοῦντος;

ΚΡΙΤΩΝ. Δῆλον ὅτι εἰς τὸ σῶμα· τοῦτο γὰρ
διολλύει.

ΣΩΚΡΑΤΗΣ. Καλῶς λέγεις. οὐκοῦν καὶ τἆλλα,
ὦ Κρίτων, οὕτως, ἵνα μὴ πάντα διίωμεν, καὶ δὴ
καὶ περὶ τῶν δικαίων καὶ ἀδίκων καὶ αἰσχρῶν καὶ
καλῶν καὶ ἀγαθῶν καὶ κακῶν, περὶ ὧν νῦν ἡ
βουλὴ ἡμῖν ἐστιν, πότερον τῇ τῶν πολλῶν δόξῃ
D δεῖ ἡμᾶς ἕπεσθαι καὶ φοβεῖσθαι αὐτὴν ἢ τῇ τοῦ
ἑνός, εἴ τίς ἐστιν ἐπαΐων, ὃν δεῖ καὶ αἰσχύνεσθαι
καὶ φοβεῖσθαι μᾶλλον ἢ ξύμπαντας τοὺς ἄλλους;
ᾧ εἰ μὴ ἀκολουθήσομεν, διαφθεροῦμεν ἐκεῖνο καὶ

[1] Schanz, following Burges, brackets καὶ τοὺς ἐπαίνους.

business, does he pay attention to every man's praise
and blame and opinion or to those of one man only
who is a physician or a trainer?

CRITO.   To those of one man only.

SOCRATES.   Then he ought to fear the blame and
welcome the praise of that one man and not of the
multitude.

CRITO.   Obviously.

SOCRATES.   And he must act and exercise and eat
and drink as the one man who is his director and
who knows the business thinks best rather than as
all the others think.

CRITO.   That is true.

SOCRATES.   Well then; if he disobeys the one man
and disregards his opinion and his praise, but regards
the words of the many who have no special knowledge, will he not come to harm?

CRITO.   Of course he will.

SOCRATES.   And what is this harm?   In what
direction and upon what part of the one who
disobeys does it act?

CRITO.   Evidently upon his body; for that is what
it ruins.

SOCRATES.   Right.   Then in other matters, not to
enumerate them all, in questions of right and
wrong and disgraceful and noble and good and bad,
which we are now considering, ought we to follow
and fear the opinion of the many or that of the one,
if there is anyone who knows about them, whom we
ought to revere and fear more than all the others?
And if we do not follow him, we shall injure and
cripple that which we used to say is benefited by

λωβησόμεθα, ὃ τῷ μὲν δικαίῳ βέλτιον ἐγίγνετο,
τῷ δὲ ἀδίκῳ ἀπώλλυτο. ἢ οὐδέν ἐστι τοῦτο;

ΚΡΙΤΩΝ. Οἶμαι ἔγωγε, ὦ Σώκρατες.

8. ΣΩΚΡΑΤΗΣ. Φέρε δή, ἐὰν τὸ ὑπὸ τοῦ ὑγιεινοῦ
μὲν βέλτιον γιγνόμενον, ὑπὸ τοῦ νοσώδους δὲ
διαφθειρόμενον διολέσωμεν πειθόμενοι μὴ τῇ τῶν
Ε ἐπαϊόντων δόξῃ, ἆρα βιωτὸν ἡμῖν ἐστιν διεφθαρμένου αὐτοῦ; ἔστι δέ που τοῦτο σῶμα· ἢ οὐχί;

ΚΡΙΤΩΝ. Ναί.

ΣΩΚΡΑΤΗΣ. Ἆρ' οὖν βιωτὸν ἡμῖν ἐστιν μετὰ
μοχθηροῦ καὶ διεφθαρμένου σώματος;

ΚΡΙΤΩΝ. Οὐδαμῶς.

ΣΩΚΡΑΤΗΣ. Ἀλλὰ μετ' ἐκείνου ἆρ' ἡμῖν βιωτὸν
διεφθαρμένου, ᾧ τὸ ἄδικον μὲν λωβᾶται, τὸ δὲ
δίκαιον ὀνίνησιν; ἢ φαυλότερον ἡγούμεθα εἶναι
τοῦ σώματος ἐκεῖνο, ὅ τί ποτ' ἐστὶ τῶν ἡμετέρων,
48 περὶ ὃ ἥ τε ἀδικία καὶ ἡ δικαιοσύνη ἐστίν;

ΚΡΙΤΩΝ. Οὐδαμῶς.

ΣΩΚΡΑΤΗΣ. Ἀλλὰ τιμιώτερον;

ΚΡΙΤΩΝ. Πολύ γε.

ΣΩΚΡΑΤΗΣ. Οὐκ ἄρα, ὦ βέλτιστε, πάνυ ἡμῖν
οὕτω φροντιστέον, τί ἐροῦσιν οἱ πολλοὶ ἡμᾶς,
ἀλλ' ὅ τι ὁ ἐπαΐων περὶ τῶν δικαίων καὶ ἀδίκων,
ὁ εἷς, καὶ αὐτὴ ἡ ἀλήθεια. ὥστε πρῶτον μὲν
ταύτῃ οὐκ ὀρθῶς εἰσηγεῖ, εἰσηγούμενος τῆς τῶν
πολλῶν δόξης δεῖν ἡμᾶς φροντίζειν περὶ τῶν
δικαίων καὶ καλῶν καὶ ἀγαθῶν καὶ τῶν ἐναντίων.
Β ἀλλὰ μὲν δή, φαίη γ' ἄν τις, οἷοί τέ εἰσιν ἡμᾶς οἱ
πολλοὶ ἀποκτιννύναι.

ΚΡΙΤΩΝ. Δῆλα δὴ καὶ ταῦτα· φαίη γὰρ ἄν,[1] ὦ
Σώκρατες.

---

[1] φαίη γὰρ ἄν bracketed by Schanz.

the right and is ruined by the wrong. Or is there nothing in this?

CRITO. I think it is true, Socrates.

SOCRATES. Well then, if through yielding to the opinion of the ignorant we ruin that which is benefited by health and injured by disease, is life worth living for us when that is ruined? And that is the body, is it not?

CRITO. Yes.

SOCRATES. Then is life worth living when the body is worthless and ruined?

CRITO. Certainly not.

SOCRATES. But is it worth living when that is ruined which is injured by the wrong and improved by the right? Or do we think that part of us, whatever it is, which is concerned with right and wrong, is less important than the body?

CRITO. By no means.

SOCRATES. But more important?

CRITO. Much more.

SOCRATES. Then, most excellent friend, we must not consider at all what the many will say of us, but what he who knows about right and wrong, the one man, and truth herself will say. And so you introduced the discussion wrongly in the first place, when you began by saying we ought to consider the opinion of the multitude about the right and the noble and the good and their opposites. But it might, of course, be said that the multitude can put us to death.

CRITO. That is clear, too. It would be said, Socrates.

ΣΩΚΡΑΤΗΣ. Ἀληθῆ λέγεις.[1] ἀλλ', ὦ θαυμάσιε, οὗτός τε ὁ λόγος ὃν διεληλύθαμεν, ἔμοιγε δοκεῖ ἔτι ὅμοιος εἶναι καὶ πρότερον·[2] καὶ τόνδε αὖ σκόπει, εἰ ἔτι μένει ἡμῖν ἢ οὔ, ὅτι οὐ τὸ ζῆν περὶ πλείστου ποιητέον, ἀλλὰ τὸ εὖ ζῆν.

ΚΡΙΤΩΝ. Ἀλλὰ μένει.

ΣΩΚΡΑΤΗΣ. Τὸ δὲ εὖ καὶ καλῶς καὶ δικαίως ὅτι ταὐτόν ἐστιν, μένει ἢ οὐ μένει;

ΚΡΙΤΩΝ. Μένει.

9. ΣΩΚΡΑΤΗΣ. Οὐκοῦν ἐκ τῶν ὁμολογουμένων τοῦτο σκεπτέον, πότερον δίκαιον ἐμὲ ἐνθένδε C πειρᾶσθαι ἐξιέναι μὴ ἀφιέντων Ἀθηναίων ἢ οὐ δίκαιον· καὶ ἐὰν μὲν φαίνηται δίκαιον, πειρώμεθα, εἰ δὲ μή, ἐῶμεν. ἃς δὲ σὺ λέγεις τὰς σκέψεις περί τε ἀναλώσεως χρημάτων καὶ δόξης καὶ παίδων τροφῆς, μὴ ὡς ἀληθῶς ταῦτα, ὦ Κρίτων, σκέμματα ᾖ τῶν ῥᾳδίως ἀποκτιννύντων καὶ ἀναβιωσκομένων γ' ἄν, εἰ οἷοί τ' ἦσαν, οὐδενὶ ξὺν νῷ, τούτων τῶν πολλῶν. ἡμῖν δ', ἐπειδὴ ὁ λόγος οὕτως αἱρεῖ, μὴ οὐδὲν ἄλλο σκεπτέον ᾖ ἢ ὅπερ νῦν δὴ ἐλέγομεν, πότερον δίκαια πράξομεν καὶ χρήματα τελοῦντες D τούτοις τοῖς ἐμὲ ἐνθένδε ἐξάξουσιν καὶ χάριτας, καὶ αὐτοὶ ἐξάγοντές τε καὶ ἐξαγόμενοι, ἢ τῇ ἀληθείᾳ ἀδικήσομεν πάντα ταῦτα ποιοῦντες· κἂν φαινώμεθα ἄδικα αὐτὰ ἐργαζόμενοι, μὴ οὐ δέῃ ὑπολογίζεσθαι οὔτ' εἰ ἀποθνήσκειν δεῖ παραμένοντας καὶ ἡσυχίαν ἄγοντας, οὔτε ἄλλο ὁτιοῦν πάσχειν πρὸ τοῦ ἀδικεῖν.

[1] Schanz gives ἀληθῆ λέγεις to Crito.

[2] The usual reading, ἔμοιγε δοκεῖ ὅμοιος εἶναι τῷ καὶ πρότερον was corrected by Schanz, who follows a quotation of the passage by Priscian.

SOCRATES. That is true. But, my friend, the argument we have just finished seems to me still much the same as before ; and now see whether we still hold to this, or not, that it is not living, but living well which we ought to consider most important.

CRITO. We do hold to it.

SOCRATES. And that living well and living rightly are the same thing, do we hold to that, or not ?

CRITO. We do.

SOCRATES. Then we agree that the question is whether it is right for me to try to escape from here without the permission of the Athenians, or not right. And if it appears to be right, let us try it, and if not, let us give it up. But the considerations you suggest, about spending money, and reputation, and bringing up my children, these are really, Crito, the reflections of those who lightly put men to death, and would bring them to life again, if they could, without any sense, I mean the multitude. But we, since our argument so constrains us, must consider only the question we just broached, whether we shall be doing right in giving money and thanks to these men who will help me to escape, and in escaping or aiding the escape ourselves, or shall in truth be doing wrong, if we do all these things. And if it appears that it is wrong for us to do them, it may be that we ought not to consider either whether we must die if we stay here and keep quiet or whether we must endure anything else whatsoever, but only the question of doing wrong.

ΚΡΙΤΩΝ. Καλῶς μέν μοι δοκεῖς λέγειν, ὦ Σώκρατες. ὅρα δέ, τί δρῶμεν.

ΣΩΚΡΑΤΗΣ. Σκοπῶμεν, ὦ ἀγαθέ, κοινῇ, καὶ εἴ πῃ ἔχεις ἀντιλέγειν ἐμοῦ λέγοντος, ἀντίλεγε, καί E σοι πείσομαι· εἰ δὲ μή, παῦσαι ἤδη, ὦ μακάριε, πολλάκις μοι λέγων τὸν αὐτὸν λόγον, ὡς χρὴ ἐνθένδε ἀκόντων Ἀθηναίων ἐμὲ ἀπιέναι· ὡς ἐγὼ περὶ πολλοῦ ποιοῦμαι πείσας σε ταῦτα πράττειν, ἀλλὰ μὴ ἄκοντος. ὅρα δὲ δὴ τῆς σκέψεως τὴν ἀρχήν, ἐάν σοι ἱκανῶς λέγηται, καὶ πειρῶ ἀποκρί-
49 νεσθαι τὸ ἐρωτώμενον, ᾗ ἂν μάλιστα οἴῃ.

ΚΡΙΤΩΝ. Ἀλλὰ πειράσομαι.

10. ΣΩΚΡΑΤΗΣ. Οὐδενὶ τρόπῳ φαμὲν ἑκόντας ἀδικητέον εἶναι, ἢ τινὶ μὲν ἀδικητέον τρόπῳ, τινὶ δὲ οὔ; ἢ οὐδαμῶς τό γε ἀδικεῖν οὔτε ἀγαθὸν οὔτε καλόν, ὡς πολλάκις ἡμῖν καὶ ἐν τῷ ἔμπροσθεν χρόνῳ ὡμολογήθη;[1] ἢ πᾶσαι ἡμῖν ἐκεῖναι αἱ πρόσθεν ὁμολογίαι ἐν ταῖσδε ταῖς ὀλίγαις ἡμέραις ἐκκεχυμέναι εἰσίν, καὶ πάλαι, ὦ Κρίτων, ἄρα
B τηλικοίδε[2] ἄνδρες πρὸς ἀλλήλους σπουδῇ διαλεγόμενοι ἐλάθομεν ἡμᾶς αὐτοὺς παίδων οὐδὲν διαφέροντες; ἢ παντὸς μᾶλλον οὕτως ἔχει, ὥσπερ τότε ἐλέγετο ἡμῖν, εἴτε φασὶν οἱ πολλοὶ εἴτε μή, καὶ εἴτε δεῖ ἡμᾶς ἔτι τῶνδε χαλεπώτερα πάσχειν εἴτε καὶ πρᾳότερα, ὅμως τό γε ἀδικεῖν τῷ ἀδικοῦντι καὶ κακὸν καὶ αἰσχρὸν τυγχάνει ὂν παντὶ τρόπῳ; φαμὲν ἢ οὔ;

ΚΡΙΤΩΝ. Φαμέν.

ΣΩΚΡΑΤΗΣ. Οὐδαμῶς ἄρα δεῖ ἀδικεῖν.

---

[1] The words ὅπερ καὶ ἄρτι ἐλέγετο, "as has just been said, too," follow in the MSS. but are omitted by Schanz and others.   [2] τηλικοίδε γέροντες MSS.

CRITO. I think what you say is right, Socrates; but think what we should do.

SOCRATES. Let us, my good friend, investigate in common, and if you can contradict anything I say, do so, and I will yield to your arguments; but if you cannot, my dear friend, stop at once saying the same thing to me over and over, that I ought to go away from here without the consent of the Athenians; for I am anxious to act in this matter with your approval, and not contrary to your wishes. Now see if the beginning of the investigation satisfies you, and try to reply to my questions to the best of your belief.

CRITO. I will try.

SOCRATES. Ought we in no way to do wrong intentionally, or should we do wrong in some ways but not in others? Or, as we often agreed in former times, is it never right or honourable to do wrong? Or have all those former conclusions of ours been overturned in these few days, and have we old men, seriously conversing with each other, failed all along to see that we were no better than children? Or is not what we used to say most certainly true, whether the world agree or not? And whether we must endure still more grievous sufferings than these, or lighter ones, is not wrongdoing inevitably an evil and a disgrace to the wrongdoer? Do we believe this or not?

CRITO. We do.

SOCRATES. Then we ought not to do wrong at all.

ΚΡΙΤΩΝ. Οὐ δῆτα.

ΣΩΚΡΑΤΗΣ. Οὐδὲ ἀδικούμενον ἄρα ἀνταδικεῖν, ὡς οἱ πολλοὶ οἴονται, ἐπειδή γε οὐδαμῶς δεῖ ἀδικεῖν.

C   ΚΡΙΤΩΝ. Οὐ φαίνεται.

ΣΩΚΡΑΤΗΣ. Τί δὲ δή; κακουργεῖν δεῖ, ὦ Κρίτων, ἢ οὔ;

ΚΡΙΤΩΝ. Οὐ δεῖ δή που, ὦ Σώκρατες.

ΣΩΚΡΑΤΗΣ. Τί δέ; ἀντικακουργεῖν κακῶς πάσχοντα, ὡς οἱ πολλοί φασιν, δίκαιον ἢ οὐ δίκαιον;

ΚΡΙΤΩΝ. Οὐδαμῶς.

ΣΩΚΡΑΤΗΣ. Τὸ γάρ που κακῶς ποιεῖν ἀνθρώπους τοῦ ἀδικεῖν οὐδὲν διαφέρει.

ΚΡΙΤΩΝ. Ἀληθῆ λέγεις.

ΣΩΚΡΑΤΗΣ. Οὔτε ἄρα ἀνταδικεῖν δεῖ οὔτε κακῶς ποιεῖν οὐδένα ἀνθρώπων, οὐδ' ἂν ὁτιοῦν πάσχῃ
D ὑπ' αὐτῶν. καὶ ὅρα, ὦ Κρίτων, ταῦτα καθομολογῶν, ὅπως μὴ παρὰ δόξαν ὁμολογῇς. οἶδα γάρ, ὅτι ὀλίγοις τισὶ ταῦτα καὶ δοκεῖ καὶ δόξει. οἷς οὖν οὕτω δέδοκται καὶ οἷς μή, τούτοις οὐκ ἔστι κοινὴ βουλή, ἀλλὰ ἀνάγκη τούτους ἀλλήλων καταφρονεῖν, ὁρῶντας τὰ ἀλλήλων βουλεύματα. σκόπει δὴ οὖν καὶ σὺ εὖ μάλα, πότερον κοινωνεῖς καὶ ξυνδοκεῖ σοι, καὶ ἀρχώμεθα ἐντεῦθεν βουλευόμενοι, ὡς οὐδέποτε ὀρθῶς ἔχοντος οὔτε τοῦ ἀδικεῖν οὔτε τοῦ ἀνταδικεῖν οὔτε κακῶς πάσχοντα ἀμύνεσθαι ἀντιδρῶντα κακῶς· ἢ ἀφίστασαι καὶ οὐ
E κοινωνεῖς τῆς ἀρχῆς; ἐμοὶ μὲν γὰρ καὶ πάλαι οὕτω καὶ νῦν ἔτι δοκεῖ, σοὶ δὲ εἴ πῃ ἄλλῃ δέδοκται, λέγε καὶ δίδασκε. εἰ δ' ἐμμένεις τοῖς πρόσθε, τὸ μετὰ τοῦτο ἄκουε.

CRITO. Why, no.

SOCRATES. And we ought not even to requite wrong with wrong, as the world thinks, since we must not do wrong at all.

CRITO. Apparently not.

SOCRATES. Well, Crito, ought one to do evil or not?

CRITO. Certainly not, Socrates.

SOCRATES. Well, then, is it right to requite evil with evil, as the world says it is, or not right?

CRITO. Not right, certainly.

SOCRATES. For doing evil to people is the same thing as wronging them.

CRITO. That is true.

SOCRATES. Then we ought neither to requite wrong with wrong nor to do evil to anyone, no matter what he may have done to us. And be careful, Crito, that you do not, in agreeing to this, agree to something you do not believe; for I know that there are few who believe or ever will believe this. Now those who believe this, and those who do not, have no common ground of discussion, but they must necessarily, in view of their opinions, despise one another. Do you therefore consider very carefully whether you agree and share in this opinion, and let us take as the starting point of our discussion the assumption that it is never right to do wrong or to requite wrong with wrong, or when we suffer evil to defend ourselves by doing evil in return. Or do you disagree and refuse your assent to this starting point? For I have long held this belief and I hold it yet, but if you have reached any other conclusion, speak and explain it to me. If you still hold to our former opinion, hear the next point.

ΚΡΙΤΩΝ. Ἀλλ' ἐμμένω τε καὶ ξυνδοκεῖ μοι· ἀλλὰ λέγε.

ΣΩΚΡΑΤΗΣ. Λέγω δὴ αὖ τὸ μετὰ τοῦτο, μᾶλλον δ' ἐρωτῶ· πότερον ἃ ἄν τις ὁμολογήσῃ τῳ δίκαια ὄντα ποιητέον ἢ ἐξαπατητέον;

ΚΡΙΤΩΝ. Ποιητέον.

11. ΣΩΚΡΑΤΗΣ. Ἐκ τούτων δὴ ἄθρει. ἀπιόντες
50 ἐνθένδε ἡμεῖς μὴ πείσαντες τὴν πόλιν πότερον κακῶς τινας ποιοῦμεν, καὶ ταῦτα οὓς ἥκιστα δεῖ, ἢ οὔ; καὶ ἐμμένομεν οἷς ὡμολογήσαμεν δικαίοις οὖσιν ἢ οὔ;

ΚΡΙΤΩΝ. Οὐκ ἔχω, ὦ Σώκρατες, ἀποκρίνασθαι πρὸς ὃ ἐρωτᾷς· οὐ γὰρ ἐννοῶ.

ΣΩΚΡΑΤΗΣ. Ἀλλ' ὧδε σκόπει. εἰ μέλλουσιν ἡμῖν ἐνθένδε εἴτε ἀποδιδράσκειν, εἴθ' ὅπως δεῖ ὀνομάσαι τοῦτο, ἐλθόντες οἱ νόμοι καὶ τὸ κοινὸν τῆς πόλεως ἐπιστάντες ἔροιντο· εἰπέ μοι, ὦ Σώκρατες, τί ἐν νῷ ἔχεις ποιεῖν; ἄλλο τι ἢ τούτῳ τῷ ἔργῳ, ᾧ ἐπιχειρεῖς, διανοεῖ τούς
B τε νόμους ἡμᾶς ἀπολέσαι καὶ ξύμπασαν τὴν πόλιν τὸ σὸν μέρος; ἢ δοκεῖ σοι οἷόν τε ἔτι ἐκείνην τὴν πόλιν εἶναι καὶ μὴ ἀνατετράφθαι, ἐν ᾗ αἱ γενόμεναι δίκαι μηδὲν ἰσχύουσιν, ἀλλὰ ὑπὸ ἰδιωτῶν ἄκυροί τε γίγνονται καὶ διαφθείρονται; τί ἐροῦμεν, ὦ Κρίτων, πρὸς ταῦτα καὶ ἄλλα τοιαῦτα; πολλὰ γὰρ ἄν τις ἔχοι, ἄλλως τε καὶ ῥήτωρ, εἰπεῖν ὑπὲρ τούτου τοῦ νόμου ἀπολλυμένου, ὃς τὰς δίκας τὰς δικασθείσας προστάττει κυρίας εἶναι. ἢ ἐροῦμεν πρὸς αὐτούς,
C ὅτι ἠδίκει γὰρ ἡμᾶς ἡ πόλις καὶ οὐκ ὀρθῶς τὴν δίκην ἔκρινεν; ταῦτα ἢ τί ἐροῦμεν;

ΚΡΙΤΩΝ. Ταῦτα νὴ Δία, ὦ Σώκρατες.

CRITO

CRITO. I do hold to it and I agree with you; so go on.

SOCRATES. Now the next thing I say, or rather ask, is this: "ought a man to do what he has agreed to do, provided it is right, or may he violate his agreements?"

CRITO. He ought to do it.

SOCRATES. Then consider whether, if we go away from here without the consent of the state, we are doing harm to the very ones to whom we least ought to do harm, or not, and whether we are abiding by what we agreed was right, or not.

CRITO. I cannot answer your question, Socrates, for I do not understand.

SOCRATES. Consider it in this way. If, as I was on the point of running away (or whatever it should be called), the laws and the commonwealth should come to me and ask, "Tell me, Socrates, what have you in mind to do? Are you not intending by this thing you are trying to do, to destroy us, the laws, and the entire state, so far as in you lies? Or do you think that state can exist and not be overturned, in which the decisions reached by the courts have no force but are made invalid and annulled by private persons?" What shall we say, Crito, in reply to this question and others of the same kind? For one might say many things, especially if one were an orator, about the destruction of that law which provides that the decisions reached by the courts shall be valid. Or shall we say to them, "The state wronged me and did not judge the case rightly"? Shall we say that, or what?

CRITO. That is what we shall say, by Zeus, Socrates.

12. ΣΩΚΡΑΤΗΣ. Τί οὖν, ἂν εἴπωσιν οἱ νόμοι·
ὦ Σώκρατες, ἦ καὶ ταῦτα ὡμολόγητο ἡμῖν τε
καὶ σοί, ἦ ἐμμένειν ταῖς δίκαις αἷς ἂν ἡ πόλις
δικάζῃ; εἰ οὖν αὐτῶν θαυμάζοιμεν λεγόντων,
ἴσως ἂν εἴποιεν ὅτι ὦ Σώκρατες, μὴ θαύμαζε
τὰ λεγόμενα, ἀλλ' ἀποκρίνου, ἐπειδὴ καὶ εἴωθας
χρῆσθαι τῷ ἐρωτᾶν τε καὶ ἀποκρίνεσθαι. φέρε
D γάρ, τί ἐγκαλῶν ἡμῖν καὶ τῇ πόλει ἐπιχειρεῖς
ἡμᾶς ἀπολλύναι; οὐ πρῶτον μέν σε ἐγεννήσαμεν
ἡμεῖς, καὶ δι' ἡμῶν ἐλάμβανεν τὴν μητέρα σου
ὁ πατὴρ καὶ ἐφύτευσέν σε; φράσον οὖν, τούτοις
ἡμῶν, τοῖς νόμοις [1] τοῖς περὶ τοὺς γάμους, μέμφει
τι, ὡς οὐ καλῶς ἔχουσιν; οὐ μέμφομαι, φαίην
ἄν. ἀλλὰ τοῖς περὶ τὴν τοῦ γενομένου τροφήν
τε καὶ παιδείαν, ἐν ᾗ καὶ σὺ ἐπαιδεύθης; ἢ οὐ
καλῶς προσέταττον ἡμῶν οἱ ἐπὶ τούτοις τεταγμένοι νόμοι,[2] παραγγέλλοντες τῷ πατρὶ τῷ
σῷ σε ἐν μουσικῇ καὶ γυμναστικῇ παιδεύειν;
E καλῶς, φαίην ἄν. εἶεν. ἐπειδὴ δὲ ἐγένου τε
καὶ ἐξετράφης καὶ ἐπαιδεύθης, ἔχοις ἂν εἰπεῖν
πρῶτον μὲν ὡς οὐχὶ ἡμέτερος ἦσθα καὶ ἔκγονος
καὶ δοῦλος, αὐτός τε καὶ οἱ σοὶ πρόγονοι; καὶ
εἰ τοῦθ' οὕτως ἔχει, ἆρ' ἐξ ἴσου οἴει εἶναι σοὶ
τὸ δίκαιον καὶ ἡμῖν, καὶ ἅττ' ἂν ἡμεῖς σε
ἐπιχειρῶμεν ποιεῖν, καὶ σοὶ ταῦτα ἀντιποιεῖν
οἴει δίκαιον εἶναι; ἢ πρὸς μὲν ἄρα σοι τὸν πατέρα
οὐκ ἐξ ἴσου ἦν τὸ δίκαιον καὶ πρὸς τὸν δεσπότην,
εἴ σοι ὢν ἐτύγχανεν, ὥστε, ἅπερ πάσχοις, ταῦτα
καὶ ἀντιποιεῖν, οὔτε κακῶς ἀκούοντα ἀντιλέγειν
51 οὔτε τυπτόμενον ἀντιτύπτειν οὔτε ἄλλα τοιαῦτα
πολλά· πρὸς δὲ τὴν πατρίδα ἄρα καὶ τοὺς νόμους

[1] Schanz omits τοῖς νόμοις.   [2] Schanz omits νόμοι.

SOCRATES. What then if the laws should say, "Socrates, is this the agreement you made with us, or did you agree to abide by the verdicts pronounced by the state?" Now if I were surprised by what they said, perhaps they would continue, "Don't be surprised at what we say, Socrates, but answer, since you are in the habit of employing the method of question and answer. Come, what fault do you find with us and the state, that you are trying to destroy us? In the first place, did we not bring you forth? Is it not through us that your father married your mother and begat you? Now tell us, have you any fault to find with those of us who are the laws of marriage?"

"I find no fault," I should say. "Or with those that have to do with the nurture of the child after he is born and with his education which you, like others, received? Did those of us who are assigned to these matters not give good directions when we told your father to educate you in music and gymnastics?" "You did," I should say. "Well then, when you were born and nurtured and educated, could you say to begin with that you were not our offspring and our slave, you yourself and your ancestors? And if this is so, do you think right as between you and us rests on a basis of equality, so that whatever we undertake to do to you it is right for you to retaliate? There was no such equality of right between you and your father or your master, if you had one, so that whatever treatment you received you might return it, answering them if you were reviled, or striking back if you were struck, and the like; and do you think that it will be proper for

ἔσται¹ σοι, ὥστε, ἐάν σε ἐπιχειρῶμεν ἡμεῖς
ἀπολλύναι δίκαιον ἡγούμενοι εἶναι, καὶ σὺ δὲ
ἡμᾶς τοὺς νόμους καὶ τὴν πατρίδα, καθ' ὅσον
δύνασαι, ἐπιχειρήσεις ἀνταπολλύναι, καὶ φήσεις
ταῦτα ποιῶν δίκαια πράττειν, ὁ τῇ ἀληθείᾳ τῆς
ἀρετῆς ἐπιμελόμενος; ἢ οὕτως εἶ σοφός, ὥστε
λέληθέν σε, ὅτι μητρός τε καὶ πατρὸς καὶ τῶν
ἄλλων προγόνων ἁπάντων τιμιώτερόν ἐστιν ἡ
B πατρὶς καὶ σεμνότερον καὶ ἁγιώτερον καὶ ἐν μεί-
ζονι μοίρᾳ καὶ παρὰ θεοῖς καὶ παρ' ἀνθρώποις τοῖς
νοῦν ἔχουσι, καὶ σέβεσθαι δεῖ καὶ μᾶλλον ὑπείκειν
καὶ θωπεύειν πατρίδα χαλεπαίνουσαν ἢ πατέρα,
καὶ ἢ πείθειν ἢ ποιεῖν ἃ ἂν κελεύῃ, καὶ πάσχειν,
ἐάν τι προστάττῃ παθεῖν, ἡσυχίαν ἄγοντα, ἐάν
τε τύπτεσθαι ἐάν τε δεῖσθαι, ἐάν τε εἰς πόλεμον
ἄγῃ τρωθησόμενον ἢ ἀποθανούμενον, ποιητέον
ταῦτα, καὶ τὸ δίκαιον οὕτως ἔχει, καὶ οὐχὶ
ὑπεικτέον οὐδὲ ἀναχωρητέον οὐδὲ λειπτέον τὴν
τάξιν, ἀλλὰ καὶ ἐν πολέμῳ καὶ ἐν δικαστηρίῳ
C καὶ πανταχοῦ ποιητέον ἃ ἂν κελεύῃ ἡ πόλις
καὶ ἡ πατρίς, ἢ πείθειν αὐτὴν ᾗ τὸ δίκαιον
πέφυκε, βιάζεσθαι δὲ οὐχ ὅσιον οὔτε μητέρα
οὔτε πατέρα, πολὺ δὲ τούτων ἔτι ἧττον τὴν
πατρίδα; τί φήσομεν πρὸς ταῦτα, ὦ Κρίτων;
ἀληθῆ λέγειν τοὺς νόμους ἢ οὔ;

ΚΡΙΤΩΝ. Ἔμοιγε δοκεῖ.

13. ΣΩΚΡΑΤΗΣ. Σκόπει τοίνυν, ὦ Σώκρατες,
φαῖεν ἂν ἴσως οἱ νόμοι, εἰ ἡμεῖς ταῦτα ἀληθῆ
λέγομεν, ὅτι οὐ δίκαια ἡμᾶς ἐπιχειρεῖς δρᾶν ἃ
νῦν ἐπιχειρεῖς. ἡμεῖς γάρ σε γεννήσαντες, ἐκθρέ-
ψαντες, παιδεύσαντες, μεταδόντες ἁπάντων ὧν

¹ So Schanz, ἐξέσται BCE.

you to act so toward your country and the laws, so that if we undertake to destroy you, thinking it is right, you will undertake in return to destroy us laws and your country, so far as you are able, and will say that in doing this you are doing right, you who really care for virtue? Or is your wisdom such that you do not see that your country is more precious and more to be revered and is holier and in higher esteem among the gods and among men of understanding than your mother and your father and all your ancestors, and that you ought to show to her more reverence and obedience and humility when she is angry than to your father, and ought either to convince her by persuasion or to do whatever she commands, and to suffer, if she commands you to suffer, in silence, and if she orders you to be scourged or imprisoned or if she leads you to war to be wounded or slain, her will is to be done, and this is right, and you must not give way or draw back or leave your post, but in war and in court and everywhere, you must do whatever the state, your country, commands, or must show her by persuasion what is really right, but that it is impious to use violence against either your father or your mother, and much more impious to use it against your country?" What shall we reply to this, Crito, that the laws speak the truth, or not?

CRITO. I think they do.

SOCRATES. "Observe then, Socrates," perhaps the laws would say, "that if what we say is true, what you are now undertaking to do to us is not right. For we brought you into the world, nurtured you, and gave a share of all the good things we could to

D οἷοί τ᾽ ἦμεν καλῶν σοὶ καὶ τοῖς ἄλλοις πᾶσιν
πολίταις, ὅμως προαγορεύομεν τῷ ἐξουσίαν
πεποιηκέναι Ἀθηναίων τῷ βουλομένῳ, ἐπειδὰν
δοκιμασθῇ καὶ ἴδῃ τὰ ἐν τῇ πόλει πράγματα
καὶ ἡμᾶς τοὺς νόμους, ᾧ ἂν μὴ ἀρέσκωμεν ἡμεῖς,
ἐξεῖναι λαβόντα τὰ αὑτοῦ ἀπιέναι ὅποι ἂν
βούληται. καὶ οὐδεὶς ἡμῶν τῶν νόμων ἐμποδών
ἐστιν οὐδ᾽ ἀπαγορεύει, ἐάν τε τις βούληται ὑμῶν
εἰς ἀποικίαν ἰέναι, εἰ μὴ ἀρέσκομεν ἡμεῖς τε
καὶ ἡ πόλις, ἐάν τε μετοικεῖν ἄλλοσέ ποι ἐλθών,
ἰέναι ἐκεῖσε ὅποι ἂν βούληται, ἔχοντα τὰ αὑτοῦ.

E ὃς δ᾽ ἂν ὑμῶν παραμείνῃ, ὁρῶν ὃν τρόπον ἡμεῖς
τάς τε δίκας δικάζομεν καὶ τἆλλα τὴν πόλιν
διοικοῦμεν, ἤδη φαμὲν τοῦτον ὡμολογηκέναι
ἔργῳ ἡμῖν ἃ ἂν ἡμεῖς κελεύωμεν ποιήσειν
ταῦτα, καὶ τὸν μὴ πειθόμενον τριχῇ φαμεν
ἀδικεῖν, ὅτι τε γεννηταῖς οὖσιν ἡμῖν οὐ πείθεται,
καὶ ὅτι τροφεῦσι, καὶ ὅτι ὁμολογήσας ἡμῖν
πείθεσθαι οὔτε πείθεται οὔτε πείθει ἡμᾶς, εἰ

52 μὴ καλῶς τι ποιοῦμεν, προτιθέντων ἡμῶν καὶ
οὐκ ἀγρίως ἐπιταττόντων ποιεῖν ἃ ἂν κελεύωμεν,
ἀλλὰ ἐφιέντων δυοῖν θάτερα, ἢ πείθειν ἡμᾶς
ἢ ποιεῖν, τούτων οὐδέτερα ποιεῖ.

14. Ταύταις δή φαμεν καὶ σέ, ὦ Σώκρατες,[1]
ταῖς αἰτίαις ἐνέξεσθαι, εἴπερ ποιήσεις ἃ ἐπινοεῖς,
καὶ οὐχ ἥκιστα Ἀθηναίων σέ, ἀλλ᾽ ἐν τοῖς
μάλιστα. εἰ οὖν ἐγὼ εἴποιμι· διὰ τί δή; ἴσως
ἄν μου δικαίως καθάπτοιντο λέγοντες, ὅτι ἐν
τοῖς μάλιστα Ἀθηναίων ἐγὼ αὐτοῖς ὡμολογηκὼς
τυγχάνω ταύτην τὴν ὁμολογίαν. φαῖεν γὰρ ἂν

B ὅτι ὦ Σώκρατες, μεγάλα ἡμῖν τούτων τεκμήριά

---

[1] Schanz omits ὦ and brackets Σώκρατες.

you and all the citizens. Yet we proclaim, by having offered the opportunity to any of the Athenians who wishes to avail himself of it, that anyone who is not pleased with us when he has become a man and has seen the administration of the city and us, the laws, may take his goods and go away wherever he likes. And none of us stands in the way or forbids any of you to take his goods and go away wherever he pleases, if we and the state do not please him, whether it be to an Athenian colony or to a foreign country where he will live as an alien. But we say that whoever of you stays here, seeing how we administer justice and how we govern the state in other respects, has thereby entered into an agreement with us to do what we command; and we say that he who does not obey does threefold wrong, because he disobeys us who are his parents, because he disobeys us who nurtured him, and because after agreeing to obey us he neither obeys us nor convinces us that we are wrong, though we give him the opportunity and do not roughly order him to do what we command, but when we allow him a choice of two things, either to convince us of error or to do our bidding, he does neither of these things."

"We say that you, Socrates, will be exposed to these reproaches, if you do what you have in mind, and you not least of the Athenians but more than most others." If then I should say, "How so?" perhaps they might retort with justice that I had made this agreement with them more emphatically than most other Athenians. For they would say, "Socrates, we have strong evidence that we and the city pleased you; for you would never have stayed in

ἐστιν, ὅτι σοι καὶ ἡμεῖς ἠρέσκομεν καὶ ἡ πόλις·
οὐ γὰρ ἄν ποτε τῶν ἄλλων Ἀθηναίων ἁπάντων
διαφερόντως ἐν αὐτῇ ἐπεδήμεις, εἰ μή σοι διαφερόντως ἤρεσκεν, καὶ οὔτ' ἐπὶ θεωρίαν πώποτ'
ἐκ τῆς πόλεως ἐξῆλθες[1] οὔτε ἄλλοσε οὐδαμόσε,
εἰ μή ποι στρατευσόμενος, οὔτε ἄλλην ἀποδημίαν
ἐποιήσω πώποτε, ὥσπερ οἱ ἄλλοι ἄνθρωποι,
οὐδ' ἐπιθυμία σε ἄλλης πόλεως οὐδὲ ἄλλων
νόμων ἔλαβεν εἰδέναι, ἀλλὰ ἡμεῖς σοι ἱκανοὶ
ἦμεν καὶ ἡ ἡμετέρα πόλις· οὕτω σφόδρα ἡμᾶς
C ᾑροῦ, καὶ ὡμολόγεις καθ' ἡμᾶς πολιτεύεσθαι,
τά τε ἄλλα καὶ παῖδας ἐν αὐτῇ ἐποιήσω, ὡς
ἀρεσκούσης σοι τῆς πόλεως. ἔτι τοίνυν ἐν αὐτῇ
τῇ δίκῃ ἐξῆν σοι φυγῆς τιμήσασθαι, εἰ ἐβούλου,
καὶ ὅπερ νῦν ἀκούσης τῆς πόλεως ἐπιχειρεῖς,
τότε ἑκούσης ποιῆσαι. σὺ δὲ τότε μὲν ἐκαλλω-
πίζου ὡς οὐκ ἀγανακτῶν, εἰ δέοι τεθνάναι σε,
ἀλλὰ ᾑροῦ, ὡς ἔφησθα, πρὸ τῆς φυγῆς θάνατον·
νῦν δὲ οὔτ' ἐκείνους τοὺς λόγους αἰσχύνει, οὔτε
ἡμῶν τῶν νόμων ἐντρέπει, ἐπιχειρῶν διαφθεῖραι,
D πράττεις τε ἅπερ ἄν δοῦλος φαυλότατος πράξειεν,
ἀποδιδράσκειν ἐπιχειρῶν παρὰ τὰς ξυνθήκας τε
καὶ τὰς ὁμολογίας, καθ' ἃς ἡμῖν ξυνέθου πολιτεύεσθαι. πρῶτον μὲν οὖν ἡμῖν τοῦτ' αὐτὸ
ἀπόκριναι, εἰ ἀληθῆ λέγομεν φάσκοντές σε
ὡμολογηκέναι πολιτεύεσθαι καθ' ἡμᾶς ἔργῳ,
ἀλλ' οὐ λόγῳ, ἢ οὐκ ἀληθῆ. τί φῶμεν πρὸς
ταῦτα, ὦ Κρίτων; ἄλλο τι ἢ ὁμολογῶμεν;

ΚΡΙΤΩΝ. Ἀνάγκη, ὦ Σώκρατες.

---

[1] The words ὅτι μὴ ἅπαξ εἰς Ἰσθμόν, "except once to the
Isthmus," after ἐξῆλθες are omitted by Schanz and others as
an early interpolation.

it more than all other Athenians if you had not been better pleased with it than they; you never went out from the city to a festival, or anywhere else, except on military service, and you never made any other journey, as other people do, and you had no wish to know any other city or other laws, but you were contented with us and our city. So strongly did you prefer us and agree to live in accordance with us; and besides, you begat children in the city, showing that it pleased you. And moreover even at your trial you might have offered exile as your penalty, if you wished, and might have done with the state's consent what you are now undertaking to do without it. But you then put on airs and said you were not disturbed if you must die, and you preferred, as you said, death to exile. And now you are not ashamed to think of those words and you do not respect us, the laws, since you are trying to bring us to naught; and you are doing what the meanest slave would do, since you are trying to run away contrary to the compacts and agreements you made with us that you would live in accordance with us. First then, answer this question, whether we speak the truth or not when we say that you agreed, not in word, but by your acts, to live in accordance with us." What shall we say to this, Crito? Must we not agree that it is true?

CRITO. We must, Socrates.

PLATO

ΣΩΚΡΑΤΗΣ. Ἄλλο τι οὖν, ἂν φαῖεν, ἢ ξυνθήκας
E τὰς πρὸς ἡμᾶς αὐτοὺς καὶ ὁμολογίας παραβαίνεις,
οὐχ ὑπὸ ἀνάγκης ὁμολογήσας οὐδὲ ἀπατηθεὶς
οὐδὲ ἐν ὀλίγῳ χρόνῳ ἀναγκασθεὶς βουλεύσασθαι,
ἀλλ' ἐν ἔτεσιν ἑβδομήκοντα, ἐν οἷς ἐξῆν σοι
ἀπιέναι, εἰ μὴ ἠρέσκομεν ἡμεῖς μηδὲ δίκαιαι
ἐφαίνοντό σοι αἱ ὁμολογίαι εἶναι· σὺ δὲ οὔτε
Λακεδαίμονα προῃροῦ οὔτε Κρήτην, ἃς δὴ ἑκάστοτε φὴς εὐνομεῖσθαι, οὔτε ἄλλην οὐδεμίαν τῶν
53 Ἑλληνίδων πόλεων οὐδὲ τῶν βαρβαρικῶν, ἀλλὰ
ἐλάττω ἐξ αὐτῆς ἀπεδήμησας ἢ οἱ χωλοί τε καὶ
τυφλοὶ καὶ οἱ ἄλλοι ἀνάπηροι· οὕτω σοι διαφερόντως τῶν ἄλλων Ἀθηναίων ἤρεσκεν ἡ πόλις τε
καὶ ἡμεῖς οἱ νόμοι δῆλον ὅτι· τίνι γὰρ ἂν πόλις
ἀρέσκοι ἄνευ νόμων;[1] νῦν δὲ δὴ οὐκ ἐμμενεῖς τοῖς
ὡμολογημένοις; ἐὰν ἡμῖν γε πείθῃ, ὦ Σώκρατες·
καὶ οὐ καταγέλαστός γε ἔσει ἐκ τῆς πόλεως
ἐξελθών.

15. Σκόπει γὰρ δή, ταῦτα παραβὰς καὶ ἐξαμαρ-
τάνων τι τούτων τί ἀγαθὸν ἐργάσει σαυτὸν ἢ
B τοὺς ἐπιτηδείους τοὺς σαυτοῦ. ὅτι μὲν γὰρ
κινδυνεύσουσί γέ σου οἱ ἐπιτήδειοι καὶ αὐτοὶ
φεύγειν καὶ στερηθῆναι τῆς πόλεως ἢ τὴν οὐσίαν
ἀπολέσαι, σχεδόν τι δῆλον· αὐτὸς δὲ πρῶτον
μὲν ἐὰν εἰς τῶν ἐγγύτατά τινα πόλεων ἔλθῃς,
ἢ Θήβαζε ἢ Μέγαράδε—εὐνομοῦνται γὰρ ἀμφότεραι—πολέμιος ἥξεις, ὦ Σώκρατες, τῇ τούτων
πολιτείᾳ, καὶ ὅσοιπερ κήδονται τῶν αὐτῶν πόλεων,
ὑποβλέψονταί σε διαφθορέα ἡγούμενοι τῶν νόμων,
C καὶ βεβαιώσεις τοῖς δικασταῖς τὴν δόξαν, ὥστε

---

[1] Schanz omits δῆλον ὅτι . . . νόμων, "evidently; for who
would be pleased with a city apart from its laws?"

SOCRATES. "Are you then," they would say, "not breaking your compacts and agreements with us, though you were not led into them by compulsion or fraud, and were not forced to make up your mind in a short time, but had seventy years, in which you could have gone away, if we did not please you and if you thought the agreements were unfair? But you preferred neither Lacedaemon nor Crete, which you are always saying are well governed, nor any other of the Greek states, or of the foreign ones, but you went away from this city less than the lame and the blind and the other cripples. So much more than the other Athenians were you satisfied with the city and evidently therefore with us, its laws; for who would be pleased with a city apart from its laws? And now will you not abide by your agreement? You will if you take our advice, Socrates; and you will not make yourself ridiculous by going away from the city.

"For consider. By transgressing in this way and committing these errors, what good will you do to yourself or any of your friends? For it is pretty clear that your friends also will be exposed to the risk of banishment and the loss of their homes in the city or of their property. And you yourself, if you go to one of the nearest cities, to Thebes or Megara—for both are well governed—will go as an enemy, Socrates, to their government, and all who care for their own cities will look askance at you, and will consider you a destroyer of the laws, and you will confirm the

δοκεῖν ὀρθῶς τὴν δίκην δικάσαι· ὅστις γὰρ
νόμων διαφθορεύς ἐστιν, σφόδρα που δόξειεν
ἂν νέων γε καὶ ἀνοήτων ἀνθρώπων διαφθορεὺς
εἶναι. πότερον οὖν φεύξει τάς τε εὐνομουμένας
πόλεις καὶ τῶν ἀνδρῶν τοὺς κοσμιωτάτους; καὶ
τοῦτο ποιοῦντι ἆρα ἄξιόν σοι ζῆν ἔσται; ἢ
πλησιάσεις τούτοις καὶ ἀναισχυντήσεις διαλεγόμενος—τίνας λόγους, ὦ Σώκρατες; ἢ οὕσπερ
ἐνθάδε, ὡς ἡ ἀρετὴ καὶ ἡ δικαιοσύνη πλείστου
ἄξιον τοῖς ἀνθρώποις καὶ τὰ νόμιμα καὶ οἱ
νόμοι; καὶ οὐκ οἴει ἄσχημον ἂν φανεῖσθαι τὸ
D τοῦ Σωκράτους πρᾶγμα; οἴεσθαί γε χρή. ἀλλ'
ἐκ μὲν τούτων τῶν τόπων ἀπαρεῖς, ἥξεις δὲ
εἰς Θετταλίαν παρὰ τοὺς ξένους τοὺς Κρίτωνος·
ἐκεῖ γὰρ δὴ πλείστη ἀταξία καὶ ἀκολασία, καὶ
ἴσως ἂν ἡδέως σου ἀκούοιεν, ὡς γελοίως ἐκ τοῦ
δεσμωτηρίου ἀπεδίδρασκες σκευήν τέ τινα περι-
θέμενος, ἢ διφθέραν λαβὼν ἢ ἄλλα οἷα δὴ
εἰώθασιν ἐνσκευάζεσθαι οἱ ἀποδιδράσκοντες, καὶ
τὸ σχῆμα τὸ σαυτοῦ μεταλλάξας· ὅτι δὲ γέρων
ἀνὴρ σμικροῦ χρόνου τῷ βίῳ λοιποῦ ὄντος, ὡς
E τὸ εἰκός, ἐτόλμησας οὕτως αἰσχρῶς ἐπιθυμεῖν
ζῆν, νόμους τοὺς μεγίστους παραβάς, οὐδεὶς ὃς
ἐρεῖ; ἴσως, ἂν μή τινα λυπῇς· εἰ δὲ μή, ἀκούσει,
ὦ Σώκρατες, πολλὰ καὶ ἀνάξια σαυτοῦ. ὑπερχό-
μενος δὴ βιώσει πάντας ἀνθρώπους καὶ δουλεύων[1]
τί ποιῶν ἢ εὐωχούμενος ἐν Θετταλίᾳ,[2] ὥσπερ
ἐπὶ δεῖπνον ἀποδεδημηκὼς εἰς Θετταλίαν; λόγοι
δὲ ἐκεῖνοι οἱ περὶ δικαιοσύνης τε καὶ τῆς ἄλλης
54 ἀρετῆς ποῦ ἡμῖν ἔσονται; ἀλλὰ δὴ τῶν παίδων

---

[1] Schanz omits δουλεύων, "being a slave."
[2] Schanz omits ἐν Θετταλίᾳ.

judges in their opinion, so that they will think their verdict was just. For he who is destroyer of the laws might certainly be regarded as a destroyer of young and thoughtless men. Will you then avoid the well-governed cities and the most civilised men ? And if you do this will your life be worth living ? Or will you go to them and have the face to carry on—what kind of conversation, Socrates ? The same kind you carried on here, saying that virtue and justice and lawful things and the laws are the most precious things to men ? And do you not think that the conduct of Socrates would seem most disgraceful ? You cannot help thinking so. Or you will keep away from these places and go to Crito's friends in Thessaly ; for there great disorder and lawlessness prevail, and perhaps they would be amused to hear of the ludicrous way in which you ran away from prison by putting on a disguise, a peasant's leathern cloak or some of the other things in which runaways dress themselves up, and changing your appearance. But will no one say that you, an old man, who had probably but a short time yet to live, clung to life with such shameless greed that you transgressed the highest laws ? Perhaps not, if you do not offend anyone ; but if you do, Socrates, you will have to listen to many things that would be a disgrace to you. So you will live as an inferior and a slave to everyone. And what will you do except feast in Thessaly, as if you had gone to Thessaly to attend a banquet ? What will become of our conversations about justice and virtue ? But

PLATO

ἕνεκα βούλει ζῆν, ἵνα αὐτοὺς ἐκθρέψῃς καὶ
παιδεύσῃς; τί δέ; εἰς Θετταλίαν αὐτοὺς ἀγαγὼν
θρέψεις τε καὶ παιδεύσεις, ξένους ποιήσας, ἵνα
καὶ τοῦτο ἀπολαύσωσιν; ἢ τοῦτο μὲν οὔ, αὐτοῦ
δὲ τρεφόμενοι σοῦ ζῶντος βέλτιον θρέψονται
καὶ παιδεύσονται, μὴ ξυνόντος σοῦ αὐτοῖς; οἱ
γὰρ ἐπιτήδειοι οἱ σοὶ ἐπιμελήσονται[1] αὐτῶν.
πότερον ἐὰν εἰς Θετταλίαν ἀποδημήσῃς, ἐπιμελήσονται, ἐὰν δὲ εἰς Ἅιδου ἀποδημήσῃς, οὐχὶ
ἐπιμελήσονται; εἴπερ γέ τι ὄφελος αὐτῶν ἐστιν
B τῶν σοι φασκόντων ἐπιτηδείων εἶναι, οἴεσθαί γε
χρή.

16. 'Ἀλλ', ὦ Σώκρατες, πειθόμενος ἡμῖν τοῖς
σοῖς τροφεῦσι μήτε παῖδας περὶ πλείονος ποιοῦ
μήτε τὸ ζῆν μήτε ἄλλο μηδὲν πρὸ τοῦ δικαίου, ἵνα
εἰς Ἅιδου ἐλθὼν ἔχῃς πάντα ταῦτα ἀπολογήσασθαι τοῖς ἐκεῖ ἄρχουσιν· οὔτε γὰρ ἐνθάδε σοι
φαίνεται ταῦτα πράττοντι ἄμεινον εἶναι οὐδὲ
δικαιότερον οὐδὲ ὁσιώτερον, οὐδὲ ἄλλῳ τῶν σῶν
οὐδενί, οὔτε ἐκεῖσε ἀφικομένῳ ἄμεινον ἔσται.
ἀλλὰ νῦν μὲν ἠδικημένος ἄπει, ἐὰν ἀπίῃς, οὐχ
C ὑφ' ἡμῶν τῶν νόμων ἀλλὰ ὑπὸ ἀνθρώπων· ἐὰν
δὲ ἐξέλθῃς οὕτως αἰσχρῶς ἀνταδικήσας τε καὶ
ἀντικακουργήσας, τὰς σαυτοῦ ὁμολογίας τε καὶ
ξυνθήκας τὰς πρὸς ἡμᾶς παραβὰς καὶ κακὰ
ἐργασάμενος τούτους οὓς ἥκιστα ἔδει, σαυτόν τε
καὶ φίλους καὶ πατρίδα καὶ ἡμᾶς, ἡμεῖς τέ σοι
χαλεπανοῦμεν ζῶντι, καὶ ἐκεῖ οἱ ἡμέτεροι ἀδελφοὶ
οἱ ἐν Ἅιδου νόμοι οὐκ εὐμενῶς σε ὑποδέξονται,
εἰδότες ὅτι καὶ ἡμᾶς ἐπεχείρησας ἀπολέσαι

---

[1] Schanz omits ἐπιμελήσονται here and also the punctuation
after αὐτῶν, making one long interrogative sentence.

perhaps you wish to live for the sake of your
children, that you may bring them up and educate
them? How so? Will you take them to Thessaly
to be brought up and educated, making exiles of
them, that you may give them that blessing also?
Or perhaps you will not do that, but if they are
brought up here while you are living, will they be
better brought up and educated if you are not with
them than if you were dead? Oh yes! your friends
will care for them. Will they care for them if you
go away to Thessaly and not if you go away to the
dwellings of the dead? If those who say they are
your friends are of any use, we must believe they will
care for them in both cases alike.

"Ah, Socrates, be guided by us who tended your
infancy. Care neither for your children nor for
life nor for anything else more than for the right,
that when you come to the home of the dead, you
may have all these things to say in your own
defence. For clearly if you do this thing it will
not be better for you here, or more just or holier,
no, nor for any of your friends, and neither will it
be better when you reach that other abode. Now,
however, you will go away wronged, if you do go
away, not by us, the laws, but by men; but if you
escape after so disgracefully requiting wrong with
wrong and evil with evil, breaking your compacts
and agreements with us, and injuring those whom
you least ought to injure—yourself, your friends,
your country and us—we shall be angry with you
while you live, and there our brothers, the laws in
Hades' realm, will not receive you graciously; for
they will know that you tried, so far as in you lay,

PLATO

τὸ σὸν μέρος. ἀλλὰ μή σε πείσῃ Κρίτων ποιεῖν
D ἃ λέγει μᾶλλον ἢ ἡμεῖς.

17. Ταῦτα, ὦ φίλε ἑταῖρε Κρίτων,[1] εὖ ἴσθι ὅτι
ἐγὼ δοκῶ ἀκούειν, ὥσπερ οἱ κορυβαντιῶντες τῶν
αὐλῶν δοκοῦσιν ἀκούειν, καὶ ἐν ἐμοὶ αὕτη ἡ ἠχὴ
τούτων τῶν λόγων βομβεῖ καὶ ποιεῖ μὴ δύνασθαι
τῶν ἄλλων ἀκούειν· ἀλλὰ ἴσθι, ὅσα γε τὰ νῦν
ἐμοὶ δοκοῦντα, ἐὰν λέγῃς παρὰ ταῦτα, μάτην
ἐρεῖς· ὅμως μέντοι εἴ τι οἴει πλέον ποιήσειν,
λέγε.

ΚΡΙΤΩΝ. Ἀλλ᾽, ὦ Σώκρατες, οὐκ ἔχω λέγειν.

E   ΣΩΚΡΑΤΗΣ. Ἔα τοίνυν, ὦ Κρίτων, καὶ πράτ-
τωμεν ταύτῃ, ἐπειδὴ ταύτῃ ὁ θεὸς ὑφηγεῖται.

[1] Schanz follows Cobet and Naber in omitting Κρίτων.

to destroy us. Do not let Crito persuade you to do what he says, but take our advice."

Be well assured, my dear friend, Crito, that this is what I seem to hear, as the frenzied dervishes of Cybele seem to hear the flutes, and this sound of these words re-echoes within me and prevents my hearing any other words. And be assured that, so far as I now believe, if you argue against these words you will speak in vain. Nevertheless, if you think you can accomplish anything, speak.

CRITO. No, Socrates, I have nothing to say.

SOCRATES. Then, Crito, let it be, and let us act in this way, since it is in this way that God leads us.

PHAEDO

INTRODUCTION TO THE *PHAEDO*

THE *Phaedo*, like the *Crito*, has for its scene the prison of Socrates, though the dialogue is here supposed to be reported by one who was present, not actually carried on in the presence of the reader. The immediate purpose of the dialogue seems to be to show that the philosopher will be glad to die ; and this purpose is never lost sight of, for it appears toward the end, as at the beginning. In order, however, to prove that willingness to die is rational, it is necessary to prove that the soul will continue to exist after the death of the body, and thus the original statement that the philosopher will be glad to die leads to the proof of a far more important truth. The commonly accepted statement that the real subject of the *Phaedo* is the immortality of the soul has certainly some justification. In order, however, to prove that the soul is immortal the theory is advanced that generation proceeds from opposite to opposite by alternation, that life proceeds from death as death from life, and that therefore the soul must exist after death as before birth. Again, all sensible objects are referable to certain types, of which they are likenesses. These types must be known to us before we can refer objects to them, and we have not seen or learned the types in this life ; we must therefore have seen them before this life began ; our knowledge is thus seen to be reminiscence of knowledge

gained before our birth. All this proves, however, only that the soul existed for a probably very long time before our birth and continues to exist for a probably very long time after our death, but not that it is immortal and indestructible. This objection leads to the discussion of causation and to the conclusion that "the ideas are the sole causes of all things and the sole objects of knowledge." The idea inherent in soul is life, and since ideas are so connected with particulars that no particular can admit an idea directly contrary to its own inherent idea, the soul cannot admit death. The proof of the immortality of the soul has been reached by proving the everlasting truth of the ideas. This last is the most important part of the *Phaedo*, so far as the development of Plato's system of philosophy is concerned, though it is introduced as a means for proving the immortality of the soul, just as the immortality of the soul is proved in order to show that the true philosopher will not fear, but welcome, death.[1]

This dialogue, then, establishes the doctrine of the real existence of ideas as the sole objects of knowledge and also shows how that doctrine is necessary to human happiness, because it serves to prove that the soul is immortal. The ordinary human being is little interested in metaphysical speculation, but greatly interested in his own future; he will therefore pay attention to metaphysical theory if it is so presented as to seem to affect his happiness. The *Phaedo*, by applying the doctrine of ideas to prove

---

[1] This brief discussion of the contents and purpose of the *Phaedo* is for the most part derived from the introduction to R. D. Archer-Hind's excellent edition, to which the reader is referred for a more complete exposition.

the immortality of the soul, tends to popularise the doctrine of ideas, and this may have been the ultimate purpose of Plato in writing the dialogue ; but that he was also fully in earnest in his belief in the immortality of the soul, and that the proof of immortality was an important part of his purpose in writing the dialogue, cannot be doubted.

In composition the *Phaedo* is elaborate without being complicated. The dramatic setting serves here, as in the *Crito*, as an appropriate introduction to a discourse on immortality and offers an opportunity to portray the gentle, genial nature, the kindly humour, and the calm, untroubled courage of Socrates ; it also marks the divisions between the various parts of the discussion, and offers relief to the mind of the reader who is wearied by close application to serious argument. Those who take part in the conversation are admirably characterised ; this is especially true of the two Thebans, Simmias and Cebes, who play the most important parts after Socrates himself. Both are eager searchers after truth, and both are evidently highly regarded by Socrates—were, in other words, at least respected by Plato ; but Simmias appears as a man of somewhat vague notions, inclined to mysticism, and somewhat lacking in keenness, while Cebes is clear-sighted, sharp, and keen, tenacious of his opinion, but quick to see when an opinion is no longer tenable. These distinguishing traits are drawn with few lines, but the few are masterly. The beautiful imaginative description of the life of souls in the other world is not merely a picturesque addition to the variety of the composition ; it teaches us how Plato believed that right and wrong actions were rewarded or

punished. Quite different imagery is employed for the same end in the *Phaedrus*, but in both dialogues the justice of the treatment accorded the souls is made clear, and in both the importance of conduct in this life is emphasised, though this emphasis is stronger in the *Phaedo*, as is natural in view of the dramatic setting.

The number of persons mentioned in the *Phaedo* is considerable.

Echecrates of Phlius was one of the last of the Pythagoreans; we know of no particular reason why he is introduced into this dialogue, unless it be that, as a Pythagorean, he might naturally be in sympathy with the doctrine of ideas. Of his personal relations to Socrates nothing is known. Phaedo, of Elis, was taken prisoner in 401 B.C. and brought to Athens, where he was, according to Aulus Gellius (ii., 18), ransomed by Cebes. After the death of Socrates he returned to Elis and founded the Elean school of philosophy, which was afterwards moved to Eretria by Menedemus and known as the Eretrian school. Phaedo wrote several dialogues, but virtually nothing is known of his doctrines. He seems to have been highly esteemed by Socrates and his followers. Apollodorus of Phalerum is of no philosophical importance. He is mentioned several times by Plato and Xenophon as an ardent admirer and constant companion of Socrates, and a man of impulsive, unrestrained disposition. Simmias and Cebes were both Thebans, warm personal friends, and equally devoted to Socrates; both offered money to secure the release of Socrates from prison (*Crito*, 45 B). The composition preserved under the name of *Pinax* or *Tablet* of Cebes is certainly spurious. Crito appears

here, as in the dialogue that bears his name, as the old and tried friend of Socrates. The others who are mentioned as companions of Socrates in his last hours are Critobulus, the son of Crito; Hermogenes, probably the son of Hipponicus and then identical with a speaker in the *Cratylus*; Epigenes, son of Antiphon; Aeschines, a well-known follower of Socrates, author of several dialogues; Antisthenes, founder of the Cynic school; Ctesippus, a youth mentioned also in the *Euthydemus* and the *Lysis*; Menexenus, son of Demophon and an admirer of Ctesippus; his name is given to one of Plato's dialogues; Phaedonides, a Theban; Euclides of Megara, founder of the Megarian school; and Terpsion, also a Megarian. Evenus, mentioned in 60 D, was a Parian sophist and poet.

The most important separate editions of the *Phaedo* are those of Geddes, W. Wagner, Wohlrab, Schanz, Hirschig, Burnet, and Archer-Hind. The introduction and commentary in the last-named edition are of special importance.

ΦΑΙΔΩΝ

Η ΠΕΡΙ ΨΥΧΗΣ, ΗΘΙΚΟΣ

ΤΑ ΤΟΥ ΔΙΑΛΟΓΟΥ ΠΡΟΣΩΠΑ

ΕΧΕΚΡΑΤΗΣ, ΦΑΙΔΩΝ, ΑΠΟΛΛΟΔΩΡΟΣ, ΣΩΚΡΑΤΗΣ, ΚΕΒΗΣ, ΣΙΜΜΙΑΣ, ΚΡΙΤΩΝ, Ο ΤΩΝ ΕΝΔΕΚΑ ΥΠΗΡΕΤΗΣ

St. I.
p. 57

A   1. ΕΧΕΚΡΑΤΗΣ. Αὐτός, ὦ Φαίδων, παρεγένου Σωκράτει ἐκείνῃ τῇ ἡμέρᾳ, ᾗ τὸ φάρμακον ἔπιεν ἐν τῷ δεσμωτηρίῳ, ἢ ἄλλου του ἤκουσας;

ΦΑΙΔΩΝ. Αὐτός, ὦ Ἐχέκρατες.

ΕΧΕΚΡΑΤΗΣ. Τί οὖν δή ἐστιν ἄττα εἶπεν ὁ ἀνὴρ πρὸ τοῦ θανάτου; καὶ πῶς ἐτελεύτα; ἡδέως γὰρ ἂν ἐγὼ ἀκούσαιμι. καὶ γὰρ οὔτε τῶν πολιτῶν Φλιασίων οὐδεὶς πάνυ τι ἐπιχωριάζει τὰ νῦν Ἀθήναζε, οὔτε τις ξένος ἀφῖκται χρόνου συχνοῦ

B   ἐκεῖθεν, ὅστις ἂν ἡμῖν σαφές τι ἀγγεῖλαι οἷός τ' ἦν περὶ τούτων, πλήν γε δὴ ὅτι φάρμακον πιὼν ἀποθάνοι· τῶν δὲ ἄλλων οὐδὲν εἶχεν φράζειν.

58   ΦΑΙΔΩΝ. Οὐδὲ τὰ περὶ τῆς δίκης ἄρα ἐπύθεσθε ὃν τρόπον ἐγένετο;

ΕΧΕΚΡΑΤΗΣ. Ναί, ταῦτα μὲν ἡμῖν ἤγγειλέ τις, καὶ ἐθαυμάζομέν γε, ὅτι πάλαι γενομένης αὐτῆς πολλῷ ὕστερον φαίνεται ἀποθανών. τί οὖν ἦν τοῦτο, ὦ Φαίδων;

ΦΑΙΔΩΝ. Τύχη τις αὐτῷ, ὦ Ἐχέκρατες, συνέβη· ἔτυχε γὰρ τῇ προτεραίᾳ τῆς δίκης ἡ πρύμνα

PHAEDO

[OR ON THE SOUL; ETHICAL]

CHARACTERS

ECHECRATES, PHAEDO, APOLLODORUS, SOCRATES, CEBES, SIMMIAS, CRITO, *the Servant of the Eleven.*

ECHECRATES. Were you with Socrates yourself, Phaedo, on the day when he drank the poison in prison, or did you hear about it from someone else?

PHAEDO. I was there myself, Echecrates.

ECHECRATES. Then what did he say before his death? and how did he die? I should like to hear, for nowadays none of the Phliasians go to Athens at all, and no stranger has come from there for a long time, who could tell us anything definite about this matter, except that he drank poison and died, so we could learn no further details.

PHAEDO. Did you not even hear about the trial and how it was conducted?

ECHECRATES. Yes, some one told us about that, and we wondered that although it took place a long time ago, he was put to death much later. Now why was that, Phaedo?

PHAEDO. It was a matter of chance, Echecrates. It happened that the stern of the ship which the

201

ἐστεμμένη τοῦ πλοίου, ὃ εἰς Δῆλον Ἀθηναῖοι
πέμπουσιν.

ΕΧΕΚΡΑΤΗΣ. Τοῦτο δὲ δὴ τί ἐστιν;

ΦΑΙΔΩΝ. Τοῦτ' ἔστι τὸ πλοῖον, ὥς φασιν
Ἀθηναῖοι, ἐν ᾧ Θησεύς ποτε εἰς Κρήτην τοὺς δὶς
B ἑπτὰ ἐκείνους ᾤχετο ἄγων καὶ ἔσωσέ τε καὶ αὐτὸς
ἐσώθη. τῷ οὖν Ἀπόλλωνι εὔξαντο, ὡς λέγεται,
τότε, εἰ σωθεῖεν, ἑκάστου ἔτους θεωρίαν ἀπάξειν
εἰς Δῆλον· ἣν δὴ ἀεὶ καὶ νῦν ἔτι ἐξ ἐκείνου κατ'
ἐνιαυτὸν τῷ θεῷ πέμπουσιν. ἐπειδὰν οὖν ἄρξωνται
τῆς θεωρίας, νόμος ἐστὶν αὐτοῖς ἐν τῷ χρόνῳ
τούτῳ καθαρεύειν τὴν πόλιν καὶ δημοσίᾳ μηδένα
ἀποκτιννύναι, πρὶν ἂν εἰς Δῆλόν τε ἀφίκηται
τὸ πλοῖον καὶ πάλιν δεῦρο· τοῦτο δ' ἐνίοτε ἐν
πολλῷ χρόνῳ γίγνεται, ὅταν τύχωσιν ἄνεμοι
C ἀπολαβόντες αὐτούς. ἀρχὴ δ' ἐστὶ τῆς θεωρίας,
ἐπειδὰν ὁ ἱερεὺς τοῦ Ἀπόλλωνος στέψῃ τὴν
πρύμναν τοῦ πλοίου· τοῦτο δ' ἔτυχεν, ὥσπερ
λέγω, τῇ προτεραίᾳ τῆς δίκης γεγονός. διὰ ταῦτα
καὶ πολὺς χρόνος ἐγένετο τῷ Σωκράτει ἐν τῷ
δεσμωτηρίῳ ὁ μεταξὺ τῆς δίκης τε καὶ θανάτου.

2. ΕΧΕΚΡΑΤΗΣ. Τί δὲ δὴ τὰ περὶ αὐτὸν τὸν
θάνατον, ὦ Φαίδων; τί ἦν τὰ λεχθέντα καὶ
πραχθέντα, καὶ τίνες οἱ παραγενόμενοι τῶν ἐπιτηδείων τῷ ἀνδρί; ἢ οὐκ εἴων οἱ ἄρχοντες παρεῖναι,
ἀλλ' ἔρημος ἐτελεύτα φίλων;

D ΦΑΙΔΩΝ. Οὐδαμῶς, ἀλλὰ παρῆσάν τινες καὶ
πολλοί γε.

ΕΧΕΚΡΑΤΗΣ. Ταῦτα δὴ πάντα προθυμήθητι ὡς
σαφέστατα ἡμῖν ἀπαγγεῖλαι, εἰ μή τίς σοι
ἀσχολία τυγχάνει οὖσα.

ΦΑΙΔΩΝ. Ἀλλὰ σχολάζω γε καὶ πειράσομαι

Athenians send to Delos was crowned on the day before the trial.

ECHECRATES. What ship is this?

PHAEDO. This is the ship, as the Athenians say, in which Theseus once went to Crete with the fourteen youths and maidens, and saved them and himself. Now the Athenians made a vow to Apollo, as the story goes, that if they were saved they would send a mission every year to Delos. And from that time even to the present day they send it annually in honour of the god. Now it is their law that after the mission begins the city must be pure and no one may be publicly executed until the ship has gone to Delos and back; and sometimes, when contrary winds detain it, this takes a long time. The beginning of the mission is when the priest of Apollo crowns the stern of the ship; and this took place, as I say, on the day before the trial. For that reason Socrates passed a long time in prison between his trial and his death.

ECHECRATES. What took place at his death, Phaedo? What was said and done? And which of his friends were with him? Or did the authorities forbid them to be present, so that he died without his friends?

PHAEDO. Not at all. Some were there, in fact, a good many.

ECHECRATES. Be so good as to tell us as exactly as you can about all these things, if you are not too busy.

PHAEDO. I am not busy and I will try to tell

ὑμῖν διηγήσασθαι· καὶ γὰρ τὸ μεμνῆσθαι Σωκράτους καὶ αὐτὸν λέγοντα καὶ ἄλλου ἀκούοντα
ἔμοιγε ἀεὶ πάντων ἥδιστον.

ΕΧΕΚΡΑΤΗΣ. Ἀλλὰ μήν, ὦ Φαίδων, καὶ τοὺς
ἀκουσομένους γε τοιούτους ἑτέρους ἔχεις· ἀλλὰ
πειρῶ ὡς ἂν δύνῃ ἀκριβέστατα διεξελθεῖν πάντα.

Ε   ΦΑΙΔΩΝ. Καὶ μὴν ἔγωγε θαυμάσια ἔπαθον
παραγενόμενος. οὔτε γὰρ ὡς θανάτῳ παρόντα με
ἀνδρὸς ἐπιτηδείου ἔλεος εἰσῄει· εὐδαίμων γάρ μοι
ἀνὴρ ἐφαίνετο, ὦ Ἐχέκρατες, καὶ τοῦ τρόπου καὶ
τῶν λόγων, ὡς ἀδεῶς καὶ γενναίως ἐτελεύτα, ὥστε
μοι ἐκεῖνον παρίστασθαι μηδ' εἰς Ἅιδου ἰόντα
ἄνευ θείας μοίρας ἰέναι, ἀλλὰ καὶ ἐκεῖσε ἀφικό-
59 μενον εὖ πράξειν, εἴπερ τις πώποτε καὶ ἄλλος.
διὰ δὴ ταῦτα οὐδὲν πάνυ μοι ἐλεεινὸν εἰσῄει,
ὡς εἰκὸς ἂν δόξειεν εἶναι παρόντι πένθει· οὔτε αὖ
ἡδονὴ ὡς ἐν φιλοσοφίᾳ ἡμῶν ὄντων, ὥσπερ
εἰώθειμεν· καὶ γὰρ οἱ λόγοι τοιοῦτοί τινες ἦσαν·
ἀλλ' ἀτεχνῶς ἄτοπόν τί μοι πάθος παρῆν καί τις
ἀήθης κρᾶσις ἀπό τε τῆς ἡδονῆς συγκεκραμένη
ὁμοῦ καὶ ἀπὸ τῆς λύπης, ἐνθυμουμένῳ ὅτι
αὐτίκα ἐκεῖνος ἔμελλε τελευτᾶν. καὶ πάντες οἱ
παρόντες σχεδόν τι οὕτω διεκείμεθα, ὁτὲ μὲν
γελῶντες, ἐνίοτε δὲ δακρύοντες, εἷς δὲ ἡμῶν καὶ
διαφερόντως, Ἀπολλόδωρος· οἶσθα γάρ που τὸν
Β ἄνδρα καὶ τὸν τρόπον αὐτοῦ.

ΕΧΕΚΡΑΤΗΣ. Πῶς γὰρ οὔ;

ΦΑΙΔΩΝ. Ἐκεῖνός τε τοίνυν παντάπασιν οὕτως
εἶχεν, καὶ αὐτὸς ἔγωγε ἐτεταράγμην καὶ οἱ ἄλλοι.

ΕΧΕΚΡΑΤΗΣ. Ἔτυχον δέ, ὦ Φαίδων, τίνες παραγενόμενοι;

ΦΑΙΔΩΝ. Οὗτός τε δὴ ὁ Ἀπολλόδωρος τῶν

you. It is always my greatest pleasure to be reminded of Socrates whether by speaking of him myself or by listening to someone else.

ECHECRATES. Well, Phaedo, you will have hearers who feel as you do ; so try to tell us everything as accurately as you can.

PHAEDO. For my part, I had strange emotions when I was there. For I was not filled with pity as I might naturally be when present at the death of a friend ; since he seemed to me to be happy, both in his bearing and his words, he was meeting death so fearlessly and nobly. And so I thought that even in going to the abode of the dead he was not going without the protection of the gods, and that when he arrived there it would be well with him, if it ever was well with anyone. And for this reason I was not at all filled with pity, as might seem natural when I was present at a scene of mourning ; nor on the other hand did I feel pleasure because we were occupied with philosophy, as was our custom—and our talk was of philosophy ;—but a very strange feeling came over me, an unaccustomed mixture of pleasure and of pain together, when I thought that Socrates was presently to die. And all of us who were there were in much the same condition, sometimes laughing and sometimes weeping ; especially one of us, Apollodorus ; you know him and his character.

ECHECRATES. To be sure I do.

PHAEDO. He was quite unrestrained, and I was much agitated myself, as were the others.

ECHECRATES. Who were these, Phaedo ?

PHAEDO. Of native Athenians there was this

ἐπιχωρίων παρῆν καὶ ὁ Κριτόβουλος καὶ ὁ πατὴρ
αὐτοῦ, καὶ ἔτι Ἑρμογένης καὶ Ἐπιγένης καὶ
Αἰσχίνης καὶ Ἀντισθένης· ἦν δὲ καὶ Κτήσιππος
ὁ Παιανιεὺς καὶ Μενέξενος καὶ ἄλλοι τινὲς τῶν
ἐπιχωρίων· Πλάτων δέ, οἶμαι, ἠσθένει.

C   ΕΧΕΚΡΑΤΗΣ.   Ξένοι δέ τινες παρῆσαν;

ΦΑΙΔΩΝ.   Ναί, Σιμμίας τέ γε ὁ Θηβαῖος καὶ
Κέβης καὶ Φαιδωνίδης καὶ Μεγαρόθεν Εὐκλείδης
τε καὶ Τερψίων.

ΕΧΕΚΡΑΤΗΣ.   Τί δέ; Ἀρίστιππος καὶ Κλεόμβροτος[1] παρεγένοντο;

ΦΑΙΔΩΝ.   Οὐ δῆτα· ἐν Αἰγίνῃ γὰρ ἐλέγοντο
εἶναι.

ΕΧΕΚΡΑΤΗΣ.   Ἄλλος δέ τις παρῆν;

ΦΑΙΔΩΝ.   Σχεδόν τι οἶμαι τούτους παραγενέ-
σθαι.

ΕΧΕΚΡΑΤΗΣ.   Τί οὖν δή; τίνες, φής, ἦσαν οἱ
λόγοι;

3. ΦΑΙΔΩΝ.   Ἐγώ σοι ἐξ ἀρχῆς πάντα πειράσομαι διηγήσασθαι. ἀεὶ γὰρ δὴ καὶ τὰς πρόσθεν
D ἡμέρας εἰώθειμεν φοιτᾶν καὶ ἐγὼ καὶ οἱ ἄλλοι
παρὰ τὸν Σωκράτη, συλλεγόμενοι ἕωθεν εἰς τὸ
δικαστήριον, ἐν ᾧ καὶ ἡ δίκη ἐγένετο· πλησίον
γὰρ ἦν τοῦ δεσμωτηρίου. περιεμένομεν οὖν
ἑκάστοτε, ἕως ἀνοιχθείη τὸ δεσμωτήριον, διατρίβοντες μετ᾽ ἀλλήλων· ἀνεῴγετο γὰρ οὐ πρῴ·
ἐπειδὴ δὲ ἀνοιχθείη, εἰσῇμεν παρὰ τὸν Σωκράτη
καὶ τὰ πολλὰ διημερεύομεν μετ᾽ αὐτοῦ. καὶ δὴ καὶ
τότε πρωιαίτερον συνελέγημεν. τῇ γὰρ προτεραίᾳ[2]

---

[1] Schanz, after Cobet, inserts οὐ after Κλεόμβροτος.
[2] After προτεραίᾳ the MSS. read ἡμέρᾳ, which Hermann,
followed by Schanz and others, brackets.

Apollodorus, and Critobulus and his father, and Hermogenes and Epiganes and Aeschines and Antisthenes; and Ctesippus the Paeanian was there too, and Menexenus and some other Athenians. But Plato, I think, was ill.

ECHECRATES. Were any foreigners there?

PHAEDO. Yes, Simmias of Thebes and Cebes and Phaedonides, and from Megara Euclides and Terpsion.

ECHECRATES. What? Were Aristippus and Cleombrotus there?

PHAEDO. No. They were said to be in Aegina.

ECHECRATES. Was anyone else there?

PHAEDO. I think these were about all.

ECHECRATES. Well then, what was the conversation?

PHAEDO. I will try to tell you everything from the beginning. On the previous days I and the others had always been in the habit of visiting Socrates. We used to meet at daybreak in the court where the trial took place, for it was near the prison; and every day we used to wait about, talking with each other, until the prison was opened, for it was not opened early; and when it was opened, we went in to Socrates and passed most of the day with him. On that day we came together earlier; for the day before, when we left the prison

Ε ἐπειδὴ ἐξήλθομεν ἐκ τοῦ δεσμωτηρίου ἑσπέρας, ἐπυθόμεθα ὅτι τὸ πλοῖον ἐκ Δήλου ἀφιγμένον εἴη. παρηγγείλαμεν οὖν ἀλλήλοις ἥκειν ὡς πρωϊαίτατα εἰς τὸ εἰωθός. καὶ ἥκομεν καὶ ἡμῖν ἐξελθὼν ὁ θυρωρός, ὅσπερ εἰώθει ὑπακούειν, εἶπεν περιμένειν καὶ μὴ πρότερον παριέναι, ἕως ἂν αὐτὸς κελεύσῃ. Λύουσι γάρ, ἔφη, οἱ ἕνδεκα Σωκράτη καὶ παραγγέλλουσιν ὅπως ἂν τῇδε τῇ ἡμέρᾳ τελευτήσῃ. οὐ πολὺν δ᾽ οὖν χρόνον ἐπισχὼν ἧκεν καὶ
60 ἐκέλευσεν ἡμᾶς εἰσιέναι. εἰσελθόντες οὖν κατελαμβάνομεν τὸν μὲν Σωκράτη ἄρτι λελυμένον, τὴν δὲ Ξανθίππην—γιγνώσκεις γάρ—ἔχουσάν τε τὸ παιδίον αὐτοῦ καὶ παρακαθημένην. ὡς οὖν εἶδεν ἡμᾶς ἡ Ξανθίππη, ἀνευφήμησέ τε καὶ τοιαῦτ᾽ ἄττα εἶπεν, οἷα δὴ εἰώθασιν αἱ γυναῖκες, ὅτι Ὦ Σώκρατες, ὕστατον δή σε προσεροῦσι νῦν οἱ ἐπιτήδειοι καὶ σὺ τούτους. καὶ ὁ Σωκράτης βλέψας εἰς τὸν Κρίτωνα· Ὦ Κρίτων, ἔφη, ἀπαγέτω τις αὐτὴν οἴκαδε. καὶ ἐκείνην μὲν ἀπῆγόν τινες τῶν τοῦ Κρίτωνος βοῶσάν
Β τε καὶ κοπτομένην· ὁ δὲ Σωκράτης ἀνακαθιζόμενος εἰς τὴν κλίνην συνέκαμψέ τε τὸ σκέλος καὶ ἐξέτριψε τῇ χειρί, καὶ τρίβων ἅμα· Ὡς ἄτοπον, ἔφη, ὦ ἄνδρες, ἔοικέ τι εἶναι τοῦτο, ὃ καλοῦσιν οἱ ἄνθρωποι ἡδύ· ὡς θαυμασίως πέφυκε πρὸς τὸ δοκοῦν ἐναντίον εἶναι, τὸ λυπηρόν, τῷ ἅμα μὲν αὐτὼ μὴ ἐθέλειν παραγίγνεσθαι τῷ ἀνθρώπῳ, ἐὰν δέ τις διώκῃ τὸ ἕτερον καὶ λαμβάνῃ, σχεδόν τι ἀναγκάζεσθαι λαμβάνειν καὶ τὸ ἕτερον, ὥσπερ ἐκ μιᾶς κορυφῆς συνημμένω δύ᾽ ὄντε. καὶ
C μοι δοκεῖ, ἔφη, εἰ ἐνενόησεν αὐτὰ Αἴσωπος, μῦθον ἂν συνθεῖναι, ὡς ὁ θεὸς βουλόμενος αὐτὰ

in the evening we heard that the ship had arrived
from Delos. So we agreed to come to the usual
place as early in the morning as possible. And we
came, and the jailer who usually answered the door
came out and told us to wait and not go in until he
told us. "For," he said, "the eleven are releasing
Socrates from his fetters and giving directions how
he is to die to-day." So after a little delay he came
and told us to go in. We went in then and found
Socrates just released from his fetters and Xanthippe
—you know her—with his little son in her arms,
sitting beside him. Now when Xanthippe saw us,
she cried out and said the kind of thing that women
always do say : "Oh Socrates, this is the last time
now that your friends will speak to you or you to
them." And Socrates glanced at Crito and said,
"Crito, let somebody take her home." And some
of Crito's people took her away wailing and beating
her breast. But Socrates sat up on his couch and
bent his leg and rubbed it with his hand, and while
he was rubbing it, he said, "What a strange thing,
my friends, that seems to be which men call
pleasure ! How wonderfully it is related to that
which seems to be its opposite, pain, in that they
will not both come to a man at the same time, and
yet if he pursues the one and captures it, he is
generally obliged to take the other also, as if the
two were joined together in one head. And I
think," he said, "if Aesop had thought of them,
he would have made a fable telling how they were
at war and god wished to reconcile them, and when

διαλλάξαι πολεμοῦντα, ἐπειδὴ οὐκ ἐδύνατο,
συνῆψεν εἰς ταὐτὸν αὐτοῖς τὰς κορυφάς, καὶ διὰ
ταῦτα ᾧ ἂν τὸ ἕτερον παραγένηται ἐπακολουθεῖ
ὕστερον καὶ τὸ ἕτερον. ὥσπερ οὖν καὶ αὐτῷ μοι
ἔοικεν, ἐπειδὴ ὑπὸ τοῦ δεσμοῦ ἦν ἐν τῷ σκέλει τὸ
ἀλγεινόν, ἥκειν δὴ φαίνεται ἐπακολουθοῦν τὸ ἡδύ.

4. Ὁ οὖν Κέβης ὑπολαβών· Νὴ τὸν Δία,
ὦ Σώκρατες, ἔφη, εὖ γ᾽ ἐποίησας ἀναμνήσας
D με. περὶ γάρ τοι τῶν ποιημάτων ὧν πεποίηκας
ἐντείνας τοὺς τοῦ Αἰσώπου λόγους καὶ τὸ εἰς
τὸν Ἀπόλλω προοίμιον καὶ ἄλλοι τινές με ἤδη
ἤροντο, ἀτὰρ καὶ Εὔηνος πρῴην, ὅ τι ποτὲ
διανοηθείς, ἐπειδὴ δεῦρο ἦλθες, ἐποίησας αὐτά,
πρότερον οὐδὲν πώποτε ποιήσας. εἰ οὖν τί σοι
μέλει τοῦ ἔχειν ἐμὲ Εὐήνῳ ἀποκρίνασθαι, ὅταν
με αὖθις ἐρωτᾷ, εὖ οἶδα γάρ, ὅτι ἐρήσεται,
εἰπέ, τί χρὴ λέγειν. Λέγε τοίνυν, ἔφη, αὐτῷ, ὦ
Κέβης, τἀληθῆ, ὅτι οὐκ ἐκείνῳ βουλόμενος οὐδὲ
τοῖς ποιήμασιν αὐτοῦ ἀντίτεχνος εἶναι ἐποίησα
E ταῦτα· ᾔδειν γὰρ ὡς οὐ ῥᾴδιον εἴη· ἀλλ᾽ ἐνυπνίων
τινῶν ἀποπειρώμενος τί λέγει, καὶ ἀφοσιούμενος,
εἰ πολλάκις ταύτην τὴν μουσικήν μοι ἐπιτάττοι
ποιεῖν. ἦν γὰρ δὴ ἄττα τοιάδε· πολλάκις μοι
φοιτῶν τὸ αὐτὸ ἐνύπνιον ἐν τῷ παρελθόντι βίῳ,
ἄλλοτ᾽ ἐν ἄλλῃ ὄψει φαινόμενον, τὰ αὐτὰ δὲ
λέγον, ὦ Σώκρατες, ἔφη, μουσικὴν ποίει καὶ
ἐργάζου. καὶ ἐγὼ ἔν γε τῷ πρόσθεν χρόνῳ
ὅπερ ἔπραττον τοῦτο ὑπελάμβανον αὐτό μοι
61 παρακελεύεσθαί τε καὶ ἐπικελεύειν, ὥσπερ οἱ
τοῖς θέουσι διακελευόμενοι, καὶ ἐμοὶ οὕτω τὸ
ἐνύπνιον, ὅπερ ἔπραττον, τοῦτο ἐπικελεύειν, μουσικὴν ποιεῖν, ὡς φιλοσοφίας μὲν οὔσης μεγίστης

he could not do that, he fastened their heads together, and for that reason, when one of them comes to anyone, the other follows after. Just so it seems that in my case, after pain was in my leg on account of the fetter, pleasure appears to have come following after."

Here Cebes interrupted and said, "By Zeus, Socrates, I am glad you reminded me. Several others have asked about the poems you have composed, the metrical versions of Aesop's fables and the hymn to Apollo, and Evenus asked me the day before yesterday why you who never wrote any poetry before, composed these verses after you came to prison. Now, if you care that I should be able to answer Evenus when he asks me again—and I know he will ask me—tell me what to say."

"Then tell him, Cebes," said he, "the truth, that I composed these verses not because I wished to rival him or his poems, for I knew that would not be easy, but because I wished to test the meaning of certain dreams, and to make sure that I was neglecting no duty in case their repeated commands meant that I must cultivate the Muses in this way. They were something like this. The same dream came to me often in my past life, sometimes in one form and sometimes in another, but always saying the same thing: 'Socrates,' it said, 'make music and work at it.' And I formerly thought it was urging and encouraging me to do what I was doing already and that just as people encourage runners by cheering, so the dream was encouraging me to do what I was doing, that is, to make music, because philosophy was the

μουσικῆς, ἐμοῦ δὲ τοῦτο πράττοντος· νῦν δ'
ἐπειδὴ ἥ τε δίκη ἐγένετο καὶ ἡ τοῦ θεοῦ ἑορτὴ
διεκώλυέ με ἀποθνῄσκειν, ἔδοξε χρῆναι, εἰ ἄρα
πολλάκις μοι προστάττοι τὸ ἐνύπνιον ταύτην
τὴν δημώδη μουσικὴν ποιεῖν, μὴ ἀπειθῆσαι αὐτῷ,
ἀλλὰ ποιεῖν. ἀσφαλέστερον γὰρ εἶναι μὴ ἀπιέναι
B πρὶν ἀφοσιώσασθαι ποιήσαντα ποιήματα πειθόμενον τῷ ἐνυπνίῳ. οὕτω δὴ πρῶτον μὲν εἰς τὸν
θεὸν ἐποίησα, οὗ ἦν ἡ παροῦσα θυσία· μετὰ δὲ
τὸν θεόν, ἐννοήσας ὅτι τὸν ποιητὴν δέοι, εἴπερ
μέλλοι ποιητὴς εἶναι, ποιεῖν μύθους, ἀλλ' οὐ
λόγους, καὶ αὐτὸς οὐκ ἦ μυθολογικός, διὰ ταῦτα
δὴ οὓς προχείρους εἶχον καὶ ἠπιστάμην μύθους
τοὺς Αἰσώπου, τούτους ἐποίησα, οἷς πρώτοις
ἐνέτυχον.

5. Ταῦτα οὖν, ὦ Κέβης, Εὐήνῳ φράζε, καὶ
ἐρρῶσθαι καί, ἂν σωφρονῇ, ἐμὲ διώκειν ὡς
C τάχιστα. ἄπειμι δέ, ὡς ἔοικε, τήμερον· κελεύουσι
γὰρ Ἀθηναῖοι. καὶ ὁ Σιμμίας· Οἷον παρακε-
λεύει, ἔφη, τοῦτο, ὦ Σώκρατες, Εὐήνῳ; πολλὰ
γὰρ ἤδη ἐντετύχηκα τῷ ἀνδρί· σχεδὸν οὖν, ἐξ
ὧν ἐγὼ ᾔσθημαι, οὐδ' ὁπωστιοῦν σοι ἑκὼν
εἶναι πείσεται. Τί δαί; ἦ δ' ὅς, οὐ φιλόσοφος
Εὔηνος; Ἔμοιγε δοκεῖ, ἔφη ὁ Σιμμίας. Ἐθε-
λήσει τοίνυν καὶ Εὔηνος καὶ πᾶς ὅτῳ ἀξίως
τούτου τοῦ πράγματος μέτεστιν. οὐ μέντοι ἴσως
βιάσεται αὑτόν· οὐ γάρ φασι θεμιτὸν εἶναι.
D καὶ ἅμα λέγων ταῦτα καθῆκε τὰ σκέλη ἐπὶ τὴν
γῆν, καὶ καθεζόμενος οὕτως ἤδη τὰ λοιπὰ διελέγετο. ἤρετο οὖν αὐτὸν ὁ Κέβης· Πῶς τοῦτο

greatest kind of music and I was working at that. But now, after the trial and while the festival of the god delayed my execution, I thought, in case the repeated dream really meant to tell me to make this which is ordinarily called music, I ought to do so and not to disobey. For I thought it was safer not to go hence before making sure that I had done what I ought, by obeying the dream and composing verses. So first I composed a hymn to the god whose festival it was ; and after the god, considering that a poet, if he is really to be a poet, must compose myths and not speeches, since I was not a maker of myths, I took the myths of Aesop, which I had at hand and knew, and turned into verse the first I came upon. So tell Evenus that, Cebes, and bid him farewell, and tell him, if he is wise, to come after me as quickly as he can. I, it seems, am going to-day ; for that is the order of the Athenians."

And Simmias said, "What a message that is, Socrates, for Evenus! I have met him often, and from what I have seen of him, I should say that he will not take your advice in the least if he can help it."

"Why so?" said he. "Is not Evenus a philosopher?"

"I think so," said Simmias.

"Then Evenus will take my advice, and so will every man who has any worthy interest in philosophy. Perhaps, however, he will not take his own life, for they say that is not permitted." And as he spoke he put his feet down on the ground and remained sitting in this way through the rest of the conversation.

Then Cebes asked him : "What do you mean by

λέγεις, ὦ Σώκρατες, τὸ μὴ θεμιτὸν εἶναι ἑαυτὸν
βιάζεσθαι, ἐθέλειν δ᾽ ἂν τῷ ἀποθνῄσκοντι τὸν
φιλόσοφον ἕπεσθαι ; Τί δέ, ὦ Κέβης ; οὐκ
ἀκηκόατε σύ τε καὶ Σιμμίας περὶ τῶν τοιούτων
Φιλολάῳ συγγεγονότες ; Οὐδέν γε σαφές, ὦ
Σώκρατες. Ἀλλὰ μὴν καὶ ἐγὼ ἐξ ἀκοῆς περὶ
αὐτῶν λέγω· ἃ μὲν οὖν τυγχάνω ἀκηκοώς, φθόνος
οὐδεὶς λέγειν. καὶ γὰρ ἴσως καὶ μάλιστα πρέπει
E μέλλοντα ἐκεῖσε ἀποδημεῖν διασκοπεῖν τε καὶ
μυθολογεῖν περὶ τῆς ἀποδημίας τῆς ἐκεῖ,[1] ποίαν
τινὰ αὐτὴν οἰόμεθα εἶναι· τί γὰρ ἄν τις καὶ ποιοῖ
ἄλλο ἐν τῷ μέχρι ἡλίου δυσμῶν χρόνῳ;

6. Κατὰ τί δὴ οὖν ποτε οὔ φασι θεμιτὸν εἶναι
αὐτὸν ἑαυτὸν ἀποκτιννύναι, ὦ Σώκρατες; ἤδη
γὰρ ἔγωγε, ὅπερ νῦν δὴ σὺ ἤρου, καὶ Φιλολάου
ἤκουσα, ὅτε παρ᾽ ἡμῖν διῃτᾶτο, ἤδη δὲ καὶ ἄλλων
τινῶν, ὡς οὐ δέοι τοῦτο ποιεῖν· σαφὲς δὲ περὶ
62 αὐτῶν οὐδενὸς πώποτε οὐδὲν ἀκήκοα. Ἀλλὰ
προθυμεῖσθαι χρή, ἔφη· τάχα γὰρ ἂν καὶ
ἀκούσαις. ἴσως μέντοι θαυμαστόν σοι φανεῖται,
εἰ τοῦτο μόνον τῶν ἄλλων ἁπάντων ἁπλοῦν
ἐστιν καὶ οὐδέποτε τυγχάνει τῷ ἀνθρώπῳ,
ὥσπερ καὶ τἆλλα,[2] ἔστιν ὅτε καὶ οἷς βέλτιον
τεθνάναι ἢ ζῆν· οἷς δὲ βέλτιον τεθνάναι, θαυμαστὸν ἴσως σοι φαίνεται, εἰ τούτοις τοῖς ἀνθρώποις μὴ ὅσιον αὐτοὺς ἑαυτοὺς εὖ ποιεῖν, ἀλλὰ
ἄλλον δεῖ περιμένειν εὐεργέτην. καὶ ὁ Κέβης
ἠρέμα ἐπιγελάσας· Ἴττω Ζεύς, ἔφη τῇ αὑτοῦ
φωνῇ εἰπών. Καὶ γὰρ ἂν δόξειεν, ἔφη ὁ

[1] Schanz brackets τῆς ἐκεῖ.
[2] Schanz, following Forster, puts a period after τἆλλα and
inserts ἀλλά.

214

this, Socrates, that it is not permitted to take one's life, but that the philosopher would desire to follow after the dying?"

"How is this, Cebes? Have you and Simmias, who are pupils of Philolaus, not heard about such things?"

"Nothing definite, Socrates."

"I myself speak of them only from hearsay; but I have no objection to telling what I have heard. And indeed it is perhaps especially fitting, as I am going to the other world, to tell stories about the life there and consider what we think about it; for what else could one do in the time between now and sunset?"

"Why in the world do they say that it is not permitted to kill oneself, Socrates? I heard Philolaus, when he was living in our city, say the same thing you just said, and I have heard it from others, too, that one must not do this; but I never heard anyone say anything definite about it."

"You must have courage," said he, "and perhaps you might hear something. But perhaps it will seem strange to you that this alone of all laws is without exception, and it never happens to mankind, as in other matters, that only at some times and for some persons it is better to die than to live; and it will perhaps seem strange to you that these human beings for whom it is better to die cannot without impiety do good to themselves, but must wait for some other benefactor."

And Cebes, smiling gently, said, "Gawd knows it doos," speaking in his own dialect.

"It would seem unreasonable, if put in this way,"

B Σωκράτης, οὕτω γ᾽ εἶναι ἄλογον· οὐ μέντοι
ἀλλ᾽ ἴσως γ᾽ ἔχει τινὰ λόγον. ὁ μὲν οὖν ἐν
ἀπορρήτοις λεγόμενος περὶ αὐτῶν λόγος, ὡς ἔν
τινι φρουρᾷ ἐσμεν οἱ ἄνθρωποι καὶ οὐ δεῖ δὴ
ἑαυτὸν ἐκ ταύτης λύειν οὐδ᾽ ἀποδιδράσκειν, μέγας
τέ τίς μοι φαίνεται καὶ οὐ ῥᾴδιος διιδεῖν· οὐ
μέντοι ἀλλὰ τόδε γέ μοι δοκεῖ, ὦ Κέβης, εὖ
λέγεσθαι, τὸ θεοὺς εἶναι ἡμῶν τοὺς ἐπιμελου-
μένους καὶ ἡμᾶς τοὺς ἀνθρώπους ἓν τῶν κτημάτων
τοῖς θεοῖς εἶναι· ἢ σοὶ οὐ δοκεῖ οὕτως; Ἔμοιγε,
C φησὶν ὁ Κέβης. Οὐκοῦν, ἦ δ᾽ ὅς, καὶ σὺ ἂν
τῶν σαυτοῦ κτημάτων εἴ τι αὐτὸ ἑαυτὸ ἀπο-
κτιννύοι, μὴ σημήναντός σου ὅτι βούλει αὐτὸ
τεθνάναι, χαλεπαίνοις ἂν αὐτῷ, καὶ εἴ τινα
ἔχοις τιμωρίαν, τιμωροῖο ἄν; Πάνυ γ᾽, ἔφη.
Ἴσως τοίνυν ταύτῃ οὐκ ἄλογον, μὴ πρότερον
αὑτὸν ἀποκτιννύναι δεῖν, πρὶν ἂν ἀνάγκην τινὰ
θεὸς ἐπιπέμψῃ, ὥσπερ καὶ τὴν νῦν ἡμῖν παροῦσαν.

7. Ἀλλ᾽ εἰκός, ἔφη ὁ Κέβης, τοῦτό γε
φαίνεται. ὃ μέντοι νῦν δὴ ἔλεγες, τὸ τοὺς φιλο-
σόφους ῥᾳδίως ἂν ἐθέλειν ἀποθνήσκειν, ἔοικεν
D τοῦτο, ὦ Σώκρατες, ἀτόπῳ, εἴπερ ὃ νῦν δὴ
ἐλέγομεν εὐλόγως ἔχει, τὸ θεόν τε εἶναι τὸν
ἐπιμελούμενον ἡμῶν καὶ ἡμᾶς ἐκείνου κτήματα
εἶναι. τὸ γὰρ μὴ ἀγανακτεῖν τοὺς φρονιμωτάτους
ἐκ ταύτης τῆς θεραπείας ἀπιόντας, ἐν ᾗ ἐπιστα-
τοῦσιν αὐτῶν οἵπερ ἄριστοί εἰσιν τῶν ὄντων
ἐπιστάται, θεοί, οὐκ ἔχει λόγον. οὐ γάρ που
αὐτός γε αὑτοῦ οἴεται ἄμεινον ἐπιμελήσεσθαι
ἐλεύθερος γενόμενος· ἀλλ᾽ ἀνόητος μὲν ἄνθρωπος
τάχ᾽ ἂν οἰηθείη ταῦτα, φευκτέον εἶναι ἀπὸ τοῦ

said Socrates, "but perhaps there is some reason in it. Now the doctrine that is taught in secret about this matter, that we men are in a kind of prison and must not set ourselves free or run away, seems to me to be weighty and not easy to understand. But this at least, Cebes, I do believe is sound, that the gods are our guardians and that we men are one of the chattels of the gods. Do you not believe this?"

"Yes," said Cebes, "I do."

"Well then," said he, "if one of your chattels should kill itself when you had not indicated that you wished it to die, would you be angry with it and punish it if you could?"

"Certainly," he replied.

"Then perhaps from this point of view it is not unreasonable to say that a man must not kill himself until god sends some necessity upon him, such as has now come upon me."

"That," said Cebes, "seems sensible. But what you said just now, Socrates, that philosophers ought to be ready and willing to die, that seems strange if we were right just now in saying that god is our guardian and we are his possessions. For it is not reasonable that the wisest men should not be troubled when they leave that service in which the gods, who are the best overseers in the world, are watching over them. A wise man certainly does not think that when he is free he can take better care of himself than they do. A foolish man might perhaps think so, that he ought to run away from his master, and he would not consider that he must not run

E δεσπότου,[1] καὶ οὐκ ἂν λογίζοιτο, ὅτι οὐ δεῖ
ἀπό γε τοῦ ἀγαθοῦ φεύγειν, ἀλλ' ὅ τι μάλιστα
παραμένειν, διὸ ἀλογίστως ἂν φεύγοι, ὁ δὲ νοῦν
ἔχων ἐπιθυμοῖ που ἂν ἀεὶ εἶναι παρὰ τῷ αὑτοῦ
βελτίονι. καίτοι οὕτως, ὦ Σώκρατες, τοὐναντίον
εἶναι εἰκὸς ἢ ὃ νῦν δὴ ἐλέγετο· τοὺς μὲν γὰρ
φρονίμους ἀγανακτεῖν ἀποθνήσκοντας πρέπει,
τοὺς δ' ἄφρονας χαίρειν. ἀκούσας οὖν ὁ Σω-
63 κράτης ἡσθῆναί τέ μοι ἔδοξε τῇ τοῦ Κέβητος
πραγματείᾳ, καὶ ἐπιβλέψας εἰς ἡμᾶς· Ἀεί τοι,
ἔφη, ὁ Κέβης λόγους τινὰς ἀνερευνᾷ, καὶ οὐ
πάνυ εὐθέως ἐθέλει πείθεσθαι, ὅ τι ἄν τις εἴπῃ.
καὶ ὁ Σιμμίας· Ἀλλὰ μήν, ἔφη, ὦ Σώκρατες,
νῦν γέ μοι δοκεῖ τι καὶ αὐτῷ λέγειν Κέβης·
τί γὰρ ἂν βουλόμενοι ἄνδρες σοφοὶ ὡς ἀληθῶς
δεσπότας ἀμείνους αὑτῶν φεύγοιεν καὶ ῥᾳδίως
ἀπαλλάττοιντο αὐτῶν; καί μοι δοκεῖ Κέβης εἰς
σὲ τείνειν τὸν λόγον, ὅτι οὕτω ῥᾳδίως φέρεις
καὶ ἡμᾶς ἀπολείπων καὶ ἄρχοντας ἀγαθούς, ὡς
B αὐτὸς ὁμολογεῖς, θεούς. Δίκαια, ἔφη, λέγετε.
οἶμαι γὰρ ὑμᾶς λέγειν, ὅτι χρή με πρὸς ταῦτα
ἀπολογήσασθαι ὥσπερ ἐν δικαστηρίῳ. Πάνυ
μὲν οὖν, ἔφη ὁ Σιμμίας.

8. Φέρε δή, ἦ δ' ὅς, πειραθῶ πιθανώτερον
πρὸς ὑμᾶς ἀπολογήσασθαι ἢ πρὸς τοὺς δικαστάς.
ἐγὼ γάρ, ἔφη, ὦ Σιμμία τε καὶ Κέβης, εἰ
μὲν μὴ ᾤμην ἥξειν πρῶτον μὲν παρὰ θεοὺς
ἄλλους σοφούς τε καὶ ἀγαθούς, ἔπειτα καὶ παρ'
ἀνθρώπους τετελευτηκότας ἀμείνους τῶν ἐνθάδε,
ἠδίκουν ἂν οὐκ ἀγανακτῶν τῷ θανάτῳ· νῦν δὲ
C εὖ ἴστε, ὅτι παρ' ἄνδρας τε ἐλπίζω ἀφίξεσθαι

[1] Schanz brackets φευκτέον . . . δεσπότου.

away from a good master, but ought to stay with him as long as possible; and so he might thoughtlessly run away; but a man of sense would wish to be always with one who is better than himself. And yet, Socrates, if we look at it in this way, the contrary of what we just said seems natural; for the wise ought to be troubled at dying and the foolish to rejoice."

When Socrates heard this I thought he was pleased by Cebes' earnestness, and glancing at us, he said, "Cebes is always on the track of arguments and will not be easily convinced by whatever anyone says."

And Simmias said, "Well, Socrates, this time I think myself that Cebes is right. For why should really wise men run away from masters who are better than they and lightly separate themselves from them? And it strikes me that Cebes is aiming his argument at you, because you are so ready to leave us and the gods, who are, as you yourself agree, good rulers."

"You have a right to say that," he replied; "for I think you mean that I must defend myself against this accusation, as if we were in a law court."

"Precisely," said Simmias.

"Well, then," said he, "I will try to make a more convincing defence than I did before the judges. For if I did not believe," said he, "that I was going to other wise and good gods, and, moreover, to men who have died, better men than those here, I should be wrong in not grieving at death. But as it is, you may rest assured that I expect to go to good men, though I should not care to assert this positively; but I would

ἀγαθούς· καὶ τοῦτο μὲν οὐκ ἂν πάνυ διισχυρι-
σαίμην· ὅτι μέντοι παρὰ θεοὺς δεσπότας πάνυ
ἀγαθοὺς ἥξειν,[1] εὖ ἴστε ὅτι, εἴπερ τι ἄλλο
τῶν τοιούτων, διισχυρισαίμην ἂν καὶ τοῦτο.
ὥστε διὰ ταῦτα οὐχ ὁμοίως ἀγανακτῶ, ἀλλ᾽
εὔελπίς εἰμι εἶναί τι τοῖς τετελευτηκόσι, καί,
ὥσπερ γε καὶ πάλαι λέγεται, πολὺ ἄμεινον τοῖς
ἀγαθοῖς ἢ τοῖς κακοῖς. Τί οὖν, ἔφη ὁ Σιμμίας,
ὦ Σώκρατες; αὐτὸς ἔχων τὴν διάνοιαν ταύτην
D ἐν νῷ ἔχεις ἀπιέναι, ἢ κἂν ἡμῖν μεταδοίης; κοινὸν
γὰρ δὴ ἔμοιγε δοκεῖ καὶ ἡμῖν εἶναι ἀγαθὸν
τοῦτο, καὶ ἅμα σοι ἀπολογία ἐστίν, ἐὰν ἅπερ
λέγεις ἡμᾶς πείσῃς. Ἀλλὰ πειράσομαι, ἔφη.
πρῶτον δὲ Κρίτωνα τόνδε σκεψώμεθα, τί ἐστιν
ὃ βούλεσθαί μοι δοκεῖ πάλαι εἰπεῖν. Τί, ὦ
Σώκρατες, ἔφη ὁ Κρίτων, ἄλλο γε ἢ πάλαι
μοι λέγει ὁ μέλλων σοι δώσειν τὸ φάρμακον,
ὅτι χρή σοι φράζειν ὡς ἐλάχιστα διαλέγεσθαι,
φησὶ γὰρ θερμαίνεσθαι μᾶλλον διαλεγομένους,
δεῖν δὲ οὐδὲν τοιοῦτον προσφέρειν τῷ φαρμάκῳ·
E εἰ δὲ μή, ἐνίοτε ἀναγκάζεσθαι καὶ δὶς καὶ τρὶς
πίνειν τούς τι τοιοῦτον ποιοῦντας. καὶ ὁ Σω-
κράτης· Ἔα, ἔφη, χαίρειν αὐτόν· ἀλλὰ μόνον
τὸ ἑαυτοῦ[2] παρασκευαζέτω ὡς καὶ δὶς δώσων,
ἐὰν δὲ δέῃ, καὶ τρίς. Ἀλλὰ σχεδὸν μέν τι
ἤδη, ἔφη ὁ Κρίτων· ἀλλά μοι πάλαι[3] πράγματα παρέχει. Ἔα αὐτόν, ἔφη. ἀλλ᾽ ὑμῖν
δὴ τοῖς δικασταῖς βούλομαι ἤδη τὸν λόγον
ἀποδοῦναι, ὥς μοι φαίνεται εἰκότως ἀνὴρ τῷ
ὄντι ἐν φιλοσοφίᾳ διατρίψας τὸν βίον θαρρεῖν

---

[1] Schanz brackets ἥξειν, following Hirschig.
[2] Schanz brackets τὸ ἑαυτοῦ.   [3] Schanz brackets πάλαι.

assert as positively as anything about such matters that I am going to gods who are good masters. And therefore, so far as that is concerned, I not only do not grieve, but I have great hopes that there is something in store for the dead, and, as has been said of old, something better for the good than for the wicked."

"Well," said Simmias, "do you intend to go away, Socrates, and keep your opinion to yourself, or would you let us share it? It seems to me that this is a good which belongs in common to us also, and at the same time, if you convince us by what you say, that will serve as your defence."

"I will try," he replied. "But first let us ask Crito there what he wants. He has apparently been trying to say something for a long time."

"Only, Socrates," said Crito, "that the man who is to administer the poison to you has been telling me for some time to warn you to talk as little as possible. He says people get warm when they talk and heat has a bad effect on the action of the poison; so sometimes he has to make those who talk too much drink twice or even three times."

And Socrates said: "Never mind him. Just let him do his part and prepare to give it twice or even, if necessary, three times."

"I was pretty sure that was what you would say," said Crito, "but he has been bothering me for a long time."

"Never mind him," said Socrates. "I wish now to explain to you, my judges, the reason why I think a man who has really spent his life in philosophy is

64 μέλλων ἀποθανεῖσθαι καὶ εὔελπις εἶναι ἐκεῖ
μέγιστα οἴσεσθαι ἀγαθά, ἐπειδὰν τελευτήσῃ·
πῶς ἂν οὖν δὴ τοῦθ' οὕτως ἔχοι, ὦ Σιμμία τε
καὶ Κέβης, ἐγὼ πειράσομαι φράσαι.

9. Κινδυνεύουσι γὰρ ὅσοι τυγχάνουσιν ὀρθῶς
ἁπτόμενοι φιλοσοφίας λεληθέναι τοὺς ἄλλους,
ὅτι οὐδὲν ἄλλο αὐτοὶ ἐπιτηδεύουσιν ἢ ἀποθνῄσκειν τε καὶ τεθνάναι. εἰ οὖν τοῦτο ἀληθές,
ἄτοπον δήπου ἂν εἴη προθυμεῖσθαι μὲν ἐν παντὶ
τῷ βίῳ μηδὲν ἄλλο ἢ τοῦτο, ἥκοντος δὲ δὴ αὐτοῦ
ἀγανακτεῖν, ὃ πάλαι προεθυμοῦντό τε καὶ ἐπετή-
δευον. καὶ ὁ Σιμμίας γελάσας· Νὴ τὸν Δία,
B ἔφη, ὦ Σώκρατες, οὐ πάνυ γέ με νῦν γελα-
σείοντα ἐποίησας γελάσαι. οἶμαι γὰρ ἂν δὴ
τοὺς πολλοὺς αὐτὸ τοῦτο ἀκούσαντας δοκεῖν
εὖ πάνυ εἰρῆσθαι εἰς τοὺς φιλοσοφοῦντας καὶ
ξυμφάναι ἂν τοὺς μὲν παρ' ἡμῖν ἀνθρώπους
καὶ πάνυ, ὅτι τῷ ὄντι οἱ φιλοσοφοῦντες θανατῶσι
καὶ σφᾶς γε οὐ λελήθασιν, ὅτι ἄξιοί εἰσιν τοῦτο
πάσχειν. Καὶ ἀληθῆ γ' ἂν λέγοιεν, ὦ Σιμμία,
πλήν γε τοῦ σφᾶς μὴ λεληθέναι. λέληθεν
γὰρ αὐτοὺς ᾗ τε θανατῶσι καὶ ᾗ ἄξιοί εἰσιν
θανάτου καὶ οἵου θανάτου οἱ ὡς ἀληθῶς φιλό-
C σοφοι. εἴπωμεν γάρ, ἔφη, πρὸς ἡμᾶς αὐτούς,
χαίρειν εἰπόντες ἐκείνοις· ἡγούμεθά τι τὸν
θάνατον εἶναι; Πάνυ γε, ἔφη ὑπολαβὼν ὁ
Σιμμίας. Ἆρα μὴ ἄλλο τι ἢ τὴν τῆς ψυχῆς
ἀπὸ τοῦ σώματος ἀπαλλαγήν; καὶ εἶναι τοῦτο
τὸ τεθνάναι, χωρὶς μὲν ἀπὸ τῆς ψυχῆς ἀπαλλαγὲν
αὐτὸ καθ' αὑτὸ τὸ σῶμα γεγονέναι, χωρὶς δὲ
τὴν ψυχὴν ἀπὸ τοῦ σώματος ἀπαλλαγεῖσαν

naturally of good courage when he is to die, and has strong hopes that when he is dead he will attain the greatest blessings in that other land. So I will try to tell you, Simmias, and Cebes, how this would be.

"Other people are likely not to be aware that those who pursue philosophy aright study nothing but dying and being dead. Now if this is true, it would be absurd to be eager for nothing but this all their lives, and then to be troubled when that came for which they had all along been eagerly practising."

And Simmias laughed and said, " By Zeus, Socrates, I don't feel much like laughing just now, but you made me laugh. For I think the multitude, if they heard what you just said about the philosophers, would say you were quite right, and our people at home would agree entirely with you that philosophers desire death, and they would add that they know very well that the philosophers deserve it."

" And they would be speaking the truth, Simmias, except in the matter of knowing very well. For they do not know in what way the real philosophers desire death, nor in what way they deserve death, nor what kind of a death it is. Let us then," said he, "speak with one another, paying no further attention to them. Do we think there is such a thing as death ? "

"Certainly," replied Simmias.

"We believe, do we not, that death is the separation of the soul from the body, and that the state of being dead is the state in which the body is separated from the soul and exists alone by itself and the soul is separated from the body and exists

αὐτὴν καθ' αὑτὴν εἶναι; ἆρα μὴ ἄλλο τι ἢ[1]
θάνατος ἢ τοῦτο; Οὔκ, ἀλλὰ τοῦτο, ἔφη.
Σκέψαι δή, ὦ ἀγαθέ, ἐὰν ἄρα καὶ σοὶ ξυνδοκῇ

D ἅπερ ἐμοί. ἐκ γὰρ τούτων μᾶλλον οἶμαι ἡμᾶς
εἴσεσθαι περὶ ὧν σκοποῦμεν. φαίνεταί σοι φιλοσόφου ἀνδρὸς εἶναι ἐσπουδακέναι περὶ τὰς ἡδονὰς
καλουμένας τὰς τοιάσδε, οἷον σίτων τε καὶ
ποτῶν; Ἥκιστα, ὦ Σώκρατες, ἔφη ὁ Σιμμίας.
Τί δέ; τὰς τῶν ἀφροδισίων; Οὐδαμῶς. Τί δέ;
τὰς ἄλλας τὰς περὶ τὸ σῶμα θεραπείας δοκεῖ σοι
ἐντίμους ἡγεῖσθαι ὁ τοιοῦτος; οἷον ἱματίων διαφε-
ρόντων κτήσεις καὶ ὑποδημάτων καὶ τοὺς ἄλλους
καλλωπισμοὺς τοὺς περὶ τὸ σῶμα πότερον τιμᾶν

E δοκεῖ σοι ἢ ἀτιμάζειν, καθ' ὅσον μὴ πολλὴ
ἀνάγκη μετέχειν αὐτῶν; Ἀτιμάζειν ἔμοιγε δοκεῖ,
ἔφη, ὅ γε ὡς ἀληθῶς φιλόσοφος. Οὐκοῦν ὅλως
δοκεῖ σοι, ἔφη, ἡ τοῦ τοιούτου πραγματεία
οὐ περὶ τὸ σῶμα εἶναι, ἀλλὰ καθ' ὅσον δύναται
ἀφεστάναι αὐτοῦ, πρὸς δὲ τὴν ψυχὴν τετράφθαι;
Ἔμοιγε. Ἆρ' οὖν πρῶτον μὲν ἐν τοῖς τοιούτοις
δῆλός ἐστιν ὁ φιλόσοφος ἀπολύων ὅ τι μάλιστα

65 τὴν ψυχὴν ἀπὸ τῆς τοῦ σώματος κοινωνίας
διαφερόντως τῶν ἄλλων ἀνθρώπων; Φαίνεται.
Καὶ δοκεῖ γε δήπου, ὦ Σιμμία, τοῖς πολλοῖς
ἀνθρώποις, ᾧ μηδὲν ἡδὺ τῶν τοιούτων μηδὲ
μετέχει αὐτῶν, οὐκ ἄξιον εἶναι ζῆν, ἀλλ' ἐγγύς
τι τείνειν τοῦ τεθνάναι ὁ μηδὲν φροντίζων τῶν
ἡδονῶν αἳ διὰ τοῦ σώματός εἰσιν. Πάνυ μὲν
οὖν ἀληθῆ λέγεις.

---

[1] Schanz brackets ἢ.

alone by itself? Is death anything other than this?"
"No, it is this," said he.

"Now, my friend, see if you agree with me ; for, if you do, I think we shall get more light on our subject. Do you think a philosopher would be likely to care much about the so-called pleasures, such as eating and drinking?"

"By no means, Socrates," said Simmias.

"How about the pleasures of love?"

"Certainly not."

"Well, do you think such a man would think much of the other cares of the body—I mean such as the possession of fine clothes and shoes and the other personal adornments? Do you think he would care about them or despise them, except so far as it is necessary to have them?"

"I think the true philosopher would despise them," he replied.

"Altogether, then, you think that such a man would not devote himself to the body, but would, so far as he was able, turn away from the body and concern himself with the soul?"

"Yes."

"To begin with, then, it is clear that in such matters the philosopher, more than other men, separates the soul from communion with the body?"

"It is."

"Now certainly most people think that a man who takes no pleasure and has no part in such things doesn't deserve to live, and that one who cares nothing for the pleasures of the body is about as good as dead."

"That is very true."

10. Τί δὲ δὴ περὶ αὐτὴν τὴν τῆς φρονήσεως κτῆσιν; πότερον ἐμπόδιον τὸ σῶμα ἢ οὔ, ἐάν τις αὐτὸ ἐν τῇ ζητήσει κοινωνὸν συμπαραλαμβάνῃ;

B οἷον τὸ τοιόνδε λέγω· ἆρα ἔχει ἀλήθειάν τινα ὄψις τε καὶ ἀκοὴ τοῖς ἀνθρώποις, ἢ τά γε τοιαῦτα καὶ οἱ ποιηταὶ ἡμῖν ἀεὶ θρυλοῦσιν, ὅτι οὔτ᾽ ἀκούομεν ἀκριβὲς οὐδὲν οὔτε ὁρῶμεν; καίτοι εἰ αὗται τῶν περὶ τὸ σῶμα αἰσθήσεων μὴ ἀκριβεῖς εἰσιν μηδὲ σαφεῖς, σχολῇ αἵ γε ἄλλαι· πᾶσαι γάρ που τούτων φαυλότεραί εἰσιν· ἢ σοὶ οὐ δοκοῦσιν; Πάνυ μὲν οὖν, ἔφη. Πότε οὖν, ἦ δ᾽ ὅς, ἡ ψυχὴ τῆς ἀληθείας ἅπτεται; ὅταν μὲν γὰρ μετὰ τοῦ σώματος ἐπιχειρῇ τι σκοπεῖν, δῆλον ὅτι τότε ἐξαπατᾶται ὑπ᾽ αὐτοῦ.

C Ἀληθῆ λέγεις. Ἆρ᾽ οὖν οὐκ ἐν τῷ λογίζεσθαι, εἴπερ που ἄλλοθι, κατάδηλον αὐτῇ γίγνεταί τι τῶν ὄντων; Ναί. Λογίζεται δέ γέ που τότε κάλλιστα, ὅταν αὐτὴν τούτων μηδὲν παραλυπῇ, μήτε ἀκοὴ μήτε ὄψις μήτε ἀλγηδὼν μηδέ τις ἡδονή, ἀλλ᾽ ὅ τι μάλιστα αὐτὴ καθ᾽ αὑτὴν γίγνηται ἐῶσα χαίρειν τὸ σῶμα, καὶ καθ᾽ ὅσον δύναται μὴ κοινωνοῦσα αὐτῷ μηδ᾽ ἁπτομένη ὀρέγηται τοῦ ὄντος. Ἔστι ταῦτα. Οὐκοῦν καὶ ἐνταῦθα

D ἡ τοῦ φιλοσόφου ψυχὴ μάλιστα ἀτιμάζει τὸ σῶμα καὶ φεύγει ἀπ᾽ αὐτοῦ, ζητεῖ δὲ αὐτὴ καθ᾽ αὑτὴν γίγνεσθαι; Φαίνεται. Τί δὲ δὴ τὰ τοιάδε, ὦ Σιμμία; φαμέν τι εἶναι δίκαιον αὐτὸ ἢ οὐδέν; Φαμὲν μέντοι νὴ Δία. Καὶ

"Now, how about the acquirement of pure knowledge? Is the body a hindrance or not, if it is made to share in the search for wisdom? What I mean is this: Have the sight and hearing of men any truth in them, or is it true, as the poets are always telling us, that we neither hear nor see anything accurately? And yet if these two physical senses are not accurate or exact, the rest are not likely to be, for they are inferior to these. Do you not think so?"

"Certainly I do," he replied.

"Then," said he, "when does the soul attain to truth? For when it tries to consider anything in company with the body, it is evidently deceived by it."

"True."

"In thought, then, if at all, something of the realities becomes clear to it?"

"Yes."

"But it thinks best when none of these things troubles it, neither hearing nor sight, nor pain nor any pleasure, but it is, so far as possible, alone by itself, and takes leave of the body, and avoiding, so far as it can, all association or contact with the body, reaches out toward the reality."

"That is true."

"In this matter also, then, the soul of the philosopher greatly despises the body and avoids it and strives to be alone by itself?"

"Evidently."

"Now how about such things as this, Simmias? Do we think there is such a thing as absolute justice, or not?"

"We certainly think there is."

καλόν γέ τι καὶ ἀγαθόν; Πῶς δ' οὔ; Ἤδη
οὖν πώποτέ τι τῶν τοιούτων τοῖς ὀφθαλμοῖς
εἶδες; Οὐδαμῶς, ἦ δ' ὅς. 'Αλλ' ἄλλη τινὶ
αἰσθήσει τῶν διὰ τοῦ σώματος ἐφήψω αὐτῶν;
λέγω δὲ περὶ πάντων, οἷον μεγέθους πέρι, ὑγιείας,
ἰσχύος, καὶ τῶν ἄλλων ἑνὶ λόγῳ ἁπάντων τῆς
E οὐσίας, ὃ τυγχάνει ἕκαστον ὄν· ἆρα διὰ τοῦ
σώματος αὐτῶν τὸ ἀληθέστατον θεωρεῖται, ἢ
ὧδε ἔχει· ὃς ἂν μάλιστα ἡμῶν καὶ ἀκριβέστατα
παρασκευάσηται αὐτὸ ἕκαστον διανοηθῆναι περὶ
οὗ σκοπεῖ, οὗτος ἂν ἐγγύτατα ἴοι τοῦ γνῶναι
ἕκαστον; Πάνυ μὲν οὖν. 'Αρ' οὖν ἐκεῖνος ἂν
τοῦτο ποιήσειε καθαρώτατα, ὅστις ὅτι μάλιστα
αὐτῇ τῇ διανοίᾳ ἴοι ἐφ' ἕκαστον, μήτε τὴν ὄψιν
παρατιθέμενος ἐν τῷ διανοεῖσθαι μήτε τινὰ ἄλλην
66 αἴσθησιν ἐφέλκων μηδεμίαν μετὰ τοῦ λογισμοῦ,
ἀλλ' αὐτῇ καθ' αὑτὴν εἰλικρινεῖ τῇ διανοίᾳ
χρώμενος αὐτὸ καθ' αὑτὸ εἰλικρινὲς ἕκαστον
ἐπιχειροῖ θηρεύειν τῶν ὄντων, ἀπαλλαγεὶς ὅτι
μάλιστα ὀφθαλμῶν τε καὶ ὤτων καὶ ὡς ἔπος
εἰπεῖν ξύμπαντος τοῦ σώματος, ὡς ταράττοντος
καὶ οὐκ ἐῶντος τὴν ψυχὴν κτήσασθαι ἀλήθειάν
τε καὶ φρόνησιν, ὅταν κοινωνῇ, ἆρ' οὐχ οὗτός
ἐστιν, ὦ Σιμμία, εἴπερ τις καὶ ἄλλος, ὁ τευξόμενος
τοῦ ὄντος; Ὑπερφυῶς, ἔφη ὁ Σιμμίας, ὡς ἀληθῆ
λέγεις, ὦ Σώκρατες.

B   11. Οὐκοῦν ἀνάγκη, ἔφη, ἐκ πάντων τούτων
παρίστασθαι δόξαν τοιάνδε τινὰ τοῖς γνησίως
φιλοσόφοις, ὥστε καὶ πρὸς ἀλλήλους τοιαῦτα
ἄττα λέγειν, ὅτι κινδυνεύει τοι ὥσπερ ἀτραπός
τις ἐκφέρειν ἡμᾶς, ὅτι, ἕως ἂν τὸ σῶμα ἔχωμεν
μετὰ τοῦ λόγου ἐν τῇ σκέψει, καὶ συμπεφυρμένη

" And absolute beauty and goodness."

" Of course."

" Well, did you ever see anything of that kind with your eyes ? "

" Certainly not," said he.

" Or did you ever reach them with any of the bodily senses ? I am speaking of all such things, as size, health, strength, and in short the essence or underlying quality of everything. Is their true nature contemplated by means of the body ? Is it not rather the case that he who prepares himself most carefully to understand the true essence of each thing that he examines would come nearest to the knowledge of it ? "

" Certainly."

" Would not that man do this most perfectly who approaches each thing, so far as possible, with the reason alone, not introducing sight into his reasoning nor dragging in any of the other senses along with his thinking, but who employs pure, absolute reason in his attempt to search out the pure, absolute essence of things, and who removes himself, so far as possible, from eyes and ears, and, in a word, from his whole body, because he feels that its companionship disturbs the soul and hinders it from attaining truth and wisdom? Is not this the man, Simmias, if anyone, to attain to the knowledge of reality ? "

" That is true as true can be, Socrates," said Simmias.

" Then," said he, " all this must cause good lovers of wisdom to think and say one to the other something like this : ' There seems to be a short cut which leads us and our argument to the conclusion in our search that so long as we have the body, and the

ἦ ἡμῶν ἡ ψυχὴ μετὰ τοιούτου κακοῦ, οὐ μή
ποτε κτησώμεθα ἱκανῶς οὗ ἐπιθυμοῦμεν· φαμὲν
δὲ τοῦτο εἶναι τὸ ἀληθές. μυρίας μὲν γὰρ ἡμῖν
ἀσχολίας παρέχει τὸ σῶμα διὰ τὴν ἀναγκαίαν
C τροφήν· ἔτι δὲ ἄν τινες νόσοι προσπέσωσιν,
ἐμποδίζουσιν ἡμῶν τὴν τοῦ ὄντος θήραν. ἐρώτων
δὲ καὶ ἐπιθυμιῶν καὶ φόβων καὶ εἰδώλων παντο-
δαπῶν καὶ φλυαρίας ἐμπίμπλησιν ἡμᾶς πολλῆς,
ὥστε τὸ λεγόμενον ὡς ἀληθῶς τῷ ὄντι ὑπ' αὐτοῦ
οὐδὲ φρονῆσαι ἡμῖν ἐγγίγνεται οὐδέποτε οὐδέν.
καὶ γὰρ πολέμους καὶ στάσεις καὶ μάχας οὐδὲν
ἄλλο παρέχει ἢ τὸ σῶμα καὶ αἱ τούτου ἐπιθυμίαι.
διὰ γὰρ τὴν τῶν χρημάτων κτῆσιν πάντες οἱ
πόλεμοι γίγνονται, τὰ δὲ χρήματα ἀναγκαζόμεθα
D κτᾶσθαι διὰ τὸ σῶμα, δουλεύοντες τῇ τούτου
θεραπείᾳ· καὶ ἐκ τούτου ἀσχολίαν ἄγομεν φιλοσοφίας πέρι διὰ πάντα ταῦτα. τὸ δ' ἔσχατον πάντων,
ὅτι, ἐάν τις ἡμῖν καὶ σχολὴ γένηται ἀπ' αὐτοῦ
καὶ τραπώμεθα πρὸς τὸ σκοπεῖν τι, ἐν ταῖς
ζητήσεσιν αὖ πανταχοῦ παραπῖπτον θόρυβον
παρέχει καὶ ταραχὴν καὶ ἐκπλήττει, ὥστε μὴ
δύνασθαι ὑπ' αὐτοῦ καθορᾶν τἀληθές, ἀλλὰ τῷ
ὄντι ἡμῖν δέδεικται ὅτι, εἰ μέλλομέν ποτε καθαρῶς
τι εἴσεσθαι, ἀπαλλακτέον αὐτοῦ καὶ αὐτῇ τῇ
E ψυχῇ θεατέον αὐτὰ τὰ πράγματα· καὶ τότε, ὡς
ἔοικεν, ἡμῖν ἔσται οὗ ἐπιθυμοῦμέν τε καί φαμεν
ἐρασταὶ εἶναι, φρονήσεως, ἐπειδὰν τελευτήσωμεν,
ὡς ὁ λόγος σημαίνει, ζῶσιν δὲ οὔ. εἰ γὰρ μὴ
οἷόν τε μετὰ τοῦ σώματος μηδὲν καθαρῶς γνῶναι,
δυοῖν θάτερον, ἢ οὐδαμοῦ ἔστιν κτήσασθαι τὸ εἰδέναι ἢ τελευτήσασιν· τότε γὰρ αὐτὴ καθ' αὑτὴν ἡ
67 ψυχὴ ἔσται χωρὶς τοῦ σώματος, πρότερον δ' οὔ.

soul is contaminated by such an evil, we shall never
attain completely what we desire, that is, the truth.
For the body keeps us constantly busy by reason of
its need of sustenance; and moreover, if diseases
come upon it they hinder our pursuit of the truth.
And the body fills us with passions and desires and
fears, and all sorts of fancies and foolishness, so
that, as they say, it really and truly makes it
impossible for us to think at all. The body and its
desires are the only cause of wars and factions and
battles; for all wars arise for the sake of gaining
money, and we are compelled to gain money for the
sake of the body. We are slaves to its service. And
so, because of all these things, we have no leisure for
philosophy. But the worst of all is that if we do get
a bit of leisure and turn to philosophy, the body is
constantly breaking in upon our studies and disturb-
ing us with noise and confusion, so that it prevents
our beholding the truth, and in fact we perceive
that, if we are ever to know anything absolutely, we
must be free from the body and must behold the
actual realities with the eye of the soul alone. And
then, as our argument shows, when we are dead we
are likely to possess the wisdom which we desire and
claim to be enamoured of, but not while we live.
For, if pure knowledge is impossible while the body
is with us, one of two thing must follow, either it
cannot be acquired at all or only when we are dead;
for then the soul will be by itself apart from the
body, but not before. And while we live, we shall,

καὶ ἐν ᾧ ἂν ζῶμεν, οὕτως, ὡς ἔοικεν, ἐγγυτάτω
ἐσόμεθα τοῦ εἰδέναι, ἐὰν ὅ τι μάλιστα μηδὲν
ὁμιλῶμεν τῷ σώματι μηδὲ κοινωνῶμεν, ὅ τι μὴ
πᾶσα ἀνάγκη, μηδὲ ἀναπιμπλώμεθα τῆς τούτου
φύσεως, ἀλλὰ καθαρεύωμεν ἀπ' αὐτοῦ, ἕως ἂν
ὁ θεὸς αὐτὸς ἀπολύσῃ ἡμᾶς· καὶ οὕτω μὲν καθαροὶ
ἀπαλλαττόμενοι τῆς τοῦ σώματος ἀφροσύνης,
ὡς τὸ εἰκός, μετὰ τοιούτων τε ἐσόμεθα καὶ
γνωσόμεθα δι' ἡμῶν αὐτῶν πᾶν τὸ εἰλικρινές·
B τοῦτο δ' ἐστὶν ἴσως τὸ ἀληθές. μὴ καθαρῷ
γὰρ καθαροῦ ἐφάπτεσθαι μὴ οὐ θεμιτὸν ᾖ.
τοιαῦτα οἶμαι, ὦ Σιμμία, ἀναγκαῖον εἶναι πρὸς
ἀλλήλους λέγειν τε καὶ δοξάζειν πάντας τοὺς
ὀρθῶς φιλομαθεῖς. ἢ οὐ δοκεῖ σοι οὕτως; Παντός
γε μᾶλλον, ὦ Σώκρατες.

12. Οὐκοῦν, ἔφη ὁ Σωκράτης, εἰ ταῦτα ἀληθῆ, ὦ
ἑταῖρε, πολλὴ ἐλπὶς ἀφικομένῳ οἷ ἐγὼ πορεύομαι,
ἐκεῖ ἱκανῶς, εἴπερ που ἄλλοθι, κτήσασθαι τοῦτο
οὗ ἕνεκα ἡ πολλὴ πραγματεία ἡμῖν ἐν τῷ παρελθόντι βίῳ γέγονεν, ὥστε ἥ γε ἀποδημία ἡ νῦν μοι
C προστεταγμένη μετὰ ἀγαθῆς ἐλπίδος γίγνεται καὶ
ἄλλῳ ἀνδρί, ὃς ἡγεῖταί οἱ παρεσκευάσθαι τὴν
διάνοιαν ὥσπερ κεκαθαρμένην. Πάνυ μὲν οὖν,
ἔφη ὁ Σιμμίας. Κάθαρσις δὲ εἶναι ἆρα οὐ τοῦτο
ξυμβαίνει, ὅπερ πάλαι ἐν τῷ λόγῳ λέγεται, τὸ
χωρίζειν ὅ τι μάλιστα ἀπὸ τοῦ σώματος τὴν ψυχὴν
καὶ ἐθίσαι αὐτὴν καθ' αὑτὴν πανταχόθεν ἐκ τοῦ
σώματος συναγείρεσθαί τε καὶ ἀθροίζεσθαι, καὶ
οἰκεῖν κατὰ τὸ δυνατὸν καὶ ἐν τῷ νῦν παρόντι
D καὶ ἐν τῷ ἔπειτα μόνην καθ' αὑτήν, ἐκλυομένην
ὥσπερ ἐκ δεσμῶν ἐκ τοῦ σώματος; Πάνυ μὲν

I think, be nearest to knowledge when we avoid, so far as possible, intercourse and communion with the body, except what is absolutely necessary, and are not filled with its nature, but keep ourselves pure from it until God himself sets us free. And in this way, freeing ourselves from the foolishness of the body and being pure, we shall, I think, be with the pure and shall know of ourselves all that is pure,—and that is, perhaps, the truth. For it cannot be that the impure attain the pure.' Such words as these, I think, Simmias, all who are rightly lovers of knowledge must say to each other and such must be their thoughts. Do you not agree ? "

" Most assuredly, Socrates."

" Then," said Socrates, " if this is true, my friend, I have great hopes that when I reach the place to which I am going, I shall there, if anywhere, attain fully to that which has been my chief object in my past life, so that the journey which is now imposed upon me is begun with good hope ; and the like hope exists for every man who thinks that his mind has been purified and made ready."

" Certainly," said Simmias.

" And does not the purification consist in this which has been mentioned long ago in our discourse, in separating, so far as possible, the soul from the body and teaching the soul the habit of collecting and bringing itself together from all parts of the body, and living, so far as it can, both now and hereafter, alone by itself, freed from the body as from fetters ? "

" Certainly," said he.

οὖν, ἔφη. Οὐκοῦν τοῦτό γε θάνατος ὀνομάζεται,
λύσις καὶ χωρισμὸς ψυχῆς ἀπὸ σώματος; Παντάπασί γε, ἦ δ᾽ ὅς. Λύειν δέ γε αὐτήν, ὥς φαμεν,
προθυμοῦνται ἀεὶ μάλιστα καὶ μόνοι οἱ φιλοσοφοῦντες ὀρθῶς, καὶ τὸ μελέτημα αὐτὸ τοῦτό ἐστιν
τῶν φιλοσόφων, λύσις καὶ χωρισμὸς ψυχῆς ἀπὸ
σώματος, ἢ οὔ; Φαίνεται. Οὐκοῦν, ὅπερ ἐν ἀρχῇ
ἔλεγον, γέλοιον ἂν εἴη ἄνδρα παρασκευάζονθ᾽
ἑαυτὸν ἐν τῷ βίῳ ὅ τι ἐγγυτάτω ὄντα τοῦ
E τεθνάναι οὕτω ζῆν, κἄπειθ᾽ ἥκοντος αὐτῷ τούτου ἀγανακτεῖν.[1] οὐ γέλοιον; Πῶς δ᾽ οὔ; Τῷ
ὄντι ἄρα, ἔφη, ὦ Σιμμία, οἱ ὀρθῶς φιλοσοφοῦντες ἀποθνῄσκειν μελετῶσι, καὶ τὸ τεθνάναι
ἥκιστα αὐτοῖς ἀνθρώπων φοβερόν. ἐκ τῶνδε δὲ
σκόπει. εἰ γὰρ διαβέβληνται μὲν πανταχῇ τῷ
σώματι, αὐτὴν δὲ καθ᾽ αὑτὴν ἐπιθυμοῦσι τὴν
ψυχὴν ἔχειν, τούτου δὲ γιγνομένου εἰ φοβοῖντο
καὶ ἀγανακτοῖεν, οὐ πολλὴ ἂν ἀλογία εἴη, εἰ
μὴ ἄσμενοι ἐκεῖσε ἴοιεν, οἷ ἀφικομένοις ἐλπίς
68 ἐστιν οὗ διὰ βίου ἤρων τυχεῖν· ἤρων δὲ φρονήσεως·
ᾧ τε διεβέβληντο, τούτου ἀπηλλάχθαι συνόντος
αὐτοῖς; ἢ ἀνθρωπίνων μὲν παιδικῶν καὶ γυναικῶν
καὶ υἱέων ἀποθανόντων πολλοὶ δὴ ἑκόντες
ἠθέλησαν εἰς Ἅιδου ἐλθεῖν, ὑπὸ ταύτης ἀγόμενοι
τῆς ἐλπίδος, τῆς τοῦ ὄψεσθαί τε ἐκεῖ ὧν ἐπεθύ-
μουν καὶ συνέσεσθαι· φρονήσεως δὲ ἄρα τις
τῷ ὄντι ἐρῶν, καὶ λαβὼν σφόδρα τὴν αὐτὴν
ταύτην ἐλπίδα, μηδαμοῦ ἄλλοθι ἐντεύξεσθαι αὐτῇ
B ἀξίως λόγου ἢ ἐν Ἅιδου, ἀγανακτήσει τε ἀπο-
θνῄσκων καὶ οὐκ ἄσμενος εἶσιν αὐτόσε; οἴεσθαί

---

[1] After ἀγανακτεῖν BT read οὐ γέλοιον; Schanz brackets
these words. Burnet reads γέλοιον·, giving it to Simmias.

" Well, then, this is what we call death, is it not, a release and separation from the body?"

" Exactly so," said he.

" But, as we hold, the true philosophers and they alone are always most eager to release the soul, and just this—the release and separation of the soul from the body—is their study, is it not?"

" Obviously."

" Then, as I said in the beginning, it would be absurd if a man who had been all his life fitting himself to live as nearly in a state of death as he could, should then be disturbed when death came to him. Would it not be absurd?"

" Of course."

" In fact, then, Simmias," said he, " the true philosophers practise dying, and death is less terrible to them than to any other men. Consider it in this way. They are in every way hostile to the body and they desire to have the soul apart by itself alone. Would it not be very foolish if they should be frightened and troubled when this very thing happens, and if they should not be glad to go to the place where there is hope of attaining what they longed for all through life—and they longed for wisdom—and of escaping from the companionship of that which they hated? When human loves or wives or sons have died, many men have willingly gone to the other world led by the hope of seeing there those whom they longed for, and of being with them; and shall he who is really in love with wisdom and has a firm belief that he can find it nowhere else than in the other world grieve when he dies and not be glad to go there? We cannot

γε χρή, ἐὰν τῷ ὄντι γε ᾖ, ὦ ἑταῖρε, φιλόσοφος·
σφόδρα γὰρ αὐτῷ ταῦτα δόξει, μηδαμοῦ ἄλλοθι
καθαρῶς ἐντεύξεσθαι φρονήσει ἀλλ' ἢ ἐκεῖ. εἰ
δὲ τοῦτο οὕτως ἔχει, ὅπερ ἄρτι ἔλεγον, οὐ πολλὴ
ἂν ἀλογία εἴη, εἰ φοβοῖτο τὸν θάνατον ὁ τοιοῦτος;
Πολλὴ μέντοι νὴ Δία, ἦ δ' ὅς.

13. Οὐκοῦν ἱκανόν σοι τεκμήριον, ἔφη, τοῦτο
ἀνδρὸς ὃν ἂν ἴδῃς ἀγανακτοῦντα μέλλοντα ἀποθανεῖσθαι, ὅτι οὐκ ἄρ' ἦν φιλόσοφος, ἀλλά τις
C φιλοσώματος; ὁ αὐτὸς δέ που οὗτος τυγχάνει ὢν
καὶ φιλοχρήματος καὶ φιλότιμος, ἤτοι τὰ ἕτερα
τούτων ἢ ἀμφότερα. Πάνυ, ἔφη, ἔχει οὕτως, ὡς
λέγεις. Ἆρ' οὖν, ἔφη, ὦ Σιμμία, οὐ καὶ ἡ ὀνομα-
ζομένη ἀνδρεία τοῖς οὕτω διακειμένοις μάλιστα
προσήκει; Πάντως δήπου, ἔφη. Οὐκοῦν καὶ ἡ
σωφροσύνη, ἣν καὶ οἱ πολλοὶ ὀνομάζουσι σωφροσύνην, τὸ περὶ τὰς ἐπιθυμίας μὴ ἐπτοῆσθαι, ἀλλ'
ὀλιγώρως ἔχειν καὶ κοσμίως, ἆρ' οὐ τούτοις μόνοις
προσήκει τοῖς μάλιστα τοῦ σώματος ὀλιγωροῦσίν
D τε καὶ ἐν φιλοσοφίᾳ ζῶσιν; Ἀνάγκη, ἔφη. Εἰ
γὰρ ἐθέλεις, ἦ δ' ὅς, ἐννοῆσαι τήν γε τῶν ἄλλων
ἀνδρείαν τε καὶ σωφροσύνην, δόξει σοι εἶναι
ἄτοπος. Πῶς δή, ὦ Σώκρατες; Οἶσθα, ἦ δ' ὅς,
ὅτι τὸν θάνατον ἡγοῦνται πάντες οἱ ἄλλοι τῶν
μεγάλων κακῶν; Καὶ μάλ', ἔφη. Οὐκοῦν φόβῳ
μειζόνων κακῶν ὑπομένουσιν αὐτῶν οἱ ἀνδρεῖοι
τὸν θάνατον, ὅταν ὑπομένωσιν; Ἔστι ταῦτα. Τῷ
δεδιέναι ἄρα καὶ δέει ἀνδρεῖοί εἰσι πάντες πλὴν οἱ

think that, my friend, if he is really a philosopher;
for he will confidently believe that he will find pure
wisdom nowhere else than in the other world.   And
if this is so, would it not be very foolish for such a
man to fear death?"

"Very foolish, certainly," said he.

"Then is it not," said Socrates, "a sufficient
indication, when you see a man troubled because he
is going to die, that he was not a lover of wisdom but
a lover of the body?   And this same man is also
a lover of money and of honour, one or both."

"Certainly," said he, "it is as you say."

"Then, Simmias," he continued, "is not that
which is called courage especially characteristic of
philosophers?"

"By all means," said he.

"And self-restraint—that which is commonly called
self-restraint, which consists in not being excited by
the passions and in being superior to them and
acting in a seemly way—is not that characteristic of
those alone who despise the body and pass their
lives in philosophy?"

"Necessarily," said he.

"For," said Socrates, "if you care to consider
the courage and the self-restraint of other men, you
will see that they are absurd."

"How so, Socrates?"

"You know, do you not, that all other men count
death among the great evils?"

"They certainly do."

"And do not brave men face death—when they
do face it—through fear of greater evils?"

"That is true."

"Then all except philosophers are brave through

φιλόσοφοι. καίτοι ἄλογόν γε δέει τινὰ καὶ δειλίᾳ

E ἀνδρεῖον εἶναι. Πάνυ μὲν οὖν. Τί δὲ οἱ κόσμιοι
αὐτῶν; οὐ ταὐτὸν τοῦτο πεπόνθασιν· ἀκολασίᾳ
τινὶ σώφρονές εἰσιν; καίτοι φαμέν γε ἀδύνατον
εἶναι, ἀλλ' ὅμως αὐτοῖς συμβαίνει τούτῳ ὅμοιον
τὸ πάθος τὸ περὶ ταύτην τὴν εὐήθη σωφροσύνην·
φοβούμενοι γὰρ ἑτέρων ἡδονῶν στερηθῆναι καὶ
ἐπιθυμοῦντες ἐκείνων, ἄλλων ἀπέχονται ὑπ'
ἄλλων κρατούμενοι. καίτοι καλοῦσί γε ἀκολασίαν

69 τὸ ὑπὸ τῶν ἡδονῶν ἄρχεσθαι· ἀλλ' ὅμως συμβαίνει
αὐτοῖς κρατουμένοις ὑφ' ἡδονῶν κρατεῖν ἄλλων[1]
ἡδονῶν. τοῦτο δ' ὅμοιόν ἐστιν ᾧ νῦν δὴ ἐλέγετο,
τῷ τρόπον τινὰ δι' ἀκολασίαν αὐτοὺς σεσω-
φρονίσθαι. Ἔοικε γάρ. Ὦ μακάριε Σιμμία,
μὴ γὰρ οὐχ αὕτη ᾖ ἡ ὀρθὴ πρὸς ἀρετὴν ἀλλαγή,
ἡδονὰς πρὸς ἡδονὰς καὶ λύπας πρὸς λύπας καὶ
φόβον πρὸς φόβον καταλλάττεσθαι, καὶ μείζω
πρὸς ἐλάττω, ὥσπερ νομίσματα, ἀλλ' ᾖ ἐκεῖνο
μόνον τὸ νόμισμα ὀρθόν, ἀντὶ οὗ δεῖ ἅπαντα

B ταῦτα καταλλάττεσθαι, φρόνησις, καὶ τούτου
μὲν πάντα καὶ μετὰ τούτου ὠνούμενά τε καὶ
πιπρασκόμενα τῷ ὄντι ᾖ καὶ ἀνδρεία καὶ σωφροσύνη καὶ δικαιοσύνη καὶ ξυλλήβδην ἀληθὴς
ἀρετὴ μετὰ φρονήσεως, καὶ προσγιγνομένων καὶ
ἀπογιγνομένων καὶ ἡδονῶν καὶ φόβων καὶ τῶν
ἄλλων πάντων τῶν τοιούτων· χωριζόμενα δὲ
φρονήσεως καὶ ἀλλαττόμενα ἀντὶ ἀλλήλων μὴ
σκιαγραφία τις ᾖ ἡ τοιαύτη ἀρετὴ καὶ τῷ ὄντι
ἀνδραποδώδης τε καὶ οὐδὲν ὑγιὲς οὐδ' ἀληθὲς
ἔχῃ, τὸ δ' ἀληθὲς τῷ ὄντι ᾖ κάθαρσίς τις

[1] Schanz brackets ἄλλων.

fear. And yet it is absurd to be brave through fear and cowardice."

"Very true."

"And how about those of seemly conduct? Is their case not the same? They are self-restrained because of a kind of self-indulgence. We say, to be sure, that this is impossible, nevertheless their foolish self-restraint amounts to little more than this; for they fear that they may be deprived of certain pleasures which they desire, and so they refrain from some because they are under the sway of others. And yet being ruled by pleasures is called self-indulgence. Nevertheless they conquer pleasures because they are conquered by other pleasures. Now this is about what I said just now, that they are self-restrained by a kind of self-indulgence."

"So it seems."

"My dear Simmias, I suspect that this is not the right way to purchase virtue, by exchanging pleasures for pleasures, and pains for pains, and fear for fear, and greater for less, as if they were coins, but the only right coinage, for which all those things must be exchanged and by means of and with which all these things are to be bought and sold, is in fact wisdom; and courage and self-restraint and justice and, in short, true virtue exist only with wisdom, whether pleasures and fears and other things of that sort are added or taken away. And virtue which consists in the exchange of such things for each other without wisdom, is but a painted imitation of virtue and is really slavish and has nothing healthy or true in it; but truth is in

PLATO

C τῶν τοιούτων πάντων, καὶ ἡ σωφροσύνη καὶ ἡ δικαιοσύνη καὶ ἀνδρεία καὶ αὐτὴ ἡ φρόνησις μὴ καθαρμός τις ᾖ. καὶ κινδυνεύουσι καὶ οἱ τὰς τελετὰς ἡμῖν οὗτοι καταστήσαντες οὐ φαῦλοι εἶναι, ἀλλὰ τῷ ὄντι πάλαι αἰνίττεσθαι ὅτι ὃς ἂν ἀμύητος καὶ ἀτέλεστος εἰς Ἅιδου ἀφίκηται, ἐν βορβόρῳ κείσεται, ὁ δὲ κεκαθαρμένος τε καὶ τετελεσμένος ἐκεῖσε ἀφικόμενος μετὰ θεῶν οἰκήσει. εἰσὶν γὰρ δή, ὥς φασιν οἱ περὶ τὰς τελετάς, ναρθηκοφόροι μὲν πολλοί, βάκχοι δέ τε παῦροι.

D οὗτοι δ' εἰσὶν κατὰ τὴν ἐμὴν δόξαν οὐκ ἄλλοι ἢ οἱ πεφιλοσοφηκότες ὀρθῶς. ὧν δὴ καὶ ἐγὼ κατά γε τὸ δυνατὸν οὐδὲν ἀπέλιπον ἐν τῷ βίῳ, ἀλλὰ παντὶ τρόπῳ προυθυμήθην γενέσθαι· εἰ δ' ὀρθῶς προυθυμήθην καί τι ἠνύσαμεν, ἐκεῖσε ἐλθόντες τὸ σαφὲς εἰσόμεθα, ἂν θεὸς ἐθέλῃ, ὀλίγον ὕστερον, ὡς ἐμοὶ δοκεῖ. ταῦτ' οὖν ἐγώ, ἔφη, ὦ Σιμμία τε καὶ Κέβης, ἀπολογοῦμαι, ὡς εἰκότως ὑμᾶς τε ἀπολείπων καὶ τοὺς ἐνθάδε δεσπότας οὐ χαλεπῶς

E φέρω οὐδ' ἀγανακτῶ, ἡγούμενος κἀκεῖ οὐδὲν ἧττον ἢ ἐνθάδε δεσπόταις τε ἀγαθοῖς ἐντεύξεσθαι καὶ ἑταίροις·[1] εἴ τι οὖν ὑμῖν πιθανώτερός εἰμι ἐν τῇ ἀπολογίᾳ ἢ τοῖς Ἀθηναίων δικασταῖς, εὖ ἂν ἔχοι.

14. Εἰπόντος δὴ τοῦ Σωκράτους ταῦτα ὑπολαβὼν ὁ Κέβης ἔφη· Ὦ Σώκρατες, τὰ μὲν ἄλλα

70 ἔμοιγε δοκεῖ καλῶς λέγεσθαι, τὰ δὲ περὶ τῆς ψυχῆς πολλὴν ἀπιστίαν παρέχει τοῖς ἀνθρώποις, μὴ ἐπειδὰν ἀπαλλαγῇ τοῦ σώματος, οὐδαμοῦ ἔτι ᾖ,

---

[1] After ἑταίροις, the MSS. read τοῖς δὲ πολλοῖς ἀπιστίαν παρέχει, "but the many do not believe this." Ast, followed by Schanz and Burnet, omits.

fact a purification from all these things, and self-restraint and justice and courage and wisdom itself are a kind of purification. And I fancy that those men who established the mysteries were not unenlightened, but in reality had a hidden meaning when they said long ago that whoever goes uninitiated and unsanctified to the other world will lie in the mire, but he who arrives there initiated and purified will dwell with the gods. For as they say in the mysteries, ' the thyrsus-bearers are many, but the mystics few' ; and these mystics are, I believe, those who have been true philosophers. And I in my life have, so far as I could, left nothing undone, and have striven in every way to make myself one of them. But whether I have striven aright and have met with success, I believe I shall know clearly, when I have arrived there, very soon, if it is God's will. This then, Simmias and Cebes, is the defence I offer to show that it is reasonable for me not to be grieved or troubled at leaving you and the rulers I have here, because I believe that there, no less than here, I shall find good rulers and friends. If now I am more successful in convincing you by my defence than I was in convincing my Athenian judges, it is well."

When Socrates had finished, Cebes answered and said : "Socrates, I agree to the other things you say, but in regard to the soul men are very prone to disbelief. They fear that when the soul leaves the body it no longer exists anywhere, and that on the

ἀλλ' ἐκείνῃ τῇ ἡμέρᾳ διαφθείρηταί τε καὶ ἀπολλύηται, ᾗ ἂν ὁ ἄνθρωπος ἀποθνήσκῃ· εὐθὺς
ἀπαλλαττομένη τοῦ σώματος καὶ ἐκβαίνουσα
ὥσπερ πνεῦμα ἢ καπνὸς διασκεδασθεῖσα οἴχηται
διαπτομένη καὶ οὐδὲν ἔτι οὐδαμοῦ ᾖ.[1] ἐπεί,
εἴπερ εἴη που αὐτὴ καθ' αὑτὴν συνηθροισμένη καὶ
ἀπηλλαγμένη τούτων τῶν κακῶν ὧν σὺ νῦν δὴ
B διῆλθες, πολλὴ ἂν ἐλπὶς εἴη καὶ καλή, ὦ Σώκρατες, ὡς ἀληθῆ ἐστιν ἃ σὺ λέγεις· ἀλλὰ τοῦτο
δὴ ἴσως οὐκ ὀλίγης παραμυθίας δεῖται καὶ
πίστεως, ὡς ἔστι τε ἡ ψυχὴ ἀποθανόντος τοῦ
ἀνθρώπου καί τινα δύναμιν ἔχει καὶ φρόνησιν.
Ἀληθῆ, ἔφη, λέγεις, ὁ Σωκράτης, ὦ Κέβης·
ἀλλὰ τί δὴ ποιῶμεν; ἢ περὶ αὐτῶν τούτων βούλει
διαμυθολογῶμεν, εἴτε εἰκὸς οὕτως ἔχειν εἴτε μή;
Ἔγωγε οὖν, ἔφη ὁ Κέβης, ἡδέως ἂν ἀκούσαιμι
ἥντινα δόξαν ἔχεις περὶ αὐτῶν. Οὔκουν γ' ἂν
οἶμαι, ἦ δ' ὃς ὁ Σωκράτης, εἰπεῖν τινα νῦν
C ἀκούσαντα, οὐδ' εἰ κωμῳδοποιὸς εἴη, ὡς ἀδολεσχῶ
καὶ οὐ περὶ προσηκόντων τοὺς λόγους ποιοῦμαι.
εἰ οὖν δοκεῖ, χρὴ διασκοπεῖσθαι.

15. Σκεψώμεθα δὲ αὐτὸ τῇδέ πῃ, εἴτ' ἄρα ἐν
Ἅιδου εἰσὶν αἱ ψυχαὶ τελευτησάντων τῶν ἀνθρώπων εἴτε καὶ οὔ. παλαιὸς μὲν οὖν ἔστι τις λόγος, οὗ
μεμνήμεθα, ὡς εἰσὶν ἐνθένδε ἀφικόμεναι ἐκεῖ, καὶ
πάλιν γε δεῦρο ἀφικνοῦνται καὶ γίγνονται ἐκ τῶν
τεθνεώτων· καὶ εἰ τοῦθ' οὕτως ἔχει, πάλιν γίγνεσθαι ἐκ τῶν ἀποθανόντων τοὺς ζῶντας, ἄλλο τι ἢ
D εἶεν ἂν αἱ ψυχαὶ ἡμῶν ἐκεῖ; οὐ γὰρ ἄν που πάλιν
ἐγίγνοντο μὴ οὖσαι, καὶ τοῦτο ἱκανὸν τεκμήριον
τοῦ ταῦτ' εἶναι, εἰ τῷ ὄντι φανερὸν γίγνοιτο, ὅτι

[1] Schanz and Burnet bracket οἴχηται . . . ᾖ.

day when the man dies it is destroyed and perishes, and when it leaves the body and departs from it, straightway it flies away and is no longer anywhere, scattering like a breath or smoke. If it exists anywhere by itself as a unit, freed from these evils which you have enumerated just now, there would be good reason for the blessed hope, Socrates, that what you say is true. But perhaps no little argument and proof is required to show that when a man is dead the soul still exists and has any power and intelligence."

"What you say, Cebes, is true," said Socrates. "Now what shall we do? Do you wish to keep on conversing about this to see whether it is probable or not?"

"I do," said Cebes. "I should like to hear what you think about it."

"Well," said Socrates, "I do not believe anyone who heard us now, even if he were a comic poet, would say that I am chattering and talking about things which do not concern me. So if you like, let us examine the matter to the end.

"Let us consider it by asking whether the souls of men who have died are in the nether world or not. There is an ancient tradition, which we remember, that they go there from here and come back here again and are born from the dead. Now if this is true, if the living are born again from the dead, our souls would exist there, would they not? For they could not be born again if they did not exist, and this would be a sufficient proof that they exist, if it should really be made evident that the

οὐδαμόθεν ἄλλοθεν γίγνονται οἱ ζῶντες ἢ ἐκ τῶν
τεθνεώτων· εἰ δὲ μὴ ἔστι τοῦτο, ἄλλου ἄν του
δέοι λόγου. Πάνυ μὲν οὖν, ἔφη ὁ Κέβης. Μὴ
τοίνυν κατ᾽ ἀνθρώπων, ἢ δ᾽ ὅς, σκόπει μόνον
τοῦτο, εἰ βούλει ῥᾷον μαθεῖν, ἀλλὰ καὶ κατὰ ζῴων
πάντων καὶ φυτῶν, καὶ ξυλλήβδην ὅσαπερ ἔχει
γένεσιν, περὶ πάντων εἰδῶμεν, ἆρ᾽ οὑτωσὶ γίγνεται
E πάντα, οὐκ ἄλλοθεν ἢ ἐκ τῶν ἐναντίων τὰ ἐναντία,
ὅσοις τυγχάνει ὂν τοιοῦτόν τι, οἷον τὸ καλὸν τῷ
αἰσχρῷ ἐναντίον που καὶ δίκαιον ἀδίκῳ, καὶ ἄλλα
δὴ μυρία οὕτως ἔχει. τοῦτο οὖν σκεψώμεθα, ἆρα
ἀναγκαῖον, ὅσοις ἔστι τι ἐναντίον, μηδαμόθεν
ἄλλοθεν αὐτὸ γίγνεσθαι ἢ ἐκ τοῦ αὐτῷ ἐναντίου.
οἷον ὅταν μεῖζόν τι γίγνηται, ἀνάγκη που ἐξ
ἐλάττονος ὄντος πρότερον ἔπειτα μεῖζον γίγνεσθαι; Ναί. Οὐκοῦν κἂν ἔλαττον γίγνηται, ἐκ
71 μείζονος ὄντος πρότερον ὕστερον ἔλαττον γενήσεται; Ἔστιν οὕτω, ἔφη. Καὶ μὴν ἐξ ἰσχυρο-
τέρου τὸ ἀσθενέστερον καὶ ἐκ βραδυτέρου τὸ
θᾶττον; Πάνυ γε. Τί δέ; ἄν τι χεῖρον γίγνηται, οὐκ ἐξ ἀμείνονος, καὶ ἂν δικαιότερον, ἐξ
ἀδικωτέρου; Πῶς γὰρ οὔ; Ἱκανῶς οὖν, ἔφη,
ἔχομεν τοῦτο, ὅτι πάντα οὕτω γίγνεται, ἐξ
ἐναντίων τὰ ἐναντία πράγματα; Πάνυ γε.
Τί δ᾽ αὖ; ἔστι τι καὶ τοιόνδε ἐν αὐτοῖς, οἷον

living are born only from the dead. But if this
is not so, then some other argument would be
needed."

"Certainly," said Cebes.

"Now," said he, "if you wish to find this out
easily, do not consider the question with regard
to men only, but with regard to all animals and
plants, and, in short, to all things which may be said
to have birth. Let us see with regard to all these,
whether it is true that they are all born or generated
only from their opposites, in case they have opposites,
as for instance, the noble is the opposite of the disgraceful, the just of the unjust, and there are countless other similar pairs. Let us consider the question
whether it is inevitable that everything which has
an opposite be generated from its opposite and from
it only. For instance, when anything becomes
greater it must inevitably have been smaller and
then have become greater."

"Yes."

"And if it becomes smaller, it must have been
greater and then have become smaller?"

"That is true," said he.

"And the weaker is generated from the stronger,
and the slower from the quicker?"

"Certainly."

"And the worse from the better and the more
just from the more unjust?"

"Of course."

"Then," said he, "we have this fact sufficiently
established, that all things are generated in this
way, opposites from opposites?"

"Certainly."

"Now then, is there between all these pairs of

μεταξὺ ἀμφοτέρων πάντων τῶν ἐναντίων δυοῖν
B ὄντοιν δύο γενέσεις, ἀπὸ μὲν τοῦ ἑτέρου ἐπὶ τὸ
ἕτερον, ἀπὸ δ' αὖ τοῦ ἑτέρου πάλιν ἐπὶ τὸ ἕτερον·
μείζονος μὲν πράγματος καὶ ἐλάττονος μεταξὺ
αὔξησις καὶ φθίσις, καὶ καλοῦμεν οὕτω τὸ μὲν
αὐξάνεσθαι, τὸ δὲ φθίνειν; Ναί, ἔφη. Οὐκοῦν
καὶ διακρίνεσθαι καὶ συγκρίνεσθαι, καὶ ψύχεσθαι
καὶ θερμαίνεσθαι, καὶ πάντα οὕτω, κἂν εἰ μὴ
χρώμεθα τοῖς ὀνόμασιν ἐνιαχοῦ, ἀλλ' ἔργῳ γοῦν
πανταχοῦ οὕτως ἔχειν ἀναγκαῖον, γίγνεσθαί τε
αὐτὰ ἐξ ἀλλήλων γένεσίν τε εἶναι ἐξ ἑκατέρου[1]
εἰς ἄλληλα; Πάνυ μὲν οὖν, ἦ δ' ὅς.
C   16. Τί οὖν; ἔφη. τῷ ζῆν ἐστί τι ἐναντίον,
ὥσπερ τῷ ἐγρηγορέναι τὸ καθεύδειν; Πάνυ μὲν
οὖν, ἔφη. Τί; Τὸ τεθνάναι, ἔφη. Οὐκοῦν ἐξ
ἀλλήλων τε γίγνεται ταῦτα, εἴπερ ἐναντία
ἐστιν, καὶ αἱ γενέσεις εἰσὶν αὐτοῖν μεταξὺ δύο
δυοῖν ὄντοιν; Πῶς γὰρ οὔ; Τὴν μὲν τοίνυν
ἑτέραν συζυγίαν ὧν νῦν δὴ ἔλεγον ἐγώ σοι, ἔφη,
Ἐρῶ, ὁ Σωκράτης, καὶ αὐτὴν καὶ τὰς γενέσεις·
σὺ δέ μοι τὴν ἑτέραν. λέγω δὲ τὸ μὲν καθεύδειν,
τὸ δὲ ἐγρηγορέναι, καὶ ἐκ τοῦ καθεύδειν τὸ
ἐγρηγορέναι γίγνεσθαι καὶ ἐκ τοῦ ἐγρηγορέναι τὸ
D καθεύδειν, καὶ τὰς γενέσεις αὐτοῖν τὴν μὲν καταδαρθάνειν εἶναι, τὴν δ' ἀνεγείρεσθαι. ἱκανῶς σοι,
ἔφη, ἦ οὔ; Πάνυ μὲν οὖν. Λέγε δή μοι καὶ

[1] Schanz brackets ἐξ ἑκατέρου.

opposites what may be called two kinds of generation, from one to the other and back again from the
other to the first? Between a larger thing and a
smaller thing there is increment and diminution and
we call one increasing and the other decreasing,
do we not?"

"Yes," said he.

"And similarly analysing and combining, and cool-
ing and heating, and all opposites in the same way.
Even if we do not in every case have the words to
express it, yet in fact is it not always inevitable that
there is a process of generation from each to the
other?"

"Certainly," said he.

"Well then," said Socrates, "is there anything that
is the opposite of living, as being awake is the
opposite of sleeping?"

"Certainly," said Cebes.

"What?"

"Being dead," said he.

"Then these two are generated from each other,
and as they are two, so the processes between them
are two; is it not so?"

"Of course."

"Now," said Socrates, "I will tell about one of the
two pairs of which I just spoke to you and its inter-
mediate processes; and do you tell me about the
other. I say one term is sleeping and the other is
being awake, and being awake is generated from
sleeping, and sleeping from being awake, and the
processes of generation are, in the latter case, falling
asleep, and in the former, waking up. Do you agree,
or not?"

"Certainly."

σύ, ἔφη, οὕτω περὶ ζωῆς καὶ θανάτου. οὐκ
ἐναντίον μὲν φὴς τῷ ζῆν τὸ τεθνάναι εἶναι;
Ἔγωγε. Γίγνεσθαι δὲ ἐξ ἀλλήλων; Ναί. Ἐξ
οὖν τοῦ ζῶντος τί τὸ γιγνόμενον; Τὸ τεθνηκός,
ἔφη. Τί δέ, ἦ δ᾽ ὅς, ἐκ τοῦ τεθνεῶτος;
Ἀναγκαῖον, ἔφη, ὁμολογεῖν ὅτι τὸ ζῶν. Ἐκ τῶν
τεθνεώτων ἄρα, ὦ Κέβης, τὰ ζῶντά τε καὶ οἱ
E ζῶντες γίγνονται; Φαίνεται, ἔφη. Εἰσὶν ἄρα,
ἔφη, αἱ ψυχαὶ ἡμῶν ἐν Ἅιδου. Ἔοικεν. Οὐκοῦν
καὶ τοῖν γενεσέοιν τοῖν περὶ ταῦτα ἥ γ᾽ ἑτέρα
σαφὴς οὖσα τυγχάνει; τὸ γὰρ ἀποθνήσκειν σαφὲς
δήπου, ἢ οὔ; Πάνυ μὲν οὖν, ἔφη. Πῶς οὖν, ἦ δ᾽
ὅς, ποιήσομεν; οὐκ ἀνταποδώσομεν τὴν ἐναντίαν
γένεσιν, ἀλλὰ ταύτῃ χωλὴ ἔσται ἡ φύσις; ἢ
ἀνάγκη ἀποδοῦναι τῷ ἀποθνήσκειν ἐναντίαν τινὰ
γένεσιν; Πάντως που, ἔφη. Τίνα ταύτην; Τὸ
ἀναβιώσκεσθαι. Οὐκοῦν, ἦ δ᾽ ὅς, εἴπερ ἔστι τὸ
72 ἀναβιώσκεσθαι, ἐκ τῶν τεθνεώτων ἂν εἴη γένεσις
εἰς τοὺς ζῶντας αὕτη, τὸ ἀναβιώσκεσθαι; Πάνυ
γε. Ὁμολογεῖται ἄρα ἡμῖν καὶ ταύτῃ τοὺς
248

"Now do you," said he, "tell me in this way about life and death. Do you not say that living is the opposite of being dead?"

"I do."

"And that they are generated one from the other?"

"Yes."

"Now what is it which is generated from the living?"

"The dead," said he.

"And what," said Socrates, "from the dead?"

"I can say only one thing—the living."

"From the dead, then, Cebes, the living, both things and persons, are generated?"

"Evidently," said he.

"Then," said Socrates, "our souls exist in the other world."

"So it seems."

"And of the two processes of generation between these two, the one is plain to be seen; for surely dying is plain to be seen, is it not?"

"Certainly," said he.

"Well then," said Socrates, "what shall we do next? Shall we deny the opposite process, and shall nature be one-sided in this instance? Or must we grant that there is some process of generation the opposite of dying?"

"Certainly we must," said he.

"What is this process?"

"Coming to life again."

"Then," said Socrates, "if there be such a thing as coming to life again, this would be the process of generation from the dead to the living?"

"Certainly."

"So by this method also we reach the conclusion

ζῶντας ἐκ τῶν τεθνεώτων γεγονέναι οὐδὲν ἧττον
ἢ τοὺς τεθνεῶτας ἐκ τῶν ζώντων· τούτου δὲ ὄντος
ἱκανόν που ἐδόκει τεκμήριον εἶναι ὅτι ἀναγκαῖον
τὰς τῶν τεθνεώτων ψυχὰς εἶναί που, ὅθεν δὴ
πάλιν γίγνεσθαι. Δοκεῖ μοι, ἔφη, ὦ Σώκρατες,
ἐκ τῶν ὡμολογημένων ἀναγκαῖον οὕτως ἔχειν.

17. Ἰδὲ τοίνυν οὕτως, ἔφη, ὦ Κέβης, ὅτι οὐδ'
ἀδίκως ὡμολογήκαμεν, ὡς ἐμοὶ δοκεῖ. εἰ γὰρ
B μὴ ἀεὶ ἀνταποδιδοίη τὰ ἕτερα τοῖς ἑτέροις γιγνόμενα ὡσπερεὶ κύκλῳ περιιόντα, ἀλλ' εὐθεῖά τις εἴη
ἡ γένεσις ἐκ τοῦ ἑτέρου μόνον εἰς τὸ καταντικρὺ
καὶ μὴ ἀνακάμπτοι πάλιν ἐπὶ τὸ ἕτερον μηδὲ
καμπὴν ποιοῖτο, οἶσθ' ὅτι πάντα τελευτῶντα τὸ
αὐτὸ σχῆμα ἂν σχοίη καὶ τὸ αὐτὸ πάθος ἂν πάθοι
καὶ παύσαιτο γιγνόμενα; Πῶς λέγεις; ἔφη. Οὐδὲν
χαλεπόν, ἦ δ' ὅς, ἐννοῆσαι ὃ λέγω· ἀλλ' οἷον
εἰ τὸ καταδαρθάνειν μὲν εἴη, τὸ δ' ἀνεγείρεσθαι
μὴ ἀνταποδιδοίη γιγνόμενον ἐκ τοῦ καθεύδοντος,
C οἶσθ' ὅτι τελευτῶντα πάντ' ἂν λῆρον τὸν Ἐνδυ-
μίωνα ἀποδείξειεν καὶ οὐδαμοῦ ἂν φαίνοιτο διὰ τὸ
καὶ τἆλλα πάντα ταὐτὸν ἐκείνῳ πεπονθέναι,
καθεύδειν. κἂν εἰ συγκρίνοιτο μὲν πάντα, δια-
κρίνοιτο δὲ μή, ταχὺ ἂν τὸ τοῦ Ἀναξαγόρου γεγονὸς εἴη, ὁμοῦ πάντα χρήματα. ὡσαύτως δέ, ὦ
φίλε Κέβης, εἰ ἀποθνήσκοι μὲν πάντα, ὅσα τοῦ
ζῆν μεταλάβοι, ἐπειδὴ δὲ ἀποθάνοι, μένοι ἐν τούτῳ
τῷ σχήματι τὰ τεθνεῶτα καὶ μὴ πάλιν ἀναβιώ-
σκοιτο, ἆρ' οὐ πολλὴ ἀνάγκη τελευτῶντα πάντα
D τεθνάναι καὶ μηδὲν ζῆν; εἰ γὰρ ἐκ μὲν τῶν ἄλλων
τὰ ζῶντα γίγνοιτο, τὰ δὲ ζῶντα θνῄσκοι, τίς

that the living are generated from the dead, just as much as the dead from the living ; and since this is the case, it seems to me to be a sufficient proof that the souls of the dead exist somewhere, whence they come back to life."

" I think, Socrates, that results necessarily from our previous admissions."

" Now here is another method, Cebes, to prove, as it seems to me, that we were right in making those admissions. For if generation did not proceed from opposite to opposite and back again, going round, as it were in a circle, but always went forward in a straight line without turning back or curving, then, you know, in the end all things would have the same form and be acted upon in the same way and stop being generated at all."

" What do you mean ? " said he.

" It is not at all hard," said Socrates, " to understand what I mean. For example, if the process of falling asleep existed, but not the opposite process of waking from sleep, in the end, you know, that would make the sleeping Endymion mere nonsense ; he would be nowhere, for everything else would be in the same state as he, sound asleep. Or if all things were mixed together and never separated, the saying of Anaxagoras, ' all things are chaos,' would soon come true. And in like manner, my dear Cebes, if all things that have life should die, and, when they had died, the dead should remain in that condition, is it not inevitable that at last all things would be dead and nothing alive ? For if the living were generated from any other things than from the dead, and the living were to die, is

PLATO

μηχανὴ μὴ οὐ πάντα καταναλωθῆναι εἰς τὸ τεθνάναι; Οὐδὲ μία μοι δοκεῖ, ἔφη ὁ Κέβης, ὦ Σώκρατες, ἀλλά μοι δοκεῖς παντάπασιν ἀληθῆ λέγειν. Ἔστιν γάρ, ἔφη, ὦ Κέβης, ὡς ἐμοὶ δοκεῖ, παντὸς μᾶλλον οὕτω, καὶ ἡμεῖς αὐτὰ ταῦτα οὐκ ἐξαπατώμενοι ὁμολογοῦμεν, ἀλλ᾽ ἔστι τῷ ὄντι καὶ τὸ ἀναβιώσκεσθαι καὶ ἐκ τῶν τεθνεώτων τοὺς ζῶντας γίγνεσθαι καὶ τὰς τῶν τεθνεώτων ψυχὰς E εἶναι.[1]

18. Καὶ μήν, ἔφη ὁ Κέβης ὑπολαβών, καὶ κατ᾽ ἐκεῖνόν γε τὸν λόγον ὦ Σώκρατες, εἰ ἀληθής ἐστιν, ὃν σὺ εἴωθας θαμὰ λέγειν, ὅτι ἡμῖν ἡ μάθησις οὐκ ἄλλο τι ἢ ἀνάμνησις τυγχάνει οὖσα, καὶ κατὰ τοῦτον ἀνάγκη που ἡμᾶς ἐν προτέρῳ τινὶ χρόνῳ μεμαθηκέναι ἃ νῦν ἀναμιμνησκόμεθα. τοῦτο δὲ ἀδύνατον, εἰ μὴ ἦν 73 που ἡμῖν ἡ ψυχὴ πρὶν ἐν τῷδε τῷ ἀνθρωπίνῳ εἴδει γενέσθαι· ὥστε καὶ ταύτῃ ἀθάνατον ἡ ψυχή τι ἔοικεν εἶναι. Ἀλλά, ὦ Κέβης, ἔφη ὁ Σιμμίας ὑπολαβών, ποῖαι τούτων αἱ ἀποδείξεις; ὑπόμνησόν με· οὐ γὰρ σφόδρα ἐν τῷ παρόντι μέμνημαι. Ἑνὶ μὲν λόγῳ, ἔφη ὁ Κέβης, καλλίστῳ, ὅτι ἐρωτώμενοι οἱ ἄνθρωποι, ἐάν τις καλῶς ἐρωτᾷ, αὐτοὶ λέγουσιν πάντα ᾗ ἔχει· καίτοι εἰ μὴ ἐτύγχανεν αὐτοῖς ἐπιστήμη ἐνοῦσα καὶ ὀρθὸς λόγος, οὐκ ἂν οἷοί τ᾽ ἦσαν τοῦτο ποιῆσαι. ἔπειτα ἐάν τις ἐπὶ τὰ διαγράμματα B ἄγῃ ἢ ἄλλο τι τῶν τοιούτων, ἐνταῦθα σαφέστατα κατηγορεῖ, ὅτι τοῦτο οὕτως ἔχει. Εἰ δὲ μὴ

---

[1] After εἶναι the MSS. read καὶ ταῖς μέν γε ἀγαθαῖς ἄμεινον εἶναι, ταῖς δὲ κακαῖς κάκιον, "and that the good fare better and the bad worse." Bracketed by Stallbaum, followed by Schanz, Burnet, and others.

there any escape from the final result that all things would be swallowed up in death?"

"I see none, Socrates," said Cebes. "What you say seems to be perfectly true."

"I think, Cebes," said he, "it is absolutely so, and we are not deluded in making these admissions, but the return to life is an actual fact, and it is a fact that the living are generated from the dead and that the souls of the dead exist."

"And besides," Cebes rejoined, "if it is true, Socrates, as you are fond of saying, that our learning is nothing else than recollection, then this would be an additional argument that we must necessarily have learned in some previous time what we now remember. But this is impossible if our soul did not exist somewhere before being born in this human form; and so by this argument also it appears that the soul is immortal."

"But, Cebes," said Simmias, "what were the proofs of this? Remind me; for I do not recollect very well just now."

"Briefly," said Cebes, "a very good proof is this: When people are questioned, if you put the questions well, they answer correctly of themselves about everything; and yet if they had not within them some knowledge and right reason, they could not do this. And that this is so is shown most clearly if you take them to mathematical diagrams or anything of that sort."

"And if you are not convinced in that way,

PLATO

ταύτῃ γε, ἔφη, πείθει, ὦ Σιμμία, ὁ Σωκράτης,
σκέψαι, ἂν τῇδέ πῃ σοι σκοπουμένῳ συνδόξῃ.
ἀπιστεῖς γὰρ δή, πῶς ἡ καλουμένη μάθησις
ἀνάμνησίς ἐστιν; Ἀπιστῶ μέν σοι ἔγωγε, ἦ δ᾽
ὃς ὁ Σιμμίας, οὔ, αὐτὸ δὲ τοῦτο, ἔφη, δέομαι
μαθεῖν περὶ οὗ ὁ λόγος, ἀναμνησθῆναι. καὶ σχεδόν
γε ἐξ ὧν Κέβης ἐπεχείρησε λέγειν ἤδη μέμνημαι
καὶ πείθομαι· οὐδὲν μέντ᾽ ἂν ἧττον ἀκούοιμι νῦν,
C πῇ σὺ ἐπεχείρησας λέγειν. Τῇδ᾽ ἔγωγε, ἦ δ᾽
ὅς. ὁμολογοῦμεν γὰρ δήπου, εἴ τίς τι ἀνα-
μνησθήσεται, δεῖν αὐτὸν τοῦτο πρότερόν ποτε
ἐπίστασθαι. Πάνυ γ᾽, ἔφη. Ἆρ᾽ οὖν καὶ τόδε
ὁμολογοῦμεν, ὅταν ἐπιστήμη παραγίγνηται τρόπῳ
τοιούτῳ, ἀνάμνησιν εἶναι; λέγω δέ τινα τρόπον
τόνδε· ἐάν τίς τι[1] ἢ ἰδὼν ἢ ἀκούσας ἤ τινα
ἄλλην αἴσθησιν λαβὼν μὴ μόνον ἐκεῖνο γνῷ,
ἀλλὰ καὶ ἕτερον ἐννοήσῃ, οὗ μὴ ἡ αὐτὴ ἐπιστήμη,
ἀλλ᾽ ἄλλη, ἆρα οὐχὶ τοῦτο δικαίως ἐλέγομεν ὅτι
D ἀνεμνήσθη, οὗ τὴν ἔννοιαν ἔλαβεν; Πῶς λέγεις;
Οἷον τὰ τοιάδε· ἄλλη που ἐπιστήμη ἀνθρώπου
καὶ λύρας. Πῶς γὰρ οὔ; Οὐκοῦν οἶσθα, ὅτι
οἱ ἐρασταί, ὅταν ἴδωσιν λύραν ἢ ἱμάτιον ἢ
ἄλλο τι οἷς τὰ παιδικὰ αὐτῶν εἴωθε χρῆσθαι,
πάσχουσι τοῦτο· ἔγνωσάν τε τὴν λύραν καὶ ἐν
τῇ διανοίᾳ ἔλαβον τὸ εἶδος τοῦ παιδός, οὗ ἦν ἡ
λύρα; τοῦτο δέ ἐστιν ἀνάμνησις· ὥσπερ καὶ
Σιμμίαν τις ἰδὼν πολλάκις Κέβητος ἀνεμνήσθη,
καὶ ἄλλα που μυρία τοιαῦτ᾽ ἂν εἴη. Μυρία
μέντοι νὴ Δία, ἔφη ὁ Σιμμίας. Οὐκοῦν, ἦ δ᾽
E ὅς, τὸ τοιοῦτον ἀνάμνησίς τίς ἐστι; μάλιστα

---

[1] After τι BCD read πρότερον, which Schanz brackets. T
reads τι ἕτερόν τι, Burnet τι ἕτερον.

Simmias," said Socrates, "see if you don't agree
when you look at it in this way. You are incredulous, are you not, how that which is called
learning can be recollection?"

"I am not incredulous," said Simmias, "but I
want just what we are talking about, recollection.
And from what Cebes undertook to say I already
begin to recollect and be convinced; nevertheless,
I should like to hear what you were going to say."

"It was this," said he. "We agree, I suppose,
that if anyone is to remember anything, he must
know it at some previous time?"

"Certainly," said he.

"Then do we agree to this also, that when
knowledge comes in such a way, it is recollection?
What I mean is this: If a man, when he has heard
or seen or in any other way perceived a thing, knows
not only that thing, but also has a perception of
some other thing, the knowledge of which is not the
same, but different, are we not right in saying that he
recollects the thing of which he has the perception?"

"What do you mean?"

"Let me give an example. Knowledge of a man
is different from knowledge of a lyre."

"Of course."

"Well, you know that a lover when he sees a lyre
or a cloak or anything else which his beloved is wont
to use, perceives the lyre and in his mind receives an
image of the boy to whom the lyre belongs, do you
not? But this is recollection, just as when one sees
Simmias, one often remembers Cebes, and I could
cite countless such examples."

"To be sure you could," said Simmias.

"Now," said he, "is that sort of thing a kind of

μέντοι, ὅταν τις τοῦτο πάθῃ περὶ ἐκεῖνα, ἃ ὑπὸ
χρόνου καὶ τοῦ μὴ ἐπισκοπεῖν ἤδη ἐπελέληστο;
Πάνυ μὲν οὖν, ἔφη. Τί δέ; ἦ δ' ὅς· ἔστιν
ἵππον γεγραμμένον ἰδόντα καὶ λύραν γεγραμμένην
ἀνθρώπου ἀναμνησθῆναι, καὶ Σιμμίαν ἰδόντα
γεγραμμένον Κέβητος ἀναμνησθῆναι; Πάνυ γε.
Οὐκοῦν καὶ Σιμμίαν ἰδόντα γεγραμμένον αὐτοῦ
74 Σιμμίου ἀναμνησθῆναι; Ἔστι μέντοι, ἔφη.

19. Ἆρ' οὖν οὐ κατὰ πάντα ταῦτα συμβαίνει
τὴν ἀνάμνησιν εἶναι μὲν ἀφ' ὁμοίων, εἶναι δὲ καὶ
ἀπὸ ἀνομοίων; Συμβαίνει. Ἀλλ' ὅταν γε ἀπὸ
τῶν ὁμοίων ἀναμιμνήσκηταί τίς τι, ἆρ' οὐκ ἀναγκαῖον τόδε προσπάσχειν, ἐννοεῖν εἴτε τι ἐλλείπει
τοῦτο κατὰ τὴν ὁμοιότητα εἴτε μὴ ἐκείνου οὗ
ἀνεμνήσθη; Ἀνάγκη, ἔφη. Σκόπει δή, ἦ δ' ὅς,
εἰ ταῦτα οὕτως ἔχει. φαμέν πού τι εἶναι ἴσον,
οὐ ξύλον λέγω ξύλῳ οὐδὲ λίθον λίθῳ οὐδ' ἄλλο
τῶν τοιούτων οὐδέν, ἀλλὰ παρὰ ταῦτα πάντα
ἕτερόν τι, αὐτὸ τὸ ἴσον· φῶμέν τι εἶναι ἢ μηδέν;
B Φῶμεν μέντοι νὴ Δί', ἔφη ὁ Σιμμίας, θαυμαστῶς
γε. Ἦ καὶ ἐπιστάμεθα αὐτὸ ὃ ἔστιν; Πάνυ γε,
ἦ δ' ὅς. Πόθεν λαβόντες αὐτοῦ τὴν ἐπιστήμην;
ἆρ' οὐκ ἐξ ὧν νῦν δὴ ἐλέγομεν, ἢ ξύλα ἢ λίθους
ἢ ἄλλα ἄττα ἰδόντες ἴσα, ἐκ τούτων ἐκεῖνο

recollection ? Especially when it takes place with regard to things which have already been forgotten through time and inattention ? "

" Certainly," he replied.

" Well, then," said Socrates, " can a person on seeing a picture of a horse or of a lyre be reminded of a man, or on seeing a picture of Simmias be reminded of Cebes ? "

" Surely."

" And on seeing a picture of Simmias he can be reminded of Simmias himself ? "

" Yes," said he.

" All these examples show, then, that recollection is caused by like things and also by unlike things, do they not ? "

" Yes."

" And when one has a recollection of anything caused by like things, will he not also inevitably consider whether this recollection offers a perfect likeness of the thing recollected, or not ? "

" Inevitably," he replied.

" Now see," said he, " if this is true. We say there is such a thing as equality. I do not mean one piece of wood equal to another, or one stone to another, or anything of that sort, but something beyond that—equality in the abstract. Shall we say there is such a thing, or not ? "

" We shall say that there is," said Simmias, " most decidedly."

" And do we know what it is ? "

" Certainly," said he.

" Whence did we derive the knowledge of it ? Is it not from the things we were just speaking of ? Did we not, by seeing equal pieces of wood

ἐνενοήσαμεν, ἕτερον ὂν τούτων; ἢ οὐχ ἕτερόν σοι
φαίνεται; σκόπει δὲ καὶ τῇδε. ἆρ' οὐ λίθοι μὲν
ἴσοι καὶ ξύλα ἐνίοτε ταὐτὰ ὄντα τῷ μὲν ἴσα
φαίνεται, τῷ δ' οὔ; Πάνυ μὲν οὖν. Τί δέ;
αὐτὰ τὰ ἴσα ἔστιν ὅτε ἄνισά σοι ἐφάνη, ἢ ἡ
C ἰσότης ἀνισότης; Οὐδεπώποτέ γε, ὦ Σώκρατες.
Οὐ ταὐτὸν ἄρα ἐστίν, ἦ δ' ὅς, ταῦτά τε τὰ ἴσα
καὶ αὐτὸ τὸ ἴσον. Οὐδαμῶς μοι φαίνεται, ὦ
Σώκρατες. Ἀλλὰ μὴν ἐκ τούτων γ', ἔφη, τῶν
ἴσων, ἑτέρων ὄντων ἐκείνου τοῦ ἴσου, ὅμως αὐτοῦ
τὴν ἐπιστήμην ἐννενόηκάς τε καὶ εἴληφας; Ἀληθέστατα, ἔφη, λέγεις. Οὐκοῦν ἢ ὁμοίου ὄντος
τούτοις ἢ ἀνομοίου; Πάνυ γε. Διαφέρει δέ γε,
ἦ δ' ὅς, οὐδέν· ἕως ἂν ἄλλο ἰδὼν ἀπὸ ταύτης τῆς
D ὄψεως ἄλλο ἐννοήσῃς, εἴτε ὅμοιον εἴτε ἀνόμοιον,
ἀναγκαῖον, ἔφη, αὐτὸ ἀνάμνησιν γεγονέναι. Πάνυ
μὲν οὖν. Τί δέ; ἦ δ' ὅς· ἦ πάσχομέν τι τοιοῦτον περὶ τὰ ἐν τοῖς ξύλοις τε καὶ οἷς νῦν δὴ
ἐλέγομεν τοῖς ἴσοις; ἆρα φαίνεται ἡμῖν οὕτως ἴσα
εἶναι ὥσπερ αὐτὸ ὃ ἔστιν ἴσον, ἢ ἐνδεῖ τι ἐκείνῳ
τῷ τοιοῦτον εἶναι οἷον τὸ ἴσον, ἢ οὐδέν; Καὶ
πολύ γε, ἔφη, ἐνδεῖ. Οὐκοῦν ὁμολογοῦμεν, ὅταν
τίς τι ἰδὼν ἐννοήσῃ, ὅτι βούλεται μὲν τοῦτο, ὃ

or stones or other things, derive from them a knowledge of abstract equality, which is another thing ? Or do you not think it is another thing ? Look at the matter in this way. Do not equal stones and pieces of wood, though they remain the same, sometimes appear to us equal in one respect and unequal in another ? "

" Certainly."

" Well, then, did absolute equals ever appear to you unequal or equality inequality ? "

" No, Socrates, never."

" Then," said he, " those equals are not the same as equality in the abstract."

" Not at all, I should say, Socrates."

" But from those equals," said he, " which are not the same as abstract equality, you have nevertheless conceived and acquired knowledge of it ? "

" Very true," he replied.

" And it is either like them or unlike them ? "

" Certainly."

" It makes no difference," said he. " Whenever the sight of one thing brings you a perception of another, whether they be like or unlike, that must necessarily be recollection."

" Surely."

" Now then," said he, " do the equal pieces of wood and the equal things of which we were speaking just now affect us in this way : Do they seem to us to be equal as abstract equality is equal, or do they somehow fall short of being like abstract equality ? "

" They fall very far short of it," said he.

" Do we agree, then, that when anyone on seeing a thing thinks, ' This thing that I see aims at being

νῦν ἐγὼ ὁρῶ, εἶναι οἷον ἄλλο τι τῶν ὄντων, ἐνδεῖ
E δὲ καὶ οὐ δύναται τοιοῦτον εἶναι οἷον ἐκεῖνο, ἀλλ'
ἔστιν φαυλότερον, ἀναγκαῖόν που τὸν τοῦτο
ἐννοοῦντα τυχεῖν προειδότα ἐκεῖνο ᾧ φησιν αὐτὸ
προσεοικέναι μέν, ἐνδεεστέρως δὲ ἔχειν; Ἀνάγκη. Τί οὖν; τοιοῦτον πεπόνθαμεν καὶ ἡμεῖς,
ἢ οὔ, περί τε τὰ ἴσα καὶ αὐτὸ τὸ ἴσον; Παντάπασί γε. Ἀναγκαῖον ἄρα ἡμᾶς προειδέναι τὸ
75 ἴσον πρὸ ἐκείνου τοῦ χρόνου, ὅτε τὸ πρῶτον
ἰδόντες τὰ ἴσα ἐνενοήσαμεν, ὅτι ὀρέγεται μὲν
πάντα ταῦτα εἶναι οἷον τὸ ἴσον, ἔχει δὲ ἐνδεεστέρως. Ἔστι ταῦτα. Ἀλλὰ μὴν καὶ τόδε
ὁμολογοῦμεν, μὴ ἄλλοθεν αὐτὸ ἐννενοηκέναι μηδὲ
δυνατὸν εἶναι ἐννοῆσαι, ἀλλ' ἢ ἐκ τοῦ ἰδεῖν ἢ
ἅψασθαι ἢ ἔκ τινος ἄλλης τῶν αἰσθήσεων· ταὐτὸν
δὲ πάντα ταῦτα λέγω. Ταὐτὸν γάρ ἐστιν, ὦ
Σώκρατες, πρός γε ὃ βούλεται δηλῶσαι ὁ λόγος.
Ἀλλὰ μὲν δὴ ἔκ γε τῶν αἰσθήσεων δεῖ ἐννοῆσαι,
B ὅτι πάντα τὰ ἐν ταῖς αἰσθήσεσιν ἐκείνου τε ὀρέγεται τοῦ ὃ ἔστιν ἴσον, καὶ αὐτοῦ ἐνδεέστερά
ἐστιν· ἢ πῶς λέγομεν; Οὕτως. Πρὸ τοῦ ἄρα
ἄρξασθαι ἡμᾶς ὁρᾶν καὶ ἀκούειν καὶ τἆλλα
αἰσθάνεσθαι τυχεῖν ἔδει που εἰληφότας ἐπιστήμην
αὐτοῦ τοῦ ἴσου ὅ τι ἔστιν, εἰ ἐμέλλομεν τὰ ἐκ τῶν
αἰσθήσεων ἴσα ἐκεῖσε ἀνοίσειν, ὅτι προθυμεῖται
μὲν πάντα τοιαῦτ' εἶναι οἷον ἐκεῖνο, ἔστιν δὲ αὐτοῦ
φαυλότερα.[1] Ἀνάγκη ἐκ τῶν προειρημένων, ὦ
Σώκρατες. Οὐκοῦν γενόμενοι εὐθὺς ἑωρῶμέν τε

---

[1] Schanz brackets ὅτι προθυμεῖται . . . φαυλότερα.

like some other thing that exists, but falls short and is unable to be like that thing, but is inferior to it,' he who thinks thus must of necessity have previous knowledge of the thing which he says the other resembles but falls short of?"

"We must."

"Well then, is this just what happened to us with regard to the equal things and equality in the abstract?"

"It certainly is."

"Then we must have had knowledge of equality before the time when we first saw equal things and thought, 'All these things are aiming to be like equality but fall short.' "

"That is true."

"And we agree, also, that we have not gained knowledge of it, and that it is impossible to gain this knowledge, except by sight or touch or some other of the senses? I consider that all the senses are alike."

"Yes, Socrates, they are all alike, for the purposes of our argument."

"Then it is through the senses that we must learn that all sensible objects strive after absolute equality and fall short of it. Is that our view?"

"Yes."

"Then before we began to see or hear or use the other senses we must somewhere have gained a knowledge of abstract or absolute equality, if we were to compare with it the equals which we perceive by the senses, and see that all such things yearn to be like abstract equality but fall short of it."

"That follows necessarily from what we have said before, Socrates."

καὶ ἠκούομεν καὶ τὰς ἄλλας αἰσθήσεις εἴχομεν;

C Πάνυ γε. Ἔδει δέ γε, φαμέν, πρὸ τούτων τὴν τοῦ ἴσου ἐπιστήμην εἰληφέναι; Ναί. Πρὶν γενέσθαι ἄρα, ὡς ἔοικεν, ἀνάγκη ἡμῖν αὐτὴν εἰληφέναι. Ἔοικεν.

20. Οὐκοῦν εἰ μὲν λαβόντες αὐτὴν πρὸ τοῦ γενέσθαι ἔχοντες ἐγενόμεθα, ἠπιστάμεθα καὶ πρὶν γενέσθαι καὶ εὐθὺς γενόμενοι οὐ μόνον τὸ ἴσον καὶ τὸ μεῖζον καὶ τὸ ἔλαττον ἀλλὰ καὶ ξύμπαντα τὰ τοιαῦτα; οὐ γὰρ περὶ τοῦ ἴσου νῦν ὁ λόγος ἡμῖν μᾶλλόν τι ἢ καὶ περὶ αὐτοῦ τοῦ καλοῦ, καὶ αὐτοῦ τοῦ ἀγαθοῦ καὶ δικαίου καὶ ὁσίου, καί, ὅπερ λέγω,

D περὶ ἁπάντων οἷς ἐπισφραγιζόμεθα τὸ ὃ ἔστι, καὶ ἐν ταῖς ἐρωτήσεσιν ἐρωτῶντες καὶ ἐν ταῖς ἀποκρίσεσιν ἀποκρινόμενοι. ὥστε ἀναγκαῖον ἡμῖν τούτων πάντων τὰς ἐπιστήμας πρὸ τοῦ γενέσθαι εἰληφέναι. Ἔστι ταῦτα. Καὶ εἰ μέν γε λαβόντες ἑκάστοτε μὴ ἐπιλελήσμεθα, εἰδότας ἀεὶ γίγνεσθαι καὶ διὰ βίου εἰδέναι· τὸ γὰρ εἰδέναι τοῦτ᾽ ἐστίν, λαβόντα του ἐπιστήμην ἔχειν καὶ μὴ ἀπολωλεκέναι· ἢ οὐ τοῦτο λήθην λέγομεν, ὦ Σιμμία, ἐπιστήμης ἀποβολήν; Πάν-

E τως δήπου, ἔφη, ὦ Σώκρατες. Εἰ δέ γε, οἶμαι, λαβόντες πρὶν γενέσθαι γιγνόμενοι ἀπωλέσαμεν, ὕστερον δὲ ταῖς αἰσθήσεσι χρώμενοι περὶ αὐτὰ ἐκείνας ἀναλαμβάνομεν τὰς ἐπιστήμας, ἅς ποτε

" And we saw and heard and had the other senses as soon as we were born ? "

" Certainly."

" But, we say, we must have acquired a knowledge of equality before we had these senses ? "

" Yes."

" Then it appears that we must have acquired it before we were born."

" It does."

" Now if we had acquired that knowledge before we were born, and were born with it, we knew before we were born and at the moment of birth not only the equal and the greater and the less, but all such abstractions ? For our present argument is no more concerned with the equal than with absolute beauty and the absolute good and the just and the holy, and, in short, with all those things which we stamp with the seal of ' absolute ' in our dialectic process of questions and answers ; so that we must necessarily have acquired knowledge of all these before our birth."

" That is true."

" And if after acquiring it we have not, in each case, forgotten it, we must always be born knowing these things, and must know them throughout our life ; for to know is to have acquired knowledge and to have retained it without losing it, and the loss of knowledge is just what we mean when we speak of forgetting, is it not, Simmias ? "

" Certainly, Socrates," said he.

" But, I suppose, if we acquired knowledge before we were born and lost it at birth, but afterwards by the use of our senses regained the knowledge which we had previously possessed, would not the process

PLATO

καὶ πρὶν εἴχομεν, ἆρ' οὐχ ὃ καλοῦμεν μανθάνειν οἰκείαν ἐπιστήμην ἀναλαμβάνειν ἂν εἴη;
τοῦτο δέ που ἀναμιμνήσκεσθαι λέγοντες ὀρθῶς ἂν
λέγοιμεν; Πάνυ γε. Δυνατὸν γὰρ δὴ τοῦτό
76 γε ἐφάνη, αἰσθόμενόν τι ἢ ἰδόντα ἢ ἀκούσαντα ἤ
τινα ἄλλην αἴσθησιν λαβόντα ἕτερόν τι ἀπὸ
τούτου ἐννοῆσαι, ὃ ἐπελέληστο, ᾧ τοῦτο ἐπλη-
σίαζεν ἀνόμοιον ὂν ἢ ὅμοιον· ὥστε, ὅπερ λέγω,
δυοῖν τὰ ἕτερα, ἤτοι ἐπιστάμενοί γε αὐτὰ γεγόναμεν καὶ ἐπιστάμεθα διὰ βίου πάντες, ἢ ὕστερον,
οὕς φαμεν μανθάνειν, οὐδὲν ἀλλ' ἢ ἀναμιμνήσκονται οὗτοι, καὶ ἡ μάθησις ἀνάμνησις ἂν εἴη.
Καὶ μάλα δὴ οὕτως ἔχει, ὦ Σώκρατες.

21. Πότερον οὖν αἱρεῖ, ὦ Σιμμία, ἐπισταμέ-
B νους ἡμᾶς γεγονέναι, ἢ ἀναμιμνήσκεσθαι ὕστερον
ὧν πρότερον ἐπιστήμην εἰληφότες ἦμεν; Οὐκ
ἔχω, ὦ Σώκρατες, ἐν τῷ παρόντι ἑλέσθαι. Τί
δὲ τόδε; ἔχεις ἑλέσθαι, καὶ πῇ σοι δοκεῖ περὶ
αὐτοῦ· ἀνὴρ ἐπιστάμενος περὶ ὧν ἐπίσταται
ἔχοι ἂν δοῦναι λόγον ἢ οὔ; Πολλὴ ἀνάγκη,
ἔφη, ὦ Σώκρατες. Ἦ καὶ δοκοῦσί σοι πάντες
ἔχειν διδόναι λόγον περὶ τούτων ὧν νῦν δὴ
ἐλέγομεν; Βουλοίμην μέντ' ἄν, ἔφη ὁ Σιμμίας·
ἀλλὰ πολὺ μᾶλλον φοβοῦμαι, μὴ αὔριον
τηνικάδε οὐκέτι ᾖ ἀνθρώπων οὐδεὶς ἀξίως οἷός τε
C τοῦτο ποιῆσαι. Οὐκ ἄρα δοκοῦσί σοι ἐπίστασθαί
γε, ἔφη, ὦ Σιμμία, πάντες αὐτά; Οὐδαμῶς.

264

which we call learning really be recovering knowledge which is our own? And should we be right
in calling this recollection?"

"Assuredly."

"For we found that it is possible, on perceiving a
thing by the sight or the hearing or any other sense,
to call to mind from that perception another thing
which had been forgotten, which was associated
with the thing perceived, whether like it or unlike
it; so that, as I said, one of two things is true, either
we are all born knowing these things and know
them all our lives, or afterwards, those who are said
to learn merely remember, and learning would then
be recollection."

"That is certainly true, Socrates."

"Which then do you choose, Simmias? Were we
born with the knowledge, or do we recollect afterwards things of which we had acquired knowledge
before our birth?"

"I cannot choose at this moment, Socrates."

"How about this question? You can choose and
you have some opinion about it: When a man knows,
can he give an account of what he knows or not?"

"Certainly he can, Socrates."

"And do you think that everybody can give an
account of the matters about which we have just been
talking?"

"I wish they might," said Simmias; "but on the
contrary I fear that to-morrow, at this time, there
will be no longer any man living who is able to do so
properly."

"Then, Simmias, you do not think all men know
these things?"

"By no means."

Ἀναμιμνήσκονται ἄρα ἅ ποτε ἔμαθον; Ἀνάγκη.
Πότε λαβοῦσαι αἱ ψυχαὶ ἡμῶν τὴν ἐπιστήμην
αὐτῶν; οὐ γὰρ δὴ ἀφ' οὗ γε ἄνθρωποι γεγόναμεν.
Οὐ δῆτα. Πρότερον ἄρα. Ναί. Ἦσαν ἄρα,
ὦ Σιμμία, αἱ ψυχαὶ καὶ πρότερον, πρὶν εἶναι
ἐν ἀνθρώπου εἴδει, χωρὶς σωμάτων, καὶ φρόνησιν
εἶχον. Εἰ μὴ ἄρα γιγνόμενοι λαμβάνομεν, ὦ
Σώκρατες, ταύτας τὰς ἐπιστήμας· οὗτος γὰρ
D λείπεται ἔτι ὁ χρόνος. Εἶεν, ὦ ἑταῖρε· ἀπόλλυμεν δὲ αὐτὰς ἐν ποίῳ ἄλλῳ χρόνῳ; οὐ γὰρ
δὴ ἔχοντές γε αὐτὰς γιγνόμεθα, ὡς ἄρτι ὡμολογή-
σαμεν· ἢ ἐν τούτῳ ἀπόλλυμεν, ἐν ᾧπερ καὶ
λαμβάνομεν; ἢ ἔχεις ἄλλον τινὰ εἰπεῖν χρόνον;
Οὐδαμῶς, ὦ Σώκρατες, ἀλλὰ ἔλαθον ἐμαυτὸν
οὐδὲν εἰπών.

22. Ἆρ' οὖν οὕτως ἔχει, ἔφη, ἡμῖν, ὦ Σιμμία;
εἰ μὲν ἔστιν ἃ θρυλοῦμεν ἀεί, καλόν τε καὶ
ἀγαθὸν καὶ πᾶσα ἡ τοιαύτη οὐσία, καὶ ἐπὶ
ταύτην τὰ ἐκ τῶν αἰσθήσεων πάντα ἀναφέ-
E ρομεν, ὑπάρχουσαν πρότερον ἀνευρίσκοντες ἡμετέραν οὖσαν, καὶ ταῦτα ἐκείνῃ ἀπεικάζομεν,
ἀναγκαῖον, οὕτως ὥσπερ καὶ ταῦτα ἔστιν, οὕτως
καὶ τὴν ἡμετέραν ψυχὴν εἶναι καὶ πρὶν γεγονέναι
ἡμᾶς· εἰ δὲ μὴ ἔστι ταῦτα, ἄλλως ἂν ὁ λόγος
οὗτος εἰρημένος εἴη; ἆρ' οὕτως ἔχει, καὶ ἴση
ἀνάγκη ταῦτά τε εἶναι καὶ τὰς ἡμετέρας ψυχὰς
πρὶν καὶ ἡμᾶς γεγονέναι, καὶ εἰ μὴ ταῦτα, οὐδὲ

" Then they recollect the things they once learned ? "

" Necessarily."

" When did our souls acquire the knowledge of them ? Surely not after we were born as human beings."

" Certainly not."

" Then previously."

" Yes."

" Then, Simmias, the souls existed previously, before they were in human form, apart from bodies, and they had intelligence."

" Unless, Socrates, we acquire these ideas at the moment of birth ; for that time still remains."

" Very well, my friend. But at what other time do we lose them ? For we are surely not born with them, as we just now agreed. Do we lose them at the moment when we receive them, or have you some other time to suggest ? "

" None whatever, Socrates. I did not notice that I was talking nonsense."

" Then, Simmias," said he, " is this the state of the case ? If, as we are always saying, the beautiful exists, and the good, and every essence of that kind, and if we refer all our sensations to these, which we find existed previously and are now ours, and compare our sensations with these, is it not a necessary inference that just as these abstractions exist, so our souls existed before we were born ; and if these abstractions do not exist, our argument is of no force ? Is this the case, and is it equally certain that provided these things exist our souls also existed before we were born, and that if these do not exist, neither did our souls ? "

τάδε; Ὑπερφυῶς, ὦ Σώκρατες, ἔφη ὁ Σιμμίας, δοκεῖ μοι ἡ αὐτὴ ἀνάγκη εἶναι, καὶ εἰς καλόν γε καταφεύγει ὁ λόγος εἰς τὸ ὁμοίως εἶναι τήν

77 τε ψυχὴν ἡμῶν πρὶν γενέσθαι ἡμᾶς καὶ τὴν οὐσίαν, ἣν σὺ λέγεις. οὐ γὰρ ἔχω ἔγωγε οὐδὲν οὕτω μοι ἐναργὲς ὂν ὡς τοῦτο, τὸ πάντα τὰ τοιαῦτ᾽ εἶναι ὡς οἷόν τε μάλιστα, καλόν τε καὶ ἀγαθὸν καὶ τἆλλα πάντα ἃ σὺ νῦν δὴ ἔλεγες· καὶ ἐμοὶ δοκεῖ ἱκανῶς ἀποδέδεικται. Τί δὲ δὴ Κέβητι; ἔφη ὁ Σωκράτης· δεῖ γὰρ καὶ Κέβητα πείθειν. Ἱκανῶς, ἔφη ὁ Σιμμίας, ὡς ἔγωγε οἶμαι· καίτοι καρτερώτατος ἀνθρώπων ἐστὶν πρὸς τὸ ἀπιστεῖν τοῖς λόγοις· ἀλλ᾽ οἶμαι οὐκ ἐνδεῶς τοῦτο πεπεῖσθαι αὐτόν, ὅτι πρὶν

B γενέσθαι ἡμᾶς ἦν ἡμῶν ἡ ψυχή.

23. Εἰ μέντοι καὶ ἐπειδὰν ἀποθάνωμεν ἔτι ἔσται, οὐδὲ αὐτῷ μοι δοκεῖ, ἔφη, ὦ Σώκρατες, ἀποδεδεῖχθαι, ἀλλ᾽ ἔτι ἐνέστηκεν, ὃ νῦν δὴ Κέβης ἔλεγε, τὸ τῶν πολλῶν, ὅπως μὴ ἀποθνῄσκοντος τοῦ ἀνθρώπου διασκεδάννυται ἡ ψυχὴ καὶ αὐτῇ τοῦ εἶναι τοῦτο τέλος ᾖ. τί γὰρ κωλύει γίγνεσθαι μὲν αὐτὴν καὶ ξυνίστασθαι ἄλλοθέν ποθεν καὶ εἶναι πρὶν καὶ εἰς ἀνθρώπειον σῶμα ἀφικέσθαι, ἐπειδὰν δὲ ἀφίκηται καὶ ἀπαλλάττηται τούτου, τότε καὶ αὐτὴν τελευτᾶν καὶ διαφθείρεσθαι;

C Εὖ λέγεις, ἔφη, ὦ Σιμμία, ὁ Κέβης. φαίνεται γὰρ ὥσπερ ἥμισυ ἀποδεδεῖχθαι οὗ δεῖ, ὅτι πρὶν γενέσθαι ἡμᾶς ἦν ἡμῶν ἡ ψυχή· δεῖ δὲ προσαποδεῖξαι ὅτι καὶ ἐπειδὰν ἀποθάνωμεν οὐδὲν ἧττον ἔσται ἢ πρὶν γενέσθαι, εἰ μέλλει τέλος ἡ ἀπόδειξις ἔχειν. Ἀποδέδεικται μέν, ἔφη, ὦ Σιμμία τε καὶ Κέβης, ὁ Σωκράτης,

"Socrates, it seems to me that there is absolutely the same certainty, and our argument comes to the excellent conclusion that our soul existed before we were born, and that the essence of which you speak likewise exists. For there is nothing so clear to me as this, that all such things, the beautiful, the good, and all the others of which you were speaking just now, have a most real existence. And I think the proof is sufficient."

"But how about Cebes?" said Socrates. "For Cebes must be convinced, too."

"He is fully convinced, I think," said Simmias; "and yet he is the most obstinately incredulous of mortals. Still, I believe he is quite convinced of this, that our soul existed before we were born. However, that it will still exist after we die does not seem even to me to have been proved, Socrates, but the common fear, which Cebes mentioned just now, that when a man dies the soul is dispersed and this is the end of his existence, still remains. For assuming that the soul comes into being and is brought together from some source or other and exists before it enters into a human body, what prevents it, after it has entered into and left that body, from coming to an end and being destroyed itself?"

"You are right, Simmias," said Cebes. "It seems to me that we have proved only half of what is required, namely, that our soul existed before our birth. But we must also show that it exists after we are dead as well as before our birth, if the proof is to be perfect."

"It has been shown, Simmias and Cebes, already," said Socrates, "if you will combine this conclusion

καὶ νῦν, εἰ θέλετε συνθεῖναι τοῦτόν τε τὸν
λόγον εἰς ταὐτὸν καὶ ὃν πρὸ τούτου ὡμολογήσαμεν, τὸ γίγνεσθαι πᾶν τὸ ζῶν ἐκ τοῦ τεθνεῶτος.
εἰ γὰρ ἔστιν μὲν ἡ ψυχὴ καὶ πρότερον, ἀνάγκη
D δὲ αὐτῇ εἰς τὸ ζῆν ἰούσῃ τε καὶ γιγνομένῃ
μηδαμόθεν ἄλλοθεν ἢ ἐκ θανάτου καὶ τοῦ τεθνάναι
γίγνεσθαι, πῶς οὐκ ἀνάγκη αὐτήν, καὶ ἐπειδὰν
ἀποθάνῃ εἶναι, ἐπειδή γε δεῖ αὖθις αὐτὴν γίγνεσθαι; ἀποδέδεικται μὲν οὖν ὅπερ λέγετε καὶ νῦν.

24. Ὅμως δέ μοι δοκεῖς σύ τε καὶ Σιμμίας
ἡδέως ἂν καὶ τοῦτον διαπραγματεύσασθαι τὸν
λόγον ἔτι μᾶλλον, καὶ δεδιέναι τὸ τῶν παίδων,
μὴ ὡς ἀληθῶς ὁ ἄνεμος αὐτὴν ἐκβαίνουσαν ἐκ
τοῦ σώματος διαφυσᾷ καὶ διασκεδάννυσιν, ἄλλως
E τε καὶ ὅταν τύχῃ τις μὴ ἐν νηνεμίᾳ, ἀλλ' ἐν
μεγάλῳ τινὶ πνεύματι ἀποθνήσκων. καὶ ὁ Κέβης
ἐπιγελάσας· Ὡς δεδιότων, ἔφη, ὦ Σώκρατες,
πειρῶ ἀναπείθειν· μᾶλλον δὲ μὴ ὡς ἡμῶν δεδιότων, ἀλλ' ἴσως ἔνι τις καὶ ἐν ἡμῖν παῖς, ὅστις
τὰ τοιαῦτα φοβεῖται· τοῦτον οὖν πειρώμεθα
πείθειν μὴ δεδιέναι τὸν θάνατον ὥσπερ τὰ μορμο-
λύκεια. Ἀλλὰ χρή, ἔφη ὁ Σωκράτης, ἐπᾴδειν αὐτῷ ἑκάστης ἡμέρας, ἕως ἂν ἐξεπᾴσητε.

78 Πόθεν οὖν, ἔφη, ὦ Σώκρατες, τῶν τοιούτων
ἀγαθὸν ἐπῳδὸν ληψόμεθα, ἐπειδὴ σύ, ἔφη, ἡμᾶς
ἀπολείπεις; Πολλὴ μὲν ἡ Ἑλλάς, ἔφη, ὦ Κέβης,
ἐν ᾗ ἔνεισί που ἀγαθοὶ ἄνδρες, πολλὰ δὲ καὶ
τὰ τῶν βαρβάρων γένη, οὓς πάντας χρὴ διερευ-
νᾶσθαι ζητοῦντας τοιοῦτον ἐπῳδόν, μήτε χρημάτων φειδομένους μήτε πόνων, ὡς οὐκ ἔστιν εἰς
ὅ τι ἂν ἀναγκαιότερον ἀναλίσκοιτε χρήματα.
ζητεῖν δὲ χρὴ καὶ αὐτοὺς μετ' ἀλλήλων· ἴσως

with the one we reached before, that every living being is born from the dead. For if the soul exists before birth, and, when it comes into life and is born, cannot be born from anything else than death and a state of death, must it not also exist after dying, since it must be born again? So the proof you call for has already been given. However, I think you and Simmias would like to carry on this discussion still further. You have the childish fear that when the soul goes out from the body the wind will really blow it away and scatter it, especially if a man happens to die in a high wind and not in calm weather."

And Cebes laughed and said, "Assume that we have that fear, Socrates, and try to convince us; or rather, do not assume that we are afraid, but perhaps there is a child within us, who has such fears. Let us try to persuade him not to fear death as if it were a hobgoblin."

"Ah," said Socrates, "you must sing charms to him every day until you charm away his fear."

"Where then, Socrates," said he, "shall we find a good singer of such charms, since you are leaving us?"

"Hellas, Cebes," he replied, "is a large country, in which there are many good men, and there are many foreign peoples also. You ought to search through all of them in quest of such a charmer, sparing neither money nor toil, for there is no greater need for which you could spend your money. And you must seek among yourselves, too, for

γὰρ ἂν οὐδὲ ῥᾳδίως εὕροιτε μᾶλλον ὑμῶν δυναμένους τοῦτο ποιεῖν. Ἀλλὰ ταῦτα μὲν δή, ἔφη,
ὑπάρξει, ὁ Κέβης· ὅθεν δὲ ἀπελίπομεν, ἐπανέλ-
B θωμεν, εἴ σοι ἡδομένῳ ἐστίν. Ἀλλὰ μὴν ἡδομένῳ γε· πῶς γὰρ οὐ μέλλει; Καλῶς, ἔφη, λέγεις.
25. Οὐκοῦν τοιόνδε τι, ἦ δ' ὃς ὁ Σωκράτης,
δεῖ ἡμᾶς ἐρέσθαι ἑαυτούς, τῷ ποίῳ τινὶ ἄρα
προσήκει τοῦτο τὸ πάθος πάσχειν, τὸ διασκεδάν-
νυσθαι, καὶ ὑπὲρ τοῦ ποίου τινὸς δεδιέναι μὴ
πάθῃ αὐτό, καὶ τῷ ποίῳ τινὶ οὔ· καὶ μετὰ τοῦτο
αὖ ἐπισκέψασθαι, πότερον ἡ ψυχή ἐστιν, καὶ ἐκ
τούτων θαρρεῖν ἢ δεδιέναι ὑπὲρ τῆς ἡμετέρας
ψυχῆς; Ἀληθῆ, ἔφη, λέγεις. Ἆρ' οὖν τῷ μὲν
C συντεθέντι τε καὶ συνθέτῳ ὄντι φύσει προσήκει
τοῦτο πάσχειν, διαιρεθῆναι ταύτῃ ᾗπερ συνε-
τέθη· εἰ δέ τι τυγχάνει ὂν ἀξύνθετον, τούτῳ μόνῳ
προσήκει μὴ πάσχειν ταῦτα, εἴπερ τῳ ἄλλῳ;
Δοκεῖ μοι, ἔφη, οὕτως ἔχειν, ὁ Κέβης. Οὐκοῦν
ἅπερ ἀεὶ κατὰ ταὐτὰ καὶ ὡσαύτως ἔχει, ταῦτα
μάλιστα εἰκὸς εἶναι τὰ ἀξύνθετα, ἃ δὲ ἄλλοτ'
ἄλλως καὶ μηδέποτε κατὰ ταὐτά, ταῦτα δὲ
εἶναι τὰ σύνθετα; Ἔμοιγε δοκεῖ οὕτως. Ἴωμεν
δή, ἔφη, ἐπὶ ταὐτὰ ἐφ' ἅπερ ἐν τῷ ἔμπροσθεν
D λόγῳ. αὐτὴ ἡ οὐσία ἧς λόγον δίδομεν τὸ εἶναι
καὶ ἐρωτῶντες καὶ ἀποκρινόμενοι, πότερον ὡσαύτως ἀεὶ ἔχει κατὰ ταὐτὰ ἢ ἄλλοτ' ἄλλως; αὐτὸ
τὸ ἴσον, αὐτὸ τὸ καλόν, αὐτὸ ἕκαστον ὃ ἔστιν,
τὸ ὄν, μή ποτε μεταβολὴν καὶ ἡντινοῦν ἐνδέχεται;
ἢ ἀεὶ αὐτῶν ἕκαστον ὃ ἔστι, μονοειδὲς ὂν αὐτὸ

perhaps you would hardly find others better able to do this than you."

"That," said Cebes, "shall be done. But let us return to the point where we left off, if you are willing."

"Oh, I am willing, of course."

"Good," said he.

"Well then," said Socrates, "must we not ask ourselves some such question as this? What kind of thing naturally suffers dispersion, and for what kind of thing might we naturally fear it, and again what kind of thing is not liable to it? And after this must we not inquire to which class the soul belongs and base our hopes or fears for our souls upon the answers to these questions?"

"You are quite right," he replied.

"Now is not that which is compounded and composite naturally liable to be decomposed, in the same way in which it was compounded? And if anything is uncompounded is not that, if anything, naturally unlikely to be decomposed?"

"I think," said Cebes, "that is true."

"Then it is most probable that things which are always the same and unchanging are the uncompounded things and the things that are changing and never the same are the composite things?"

"Yes, I think so."

"Let us then," said he, "turn to what we were discussing before. Is the absolute essence, which we in our dialectic process of question and answer call true being, always the same or is it liable to change? Absolute equality, absolute beauty, any absolute existence, true being—do they ever admit of any change whatsoever? Or does each absolute essence,

καθ᾽ αὑτό, ὡσαύτως κατὰ ταὐτὰ ἔχει καὶ οὐδέποτε
οὐδαμῇ οὐδαμῶς ἀλλοίωσιν οὐδεμίαν ἐνδέχεται;
Ὡσαύτως, ἔφη, ἀνάγκη, ὁ Κέβης, κατὰ ταὐτὰ
E ἔχειν, ὦ Σώκρατες. Τί δὲ τῶν πολλῶν, οἷον
ἀνθρώπων ἢ ἵππων ἢ ἱματίων ἢ ἄλλων ὡντινωνοῦν
τοιούτων, ἢ ἴσων ἢ καλῶν ἢ πάντων τῶν ἐκείνοις
ὁμωνύμων; ἆρα κατὰ ταὐτὰ ἔχει, ἢ πᾶν τοὐναντίον ἐκείνοις οὔτε αὐτὰ αὑτοῖς οὔτε ἀλλήλοις
οὐδέποτε, ὡς ἔπος εἰπεῖν, οὐδαμῶς κατὰ ταὐτά;
Οὕτως, ἔφη ὁ Κέβης· οὐδέποτε ὡσαύτως ἔχει.
79 Οὐκοῦν τούτων μὲν κἂν ἅψαιο κἂν ἴδοις κἂν
ταῖς ἄλλαις αἰσθήσεσιν αἴσθοιο, τῶν δὲ κατὰ
ταὐτὰ ἐχόντων οὐκ ἔστιν ὅτῳ ποτ᾽ ἂν ἄλλῳ
ἐπιλάβοιο ἢ τῷ τῆς διανοίας λογισμῷ, ἀλλ᾽
ἐστὶν ἀειδῆ τὰ τοιαῦτα καὶ οὐχ ὁρατά; Παντάπασιν, ἔφη, ἀληθῆ λέγεις.

26. Θῶμεν οὖν βούλει, ἔφη, δύο εἴδη τῶν ὄντων,
τὸ μὲν ὁρατόν, τὸ δὲ ἀειδές; Θῶμεν, ἔφη. Καὶ
τὸ μὲν ἀειδὲς ἀεὶ κατὰ ταὐτὰ ἔχον, τὸ δὲ ὁρατὸν
μηδέποτε κατὰ ταὐτά; Καὶ τοῦτο, ἔφη, θῶμεν.
B Φέρε δή, ἦ δ᾽ ὅς, ἄλλο τι ἡμῶν αὐτῶν τὸ μὲν
σῶμά ἐστι, τὸ δὲ ψυχή; Οὐδὲν ἄλλο, ἔφη.
Ποτέρῳ οὖν ὁμοιότερον τῷ εἴδει φαῖμεν ἂν εἶναι
καὶ ξυγγενέστερον τὸ σῶμα; Παντί, ἔφη, τοῦτό
γε δῆλον, ὅτι τῷ ὁρατῷ. Τί δὲ ἡ ψυχή; ὁρατὸν
ἢ ἀειδές; Οὐχ ὑπ᾽ ἀνθρώπων γε, ὦ Σώκρατες,

since it is uniform and exists by itself, remain the same and never in any way admit of any change?"

"It must," said Cebes, "necessarily remain the same, Socrates."

"But how about the many things, for example, men, or horses, or cloaks, or any other such things, which bear the same names as the absolute essences and are called beautiful or equal or the like? Are they always the same? Or are they, in direct opposition to the essences, constantly changing in themselves, unlike each other, and, so to speak, never the same?"

"The latter," said Cebes; "they are never the same."

"And. you can see these and touch them and perceive them by the other senses, whereas the things which are always the same can be grasped only by the reason, and are invisible and not to be seen?"

"Certainly," said he, "that is true."

"Now," said he, "shall we assume two kinds of existences, one visible, the other invisible?"

"Let us assume them," said Cebes.

"And that the invisible is always the same and the visible constantly changing?"

"Let us assume that also," said he.

"Well then," said Socrates, "are we not made up of two parts, body and soul?"

"Yes," he replied.

"Now to which class should we say the body is more similar and more closely akin?"

"To the visible," said he; "that is clear to everyone."

"And the soul? Is it visible or invisible?"

"Invisible, to man, at least, Socrates."

ἔφη. Ἀλλὰ ἡμεῖς γε τὰ ὁρατὰ καὶ τὰ μὴ τῇ τῶν ἀνθρώπων φύσει λέγομεν· ἢ ἄλλῃ τινὶ οἴει; Τῇ τῶν ἀνθρώπων. Τί οὖν περὶ ψυχῆς λέγομεν; ὁρατὸν ἢ ἀόρατον εἶναι; Οὐχ ὁρατόν. Ἀειδὲς ἄρα; Ναί. Ὁμοιότερον ἄρα ψυχὴ σώματός ἐστιν

C τῷ ἀειδεῖ, τὸ δὲ τῷ ὁρατῷ. Πᾶσα ἀνάγκη, ὦ Σώκρατες.

27. Οὐκοῦν καὶ τόδε πάλαι λέγομεν, ὅτι ἡ ψυχή, ὅταν μὲν τῷ σώματι προσχρῆται εἰς τὸ σκοπεῖν τι ἢ διὰ τοῦ ὁρᾶν ἢ διὰ τοῦ ἀκούειν ἢ δι' ἄλλης τινὸς αἰσθήσεως—τοῦτο γάρ ἐστιν τὸ διὰ τοῦ σώματος, τὸ δι' αἰσθήσεων σκοπεῖν τι—, τότε μὲν ἕλκεται ὑπὸ τοῦ σώματος εἰς τὰ οὐδέποτε κατὰ ταὐτὰ ἔχοντα, καὶ αὐτὴ πλανᾶται καὶ ταράττεται καὶ ἰλιγγιᾷ ὥσπερ μεθύουσα, ἅτε τοιούτων ἐφαπτομένη; Πάνυ γε. Ὅταν δέ γε

D αὐτὴ καθ' αὑτὴν σκοπῇ, ἐκεῖσε οἴχεται εἰς τὸ καθαρόν τε καὶ ἀεὶ ὂν καὶ ἀθάνατον καὶ ὡσαύτως ἔχον, καὶ ὡς συγγενὴς οὖσα αὐτοῦ ἀεὶ μετ' ἐκείνου τε γίγνεται, ὅτανπερ αὐτὴ καθ' αὑτὴν γένηται καὶ ἐξῇ αὐτῇ, καὶ πέπαυταί τε τοῦ πλάνου καὶ περὶ ἐκεῖνα ἀεὶ κατὰ ταὐτὰ ὡσαύτως ἔχει, ἅτε τοιούτων ἐφαπτομένη· καὶ τοῦτο αὐτῆς τὸ πάθημα φρόνησις κέκληται; Παντάπασιν, ἔφη, καλῶς καὶ ἀληθῆ λέγεις, ὦ Σώκρατες. Ποτέρῳ οὖν αὖ σοι δοκεῖ τῷ εἴδει καὶ ἐκ τῶν ἔμπροσθεν καὶ ἐκ

"But we call things visible and invisible with reference to human vision, do we not?"

"Yes, we do."

"Then what do we say about the soul? Can it be seen or not?"

"It cannot be seen."

"Then it is invisible?"

"Yes."

"Then the soul is more like the invisible than the body is, and the body more like the visible."

"Necessarily, Socrates."

"Now we have also been saying for a long time, have we not, that, when the soul makes use of the body for any inquiry, either through seeing or hearing or any of the other senses—for inquiry through the body means inquiry through the senses,—then it is dragged by the body to things which never remain the same, and it wanders about and is confused and dizzy like a drunken man because it lays hold upon such things?"

"Certainly."

"But when the soul inquires alone by itself, it departs into the realm of the pure, the everlasting, the immortal and the changeless, and being akin to these it dwells always with them whenever it is by itself and is not hindered, and it has rest from its wanderings and remains always the same and unchanging with the changeless, since it is in communion therewith. And this state of the soul is called wisdom. Is it not so?"

"Socrates," said he, "what you say is perfectly right and true."

"And now again, in view of what we said before and of what has just been said, to which

E τῶν νῦν λεγομένων ψυχὴ ὁμοιότερον εἶναι καὶ
ξυγγενέστερον; Πᾶς ἄν μοι δοκεῖ, ἦ δ᾽ ὅς, συγχωρῆσαι, ὦ Σώκρατες, ἐκ ταύτης τῆς μεθόδου,
καὶ ὁ δυσμαθέστατος, ὅτι ὅλῳ καὶ παντὶ ὁμοιό-
τερόν ἐστι ψυχὴ τῷ ἀεὶ ὡσαύτως ἔχοντι μᾶλλον
ἢ τῷ μή. Τί δὲ τὸ σῶμα; Τῷ ἑτέρῳ.

28. Ὅρα δὴ καὶ τῇδε, ὅτι, ἐπειδὰν ἐν τῷ
80 αὐτῷ ὦσι ψυχὴ καὶ σῶμα, τῷ μὲν δουλεύειν καὶ
ἄρχεσθαι ἡ φύσις προστάττει, τῇ δὲ ἄρχειν καὶ
δεσπόζειν· καὶ κατὰ ταῦτα αὖ πότερόν σοι δοκεῖ
ὅμοιον τῷ θείῳ εἶναι καὶ πότερον τῷ θνητῷ; ἢ οὐ
δοκεῖ σοι τὸ μὲν θεῖον οἷον ἄρχειν τε καὶ ἡγεμονεύειν πεφυκέναι, τὸ δὲ θνητὸν ἄρχεσθαί τε καὶ
δουλεύειν; Ἔμοιγε. Ποτέρῳ οὖν ἡ ψυχὴ ἔοικεν;
Δῆλα δή, ὦ Σώκρατες, ὅτι ἡ μὲν ψυχὴ τῷ θείῳ,
τὸ δὲ σῶμα τῷ θνητῷ. Σκόπει δή, ἔφη, ὦ
Κέβης, εἰ ἐκ πάντων τῶν εἰρημένων τάδε ἡμῖν
15 ξυμβαίνει, τῷ μὲν θείῳ καὶ ἀθανάτῳ καὶ νοητῷ
καὶ μονοειδεῖ καὶ ἀδιαλύτῳ καὶ ἀεὶ ὡσαύτως
κατὰ ταὐτὰ ἔχοντι ἑαυτῷ ὁμοιότατον εἶναι ψυχήν, τῷ δὲ ἀνθρωπίνῳ καὶ θνητῷ καὶ πολυειδεῖ
καὶ ἀνοήτῳ καὶ διαλυτῷ καὶ μηδέποτε κατὰ ταὐτὰ
ἔχοντι ἑαυτῷ ὁμοιότατον αὖ εἶναι σῶμα. ἔχομέν
τι παρὰ ταῦτα ἄλλο λέγειν, ὦ φίλε Κέβης, ἢ οὐχ
οὕτως ἔχει; Οὐκ ἔχομεν.

29. Τί οὖν; τούτων οὕτως ἐχόντων ἆρ᾽ οὐχὶ
σώματι μὲν ταχὺ διαλύεσθαι προσήκει, ψυχῇ δὲ
αὖ τὸ παράπαν ἀδιαλύτῳ εἶναι ἢ ἐγγύς τι τού-

class do you think the soul has greater likeness and kinship?"

"I think, Socrates," said he, "that anyone, even the dullest, would agree, after this argument that the soul is infinitely more like that which is always the same than that which is not."

"And the body?"

"Is more like the other."

"Consider, then, the matter in another way. When the soul and the body are joined together, nature directs the one to serve and be ruled, and the other to rule and be master. Now this being the case, which seems to you like the divine, and which like the mortal? Or do you not think that the divine is by nature fitted to rule and lead, and the mortal to obey and serve?"

"Yes, I think so."

"Which, then, does the soul resemble?"

"Clearly, Socrates, the soul is like the divine and the body like the mortal."

"Then see, Cebes, if this is not the conclusion from all that we have said, that the soul is most like the divine and immortal and intellectual and uniform and indissoluble and ever unchanging, and the body, on the contrary, most like the human and mortal and multiform and unintellectual and dissoluble and ever changing. Can we say anything, my dear Cebes, to show that this is not so?"

"No, we cannot."

"Well then, since this is the case, is it not natural for the body to meet with speedy dissolution and for the soul, on the contrary, to be entirely indissoluble, or nearly so?"

PLATO

C του; Πῶς γὰρ οὔ; Ἐννοεῖς οὖν, ἔφη, ὅτι, ἐπειδὰν
ἀποθάνῃ ὁ ἄνθρωπος, τὸ μὲν ὁρατὸν αὐτοῦ, τὸ
σῶμα, καὶ ἐν ὁρατῷ κείμενον, ὃ δὴ νεκρὸν καλοῦμεν, ᾧ προσήκει διαλύεσθαι καὶ διαπίπτειν, οὐκ
εὐθὺς τούτων οὐδὲν πέπονθεν, ἀλλ' ἐπιεικῶς
συχνὸν ἐπιμένει χρόνον, ἐὰν μέν τις καὶ χαριέντως
ἔχων τὸ σῶμα τελευτήσῃ καὶ ἐν τοιαύτῃ ὥρᾳ, καὶ
πάνυ μάλα. συμπεσὸν γὰρ τὸ σῶμα καὶ ταρι-
χευθέν, ὥσπερ οἱ ἐν Αἰγύπτῳ ταριχευθέντες,
ὀλίγου ὅλον μένει ἀμήχανον ὅσον χρόνον.[1] ἔνια
D δὲ μέρη τοῦ σώματος, καὶ ἂν σαπῇ, ὀστᾶ τε καὶ
νεῦρα καὶ τὰ τοιαῦτα πάντα, ὅμως ὡς ἔπος εἰπεῖν
ἀθάνατά ἐστιν· ἢ οὔ; Ναί. Ἡ δὲ ψυχὴ ἄρα, τὸ
ἀειδές, τὸ εἰς τοιοῦτον τόπον ἕτερον οἰχόμενον
γενναῖον καὶ καθαρὸν καὶ ἀειδῆ, εἰς Ἅιδου ὡς
ἀληθῶς, παρὰ τὸν ἀγαθὸν καὶ φρόνιμον θεόν, οἷ,
ἂν θεὸς ἐθέλῃ, αὐτίκα καὶ τῇ ἐμῇ ψυχῇ ἰτέον,
αὕτη δὲ δὴ ἡμῖν ἡ τοιαύτη καὶ οὕτω πεφυκυῖα
ἀπαλλαττομένη τοῦ σώματος εὐθὺς διαπέφυσηται
καὶ ἀπόλωλεν, ὥς φασιν οἱ πολλοὶ ἄνθρωποι;
E πολλοῦ γε δεῖ, ὦ φίλε Κέβης τε καὶ Σιμμία,
ἀλλὰ πολλῷ μᾶλλον ὧδ' ἔχει· ἐὰν μὲν καθαρὰ
ἀπαλλάττηται, μηδὲν τοῦ σώματος ξυνεφέλκουσα,
ἅτε οὐδὲν κοινωνοῦσα αὐτῷ ἐν τῷ βίῳ ἑκοῦσα
εἶναι, ἀλλὰ φεύγουσα αὐτὸ καὶ συνηθροισμένη[2]
αὐτὴ εἰς ἑαυτήν, ἅτε μελετῶσα ἀεὶ τοῦτο—τοῦτο
δὲ οὐδὲν ἄλλο ἐστὶν ἢ ὀρθῶς φιλοσοφοῦσα καὶ τῷ
81 ὄντι τεθνάναι μελετῶσα·[3] ἢ οὐ τοῦτ' ἂν εἴη

---

[1] Schanz brackets συμπεσὸν . . . χρόνον.
[2] συνηθροισμένη αὐτὴ εἰς ἑαυτήν T Stobaeus. Schanz brackets
καὶ συνηθροισμένη. B and Schanz omit αὐτὴ εἰς ἑαυτήν.
[3] The MSS. read μελετῶσα ῥᾳδίως. Schanz brackets ῥᾳδίως.

"Of course."

"Observe," he went on, "that when a man dies, the visible part of him, the body, which lies in the visible world and which we call the corpse, which is naturally subject to dissolution and decomposition, does not undergo these processes at once, but remains for a considerable time, and even for a very long time, if death takes place when the body is in good condition, and at a favourable time of the year. For when the body is shrunk and embalmed, as is done in Egypt, it remains almost entire for an incalculable time. And even if the body decay, some parts of it, such as the bones and sinews and all that, are, so to speak, indestructible. Is not that true?"

"Yes."

"But the soul, the invisible, which departs into another place which is, like itself, noble and pure and invisible, to the realm of the god of the other world in truth, to the good and wise god, whither, if God will, my soul is soon to go,—is this soul, which has such qualities and such a nature, straightway scattered and destroyed when it departs from the body, as most men say? Far from it, dear Cebes and Simmias, but the truth is much rather this:—if it departs pure, dragging with it nothing of the body, because it never willingly associated with the body in life, but avoided it and gathered itself into itself alone, since this has always been its constant study—but this means nothing else than that it pursued philosophy rightly and really practised being in a state of death: or is not this the practice of death?"

PLATO

μελέτη θανάτου; Παντάπασί γε. Οὐκοῦν οὕτω
μὲν ἔχουσα εἰς τὸ ὅμοιον αὐτῇ τὸ ἀειδὲς ἀπέρχεται,
τὸ θεῖόν τε καὶ ἀθάνατον καὶ φρόνιμον, οἷ ἀφικο-
μένῃ ὑπάρχει αὐτῇ εὐδαίμονι εἶναι, πλάνης καὶ
ἀνοίας καὶ φόβων καὶ ἀγρίων ἐρώτων καὶ τῶν
ἄλλων κακῶν τῶν ἀνθρωπείων ἀπηλλαγμένῃ,
ὥσπερ δὲ λέγεται κατὰ τῶν μεμυημένων, ὡς ἀληθῶς τὸν λοιπὸν χρόνον μετὰ τῶν θεῶν διάγουσα;
οὕτω φῶμεν, ὦ Κέβης, ἢ ἄλλως;
   30. Οὕτω νὴ Δία, ἔφη ὁ Κέβης. Ἐὰν δέ γε,
B οἶμαι, μεμιασμένη καὶ ἀκάθαρτος τοῦ σώματος
ἀπαλλάττεται, ἅτε τῷ σώματι ἀεὶ ξυνοῦσα καὶ
τοῦτο θεραπεύουσα καὶ ἐρῶσα καὶ γεγοητευμένη
ὑπ' αὐτοῦ ὑπό τε τῶν ἐπιθυμιῶν καὶ ἡδονῶν,
ὥστε μηδὲν ἄλλο δοκεῖν εἶναι ἀληθὲς ἀλλ' ἢ τὸ
σωματοειδές, οὗ τις ἂν ἅψαιτο καὶ ἴδοι καὶ πίοι
καὶ φάγοι καὶ πρὸς τὰ ἀφροδίσια χρήσαιτο, τὸ δὲ
τοῖς ὄμμασι σκοτῶδες καὶ ἀειδές, νοητὸν δὲ καὶ
φιλοσοφίᾳ αἱρετόν, τοῦτο δὲ εἰθισμένη μισεῖν τε
καὶ τρέμειν καὶ φεύγειν, οὕτω δὴ ἔχουσαν οἴει
C ψυχὴν αὐτὴν καθ' αὑτὴν εἰλικρινῆ ἀπαλλάξεσθαι; Οὐδ' ὁπωστιοῦν, ἔφη. Ἀλλὰ καὶ διει-
λημμένην γε, οἶμαι, ὑπὸ τοῦ σωματοειδοῦς, ὃ
αὐτῇ ἡ ὁμιλία τε καὶ συνουσία τοῦ σώματος διὰ
τὸ ἀεὶ ξυνεῖναι καὶ διὰ τὴν πολλὴν μελέτην
ἐνεποίησε ξύμφυτον; Πάνυ γε. Ἐμβριθὲς δέ
γε, ὦ φίλε, τοῦτο οἴεσθαι χρὴ εἶναι καὶ βαρὺ καὶ
γεῶδες καὶ ὁρατόν· ὃ δὴ καὶ ἔχουσα ἡ τοιαύτη
ψυχὴ βαρύνεταί τε καὶ ἕλκεται πάλιν εἰς τὸν
ὁρατὸν τόπον, φόβῳ τοῦ ἀειδοῦς τε καὶ Ἅιδου,
D ὥσπερ λέγεται, περὶ τὰ μνήματά τε καὶ τοὺς
τάφους κυλινδουμένη, περὶ ἃ δὴ καὶ ὤφθη ἄττα

" By all means."

" Then if it is in such a condition, it goes away into that which is like itself, into the invisible, divine, immortal, and wise, and when it arrives there it is happy, freed from error and folly and fear and fierce loves and all the other human ills, and as the initiated say, lives in truth through all after time with the gods. Is this our belief, Cebes, or not?"

" Assuredly," said Cebes.

" But, I think, if when it departs from the body it is defiled and impure, because it was always with the body and cared for it and loved it and was fascinated by it and its desires and pleasures, so that it thought nothing was true except the corporeal, which one can touch and see and drink and eat and employ in the pleasures of love, and if it is accustomed to hate and fear and avoid that which is shadowy and invisible to the eyes but is intelligible and tangible to philosophy—do you think a soul in this condition will depart pure and uncontaminated?"

" By no means," said he.

"But it will be interpenetrated, I suppose, with the corporeal which intercourse and communion with the body have made a part of its nature because the body has been its constant companion and the object of its care?"

" Certainly."

" And, my friend, we must believe that the corporeal is burdensome and heavy and earthly and visible. And such a soul is weighed down by this and is dragged back into the visible world, through fear of the invisible and of the other world, and so, as they say, it flits about the monuments and the tombs, where shadowy shapes of souls have been

ψυχῶν σκιοειδῆ φαντάσματα, οἷα παρέχονται αἱ
τοιαῦται ψυχαὶ εἴδωλα, αἱ μὴ καθαρῶς ἀπολυ-
θεῖσαι, ἀλλὰ τοῦ ὁρατοῦ μετέχουσαι, διὸ καὶ
ὁρῶνται. Εἰκός γε, ὦ Σώκρατες. Εἰκὸς μέντοι,
ὦ Κέβης· καὶ οὔ τί γε τὰς τῶν ἀγαθῶν ταύτας
εἶναι, ἀλλὰ τὰς τῶν φαύλων, αἳ περὶ τὰ τοιαῦτα
ἀναγκάζονται πλανᾶσθαι δίκην τίνουσαι τῆς προτέρας τροφῆς κακῆς οὔσης· καὶ μέχρι γε τούτου
Ε πλανῶνται, ἕως ἂν τῇ τοῦ ξυνεπακολουθοῦντος
τοῦ σωματοειδοῦς ἐπιθυμίᾳ ἐνδεθῶσιν εἰς σῶμα.
31. Ἐνδοῦνται δέ, ὥσπερ εἰκός, εἰς τοιαῦτα ἤθη
ὁποῖ᾽ ἄττ᾽ ἂν καὶ μεμελετηκυῖαι τύχωσιν ἐν τῷ
βίῳ.

Τὰ ποῖα δὴ ταῦτα λέγεις, ὦ Σώκρατες; Οἷον
τοὺς μὲν γαστριμαργίας τε καὶ ὕβρεις καὶ
φιλοποσίας μεμελετηκότας καὶ μὴ διευλαβημένους,
εἰς τὰ τῶν ὄνων γένη καὶ τῶν τοιούτων θηρίων
82 εἰκὸς ἐνδύεσθαι. ἢ οὐκ οἴει; Πάνυ μὲν οὖν εἰκὸς
λέγεις. Τοὺς δέ γε ἀδικίας τε καὶ τυραννίδας
καὶ ἁρπαγὰς προτετιμηκότας εἰς τὰ τῶν λύκων
τε καὶ ἱεράκων καὶ ἰκτίνων γένη· ἢ ποῖ ἂν ἄλλοσέ
φαμεν τὰς τοιαύτας ἰέναι; Ἀμέλει, ἔφη ὁ Κέβης,
εἰς τὰ τοιαῦτα. Οὐκοῦν, ἦ δ᾽ ὅς, δῆλα δὴ καὶ
τἆλλα, ᾗ ἂν ἕκαστα ἴοι, κατὰ τὰς αὐτῶν ὁμοιότητας τῆς μελέτης; Δῆλον δή, ἔφη· πῶς δ᾽ οὔ;
Οὐκοῦν εὐδαιμονέστατοι, ἔφη, καὶ τούτων εἰσὶ
καὶ εἰς βέλτιστον τόπον ἰόντες οἱ τὴν δημοτικὴν
Β καὶ πολιτικὴν ἀρετὴν ἐπιτετηδευκότες, ἣν δὴ
καλοῦσι σωφροσύνην τε καὶ δικαιοσύνην, ἐξ ἔθους
τε καὶ μελέτης γεγονυῖαν ἄνευ φιλοσοφίας τε καὶ

seen, figures of those souls which were not set free in purity but retain something of the visible; and this is why they are seen."

"That is likely, Socrates."

"It is likely, Cebes. And it is likely that those are not the souls of the good, but those of the base, which are compelled to flit about such places as a punishment for their former evil mode of life. And they flit about until through the desire of the corporeal which clings to them they are again imprisoned in a body. And they are likely to be imprisoned in natures which correspond to the practices of their former life."

"What natures do you mean, Socrates?"

"I mean, for example, that those who have indulged in gluttony and violence and drunkenness, and have taken no pains to avoid them, are likely to pass into the bodies of asses and other beasts of that sort. Do you not think so?"

"Certainly that is very likely."

"And those who have chosen injustice and tyranny and robbery pass into the bodies of wolves and hawks and kites. Where else can we imagine that they go?"

"Beyond a doubt," said Cebes, "they pass into such creatures."

"Then," said he, "it is clear where all the others go, each in accordance with its own habits?"

"Yes," said Cebes, "of course."

"Then," said he, "the happiest of those, and those who go to the best place, are those who have practised, by nature and habit, without philosophy or reason, the social and civil virtues which are called moderation and justice?"

νοῦ; Πῇ δὴ οὗτοι εὐδαιμονέστατοι; Ὅτι τούτους
εἰκός ἐστιν εἰς τοιοῦτον πάλιν ἀφικνεῖσθαι πολι-
τικόν τε καὶ ἥμερον γένος, ἤ που μελιττῶν ἢ
σφηκῶν ἢ μυρμήκων, ἢ καὶ εἰς ταὐτόν γε πάλιν
τὸ ἀνθρώπινον γένος, καὶ γίγνεσθαι ἐξ αὐτῶν
ἄνδρας μετρίους· Εἰκός.

32. Εἰς δέ γε θεῶν γένος μὴ φιλοσοφήσαντι
καὶ παντελῶς καθαρῷ ἀπιόντι οὐ θέμις ἀφι-
C κνεῖσθαι ἀλλ' ἢ τῷ φιλομαθεῖ. ἀλλὰ τούτων
ἕνεκα, ὦ ἑταῖρε Σιμμία τε καὶ Κέβης, οἱ ὀρθῶς
φιλοσοφοῦντες ἀπέχονται τῶν κατὰ τὸ σῶμα
ἐπιθυμιῶν ἁπασῶν καὶ καρτεροῦσι καὶ οὐ
παραδιδόασιν αὐταῖς ἑαυτούς, οὔ τι οἰκοφθορίαν
τε καὶ πενίαν φοβούμενοι, ὥσπερ οἱ πολλοὶ καὶ
φιλοχρήματοι· οὐδὲ αὖ ἀτιμίαν τε καὶ ἀδοξίαν
μοχθηρίας δεδιότες, ὥσπερ οἱ φίλαρχοί τε καὶ
φιλότιμοι, ἔπειτα ἀπέχονται αὐτῶν. Οὐ γὰρ ἂν
πρέποι, ἔφη, ὦ Σώκρατες, ὁ Κέβης. Οὐ μέντοι
D μὰ Δία, ἦ δ' ὅς. Τοιγάρτοι τούτοις μὲν ἅπασιν,
ὦ Κέβης, ἐκεῖνοι, οἷς τι μέλει τῆς ἑαυτῶν ψυχῆς,
ἀλλὰ μὴ σώματι λατρεύοντες [1] ζῶσι, χαίρειν
εἰπόντες οὐ κατὰ ταὐτὰ πορεύονται αὐτοῖς, ὡς
οὐκ εἰδόσιν ὅπη ἔρχονται, αὐτοὶ δὲ ἡγούμενοι οὐ
δεῖν ἐναντία τῇ φιλοσοφίᾳ πράττειν καὶ τῇ ἐκείνης
λύσει τε καὶ καθαρμῷ ταύτῃ τρέπονται ἐκείνῃ
ἑπόμενοι, ᾗ ἐκείνη ὑφηγεῖται.

33. Πῶς, ὦ Σώκρατες; Ἐγὼ ἐρῶ, ἔφη. γιγνώ-
σκουσι γάρ, ἦ δ' ὅς, οἱ φιλομαθεῖς ὅτι παρα-
λαβοῦσα αὐτῶν τὴν ψυχὴν ἡ φιλοσοφία ἀτεχνῶς

---

[1] λατρεύοντες is an emendation proposed by Schanz for
πλάττοντες of the MSS.

" How are these happiest?"

" Don't you see? Is it not likely that they pass again into some such social and gentle species as that of bees or of wasps or ants, or into the human race again, and that worthy men spring from them?"

" Yes."

" And no one who has not been a philosopher and who is not wholly pure when he departs, is allowed to enter into the communion of the gods, but only the lover of knowledge. It is for this reason, dear Simmias and Cebes, that those who truly love wisdom refrain from all bodily desires and resist them firmly and do not give themselves up to them, not because they fear poverty or loss of property, as most men, in their love of money, do; nor is it because they fear the dishonour or disgrace of wickedness, like the lovers of honour and power, that they refrain from them."

" No, that would not be seemly for them, Socrates," said Cebes.

" Most assuredly not," said he. " And therefore those who care for their own souls, and do not live in service to the body, turn their backs upon all these men and do not walk in their ways, for they feel that they know not whither they are going. They themselves believe that philosophy, with its deliverance and purification, must not be resisted, and so they turn and follow it whithersoever it leads."

" How do they do this, Socrates?"

" I will tell you," he replied. " The lovers of knowledge," said he, "perceive that when philo-

E διαδεδεμένην ἐν τῷ σώματι καὶ προσκεκολλη-
μένην, ἀναγκαζομένην δὲ ὥσπερ διὰ εἱργμοῦ διὰ
τούτου σκοπεῖσθαι τὰ ὄντα ἀλλὰ μὴ αὐτὴν δι'
αὑτῆς, καὶ ἐν πάσῃ ἀμαθίᾳ κυλινδουμένην, καὶ
τοῦ εἱργμοῦ τὴν δεινότητα κατιδοῦσα ὅτι δι'
ἐπιθυμίας ἐστίν, ὡς ἂν μάλιστα αὐτὸς ὁ δεδεμένος
83 ξυλλήπτωρ εἴη τοῦ δεδέσθαι,—ὅπερ οὖν λέγω,
γιγνώσκουσιν οἱ φιλομαθεῖς ὅτι οὕτω παραλα-
βοῦσα ἡ φιλοσοφία ἔχουσαν αὐτῶν τὴν ψυχὴν
ἠρέμα παραμυθεῖται καὶ λύειν ἐπιχειρεῖ, ἐνδεικ-
νυμένη ὅτι ἀπάτης μὲν μεστὴ ἡ διὰ τῶν ὀμμάτων
σκέψις, ἀπάτης δὲ ἡ διὰ τῶν ὤτων καὶ τῶν
ἄλλων αἰσθήσεων, πείθουσα δὲ ἐκ τούτων μὲν
ἀναχωρεῖν, ὅσον μὴ ἀνάγκη αὐτοῖς χρῆσθαι,
αὐτὴν δὲ εἰς αὑτὴν ξυλλέγεσθαι καὶ ἀθροίζεσθαι
παρακελευομένη, πιστεύειν δὲ μηδενὶ ἄλλῳ ἀλλ'
B ἢ αὐτὴν αὑτῇ, ὅ τι ἂν νοήσῃ αὐτὴ καθ' αὑτὴν
αὐτὸ καθ' αὑτὸ τῶν ὄντων· ὅ τι δ' ἂν δι' ἄλλων
σκοπῇ ἐν ἄλλοις ὂν ἄλλο, μηδὲν ἡγεῖσθαι
ἀληθές· εἶναι δὲ τὸ μὲν τοιοῦτον αἰσθητόν τε καὶ
ὁρατόν, ὃ δὲ αὐτὴ ὁρᾷ νοητόν τε καὶ ἀειδές. ταύτῃ
οὖν τῇ λύσει οὐκ οἰομένη δεῖν ἐναντιοῦσθαι ἡ τοῦ
ὡς ἀληθῶς φιλοσόφου ψυχὴ οὕτως ἀπέχεται
τῶν ἡδονῶν τε καὶ ἐπιθυμιῶν καὶ λυπῶν καὶ
φόβων, καθ' ὅσον δύναται, λογιζομένη ὅτι, ἐπειδάν
τις σφόδρα ἡσθῇ ἢ φοβηθῇ ἢ λυπηθῇ ἢ ἐπιθυ-
μήσῃ, οὐδὲν τοσοῦτον κακὸν ἔπαθεν ἀπ' αὐτῶν ὧν
ἄν τις οἰηθείη, οἷον ἢ νοσήσας ἤ τι ἀναλώσας
C διὰ τὰς ἐπιθυμίας, ἀλλ' ὃ πάντων μέγιστόν τε
κακὸν καὶ ἔσχατόν ἐστι, τοῦτο πάσχει καὶ οὐ
λογίζεται αὐτό. Τί τοῦτο, ὦ Σώκρατες; ἔφη ὁ

sophy first takes possession of their soul it is
entirely fastened and welded to the body and is
compelled to regard realities through the body as
through prison bars, not with its own unhindered
vision, and is wallowing in utter ignorance. And
philosophy sees that the most dreadful thing about
the imprisonment is the fact that it is caused by
the lusts of the flesh, so that the prisoner is the
chief assistant in his own imprisonment. The lovers
of knowledge, then, I say, perceive that philosophy,
taking possession of the soul when it is in this state,
encourages it gently and tries to set it free, pointing
out that the eyes and the ears and the other senses
are full of deceit, and urging it to withdraw from
these, except in so far as their use is unavoidable,
and exhorting it to collect and concentrate itself
within itself, and to trust nothing except itself and
its own abstract thought of abstract existence ; and
to believe that there is no truth in that which it
sees by other means and which varies with the
various objects in which it appears, since everything
of that kind is visible and apprehended by the
senses, whereas the soul itself sees that which is
invisible and apprehended by the mind. Now the
soul of the true philosopher believes that it must
not resist this deliverance, and therefore it stands
aloof from pleasures and lusts and griefs and fears,
so far as it can, considering that when anyone has
violent pleasures or fears or griefs or lusts he suffers
from them not merely what one might think—for
example, illness or loss of money spent for his
lusts—but he suffers the greatest and most extreme
evil and does not take it into account."

" What is this evil, Socrates ? " said Cebes.

Κέβης "Οτι ψυχὴ παντὸς ἀνθρώπου ἀναγκάζεται
ἅμα τε ἡσθῆναι ἢ λυπηθῆναι σφόδρα ἐπί τῳ καὶ
ἡγεῖσθαι, περὶ ὃ ἂν μάλιστα τοῦτο πάσχῃ, τοῦτο
ἐναργέστατόν τε εἶναι καὶ ἀληθέστατον, οὐχ
οὕτως ἔχον· ταῦτα δὲ μάλιστα τὰ ὁρατά· ἢ οὔ;
D Πάνυ γε. Οὐκοῦν ἐν τούτῳ τῷ πάθει μάλιστα
καταδεῖται ψυχὴ ὑπὸ σώματος; Πῶς δή; "Οτι
ἑκάστη ἡδονὴ καὶ λύπη ὥσπερ ἧλον ἔχουσα
προσηλοῖ αὐτὴν πρὸς τὸ σῶμα καὶ προσπερονᾷ
καὶ ποιεῖ σωματοειδῆ, δοξάζουσαν ταῦτα ἀληθῆ
εἶναι ἅπερ ἂν καὶ τὸ σῶμα φῇ. ἐκ γὰρ τοῦ
ὁμοδοξεῖν τῷ σώματι καὶ τοῖς αὐτοῖς χαίρειν
ἀναγκάζεται οἶμαι ὁμότροπός τε καὶ ὁμότροφος
γίγνεσθαι καὶ οἷα μηδέποτε εἰς "Αιδου καθαρῶς
ἀφικέσθαι, ἀλλὰ ἀεὶ τοῦ σώματος ἀναπλέα ἐξιέναι,
ὥστε ταχὺ πάλιν πίπτειν εἰς ἄλλο σῶμα καὶ
E ὥσπερ σπειρομένη ἐμφύεσθαι, καὶ ἐκ τούτων
ἄμοιρος εἶναι τῆς τοῦ θείου τε καὶ καθαροῦ καὶ
μονοειδοῦς συνουσίας. Ἀληθέστατα, ἔφη, λέγεις,
ὁ Κέβης, ὦ Σώκρατες.

34. Τούτων τοίνυν ἕνεκα, ὦ Κέβης, οἱ δικαίως
φιλομαθεῖς κόσμιοί εἰσι καὶ ἀνδρεῖοι, οὐχ ὧν οἱ
84 πολλοὶ ἕνεκα· ἢ σὺ οἴει; Οὐ δῆτα ἔγωγε. Οὐ
γάρ, ἀλλ' οὕτω λογίσαιτ' ἂν ψυχὴ ἀνδρὸς φιλοσόφου, καὶ οὐκ ἂν οἰηθείη τὴν μὲν φιλοσοφίαν
χρῆναι ἑαυτὴν λύειν, λυούσης δὲ ἐκείνης αὐτὴν
ταῖς ἡδοναῖς καὶ λύπαις ἑαυτὴν πάλιν αὖ ἐγκα-
ταδεῖν καὶ ἀνήνυτον ἔργον πράττειν Πηνελόπης

"The evil is that the soul of every man, when it is greatly pleased or pained by anything, is compelled to believe that the object which caused the emotion is very distinct and very true ; but it is not. These objects are mostly the visible ones, are they not ? "

"Certainly."

"And when this occurs, is not the soul most completely put in bondage by the body ? "

"How so ? "

"Because each pleasure or pain nails it as with a nail to the body and rivets it on and makes it corporeal, so that it fancies the things are true which the body says are true. For because it has the same beliefs and pleasures as the body it is compelled to adopt also the same habits and mode of life, and can never depart in purity to the other world, but must always go away contaminated with the body ; and so it sinks quickly into another body again and grows into it, like seed that is sown. Therefore it has no part in the communion with the divine and pure and absolute."

"What you say, Socrates, is very true," said Cebes.

"This, Cebes, is the reason why the true lovers of knowledge are temperate and brave; not the world's reason. Or do you disagree ? "

"Certainly not."

"No, for the soul of the philosopher would not reason as others do, and would not think it right that philosophy should set it free, and that then when set free it should give itself again into bondage to pleasure and pain and engage in futile toil, like Penelope unweaving the web she wove. No, his

τινὰ ἐναντίως ἱστὸν μεταχειριζομένην, ἀλλὰ
γαλήνην τούτων παρασκευάζουσα, ἑπομένη τῷ
λογισμῷ καὶ ἀεὶ ἐν τούτῳ οὖσα, τὸ ἀληθὲς καὶ τὸ
θεῖον καὶ τὸ ἀδόξαστον θεωμένη καὶ ὑπ' ἐκείνου
B τρεφομένη, ζῆν τε οἴεται οὕτω δεῖν, ἕως ἂν ζῇ, καὶ
ἐπειδὰν τελευτήσῃ, εἰς τὸ ξυγγενὲς καὶ εἰς τὸ
τοιοῦτον ἀφικομένη ἀπηλλάχθαι τῶν ἀνθρωπίνων
κακῶν. ἐκ δὲ τῆς τοιαύτης τροφῆς οὐδὲν δεινὸν
μὴ φοβηθῇ,[1] ὦ Σιμμία τε καὶ Κέβης, ὅπως μὴ
διασπασθεῖσα ἐν τῇ ἀπαλλαγῇ τοῦ σώματος ὑπὸ
τῶν ἀνέμων διαφυσηθεῖσα καὶ διαπτομένη οἴχηται
καὶ οὐδὲν ἔτι οὐδαμοῦ ᾖ.

35. Σιγὴ οὖν ἐγένετο ταῦτα εἰπόντος τοῦ
C Σωκράτους ἐπὶ πολὺν χρόνον, καὶ αὐτός τε πρὸς
τῷ εἰρημένῳ λόγῳ ἦν ὁ Σωκράτης, ὡς ἰδεῖν
ἐφαίνετο, καὶ ἡμῶν οἱ πλεῖστοι. Κέβης δὲ καὶ
Σιμμίας σμικρὸν πρὸς ἀλλήλω διελεγέσθην· καὶ
ὁ Σωκράτης ἰδὼν αὐτὼ ἤρετο· Τί; ἔφη, ὑμῖν τὰ
λεχθέντα μῶν μὴ δοκεῖ ἐνδεῶς λέγεσθαι; πολλὰς
γὰρ δὴ ἔτι ἔχει ὑποψίας καὶ ἀντιλαβάς, εἴ γε δή
τις αὐτὰ μέλλει ἱκανῶς διεξιέναι. εἰ μὲν οὖν τι
ἄλλο σκοπεῖσθον, οὐδὲν λέγω· εἰ δέ τι περὶ
τούτων ἀπορεῖτον, μηδὲν ἀποκνήσητε καὶ αὐτοὶ
D εἰπεῖν καὶ διελθεῖν, εἴ πῃ ὑμῖν φαίνεται βέλτιον
ἂν λεχθῆναι, καὶ αὖ καὶ ἐμὲ συμπαραλαβεῖν, εἴ
τι μᾶλλον οἴεσθε μετ' ἐμοῦ εὐπορήσειν. καὶ ὁ
Σιμμίας ἔφη· Καὶ μήν, ὦ Σώκρατες, τἀληθῆ σοι
ἐρῶ. πάλαι γὰρ ἡμῶν ἑκάτερος ἀπορῶν τὸν ἕτερον προωθεῖ καὶ κελεύει ἐρέσθαι διὰ τὸ ἐπιθυμεῖν

---

[1] After φοβηθῇ the MSS. read ταῦτα δ' ἐπιτηδεύσασα. Ast
bracketed this and is followed by Schanz and Burnet.

soul believes that it must gain peace from these emotions, must follow reason and abide always in it, beholding that which is true and divine and not a matter of opinion, and making that its only food; and in this way it believes it must live, while life endures, and then at death pass on to that which is akin to itself and of like nature, and be free from human ills. A soul which has been nurtured in this way, Simmias and Cebes, is not likely to fear that it will be torn asunder at its departure from the body and will vanish into nothingness, blown apart by the winds, and be no longer anywhere."

When Socrates had said this there was silence for a long time, and Socrates himself was apparently absorbed in what had been said, as were also most of us. But Simmias and Cebes conversed a little with each other; and Socrates saw them and said: "Do you think there is any incompleteness in what has been said? There are still many subjects for doubt and many points open to attack, if anyone cares to discuss the matter thoroughly. If you are considering anything else, I have nothing to say; but if you are in any difficulty about these matters, do not hesitate to speak and discuss them yourselves, if you think anything better could be said on the subject, and to take me along with you in the discussion, if you think you can get on better in my company."

And Simmias said: "Socrates, I will tell you the truth. For some time each of us has been in doubt and has been egging the other on and urging him to ask a question, because we wish to hear your answer,

PLATO

μὲν ἀκοῦσαι, ὀκνεῖν δὲ ὄχλον παρέχειν, μή σοι
ἀηδὲς ᾖ διὰ τὴν παροῦσαν συμφοράν. καὶ ὃς
ἀκούσας ἐγέλασέν τε ἠρέμα καί φησιν, Βαβαί,
E ὦ Σιμμία· ἦ που χαλεπῶς ἂν τοὺς ἄλλους ἀνθρώπους πείσαιμι, ὡς οὐ συμφορὰν ἡγοῦμαι τὴν
παροῦσαν τύχην, ὅτε γε μηδ' ὑμᾶς δύναμαι
πείθειν, ἀλλὰ φοβεῖσθε, μὴ δυσκολώτερόν τι νῦν
διάκειμαι ἢ ἐν τῷ πρόσθεν βίῳ· καί, ὡς ἔοικε,
τῶν κύκνων δοκῶ φαυλότερος ὑμῖν εἶναι τὴν
μαντικήν, οἳ ἐπειδὰν αἴσθωνται ὅτι δεῖ αὐτοὺς
ἀποθανεῖν, ᾄδοντες καὶ ἐν τῷ πρόσθεν χρόνῳ,
85 τότε δὴ πλεῖστα καὶ μάλιστα ᾄδουσι, γεγηθότες
ὅτι μέλλουσι παρὰ τὸν θεὸν ἀπιέναι, οὗπέρ εἰσι
θεράποντες. οἱ δ' ἄνθρωποι διὰ τὸ αὐτῶν δέος
τοῦ θανάτου καὶ τῶν κύκνων καταψεύδονται, καί
φασιν αὐτοὺς θρηνοῦντας τὸν θάνατον ὑπὸ λύπης
ἐξᾴδειν, καὶ οὐ λογίζονται, ὅτι οὐδὲν ὄρνεον ᾄδει,
ὅταν πεινῇ ἢ ῥιγοῖ ἤ τινα ἄλλην λύπην λυπῆται,
οὐδὲ αὐτὴ ἥ τε ἀηδὼν καὶ χελιδὼν καὶ ὁ ἔποψ, ἃ
δή φασι διὰ λύπην θρηνοῦντα ᾄδειν· ἀλλ' οὔτε
ταῦτά μοι φαίνεται λυπούμενα ᾄδειν οὔτε οἱ
B κύκνοι, ἀλλ' ἅτε οἶμαι τοῦ Ἀπόλλωνος ὄντες
μαντικοί τέ εἰσι καὶ προειδότες τὰ ἐν Ἅιδου
ἀγαθὰ ᾄδουσι καὶ τέρπονται ἐκείνην τὴν ἡμέραν
διαφερόντως ἢ ἐν τῷ ἔμπροσθεν χρόνῳ. ἐγὼ δὲ
καὶ αὐτὸς ἡγοῦμαι ὁμόδουλός γε εἶναι τῶν κύκνων
καὶ ἱερὸς τοῦ αὐτοῦ θεοῦ, καὶ οὐ χεῖρον' ἐκείνων
τὴν μαντικὴν ἔχειν παρὰ τοῦ δεσπότου, οὐδὲ
δυσθυμότερον αὐτῶν τοῦ βίου ἀπαλλάττεσθαι.
ἀλλὰ τούτου γε ἕνεκα λέγειν τε χρὴ καὶ ἐρωτᾶν
ὅ τι ἂν βούλησθε, ἕως ἂν Ἀθηναίων ἐῶσιν ἄνδρες

but hesitate to trouble you, for fear that it may be disagreeable to you in your present misfortune."

And when he heard this, he laughed gently and said : "Ah, Simmias! I should have hard work to persuade other people that I do not regard my present situation as a misfortune, when I cannot even make you believe it, but you are afraid I am more churlish now than I used to be. And you seem to think I am inferior in prophetic power to the swans who sing at other times also, but when they feel that they are to die, sing most and best in their joy that they are to go to the god whose servants they are. But men, because of their own fear of death, misrepresent the swans and say that they sing for sorrow, in mourning for their own death. They do not consider that no bird sings when it is hungry or cold or has any other trouble ; no, not even the nightingale or the swallow or the hoopoe which are said to sing in lamentation. I do not believe they sing for grief, nor do the swans ; but since they are Apollo's birds, I believe they have prophetic vision, and because they have foreknowledge of the blessings in the other world they sing and rejoice on that day more than ever before. And I think that I am myself a fellow-servant of the swans, and am consecrated to the same God and have received from our master a gift of prophecy no whit inferior to theirs, and that I go out from life with as little sorrow as they. So far as this is concerned, then, speak and ask whatever questions you please, so long as the eleven of the Athenians permit."

ἕνδεκα.[1] Καλῶς, ἔφη, λέγεις, ὁ Σιμμίας· καὶ
C ἔγωγέ σοι ἐρῶ ὃ ἀπορῶ, καὶ αὖ ὅδε, ᾗ οὐκ
ἀποδέχεται τὰ εἰρημένα. ἐμοὶ γὰρ δοκεῖ, ὦ
Σώκρατες, περὶ τῶν τοιούτων ἴσως ὥσπερ καὶ σοὶ
τὸ μὲν σαφὲς εἰδέναι ἐν τῷ νῦν βίῳ ἢ ἀδύνατον
εἶναι ἢ παγχάλεπόν τι, τὸ μέντοι αὖ τὰ λεγόμενα
περὶ αὐτῶν μὴ οὐχὶ παντὶ τρόπῳ ἐλέγχειν καὶ
μὴ προαφίστασθαι, πρὶν ἂν πανταχῇ σκοπῶν
ἀπείπῃ τις, πάνυ μαλθακοῦ εἶναι ἀνδρός· δεῖν
γὰρ περὶ αὐτὰ ἕν γέ τι τούτων διαπράξασθαι,
ἢ μαθεῖν ὅπῃ ἔχει ἢ εὑρεῖν ἤ, εἰ ταῦτα ἀδύνατον,
τὸν γοῦν βέλτιστον τῶν ἀνθρωπίνων λόγων
D λαβόντα καὶ δυσεξελεγκτότατον, ἐπὶ τούτου
ὀχούμενον ὥσπερ ἐπὶ σχεδίας κινδυνεύοντα
διαπλεῦσαι τὸν βίον, εἰ μή τις δύναιτο ἀσφαλέστερον καὶ ἀκινδυνότερον ἐπὶ βεβαιοτέρου ὀχή-
ματος, λόγου θείου τινός, διαπορευθῆναι. καὶ δὴ
καὶ νῦν ἔγωγε οὐκ ἐπαισχυνθήσομαι ἐρέσθαι,
ἐπειδὴ καὶ σὺ ταῦτα λέγεις, οὐδ' ἐμαυτὸν αἰτιά-
σομαι ἐν ὑστέρῳ χρόνῳ, ὅτι νῦν οὐκ εἶπον ἃ
ἐμοὶ δοκεῖ. ἐμοὶ γάρ, ὦ Σώκρατες, ἐπειδὴ καὶ
πρὸς ἐμαυτὸν καὶ πρὸς τόνδε σκοπῶ τὰ εἰρημένα,
οὐ πάνυ φαίνεται ἱκανῶς εἰρῆσθαι.

E   36. Καὶ ὁ Σωκράτης· Ἴσως γάρ, ἔφη, ὦ
ἑταῖρε, ἀληθῆ σοι φαίνεται· ἀλλὰ λέγε, ὅπῃ δὴ
οὐχ ἱκανῶς. Ταύτῃ ἔμοιγε, ἦ δ' ὅς, ᾗ δὴ καὶ
περὶ ἁρμονίας ἄν τις καὶ λύρας τε καὶ χορδῶν
τὸν αὐτὸν τοῦτον λόγον εἴποι, ὡς ἡ μὲν ἁρμονία
ἀόρατόν τι καὶ ἀσώματον καὶ πάγκαλόν τι καὶ
86 θεῖόν ἐστιν ἐν τῇ ἡρμοσμένῃ λύρᾳ, αὐτὴ δ' ἡ λύρα

---

[1] Schanz brackets ἕως . . . ἕνδεκα.

" Good," said Simmias. " I will tell you my difficulty, and then Cebes in turn will say why he does not agree to all you have said. I think, Socrates, as perhaps you do yourself, that it is either impossible or very difficult to acquire clear knowledge about these matters in this life. And yet he is a weakling who does not test in every way what is said about them and persevere until he is worn out by studying them on every side. For he must do one of two things ; either he must learn or discover the truth about these matters, or if that is impossible, he must take whatever human doctrine is best and hardest to disprove and, embarking upon it as upon a raft, sail upon it through life in the midst of dangers, unless he can sail upon some stronger vessel, some divine revelation, and make his voyage more safely and securely. And so now I am not ashamed to ask questions, since you encourage me to do so, and I shall not have to blame myself hereafter for not saying now what I think. For, Socrates, when I examine what has been said, either alone or with Cebes, it does not seem quite satisfactory."

And Socrates replied : " Perhaps, my friend, you are right. But tell me in what respect it is not satisfactory."

" In this," said he, " that one might use the same argument about harmony and a lyre with its strings. One might say that the harmony is invisible and incorporeal, and very beautiful and divine in the well attuned lyre, but the lyre itself and its strings are bodies,

καὶ αἱ χορδαὶ σώματά τε καὶ σωματοειδῆ καὶ
ξύνθετα καὶ γεώδη ἐστὶ καὶ τοῦ θνητοῦ ξυγγενῆ. ἐπειδὰν οὖν ἢ κατάξῃ τις τὴν λύραν ἢ
διατέμῃ[1] καὶ διαρρήξῃ τὰς χορδάς, εἴ τις διισχυρί-
ζοιτο τῷ αὐτῷ λόγῳ ὥσπερ σύ, ὡς ἀνάγκη ἔτι
εἶναι τὴν ἁρμονίαν ἐκείνην καὶ μὴ ἀπολωλέναι·
οὐδεμία γὰρ μηχανὴ ἂν εἴη τὴν μὲν λύραν ἔτι
εἶναι διερρωγυιῶν τῶν χορδῶν[2] καὶ τὰς χορδὰς
θνητοειδεῖς οὔσας, τὴν δὲ ἁρμονίαν ἀπολωλέναι
B τὴν τοῦ θείου τε καὶ ἀθανάτου ὁμοφυῆ τε καὶ
ξυγγενῆ, προτέραν τοῦ θνητοῦ ἀπολομένην· ἀλλὰ
φαίη ἀνάγκη ἔτι που εἶναι αὐτὴν τὴν ἁρμονίαν,
καὶ πρότερον τὰ ξύλα καὶ τὰς χορδὰς κατασαπή-
σεσθαι, πρίν τι ἐκείνην παθεῖν, — καὶ γὰρ οὖν,
ὦ Σώκρατες, οἶμαι ἔγωγε καὶ αὐτόν σε τοῦτο
ἐντεθυμῆσθαι, ὅτι τοιοῦτόν τι μάλιστα ὑπολαμβάνομεν τὴν ψυχὴν εἶναι, ὥσπερ ἐντεταμένου τοῦ
σώματος ἡμῶν καὶ συνεχομένου ὑπὸ θερμοῦ καὶ
ψυχροῦ καὶ ξηροῦ καὶ ὑγροῦ καὶ τοιούτων τινῶν,
C κρᾶσιν εἶναι καὶ ἁρμονίαν αὐτῶν τούτων τὴν
ψυχὴν ἡμῶν, ἐπειδὰν ταῦτα καλῶς καὶ μετρίως
κραθῇ πρὸς ἄλληλα. εἰ οὖν τυγχάνει ἡ ψυχὴ
οὖσα ἁρμονία τις, δῆλον ὅτι, ὅταν χαλασθῇ τὸ
σῶμα ἡμῶν ἀμέτρως ἢ ἐπιταθῇ ὑπὸ νόσων καὶ
ἄλλων κακῶν, τὴν μὲν ψυχὴν ἀνάγκη εὐθὺς
ὑπάρχει ἀπολωλέναι, καίπερ οὖσαν θειοτάτην,
ὥσπερ καὶ αἱ ἄλλαι ἁρμονίαι αἵ τ' ἐν τοῖς
φθόγγοις καὶ αἱ ἐν τοῖς τῶν δημιουργῶν ἔργοις
πᾶσι, τὰ δὲ λείψανα τοῦ σώματος ἑκάστου πολὺν

---

[1] Schanz brackets διατέμῃ.
[2] Schanz brackets διερρωγυιῶν τῶν χορδῶν.

and corporeal and composite and earthy and akin to that which is mortal. Now if someone shatters the lyre or cuts and breaks the strings, what if he should maintain by the same argument you employed, that the harmony could not have perished and must still exist? For there would be no possibility that the lyre and its strings, which are of mortal nature, still exist after the strings are broken, and the harmony, which is related and akin to the divine and the immortal, perish before that which is mortal. He would say that the harmony must still exist somewhere, and that the wood and the strings must rot away before anything could happen to it. And I fancy, Socrates, that it must have occurred to your own mind that we believe the soul to be something after this fashion; that our body is strung and held together by heat, cold, moisture, dryness, and the like, and the soul is a mixture and a harmony of these same elements, when they are well and properly mixed. Now if the soul is a harmony, it is clear that when the body is too much relaxed or is too tightly strung by diseases or other ills, the soul must of necessity perish, no matter how divine it is, like other harmonies in sounds and in all the works of artists, and the remains of each body will endure a

PLATO

D χρόνον παραμένειν, ἕως ἂν ἢ κατακαυθῇ ἢ κατα-
σαπῇ. ὅρα οὖν πρὸς τοῦτον τὸν λόγον τί φήσομεν, ἐάν τις ἀξιοῖ κρᾶσιν οὖσαν τὴν ψυχὴν τῶν
ἐν τῷ σώματι ἐν τῷ καλουμένῳ θανάτῳ πρώτην
ἀπόλλυσθαι.

37. Διαβλέψας οὖν ὁ Σωκράτης, ὥσπερ τὰ
πολλὰ εἰώθει, καὶ μειδιάσας, Δίκαια μέντοι, ἔφη,
λέγει ὁ Σιμμίας. εἰ οὖν τις ὑμῶν εὐπορώτερος
ἐμοῦ, τί οὐκ ἀπεκρίνατο; καὶ γὰρ οὐ φαύλως
ἔοικεν ἀπτομένῳ τοῦ λόγου. δοκεῖ μέντοι μοι
E χρῆναι πρὸ τῆς ἀποκρίσεως ἔτι πρότερον Κέβητος
ἀκοῦσαι, τί αὖ ὅδε ἐγκαλεῖ τῷ λόγῳ, ἵνα χρόνου
ἐγγενομένου βουλευσώμεθα, τί ἐροῦμεν, ἔπειτα δὲ
ἀκούσαντας ἢ συγχωρεῖν αὐτοῖς, ἐάν τι δοκῶσι
προσάδειν, ἐὰν δὲ μή, οὕτως ἤδη ὑπερδικεῖν τοῦ
λόγου. ἀλλ' ἄγε, ἦ δ' ὅς, ὦ Κέβης, λέγε, τί ἦν
τὸ σὲ αὖ θρᾶττον. Λέγω δή, ἦ δ' ὃς ὁ Κέβης.
ἐμοὶ γὰρ φαίνεται ἔτι ἐν τῷ αὐτῷ ὁ λόγος εἶναι,
καί, ὅπερ ἐν τοῖς πρόσθεν ἐλέγομεν, ταὐτὸν
87 ἔγκλημα ἔχειν. ὅτι μὲν γὰρ ἦν ἡμῶν ἡ ψυχὴ καὶ
πρὶν εἰς τόδε τὸ εἶδος ἐλθεῖν, οὐκ ἀνατίθεμαι μὴ
οὐχὶ πάνυ χαριέντως, καί, εἰ μὴ ἐπαχθές ἐστιν
εἰπεῖν, πάνυ ἱκανῶς ἀποδεδεῖχθαι· ὡς δὲ καὶ
ἀποθανόντων ἡμῶν ἔτι που ἔσται, οὔ μοι δοκεῖ
τῇδε. ὡς μὲν οὐκ ἰσχυρότερον καὶ πολυχρονιώτερον ψυχὴ σώματος, οὐ συγχωρῶ τῇ Σιμμίου
ἀντιλήψει· δοκεῖ γάρ μοι πᾶσι τούτοις πάνυ πολὺ
διαφέρειν. τί οὖν, ἂν φαίη ὁ λόγος, ἔτι ἀπιστεῖς,
ἐπειδὴ ὁρᾷς ἀποθανόντος τοῦ ἀνθρώπου τό γε
B ἀσθενέστερον ἔτι ὄν; τὸ δὲ πολυχρονιώτερον οὐ
δοκεῖ σοι ἀναγκαῖον εἶναι ἔτι σῴζεσθαι ἐν τούτῳ
τῷ χρόνῳ; πρὸς δὴ τοῦτο τόδε ἐπίσκεψαι, εἴ τι

long time until they are burnt or decayed. Now what shall we say to this argument, if anyone claims that the soul, being a mixture of the elements of the body, is the first to perish in what is called death?"

Then Socrates, looking keenly at us, as he often used to do, smiled and said: "Simmias raises a fair objection. Now if any of you is readier than I, why does he not reply to him? For he seems to score a good point. However, I think before replying to him we ought to hear what fault our friend Cebes finds with our argument, that we may take time to consider what to say, and then when we have heard them, we can either agree with them, if they seem to strike the proper note, or, if they do not, we can proceed to argue in defence of our reasoning. Come, Cebes," said he, "tell us what it was that troubled you."

"Well, I will tell you," said Cebes. "The argument seems to me to be just where it was, and to be still open to the objection I made before. For I do not deny that it has been very cleverly, and, if I may say so, conclusively shown that the soul existed before it entered into this bodily form, but it does not seem to me proved that it will still exist when we are dead. I do not agree with Simmias' objection, that the soul is not stronger and more lasting than the body, for I think it is far superior in all such respects. 'Why then,' the argument might say, 'do you still disbelieve, when you see that after a man dies the weaker part still exists? Do you not think the stronger part must necessarily be preserved during the same length of time?' Now see if my

λέγω· εἰκόνος γάρ τινος, ὡς ἔοικεν, κἀγὼ ὥσπερ
Σιμμίας δέομαι. ἐμοὶ γὰρ δοκεῖ ὁμοίως λέγεσθαι
ταῦτα, ὥσπερ ἄν τις περὶ ἀνθρώπου ὑφάντου
πρεσβύτου ἀποθανόντος λέγοι τοῦτον τὸν λόγον,
ὅτι οὐκ ἀπόλωλεν ὁ ἄνθρωπος, ἀλλ' ἔστι που
σῶς,¹ τεκμήριον δὲ παρέχοιτο θοἰμάτιον ὃ ἠμπεί-
χετο αὐτὸς ὑφηνάμενος, ὅτι ἐστὶ σῶν καὶ οὐκ
ἀπόλωλεν, καὶ εἴ τις ἀπιστοίη αὐτῷ, ἀνερωτώῃ
C πότερον πολυχρονιώτερόν ἐστι τὸ γένος ἀνθρώπου
ἢ ἱματίου ἐν χρείᾳ τε ὄντος καὶ φορουμένου, ἀπο-
κριναμένου δέ τινος ὅτι πολὺ τὸ τοῦ ἀνθρώπου,
οἴοιτο ἀποδεδεῖχθαι ὅτι παντὸς ἄρα μᾶλλον ὅ
γε ἄνθρωπος σῶς ἐστιν, ἐπειδὴ τό γε ὀλιγοχρονιώ-
τερον οὐκ ἀπόλωλεν. τὸ δ' οἶμαι, ὦ Σιμμία,
οὐχ οὕτως ἔχει· σκόπει γὰρ καὶ σὺ ἃ λέγω.
πᾶς γὰρ ἂν ὑπολάβοι ὅτι εὔηθες λέγει ὁ τοῦτο
λέγων· ὁ γὰρ ὑφάντης οὗτος πολλὰ κατατρίψας
τοιαῦτα ἱμάτια καὶ ὑφηνάμενος ἐκείνων μὲν
D ὕστερος ἀπόλωλεν πολλῶν ὄντων, τοῦ δὲ τελευ-
ταίου οἶμαι πρότερος, καὶ οὐδέν τι μᾶλλον τούτου
ἕνεκα ἄνθρωπός ἐστιν ἱματίου φαυλότερον οὐδ'
ἀσθενέστερον. τὴν αὐτὴν δὲ οἶμαι εἰκόνα δέξαιτ'
ἂν ψυχὴ πρὸς σῶμα, καί τις λέγων αὐτὰ ταῦτα
περὶ αὐτῶν μέτρι' ἄν μοι φαίνοιτο λέγειν, ὡς ἡ
μὲν ψυχὴ πολυχρόνιόν ἐστι, τὸ δὲ σῶμα ἀσθενέστερον καὶ ὀλιγοχρονιώτερον· ἀλλὰ γὰρ ἂν φαίη
ἑκάστην τῶν ψυχῶν πολλὰ σώματα κατατρίβειν,
ἄλλως τε καὶ εἰ πολλὰ ἔτη βιῴη· εἰ γὰρ ῥέοι τὸ
σῶμα καὶ ἀπολλύοιτο ἔτι ζῶντος τοῦ ἀνθρώπου,
E ἀλλ' ἡ ψυχὴ ἀεὶ τὸ κατατριβόμενον ἀνυφαίνοι,

¹ σῶς Schanz, after Forster; ἴσως BCDE.

reply to this has any sense. I think I may, like Simmias, best express myself in a figure. It seems to me that it is much as if one should say about an old weaver who had died, that the man had not perished but was safe and sound somewhere, and should offer as a proof of this the fact that the cloak which the man had woven and used to wear was still whole and had not perished. Then if anyone did not believe him, he would ask which lasts longer, a man or a cloak that is in use and wear, and when the answer was given that a man lasts much longer, he would think it had been proved beyond a doubt that the man was safe, because that which was less lasting had not perished.

"But I do not think he is right, Simmias, and I ask you especially to notice what I say. Anyone can understand that a man who says this is talking nonsense. For the weaver in question wove and wore out many such cloaks and lasted longer than they, though they were many, but perished, I suppose, before the last one. Yet a man is not feebler or weaker than a cloak on that account at all. And I think the same figure would apply to the soul and the body and it would be quite appropriate to say in like manner about them, that the soul lasts a long time, but the body lasts a shorter time and is weaker. And one might go on to say that each soul wears out many bodies, especially if the man lives many years. For if the body is constantly changing and being destroyed while the man still lives, and the soul is always weaving anew that which wears out, then

ἀναγκαῖον μέντ᾽ ἂν εἴη, ὁπότε ἀπολλύοιτο ἡ
ψυχή, τὸ τελευταῖον ὕφασμα τυχεῖν αὐτὴν
ἔχουσαν καὶ τούτου μόνου προτέραν ἀπόλλυσθαι,
ἀπολομένης δὲ τῆς ψυχῆς τότ᾽ ἤδη τὴν φύσιν τῆς
ἀσθενείας ἐπιδεικνύοι τὸ σῶμα καὶ ταχὺ σαπὲν
διοίχοιτο. ὥστε τούτῳ τῷ λόγῳ οὔπω ἄξιον
πιστεύσαντα θαρρεῖν, ὡς, ἐπειδὰν ἀποθάνωμεν,
88 ἔτι που ἡμῶν ἡ ψυχὴ ἔσται. εἰ γάρ τις καὶ πλέον
ἔτι τῷ λέγοντι ἃ σὺ λέγεις συγχωρήσειεν, δοὺς
αὐτῷ μὴ μόνον ἐν τῷ πρὶν καὶ γενέσθαι ἡμᾶς
χρόνῳ εἶναι ἡμῶν τὰς ψυχάς, ἀλλὰ μηδὲν κωλύειν
καὶ ἐπειδὰν ἀποθάνωμεν ἐνίων ἔτι εἶναι καὶ
ἔσεσθαι καὶ πολλάκις γενήσεσθαι καὶ ἀποθανεῖσθαι αὖθις· οὕτω γὰρ αὐτὸ φύσει ἰσχυρὸν εἶναι,
ὥστε πολλάκις γιγνομένην ψυχὴν ἀντέχειν· δοὺς
δὲ ταῦτα ἐκεῖνο μηκέτι συγχωροῖ, μὴ οὐ πονεῖν
αὐτὴν ἐν ταῖς πολλαῖς γενέσεσιν καὶ τελευτῶσάν
γε ἔν τινι τῶν θανάτων παντάπασιν ἀπόλλυσθαι·
B τοῦτον δὲ τὸν θάνατον καὶ ταύτην τὴν διάλυσιν
τοῦ σώματος, ἣ τῇ ψυχῇ φέρει ὄλεθρον, μηδένα
φαίη εἰδέναι· ἀδύνατον γὰρ εἶναι ὁτῳοῦν αἰσθάνεσθαι ἡμῶν· εἰ δὲ τοῦτο οὕτως ἔχει, οὐδενὶ προσήκει θάνατον θαρροῦντι μὴ οὐκ ἀνοήτως θαρρεῖν,
ὃς ἂν μὴ ἔχῃ ἀποδεῖξαι ὅτι ἔστι ψυχὴ παντάπασιν ἀθάνατόν τε καὶ ἀνώλεθρον· εἰ δὲ μή,
ἀνάγκην εἶναι ἀεὶ τὸν μέλλοντα ἀποθανεῖσθαι
δεδιέναι ὑπὲρ τῆς αὑτοῦ ψυχῆς, μὴ ἐν τῇ νῦν τοῦ
σώματος διαζεύξει παντάπασιν ἀπόληται.

38. Πάντες οὖν ἀκούσαντες εἰπόντων αὐτῶν
C ἀηδῶς διετέθημεν, ὡς ὕστερον ἐλέγομεν πρὸς
ἀλλήλους, ὅτι ὑπὸ τοῦ ἔμπροσθεν λόγου σφόδρα
πεπεισμένους ἡμᾶς πάλιν ἐδόκουν ἀναταράξαι καὶ

when the soul perishes it must necessarily have on its last garment, and this only will survive it, and when the soul has perished, then the body will at once show its natural weakness and will quickly disappear in decay. And so we are not yet justified in feeling sure, on the strength of this argument, that our souls will still exist somewhere after we are dead. For if one were to grant even more to a man who uses your argument, Socrates, and allow not only that our souls existed before we were born, but also that there is nothing to prevent some of them from continuing to exist and from being born and dying again many times after we are dead, because the soul is naturally so strong that it can endure repeated births,—even allowing this, one might not grant that it does not suffer by its many births and does not finally perish altogether in one of its deaths. But he might say that no one knows beforehand the particular death and the particular dissolution of the body which brings destruction to the soul, for none of us can perceive that. Now if this is the case, anyone who feels confident about death has a foolish confidence, unless he can show that the soul is altogether immortal and imperishable. Otherwise a man who is about to die must always fear that his soul will perish utterly in the impending dissolution of the body."

Now all of us, as we remarked to one another afterwards, were very uncomfortable when we heard what they said; for we had been thoroughly convinced by the previous argument, and now they seemed to be throwing us again into confusion and

PLATO

εἰς ἀπιστίαν καταβαλεῖν οὐ μόνον τοῖς προειρη-
μένοις λόγοις, ἀλλὰ καὶ εἰς τὰ ὕστερον μέλλοντα
ῥηθήσεσθαι, μὴ οὐδενὸς ἄξιοι εἶμεν κριταὶ ἢ καὶ
τὰ πράγματα ἄπιστα ᾖ.

ΕΧΕΚΡΑΤΗΣ. Νὴ τοὺς θεούς, ὦ Φαίδων, συγγνώμην γε ἔχω ὑμῖν. καὶ γὰρ αὐτόν με νῦν ἀκού-
σαντά σου τοιοῦτόν τι λέγειν πρὸς ἐμαυτὸν
D ἐπέρχεται· τίνι οὖν ἔτι πιστεύσομεν λόγῳ; ὡς
γὰρ σφόδρα πιθανὸς ὤν, ὃν ὁ Σωκράτης ἔλεγε
λόγον, νῦν εἰς ἀπιστίαν καταπέπτωκεν. θαυμαστῶς γάρ μου ὁ λόγος οὗτος ἀντιλαμβάνεται καὶ
νῦν καὶ ἀεί, τὸ ἁρμονίαν τινὰ ἡμῶν εἶναι τὴν
ψυχήν, καὶ ὥσπερ ὑπέμνησέν με ῥηθεὶς ὅτι καὶ
αὐτῷ μοι ταῦτα προυδέδοκτο. καὶ πάνυ δέομαι
πάλιν ὥσπερ ἐξ ἀρχῆς ἄλλου τινὸς λόγου, ὅς με
πείσει ὡς τοῦ ἀποθανόντος οὐ συναποθνῄσκει
ἡ ψυχή. λέγε οὖν πρὸς Διός, πῇ ὁ Σωκράτης
E μετῆλθε τὸν λόγον; καὶ πότερον κἀκεῖνος, ὥσπερ
ὑμᾶς φῄς, ἔνδηλός τι ἐγένετο ἀχθόμενος ἢ οὔ,
ἀλλὰ πράως ἐβοήθει τῷ λόγῳ; καὶ ἱκανῶς
ἐβοήθησεν ἢ ἐνδεῶς; πάντα ἡμῖν δίελθε ὡς δύνασαι ἀκριβέστατα.

ΦΑΙΔΩΝ. Καὶ μήν, ὦ Ἐχέκρατες, πολλάκις
θαυμάσας Σωκράτη οὐ πώποτε μᾶλλον ἠγάσθην
89 ἢ τότε παραγενόμενος. τὸ μὲν οὖν ἔχειν ὅ τι
λέγοι ἐκεῖνος, ἴσως οὐδὲν ἄτοπον· ἀλλὰ ἔγωγε
μάλιστα ἐθαύμασα αὐτοῦ πρῶτον μὲν τοῦτο, ὡς
ἡδέως καὶ εὐμενῶς καὶ ἀγαμένως τῶν νεανίσκων
τὸν λόγον ἀπεδέξατο, ἔπειτα ἡμῶν ὡς ὀξέως
ᾔσθετο ὃ πεπόνθειμεν ὑπὸ τῶν λόγων, ἔπειτα ὡς
εὖ ἡμᾶς ἰάσατο καὶ ὥσπερ πεφευγότας καὶ

306

distrust, not only in respect to the past discussion but also with regard to any future one. They made us fear that our judgment was worthless or that no certainty could be attained in these matters.

ECHECRATES. By the gods, Phaedo, I sympathise with you; for I myself after listening to you am inclined to ask myself: "What argument shall we believe henceforth? For the argument of Socrates was perfectly convincing, and now it has fallen into discredit." For the doctrine that the soul is a kind of harmony has always had (and has now) a wonderful hold upon me, and your mention of it reminded me that I had myself believed in it before. Now I must begin over again and find another argument to convince me that when a man dies his soul does not perish with him. So, for heaven's sake, tell how Socrates continued the discourse, and whether he also, as you say the rest of you did, showed any uneasiness, or calmly defended his argument. And did he defend it successfully? Tell us everything as accurately as you can.

PHAEDO. Echecrates, I have often wondered at Socrates, but never did I admire him more than then. That he had an answer ready was perhaps to be expected; but what astonished me more about him was, first, the pleasant, gentle, and respectful manner in which he listened to the young men's criticisms, secondly, his quick sense of the effect their words had upon us, and lastly, the skill with which he cured us and, as it were, recalled us from our flight and

ἡττημένους ἀνεκαλέσατο καὶ προύτρεψεν πρὸς τὸ
παρέπεσθαί τε καὶ συσκοπεῖν τὸν λόγον.

ΕΧΕΚΡΑΤΗΣ. Πῶς δή;

ΦΑΙΔΩΝ. Ἐγὼ ἐρῶ. ἔτυχον γὰρ ἐν δεξιᾷ αὐτοῦ
B καθήμενος παρὰ τὴν κλίνην ἐπὶ χαμαιζήλου τινός,
ὁ δὲ ἐπὶ πολὺ ὑψηλοτέρου ἢ ἐγώ. καταψήσας
οὖν μου τὴν κεφαλὴν καὶ συμπιέσας τὰς ἐπὶ τῷ
αὐχένι τρίχας—εἰώθει γάρ, ὁπότε τύχοι, παίζειν
μου εἰς τὰς τρίχας—Αὔριον δή, ἔφη, ἴσως, ὦ
Φαίδων, τὰς καλὰς κόμας ἀποκερεῖ. Ἔοικεν, ἦν
δ' ἐγώ, ὦ Σώκρατες. Οὔκ, ἄν γε ἐμοὶ πείθῃ.
Ἀλλὰ τί; ἦν δ' ἐγώ. Τήμερον, ἔφη, κἀγὼ τὰς
ἐμὰς καὶ σὺ ταύτας, ἐάνπερ γε ἡμῖν ὁ λόγος
τελευτήσῃ καὶ μὴ δυνώμεθα αὐτὸν ἀναβιώσασθαι.
C καὶ ἔγωγ' ἄν, εἰ σὺ εἴην καί με διαφεύγοι ὁ λόγος,
ἔνορκον ἂν ποιησαίμην ὥσπερ Ἀργεῖοι, μὴ πρότερον κομήσειν, πρὶν ἂν νικήσω ἀναμαχόμενος
τὸν Σιμμίου τε καὶ Κέβητος λόγον. Ἀλλ', ἦν δ'
ἐγώ, πρὸς δύο λέγεται οὐδ' ὁ Ἡρακλῆς οἷός τε
εἶναι. Ἀλλὰ καὶ ἐμέ, ἔφη, τὸν Ἰόλεων παρα-
κάλει, ἕως ἔτι φῶς ἐστιν. Παρακαλῶ τοίνυν,
ἔφην, οὐχ ὡς Ἡρακλῆς, ἀλλ' ὡς Ἰόλεως. Οὐδὲν
διοίσει, ἔφη.

39. Ἀλλὰ πρῶτον εὐλαβηθῶμέν τι πάθος μὴ
πάθωμεν. Τὸ ποῖον; ἦν δ' ἐγώ. Μὴ γενώ-
D μεθα, ἦ δ' ὅς, μισόλογοι, ὥσπερ οἱ μισάνθρω-
ποι γιγνόμενοι· ὡς οὐκ ἔστιν, ἔφη, ὅ τι ἄν τις
μεῖζον τούτου κακὸν πάθοι ἢ λόγους μισήσας.
γίγνεται δὲ ἐκ τοῦ αὐτοῦ τρόπου μισολογία τε καὶ
μισανθρωπία. ἥ τε γὰρ μισανθρωπία ἐνδύεται
ἐκ τοῦ σφόδρα τινὶ πιστεῦσαι ἄνευ τέχνης, καὶ

defeat and made us face about and follow him and join in his examination of the argument.

ECHECRATES.   How did he do it?

PHAEDO.   I will tell you.   I was sitting at his right hand on a low stool beside his couch, and his seat was a good deal higher than mine.   He stroked my head and gathered the hair on the back of my neck into his hand—he had a habit of playing with my hair on occasion—and said, "To-morrow, perhaps, Phaedo, you will cut off this beautiful hair."

"I suppose so, Socrates," said I.

"Not if you take my advice."

"What shall I do then?" I asked.

"You will cut it off to-day, and I will cut mine, if our argument dies and we cannot bring it to life again.   If I were you and the argument escaped me, I would take an oath, like the Argives, not to let my hair grow until I had renewed the fight and won a victory over the argument of Simmias and Cebes."

"But," I replied, "they say that even Heracles is not a match for two."

"Well," said he, "call me to help you, as your Iolaus, while there is still light."

"I call you to help, then," said I, "not as Heracles calling Iolaus, but as Iolaus calling Heracles."

"That is all one," said he.   "But first let us guard against a danger."

"Of what sort?" I asked.

"The danger of becoming misologists or haters of argument," said he, "as people become misanthropists or haters of man; for no worse evil can happen to a man than to hate argument.   Misology and misanthropy arise from similar causes.   For misanthropy arises from trusting someone implicitly without

PLATO

ἡγήσασθαι παντάπασί τε ἀληθῆ εἶναι καὶ ὑγιῆ
καὶ πιστὸν τὸν ἄνθρωπον, ἔπειτα ὀλίγον ὕστερον
εὑρεῖν τοῦτον πονηρόν τε καὶ ἄπιστον καὶ αὖθις
ἕτερον· καὶ ὅταν τοῦτο πολλάκις πάθῃ τις καὶ
ὑπὸ τούτων μάλιστα οὓς ἂν ἡγήσαιτο οἰκειοτά-
E τους τε καὶ ἑταιροτάτους, τελευτῶν δὴ θαμὰ
προσκρούων μισεῖ τε πάντας καὶ ἡγεῖται οὐδενὸς
οὐδὲν ὑγιὲς εἶναι τὸ παράπαν. ἢ οὐκ ᾔσθησαι σὺ
τοῦτο γιγνόμενον; Πάνυ γε, ἦν δ' ἐγώ. Οὐκοῦν,
ἢ δ' ὅς, αἰσχρόν,[1] καὶ δῆλον ὅτι ἄνευ τέχνης
τῆς περὶ τἀνθρώπεια ὁ τοιοῦτος χρῆσθαι ἐπιχειρεῖ
τοῖς ἀνθρώποις; εἰ γάρ που μετὰ τέχνης ἐχρῆτο,
ὥσπερ ἔχει, οὕτως ἂν ἡγήσατο, τοὺς μὲν χρηστοὺς
90 καὶ πονηροὺς σφόδρα ὀλίγους εἶναι ἑκατέρους, τοὺς
δὲ μεταξὺ πλείστους. Πῶς λέγεις; ἔφην ἐγώ.
Ὥσπερ, ἦ δ' ὅς, περὶ τῶν σφόδρα σμικρῶν καὶ
μεγάλων· οἴει τι σπανιώτερον εἶναι ἢ σφόδρα
μέγαν ἢ σφόδρα σμικρὸν ἐξευρεῖν ἄνθρωπον ἢ κύνα
ἢ ἄλλο ὁτιοῦν; ἢ αὖ ταχὺν ἢ βραδὺν ἢ αἰσχρὸν
ἢ καλὸν ἢ λευκὸν ἢ μέλανα; ἢ οὐκ ᾔσθησαι
ὅτι πάντων τῶν τοιούτων τὰ μὲν ἄκρα τῶν
ἐσχάτων σπάνια καὶ ὀλίγα, τὰ δὲ μεταξὺ ἄφθονα
καὶ πολλά; Πάνυ γε, ἦν δ' ἐγώ. Οὐκοῦν οἴει,
B ἔφη, εἰ πονηρίας ἀγὼν προτεθείη, πάνυ ἂν ὀλίγους καὶ ἐνταῦθα τοὺς πρώτους φανῆναι; Εἰκός
γε, ἦν δ' ἐγώ. Εἰκὸς γάρ, ἔφη. ἀλλὰ ταύτῃ

[1] Schanz brackets αἰσχρόν.

310

sufficient knowledge. You think the man is perfectly true and sound and trustworthy, and afterwards
you find him base and false. Then you have the
same experience with another person. By the time
this has happened to a man a good many times,
especially if it happens among those whom he might
regard as his nearest and dearest friends, he ends by
being in continual quarrels and by hating everybody
and thinking there is nothing sound in anyone at all.
Have you not noticed this?"

"Certainly," said I.

"Well," he went on, "is it not disgraceful, and is
it not plain that such a man undertakes to consort
with men when he has no knowledge of human
nature? For if he had knowledge when he .dealt
with them, he would think that the good and the
bad are both very few and those between the two
are very many, for that is the case."

"What do you mean?"

"I mean just what I might say about the large
and small. Do you think there is anything more
unusual than to find a very large or a very small man,
or dog, or other creature, or again, one that is very
quick or slow, very ugly or beautiful, very black or
white? Have you not noticed that the extremes in
all these instances are rare and few, and the examples
between the extremes are very many?"

"To be sure," said I.

"And don't you think," said he, "that if there
were to be a competition in rascality, those who
excelled would be very few in that also?"

"Very likely," I replied.

"Yes, very likely," he said. "But it is not in that

μὲν οὐχ ὅμοιοι οἱ λόγοι τοῖς ἀνθρώποις, ἀλλὰ
σοῦ νῦν δὴ προάγοντος ἐγὼ ἐφεσπόμην, ἀλλ'
ἐκείνῃ, ἐπειδάν τις πιστεύσῃ λόγῳ τινὶ ἀληθεῖ
εἶναι ἄνευ τῆς περὶ τοὺς λόγους τέχνης, κἄπειτα ὀλίγον ὕστερον αὐτῷ δόξῃ ψευδὴς εἶναι
ἐνίοτε μὲν ὤν, ἐνίοτε δ' οὐκ ὤν, καὶ αὖθις ἕτερος
καὶ ἕτερος· καὶ μάλιστα δὴ οἱ περὶ τοὺς ἀντι-
C λογικοὺς λόγους διατρίψαντες οἶσθ' ὅτι τελευτῶντες οἴονται σοφώτατοι γεγονέναι τε καὶ
κατανενοηκέναι μόνοι ὅτι οὔτε τῶν πραγμάτων
οὐδενὸς οὐδὲν ὑγιὲς οὐδὲ βέβαιον οὔτε τῶν λόγων,
ἀλλὰ πάντα τὰ ὄντα ἀτεχνῶς ὥσπερ ἐν Εὐρίπῳ
ἄνω καὶ κάτω στρέφεται καὶ χρόνον οὐδένα ἐν
οὐδενὶ μένει. Πάνυ μὲν οὖν, ἔφην ἐγώ, ἀληθῆ
λέγεις. Οὐκοῦν, ὦ Φαίδων, ἔφη, οἰκτρὸν ἂν εἴη
τὸ πάθος, εἰ ὄντος δή τινος ἀληθοῦς καὶ βε-
βαίου λόγου καὶ δυνατοῦ κατανοῆσαι, ἔπειτα
D διὰ τὸ παραγίγνεσθαι τοιουτοισὶ λόγοις τοῖς
αὐτοῖς τοτὲ μὲν δοκοῦσιν ἀληθέσιν εἶναι, τοτὲ δὲ
μή, μὴ ἑαυτόν τις αἰτιῷτο μηδὲ τὴν ἑαυτοῦ
ἀτεχνίαν, ἀλλὰ τελευτῶν διὰ τὸ ἀλγεῖν ἄσμενος
ἐπὶ τοὺς λόγους ἀφ' ἑαυτοῦ τὴν αἰτίαν ἀπώσαιτο
καὶ ἤδη τὸν λοιπὸν βίον μισῶν τε καὶ λοιδορῶν
διατελοῖ, τῶν δὲ ὄντων τῆς ἀληθείας τε καὶ
ἐπιστήμης στερηθείη. Νὴ τὸν Δία, ἦν δ' ἐγώ,
οἰκτρὸν δῆτα.

40. Πρῶτον μὲν τοίνυν, ἔφη, τοῦτο εὐλαβη-
E θῶμεν καὶ μὴ παρίωμεν εἰς τὴν ψυχήν, ὡς τῶν
λόγων κινδυνεύει οὐδὲν ὑγιὲς εἶναι, ἀλλὰ πολὺ
μᾶλλον, ὅτι ἡμεῖς οὔπω ὑγιῶς ἔχομεν, ἀλλὰ
ἀνδριστέον καὶ προθυμητέον ὑγιῶς ἔχειν, σοὶ μὲν
οὖν καὶ τοῖς ἄλλοις καὶ τοῦ ἔπειτα βίου παντὸς

respect that arguments are like men; I was merely
following your lead in discussing that. The similarity
lies in this: when a man without proper knowledge
concerning arguments has confidence in the truth of
an argument and afterwards thinks that it is false,
whether it really is so or not, and this happens again
and again; then you know, those men especially who
have spent their time in disputation come to believe
that they are the wisest of men and that they alone
have discovered that there is nothing sound or sure
in anything, whether argument or anything else, but
all things go up and down, like the tide in the
Euripus, and nothing is stable for any length of
time."

"Certainly," I said, "that is very true."

"Then, Phaedo," he said, "if there is any system of
argument which is true and sure and can be learned,
it would be a sad thing if a man, because he has met
with some of those arguments which seem to be
sometimes true and sometimes false, should then not
blame himself or his own lack of skill, but should
end, in his vexation, by throwing the blame gladly
upon the arguments and should hate and revile them
all the rest of his life, and be deprived of the truth
and knowledge of reality."

"Yes, by Zeus," I said, "it would be sad."

"First, then," said he, "let us be on our guard
against this, and let us not admit into our souls the
notion that there is no soundness in arguments at all.
Let us far rather assume that we ourselves are not
yet in sound condition and that we must strive manfully and eagerly to become so, you and the others

91 ἕνεκα, ἐμοὶ δὲ αὐτοῦ ἕνεκα τοῦ θανάτου· ὡς
κινδυνεύω ἔγωγε ἐν τῷ παρόντι περὶ αὐτοῦ τούτου
οὐ φιλοσόφως ἔχειν, ἀλλ' ὥσπερ οἱ πάνυ ἀπαί-
δευτοι φιλονείκως. καὶ γὰρ ἐκεῖνοι ὅταν περί του
ἀμφισβητῶσιν, ὅπῃ μὲν ἔχει περὶ ὧν ἂν ὁ λόγος
ᾖ οὐ φροντίζουσιν, ὅπως δὲ ἃ αὐτοὶ ἔθεντο
ταῦτα δόξει τοῖς παροῦσιν, τοῦτο προθυμοῦνται.
καὶ ἐγώ μοι δοκῶ ἐν τῷ παρόντι τοσοῦτον μόνον
ἐκείνων διοίσειν· οὐ γὰρ ὅπως τοῖς παροῦσιν ἃ
ἐγὼ λέγω δόξει ἀληθῆ εἶναι προθυμηθήσομαι, εἰ
μὴ εἴη πάρεργον, ἀλλ' ὅπως αὐτῷ ἐμοὶ ὅ τι
B μάλιστα δόξει οὕτως ἔχειν. λογίζομαι γάρ, ὦ
φίλε ἑταῖρε· θέασαι ὡς πλεονεκτικῶς· εἰ μὲν
τυγχάνει ἀληθῆ ὄντα ἃ λέγω, καλῶς δὴ ἔχει τὸ
πεισθῆναι· εἰ δὲ μηδέν ἐστι τελευτήσαντι, ἀλλ'
οὖν τοῦτόν γε τὸν χρόνον αὐτὸν τὸν πρὸ τοῦ
θανάτου ἧττον τοῖς παροῦσιν ἀηδὴς ἔσομαι
ὀδυρόμενος. ἡ δὲ ἄγνοιά μοι αὕτη οὐ ξυνδιατελεῖ,
κακὸν γὰρ ἂν ἦν, ἀλλ' ὀλίγον ὕστερον ἀπολεῖ-
ται. παρεσκευασμένος δή, ἔφη, ὦ Σιμμία τε καὶ
Κέβης, οὑτωσὶ ἔρχομαι ἐπὶ τὸν λόγον· ὑμεῖς
C μέντοι, ἂν ἐμοὶ πείθησθε, σμικρὸν φροντίσαντες
Σωκράτους, τῆς δὲ ἀληθείας πολὺ μᾶλλον, ἐὰν
μέν τι ὑμῖν δοκῶ ἀληθὲς λέγειν, συνομολογήσατε,
εἰ δὲ μή, παντὶ λόγῳ ἀντιτείνετε, ὅπως μὴ ἐγὼ
ὑπὸ προθυμίας ἅμα ἐμαυτόν τε καὶ ὑμᾶς ἐξα-
πατήσας ὥσπερ μέλιττα τὸ κέντρον ἐγκαταλιπὼν
οἰχήσομαι.

41. Ἀλλ' ἰτέον, ἔφη. πρῶτόν με ὑπομνή-
σατε ἃ ἐλέγετε, ἐὰν μὴ φαίνωμαι μεμνημένος.
Σιμμίας μὲν γάρ, ὡς ἐγᾦμαι, ἀπιστεῖ τε καὶ
φοβεῖται, μὴ ἡ ψυχὴ ὅμως καὶ θειότερον καὶ

for the sake of all your future life, and I because of my impending death; for I fear that I am not just now in a philosophical frame of mind as regards this particular question, but am contentious, like quite uncultured persons. For when they argue about anything, they do not care what the truth is in the matters they are discussing, but are eager only to make their own views seem true to their hearers. And I fancy I differ from them just now only to this extent: I shall not be eager to make what I say seem true to my hearers, except as a secondary matter, but shall be very eager to make myself believe it. For see, my friend, how selfish my attitude is. If what I say is true, I am the gainer by believing it; and if there be nothing for me after death, at any rate I shall not be burdensome to my friends by my lamentations in these last moments. And this ignorance of mine will not last, for that would be an evil, but will soon end. So," he said, " Simmias and Cebes, I approach the argument with my mind thus prepared. But you, if you do as I ask, will give little thought to Socrates and much more to the truth; and if you think what I say is true, agree to it, and if not, oppose me with every argument you can muster, that I may not in my eagerness deceive myself and you alike and go away, like a bee, leaving my sting sticking in you.

"But we must get to work," he said. "First refresh my memory, if I seem to have forgotten anything. Simmias, I think, has doubts and fears that the soul, though more divine and excellent than the

D κάλλιον ὂν τοῦ σώματος προαπολλύηται ἐν
ἁρμονίας εἴδει οὖσα· Κέβης δέ μοι ἔδοξε τοῦτο
μὲν ἐμοὶ συγχωρεῖν, πολυχρονιώτερόν γε εἶναι
ψυχὴν σώματος, ἀλλὰ τόδε ἄδηλον παντί, μὴ
πολλὰ δὴ σώματα καὶ πολλάκις κατατρίψασα
ἡ ψυχὴ τὸ τελευταῖον σῶμα καταλιποῦσα νῦν
αὐτὴ ἀπολλύηται, καὶ ᾖ αὐτὸ τοῦτο θάνατος,
ψυχῆς ὄλεθρος, ἐπεὶ σῶμά γε ἀεὶ ἀπολλύμενον
οὐδὲν παύεται. ἆρα ἄλλ' ἢ ταῦτ' ἐστίν, ὦ Σιμμία τε καὶ Κέβης, ἃ δεῖ ἡμᾶς ἐπισκοπεῖσθαι;
E συνωμολογείτην δὴ ταῦτ' εἶναι ἄμφω. Πότερον
οὖν, ἔφη, πάντας τοὺς ἔμπροσθε λόγους οὐκ
ἀποδέχεσθε, ἢ τοὺς μέν, τοὺς δ' οὔ; Τοὺς μέν,
ἐφάτην, τοὺς δ' οὔ. Τί οὖν, ἦ δ' ὅς, περὶ
ἐκείνου τοῦ λόγου λέγετε, ἐν ᾧ ἔφαμεν τὴν
μάθησιν ἀνάμνησιν εἶναι, καὶ τούτου οὕτως
ἔχοντος ἀναγκαίως ἔχειν ἄλλοθι πρότερον ἡμῶν
92 εἶναι τὴν ψυχήν, πρὶν ἐν τῷ σώματι ἐνδεθῆναι;
Ἐγὼ μέν, ἔφη ὁ Κέβης, καὶ τότε θαυμαστῶς
ὡς ἐπείσθην ὑπ' αὐτοῦ καὶ νῦν ἐμμένω ὡς οὐδενὶ
λόγῳ. Καὶ μήν, ἔφη ὁ Σιμμίας, καὶ αὐτὸς
οὕτως ἔχω, καὶ πάνυ ἂν θαυμάζοιμι, εἴ μοι περὶ
γε τούτου ἄλλα ποτὲ δόξειεν. καὶ ὁ Σωκράτης·
Ἀλλὰ ἀνάγκη σοι, ἔφη, ὦ ξένε Θηβαῖε, ἄλλα
δοξάσαι, ἐάνπερ μείνῃ ἥδε ἡ οἴησις, τὸ ἁρμονίαν
μὲν εἶναι σύνθετον πρᾶγμα, ψυχὴν δὲ ἁρμονίαν
τινὰ ἐκ τῶν κατὰ τὸ σῶμα ἐντεταμένων συγκεῖ-
B σθαι. οὐ γάρ που ἀποδέξει γε σαυτοῦ λέγοντος,
ὡς πρότερον ἦν ἁρμονία συγκειμένη, πρὶν ἐκεῖνα
εἶναι, ἐξ ὧν ἔδει αὐτὴν συντεθῆναι. ἢ ἀποδέξει;
Οὐδαμῶς, ἔφη, ὦ Σώκρατες. Αἰσθάνει οὖν,
ἦ δ' ὅς, ὅτι ταῦτά σοι συμβαίνει λέγειν, ὅταν

body, may perish first, being of the nature of a harmony. And, Cebes, I believe, granted that the soul is more lasting than the body, but said that no one could know that the soul, after wearing out many bodies, did not at last perish itself upon leaving the body; and that this was death—the destruction of the soul, since the body is continually being destroyed. Are those the points, Simmias and Cebes, which we must consider?"

They both agreed that these were the points.

"Now," said he, "do you reject all of our previous arguments, or only some of them?"

"Only some of them," they replied.

"What do you think," he asked, "about the argument in which we said that learning is recollection and that, since this is so, our soul must necessarily have been somewhere before it was imprisoned in the body?"

"I," said Cebes, "was wonderfully convinced by it at the time and I still believe it more firmly than any other argument."

"And I too," said Simmias, "feel just as he does, and I should be much surprised if I should ever think differently on this point."

And Socrates said: "You must, my Theban friend, think differently, if you persist in your opinion that a harmony is a compound and that the soul is a harmony made up of the elements that are strung like harpstrings in the body. For surely you will not accept your own statement that a composite harmony existed before those things from which it had to be composed, will you?"

"Certainly not, Socrates."

"Then do you see," said he, "that this is just

317

φῆς μὲν εἶναι τὴν ψυχὴν πρὶν καὶ εἰς ἀνθρώπου εἶδός γε καὶ σῶμα ἀφικέσθαι, εἶναι δὲ
αὐτὴν συγκειμένην ἐκ τῶν οὐδέπω ὄντων· οὐ γὰρ
δὴ ἁρμονία γέ σοι τοιοῦτόν ἐστιν ὃ ἀπεικάζεις,
ἀλλὰ πρότερον καὶ ἡ λύρα καὶ αἱ χορδαὶ καὶ οἱ
C φθόγγοι ἔτι ἀνάρμοστοι ὄντες γίγνονται, τελευταῖον δὲ πάντων ξυνίσταται ἡ ἁρμονία καὶ πρῶτον
ἀπόλλυται. οὗτος οὖν σοι ὁ λόγος ἐκείνῳ πῶς
ξυνάσεται; Οὐδαμῶς, ἔφη ὁ Σιμμίας. Καὶ μήν,
ἦ δ' ὅς, πρέπει γε εἴπερ τῳ ἄλλῳ λόγῳ ξυνῳδῷ
εἶναι καὶ τῷ περὶ ἁρμονίας. Πρέπει γάρ, ἔφη
ὁ Σιμμίας. Οὗτος τοίνυν, ἔφη, σοὶ οὐ ξυνῳδός·
ἀλλ' ὅρα, πότερον αἱρεῖ τῶν λόγων, τὴν μάθησιν
ἀνάμνησιν εἶναι ἢ ψυχὴν ἁρμονίαν; Πολὺ μᾶλλον, ἔφη, ἐκεῖνον, ὦ Σώκρατες. ὅδε μὲν γάρ
μοι γέγονεν ἄνευ ἀποδείξεως μετὰ εἰκότος τινὸς
D καὶ εὐπρεπείας, ὅθεν καὶ τοῖς πολλοῖς δοκεῖ
ἀνθρώποις· ἐγὼ δὲ τοῖς διὰ τῶν εἰκότων τὰς
ἀποδείξεις ποιουμένοις λόγοις ξύνοιδα οὖσιν ἀλα-
ζόσιν, καὶ ἄν τις αὐτοὺς μὴ φυλάττηται, εὖ
μάλα ἐξαπατῶσι, καὶ ἐν γεωμετρίᾳ καὶ ἐν τοῖς
ἄλλοις ἅπασιν. ὁ δὲ περὶ τῆς ἀναμνήσεως καὶ
μαθήσεως λόγος δι' ὑποθέσεως ἀξίας ἀποδέξασθαι
εἴρηται. ἐρρήθη γάρ που οὕτως ἡμῶν εἶναι ἡ
ψυχὴ καὶ πρὶν εἰς σῶμα ἀφικέσθαι, ὥσπερ αὐτὴ
ἐστιν ἡ οὐσία ἔχουσα τὴν ἐπωνυμίαν τὴν τοῦ ὃ
E ἔστιν. ἐγὼ δὲ ταύτην, ὡς ἐμαυτὸν πείθω, ἱκανῶς
τε καὶ ὀρθῶς ἀποδέδεγμαι. ἀνάγκη οὖν μοι, ὡς
ἔοικε, διὰ ταῦτα μήτε ἐμαυτοῦ μήτε ἄλλου
ἀποδέχεσθαι λέγοντος, ὡς ψυχή ἐστιν ἁρμονία.

what you say when you assert that the soul exists before it enters into the form and body of a man, and that it is composed of things that do not yet exist? For harmony is not what your comparison assumes it to be. The lyre and the strings and the sounds come into being in a tuneless condition, and the harmony is the last of all to be composed and the first to perish. So how can you bring this theory into harmony with the other?"

"I cannot at all," said Simmias.

"And yet," said Socrates, "there ought to be harmony between it and the theory about harmony above all others."

"Yes, there ought," said Simmias.

"Well," said he, "there is no harmony between the two theories. Now which do you prefer, that knowledge is recollection or that the soul is a harmony?"

"The former, decidedly, Socrates," he replied. "For this other came to me without demonstration; it merely seemed probable and attractive, which is the reason why many men hold it. I am conscious that those arguments which base their demonstrations on mere probability are deceptive, and if we are not on our guard against them they deceive us greatly, in geometry and in all other things. But the theory of recollection and knowledge has been established by a sound course of argument. For we agreed that our soul before it entered into the body existed just as the very essence which is called the absolute exists. Now I am persuaded that I have accepted this essence on sufficient and right grounds. I cannot therefore accept from myself or anyone else the statement that the soul is a harmony."

42. Τί δέ, ἦ δ' ὅς, ὦ Σιμμία, τῇδε; δοκεῖ σοι
ἁρμονίᾳ ἢ ἄλλῃ τινὶ συνθέσει προσήκειν ἄλλως
93 πως ἔχειν ἢ ὡς ἂν ἐκεῖνα ἔχῃ, ἐξ ὧν ἂν συγ-
κέηται; Οὐδαμῶς. Οὐδὲ μὴν ποιεῖν τι, ὡς
ἐγῷμαι, οὐδέ τι πάσχειν ἄλλο παρ' ἃ ἂν ἐκεῖνα ἢ
ποιῇ ἢ πάσχῃ; Συνέφη. Οὐκ ἄρα ἡγεῖσθαί γε
προσήκει ἁρμονίαν τούτων, ἐξ ὧν ἂν συντεθῇ,
ἀλλ' ἕπεσθαι. Συνεδόκει. Πολλοῦ ἄρα δεῖ
ἐναντία γε ἁρμονία κινηθῆναι ἢ φθέγξασθαι ἤ τι
ἄλλο ἐναντιωθῆναι τοῖς αὑτῆς μέρεσιν. Πολλοῦ
μέντοι, ἔφη. Τί δέ; οὐχ οὕτως ἁρμονία πέφυκεν
εἶναι ἑκάστη ἁρμονία, ὡς ἂν ἁρμοσθῇ; Οὐ
μανθάνω, ἔφη. Οὐχί, ἦ δ' ὅς, ἂν μὲν μᾶλλον
B ἁρμοσθῇ καὶ ἐπὶ πλέον, εἴπερ ἐνδέχεται τοῦτο
γίγνεσθαι, μᾶλλόν τε ἂν ἁρμονία εἴη καὶ πλείων,
εἰ δ' ἧττόν τε καὶ ἐπ' ἔλαττον, ἧττόν τε καὶ
ἐλάττων; Πάνυ γε. Ἦ οὖν ἔστι τοῦτο περὶ
ψυχήν, ὥστε καὶ κατὰ τὸ σμικρότατον ἑτέραν
ἑτέρας ψυχῆς ἐπὶ πλέον καὶ μᾶλλον ἢ ἐπ'
ἔλαττον καὶ ἧττον αὐτὸ τοῦτο εἶναι, ψυχήν;
Οὐδ' ὁπωστιοῦν, ἔφη. Φέρε δή, ἔφη, πρὸς Διός·
λέγεται ψυχὴ ἡ μὲν νοῦν τε ἔχειν καὶ ἀρετὴν
καὶ εἶναι ἀγαθή, ἡ δὲ ἄνοιάν τε καὶ μοχ-

" Here is another way of looking at it, Simmias,"
said he. " Do you think a harmony or any other
composite thing can be in any other state than that
in which the elements are of which it is composed ? "

" Certainly not."

" And it can neither do nor suffer anything other
than they do or suffer ? "

He agreed.

" Then a harmony cannot be expected to lead the
elements of which it is composed, but to follow
them."

He assented.

" A harmony, then, is quite unable to move or
make a sound or do anything else that is opposed to
its component parts."

" Quite unable," said he.

" Well then, is not every harmony by nature a
harmony according as it is harmonised ? "

" I do not understand," said Simmias.

" Would it not," said Socrates, " be more completely
a harmony and a greater harmony if it were harmonised more fully and to a greater extent, assuming
that to be possible, and less completely a harmony
and a lesser harmony if less completely harmonised
and to a less extent ? "

" Certainly."

" Is this true of the soul ? Is one soul even in
the slightest degree more completely and to a greater
extent a soul than another, or less completely and
to a less extent ? "

" Not in the least," said he.

" Well now," said he, " one soul is said to possess
sense and virtue and to be good, and another to

θηρίαν καὶ εἶναι κακή; καὶ ταῦτα ἀληθῶς
C λέγεται; Ἀληθῶς μέντοι. Τῶν οὖν θεμένων
ψυχὴν ἁρμονίαν εἶναι τί τις φήσει ταῦτα ὄντα
εἶναι ἐν ταῖς ψυχαῖς, τήν τε ἀρετὴν καὶ τὴν
κακίαν; πότερον ἁρμονίαν αὖ τινα ἄλλην καὶ
ἀναρμοστίαν; καὶ τὴν μὲν ἡρμόσθαι, τὴν ἀγαθήν,
καὶ ἔχειν ἐν αὑτῇ ἁρμονίᾳ οὔσῃ ἄλλην ἁρμονίαν,
τὴν δὲ ἀνάρμοστον αὐτήν τε εἶναι καὶ οὐκ ἔχειν ἐν
αὑτῇ ἄλλην; Οὐκ ἔχω ἔγωγ᾽, ἔφη ὁ Σιμμίας,
εἰπεῖν· δῆλον δ᾽ ὅτι τοιαῦτ᾽ ἄττ᾽ ἂν λέγοι ὁ
ἐκεῖνο ὑποθέμενος. Ἀλλὰ προωμολόγηται, ἔφη,
D μηδὲν μᾶλλον μηδ᾽ ἧττον ἑτέραν ἑτέρας ψυχὴν ψυχῆς εἶναι· τοῦτο δ᾽ ἔστι τὸ ὁμολόγημα,
μηδὲν μᾶλλον μηδ᾽ ἐπὶ πλέον μηδ᾽ ἧττον μηδ᾽
ἐπ᾽ ἔλαττον ἑτέραν ἑτέρας ἁρμονίαν εἶναι. ἦ
γάρ; Πάνυ γε. Τὴν δέ γε μηδὲν μᾶλλον μηδὲ
ἧττον ἁρμονίαν οὖσαν μήτε μᾶλλον μήτε ἧττον
ἡρμόσθαι· ἔστιν οὕτως; Ἔστιν. Ἡ δὲ μήτε
μᾶλλον μήτε ἧττον ἡρμοσμένη ἔστιν ὅ τι πλέον
ἢ ἔλαττον ἁρμονίας μετέχει, ἢ τὸ ἴσον; Τὸ ἴσον.
Οὐκοῦν ψυχὴ ἐπειδὴ οὐδὲν μᾶλλον οὐδ᾽ ἧττον
E ἄλλη ἄλλης αὐτὸ τοῦτο ψυχή ἐστιν, οὐδὲ δὴ
μᾶλλον οὐδὲ ἧττον ἥρμοσται; Οὕτω. Τοῦτο δέ
γε πεπονθυῖα οὐδὲν πλέον ἀναρμοστίας οὐδὲ
ἁρμονίας μετέχοι ἄν; Οὐ γὰρ οὖν. Τοῦτο δ᾽
αὖ πεπονθυῖα ἆρ᾽ ἄν τι πλέον κακίας ἢ ἀρετῆς
μετέχοι ἑτέρα ἑτέρας, εἴπερ ἡ μὲν κακία ἀναρ-
μοστία, ἡ δὲ ἀρετὴ ἁρμονία εἴη; Οὐδὲν πλέον.
Μᾶλλον δέ γέ που, ὦ Σιμμία, κατὰ τὸν ὀρθὸν
94 λόγον κακίας οὐδεμία ψυχὴ μεθέξει, εἴπερ ἁρ-

possess folly and wickedness and to be bad; and is this true?" "Yes, it is true."

"Now what will those who assume that the soul is a harmony say that these things—the virtue and the wickedness—in the soul are? Will they say that this is another kind of harmony and a discord, and that the soul, which is itself a harmony, has within it another harmony and that the other soul is discordant and has no other harmony within it?"

"I cannot tell," replied Simmias, "but evidently those who make that assumption would say something of that sort."

"But we agreed," said Socrates, "that one soul is no more or less a soul than another; and that is equivalent to an agreement that one is no more and to no greater extent, and no less and to no less extent, a harmony than another, is it not?" "Certainly."

"And that which is no more or less a harmony, is no more or less harmonised. Is that so?" "Yes."

"But has that which is no more and no less harmonised any greater or any less amount of harmony, or an equal amount?" "An equal amount."

"Then a soul, since it is neither more nor less a soul than another, is neither more nor less harmonised."

"That is so."

"And therefore can have no greater amount of discord or of harmony?" "No."

"And therefore again one soul can have no greater amount of wickedness or virtue than another, if wickedness is discord and virtue harmony?" "It cannot."

"Or rather, to speak exactly, Simmias, no soul will have any wickedness at all, if the soul is a harmony;

μονία ἐστίν· ἁρμονία γὰρ δήπου παντελῶς αὐτὸ
τοῦτο οὖσα ἁρμονία ἀναρμοστίας οὔποτ' ἂν
μετάσχοι. Οὐ μέντοι. Οὐδέ γε δήπου ψυχή,
οὖσα παντελῶς ψυχή, κακίας. Πῶς γὰρ ἔκ
γε τῶν προειρημένων; Ἐκ τούτου ἄρα τοῦ λόγου
ἡμῖν πᾶσαι ψυχαὶ πάντων ζῴων ὁμοίως ἀγαθαὶ
ἔσονται, εἴπερ ὁμοίως πεφύκασιν αὐτὸ τοῦτο,
ψυχαί, εἶναι. Ἔμοιγε δοκεῖ, ἔφη, ὦ Σώκρατες.
B Ἦ καὶ καλῶς δοκεῖ, ἦ δ' ὅς, οὕτω λέγεσθαι,
καὶ πάσχειν ἂν ταῦτα ὁ λόγος, εἰ ὀρθὴ ἡ ὑπό-
θεσις ἦν, τὸ ψυχὴν ἁρμονίαν εἶναι; Οὐδ' ὁπωστιοῦν, ἔφη.

43. Τί δέ; ἦ δ' ὅς· τῶν ἐν ἀνθρώπῳ πάντων ἔσθ' ὅ τι ἄλλο λέγεις ἄρχειν ἢ ψυχὴν
ἄλλως τε καὶ φρόνιμον; Οὐκ ἔγωγε. Πότερον
συγχωροῦσαν[1] τοῖς κατὰ τὸ σῶμα πάθεσιν ἢ καὶ[2]
ἐναντιουμένην; λέγω δὲ τὸ τοιόνδε, οἷον[3] καύματος
ἐνόντος καὶ δίψους ἐπὶ τοὐναντίον ἕλκειν, τὸ μὴ
πίνειν, καὶ πείνης ἐνούσης ἐπὶ τὸ μὴ ἐσθίειν, καὶ
ἄλλα μυρία που ὁρῶμεν ἐναντιουμένην τὴν ψυχὴν
C τοῖς κατὰ τὸ σῶμα· ἢ οὔ; Πάνυ μὲν οὖν.
Οὐκοῦν αὖ ὡμολογήσαμεν ἐν τοῖς πρόσθεν μή-
ποτ' ἂν αὐτήν, ἁρμονίαν γε οὖσαν, ἐναντία
ᾄδειν οἷς ἐπιτείνοιτο καὶ χαλῷτο καὶ πάλλοιτο
καὶ ἄλλο ὁτιοῦν πάθος πάσχοι ἐκεῖνα ἐξ ὧν
τυγχάνει οὖσα, ἀλλ' ἕπεσθαι ἐκείνοις καὶ οὔποτ'

---

[1] Schanz brackets συγχωροῦσαν.
[2] Schanz omits ἢ καί.
[3] οἷον Stobaeus. ὡσεὶ CDE, bracketed by Schanz.

for if a harmony is entirely harmony, it could have no part in discord."

"Certainly not."

"Then the soul, being entirely soul, could have no part in wickedness."

"How could it, if what we have said is right?"

"According to this argument, then, if all souls are by nature equally souls, all souls of all living creatures will be equally good."

"So it seems, Socrates," said he.

"And," said Socrates, "do you think that this is true and that our reasoning would have come to this end, if the theory that the soul is a harmony were correct?"

"Not in the least," he replied.

"Well," said Socrates, "of all the parts that make up a man, do you think any is ruler except the soul, especially if it be a wise one?"

"No, I do not."

"Does it yield to the feelings of the body or oppose them? I mean, when the body is hot and thirsty, does not the soul oppose it and draw it away from drinking, and from eating when it is hungry, and do we not see the soul opposing the body in countless other ways?"

"Certainly."

"Did we not agree in our previous discussion that it could never, if it be a harmony, give forth a sound at variance with the tensions and relaxations and vibrations and other conditions of the elements which compose it, but that it would follow them and never lead them?"

ἂν ἡγεμονεύειν; Ὡμολογήσαμεν, ἔφη· πῶς γὰρ
οὔ; Τί οὖν; νῦν οὐ πᾶν τοὐναντίον ἡμῖν φαίνεται ἐργαζομένη, ἡγεμονεύουσά τε ἐκείνων
πάντων ἐξ ὧν φησί τις αὐτὴν εἶναι, καὶ ἐναντιου-
D μένη ὀλίγου πάντα διὰ παντὸς τοῦ βίου καὶ
δεσπόζουσα πάντας τρόπους, τὰ μὲν χαλεπώτερον
κολάζουσα καὶ μετ' ἀλγηδόνων, τά τε κατὰ τὴν
γυμναστικὴν καὶ τὴν ἰατρικήν, τὰ δὲ πραότερον,
καὶ τὰ μὲν ἀπειλοῦσα, τὰ δὲ νουθετοῦσα, ταῖς
ἐπιθυμίαις καὶ ὀργαῖς καὶ φόβοις ὡς ἄλλη οὖσα
ἄλλῳ πράγματι διαλεγομένη; οἷόν που καὶ
Ὅμηρος ἐν Ὀδυσσείᾳ πεποίηκεν, οὗ λέγει τὸν
Ὀδυσσέα·

στῆθος δὲ πλήξας κραδίην ἠνίπαπε μύθῳ·
τέτλαθι δή, κραδίη· καὶ κύντερον ἄλλο ποτ'
ἔτλης.

E ἆρ' οἴει αὐτὸν ταῦτα ποιῆσαι διανοούμενον ὡς
ἁρμονίας αὐτῆς οὔσης καὶ οἵας ἄγεσθαι ὑπὸ τῶν
τοῦ σώματος παθῶν, ἀλλ' οὐχ οἵας ἄγειν τε
ταῦτα καὶ δεσπόζειν, καὶ οὔσης αὐτῆς πολὺ
θειοτέρου τινὸς πράγματος ἢ καθ' ἁρμονίαν;
Νὴ Δία, ὦ Σώκρατες, ἔμοιγε δοκεῖ. Οὐκ ἄρα,
ὦ ἄριστε, ἡμῖν οὐδαμῇ καλῶς ἔχει ψυχὴν
ἁρμονίαν τινὰ φάναι εἶναι· οὔτε γὰρ ἄν, ὡς
95 ἔοικεν, Ὁμήρῳ θείῳ ποιητῇ ὁμολογοῖμεν οὔτε
αὐτοὶ ἡμῖν αὐτοῖς. Ἔχειν οὕτως ἔφη.

44. Εἶεν δή, ἦ δ' ὃς ὁ Σωκράτης, τὰ μὲν
Ἁρμονίας ἡμῖν τῆς Θηβαϊκῆς ἵλεά πως, ὡς ἔοικε,
μετρίως γέγονεν· τί δὲ δὴ τὰ Κάδμου, ἔφη, ὦ

" Yes," he replied, " we did, of course."

" Well then, do we not now find that the soul acts in exactly the opposite way, leading those elements of which it is said to consist and opposing them in almost everything through all our life, and tyrannising over them in every way, sometimes inflicting harsh and painful punishments (those of gymnastics and medicine), and sometimes milder ones, sometimes threatening and sometimes admonishing, in short, speaking to the desires and passions and fears as if it were distinct from them and they from it, as Homer has shown in the *Odyssey* [1] when he says of Odysseus :

He smote his breast, and thus he chid his heart :
' Endure it, heart, thou didst bear worse than this ' ?

Do you suppose that, when he wrote those words, he thought of the soul as a harmony which would be led by the conditions of the body, and not rather as something fitted to lead and rule them, and itself a far more divine thing than a harmony ? "

" By Zeus, Socrates, the latter, I think."

" Then, my good friend, it will never do for us to say that the soul is a harmony ; for we should, it seems, agree neither with Homer, the divine poet, nor with ourselves."

" That is true," said he.

" Very well," said Socrates, " Harmonia, the Theban goddess, has, it seems, been moderately

---

[1] *Odyssey* xx, 17, 18. Bryant's translation.

Κέβης, πῶς ἱλασόμεθα καὶ τίνι λόγῳ; Σὺ μοι δοκεῖς, ἔφη ὁ Κέβης, ἐξευρήσειν· τουτονὶ γοῦν τὸν λόγον τὸν πρὸς τὴν ἁρμονίαν θαυμαστῶς μοι εἶπες ὡς παρὰ δόξαν. Σιμμίου γὰρ λέγοντος ὅ τι ἠπόρει, πάνυ ἐθαύμαζον, εἴ τι ἕξει τις χρήσασθαι

B τῷ λόγῳ αὐτοῦ· πάνυ μὲν οὖν μοι ἀτόπως ἔδοξεν εὐθὺς τὴν πρώτην ἔφοδον οὐ δέξασθαι τοῦ σοῦ λόγου. ταὐτὰ δὴ οὐκ ἂν θαυμάσαιμι καὶ τὸν τοῦ Κάδμου λόγον εἰ πάθοι. Ὦ 'γαθέ, ἔφη ὁ Σωκράτης, μὴ μέγα λέγε, μή τις ἡμῶν βασκανία περιτρέψῃ τὸν λόγον τὸν μέλλοντα ἔσεσθαι.[1] ἀλλὰ δὴ ταῦτα μὲν τῷ θεῷ μελήσει, ἡμεῖς δὲ Ὁμηρικῶς ἐγγὺς ἰόντες πειρώμεθα, εἰ ἄρα τι λέγεις. ἔστι δὲ δὴ τὸ κεφάλαιον ὧν ζητεῖς· ἀξιοῖς ἐπιδειχθῆναι ἡμῶν τὴν ψυχὴν ἀνώλεθρόν

C τε καὶ ἀθάνατον οὖσαν, εἰ φιλόσοφος ἀνὴρ μέλλων ἀποθανεῖσθαι, θαρρῶν τε καὶ ἡγούμενος ἀποθανὼν ἐκεῖ εὖ πράξειν διαφερόντως ἢ εἰ ἐν ἄλλῳ βίῳ βιοὺς ἐτελεύτα, μὴ ἀνόητόν τε καὶ ἠλίθιον θάρρος θαρρήσει. τὸ δὲ ἀποφαίνειν, ὅτι ἰσχυρόν τί ἐστιν ἡ ψυχὴ καὶ θεοειδὲς καὶ ἦν ἔτι πρότερον, πρὶν ἡμᾶς ἀνθρώπους γενέσθαι, οὐδὲν κωλύειν φὴς πάντα ταῦτα μηνύειν ἀθανασίαν μὲν μή, ὅτι δὲ πολυχρόνιόν τέ ἐστιν ψυχὴ καὶ ἦν που πρότερον ἀμήχανον ὅσον χρόνον καὶ ᾔδει τε καὶ ἔπραττεν πολλὰ ἄττα· ἀλλὰ γὰρ οὐδέν τι μᾶλλον

D ἦν ἀθάνατον, ἀλλὰ καὶ αὐτὸ τὸ εἰς ἀνθρώπου σῶμα ἐλθεῖν ἀρχὴ ἦν αὐτῇ ὀλέθρου, ὥσπερ νόσος· καὶ ταλαιπωρουμένη τε δὴ τοῦτον τὸν βίον ζώη καὶ τελευτῶσά γε ἐν τῷ καλουμένῳ θανάτῳ

---

[1] Schanz, following Hermann, brackets ἔσεσθαι.

gracious to us; but how, Cebes, and by what argument can we find grace in the sight of Cadmus?"

"I think," said Cebes, "you will find a way. At any rate, you conducted this argument against harmony wonderfully and better than I expected. For when Simmias was telling of his difficulty, I wondered if anyone could make head against his argument; so it seemed to me very remarkable that it could not withstand the first attack of your argument. Now I should not be surprised if the argument of Cadmus met with the same fate.

"My friend," said Socrates, "do not be boastful, lest some evil eye put to rout the argument that is to come. That, however, is in the hands of God. Let us, in Homeric fashion, 'charge the foe' and test the worth of what you say. Now the sum total of what you seek is this: You demand a proof that our soul is indestructible and immortal, if the philosopher, who is confident in the face of death and who thinks that after death he will fare better in the other world than if he had lived his life differently, is not to find his confidence senseless and foolish. And although we show that the soul is strong and godlike and existed before we men were born as men, all this, you say, may bear witness not to immortality, but only to the fact that the soul lasts a long while, and existed somewhere an immeasurably long time before our birth, and knew and did various things; yet it was none the more immortal for all that, but its very entrance into the human body was the beginning of its dissolution, a disease, as it were; and it lives in toil through this life and finally

ἀπολλύοιτο. διαφέρειν[1] δὲ δὴ φῂς οὐδέν, εἴτε
ἅπαξ εἰς σῶμα ἔρχεται εἴτε πολλάκις, πρός γε τὸ
ἕκαστον ἡμῶν φοβεῖσθαι· προσήκειν[2] γὰρ φοβεῖσθαι, εἰ μὴ ἀνόητος εἴη, τῷ μὴ εἰδότι μηδὲ ἔχοντι
λόγον διδόναι, ὡς ἀθάνατόν ἐστι. τοιαῦτ' ἄττα
E ἐστίν, οἶμαι, ὦ Κέβης, ἃ λέγεις· καὶ ἐξεπίτηδες
πολλάκις ἀναλαμβάνω, ἵνα μή τι διαφύγῃ ἡμᾶς,
εἴ τέ τι βούλει, προσθῇς ἢ ἀφέλῃς. καὶ ὁ Κέβης·
Ἀλλ' οὐδὲν ἔγωγε ἐν τῷ παρόντι, ἔφη, οὔτε
ἀφελεῖν οὔτε προσθεῖναι δέομαι· ἔστι δὲ ταῦτα, ἃ
λέγω.

45. Ὁ οὖν Σωκράτης συχνὸν χρόνον ἐπισχὼν
καὶ πρὸς ἑαυτόν τι σκεψάμενος, Οὐ φαῦλον
πρᾶγμα, ἔφη, ὦ Κέβης, ζητεῖς· ὅλως γὰρ δεῖ
περὶ γενέσεως καὶ φθορᾶς τὴν αἰτίαν διαπραγ-
96 ματεύσασθαι. ἐγὼ οὖν σοι δίειμι περὶ αὐτῶν,
ἐὰν βούλῃ, τά γε ἐμὰ πάθη· ἔπειτα ἄν τί σοι
χρήσιμον φαίνηται ὧν ἂν λέγω, πρὸς τὴν πειθὼ
περὶ ὧν λέγεις χρήσει. Ἀλλὰ μήν, ἔφη ὁ
Κέβης, βούλομαί γε. Ἄκουε τοίνυν ὡς ἐροῦν-
τος. ἐγὼ γάρ, ἔφη, ὦ Κέβης, νέος ὢν θαυμαστῶς ὡς ἐπεθύμησα ταύτης τῆς σοφίας, ἣν δὴ
καλοῦσι περὶ φύσεως ἱστορίαν. ὑπερήφανος γάρ
μοι ἐδόκει εἶναι, εἰδέναι τὰς αἰτίας ἑκάστου, διὰ τί
γίγνεται ἕκαστον καὶ διὰ τί ἀπόλλυται καὶ διὰ τί
B ἔστι· καὶ πολλάκις ἐμαυτὸν ἄνω κάτω μετέβαλ-
λον σκοπῶν πρῶτον τὰ τοιάδε, ἆρ' ἐπειδὰν τὸ
θερμὸν καὶ τὸ ψυχρὸν[3] σηπεδόνα τινὰ λάβῃ, ὥς

---

[1] Schanz reads διαφέρει.
[2] Schanz reads προσήκει.
[3] τὸ θερμὸν καὶ τὸ ψυχρὸν Eb Stobaeus. τὸ θερμὸν καὶ ψυχρὸν BD, Schanz brackets ψυχρὸν.

perishes in what we call death. Now it makes no difference, you say, whether a soul enters into a body once or many times, so far as the fear each of us feels is concerned; for anyone, unless he is a fool, must fear, if he does not know and cannot prove that the soul is immortal. That, Cebes, is, I think, about what you mean. And I restate it purposely that nothing may escape us and that you may, if you wish, add or take away anything."

And Cebes said, "I do not at present wish to take anything away or to add anything. You have expressed my meaning."

Socrates paused for some time and was absorbed in thought. Then he said: "It is no small thing that you seek; for the cause of generation and decay must be completely investigated. Now I will tell you my own experience in the matter, if you wish; then if anything I say seems to you to be of any use, you can employ it for the solution of your difficulty."

"Certainly," said Cebes, "I wish to hear your experiences."

"Listen then, and I will tell you. When I was young, Cebes, I was tremendously eager for the kind of wisdom which they call investigation of nature. I thought it was a glorious thing to know the causes of everything, why each thing comes into being and why it perishes and why it exists; and I was always unsettling myself with such questions as these: Do heat and cold, by a sort of fermentation, bring about the organisation of animals, as some people say? Is

τινες ἔλεγον, τότε δὴ τὰ ζῷα συντρέφεται· καὶ
πότερον τὸ αἷμά ἐστιν ᾧ φρονοῦμεν, ἢ ὁ ἀὴρ ἢ τὸ
πῦρ, ἢ τούτων μὲν οὐδέν, ὁ δ' ἐγκέφαλός ἐστιν ὁ
τὰς αἰσθήσεις παρέχων τοῦ ἀκούειν καὶ ὁρᾶν καὶ
ὀσφραίνεσθαι, ἐκ τούτων δὲ γίγνοιτο μνήμη καὶ
δόξα, ἐκ δὲ μνήμης καὶ δόξης λαβούσης τὸ ἠρεμεῖν
κατὰ ταῦτα γίγνεσθαι ἐπιστήμην· καὶ αὖ τούτων
C τὰς φθορὰς σκοπῶν, καὶ τὰ περὶ τὸν οὐρανὸν καὶ
τὴν γῆν πάθη, τελευτῶν οὕτως ἐμαυτῷ ἔδοξα πρὸς
ταύτην τὴν σκέψιν ἀφυὴς εἶναι, ὡς οὐδὲν χρῆμα.
τεκμήριον δέ σοι ἐρῶ ἱκανόν· ἐγὼ γὰρ ἃ καὶ
πρότερον σαφῶς ἠπιστάμην, ὥς γε ἐμαυτῷ καὶ
τοῖς ἄλλοις ἐδόκουν, τότε ὑπὸ ταύτης τῆς σκέψεως
οὕτω σφόδρα ἐτυφλώθην, ὥστε ἀπέμαθον καὶ ἃ
πρὸ τοῦ ᾤμην εἰδέναι, περὶ ἄλλων τε πολλῶν καὶ
διὰ τί ἄνθρωπος αὐξάνεται. τοῦτο γὰρ ᾤμην πρὸ
τοῦ παντὶ δῆλον εἶναι, ὅτι διὰ τὸ ἐσθίειν καὶ
D πίνειν· ἐπειδὰν γὰρ ἐκ τῶν σιτίων ταῖς μὲν σαρξὶ
σάρκες προσγένωνται, τοῖς δὲ ὀστέοις ὀστᾶ, καὶ
οὕτω κατὰ τὸν αὐτὸν λόγον καὶ τοῖς ἄλλοις τὰ
αὐτῶν οἰκεῖα ἑκάστοις προσγένηται, τότε δὴ τὸν
ὀλίγον ὄγκον ὄντα ὕστερον πολὺν γεγονέναι, καὶ
οὕτω γίγνεσθαι τὸν σμικρὸν ἄνθρωπον μέγαν·
οὕτως τότε ᾤμην· οὐ δοκῶ σοι μετρίως; Ἔμοιγε,
ἔφη ὁ Κέβης. Σκέψαι δὴ καὶ τάδε ἔτι. ᾤμην
γὰρ ἱκανῶς μοι δοκεῖν, ὁπότε τις φαίνοιτο ἄνθρωπος παραστὰς μέγας σμικρῷ μείζων εἶναι αὐτῇ τῇ
E κεφαλῇ, καὶ ἵππος ἵππου· καὶ ἔτι γε τούτων
ἐναργέστερα, τὰ δέκα μοι ἐδόκει τῶν ὀκτὼ πλέονα
εἶναι διὰ τὸ δύο αὐτοῖς προσθεῖναι, καὶ τὸ δίπηχυ
τοῦ πηχυαίου μεῖζον εἶναι διὰ τὸ ἡμίσει αὐτοῦ
ὑπερέχειν. Νῦν δὲ δή, ἔφη ὁ Κέβης, τί σοι

it the blood, or air, or fire by which we think? Or
is it none of these, and does the brain furnish the
sensations of hearing and sight and smell, and do
memory and opinion arise from these, and does
knowledge come from memory and opinion in a state
of rest? And again I tried to find out how these
things perish, and I investigated the phenomena of
heaven and earth until finally I made up my mind that
I was by nature totally unfitted for this kind of investigation. And I will give you a sufficient proof of
this. I was so completely blinded by these studies
that I lost the knowledge that I, and others also,
thought I had before; I forgot what I had formerly
believed I knew about many things and even about the
cause of man's growth. For I had thought previously
that it was plain to everyone that man grows through
eating and drinking; for when, from the food he
eats, flesh is added to his flesh and bones to his bones,
and in the same way the appropriate thing is added
to each of his other parts, then the small bulk
becomes greater and the small man large. That is
what I used to think. Doesn't that seem to you
reasonable?"

"Yes," said Cebes.

"Now listen to this, too. I thought I was sure
enough, when I saw a tall man standing by a short
one, that he was, say, taller by a head than the other,
and that one horse was larger by a head than another
horse; and, to mention still clearer things than those,
I thought ten were more than eight because two had
been added to the eight, and I thought a two-cubit
rule was longer than a one-cubit rule because it
exceeded it by half its length."

"And now," said Cebes, "what do you think
about them?"

δοκεῖ περὶ αὐτῶν; Πόρρω που, ἔφη, νὴ Δία
ἐμὲ εἶναι τοῦ οἴεσθαι περὶ τούτων του τὴν αἰτίαν
εἰδέναι, ὅς γε οὐκ ἀποδέχομαι ἐμαυτοῦ οὐδὲ ὡς,
ἐπειδὰν ἑνί τις προσθῇ ἕν, ἢ τὸ ἓν ᾧ προσετέθη
δύο γέγονεν, ἢ τὸ προστεθέν, ἢ τὸ προστεθὲν καὶ
97 ᾧ προσετέθη διὰ τὴν πρόσθεσιν τοῦ ἑτέρου τῷ
ἑτέρῳ δύο ἐγένετο· θαυμάζω γάρ, εἰ, ὅτε μὲν
ἑκάτερον αὐτῶν χωρὶς ἀλλήλων ἦν, ἓν ἄρα
ἑκάτερον ἦν καὶ οὐκ ἤστην τότε δύο, ἐπεὶ δ᾽
ἐπλησίασαν ἀλλήλοις, αὕτη ἄρα αἰτία αὐτοῖς
ἐγένετο δύο γενέσθαι, ἡ ξύνοδος τοῦ πλησίον
ἀλλήλων τεθῆναι. οὐδέ γε ὡς, ἐάν τις ἓν διασχίσῃ,
δύναμαι ἔτι πείθεσθαι ὡς αὕτη αὖ αἰτία γέγονεν,
ἡ σχίσις, τοῦ δύο γεγονέναι· ἐναντία γὰρ γίγνεται
B ἢ τότε αἰτία τοῦ δύο γίγνεσθαι· τότε μὲν γὰρ ὅτι
συνήγετο πλησίον ἀλλήλων καὶ προσετίθετο
ἕτερον ἑτέρῳ, νῦν δ᾽ ὅτι ἀπάγεται καὶ χωρίζεται
ἕτερον ἀφ᾽ ἑτέρου. οὐδέ γε, δι᾽ ὅ τι ἓν γίγνεται
ὡς ἐπίσταμαι ἔτι πείθω ἐμαυτόν, οὐδ᾽ ἄλλο οὐδὲν
ἑνὶ λόγῳ δι᾽ ὅ τι γίγνεται ἢ ἀπόλλυται ἢ ἔστι,
κατὰ τοῦτον τὸν τρόπον τῆς μεθόδου, ἀλλά τιν᾽
ἄλλον τρόπον αὐτὸς εἰκῇ φύρω, τοῦτον δὲ οὐδαμῇ
προσίεμαι.

46. Ἀλλ᾽ ἀκούσας μέν ποτε ἐκ βιβλίου τινός,
ὡς ἔφη, Ἀναξαγόρου ἀναγιγνώσκοντος, καὶ
C λέγοντος ὡς ἄρα νοῦς ἐστιν ὁ διακοσμῶν τε καὶ
πάντων αἴτιος, ταύτῃ δὴ τῇ αἰτίᾳ ἥσθην τε καὶ
ἔδοξέ μοι τρόπον τινὰ εὖ ἔχειν τὸ τὸν νοῦν εἶναι
πάντων αἴτιον, καὶ ἡγησάμην, εἰ τοῦθ᾽ οὕτως ἔχει,
τόν γε νοῦν κοσμοῦντα πάντα κοσμεῖν[1] καὶ ἕκα-

[1] Schanz brackets κοσμεῖν.

"By Zeus," said he, "I am far from thinking that I know the cause of any of these things, I who do not even dare to say, when one is added to one, whether the one to which the addition was made has become two, or the one which was added, or the one which was added and the one to which it was added became two by the addition of each to the other. I think it is wonderful that when each of them was separate from the other, each was one and they were not then two, and when they were brought near each other this juxtaposition was the cause of their becoming two. And I cannot yet believe that if one is divided, the division causes it to become two ; for this is the opposite of the cause which produced two in the former case ; for then two arose because one was brought near and added to another one, and now because one is removed and separated from another. And I no longer believe that I know by this method even how one is generated or, in a word, how anything is generated or is destroyed or exists, and I no longer admit this method, but have another confused way of my own.

"Then one day I heard a man reading from a book, as he said, by Anaxagoras, that it is the mind that arranges and causes all things. I was pleased with this theory of cause, and it seemed to me to be somehow right that the mind should be the cause of all things, and I thought, 'If this is so, the mind in arranging things arranges everything and establishes

στον τιθέναι ταύτη ὅπη ἂν βέλτιστα ἔχη· εἰ οὖν
τις βούλοιτο τὴν αἰτίαν εὑρεῖν περὶ ἑκάστου, ὅπη
γίγνεται ἢ ἀπόλλυται ἢ ἔστι, τοῦτο δεῖν περὶ
αὐτοῦ εὑρεῖν, ὅπη βέλτιστον αὐτῷ ἐστιν ἢ εἶναι ἢ
ἄλλο ὁτιοῦν πάσχειν ἢ ποιεῖν. ἐκ δὲ δὴ τοῦ
D λόγου τούτου οὐδὲν ἄλλο σκοπεῖν προσήκειν ἀνθρώπῳ καὶ περὶ αὐτοῦ[1] καὶ περὶ ἄλλων, ἀλλ' ἢ
τὸ ἄριστον καὶ τὸ βέλτιστον. ἀναγκαῖον δὲ εἶναι
τὸν αὐτὸν τοῦτον καὶ τὸ χεῖρον εἰδέναι· τὴν αὐτὴν
γὰρ εἶναι ἐπιστήμην περὶ αὐτῶν. ταῦτα δὴ
λογιζόμενος ἅσμενος εὑρηκέναι ᾤμην διδάσκαλον
τῆς αἰτίας περὶ τῶν ὄντων κατὰ νοῦν ἐμαυτῷ, τὸν
Ἀναξαγόραν, καί μοι φράσειν πρῶτον μέν, πότερον ἡ γῆ πλατεῖά ἐστιν ἢ στρογγύλη, ἐπειδὴ δὲ
E φράσειεν, ἐπεκδιηγήσεσθαι τὴν αἰτίαν καὶ τὴν
ἀνάγκην, λέγοντα τὸ ἄμεινον καὶ ὅτι αὐτὴν
ἄμεινον ἦν τοιαύτην εἶναι· καὶ εἰ ἐν μέσῳ φαίη
εἶναι αὐτήν, ἐπεκδιηγήσεσθαι ὡς ἄμεινον ἦν
αὐτὴν ἐν μέσῳ εἶναι· καὶ εἴ μοι ταῦτα ἀπο-
98 φαίνοιτο, παρεσκευάσμην ὡς οὐκέτι ποθεσόμενος
αἰτίας ἄλλο εἶδος. καὶ δὴ καὶ περὶ ἡλίου οὕτω
παρεσκευάσμην, ὡσαύτως πευσόμενος, καὶ σελήνης
καὶ τῶν ἄλλων ἄστρων, τάχους τε πέρι πρὸς
ἄλληλα καὶ τροπῶν καὶ τῶν ἄλλων παθημάτων,
πῆ ποτε ταῦτ' ἄμεινόν ἐστιν ἕκαστον καὶ ποιεῖν
καὶ πάσχειν ἃ πάσχει. οὐ γὰρ ἄν ποτε αὐτὸν
ᾤμην, φάσκοντά γε ὑπὸ νοῦ αὐτὰ κεκοσμῆσθαι,
ἄλλην τινὰ αὐτοῖς αἰτίαν ἐπενεγκεῖν ἢ ὅτι
βέλτιστον αὐτὰ οὕτως ἔχειν ἐστὶν ὥσπερ ἔχει·
B ἑκάστῳ οὖν αὐτὸν ἀποδιδόντα τὴν αἰτίαν καὶ

---

[1] αὐτοῦ ἐκείνου BCDE. Schanz brackets αὐτοῦ. Wohlrab
omits ἐκείνου and reads αὐτοῦ. Burnet brackets ἐκείνου.

each thing as it is best for it to be. So if anyone wishes to find the cause of the generation or destruction or existence of a particular thing, he must find out what sort of existence, or passive state of any kind, or activity is best for it. And therefore in respect to that particular thing, and other things too, a man need examine nothing but what is best and most excellent; for then he will necessarily know also what is inferior, since the science of both is the same.' As I considered these things I was delighted to think that I had found in Anaxagoras a teacher of the cause of things quite to my mind, and I thought he would tell me whether the earth is flat or round, and when he had told me that, would go on to explain the cause and the necessity of it, and would tell me the nature of the best and why it is best for the earth to be as it is; and if he said the earth was in the centre, he would proceed to show that it is best for it to be in the centre; and I had made up my mind that if he made those things clear to me, I would no longer yearn for any other kind of cause. And I had determined that I would find out in the same way about the sun and the moon and the other stars, their relative speed, their revolutions, and their other changes, and why the active or passive condition of each of them is for the best. For I never imagined that, when he said they were ordered by intelligence, he would introduce any other cause for these things than that it is best for them to be as they are. So I thought when he assigned the cause

κοινῇ πᾶσι τὸ ἑκάστῳ βέλτιστον ᾤμην καὶ τὸ
κοινὸν πᾶσιν ἐπεκδιηγήσεσθαι ἀγαθόν· καὶ οὐκ ἂν
ἀπεδόμην πολλοῦ τὰς ἐλπίδας, ἀλλὰ πάνυ σπουδῇ
λαβὼν τὰς βίβλους ὡς τάχιστα οἷός τ᾽ ἦ ἀνε-
γίγνωσκον, ἵν᾽ ὡς τάχιστα εἰδείην τὸ βέλτιστον
καὶ τὸ χεῖρον.

47. Ἀπὸ δὴ θαυμαστῆς ἐλπίδος, ὦ ἑταῖρε,
ᾠχόμην φερόμενος, ἐπειδὴ προϊὼν καὶ [1] ἀναγιγνώσκων ὁρῶ ἄνδρα τῷ μὲν νῷ οὐδὲν χρώμενον οὐδέ
C τινας αἰτίας ἐπαιτιώμενον εἰς τὸ διακοσμεῖν τὰ
πράγματα, ἀέρας δὲ καὶ αἰθέρας καὶ ὕδατα αἰτιώ-
μενον καὶ ἄλλα πολλὰ καὶ ἄτοπα. καί μοι ἔδοξεν
ὁμοιότατον πεπονθέναι ὥσπερ ἂν εἴ τις λέγων
ὅτι Σωκράτης πάντα ὅσα πράττει νῷ πράττει,
κἄπειτα ἐπιχειρήσας λέγειν τὰς αἰτίας ἑκάστων
ὧν πράττω, λέγοι πρῶτον μὲν ὅτι διὰ ταῦτα νῦν
ἐνθάδε κάθημαι, ὅτι σύγκειταί μου τὸ σῶμα ἐξ
ὀστέων καὶ νεύρων, καὶ τὰ μὲν ὀστᾶ ἐστιν στερεὰ
καὶ διαφυὰς ἔχει χωρὶς ἀπ᾽ ἀλλήλων, τὰ δὲ νεῦρα
D οἷα ἐπιτείνεσθαι καὶ ἀνίεσθαι, περιαμπέχοντα τὰ
ὀστᾶ μετὰ τῶν σαρκῶν καὶ δέρματος ὃ συνέχει
αὐτά· αἰωρουμένων οὖν τῶν ὀστέων ἐν ταῖς αὑτῶν
ξυμβολαῖς χαλῶντα καὶ συντείνοντα τὰ νεῦρα
κάμπτεσθαί που ποιεῖ οἷόν τ᾽ εἶναι ἐμὲ νῦν τὰ
μέλη, καὶ διὰ ταύτην τὴν αἰτίαν συγκαμφθεὶς
ἐνθάδε κάθημαι· καὶ αὖ περὶ τοῦ διαλέγεσθαι ὑμῖν
ἑτέρας τοιαύτας αἰτίας λέγοι, φωνάς τε καὶ ἀέρας
καὶ ἀκοὰς καὶ ἄλλα μυρία τοιαῦτα αἰτιώμενος,
E ἀμελήσας τὰς ὡς ἀληθῶς αἰτίας λέγειν ὅτι,
ἐπειδὴ Ἀθηναίοις ἔδοξε βέλτιον εἶναι ἐμοῦ
καταψηφίσασθαι, διὰ ταῦτα δὴ καὶ ἐμοὶ βέλτιον

[1] Schanz brackets καί.

338

of each thing and of all things in common he would go on and explain what is best for each and what is good for all in common. I prized my hopes very highly, and I seized the books very eagerly and read them as fast as I could, that I might know as fast as I could about the best and the worst.

" My glorious hope, my friend, was quickly snatched away from me. As I went on with my reading I saw that the man made no use of intelligence, and did not assign any real causes for the ordering of things, but mentioned as causes air and ether and water and many other absurdities. And it seemed to me it was very much as if one should say that Socrates does with intelligence whatever he does, and then, in trying to give the causes of the particular thing I do, should say first that I am now sitting here because my body is composed of bones and sinews, and the bones are hard and have joints which divide them and the sinews can be contracted and relaxed and, with the flesh and the skin which contains them all, are laid about the bones; and so, as the bones are hung loose in their ligaments, the sinews, by relaxing and contracting, make me able to bend my limbs now, and that is the cause of my sitting here with my legs bent. Or as if in the same way he should give voice and air and hearing and countless other things of the sort as causes for our talking with each other, and should fail to mention the real causes, which are, that the Athenians decided that it was best to condemn me, and therefore I have decided

αὖ δέδοκται ἐνθάδε καθῆσθαι, καὶ δικαιότερον
παραμένοντα ὑπέχειν τὴν δίκην ἣν ἂν κελεύσωσιν·
99 ἐπεὶ νὴ τὸν κύνα, ὡς ἐγῷμαι, πάλαι ἂν ταῦτα τὰ
νεῦρά τε καὶ τὰ ὀστᾶ ἢ περὶ Μέγαρα ἢ Βοιωτοὺς
ἦν, ὑπὸ δόξης φερόμενα τοῦ βελτίστου, εἰ μὴ
δικαιότερον ᾤμην καὶ κάλλιον εἶναι πρὸ τοῦ
φεύγειν τε καὶ ἀποδιδράσκειν ὑπέχειν τῇ πόλει
δίκην ἥντιν' ἂν τάττῃ. ἀλλ' αἴτια μὲν τὰ τοιαῦτα
καλεῖν λίαν ἄτοπον· εἰ δέ τις λέγοι ὅτι ἄνευ τοῦ
τὰ τοιαῦτα ἔχειν καὶ ὀστᾶ καὶ νεῦρα καὶ ὅσα ἄλλα
ἔχω, οὐκ ἂν οἷός τ' ἦν ποιεῖν τὰ δόξαντά μοι,
ἀληθῆ ἂν λέγοι· ὡς μέντοι διὰ ταῦτα ποιῶ ἃ ποιῶ
B καὶ ταῦτα νῷ πράττω, ἀλλ' οὐ τῇ τοῦ βελτίστου
αἱρέσει, πολλὴ καὶ μακρὰ ῥᾳθυμία ἂν εἴη τοῦ
λόγου. τὸ γὰρ μὴ διελέσθαι οἷόν τ' εἶναι ὅτι
ἄλλο μέν τί ἐστι τὸ αἴτιον τῷ ὄντι, ἄλλο δὲ
ἐκεῖνο ἄνευ οὗ τὸ αἴτιον οὐκ ἄν ποτ' εἴη αἴτιον· ὃ
δή μοι φαίνονται ψηλαφῶντες οἱ πολλοὶ ὥσπερ
ἐν σκότει, ἀλλοτρίῳ ὀνόματι προσχρώμενοι, ὡς
αἴτιον αὐτὸ προσαγορεύειν. διὸ δὴ καὶ ὁ μέν τις
δίνην περιτιθεὶς τῇ γῇ ὑπὸ τοῦ οὐρανοῦ μένειν δὴ
ποιεῖ τὴν γῆν, ὁ δὲ ὥσπερ καρδόπῳ πλατείᾳ
βάθρον τὸν ἀέρα ὑπερείδει· τὴν δὲ τοῦ ὡς οἷόν τε
C βέλτιστα αὐτὰ τεθῆναι δύναμιν οὕτω νῦν κεῖσθαι,
ταύτην οὔτε ζητοῦσιν οὔτε τινὰ οἴονται δαιμονίαν
ἰσχὺν ἔχειν, ἀλλὰ ἡγοῦνται τούτου Ἄτλαντα ἄν
ποτε ἰσχυρότερον καὶ ἀθανατώτερον καὶ μᾶλλον
ἅπαντα συνέχοντα ἐξευρεῖν, καὶ ὡς ἀληθῶς τὸ
ἀγαθὸν καὶ δέον ξυνδεῖν καὶ συνέχειν οὐδὲν
οἴονται. ἐγὼ μὲν οὖν τῆς τοιαύτης αἰτίας, ὅπῃ
ποτὲ ἔχει, μαθητὴς ὁτουοῦν ἥδιστ' ἂν γενοίμην·
ἐπειδὴ δὲ ταύτης ἐστερήθην καὶ οὔτ' αὐτὸς εὑρεῖν

that it was best for me to sit here and that it is right
for me to stay and undergo whatever penalty they
order. For, by the Dog, I fancy these bones and
sinews of mine would have been in Megara or Boeotia
long ago, carried thither by an opinion of what was
best, if I did not think it was better and nobler to
endure any penalty the city may inflict rather than to
escape and run away. But it is most absurd to call
things of that sort causes. If anyone were to say that
I could not have done what I thought proper if I had
not bones and sinews and other things that I have, he
would be right. But to say that those things are the
cause of my doing what I do, and that I act with
intelligence but not from the choice of what is best,
would be an extremely careless way of talking. Whoever talks in that way is unable to make a distinction
and to see that in reality a cause is one thing, and
the thing without which the cause could never be a
cause is quite another thing. And so it seems to me
that most people, when they give the name of cause
to the latter, are groping in the dark, as it were, and
are giving it a name that does not belong to it. And
so one man makes the earth stay below the heavens by
putting a vortex about it, and another regards the earth
as a flat trough supported on a foundation of air; but
they do not look for the power which causes things
to be now placed as it is best for them to be placed,
nor do they think it has any divine force, but they
think they can find a new Atlas more powerful and
more immortal and more all-embracing than this, and
in truth they give no thought to the good, which
must embrace and hold together all things. Now I
would gladly be the pupil of anyone who would
teach me the nature of such a cause; but since that

οὔτε παρ' ἄλλου μαθεῖν οἷός τε ἐγενόμην, τὸν
D δεύτερον πλοῦν ἐπὶ τὴν τῆς αἰτίας ζήτησιν ᾗ
πεπραγμάτευμαι, βούλει σοι, ἔφη, ἐπίδειξιν
ποιήσωμαι, ὦ Κέβης; Ὑπερφυῶς μὲν οὖν, ἔφη,
ὡς βούλομαι.

48. Ἔδοξε τοίνυν μοι, ἦ δ' ὅς, μετὰ ταῦτα,
ἐπειδὴ ἀπείρηκα τὰ ὄντα σκοπῶν, δεῖν εὐλαβη-
θῆναι, μὴ πάθοιμι ὅπερ οἱ τὸν ἥλιον ἐκλείποντα
θεωροῦντες καὶ σκοπούμενοι· διαφθείρονται γάρ
που ἔνιοι τὰ ὄμματα, ἐὰν μὴ ἐν ὕδατι ἤ τινι
E τοιούτῳ σκοπῶνται τὴν εἰκόνα αὐτοῦ. τοιοῦτόν
τι καὶ ἐγὼ διενοήθην, καὶ ἔδεισα, μὴ παντάπασι
τὴν ψυχὴν τυφλωθείην βλέπων πρὸς τὰ πράγματα τοῖς ὄμμασι καὶ ἑκάστῃ τῶν αἰσθήσεων
ἐπιχειρῶν ἅπτεσθαι αὐτῶν. ἔδοξε δή μοι χρῆναι
εἰς τοὺς λόγους καταφυγόντα ἐν ἐκείνοις σκοπεῖν
τῶν ὄντων τὴν ἀλήθειαν. ἴσως μὲν οὖν ᾧ εἰκάζω
100 τρόπον τινὰ οὐκ ἔοικεν. οὐ γὰρ πάνυ συγχωρῶ
τὸν ἐν τοῖς λόγοις σκοπούμενον τὰ ὄντα ἐν εἰκόσι
μᾶλλον σκοπεῖν ἢ τὸν ἐν τοῖς ἔργοις· ἀλλ' οὖν δὴ
ταύτῃ γε ὥρμησα, καὶ ὑποθέμενος ἑκάστοτε λόγον
ὃν ἂν κρίνω ἐρρωμενέστατον εἶναι, ἃ μὲν ἄν μοι
δοκῇ τούτῳ συμφωνεῖν, τίθημι ὡς ἀληθῆ ὄντα,
καὶ περὶ αἰτίας καὶ περὶ τῶν ἄλλων ἁπάντων
τῶν ὄντων, ἃ δ' ἂν μή, ὡς οὐκ ἀληθῆ. βούλομαι
δέ σοι σαφέστερον εἰπεῖν ἃ λέγω· οἶμαι γάρ σε
νῦν οὐ μανθάνειν. Οὐ μὰ τὸν Δία, ἔφη ὁ Κέβης,
οὐ σφόδρα.

B 49. Ἀλλ', ἦ δ' ὅς, ὧδε λέγω, οὐδὲν καινόν,
ἀλλ' ἅπερ ἀεὶ καὶ ἄλλοτε καὶ ἐν τῷ παρεληλυθότι
λόγῳ οὐδὲν πέπαυμαι λέγων. ἔρχομαι γὰρ δὴ
ἐπιχειρῶν σοι ἐπιδείξασθαι τῆς αἰτίας τὸ εἶδος ὃ

was denied me and I was not able to discover it myself or to learn of it from anyone else, do you wish me, Cebes," said he, "to give you an account of the way in which I have conducted my second voyage in quest of the cause?"

"I wish it with all my heart," he replied.

"After this, then," said he, "since I had given up investigating realities, I decided that I must be careful not to suffer the misfortune which happens to people who look at the sun and watch it during an eclipse. For some of them ruin their eyes unless they look at its image in water or something of the sort. I thought of that danger, and I was afraid my soul would be blinded if I looked at things with my eyes and tried to grasp them with any of my senses. So I thought I must have recourse to conceptions and examine in them the truth of realities. Now perhaps my metaphor is not quite accurate; for I do not grant in the least that he who studies realities by means of conceptions is looking at them in images any more than he who studies them in the facts of daily life. However, that is the way I began. I assume in each case some principle which I consider strongest, and whatever seems to me to agree with this, whether relating to cause or to anything else, I regard as true, and whatever disagrees with it, as untrue. But I want to tell you more clearly what I mean; for I think you do not understand now."

"Not very well, certainly," said Cebes.

"Well," said Socrates, "this is what I mean. It is nothing new, but the same thing I have always been saying, both in our previous conversation and elsewhere. I am going to try to explain to you the nature of that cause which I have been studying,

343

πεπραγμάτευμαι, καὶ εἶμι πάλιν ἐπ' ἐκεῖνα τὰ
πολυθρύλητα καὶ ἄρχομαι ἀπ' ἐκείνων, ὑποθέμενος εἶναί τι καλὸν αὐτὸ καθ' αὑτὸ καὶ ἀγαθὸν
καὶ μέγα καὶ τἆλλα πάντα· ἃ εἴ μοι δίδως τε
καὶ συγχωρεῖς εἶναι ταῦτα, ἐλπίζω σοι ἐκ τούτων τὴν αἰτίαν ἐπιδείξειν καὶ ἀνευρήσειν, ὡς
C ἀθάνατον ἡ ψυχή. Ἀλλὰ μήν, ἔφη ὁ Κέβης,
ὡς διδόντος σοι οὐκ ἂν φθάνοις περαίνων.
Σκόπει δή, ἔφη, τὰ ἑξῆς ἐκείνοις, ἐάν σοι
ξυνδοκῇ ὥσπερ ἐμοί. φαίνεται γάρ μοι, εἴ τί
ἐστιν ἄλλο καλὸν πλὴν αὐτὸ τὸ καλόν, οὐδὲ
δι' ἓν ἄλλο καλὸν εἶναι ἢ διότι μετέχει ἐκείνου
τοῦ καλοῦ· καὶ πάντα δὴ οὕτως λέγω. τῇ
τοιᾷδε αἰτίᾳ συγχωρεῖς; Συγχωρῶ," ἔφη. Οὐ
τοίνυν, ἦ δ' ὅς, ἔτι μανθάνω οὐδὲ δύναμαι τὰς
ἄλλας αἰτίας τὰς σοφὰς ταύτας γιγνώσκειν· ἀλλ'
ἐάν τίς μοι λέγῃ, δι' ὅ τι καλόν ἐστιν ὁτιοῦν, ἢ
D χρῶμα εὐανθὲς ἔχον ἢ σχῆμα ἢ ἄλλο ὁτιοῦν τῶν
τοιούτων, τὰ μὲν ἄλλα χαίρειν ἐῶ, ταράττομαι
γὰρ ἐν τοῖς ἄλλοις πᾶσι, τοῦτο δὲ ἁπλῶς καὶ
ἀτέχνως καὶ ἴσως εὐήθως ἔχω παρ' ἐμαυτῷ, ὅτι
οὐκ ἄλλο τι ποιεῖ αὐτὸ καλὸν ἢ ἡ ἐκείνου τοῦ
καλοῦ εἴτε παρουσία εἴτε κοινωνία ὅπῃ δὴ καὶ
ὅπως προσγενομένη· οὐ γὰρ ἔτι τοῦτο διισχυρί-
ζομαι, ἀλλ' ὅτι τῷ καλῷ πάντα τὰ καλὰ γίγνεται
καλά. τοῦτο γάρ μοι δοκεῖ ἀσφαλέστατον εἶναι
καὶ ἐμαυτῷ ἀποκρίνασθαι καὶ ἄλλῳ, καὶ τούτου
E ἐχόμενος ἡγοῦμαι οὐκ ἄν ποτε πεσεῖν, ἀλλ'
ἀσφαλὲς εἶναι καὶ ἐμοὶ καὶ ὁτῳοῦν ἄλλῳ ἀποκρίνασθαι, ὅτι τῷ καλῷ τὰ καλὰ καλά· ἢ οὐ
καὶ σοὶ δοκεῖ; Δοκεῖ. Καὶ μεγέθει ἄρα τὰ

and I will revert to those familiar subjects of ours as my point of departure and assume that there are such things as absolute beauty and good and greatness and the like. If you grant this and agree that these exist, I believe I shall explain cause to you and shall prove that the soul is immortal."

"You may assume," said Cebes, "that I grant it, and go on."

"Then," said he, "see if you agree with me in the next step. I think that if anything is beautiful besides absolute beauty it is beautiful for no other reason than because it partakes of absolute beauty; and this applies to everything. Do you assent to this view of cause?"

"I do," said he.

"Now I do not yet, understand," he went on, "nor can I perceive those other ingenious causes. If anyone tells me that what makes a thing beautiful is its lovely colour, or its shape or anything else of the sort, I let all that go, for all those things confuse me, and I hold simply and plainly and perhaps foolishly to this, that nothing else makes it beautiful but the presence or communion (call it which you please) of absolute beauty, however it may have been gained; about the way in which it happens, I make no positive statement as yet, but I do insist that beautiful things are made beautiful by beauty. For I think this is the safest answer I can give to myself or to others, and if I cleave fast to this, I think I shall never be overthrown, and I believe it is safe for me or anyone else to give this answer, that beautiful things are beautiful through beauty. Do you agree?"

"I do."

"And great things are great and greater things

345

μεγάλα μεγάλα καὶ τὰ μείζω μείζω, καὶ σμικρότητι τὰ ἐλάττω ἐλάττω; Ναί. Οὐδὲ σὺ ἄρ' ἂν ἀπο-
δέχοιο, εἴ τίς τινα φαίη ἕτερον ἑτέρου τῇ κεφαλῇ
μείζω εἶναι, καὶ τὸν ἐλάττω τῷ αὐτῷ τούτῳ
101 ἐλάττω, ἀλλὰ διαμαρτύροιο ἄν, ὅτι σὺ μὲν οὐδὲν
ἄλλο λέγεις ἢ ὅτι τὸ μεῖζον πᾶν ἕτερον ἑτέρου
οὐδενὶ ἄλλῳ μεῖζόν ἐστιν ἢ μεγέθει, καὶ διὰ
τοῦτο μεῖζον, διὰ τὸ μέγεθος, τὸ δὲ ἔλαττον
οὐδενὶ ἄλλῳ ἔλαττον ἢ σμικρότητι, καὶ διὰ
τοῦτο ἔλαττον, διὰ τὴν σμικρότητα, φοβούμενος
οἶμαι, μή τίς σοι ἐναντίος λόγος ἀπαντήσῃ, ἐὰν
τῇ κεφαλῇ·μείζονά τινα φῇς εἶναι καὶ ἐλάττω,
πρῶτον μὲν τῷ αὐτῷ τὸ μεῖζον μεῖζον εἶναι καὶ
τὸ ἔλαττον ἔλαττον, ἔπειτα τῇ κεφαλῇ σμικρᾷ
B οὔσῃ τὸν μείζω μείζω εἶναι, καὶ τοῦτο δὴ τέρας
εἶναι, τὸ σμικρῷ τινι μέγαν τινὰ εἶναι· ἢ οὐκ ἂν
φοβοῖο ταῦτα; Καὶ ὁ Κέβης γελάσας· Ἔγωγε,
ἔφη. Οὐκοῦν, ἦ δ' ὅς, τὰ δέκα τῶν ὀκτὼ δυοῖν
πλείω εἶναι, καὶ διὰ ταύτην τὴν αἰτίαν ὑπερ-
βάλλειν, φοβοῖο ἂν λέγειν, ἀλλὰ μὴ πλήθει καὶ
διὰ τὸ πλῆθος; καὶ τὸ δίπηχυ τοῦ πηχυαίου
ἡμίσει μεῖζον εἶναι, ἀλλ' οὐ μεγέθει; ὁ αὐτὸς γάρ
που φόβος. Πάνυ γ', ἔφη. Τί δέ; ἑνὶ ἑνὸς
προστεθέντος τὴν πρόσθεσιν αἰτίαν εἶναι τοῦ δύο
C γενέσθαι ἢ διασχισθέντος τὴν σχίσιν οὐκ εὐλα-
βοῖο ἂν λέγειν; καὶ μέγα ἂν βοῴης ὅτι οὐκ
οἶσθα ἄλλως πως ἕκαστον γιγνόμενον ἢ μετασχὸν
τῆς ἰδίας οὐσίας ἑκάστου οὗ ἂν μετάσχῃ, καὶ ἐν

greater by greatness, and smaller things smaller by smallness?"

"Yes."

"And you would not accept the statement, if you were told that one man was greater or smaller than another by a head, but you would insist that you say only that every greater thing is greater than another by nothing else than greatness, and that it is greater by reason of greatness, and that which is smaller is smaller by nothing else than smallness and is smaller by reason of smallness. For you would, I think, be afraid of meeting with the retort, if you said that a man was greater or smaller than another by a head, first that the greater is greater and the smaller is smaller by the same thing, and secondly, that the greater man is greater by a head, which is small, and that it is a monstrous thing that one is great by something that is small. Would you not be afraid of this?"

And Cebes laughed and said, "Yes, I should."

"Then," he continued, "you would be afraid to say that ten is more than eight by two and that this is the reason it is more. You would say it is more by number and by reason of number; and a two-cubit measure is greater than a one-cubit measure not by half but by magnitude, would you not? For you would have the same fear."

"Certainly," said he.

"Well, then, if one is added to one or if one is divided, you would avoid saying that the addition or the division is the cause of two? You would exclaim loudly that you know no other way by which any-thing can come into existence than by participating in the proper essence of each thing in which it

τούτοις οὐκ ἔχεις ἄλλην τινὰ αἰτίαν τοῦ δύο
γενέσθαι ἀλλ' ἢ τὴν τῆς δυάδος μετάσχεσιν, καὶ
δεῖν τούτου μετασχεῖν τὰ μέλλοντα δύο ἔσεσθαι,
καὶ μονάδος ὃ ἂν μέλλῃ ἓν ἔσεσθαι, τὰς δὲ σχίσεις
ταύτας καὶ προσθέσεις καὶ τὰς ἄλλας τὰς
τοιαύτας κομψείας ἐῴης ἂν χαίρειν, παρεὶς ἀποκρίνασθαι τοῖς σεαυτοῦ σοφωτέροις· σὺ δὲ δεδιὼς
D ἄν, τὸ λεγόμενον, τὴν σεαυτοῦ σκιὰν καὶ τὴν
ἀπειρίαν, ἐχόμενος ἐκείνου τοῦ ἀσφαλοῦς τῆς
ὑποθέσεως, οὕτως ἀποκρίναιο ἄν; εἰ δέ τις αὐτῆς
τῆς ὑποθέσεως ἔχοιτο, χαίρειν ἐῴης ἂν καὶ οὐκ
ἀποκρίναιο, ἕως ἂν τὰ ἀπ' ἐκείνης ὁρμηθέντα
σκέψαιο, εἴ σοι ἀλλήλοις συμφωνεῖ ἢ διαφωνεῖ·
ἐπειδὴ δὲ ἐκείνης αὐτῆς δέοι σε διδόναι λόγον,
ὡσαύτως ἂν διδοίης, ἄλλην αὖ ὑπόθεσιν ὑποθέμενος, ἥτις τῶν ἄνωθεν βελτίστη φαίνοιτο, ἕως
E ἐπί τι ἱκανὸν ἔλθοις, ἅμα δὲ οὐκ ἂν φύροιο ὥσπερ
οἱ ἀντιλογικοὶ περί τε τῆς ἀρχῆς διαλεγόμενος καὶ
τῶν ἐξ ἐκείνης ὡρμημένων, εἴπερ βούλοιό τι τῶν
ὄντων εὑρεῖν. ἐκείνοις μὲν γὰρ ἴσως οὐδὲ εἷς περὶ
τούτου λόγος οὐδὲ φροντίς· ἱκανοὶ γὰρ ὑπὸ σοφίας
ὁμοῦ πάντα κυκῶντες ὅμως δύνασθαι[1] αὐτοὶ
102 αὑτοῖς ἀρέσκειν· σὺ δ' εἴπερ εἶ τῶν φιλοσόφων,
οἶμαι ἂν ὡς ἐγὼ λέγω ποιοῖς. Ἀληθέστατα,
ἔφη, λέγεις, ὅ τε Σιμμίας ἅμα καὶ ὁ Κέβης.

ΕΧΕΚΡΑΤΗΣ. Νὴ Δία, ὦ Φαίδων, εἰκότως γε· θαυμαστῶς γάρ μοι δοκεῖ ὡς ἐναργῶς τῷ καὶ σμικρὸν
νοῦν ἔχοντι εἰπεῖν ἐκεῖνος ταῦτα.

ΦΑΙΔΩΝ. Πάνυ μὲν οὖν, ὦ Ἐχέκρατες, καὶ πᾶσι
τοῖς παροῦσιν ἔδοξεν.

---

[1] Schanz follows Hirschig in bracketing δύνασθαι.

participates, and therefore you accept no other cause
of the existence of two than participation in duality,
and things which are to be two must participate in
duality, and whatever is to be one must participate
in unity, and you would pay no attention to the
divisions and additions and other such subtleties,
leaving those for wiser men to explain. You would
distrust your inexperience and would be afraid, as the
saying goes, of your own shadow; so you would cling
to that safe principle of ours and would reply as I
have said. And if anyone attacked the principle,
you would pay him no attention and you would not
reply to him until you had examined the consequences to see whether they agreed with one
another or not; and when you had to give an
explanation of the principle, you would give it in the
same way by assuming some other principle which
seemed to you the best of the higher ones, and so on
until you reached one which was adequate. You
would not mix things up, as disputants do, in talking
about the beginning and its consequences, if you
wished to discover any of the realities; for perhaps
not one of them thinks or cares in the least about
these things. They are so clever that they succeed
in being well pleased with themselves even when
they mix everything up; but if you are a philosopher,
I think you will do as I have said."

"That is true," said Simmias and Cebes together.

ECHECRATES. By Zeus, Phaedo, they were right.
It seems to me that he made those matters astonish-
ingly clear, to anyone with even a little sense.

PHAEDO. Certainly, Echecrates, and all who were
there thought so, too.

ΕΧΕΚΡΑΤΗΣ. Καὶ γὰρ ἡμῖν τοῖς ἀποῦσι, νῦν δὲ ἀκούουσιν. ἀλλὰ τίνα δὴ ἦν τὰ μετὰ ταῦτα λεχθέντα;

50. ΦΑΙΔΩΝ. Ὡς μὲν ἐγὼ οἶμαι, ἐπεὶ αὐτῷ ταῦτα συνεχωρήθη, καὶ ὡμολογεῖτο εἶναί τι B ἕκαστον τῶν εἰδῶν καὶ τούτων τἆλλα μεταλαμβάνοντα αὐτῶν τούτων τὴν ἐπωνυμίαν ἴσχειν, τὸ δὴ μετὰ ταῦτα ἠρώτα· Εἰ δή, ἦ δ᾽ ὅς, ταῦτα οὕτως λέγεις, ἆρ᾽ οὐχ, ὅταν Σιμμίαν Σωκράτους φῇς μείζω εἶναι, Φαίδωνος δὲ ἐλάττω, λέγεις τότ᾽ εἶναι ἐν τῷ Σιμμίᾳ ἀμφότερα, καὶ μέγεθος καὶ σμικρότητα; Ἔγωγε. Ἀλλὰ γάρ, ἦ δ᾽ ὅς, ὁμολογεῖς τὸ τὸν Σιμμίαν ὑπερέχειν Σωκράτους οὐχ ὡς τοῖς ῥήμασι λέγεται οὕτω καὶ τὸ ἀληθὲς ἔχειν. οὐ γάρ που πεφυκέναι Σιμμίαν ὑπερέχειν C τούτῳ τῷ Σιμμίαν εἶναι, ἀλλὰ τῷ μεγέθει ὃ τυγχάνει ἔχων· οὐδ᾽ αὖ Σωκράτους ὑπερέχειν, ὅτι Σωκράτης ὁ Σωκράτης ἐστίν, ἀλλ᾽ ὅτι σμικρότητα ἔχει ὁ Σωκράτης πρὸς τὸ ἐκείνου μέγεθος; Ἀληθῆ. Οὐδέ γε αὖ ὑπὸ Φαίδωνος ὑπερέχεσθαι τῷ ὅτι Φαίδων ὁ Φαίδων ἐστίν, ἀλλ᾽ ὅτι μέγεθος ἔχει ὁ Φαίδων πρὸς τὴν Σιμμίου σμικρότητα; Ἔστι ταῦτα. Οὕτως ἄρα ὁ Σιμμίας ἐπωνυμίαν ἔχει σμικρός τε καὶ μέγας εἶναι, ἐν μέσῳ ὢν ἀμφοτέρων, D τοῦ μὲν τῷ μεγέθει ὑπερέχειν τὴν σμικρότητα ὑπέχων, τῷ δὲ τὸ μέγεθος τῆς σμικρότητος παρέχων ὑπερέχον. καὶ ἅμα μειδιάσας· Ἔοικα, ἔφη, καὶ ξυγγραφικῶς ἐρεῖν, ἀλλ᾽ οὖν ἔχει γέ που, ὡς λέγω. Συνέφη. Λέγω δὲ τοῦδ᾽ ἕνεκα,

ECHECRATES. And so do we who were not there, and are hearing about it now. But what was said after that?

PHAEDO. As I remember it, after all this had been admitted, and they had agreed that each of the abstract qualities exists and that other things which participate in these get their names from them, then Socrates asked : "Now if you assent to this, do you not, when you say that Simmias is greater than Socrates and smaller than Phaedo, say that there is in Simmias greatness and smallness?"

"Yes."

"But," said Socrates, "you agree that the statement that Simmias is greater than Socrates is not true as stated in those words. For Simmias is not greater than Socrates by reason of being Simmias, but by reason of the greatness he happens to have ; nor is he greater than Socrates because Socrates is Socrates, but because Socrates has smallness relatively to his greatness."

"True."

" And again, he is not smaller than Phaedo because Phaedo is Phaedo, but because Phaedo has greatness relatively to Simmias's smallness."

" That is true."

" Then Simmias is called small and great, when he is between the two, surpassing the smallness of the one by exceeding him in height, and granting to the other the greatness that exceeds his own smallness." And he laughed and said, " I seem to be speaking like a legal document, but it really is very much as I say."

Simmias agreed.

" I am speaking so because I want you to agree

βουλόμενος δόξαι σοὶ ὅπερ ἐμοί. ἐμοὶ γὰρ
φαίνεται οὐ μόνον αὐτὸ τὸ μέγεθος οὐδέποτ᾽
ἐθέλειν ἅμα μέγα καὶ σμικρὸν εἶναι, ἀλλὰ καὶ
τὸ ἐν ἡμῖν μέγεθος οὐδέποτε προσδέχεσθαι τὸ
σμικρὸν οὐδ᾽ ἐθέλειν ὑπερέχεσθαι, ἀλλὰ δυοῖν τὸ
ἕτερον, ἢ φεύγειν καὶ ὑπεκχωρεῖν, ὅταν αὐτῷ
E προσίῃ τὸ ἐναντίον, τὸ σμικρόν, ἢ προσελθόντος
ἐκείνου ἀπολωλέναι· ὑπομεῖναν δὲ καὶ δεξάμενον
τὴν σμικρότητα οὐκ ἐθέλειν εἶναι ἕτερον ἢ ὅπερ ἦν.
ὥσπερ ἐγὼ δεξάμενος καὶ ὑπομείνας τὴν σμικρότητα, καὶ ἔτι ὢν ὅσπερ εἰμί, οὗτος ὁ αὐτὸς
σμικρός εἰμι· ἐκεῖνο δὲ οὐ τετόλμηκεν μέγα ὂν
σμικρὸν εἶναι· ὡς δ᾽ αὕτως καὶ τὸ σμικρὸν τὸ ἐν
ἡμῖν οὐκ ἐθέλει ποτὲ μέγα γίγνεσθαι οὐδὲ εἶναι,
οὐδ᾽ ἄλλο οὐδὲν τῶν ἐναντίων, ἔτι ὂν ὅπερ ἦν
ἅμα τοὐναντίον γίγνεσθαί τε καὶ εἶναι, ἀλλ᾽ ἤτοι
103 ἀπέρχεται ἢ ἀπόλλυται ἐν τούτῳ τῷ παθήματι.
Παντάπασιν, ἔφη ὁ Κέβης, οὕτω φαίνεταί μοι.

51. Καί τις εἶπε τῶν παρόντων ἀκούσας—ὅστις
δ᾽ ἦν, οὐ σαφῶς μέμνημαι· Πρὸς θεῶν, οὐκ ἐν
τοῖς πρόσθεν ἡμῖν λόγοις αὐτὸ τὸ ἐναντίον τῶν
νυνὶ λεγομένων ὡμολογεῖτο, ἐκ τοῦ ἐλάττονος τὸ
μεῖζον γίγνεσθαι καὶ ἐκ τοῦ μείζονος τὸ ἔλαττον,
καὶ ἀτεχνῶς αὕτη εἶναι ἡ γένεσις τοῖς ἐναντίοις,
ἐκ τῶν ἐναντίων; νῦν δέ μοι δοκεῖ λέγεσθαι, ὅτι
τοῦτο οὐκ ἄν ποτε γένοιτο. καὶ ὁ Σωκράτης
παραβαλὼν τὴν κεφαλὴν καὶ ἀκούσας, Ἀνδρι-
B κῶς, ἔφη, ἀπεμνημόνευκας, οὐ μέντοι ἐννοεῖς
τὸ διαφέρον τοῦ τε νῦν λεγομένου καὶ τοῦ τότε.
τότε μὲν γὰρ ἐλέγετο ἐκ τοῦ ἐναντίου πράγματος
τὸ ἐναντίον πρᾶγμα γίγνεσθαι, νῦν δέ, ὅτι αὐτὸ
τὸ ἐναντίον ἑαυτῷ ἐναντίον οὐκ ἄν ποτε γένοιτο,

with me. I think it is evident not only that greatness itself will never be great and also small, but
that the greatness in us will never admit the small
or allow itself to be exceeded. One of two things
must take place: either it flees or withdraws when
its opposite, smallness, advances toward it, or it has
already ceased to exist by the time smallness comes
near it. But it will not receive and admit smallness,
thereby becoming other than it was. So I have
received and admitted smallness and am still the
same small person I was; but the greatness in me,
being great, has not suffered itself to become small.
In the same way the smallness in us will never
become or be great, nor will any other opposite
which is still what it was, ever become or be also its
own opposite. It either goes away or loses its
existence in the change."

"That," said Cebes, "seems to me quite evident."

Then one of those present—I don't just remember
who it was—said: "In Heaven's name, is not this
present doctrine the exact opposite of what was
admitted in our earlier discussion, that the greater is
generated from the less and the less from the greater
and that opposites are always generated from their
opposites? But now it seems to me we are saying
that this can never happen."

Socrates cocked his head on one side and listened.

"You have spoken up like a man," he said, "but
you do not observe the difference between the present
doctrine and what we said before. We said before
that in the case of concrete things opposites are
generated from opposites; whereas now we say that
the abstract concept of an opposite can never become

353

οὔτε τὸ ἐν ἡμῖν οὔτε τὸ ἐν τῇ φύσει. τότε μὲν γάρ,
ὦ φίλε, περὶ τῶν ἐχόντων τὰ ἐναντία ἐλέγομεν,
ἐπονομάζοντες αὐτὰ τῇ ἐκείνων ἐπωνυμίᾳ, νῦν δὲ
περὶ ἐκείνων αὐτῶν, ὧν ἐνόντων ἔχει τὴν ἐπωνυμίαν τὰ ὀνομαζόμενα· αὐτὰ δ' ἐκεῖνα οὐκ ἄν ποτέ
C φαμεν ἐθελῆσαι γένεσιν ἀλλήλων δέξασθαι.
καὶ ἅμα βλέψας πρὸς τὸν Κέβητα εἶπεν· Ἆρα
μή που, ὦ Κέβης, ἔφη, καὶ σέ τι τούτων
ἐτάραξεν ὧν ὅδε εἶπεν; ὁ δ' Οὐκ[1] αὖ, ἔφη ὁ
Κέβης,[2] οὕτως ἔχω· καίτοι οὔτι λέγω ὡς οὐ
πολλά με ταράττει. Συνωμολογήκαμεν ἄρα, ἦ
δ' ὅς, ἁπλῶς τοῦτο, μηδέποτε ἐναντίον ἑαυτῷ
τὸ ἐναντίον ἔσεσθαι. Παντάπασιν, ἔφη.

52. Ἔτι δή μοι καὶ τόδε σκέψαι, ἔφη, εἰ
ἄρα συνομολογήσεις. θερμόν τι καλεῖς καὶ
ψυχρόν; Ἔγωγε. Ἀρ' ὅπερ χιόνα καὶ πῦρ;
D Μὰ Δί', οὐκ ἔγωγε. Ἀλλ' ἕτερόν τι πυρὸς τὸ
θερμὸν καὶ ἕτερόν τι χιόνος τὸ ψυχρόν; Ναί.
Ἀλλὰ τόδε γ', οἶμαι, δοκεῖ σοι, οὐδέποτε χιόνα[3]
οὖσαν δεξαμένην τὸ θερμόν, ὥσπερ ἐν τοῖς
ἔμπροσθεν ἐλέγομεν, ἔτι ἔσεσθαι ὅπερ ἦν, χιόνα
καὶ θερμόν,[4] ἀλλὰ προσιόντος τοῦ θερμοῦ ἢ ὑπεκ-
χωρήσειν αὐτῷ[5] ἢ ἀπολεῖσθαι. Πάνυ γε.
Καὶ τὸ πῦρ γε αὖ προσιόντος τοῦ ψυχροῦ αὐτῷ
ἢ ὑπεξιέναι ἢ ἀπολεῖσθαι, οὐ μέντοι ποτὲ

---

[1] ὁ δ' αὖ ΒΤ. ὁ δ' οὐκ αὖ, Hermann, Schanz.
[2] Schanz brackets ὁ Κέβης.
[3] Schanz inserts χιόνα before χιόνα.
[4] Schanz brackets καὶ θερμόν.
[5] αὐτό ΒCΕ; bracketed by Schanz. αὐτῷ c, Wohlrab,
Burnet.

its own opposite, either in us or in the world about
us. Then we were talking about things which possess
opposite qualities and are called after them, but now
about those very opposites the immanence of which
gives the things their names. We say that these
latter can never be generated from each other."

At the same time he looked at Cebes and said :
" And you—are you troubled by any of our friends'
objections ? "

" No," said Cebes, " not this time ; though I confess
that objections often do trouble me."

" Well, we are quite agreed," said Socrates, " upon
this, that an opposite can never be its own opposite."

" Entirely agreed," said Cebes.

" Now," said he, " see if you agree with me in
what follows : Is there something that you call heat
and something you call cold ? "

" Yes."

" Are they the same as snow and fire ? "

" No, not at all."

" But heat is a different thing from fire and cold
differs from snow ? "

" Yes."

" Yet I fancy you believe that snow, if (to employ
the form of phrase we used before) it admits heat,
will no longer be what it was, namely snow, and also
warm, but will either withdraw when heat approaches
it or will cease to exist."

" Certainly."

" And similarly fire, when cold approaches it, will
either withdraw or perish. It will never succeed in

τολμήσειν δεξάμενον τὴν ψυχρότητα ἔτι εἶναι
E ὅπερ ἦν, πῦρ καὶ ψυχρόν.¹ Ἀληθῆ, ἔφη,
λέγεις. Ἔστιν ἄρα, ἦ δ' ὅς, περὶ ἔνια τῶν
τοιούτων, ὥστε μὴ μόνον αὐτὸ τὸ εἶδος ἀξιοῦσθαι
τοῦ αὐτοῦ ὀνόματος εἰς τὸν ἀεὶ χρόνον, ἀλλὰ καὶ
ἄλλο τι, ὃ ἔστι μὲν οὐκ ἐκεῖνο, ἔχει δὲ τὴν ἐκείνου
μορφὴν ἀεὶ ὅτανπερ ᾖ. ἔτι δὲ ἐν τοῖσδε ἴσως
ἔσται σαφέστερον ὃ λέγω. τὸ γὰρ περιττὸν ἀεί
που δεῖ τούτου τοῦ ὀνόματος τυγχάνειν, ὅπερ νῦν
λέγομεν· ἦ οὔ; Πάνυ γε. Ἆρα μόνον τῶν
ὄντων, τοῦτο γὰρ ἐρωτῶ, ἦ καὶ ἄλλο τι, ὃ ἔστι
104 μὲν οὐχ ὅπερ τὸ περιττόν, ὅμως δὲ δεῖ αὐτὸ μετὰ
τοῦ ἑαυτοῦ ὀνόματος καὶ τοῦτο καλεῖν ἀεὶ διὰ τὸ
οὕτω πεφυκέναι, ὥστε τοῦ περιττοῦ μηδέποτε
ἀπολείπεσθαι; λέγω δὲ αὐτὸ εἶναι οἷον καὶ ἡ τριὰς
πέπονθε καὶ ἄλλα πολλά. σκόπει δὲ περὶ τῆς
τριάδος. ἆρα οὐ δοκεῖ σοι τῷ τε αὐτῆς ὀνόματι
ἀεὶ προσαγορευτέα εἶναι καὶ τῷ τοῦ περιττοῦ,
ὄντος οὐχ οὕπερ τῆς τριάδος; ἀλλ' ὅμως οὕτω πως
πέφυκε καὶ ἡ τριὰς καὶ ἡ πεμπτὰς καὶ ὁ ἥμισυς
τοῦ ἀριθμοῦ ἅπας, ὥστε οὐκ ὢν ὅπερ τὸ περιττὸν
B ἀεὶ ἕκαστος αὐτῶν ἐστι περιττός· καὶ αὖ τὰ δύο
καὶ τὰ τέτταρα καὶ ἅπας ὁ ἕτερος αὖ στίχος τοῦ
ἀριθμοῦ οὐκ ὢν ὅπερ τὸ ἄρτιον ὅμως ἕκαστος
αὐτῶν ἄρτιός ἐστιν ἀεί· συγχωρεῖς ἦ οὔ; Πῶς
γὰρ οὔκ; ἔφη. Ὁ τοίνυν, ἔφη, βούλομαι δηλῶσαι, ἄθρει. ἔστιν δὲ τόδε, ὅτι φαίνεται οὐ
μόνον ἐκεῖνα τὰ ἐναντία ἄλληλα οὐ δεχόμενα,
ἀλλὰ καὶ ὅσα οὐκ ὄντ' ἀλλήλοις ἐναντία ἔχει ἀεὶ
τἀναντία, οὐδὲ ταῦτα ἔοικε δεχομένοις ἐκείνην τὴν

¹ Schanz brackets καὶ ψυχρόν.

admitting cold and being still fire, as it was before, and also cold."

"That is true," said he.

"The fact is," said he, "in some such cases, that not only the abstract idea itself has a right to the same name through all time, but also something else, which is not the idea, but which always, whenever it exists, has the form of the idea. But perhaps I can make my meaning clearer by some examples. In numbers, the odd must always have the name of odd, must it not?"

"Certainly."

"But is this the only thing so called (for this is what I mean to ask), or is there something else, which is not identical with the odd but nevertheless has a right to the name of odd in addition to its own name, because it is of such a nature that it is never separated from the odd? I mean, for instance, the number three, and there are many other examples. Take the case of three; do you not think it may always be called by its own name and also be called odd, which is not the same as three? Yet the number three and the number five and half of numbers in general are so constituted, that each of them is odd though not identified with the idea of odd. And in the same way two and four and all the other series of numbers are even, each of them, though not identical with evenness. Do you agree, or not?"

"Of course," he replied.

"Now see what I want to make plain. This is my point, that not only abstract opposites exclude each other, but all things which, although not opposites one to another, always contain opposites;

ἰδέαν ἢ ἂν τῇ ἐν αὐτοῖς οὔσῃ ἐναντία ᾖ, ἀλλ'
C ἐπιούσης αὐτῆς ἤτοι ἀπολλύμενα ἢ ὑπεκχω-
ροῦντα· ἢ οὐ φήσομεν τὰ τρία καὶ ἀπολεῖσθαι
πρότερον καὶ ἄλλο ὁτιοῦν πείσεσθαι, πρὶν ὑπομεῖναι ἔτι τρία ὄντα ἄρτια γενέσθαι; Πάνυ μὲν
οὖν, ἔφη ὁ Κέβης. Οὐδὲ μήν, ἦ δ' ὅς, ἐναντίον
γέ ἐστι δυὰς τριάδι. Οὐ γὰρ οὖν. Οὐκ ἄρα
μόνον τὰ εἴδη τὰ ἐναντία οὐχ ὑπομένει ἐπιόντα
ἄλληλα, ἀλλὰ καὶ ἄλλ' ἄττα τὰ ἐναντία οὐχ
ὑπομένει ἐπιόντα. Ἀληθέστατα, ἔφη, λέγεις.

53. Βούλει οὖν, ἦ δ' ὅς, ἐὰν οἱοί τ' ὦμεν,
ὁρισώμεθα ὁποῖα ταῦτά ἐστιν; Πάνυ γε.
D Ἀρ' οὖν, ἔφη, ὦ Κέβης, τάδε εἴη ἄν, ἃ ὅ τι ἂν
κατάσχῃ, μὴ μόνον ἀναγκάζει τὴν αὐτοῦ ἰδέαν
αὐτὸ ἴσχειν, ἀλλὰ καὶ ἐναντίου ἀεί τινος;[1] Πῶς
λέγεις; Ὥσπερ ἄρτι ἐλέγομεν. οἶσθα γὰρ δήπου, ὅτι ἃ ἂν ἡ τῶν τριῶν ἰδέα κατάσχῃ, ἀνάγκη
αὐτοῖς οὐ μόνον τρισὶν εἶναι ἀλλὰ καὶ περιττοῖς.
Πάνυ γε. Ἐπὶ τὸ τοιοῦτον δή, φαμέν, ἡ ἐναντία ἰδέα ἐκείνῃ τῇ μορφῇ, ἢ ἂν τοῦτο ἀπεργά-
ζηται, οὐδέποτ' ἂν ἔλθοι. Οὐ γάρ. Εἰργάζετο

---

[1] αὐτῷ ἀεί τινος BCDE. Stallbaum, followed by Schanz,
brackets αὐτῷ.

these also, we find, exclude the idea which is opposed to the idea contained in them, and when it approaches they either perish or withdraw. We must certainly agree that the number three will endure destruction or anything else rather than submit to becoming even, while still remaining three, must we not?"

"Certainly," said Cebes.

"But the number two is not the opposite of the number three."

"No."

"Then not only opposite ideas refuse to admit each other when they come near, but certain other things refuse to admit the approach of opposites."

"Very true," he said.

"Shall we then," said Socrates, "determine if we can, what these are?"

"Certainly."

"Then, Cebes, will they be those which always compel anything of which they take possession not only to take their form but also that of some opposite?"

"What do you mean?"

"Such things as we were speaking of just now. You know of course that those things in which the number three is an essential element must be not only three but also odd."

"Certainly."

"Now such a thing can never admit the idea which is the opposite of the concept which produces this result."

"No, it cannot."

δέ γε ἡ περιττή; Ναί. Ἐναντία δὲ ταύτῃ ἡ
E τοῦ ἀρτίου; Ναί. Ἐπὶ τὰ τρία ἄρα ἡ τοῦ
ἀρτίου ἰδέα οὐδέποτε ἥξει. Οὐ δῆτα. Ἄμοιρα
δὴ τοῦ ἀρτίου τὰ τρία. Ἄμοιρα. Ἀνάρτιος
ἄρα ἡ τριάς. Ναί. Ὃ τοίνυν ἔλεγον ὁρίσασθαι, ποῖα οὐκ ἐναντία τινὶ ὄντα ὅμως οὐ
δέχεται αὐτὸ τὸ ἐναντίον,[1] οἷον νῦν ἡ τριὰς τῷ
ἀρτίῳ οὐκ οὖσα ἐναντία οὐδέν τι μᾶλλον αὐτὸ
δέχεται, τὸ γὰρ ἐναντίον ἀεὶ αὐτῷ ἐπιφέρει, καὶ
105 ἡ δυὰς τῷ περιττῷ καὶ τὸ πῦρ τῷ ψυχρῷ καὶ ἄλλα
πάμπολλα—ἀλλ' ὅρα δή, εἰ οὕτως ὁρίζει, μὴ μόνον
τὸ ἐναντίον τὸ ἐναντίον μὴ δέχεσθαι, ἀλλὰ καὶ
ἐκεῖνο, ὃ ἂν ἐπιφέρῃ τι ἐναντίον ἐκείνῳ, ἐφ' ὅ τι ἂν
αὐτὸ ἴῃ, αὐτὸ τὸ ἐπιφέρον τὴν τοῦ ἐπιφερομένου
ἐναντιότητα μηδέποτε δέξασθαι. πάλιν δὲ ἀνα-
μιμνῄσκου· οὐ γὰρ χεῖρον πολλάκις ἀκούειν. τὰ
πέντε τὴν τοῦ ἀρτίου οὐ δέξεται, οὐδὲ τὰ δέκα τὴν
τοῦ περιττοῦ, τὸ διπλάσιον· τοῦτο μὲν οὖν καὶ
αὐτὸ ἄλλῳ οὐκ ἐναντίον, ὅμως δὲ τὴν τοῦ περιττοῦ
B οὐ δέξεται· οὐδὲ τὸ ἡμιόλιον οὐδὲ τἆλλα τὰ
τοιαῦτα,[2] τὴν τοῦ ὅλου, καὶ τριτημόριον αὖ καὶ

---

[1] Schanz, following Bekker, brackets τὸ ἐναντίον.
[2] After τοιαῦτα the MSS. read τὸ ἥμισυ. "half," which Schanz brackets.

" But the result was produced by the concept of the odd ? "

" Yes."

" And the opposite of this is the idea of the even ? "

" Yes."

" Then the idea of the even will never be admitted by the number three."

" No."

" Then three has no part in the even."

" No, it has none."

" Then the number three is uneven."

" Yes."

" Now I propose to determine what things, without being the opposites of something, nevertheless refuse to admit it, as the number three, though it is not the opposite of the idea of even, nevertheless refuses to admit it, but always brings forward its opposite against it, and as the number two brings forward the opposite of the odd and fire that of cold, and so forth, for there are plenty of examples. Now see if you accept this statement : not only will opposites not admit their opposites, but nothing which brings an opposite to that which it approaches will ever admit in itself the oppositeness of that which is brought. Now let me refresh your memory ; for there is no harm in repetition. The number five will not admit the idea of the even, nor will ten, the double of five, admit the idea of the odd. Now ten is not itself an opposite, and yet it will not admit the idea of the odd ; and so one-and-a-half and other mixed fractions and one-third and other simple frac-

πάντα τὰ τοιαῦτα, εἴπερ ἔπει τε καὶ συνδοκεῖ σοι
οὕτως. Πάνυ σφόδρα καὶ συνδοκεῖ, ἔφη, καὶ
ἕπομαι.

54. Πάλιν δή μοι, ἔφη, ἐξ ἀρχῆς λέγε. καὶ
μή μοι ὃ ἂν ἐρωτῶ ἀποκρίνου, ἀλλὰ μιμούμενος ἐμέ. λέγω δὲ παρ' ἣν τὸ πρῶτον ἔλεγον
ἀπόκρισιν, τὴν ἀσφαλῆ ἐκείνην, ἐκ τῶν νῦν
λεγομένων ἄλλην ὁρῶν ἀσφάλειαν. εἰ γὰρ ἔροιό
με, ᾧ ἂν τί[1] ἐγγένηται, θερμὸν ἔσται, οὐ τὴν
C ἀσφαλῆ σοι ἐρῶ ἀπόκρισιν ἐκείνην τὴν ἀμαθῆ,
ὅτι ᾧ ἂν θερμότης, ἀλλὰ κομψοτέραν ἐκ τῶν νῦν,
ὅτι ᾧ ἂν πῦρ· οὐδὲ ἂν ἔρῃ, ᾧ ἂν σώματι τί ἐγγένηται, νοσήσει, οὐκ ἐρῶ ὅτι ᾧ ἂν νόσος, ἀλλ' ᾧ
ἂν πυρετός· οὐδ' ᾧ ἂν ἀριθμῷ τί ἐγγένηται, περιτ-
τὸς ἔσται, οὐκ ἐρῶ ᾧ ἂν περιττότης, ἀλλ' ᾧ ἂν
μονάς, καὶ τἆλλα οὕτως. ἀλλ' ὅρα, εἰ ἤδη ἱκανῶς
οἶσθ' ὅ τι βούλομαι. Ἀλλὰ πάνυ ἱκανῶς, ἔφη.
Ἀποκρίνου δή, ᾗ δ' ὅς, ᾧ ἂν τί ἐγγένηται
σώματι, ζῶν ἔσται; Ὧι ἂν ψυχή, ἔφη. Οὐκ-
D οῦν ἀεὶ τοῦτο οὕτως ἔχει; Πῶς γὰρ οὐχί; ἡ
δ' ὅς. Ἡ ψυχὴ ἄρα ὅτι ἂν αὐτὴ κατάσχῃ, ἀεὶ
ἥκει ἐπ' ἐκεῖνο φέρουσα ζωήν; Ἥκει μέντοι,
ἔφη. Πότερον δ' ἔστι τι ζωῇ ἐναντίον ἢ οὐδέν;
Ἔστιν, ἔφη. Τί; Θάνατος. Οὐκοῦν ψυχὴ τὸ
ἐναντίον ᾧ αὐτὴ ἐπιφέρει ἀεὶ οὐ μή ποτε

---

[1] After τί the MSS. read ἐν τῷ σώματι, "in the body,"
which Schanz brackets.

tions reject the idea of the whole. Do you go with me and agree to this?"

"Yes, I agree entirely," he said, "and am with you."

"Then," said Socrates, "please begin again at the beginning. And do not answer my questions in their own words, but do as I do. I give an answer beyond that safe answer which I spoke of at first, now that I see another safe reply deduced from what has just been said. If you ask me what causes anything in which it is to be hot, I will not give you that safe but stupid answer and say that it is heat, but I can now give a more refined answer, that it is fire; and if you ask, what causes the body in which it is to be ill, I shall not say illness, but fever; and if you ask what causes a number in which it is to be odd, I shall not say oddness, but the number one, and so forth. Do you understand sufficiently what I mean?"

"Quite sufficiently," he replied.

"Now answer," said he. "What causes the body in which it is to be alive?"

"The soul," he replied.

"Is this always the case?"

"Yes," said he, "of course."

"Then if the soul takes possession of anything it always brings life to it?"

"Certainly," he said.

"Is there anything that is the opposite of life?"

"Yes," said he.

"What?"

"Death."

"Now the soul, as we have agreed before, will

δέξηται, ὡς ἐκ τῶν πρόσθεν ὡμολόγηται; Καὶ μάλα σφόδρα, ἔφη ὁ Κέβης.

55. Τί οὖν; τὸ μὴ δεχόμενον τὴν τοῦ ἀρτίου ἰδέαν τί νῦν δὴ ὠνομάζομεν; Ἀνάρτιον, ἔφη. Τὸ δὲ δίκαιον μὴ δεχόμενον καὶ ὃ ἂν μουσικὸν Ε μὴ δέχηται; Ἄμουσον, ἔφη, τὸ δὲ ἄδικον. Εἶεν· ὃ δ' ἂν θάνατον μὴ δέχηται, τί καλοῦμεν; Ἀθάνατον, ἔφη. Οὐκοῦν ἡ ψυχὴ οὐ δέχεται θάνατον; Οὔ. Ἀθάνατον ἄρα ἡ ψυχή. Ἀθάνατον. Εἶεν, ἔφη· τοῦτο μὲν δὴ ἀποδεδεῖχθαι φῶμεν· ἢ πῶς δοκεῖ; Καὶ μάλα γε ἱκανῶς, ὦ Σώκρατες. Τί οὖν, ἦ δ' ὅς, ὦ Κέβης; εἰ τῷ ἀναρτίῳ ἀναγκαῖον ἦν ἀνωλέθρῳ εἶναι, ἄλλο 106 τι τὰ τρία ἢ ἀνώλεθρα ἂν ἦν; Πῶς γὰρ οὔ; Οὐκοῦν εἰ καὶ τὸ ἄθερμον ἀναγκαῖον ἦν ἀνώλεθρον εἶναι, ὁπότε τις ἐπὶ χιόνα θερμὸν ἐπαγάγοι, ὑπεξήει ἂν ἡ χιὼν οὖσα σῶς καὶ ἄτηκτος; οὐ γὰρ ἂν ἀπώλετό γε, οὐδ' αὖ ὑπομένουσα ἐδέξατο ἂν τὴν θερμότητα. Ἀληθῆ, ἔφη, λέγεις. Ὡσαύτως, οἶμαι, κἂν εἰ τὸ ἄψυκτον ἀνώλεθρον ἦν, ὁπότε ἐπὶ τὸ πῦρ ψυχρόν τι ἐπῄει, οὔποτ' ἂν ἀπεσβέννυτο οὐδ' ἀπώλλυτο, ἀλλὰ σῶν ἂν ἀπελθὸν ᾤχετο. Ἀνάγκη, ἔφη. Β Οὐκοῦν καὶ ὧδε, ἔφη, ἀνάγκη περὶ τοῦ ἀθανάτου

never admit the opposite of that which it brings with it."

"Decidedly not," said Cebes.

"Then what do we now call that which does not admit the idea of the even?"

"Uneven," said he.

"And those which do not admit justice and music?"

"Unjust," he replied, "and unmusical."

"Well then what do we call that which does not admit death?"

"Deathless or immortal," he said.

"And the soul does not admit death?"

"No."

"Then the soul is immortal."

"Yes."

"Very well," said he. "Shall we say then that this is proved?"

"Yes, and very satisfactorily, Socrates."

"Well then, Cebes," said he, "if the odd were necessarily imperishable, would not the number three be imperishable?"

"Of course."

"And if that which is without heat were imperishable, would not snow go away whole and unmelted whenever heat was brought in conflict with snow? For it could not have been destroyed, nor could it have remained and admitted the heat."

"That is very true," he replied.

"In the same way, I think, if that which is without cold were imperishable, whenever anything cold approached fire, it would never perish or be quenched, but would go away unharmed."

"Necessarily," he said.

"And must not the same be said of that which is

εἰπεῖν; εἰ μὲν τὸ ἀθάνατον καὶ ἀνώλεθρόν
ἐστιν, ἀδύνατον ψυχῇ, ὅταν θάνατος ἐπ' αὐτὴν
ἴῃ, ἀπόλλυσθαι· θάνατον μὲν γὰρ δὴ ἐκ τῶν
προειρημένων οὐ δέξεται οὐδ' ἔσται τεθνηκυῖα,
ὥσπερ τὰ τρία οὐκ ἔσται, ἔφαμεν, ἄρτιον, οὐδέ γ'
αὖ τὸ περιττόν, οὐδὲ δὴ πῦρ ψυχρόν, οὐδέ γε ἡ ἐν
τῷ πυρὶ θερμότης. ἀλλὰ τί κωλύει, φαίη ἄν τις,
ἄρτιον μὲν τὸ περιττὸν μὴ γίγνεσθαι ἐπιόντος τοῦ
ἀρτίου, ὥσπερ ὡμολόγηται, ἀπολομένου δὲ αὐτοῦ
C ἀντ' ἐκείνου ἄρτιον γεγονέναι; τῷ ταῦτα λέγοντι
οὐκ ἂν ἔχοιμεν διαμάχεσθαι ὅτι οὐκ ἀπόλλυται·
τὸ γὰρ ἀνάρτιον οὐκ ἀνώλεθρόν ἐστιν· ἐπεὶ εἰ
τοῦτο ὡμολόγητο ἡμῖν, ῥαδίως ἂν διεμαχόμεθα
ὅτι ἐπελθόντος τοῦ ἀρτίου τὸ περιττὸν καὶ τὰ
τρία οἴχεται ἀπιόντα· καὶ περὶ πυρὸς καὶ θερμοῦ
καὶ τῶν ἄλλων οὕτως ἂν διεμαχόμεθα. ἢ οὔ;
Πάνυ μὲν οὖν. Οὐκοῦν καὶ νῦν περὶ τοῦ ἀθανάτου, εἰ μὲν ἡμῖν ὁμολογεῖται καὶ ἀνώλεθρον
εἶναι, ψυχὴ ἂν εἴη πρὸς τῷ ἀθάνατος εἶναι καὶ
D ἀνώλεθρος· εἰ δὲ μή, ἄλλου ἂν δέοι λόγου.
'Αλλ' οὐδὲν δεῖ, ἔφη, τούτου γε ἕνεκα· σχολῇ
γὰρ ἄν τι ἄλλο φθορὰν μὴ δέχοιτο, εἴ γε τὸ
ἀθάνατον ἀίδιον ὂν φθορὰν δέξεται.

56. Ὁ δέ γε θεός, οἶμαι, ἔφη ὁ Σωκράτης,
καὶ αὐτὸ τὸ τῆς ζωῆς εἶδος καὶ εἴ τι ἄλλο
ἀθάνατόν ἐστιν, παρὰ πάντων ἂν ὁμολογηθείη
μηδέποτε ἀπόλλυσθαι. Παρὰ πάντων μέντοι νὴ
Δί', ἔφη, ἀνθρώπων τέ γε καὶ ἔτι μᾶλλον, ὡς
ἐγῷμαι, παρὰ θεῶν. Ὁπότε δὴ τὸ ἀθάνατον
E καὶ ἀδιάφθορόν ἐστιν, ἄλλο τι ψυχὴ ἤ, εἰ ἀθάνατος τυγχάνει οὖσα, καὶ ἀνώλεθρος ἂν εἴη;

immortal ? If the immortal is also imperishable, it is impossible for the soul to perish when death comes against it. For, as our argument has shown, it will not admit death and will not be dead, just as the number three, we said, will not be even, and the odd will not be even, and as fire, and the heat in the fire, will not be cold. But, one might say, why is it not possible that the odd does not become even when the even comes against it (we agreed to that), but perishes, and the even takes its place ? Now we cannot silence him who raises this question by saying that it does not perish, for the odd is not imperishable. If that were conceded to us, we could easily silence him by saying that when the even approaches, the odd and the number three go away ; and we could make the corresponding reply about fire and heat and the rest, could we not ? "

" Certainly."

" And so, too, in the case of the immortal ; if it is conceded that the immortal is imperishable, the soul would be imperishable as well as immortal, but if not, further argument is needed."

" But," he said, " it is not needed, so far as that is concerned ; for surely nothing would escape destruction, if the immortal, which is everlasting, is perishable."

" All, I think," said Socrates, " would agree that God and the principle of life, and anything else that is immortal, can never perish."

" All men would, certainly," said he, " and still more, I fancy, the Gods."

" Since, then, the immortal is also indestructible, would not the soul, if it is immortal, be also imperishable ? "

Πολλὴ ἀνάγκη. Ἐπιόντος ἄρα θανάτου ἐπὶ τὸν ἄνθρωπον τὸ μὲν θνητόν, ὡς ἔοικεν, αὐτοῦ ἀποθνήσκει, τὸ δ' ἀθάνατον σῶν καὶ ἀδιάφθορον οἴχεται ἀπιόν, ὑπεκχωρῆσαν τῷ θανάτῳ. Φαίνεται. Παντὸς μᾶλλον ἄρα, ἔφη, ὦ Κέβης,
107 ψυχὴ ἀθάνατον καὶ ἀνώλεθρον, καὶ τῷ ὄντι ἔσονται ἡμῶν αἱ ψυχαὶ ἐν Ἅιδου. Οὔκουν ἔγωγε, ὦ Σώκρατες, ἔφη, ἔχω παρὰ ταῦτα ἄλλο τι λέγειν οὐδέ πῃ ἀπιστεῖν τοῖς λόγοις. ἀλλ' εἰ δή τι Σιμμίας ἤ τις ἄλλος ἔχει λέγειν, εὖ ἔχει μὴ κατασιγῆσαι· ὡς οὐκ οἶδα εἰς ὅντινά τις ἄλλον καιρὸν ἀναβάλλοιτο ἢ τὸν νῦν παρόντα, περὶ τῶν τοιούτων βουλόμενος ἤ τι εἰπεῖν ἢ ἀκοῦσαι. Ἀλλὰ μήν, ἦ δ' ὃς ὁ Σιμμίας, οὐδ' αὐτὸς ἔχω ὅπῃ ἀπιστῶ ἔκ γε τῶν λεγομένων· ὑπὸ μέντοι τοῦ μεγέθους περὶ ὧν οἱ λόγοι εἰσίν,
B καὶ τὴν ἀνθρωπίνην ἀσθένειαν ἀτιμάζων, ἀναγκάζομαι ἀπιστίαν ἔτι ἔχειν παρ' ἐμαυτῷ περὶ τῶν εἰρημένων. Οὐ μόνον γ', ἔφη, ὦ Σιμμία, ὁ Σωκράτης, ἀλλὰ[1] καὶ τὰς ὑποθέσεις τὰς πρώτας, καὶ εἰ πισταὶ ὑμῖν εἰσιν, ὅμως ἐπισκεπτέαι σαφέστερον· καὶ ἐὰν αὐτὰς ἱκανῶς διέλητε, ὡς ἐγᾦμαι, ἀκολουθήσετε τῷ λόγῳ καθ' ὅσον δυνατὸν μάλιστ' ἀνθρώπῳ ἐπακολουθῆσαι· κἂν τοῦτο αὐτὸ σαφὲς γένηται, οὐδὲν ζητήσετε περαιτέρω. Ἀληθῆ, ἔφη, λέγεις.

57. Ἀλλὰ τόδε γ', ἔφη, ὦ ἄνδρες, δίκαιον
C διανοηθῆναι ὅτι, εἴπερ ἡ ψυχὴ ἀθάνατος, ἐπιμελείας δὴ δεῖται οὐχ ὑπὲρ τοῦ χρόνου τούτου μόνον, ἐν ᾧ καλοῦμεν τὸ ζῆν, ἀλλ' ὑπὲρ τοῦ παντός, καὶ

---

[1] After ἀλλὰ the MSS. read ταῦτά τε εὖ λέγεις ; bracketed by Ast, Schanz, and others.

"Necessarily."

"Then when death comes to a man, his mortal part, it seems, dies, but the immortal part goes away unharmed and undestroyed, withdrawing from death."

"So it seems."

"Then, Cebes," said he, "it is perfectly certain that the soul is immortal and imperishable, and our souls will exist somewhere in another world."

"I," said Cebes, "have nothing more to say against that, and I cannot doubt your conclusions. But if Simmias, or anyone else, has anything to say, he would do well to speak, for I do not know to what other time than the present he could defer speaking, if he wishes to say or hear anything about those matters."

"But," said Simmias, "I don't see how I can doubt, either, as to the result of the discussion; but the subject is so great, and I have such a poor opinion of human weakness, that I cannot help having some doubt in my own mind about what has been said."

"Not only that, Simmias," said Socrates, "but our first assumptions ought to be more carefully examined, even though they seem to you to be certain. And if you analyse them completely, you will, I think, follow and agree with the argument, so far as it is possible for man to do so. And if this is made clear, you will seek no farther."

"That is true," he said.

"But my friends," he said, "we ought to bear in mind, that, if the soul is immortal, we must care for it, not only in respect to this time, which we call life,

ὁ κίνδυνος νῦν δὴ καὶ δόξειεν ἂν δεινὸς εἶναι, εἴ τις
αὐτῆς ἀμελήσει. εἰ μὲν γὰρ ἦν ὁ θάνατος τοῦ
παντὸς ἀπαλλαγή, ἕρμαιον ἂν ἦν τοῖς κακοῖς
ἀποθανοῦσι τοῦ τε σώματος ἅμ᾽ ἀπηλλάχθαι καὶ
τῆς αὐτῶν κακίας μετὰ τῆς ψυχῆς· νῦν δ᾽ ἐπειδὴ
ἀθάνατος φαίνεται οὖσα, οὐδεμία ἂν εἴη αὐτῇ
D ἄλλη ἀποφυγὴ κακῶν οὐδὲ σωτηρία πλὴν τοῦ ὡς
βελτίστην τε καὶ φρονιμωτάτην γενέσθαι. οὐδὲν
γὰρ ἄλλο ἔχουσα εἰς Ἅιδου ἡ ψυχὴ ἔρχεται πλὴν
τῆς παιδείας τε καὶ τροφῆς, ἃ δὴ καὶ μέγιστα
λέγεται ὠφελεῖν ἢ βλάπτειν τὸν τελευτήσαντα
εὐθὺς ἐν ἀρχῇ τῆς ἐκεῖσε πορείας. λέγεται δὲ
οὕτως, ὡς ἄρα τελευτήσαντα ἕκαστον ὁ ἑκάστου
δαίμων, ὅσπερ ζῶντα εἰλήχει, οὗτος ἄγειν ἐπιχειρεῖ εἰς δή τινα τόπον, οἳ δεῖ τοὺς συλ-
λεγέντας διαδικασαμένους εἰς Ἅιδου πορεύεσθαι
E μετὰ ἡγεμόνος ἐκείνου ᾧ δὴ προστέτακται
τοὺς ἐνθένδε ἐκεῖσε πορεῦσαι· τυχόντας δὲ ἐκεῖ
ὧν δεῖ τυχεῖν καὶ μείναντας ὃν χρὴ χρόνον
ἄλλος δεῦρο πάλιν ἡγεμὼν κομίζει ἐν πολλαῖς
χρόνου καὶ μακραῖς περιόδοις. ἔστι δὲ ἄρα ἡ
πορεία οὐχ ὡς ὁ Αἰσχύλου Τήλεφος λέγει·
108 ἐκεῖνος μὲν γὰρ ἁπλῆν οἶμόν φησιν εἰς Ἅιδου
φέρειν, ἡ δ᾽ οὔτε ἁπλῆ οὔτε μία φαίνεταί μοι
εἶναι. οὐδὲ γὰρ ἂν ἡγεμόνων ἔδει· οὐ γάρ πού τις
ἂν διαμάρτοι οὐδαμόσε μιᾶς ὁδοῦ οὔσης. νῦν δὲ
ἔοικε σχίσεις τε καὶ περιόδους πολλὰς ἔχειν· ἀπὸ
τῶν ὁσίων τε καὶ νομίμων τῶν ἐνθάδε τεκμαιρόμενος λέγω. ἡ μὲν οὖν κοσμία τε καὶ φρόνιμος
ψυχὴ ἕπεταί τε καὶ οὐκ ἀγνοεῖ τὰ παρόντα· ἡ δ᾽
ἐπιθυμητικῶς τοῦ σώματος ἔχουσα, ὅπερ ἐν τῷ
ἔμπροσθεν εἶπον, περὶ ἐκεῖνο πολὺν χρόνον

but in respect to all time, and if we neglect it, the danger now appears to be terrible. For if death were an escape from everything, it would be a boon to the wicked, for when they die they would be freed from the body and from their wickedness together with their souls. But now, since the soul is seen to be immortal, it cannot escape from evil or be saved in any other way than by becoming as good and wise as possible. For the soul takes with it to the other world nothing but its education and nurture, and these are said to benefit or injure the departed greatly from the very beginning of his journey thither. And so it is said that after death, the tutelary genius of each person, to whom he had been allotted in life, leads him to a place where the dead are gathered together; then they are judged and depart to the other world with the guide whose task it is to conduct thither those who come from this world; and when they have there received their due and remained through the time appointed, another guide brings them back after many long periods of time. And the journey is not as Telephus says in the play of Aeschylus; for he says a simple path leads to the lower world, but I think the path is neither simple nor single, for if it were, there would be no need of guides, since no one could miss the way to any place if there were only one road. But really there seem to be many forks of the road and many windings; this I infer from the rites and ceremonies practised here on earth. Now the orderly and wise soul follows its guide and understands its circumstances; but the soul that is desirous of the body, as I said before, flits about it, and in the visible world for a long time, and after much resist-

B ἐπτοημένη καὶ περὶ τὸν ὁρατὸν τόπον, πολλὰ
ἀντιτείνασα καὶ πολλὰ παθοῦσα, βίᾳ καὶ μόγις
ὑπὸ τοῦ προστεταγμένου δαίμονος οἴχεται ἀγομένη.
ἀφικομένην δὲ ὅθιπερ αἱ ἄλλαι, τὴν μὲν ἀκάθαρτον
καί τι πεποιηκυῖαν τοιοῦτον, ἢ φόνων ἀδίκων
ἡμμένην ἢ ἄλλ᾽ ἄττα τοιαῦτα εἰργασμένην, ἃ
τούτων ἀδελφά τε καὶ ἀδελφῶν ψυχῶν ἔργα
τυγχάνει ὄντα, ταύτην μὲν ἅπας φεύγει τε καὶ
ὑπεκτρέπεται καὶ οὔτε ξυνέμπορος οὔτε ἡγεμὼν
C ἐθέλει γίγνεσθαι, αὐτὴ δὲ πλανᾶται ἐν πάσῃ
ἐχομένη ἀπορίᾳ, ἕως ἂν δή τινες χρόνοι γένωνται,
ὧν ἐξελθόντων ὑπ᾽ ἀνάγκης φέρεται εἰς τὴν αὐτῇ
πρέπουσαν οἴκησιν· ἡ δὲ καθαρῶς τε καὶ μετρίως
τὸν βίον διεξελθοῦσα, καὶ ξυνεμπόρων καὶ
ἡγεμόνων θεῶν τυχοῦσα, ᾤκησεν τὸν αὐτῇ ἑκάστη
τόπον προσήκοντα. εἰσὶν δὲ πολλοὶ καὶ θαυ-
μαστοὶ τῆς γῆς τόποι, καὶ αὐτὴ οὔτε οἷα οὔτε ὅση
δοξάζεται ὑπὸ τῶν περὶ γῆς εἰωθότων λέγειν, ὡς
ἐγὼ ὑπό τινος πέπεισμαι.

D   58. Καὶ ὁ Σιμμίας· Πῶς ταῦτα, ἔφη, λέγεις,
ὦ Σώκρατες; περὶ γάρ τοι γῆς καὶ αὐτὸς πολλὰ
δὴ ἀκήκοα, οὐ μέντοι ταῦτα ἃ σὲ πείθει· ἡδέως
οὖν ἂν ἀκούσαιμι. Ἀλλὰ μέντοι, ὦ Σιμμία, οὐχὶ
Γλαύκου τέχνη γέ μοι δοκεῖ εἶναι διηγήσασθαι
ἅ γ᾽ ἐστίν· ὡς μέντοι ἀληθῆ, χαλεπώτερόν μοι
φαίνεται ἢ κατὰ τὴν Γλαύκου τέχνην, καὶ ἅμα
μὲν ἐγὼ ἴσως οὐδ᾽ ἂν οἷός τε εἴην, ἅμα δέ, εἰ καὶ
ἠπιστάμην, ὁ βίος μοι δοκεῖ ὁ ἐμός, ὦ Σιμμία, τῷ
μήκει τοῦ λόγου οὐκ ἐξαρκεῖ. τὴν μέντοι ἰδέαν
E τῆς γῆς, οἵαν πέπεισμαι εἶναι, καὶ τοὺς τόπους
αὐτῆς οὐδέν με κωλύει λέγειν. Ἀλλ᾽, ἔφη ὁ
Σιμμίας, καὶ ταῦτα ἀρκεῖ. Πέπεισμαι τοίνυν,

ance and many sufferings is led away with violence
and with difficulty by its appointed genius. And
when it arrives at the place where the other souls
are, the soul which is impure and has done wrong, by
committing wicked murders or other deeds akin to
those and the works of kindred souls, is avoided and
shunned by all, and no one is willing to be its companion or its guide, but it wanders about alone in utter
bewilderment, during certain fixed times, after which
it is carried by necessity to its fitting habitation. But
the soul that has passed through life in purity and
righteousness, finds gods for companions and guides,
and goes to dwell in its proper dwelling. Now there
are many wonderful regions of the earth, and the
earth itself is neither in size nor in other respects
such as it is supposed to be by those who habitually
discourse about it, as I believe on someone's
authority."

And Simmias said, " What do you mean, Socrates ?
I have heard a good deal about the earth myself, but
not what you believe ; so I should like to hear it."

" Well Simmias, I do not think I need the art of
Glaucus to tell what it is. But to prove that it is
true would, I think, be too hard for the art of Glaucus,
and perhaps I should not be able to do it ; besides,
even if I had the skill, I think my life, Simmias, will
end before the discussion could be finished. However,
there is nothing to prevent my telling what I believe
the form of the earth to be, and the regions in it."

" Well," said Simmias, " that will be enough."

" I am convinced, then," said he, " that in the first

ἦ δ' ὅς, ἐγώ, ὡς πρῶτον μέν, εἰ ἔστιν ἐν μέσῳ
τῷ οὐρανῷ περιφερὴς οὖσα, μηδὲν αὐτῇ δεῖν μήτε
109 ἀέρος πρὸς τὸ μὴ πεσεῖν μήτε ἄλλης ἀνάγκης
μηδεμιᾶς τοιαύτης, ἀλλὰ ἱκανὴν εἶναι αὐτὴν
ἴσχειν τὴν ὁμοιότητα τοῦ οὐρανοῦ αὐτοῦ ἑαυτῷ
πάντῃ καὶ τῆς γῆς αὐτῆς τὴν ἰσορροπίαν· ἰσόρ-
ροπον γὰρ πρᾶγμα ὁμοίου τινὸς ἐν μέσῳ τεθὲν
οὐχ ἕξει μᾶλλον οὐδ' ἧττον οὐδαμόσε κλιθῆναι,
ὁμοίως δ' ἔχον ἀκλινὲς μενεῖ. πρῶτον μέν, ἦ δ'
ὅς, τοῦτο πέπεισμαι. Καὶ ὀρθῶς γε, ἔφη ὁ
Σιμμίας. Ἔτι τοίνυν, ἔφη, πάμμεγά τι εἶναι
αὐτό, καὶ ἡμᾶς οἰκεῖν τοὺς μέχρι Ἡρακλείων
B στηλῶν ἀπὸ Φάσιδος ἐν σμικρῷ τινι μορίῳ, ὥσπερ
περὶ τέλμα μύρμηκας ἢ βατράχους περὶ τὴν
θάλατταν οἰκοῦντας, καὶ ἄλλους ἄλλοθι πολλοὺς
ἐν πολλοῖς τοιούτοις τόποις οἰκεῖν. εἶναι γὰρ
πανταχῇ περὶ τὴν γῆν πολλὰ κοῖλα καὶ παντοδαπὰ καὶ τὰς ἰδέας καὶ τὰ μεγέθη, εἰς ἃ ξυνερρυη-
κέναι τό τε ὕδωρ καὶ τὴν ὁμίχλην καὶ τὸν ἀέρα·
αὐτὴν δὲ τὴν γῆν καθαρὰν ἐν καθαρῷ κεῖσθαι τῷ
οὐρανῷ, ἐν ᾧπέρ ἐστι τὰ ἄστρα, ὃν δὴ αἰθέρα
C ὀνομάζειν τοὺς πολλοὺς τῶν περὶ τὰ τοιαῦτα
εἰωθότων λέγειν· οὗ δὴ ὑποστάθμην ταῦτα εἶναι,
καὶ ξυρρεῖν ἀεὶ εἰς τὰ κοῖλα τῆς γῆς. ἡμᾶς οὖν
οἰκοῦντας ἐν τοῖς κοίλοις αὐτῆς λεληθέναι, καὶ
οἴεσθαι ἄνω ἐπὶ τῆς γῆς οἰκεῖν, ὥσπερ ἂν εἴ τις
ἐν μέσῳ τῷ πυθμένι τοῦ πελάγους οἰκῶν οἴοιτό τε
ἐπὶ τῆς θαλάττης οἰκεῖν, καὶ διὰ τοῦ ὕδατος ὁρῶν
τὸν ἥλιον καὶ τὰ ἄλλα ἄστρα τὴν θάλατταν
ἡγοῖτο οὐρανὸν εἶναι, διὰ δὲ βραδυτῆτά τε καὶ
D ἀσθένειαν μηδεπώποτε ἐπὶ τὰ ἄκρα τῆς θαλάττης
ἀφιγμένος μηδὲ ἑωρακὼς εἴη, ἐκδὺς καὶ ἀνακύψας

place, if the earth is round and in the middle of the
heavens, it needs neither the air nor any other
similar force to keep it from falling, but its own
equipoise and the homogeneous nature of the heavens
on all sides suffice to hold it in place ; for a body
which is in equipoise and is placed in the centre of
something which is homogeneous cannot change its
inclination in any direction, but will remain always
in the same position.   This, then, is the first thing of
which I am convinced."

"And rightly," said Simmias.

"Secondly," said he, "I believe that the earth is
very large and that we who dwell between the
pillars of Hercules and the river Phasis live in a small
part of it about the sea, like ants or frogs about a
pond, and that many other people live in many other
such regions.   For I believe there are in all directions
on the earth many hollows of very various forms and
sizes, into which the water and mist and air have run
together ; but the earth itself is pure and is situated
in the pure heaven in which the stars are, the
heaven which those who discourse about such matters
call the ether ; the water, mist and air are the sedi-
ment of this and flow together into the hollows of
the earth.   Now we do not perceive that we live in
the hollows, but think we live on the upper surface
of the earth, just as if someone who lives in the depth
of the ocean should think he lived on the surface of
the sea, and, seeing the sun and the stars through
the water, should think the sea was the sky, and
should, by reason of sluggishness or feebleness, never
have reached the surface of the sea, and should never
have seen, by rising and lifting his head out of the

375

PLATO

ἐκ τῆς θαλάττης εἰς τὸν ἐνθάδε τόπον, ὅσῳ
καθαρώτερος καὶ καλλίων τυγχάνει ὢν τοῦ παρὰ
σφίσι, μηδὲ ἄλλου ἀκηκοὼς εἴη τοῦ ἑωρακότος.
ταὐτὸν δὴ τοῦτο καὶ ἡμᾶς πεπονθέναι· οἰκοῦντας
γὰρ ἔν τινι κοίλῳ τῆς γῆς οἴεσθαι ἐπάνω αὐτῆς
οἰκεῖν, καὶ τὸν ἀέρα οὐρανὸν καλεῖν, ὡς διὰ τούτου
οὐρανοῦ ὄντος τὰ ἄστρα χωροῦντα· τὸ δὲ εἶναι
E ταὐτόν,[1] ὑπ᾽ ἀσθενείας καὶ βραδυτῆτος οὐχ οἵους
τε εἶναι ἡμᾶς διεξελθεῖν ἐπ᾽ ἔσχατον τὸν ἀέρα·
ἐπεί, εἴ τις αὐτοῦ ἐπ᾽ ἄκρα ἔλθοι ἢ πτηνὸς
γενόμενος ἀνάπτοιτο, κατιδεῖν ἂν ἀνακύψαντα,
ὥσπερ ἐνθάδε οἱ ἐκ τῆς θαλάττης ἰχθύες ἀνακύ-
πτοντες ὁρῶσι τὰ ἐνθάδε, οὕτως ἄν τινα καὶ τὰ
ἐκεῖ κατιδεῖν, καὶ εἰ ἡ φύσις ἱκανὴ εἴη ἀνέχεσθαι
θεωροῦσα, γνῶναι ἄν, ὅτι ἐκεῖνός ἐστιν ὁ ἀληθῶς
110 οὐρανὸς καὶ τὸ ἀληθῶς φῶς καὶ ἡ ὡς ἀληθῶς γῆ.
ἥδε μὲν γὰρ ἡ γῆ καὶ οἱ λίθοι καὶ ἅπας ὁ τόπος ὁ
ἐνθάδε διεφθαρμένα ἐστὶν καὶ καταβεβρωμένα,
ὥσπερ τὰ ἐν τῇ θαλάττῃ ὑπὸ τῆς ἅλμης, καὶ οὔτε
φύεται οὐδὲν ἄξιον λόγου ἐν τῇ θαλάττῃ, οὔτε
τέλειον, ὡς ἔπος εἰπεῖν, οὐδέν ἐστι, σήραγγες δὲ
καὶ ἄμμος καὶ πηλὸς ἀμήχανος καὶ βόρβοροί
εἰσιν, ὅπου ἂν καὶ ἡ γῆ ᾖ, καὶ πρὸς τὰ παρ᾽ ἡμῖν
κάλλη κρίνεσθαι οὐδ᾽ ὁπωστιοῦν ἄξια· ἐκεῖνα δὲ
αὖ τῶν παρ᾽ ἡμῖν πολὺ ἂν ἔτι πλέον φανείη
B διαφέρειν. εἰ γὰρ δεῖ καὶ μῦθον λέγειν, ἄξιον
ἀκοῦσαι, ὦ Σιμμία, οἷα τυγχάνει τὰ ἐπὶ τῆς
γῆς ὑπὸ τῷ οὐρανῷ ὄντα. Ἀλλὰ μήν, ἔφη ὁ
Σιμμίας, ὦ Σώκρατες, ἡμεῖς γε τούτου τοῦ
μύθου ἡδέως ἂν ἀκούσαιμεν.

59. Λέγεται τοίνυν, ἔφη, ὦ ἑταῖρε, πρῶτον

---

[1] Schanz, following Rückert, brackets εἶναι ταὐτόν.

sea into our upper world, and should never have heard from anyone who had seen, how much purer and fairer it is than the world he lived in. Now I believe this is just the case with us; for we dwell in a hollow of the earth and think we dwell on its upper suface; and the air we call the heaven, and think that is the heaven in which the stars move. But the fact is the same, that by reason of feebleness and sluggishness, we are unable to attain to the upper surface of the air; for if anyone should come to the top of the air or should get wings and fly up, he could lift his head above it and see, as fishes lift their heads out of the water and see the things in our world, so he would see things in that upper world; and, if his nature were strong enough to bear the sight, he would recognise that that is the real heaven and the real light and the real earth. For this earth of ours, and the stones and the whole region where we live, are injured and corroded, as in the sea things are injured by the brine, and nothing of any account grows in the sea, and there is, one might say, nothing perfect there, but caverns and sand and endless mud and mire, where there is earth also, and there is nothing at all worthy to be compared with the beautiful things of our world. But the things in that world above would be seen to be even more superior to those in this world of ours. If I may tell a story, Simmias, about the things on the earth that is below the heaven, and what they are like, it is well worth hearing."

" By all means, Socrates," said Simmias; "we should be glad to hear this story."

"Well then, my friend," said he, " to begin with,

PLATO

μὲν εἶναι τοιαύτη ἡ γῆ αὐτὴ ἰδεῖν, εἴ τις ἄνωθεν
θεῷτο, ὥσπερ αἱ δωδεκάσκυτοι σφαῖραι, ποικίλη,
χρώμασιν διειλημμένη, ὧν καὶ τὰ ἐνθάδε εἶναι
χρώματα ὥσπερ δείγματα, οἷς δὴ οἱ γραφεῖς
C καταχρῶνται· ἐκεῖ δὲ πᾶσαν τὴν γῆν ἐκ τοιούτων
εἶναι, καὶ πολὺ ἔτι ἐκ λαμπροτέρων καὶ καθαρω-
τέρων ἢ τούτων· τὴν μὲν γὰρ ἁλουργῆ εἶναι καὶ
θαυμαστὴν τὸ κάλλος, τὴν δὲ χρυσοειδῆ, τὴν δὲ
ὅση λευκὴ γύψου ἢ χιόνος λευκοτέραν, καὶ ἐκ
τῶν ἄλλων χρωμάτων συγκειμένην ὡσαύτως, καὶ
ἔτι πλειόνων καὶ καλλιόνων ἢ ὅσα ἡμεῖς ἑωρά-
καμεν. καὶ γὰρ αὐτὰ ταῦτα τὰ κοῖλα αὐτῆς
ὕδατός τε καὶ ἀέρος ἔκπλεα ὄντα, χρώματός τι
D εἶδος παρέχεσθαι στίλβοντα ἐν τῇ τῶν ἄλλων
χρωμάτων ποικιλίᾳ, ὥστε ἕν τι αὐτῆς εἶδος
συνεχὲς ποικίλον φαντάζεσθαι. ἐν δὲ ταύτῃ οὔσῃ
τοιαύτῃ ἀνὰ λόγον τὰ φυόμενα φύεσθαι, δένδρα
τε καὶ ἄνθη καὶ τοὺς καρπούς· καὶ αὖ τὰ ὄρη
ὡσαύτως καὶ τοὺς λίθους ἔχειν ἀνὰ τὸν αὐτὸν
λόγον τήν τε λειότητα καὶ τὴν διαφάνειαν καὶ
τὰ χρώματα καλλίω· ὧν καὶ τὰ ἐνθάδε λιθίδια
εἶναι ταῦτα τὰ ἀγαπώμενα μόρια, σάρδιά τε
E καὶ ἰάσπιδας καὶ σμαράγδους καὶ πάντα τὰ
τοιαῦτα· ἐκεῖ δὲ οὐδὲν ὅ τι οὐ τοιοῦτον εἶναι καὶ
ἔτι τούτων καλλίω. τὸ δ' αἴτιον τούτου εἶναι, ὅτι
ἐκεῖνοι οἱ λίθοι εἰσὶ καθαροὶ καὶ οὐ κατεδηδεσμένοι
οὐδὲ διεφθαρμένοι ὥσπερ οἱ ἐνθάδε ὑπὸ σηπεδόνος
καὶ ἅλμης[1] ὑπὸ τῶν δεῦρο ξυνερρυηκότων, ἃ καὶ
λίθοις καὶ γῇ καὶ τοῖς ἄλλοις ζῴοις τε καὶ φυτοῖς
αἴσχη τε καὶ νόσους παρέχει. τὴν δὲ γῆν αὐτὴν
κεκοσμῆσθαι τούτοις τε ἅπασι καὶ ἔτι χρυσῷ καὶ

[1] Schanz brackets ὑπὸ σηπεδόνος καὶ ἅλμης.

378

the earth when seen from above is said to look like
those balls that are covered with twelve pieces of
leather ; it is divided into patches of various colours,
of which the colours which we see here may be
regarded as samples, such as painters use. But
there the whole earth is of such colours, and they
are much brighter and purer than ours ; for one
part is purple of wonderful beauty, and one is
golden, and one is white, whiter than chalk or
snow, and the earth is made up of the other
colours likewise, and they are more in number
and more beautiful than those which we see here.
For those very hollows of the earth which are full of
water and air, present an appearance of colour as they
glisten amid the variety of the other colours, so that
the whole produces one continuous effect of variety.
And in this fair earth the things that grow, the trees,
and flowers and fruits, are correspondingly beautiful ;
and so too the mountains and the stones are smoother,
and more transparent and more lovely in colour than
ours. In fact, our highly prized stones, sards and
jaspers, and emeralds, and other gems, are fragments
of those there, but there everything is like these or
still more beautiful. And the reason of this is that
there the stones are pure, and not corroded or defiled,
as ours are, with filth and brine by the vapours and
liquids which flow together here and which cause
ugliness and disease in earth and stones and animals
and plants. And the earth there is adorned with all
these jewels and also with gold and silver and every-

PLATO

111 ἀργύρῳ καὶ τοῖς ἄλλοις αὖ τοῖς τοιούτοις. ἐκφανῆ
γὰρ αὐτὰ πεφυκέναι, ὄντα πολλὰ πλήθει καὶ
μεγάλα καὶ πολλαχοῦ τῆς γῆς, ὥστε αὐτὴν ἰδεῖν
εἶναι θέαμα εὐδαιμόνων θεατῶν. ζῷα δ' ἐπ' αὐτῇ
εἶναι ἄλλα τε πολλὰ καὶ ἀνθρώπους, τοὺς μὲν ἐν
μεσογαίᾳ οἰκοῦντας, τοὺς δὲ περὶ τὸν ἀέρα, ὥσπερ
ἡμεῖς περὶ τὴν θάλατταν, τοὺς δ' ἐν νήσοις ἃς
περιρρεῖν τὸν ἀέρα πρὸς τῇ ἠπείρῳ οὔσας· καὶ ἑνὶ
λόγῳ, ὅπερ ἡμῖν τὸ ὕδωρ τε καὶ ἡ θάλαττά ἐστι
B πρὸς τὴν ἡμετέραν χρείαν, τοῦτο ἐκεῖ τὸν ἀέρα,
ὃ δὲ ἡμῖν ὁ ἀήρ, ἐκείνοις τὸν αἰθέρα. τὰς δὲ ὥρας
αὐτῆς κρᾶσιν ἔχειν τοιαύτην, ὥστε ἐκείνους ἀνό-
σους εἶναι καὶ χρόνον τε ζῆν πολὺ πλείω τῶν
ἐνθάδε, καὶ ὄψει καὶ ἀκοῇ καὶ φρονήσει καὶ πᾶσι
τοῖς τοιούτοις ἡμῶν ἀφεστάναι τῇ αὐτῇ ἀποστάσει,
ᾗπερ ἀήρ τε ὕδατος ἀφέστηκεν καὶ αἰθὴρ ἀέρος
πρὸς καθαρότητα. καὶ δὴ καὶ θεῶν ἄλση τε καὶ
ἱερὰ αὐτοῖς εἶναι, ἐν οἷς τῷ ὄντι οἰκητὰς θεοὺς
εἶναι, καὶ φήμας τε καὶ μαντείας καὶ αἰσθήσεις
τῶν θεῶν καὶ τοιαύτας συνουσίας γίγνεσθαι
C αὐτοῖς πρὸς αὐτούς· καὶ τόν γε ἥλιον καὶ σελήνην
καὶ ἄστρα ὁρᾶσθαι ὑπ' αὐτῶν οἷα τυγχάνει ὄντα,
καὶ τὴν ἄλλην εὐδαιμονίαν τούτων ἀκόλουθον
εἶναι.

60. Καὶ ὅλην μὲν δὴ τὴν γῆν οὕτω πεφυκέναι
καὶ τὰ περὶ τὴν γῆν· τόπους δ' ἐν αὐτῇ εἶναι κατὰ
τὰ ἔγκοιλα αὐτῆς κύκλῳ περὶ ὅλην πολλούς, τοὺς
μὲν βαθυτέρους καὶ ἀναπεπταμένους μᾶλλον ἢ ἐν
ᾧ ἡμεῖς οἰκοῦμεν, τοὺς δὲ βαθυτέρους ὄντας τὸ
αὐτῶν χάσμα ἔλαττον ἔχειν τοῦ παρ' ἡμῖν τόπου,
D ἔστι δ' οὓς καὶ βραχυτέρους τῷ βάθει τοῦ ἐνθάδε
εἶναι καὶ πλατυτέρους· τούτους δὲ πάντας ὑπὸ

thing of the sort. For there they are in plain sight, abundant and large and in many places, so that the earth is a sight to make those blessed who look upon it. And there are many animals upon it, and men also, some dwelling inland, others on the coasts of the air, as we dwell about the sea, and others on islands, which the air flows around, near the mainland ; and in short, what water and the sea are in our lives, air is in theirs, and what the air is to us, ether is to them. And the seasons are so tempered that people there have no diseases and live much longer than we, and in sight and hearing and wisdom and all such things are as much superior to us as air is purer than water or the ether than air. And they have sacred groves and temples of the gods, in which the gods really dwell, and they have intercourse with the gods by speech and prophecies and visions, and they see the sun and moon and stars as they really are, and in all other ways their blessedness is in accord with this.

"Such then is the nature of the earth as a whole, and of the things around it. But round about the whole earth, in the hollows of it, are many regions, some deeper and wider than that in which we live, some deeper but with a narrower opening than ours, and some also less in depth and wider. Now all these

γῆν εἰς ἀλλήλους συντετρῆσθαί τε πολλαχῇ καὶ
κατὰ στενότερα καὶ εὐρύτερα, καὶ διεξόδους ἔχειν,
ᾗ πολὺ μὲν ὕδωρ ῥεῖν ἐξ ἀλλήλων εἰς ἀλλήλους
ὥσπερ εἰς κρατῆρας, καὶ ἀενάων ποταμῶν ἀμήχανα
μεγέθη ὑπὸ τὴν γῆν καὶ θερμῶν ὑδάτων καὶ
ψυχρῶν, πολὺ δὲ πῦρ καὶ πυρὸς μεγάλους ποτα-
μούς, πολλοὺς δὲ ὑγροῦ πηλοῦ καὶ καθαρωτέρου
E καὶ βορβορωδεστέρου, ὥσπερ ἐν Σικελίᾳ οἱ πρὸ
τοῦ ῥύακος πηλοῦ ῥέοντες ποταμοὶ καὶ αὐτὸς ὁ
ῥύαξ· ὧν δὴ καὶ ἑκάστους τοὺς τόπους πληροῦ-
σθαι, ὡς ἂν ἑκάστοις τύχῃ ἑκάστοτε ἡ περιρροὴ
γιγνομένη. ταῦτα δὲ πάντα κινεῖν ἄνω καὶ κάτω
ὥσπερ αἰώραν τινὰ ἐνοῦσαν ἐν τῇ γῇ· ἔστι δὲ ἄρα
αὕτη ἡ αἰώρα διὰ φύσιν τοιάνδε τινά. ἔν τι τῶν
χασμάτων τῆς γῆς ἄλλως τε μέγιστον τυγχάνει
112 ὂν καὶ διαμπερὲς τετρημένον δι' ὅλης τῆς γῆς,
τοῦτο ὅπερ Ὅμηρος εἶπε, λέγων αὐτό

τῆλε μάλ', ᾗχι βάθιστον ὑπὸ χθονός ἐστι
βέρεθρον·

ὃ καὶ ἄλλοθι καὶ ἐκεῖνος καὶ ἄλλοι πολλοὶ
τῶν ποιητῶν Τάρταρον κεκλήκασιν. εἰς γὰρ
τοῦτο τὸ χάσμα συρρέουσί τε πάντες οἱ ποταμοὶ
καὶ ἐκ τούτου πάλιν ἐκρέουσιν· γίγνονται δὲ
ἕκαστοι τοιοῦτοι, δι' οἵας ἂν καὶ τῆς γῆς ῥέωσιν.
ἡ δὲ αἰτία ἐστὶν τοῦ ἐκρεῖν τε ἐντεῦθεν καὶ εἰσρεῖν
B πάντα τὰ ῥεύματα, ὅτι πυθμένα οὐκ ἔχει οὐδὲ
βάσιν τὸ ὑγρὸν τοῦτο. αἰωρεῖται δὴ καὶ κυμαίνει
ἄνω καὶ κάτω, καὶ ὁ ἀὴρ καὶ τὸ πνεῦμα τὸ περὶ
αὐτὸ ταὐτὸν ποιεῖ· ξυνέπεται γὰρ αὐτῷ καὶ ὅταν
εἰς τὸ ἐπέκεινα τῆς γῆς ὁρμήσῃ καὶ ὅταν εἰς τὸ

are connected with one another by many subterranean channels, some larger and some smaller, which are bored in all of them, and there are passages through which much water flows from one to another as into mixing bowls; and there are everlasting rivers of huge size under the earth, flowing with hot and cold water; and there is much fire, and great rivers of fire, and many streams of mud, some thinner and some thicker, like the rivers of mud that flow before the lava in Sicily, and the lava itself. These fill the various regions as they happen to flow to one or another at any time. Now a kind of oscillation within the earth moves all these up and down. And the nature of the oscillation is as follows: One of the chasms of the earth is greater than the rest, and is bored right through the whole earth; this is the one which Homer means when he says:

Far off, the lowest abyss beneath the earth; [1]

and which elsewhere he and many other poets have called Tartarus. For all the rivers flow together into this chasm and flow out of it again, and they have each the nature of the earth through which they flow. And the reason why all the streams flow in and out here is that this liquid matter has no bottom or foundation. So it oscillates and waves up and down, and the air and wind about it do the same; for they follow the liquid both when it moves toward the other side of the earth and when it moves toward this side, and

[1] Homer, *Iliad* 8, 14, Lord Derby's translation.

ἐπὶ τάδε, καὶ ὥσπερ τῶν ἀναπνεόντων ἀεὶ ἐκπνεῖ
τε καὶ ἀναπνεῖ ῥέον τὸ πνεῦμα, οὕτω καὶ ἐκεῖ
ξυναιωρούμενον τῷ ὑγρῷ τὸ πνεῦμα δεινούς τινας
ἀνέμους καὶ ἀμηχάνους παρέχεται καὶ εἰσιὸν καὶ
C ἐξιόν. ὅταν τε οὖν ὑποχωρήσῃ τὸ ὕδωρ εἰς τὸν
τόπον τὸν δὴ κάτω καλούμενον, τοῖς κατ᾽ ἐκεῖνα
τὰ ῥεύματα διὰ τῆς γῆς εἰσρεῖ τε καὶ πληροῖ αὐτὰ
ὥσπερ οἱ ἐπαντλοῦντες· ὅταν τε αὖ ἐκεῖθεν μὲν
ἀπολίπῃ, δεῦρο δὲ ὁρμήσῃ, τὰ ἐνθάδε πληροῖ
αὖθις, τὰ δὲ πληρωθέντα ῥεῖ διὰ τῶν ὀχετῶν καὶ
διὰ τῆς γῆς, καὶ εἰς τοὺς τόπους ἕκαστα ἀφικνού-
μενα, εἰς οὓς ἑκάστους ὁδοποιεῖται, θαλάττας τε
καὶ λίμνας καὶ ποταμοὺς καὶ κρήνας ποιεῖ·
ἐντεῦθεν δὲ πάλιν δυόμενα κατὰ τῆς γῆς, τὰ μὲν
D μακροτέρους τόπους περιελθόντα καὶ πλείους, τὰ
δὲ ἐλάττους καὶ βραχυτέρους, πάλιν εἰς τὸν
Τάρταρον ἐμβάλλει, τὰ μὲν πολὺ κατωτέρω ἢ
ἐπηντλεῖτο, τὰ δὲ ὀλίγον· πάντα δὲ ὑποκάτω
εἰσρεῖ τῆς ἐκροῆς. καὶ ἔνια μὲν καταντικρὺ ἢ
ἐξέπεσεν εἰσρεῖ, ἔνια δὲ κατὰ τὸ αὐτὸ μέρος· ἔστι
δὲ ἃ παντάπασιν κύκλῳ περιελθόντα, ἢ ἅπαξ ἢ
καὶ πλεονάκις περιελιχθέντα περὶ τὴν γῆν ὥσπερ
οἱ ὄφεις, εἰς τὸ δυνατὸν κάτω καθέντα πάλιν
E ἐμβάλλει. δυνατὸν δέ ἐστιν ἑκατέρωσε μέχρι τοῦ
μέσου καθιέναι, πέρα δ᾽ οὔ· ἄναντες γὰρ ἀμφοτέροις τοῖς ῥεύμασι τὸ ἑκατέρωθεν γίγνεται μέρος.

61. Τὰ μὲν οὖν δὴ ἄλλα πολλά τε καὶ μεγάλα
καὶ παντοδαπὰ ῥεύματά ἐστι· τυγχάνει δ᾽ ἄρα
ὄντα ἐν τούτοις τοῖς πολλοῖς τέτταρ᾽ ἄττα ῥεύματα,
ὧν τὸ μὲν μέγιστον καὶ ἐξωτάτω ῥέον κύκλῳ ὁ
καλούμενος Ὠκεανός ἐστιν, τούτου δὲ καταντικρὺ
καὶ ἐναντίως ῥέων Ἀχέρων, ὃς δι᾽ ἐρήμων τε

just as the breath of those who breathe blows in and out, so the wind there oscillates with the liquid and causes terrible and irresistible blasts as it rushes in and out. And when the water retires to the region which we call the lower, it flows into the rivers there and fills them up, as if it were pumped into them; and when it leaves that region and comes back to this side, it fills the rivers here; and when the streams are filled they flow through the passages and through the earth and come to the various places to which their different paths lead, where they make seas and marshes, and rivers and springs. Thence they go down again under the earth, some passing around many great regions and others around fewer and smaller places, and flow again into Tartarus, some much below the point where they were sucked out, and some only a little; but all flow in below their exit. Some flow in on the side from which they flowed out, others on the opposite side; and some pass completely around in a circle, coiling about the earth once or several times, like serpents, then descend to the lowest possible depth and fall again into the chasm. Now it is possible to go down from each side to the centre, but not beyond, for there the slope rises upward in front of the streams from either side of the earth.

" Now these streams are many and great and of all sorts, but among the many are four streams, the greatest and outermost of which is that called Oceanus, which flows round in a circle, and opposite this, flowing in the opposite direction, is Acheron, which flows through

113 τόπων ῥεῖ ἄλλων καὶ δὴ καὶ ὑπὸ γῆν ῥέων εἰς τὴν
λίμνην ἀφικνεῖται τὴν Ἀχερουσιάδα, οἷ αἱ τῶν
τετελευτηκότων ψυχαὶ τῶν πολλῶν ἀφικνοῦνται
καί τινας εἱμαρμένους χρόνους μείνασαι, αἱ μὲν
μακροτέρους, αἱ δὲ βραχυτέρους, πάλιν ἐκπέμ-
πονται εἰς τὰς τῶν ζῴων γενέσεις. τρίτος δὲ
ποταμὸς τούτων κατὰ μέσον ἐκβάλλει, καὶ ἐγγὺς
τῆς ἐκβολῆς ἐκπίπτει εἰς τόπον μέγαν πυρὶ
πολλῷ καιόμενον, καὶ λίμνην ποιεῖ μείζω τῆς παρ᾽
ἡμῖν θαλάττης, ζέουσαν ὕδατος καὶ πηλοῦ·
B ἐντεῦθεν δὲ χωρεῖ κύκλῳ θολερὸς καὶ πηλώδης,
περιελιττόμενος δὲ ἄλλοσέ τε ἀφικνεῖται καὶ παρ᾽
ἔσχατα τῆς Ἀχερουσιάδος λίμνης, οὐ συμμιγνύ-
μενος τῷ ὕδατι· περιελιχθεὶς δὲ πολλάκις ὑπὸ
γῆς ἐμβάλλει κατωτέρω τοῦ Ταρτάρου· οὗτος δ᾽
ἐστὶν ὃν ἐπονομάζουσιν Πυριφλεγέθοντα, οὗ καὶ
οἱ ῥύακες ἀποσπάσματα ἀναφυσῶσιν ὅπη ἂν
τύχωσι τῆς γῆς. τούτου δὲ αὖ καταντικρὺ ὁ
τέταρτος ἐκπίπτει εἰς τόπον πρῶτον[1] δεινόν τε καὶ
ἄγριον, ὡς λέγεται, χρῶμα δ᾽ ἔχοντα ὅλον οἷον ὁ
C κυανός, ὃν δὴ ἐπονομάζουσι Στύγιον, καὶ τὴν
λίμνην, ἣν ποιεῖ ὁ ποταμὸς ἐμβάλλων, Στύγα· ὁ
δ᾽ ἐμπεσὼν ἐνταῦθα καὶ δεινὰς δυνάμεις λαβὼν ἐν
τῷ ὕδατι, δὺς κατὰ τῆς γῆς, περιελιττόμενος
χωρεῖ ἐναντίος τῷ Πυριφλεγέθοντι καὶ ἀπαντᾷ ἐν
τῇ Ἀχερουσιάδι λίμνῃ ἐξ ἐναντίας· καὶ οὐδὲ τὸ
τούτου ὕδωρ οὐδενὶ μίγνυται, ἀλλὰ καὶ οὗτος
κύκλῳ περιελθὼν ἐμβάλλει εἰς τὸν Τάρταρον
ἐναντίος τῷ Πυριφλεγέθοντι· ὄνομα δὲ τούτῳ
ἐστίν, ὡς οἱ ποιηταὶ λέγουσιν, Κωκυτός.
D 62. Τούτων δὲ οὕτως πεφυκότων, ἐπειδὰν ἀφί-

[1] Schanz brackets πρῶτον.

various desert places and, passing under the earth, comes to the Acherusian lake. To this lake the souls of most of the dead go and, after remaining there the appointed time, which is for some longer and for others shorter, are sent back to be born again into living beings. The third river flows out between these two, and near the place whence it issues it falls into a vast region burning with a great fire and makes a lake larger than our Mediterranean sea, boiling with water and mud. Thence it flows in a circle, turbid and muddy, and comes in its winding course, among other places, to the edge of the Acherusian lake, but does not mingle with its water. Then, after winding about many times underground, it flows into Tartarus at a lower level. This is the river which is called Pyriphlegethon, and the streams of lava which spout up at various places on earth are offshoots from it. Opposite this the fourth river issues, it is said, first into a wild and awful place, which is all of a dark blue colour, like lapis lazuli. This is called the Stygian river, and the lake which it forms by flowing in is the Styx. And when the river has flowed in here and has received fearful powers into its waters, it passes under the earth and, circling round in the direction opposed to that of Pyriphlegethon, it meets it coming from the other way in the Acherusian lake. And the water of this river also mingles with no other water, but this also passes round in a circle and falls into Tartarus opposite Pyriphlegethon. And the name of this river, as the poets say, is Cocytus.

"Such is the nature of these things. Now when

κωνται οἱ τετελευτηκότες εἰς τὸν τόπον οἷ ὁ
δαίμων ἕκαστον κομίζει, πρῶτον μὲν διεδικάσαντο
οἵ τε καλῶς καὶ ὁσίως βιώσαντες καὶ οἱ μή. καὶ
οἱ μὲν ἂν δόξωσι μέσως βεβιωκέναι, πορευθέντες
ἐπὶ τὸν Ἀχέροντα, ἀναβάντες ἃ δὴ αὐτοῖς ὀχή-
ματά ἐστιν, ἐπὶ τούτων ἀφικνοῦνται εἰς τὴν λίμνην,
καὶ ἐκεῖ οἰκοῦσί τε καὶ καθαιρόμενοι τῶν τε
ἀδικημάτων διδόντες δίκας ἀπολύονται, εἴ τίς τι
E ἠδίκηκεν, τῶν τε εὐεργεσιῶν τιμὰς φέρονται κατὰ
τὴν ἀξίαν ἕκαστος· οἱ δ' ἂν δόξωσιν ἀνιάτως
ἔχειν διὰ τὰ μεγέθη τῶν ἁμαρτημάτων, ἢ ἱερο-
συλίας πολλὰς καὶ μεγάλας ἢ φόνους ἀδίκους καὶ
παρανόμους πολλοὺς ἐξειργασμένοι, ἢ ἄλλα ὅσα
τοιαῦτα τυγχάνει ὄντα, τούτους δὲ ἡ προσήκουσα
μοῖρα ῥίπτει εἰς τὸν Τάρταρον, ὅθεν οὔποτε ἐκβαί-
νουσιν. οἱ δ' ἂν ἰάσιμα μέν, μεγάλα δὲ δόξωσιν
ἡμαρτηκέναι ἁμαρτήματα, οἷον πρὸς πατέρα ἢ
μητέρα ὑπ' ὀργῆς βίαιόν τι πράξαντες, καὶ μετα-
114 μέλον αὐτοῖς τὸν ἄλλον βίον βιῶσιν, ἢ ἀνδροφόνοι
τοιούτῳ τινὶ ἄλλῳ τρόπῳ γένωνται, τούτους δὲ
ἐμπεσεῖν μὲν εἰς τὸν Τάρταρον ἀνάγκη, ἐμπεσόντας
δὲ αὐτοὺς καὶ ἐνιαυτὸν ἐκεῖ γενομένους ἐκβάλλει
τὸ κῦμα, τοὺς μὲν ἀνδροφόνους κατὰ τὸν Κωκυτόν,
τοὺς δὲ πατραλοίας καὶ μητραλοίας κατὰ τὸν
Πυριφλεγέθοντα· ἐπειδὰν δὲ φερόμενοι γένωνται
κατὰ τὴν λίμνην τὴν Ἀχερουσιάδα, ἐνταῦθα
βοῶσί τε καὶ καλοῦσιν, οἱ μὲν οὓς ἀπέκτειναν,
οἱ δὲ οὓς ὕβρισαν, καλέσαντες δ' ἱκετεύουσι καὶ
B δέονται ἐᾶσαι σφᾶς ἐκβῆναι εἰς τὴν λίμνην καὶ
δέξασθαι, καὶ ἐὰν μὲν πείσωσιν, ἐκβαίνουσί τε
καὶ λήγουσι τῶν κακῶν, εἰ δὲ μή, φέρονται αὖθις
εἰς τὸν Τάρταρον καὶ ἐκεῖθεν πάλιν εἰς τοὺς ποτα-

the dead have come to the place where each is led by his genius, first they are judged and sentenced, as they have lived well and piously, or not. And those who are found to have lived neither well nor ill, go to the Acheron and, embarking upon vessels provided for them, arrive in them at the lake; there they dwell and are purified, and if they have done any wrong they are absolved by paying the penalty for their wrong doings, and for their good deeds they receive rewards, each according to his merits. But those who appear to be incurable, on account of the greatness of their wrong-doings, because they have committed many great deeds of sacrilege, or wicked and abominable murders, or any other such crimes, are cast by their fitting destiny into Tartarus, whence they never emerge. Those, however, who are curable, but are found to have committed great sins—who have, for example, in a moment of passion done some act of violence against father or mother and have lived in repentance the rest of their lives, or who have slain some other person under similar conditions—these must needs be thrown into Tartarus, and when they have been there a year the wave casts them out, the homicides by way of Cocytus, those who have outraged their parents by way of Pyriphlegethon. And when they have been brought by the current to the Acherusian lake, they shout and cry out, calling to those whom they have slain or outraged, begging and beseeching them to be gracious and to let them come out into the lake; and if they prevail they come out and cease from their ills, but if not, they are borne away again to Tartarus and thence back into the rivers, and this goes on

μούς, καὶ ταῦτα πάσχοντες οὐ πρότερον παύονται,
πρὶν ἂν πείσωσιν οὓς ἠδίκησαν· αὕτη γὰρ ἡ δίκη
ὑπὸ τῶν δικαστῶν αὐτοῖς ἐτάχθη. οἳ δὲ δὴ ἂν
δόξωσι διαφερόντως πρὸς τὸ ὁσίως βιῶναι, οὗτοί
εἰσιν οἱ τῶνδε μὲν τῶν τόπων τῶν ἐν τῇ γῇ ἐλευ-
θερούμενοί τε καὶ ἀπαλλαττόμενοι ὥσπερ δεσμω-
C τηρίων, ἄνω δὲ εἰς τὴν καθαρὰν οἴκησιν ἀφικνού-
μενοι καὶ ἐπὶ γῆς οἰκιζόμενοι. τούτων δὲ αὐτῶν
οἱ φιλοσοφίᾳ ἱκανῶς καθηράμενοι ἄνευ τε σωμάτων
ζῶσι τὸ παράπαν εἰς τὸν ἔπειτα χρόνον, καὶ εἰς
οἰκήσεις ἔτι τούτων καλλίους ἀφικνοῦνται, ἃς
οὔτε ῥᾴδιον δηλῶσαι οὔτε ὁ χρόνος ἱκανὸς ἐν τῷ
παρόντι. ἀλλὰ τούτων δὴ ἕνεκα χρὴ ὧν διεληλύθαμεν, ὦ Σιμμία, πᾶν ποιεῖν, ὥστε ἀρετῆς καὶ
φρονήσεως ἐν τῷ βίῳ μετασχεῖν· καλὸν γὰρ τὸ
ἆθλον καὶ ἡ ἐλπὶς μεγάλη.

D 63. Τὸ μὲν οὖν τοιαῦτα διισχυρίσασθαι οὕτως
ἔχειν, ὡς ἐγὼ διελήλυθα, οὐ πρέπει νοῦν ἔχοντι
ἀνδρί· ὅτι μέντοι ἢ ταῦτ' ἐστὶν ἢ τοιαῦτ' ἄττα
περὶ τὰς ψυχὰς ἡμῶν καὶ τὰς οἰκήσεις, ἐπείπερ
ἀθάνατόν γε ἡ ψυχὴ φαίνεται οὖσα, τοῦτο καὶ
πρέπειν μοι δοκεῖ καὶ ἄξιον κινδυνεῦσαι οἰομένῳ
οὕτως ἔχειν· καλὸς γὰρ ὁ κίνδυνος· καὶ χρὴ τὰ
τοιαῦτα ὥσπερ ἐπᾴδειν ἑαυτῷ, διὸ δὴ ἔγωγε καὶ
πάλαι μηκύνω τὸν μῦθον. ἀλλὰ τούτων δὴ ἕνεκα
θαρρεῖν χρὴ περὶ τῇ ἑαυτοῦ ψυχῇ ἄνδρα, ὅστις ἐν
E τῷ βίῳ τὰς μὲν ἄλλας ἡδονὰς τὰς περὶ τὸ σῶμα
καὶ τοὺς κόσμους εἴασε χαίρειν, ὡς ἀλλοτρίους τε
ὄντας, καὶ πλέον θάτερον ἡγησάμενος ἀπεργά-
ζεσθαι, τὰς δὲ περὶ τὸ μανθάνειν ἐσπούδασέ τε
καὶ κοσμήσας τὴν ψυχὴν οὐκ ἀλλοτρίῳ ἀλλὰ τῷ
αὑτῆς κόσμῳ, σωφροσύνῃ τε καὶ δικαιοσύνῃ καὶ

until they prevail upon those whom they have wronged; for this is the penalty imposed upon them by the judges. But those who are found to have excelled in holy living are freed from these regions within the earth and are released as from prisons; they mount upward into their pure abode and dwell upon the earth. And of these, all who have duly purified themselves by philosophy live henceforth altogether without bodies, and pass to still more beautiful abodes which it is not easy to describe, nor have we now time enough.

"But, Simmias, because of all these things which we have recounted we ought to do our best to acquire virtue and wisdom in life. For the prize is fair and the hope great.

"Now it would not be fitting for a man of sense to maintain that all this is just as I have described it, but that this or something like it is true concerning our souls and their abodes, since the soul is shown to be immortal, I think he may properly and worthily venture to believe; for the venture is well worth while; and he ought to repeat such things to himself as if they were magic charms, which is the reason why I have been lengthening out the story so long. This then is why a man should be of good cheer about his soul, who in his life has rejected the pleasures and ornaments of the body, thinking they are alien to him and more likely to do him harm than good, and has sought eagerly for those of learning, and after adorning his soul with no alien ornaments, but with its own proper adornment of self-restraint and justice and

115 ἀνδρείᾳ καὶ ἐλευθερίᾳ καὶ ἀληθείᾳ, οὕτω περι-
μένει τὴν εἰς Ἅιδου πορείαν, ὡς πορευσόμενος
ὅταν ἡ εἱμαρμένη καλῇ. ὑμεῖς μὲν οὖν, ἔφη, ὦ
Σιμμία τε καὶ Κέβης καὶ οἱ ἄλλοι, εἰσαῦθις ἔν
τινι χρόνῳ ἕκαστοι πορεύσεσθε· ἐμὲ δὲ νῦν ἤδη
καλεῖ, φαίη ἂν ἀνὴρ τραγικός, ἡ εἱμαρμένη, καὶ
σχεδόν τί μοι ὥρα τραπέσθαι πρὸς τὸ λουτρόν·
δοκεῖ γὰρ δὴ βέλτιον εἶναι λουσάμενον πιεῖν τὸ
φάρμακον καὶ μὴ πράγματα ταῖς γυναιξὶ παρέχειν
νεκρὸν λούειν.

64. Ταῦτα δὴ εἰπόντος αὐτοῦ ὁ Κρίτων· Εἶεν,
B ἔφη, ὦ Σώκρατες· τί δὲ τούτοις ἢ ἐμοὶ ἐπι-
στέλλεις ἢ περὶ τῶν παίδων ἢ περὶ ἄλλου του,
ὅ τι ἄν σοι ποιοῦντες ἡμεῖς ἐν χάριτι μάλιστα
ποιοῖμεν; Ἅπερ ἀεὶ λέγω, ἔφη, ὦ Κρίτων, οὐδὲν
καινότερον· ὅτι ὑμῶν αὐτῶν ἐπιμελούμενοι ὑμεῖς
καὶ ἐμοὶ καὶ τοῖς ἐμοῖς καὶ ὑμῖν αὐτοῖς ἐν χάριτι
ποιήσετε ἅττ᾽ ἂν ποιῆτε, κἂν μὴ νῦν ὁμολογήσητε·
ἐὰν δὲ ὑμῶν μὲν αὐτῶν ἀμελῆτε καὶ μὴ θέλητε
ὥσπερ κατ᾽ ἴχνη κατὰ τὰ νῦν τε εἰρημένα καὶ τὰ
ἐν τῷ ἔμπροσθεν χρόνῳ ζῆν, οὐδὲ ἐὰν πολλὰ
C ὁμολογήσητε ἐν τῷ παρόντι καὶ σφόδρα, οὐδὲν
πλέον ποιήσετε. Ταῦτα μὲν τοίνυν προθυ-
μηθησόμεθα, ἔφη, οὕτω ποιεῖν· θάπτωμεν δέ
σε τίνα τρόπον; Ὅπως ἄν, ἔφη, βούλησθε,
ἐάνπερ γε λάβητέ με καὶ μὴ ἐκφύγω ὑμᾶς.
γελάσας δὲ ἅμα ἡσυχῇ καὶ πρὸς ἡμᾶς ἀποβλέψας
εἶπεν· Οὐ πείθω, ὦ ἄνδρες, Κρίτωνα, ὡς ἐγώ
εἰμι οὗτος Σωκράτης, ὁ νυνὶ διαλεγόμενος καὶ
διατάττων ἕκαστον τῶν λεγομένων, ἀλλ᾽ οἴεταί με
ἐκεῖνον εἶναι, ὃν ὄψεται ὀλίγον ὕστερον νεκρόν,
D καὶ ἐρωτᾷ δή, πῶς με θάπτῃ. ὅτι δὲ ἐγὼ πάλαι

courage and freedom and truth, awaits his departure
to the other world, ready to go when fate calls him.
You, Simmias and Cebes and the rest," he said, "will
go hereafter, each in his own time; but I am now
already, as a tragedian would say, called by fate, and
it is about time for me to go to the bath; for I think
it is better to bathe before drinking the poison, that
the women may not have the trouble of bathing
the corpse."

When he had finished speaking, Crito said: "Well,
Socrates, do you wish to leave any directions with us
about your children or anything else—anything we
can do to serve you?"

"What I always say, Crito," he replied, "nothing
new. If you take care of yourselves you will serve me
and mine and yourselves, whatever you do, even if
you make no promises now; but if you neglect yourselves and are not willing to live following step by
step, as it were, in the path marked out by our present
and past discussions, you will accomplish nothing,
no matter how much or how eagerly you promise
at present."

"We will certainly try hard to do as you say," he
replied. "But how shall we bury you?"

"However you please," he replied, "if you can
catch me and I do not get away from you." And he
laughed gently, and looking towards us, said: "I cannot persuade Crito, my friends, that the Socrates
who is now conversing and arranging the details of
his argument is really I; he thinks I am the one
whom he will presently see as a corpse, and he asks
how to bury me. And though I have been saying at

πολὺν λόγον πεποίημαι, ὡς, ἐπειδὰν πίω τὸ
φάρμακον, οὐκέτι ὑμῖν παραμενῶ, ἀλλ᾽ οἰχήσομαι
ἀπιὼν εἰς μακάρων δή τινας εὐδαιμονίας, ταῦτά
μοι[1] δοκῶ αὐτῷ ἄλλως λέγειν, παραμυθούμενος
ἅμα μὲν ὑμᾶς, ἅμα δ᾽ ἐμαυτόν. ἐγγυήσασθε οὖν
με πρὸς Κρίτωνα, ἔφη, τὴν ἐναντίαν ἐγγύην
ἢ ἣν οὗτος πρὸς τοὺς δικαστὰς ἠγγυᾶτο. οὗτος
μὲν γὰρ ἦ μὴν παραμενεῖν· ὑμεῖς δὲ ἦ μὴν μὴ
παραμενεῖν ἐγγυήσασθε, ἐπειδὰν ἀποθάνω, ἀλλὰ
E οἰχήσεσθαι ἀπιόντα, ἵνα Κρίτων ῥᾷον φέρῃ, καὶ
μὴ ὁρῶν μου τὸ σῶμα ἢ καιόμενον ἢ κατορυττό-
μενον ἀγανακτῇ ὑπὲρ ἐμοῦ ὡς δεινὰ πάσχοντος,
μηδὲ λέγῃ ἐν τῇ ταφῇ, ὡς ἢ προτίθεται Σωκράτη
ἢ ἐκφέρει ἢ κατορύττει. εὖ γὰρ ἴσθι, ἦ δ᾽ ὅς,
ὦ ἄριστε Κρίτων, τὸ μὴ καλῶς λέγειν οὐ μόνον
εἰς αὐτὸ τοῦτο πλημμελές, ἀλλὰ καὶ κακόν τι
ἐμποιεῖ ταῖς ψυχαῖς. ἀλλὰ θαρρεῖν τε χρὴ καὶ
φάναι τοὐμὸν σῶμα θάπτειν, καὶ θάπτειν οὕτως
116 ὅπως ἄν σοι φίλον ᾖ καὶ μάλιστα ἡγῇ νόμιμον
εἶναι.

65. Ταῦτ᾽ εἰπὼν ἐκεῖνος μὲν ἀνίστατο εἰς οἴκημά
τι ὡς λουσόμενος, καὶ ὁ Κρίτων εἵπετο αὐτῷ,
ἡμᾶς δ᾽ ἐκέλευε περιμένειν. περιεμένομεν οὖν
πρὸς ἡμᾶς αὐτοὺς διαλεγόμενοι περὶ τῶν εἰρημένων καὶ ἀνασκοποῦντες, τοτὲ δ᾽ αὖ περὶ τῆς
ξυμφορᾶς διεξιόντες, ὅση ἡμῖν γεγονυῖα εἴη,
ἀτεχνῶς ἡγούμενοι ὥσπερ πατρὸς στερηθέντες
διάξειν ὀρφανοὶ τὸν ἔπειτα βίον. ἐπειδὴ δὲ ἐλού-
B σατο καὶ ἠνέχθη παρ᾽ αὐτὸν τὰ παιδία—δύο γὰρ
αὐτῷ υἱεῖς σμικροὶ ἦσαν, εἷς δὲ μέγας—καὶ αἱ

---

[1] Schanz, following Madvig, brackets μοι.

great length that after I drink the poison I shall no longer be with you, but shall go away to the joys of the blessed you know of, he seems to think that was idle talk uttered to encourage you and myself. So," he said, " give security for me to Crito, the opposite of that which he gave the judges at my trial ; for he gave security that I would remain, but you must give security that I shall not remain when I die, but shall go away, so that Crito may bear it more easily, and may not be troubled when he sees my body being burnt or buried, or think I am undergoing terrible treatment, and may not say at the funeral that he is laying out Socrates, or following him to the grave, or burying him. For, dear Crito, you may be sure that such wrong words are not only undesirable in themselves, but they infect the soul with evil. No, you must be of good courage, and say that you bury my body,—and bury it as you think best and as seems to you most fitting."

When he had said this, he got up and went into another room to bathe ; Crito followed him, but he told us to wait. So we waited, talking over with each other and discussing the discourse we had heard, and then speaking of the great misfortune that had befallen us, for we felt that he was like a father to us and that when bereft of him we should pass the rest of our lives as orphans. And when he had bathed and his children had been brought to him —for he had two little sons and one big one—and

οἰκεῖαι γυναῖκες ἀφίκοντο, ἐκείναις ἐναντίον[1] τοῦ
Κρίτωνος διαλεχθείς τε καὶ ἐπιστείλας ἄττα
ἐβούλετο, τὰς μὲν γυναῖκας καὶ τὰ παιδία ἀπιέναι
ἐκέλευσεν, αὐτὸς δὲ ἧκε παρ' ἡμᾶς. καὶ ἦν ἤδη
ἐγγὺς ἡλίου δυσμῶν· χρόνον γὰρ πολὺν διέτριψεν
ἔνδον. ἐλθὼν δ' ἐκαθέζετο λελουμένος, καὶ οὐ
πολλὰ μετὰ ταῦτα διελέχθη, καὶ ἧκεν ὁ τῶν
C ἔνδεκα ὑπηρέτης καὶ στὰς παρ' αὐτόν· Ὦ Σώκρατες, ἔφη, οὐ καταγνώσομαί σου ὅπερ ἄλλων
καταγιγνώσκω, ὅτι μοι χαλεπαίνουσι καὶ κατα-
ρῶνται, ἐπειδὰν αὐτοῖς παραγγέλλω πίνειν τὸ
φάρμακον ἀναγκαζόντων τῶν ἀρχόντων. σὲ δὲ
ἐγὼ καὶ ἄλλως ἔγνωκα ἐν τούτῳ τῷ χρόνῳ γενναι-
ότατον καὶ πρᾳότατον καὶ ἄριστον ἄνδρα ὄντα
τῶν πώποτε δεῦρο ἀφικομένων, καὶ δὴ καὶ νῦν
εὖ οἶδ' ὅτι οὐκ ἐμοὶ χαλεπαίνεις, γιγνώσκεις γὰρ
τοὺς αἰτίους, ἀλλὰ ἐκείνοις. νῦν, οἶσθα γὰρ ἃ
ἦλθον ἀγγέλλων, χαῖρέ τε καὶ πειρῶ ὡς ῥᾷστα
D φέρειν τὰ ἀναγκαῖα. καὶ ἅμα δακρύσας μετα-
στρεφόμενος ἀπῄει. καὶ ὁ Σωκράτης ἀναβλέψας
πρὸς αὐτόν, Καὶ σύ, ἔφη, χαῖρε, καὶ ἡμεῖς
ταῦτα ποιήσομεν. καὶ ἅμα πρὸς ἡμᾶς, Ὡς
ἀστεῖος, ἔφη, ὁ ἄνθρωπος· καὶ παρὰ πάντα μοι
τὸν χρόνον προσῄει καὶ διελέγετο ἐνίοτε καὶ ἦν
ἀνδρῶν λῷστος, καὶ νῦν ὡς γενναίως με ἀπο-
δακρύει. ἀλλ' ἄγε δή, ὦ Κρίτων, πειθώμεθα
αὐτῷ, καὶ ἐνεγκάτω τις τὸ φάρμακον, εἰ τέτριπται·
εἰ δὲ μή, τριψάτω ὁ ἄνθρωπος. καὶ ὁ Κρίτων,
E Ἀλλ' οἶμαι, ἔφη, ἔγωγε, ὦ Σώκρατες, ἔτι
ἥλιον εἶναι ἐπὶ τοῖς ὄρεσιν καὶ οὔπω δεδυκέναι.

---

[1] ἐναντίον ἐκείναις, Ebd. ἐναντίον ἐκεῖναι, BD. Schanz
brackets ἐκεῖναι. ἐκείναις ἐναντίον Herrmann, Wohlrab.

the women of the family had come, he talked with
them in Crito's presence and gave them such directions as he wished; then he told the women to go
away, and he came to us. And it was now nearly sunset;
for he had spent a long time within. And he came
and sat down fresh from the bath. After that not
much was said, and the servant of the eleven came
and stood beside him and said : " Socrates, I shall not
find fault with you, as I do with others, for being
angry and cursing me, when at the behest of the
authorities, I tell them to drink the poison. No, I
have found you in all this time in every way the
noblest and gentlest and best man who has ever
come here, and now I know your anger is directed
against others, not against me, for you know who
are to blame. Now, for you know the message I
came to bring you, farewell and try to bear what
you must as easily as you can." And he burst into
tears and turned and went away. And Socrates
looked up at him and said : " Fare you well, too; I
will do as you say." And then he said to us : " How
charming the man is! Ever since I have been here
he has been coming to see me and talking with me
from time to time, and has been the best of men,
and now how nobly he weeps for me! But come,
Crito, let us obey him, and let someone bring the
poison, if it is ready ; and if not, let the man prepare
it." And Crito said : " But I think, Socrates, the sun
is still upon the mountains and has not yet set ; and

καὶ ἅμα ἐγὼ οἶδα καὶ ἄλλους πάνυ ὀψὲ πίνοντας,
ἐπειδὰν παραγγελθῇ αὐτοῖς, δειπνήσαντάς τε καὶ
πιόντας εὖ μάλα, καὶ ξυγγενομένους γ᾽ ἐνίους ὧν
ἂν τύχωσιν ἐπιθυμοῦντες. ἀλλὰ μηδὲν ἐπείγου·
ἔτι γὰρ ἐγχωρεῖ. καὶ ὁ Σωκράτης, Εἰκότως
γε, ἔφη, ὦ Κρίτων, ἐκεῖνοί τε ταῦτα ποιοῦσιν,
οὓς σὺ λέγεις, οἴονται γὰρ κερδαίνειν ταῦτα ποιή-
σαντες, καὶ ἔγωγε ταῦτα εἰκότως[1] οὐ ποιήσω·
117 οὐδὲν γὰρ οἶμαι κερδανεῖν ὀλίγον ὕστερον πιὼν
ἄλλο γε ἢ γέλωτα ὀφλήσειν παρ᾽ ἐμαυτῷ, γλιχό-
μενος τοῦ ζῆν καὶ φειδόμενος οὐδενὸς ἔτι ἐνόντος.
ἀλλ᾽ ἴθι, ἔφη, πιθοῦ καὶ μὴ ἄλλως ποίει.

66. Καὶ ὁ Κρίτων ἀκούσας ἔνευσε τῷ παιδὶ
πλησίον ἑστῶτι. καὶ ὁ παῖς ἐξελθὼν καὶ συχνὸν
χρόνον διατρίψας ἧκεν ἄγων τὸν μέλλοντα διδόναι
τὸ φάρμακον, ἐν κύλικι φέροντα τετριμμένον·
ἰδὼν δὲ ὁ Σωκράτης τὸν ἄνθρωπον, Εἶεν, ἔφη, ὦ
βέλτιστε, σὺ γὰρ τούτων ἐπιστήμων, τί χρὴ
ποιεῖν; Οὐδὲν ἄλλο, ἔφη, ἢ πιόντα περιιέναι,
B ἕως ἄν σου βάρος ἐν τοῖς σκέλεσι γένηται, ἔπειτα
κατακεῖσθαι· καὶ οὕτως αὐτὸ ποιήσει. καὶ ἅμα
ὤρεξε τὴν κύλικα τῷ Σωκράτει· καὶ ὃς λαβὼν
καὶ μάλα ἵλεως, ὦ Ἐχέκρατες, οὐδὲν τρέσας οὐδὲ
διαφθείρας οὔτε τοῦ χρώματος οὔτε τοῦ προσώ-
που, ἀλλ᾽ ὥσπερ εἰώθει ταυρηδὸν ὑποβλέψας
πρὸς τὸν ἄνθρωπον, Τί λέγεις, ἔφη, περὶ τοῦδε
τοῦ πώματος πρὸς τὸ ἀποσπεῖσαί τινι; ἔξεστιν
ἢ οὔ; Τοσοῦτον, ἔφη, ὦ Σώκρατες, τρίβομεν,
ὅσον οἰόμεθα μέτριον εἶναι πιεῖν. Μανθάνω, ἢ
C δ᾽ ὅς· ἀλλ᾽ εὔχεσθαί γέ πού τοῖς θεοῖς ἔξεστί
τε καὶ χρή, τὴν μετοίκησιν τὴν ἐνθένδε ἐκεῖσε

---

[1] Schanz brackets εἰκότως, following Hirschig.

I know that others have taken the poison very late, after the order has come to them, and in the meantime have eaten and drunk and some of them enjoyed the society of those whom they loved. Do not hurry; for there is still time."

And Socrates said: "Crito, those whom you mention are right in doing as they do, for they think they gain by it; and I shall be right in not doing as they do; for I think I should gain nothing by taking the poison a little later. I should only make myself ridiculous in my own eyes if I clung to life and spared it, when there is no more profit in it. Come," he said, "do as I ask and do not refuse."

Thereupon Crito nodded to the boy who was standing near. The boy went out and stayed a long time, then came back with the man who was to administer the poison, which he brought with him in a cup ready for use. And when Socrates saw him, he said: "Well, my good man, you know about these things; what must I do?" "Nothing," he replied, "except drink the poison and walk about till your legs feel heavy; then lie down, and the poison will take effect of itself."

At the same time he held out the cup to Socrates. He took it, and very gently, Echecrates, without trembling or changing colour or expression, but looking up at the man with wide open eyes, as was his custom, said: "What do you say about pouring a libation to some deity from this cup? May I, or not?" "Socrates," said he, "we prepare only as much as we think is enough." "I understand," said Socrates; "but I may and must pray to the gods that my departure hence be a fortunate one; so I

εὐτυχῆ γενέσθαι· ἃ δὴ καὶ ἐγὼ εὔχομαί τε καὶ γένοιτο ταύτῃ. καὶ ἅμ' εἰπὼν ταῦτα ἐπισχόμενος καὶ
μάλα εὐχερῶς καὶ εὐκόλως ἐξέπιεν. καὶ ἡμῶν οἱ
πολλοὶ τέως μὲν ἐπιεικῶς οἷοί τε ἦσαν κατέχειν
τὸ μὴ δακρύειν, ὡς δὲ εἴδομεν πίνοντά τε καὶ
πεπωκότα, οὐκέτι, ἀλλ' ἐμοῦ γε βίᾳ καὶ αὐτοῦ
ἀστακτὶ ἐχώρει τὰ δάκρυα, ὥστε ἐγκαλυψάμενος
ἀπέκλαιον ἐμαυτόν· οὐ γὰρ δὴ ἐκεῖνόν γε, ἀλλὰ
D τὴν ἐμαυτοῦ τύχην, οἵου ἀνδρὸς ἑταίρου ἐστερη-
μένος εἴην. ὁ δὲ Κρίτων ἔτι πρότερος ἐμοῦ,
ἐπειδὴ οὐχ οἷός τ' ἦν κατέχειν τὰ δάκρυα,
ἐξανέστη. Ἀπολλόδωρος δὲ καὶ ἐν τῷ ἔμπροσθεν χρόνῳ οὐδὲν ἐπαύετο δακρύων, καὶ δὴ καὶ
τότε ἀναβρυχησάμενος κλαίων καὶ[1] ἀγανακτῶν
οὐδένα ὅντινα οὐ κατέκλασε τῶν παρόντων πλήν
γε αὐτοῦ Σωκράτους. ἐκεῖνος δέ, Οἷα, ἔφη,
ποιεῖτε, ὦ θαυμάσιοι. ἐγὼ μέντοι οὐχ ἥκιστα
τούτου ἕνεκα τὰς γυναῖκας ἀπέπεμψα, ἵνα μὴ
τοιαῦτα πλημμελοῖεν· καὶ γὰρ ἀκήκοα, ὅτι ἐν
E εὐφημίᾳ χρὴ τελευτᾶν. ἀλλ' ἡσυχίαν τε ἄγετε
καὶ καρτερεῖτε. καὶ ἡμεῖς ἀκούσαντες ᾐσχύνθη-
μέν τε καὶ ἐπέσχομεν τοῦ δακρύειν. ὁ δὲ περιελ-
θών, ἐπειδὴ οἱ βαρύνεσθαι ἔφη τὰ σκέλη, κατε-
κλίθη ὕπτιος· οὕτω γὰρ ἐκέλευεν ὁ ἄνθρωπος·
καὶ ἅμα ἐφαπτόμενος αὐτοῦ οὗτος ὁ δοὺς τὸ
φάρμακον,[2] διαλιπὼν χρόνον ἐπεσκόπει τοὺς πόδας
καὶ τὰ σκέλη, κἄπειτα σφόδρα πιέσας αὐτοῦ τὸν
πόδα ἤρετο, εἰ αἰσθάνοιτο· ὁ δ' οὐκ ἔφη· καὶ μετὰ
118 τοῦτο αὖθις τὰς κνήμας· καὶ ἐπανιὼν οὕτως ἡμῖν

---

[1] Schanz brackets κλαίων καὶ.
[2] Schanz follows Upton and others in bracketing οὗτος . . .
φάρμακον.

offer this prayer, and may it be granted." With these words he raised the cup to his lips and very cheerfully and quietly drained it. Up to that time most of us had been able to restrain our tears fairly well, but when we watched him drinking and saw that he had drunk the poison, we could do so no longer, but in spite of myself my tears rolled down in floods, so that I wrapped my face in my cloak and wept for myself; for it was not for him that I wept, but for my own misfortune in being deprived of such a friend. Crito had got up and gone away even before I did, because he could not restrain his tears. But Apollodorus, who had been weeping all the time before, then wailed aloud in his grief and made us all break down, except Socrates himself. But he said, "What conduct is this, you strange men! I sent the women away chiefly for this very reason, that they might not behave in this absurd way; for I have heard that it is best to die in silence. Keep quiet and be brave.'' Then we were ashamed and controlled our tears. He walked about and, when he said his legs were heavy, lay down on his back, for such was the advice of the attendant. The man who had administered the poison laid his hands on him and after a while examined his feet and legs, then pinched his foot hard and asked if he felt it. He said "No"; then after that, his thighs; and passing upwards in

ἐπεδείκνυτο, ὅτι ψύχοιτό τε καὶ πηγνῦτο. καὶ
αὖθις[1] ἥπτετο καὶ εἶπεν ὅτι, ἐπειδὰν πρὸς τῇ
καρδίᾳ γένηται αὐτῷ, τότε οἰχήσεται. ἤδη οὖν
σχεδόν τι αὐτοῦ ἦν τὰ περὶ τὸ ἦτρον ψυχόμενα,
καὶ ἐκκαλυψάμενος, ἐνεκεκάλυπτο γάρ, εἶπεν,
ὃ δὴ τελευταῖον ἐφθέγξατο· Ὦ Κρίτων, ἔφη,
τῷ Ἀσκληπιῷ ὀφείλομεν ἀλεκτρυόνα· ἀλλὰ
ἀπόδοτε καὶ μὴ ἀμελήσητε. Ἀλλὰ ταῦτα,
ἔφη, ἔσται, ὁ Κρίτων· ἀλλ᾽ ὅρα, εἴ τι ἄλλο
λέγεις. ταῦτα ἐρομένου αὐτοῦ οὐδὲν ἔτι ἀπεκρίνατο, ἀλλ᾽ ὀλίγον χρόνον διαλιπὼν ἐκινήθη τε καὶ
ὁ ἄνθρωπος ἐξεκάλυψεν αὐτόν, καὶ ὃς τὰ ὄμματα
ἔστησεν· ἰδὼν δὲ ὁ Κρίτων συνέλαβε τὸ στόμα
καὶ τοὺς ὀφθαλμούς.

67. Ἥδε ἡ τελευτή, ὦ Ἐχέκρατες, τοῦ ἑταίρου
ἡμῖν ἐγένετο, ἀνδρός, ὡς ἡμεῖς φαῖμεν ἄν, τῶν
τότε ὧν ἐπειράθημεν ἀρίστου καὶ ἄλλως[2] φρονι-
μωτάτου καὶ δικαιοτάτου.

---

[1] αὖθις, Forster. αὐτὸς, BCDE. αὖ, Schanz.
[2] Schanz brackets ἄλλως.

this way he showed us that he was growing cold and rigid. And again he touched him and said that when it reached his heart, he would be gone. The chill had now reached the region about the groin, and uncovering his face, which had been covered, he said—and these were his last words—" Crito, we owe a cock to Aesculapius. Pay it and do not neglect it." "That," said Crito, "shall be done; but see if you have anything else to say." To this question he made no reply, but after a little while he moved; the attendant uncovered him; his eyes were fixed. And Crito when he saw it, closed his mouth and eyes.

Such was the end, Echecrates, of our friend, who was, as we may say, of all those of his time whom we have known, the best and wisest and most righteous man.

PHAEDRUS

INTRODUCTION TO THE *PHAEDRUS*

THE *Phaedrus* is pre-eminent among the dialogues of Plato for the variety of its contents and style, the richness of its imaginative description, and the sportive humour of its conversation. The chief theme of the dialogue is rhetoric, the art of speaking, a subject which formed an important part of the oral and written instruction of the sophists. Plato, and herein he agrees with the sophists, assumes that the result aimed at by rhetoric is persuasiveness, ability to lead the minds of the hearers to a particular belief or action. For the attainment of this result, the sophists claimed that knowledge of the truth concerning the subject under discussion is not essential; all that is necessary is ability to make one's conclusions seem probable. Plato shows that only the man who knows the truth can know what will seem probable; and he must also know the minds or souls to be persuaded. This he cannot do without a knowledge of the nature of the soul. Now knowledge of the truth concerning the various subjects of discourse and knowledge of all the different classes of human souls must be supplemented by knowledge of the different kinds of argument and of the various niceties of speech taught by the sophists. Only he who has acquired all this knowledge is a perfect orator, so far as perfection is attainable by man; but the acquisition

of this knowledge is a great task, which no one would undertake merely for the purpose of persuading his fellows ; a higher purpose, the perfection of his soul and the desire to serve the gods, must animate the spirit of the student of the real art of rhetoric.

But if rhetoric is the chief theme of the dialogue, it is not by any means the only theme. The rationalistic (Euhemeristic) explanation of myths is briefly discussed and rejected, the higher and lower forms of love are analysed, the nature of the soul is described in the beautiful figure of the charioteer and his two horses, and here, as in the *Phaedo*, the doctrine of ideas and its derivative, the doctrine of reminiscence, are intimately connected with the description of the life of the soul. Yet, formally, at any rate, the other subjects of the dialogue are subordinate to the discussion of rhetoric. The processes of collection and division, by which a number of particulars may be brought together under one head and a general concept may be divided, are clearly stated. The latter is of such importance in the dialectic method, which for Plato was the only correct method of reasoning, that we may well believe the discussion of rhetoric to have been undertaken in part for the purpose of giving a concise and clear statement of this principle.

In this dialogue, as in the *Phaedo*, we find the soul justly rewarded or punished for conduct in this life ; but the soul is here described as made up of a charioteer and two horses, whereas in the *Phaedo* it is one and indivisible ; but the description of the soul in the *Phaedrus* is confessedly and obviously figurative, and the simple, uniform nature of the soul

is arrived at in the *Phaedo* by serious argument. It is therefore evident that Plato did not consider the soul a composite creature, but a single being. The two horses, then, represent not distinct parts of the soul, but modes of the soul as it is affected by its contact with the body; the good horse typifies the influence of the emotions, the bad horse that of the appetites, and the charioteer is reason. It is important to bear in mind that the description of the soul in the *Phaedrus* is figurative, otherwise we are involved in hopeless confusion in any attempt to determine Plato's conception of the soul. Since the *Phaedo* and the *Phaedrus* were probably written about the same time, no real disagreement between them is to be assumed.

The first of the three discourses on love is ascribed to the famous orator, Lysias, son of Cephalus, and the question has been much discussed whether it is really a work of Lysias which Plato has inserted here. All the extant speeches of Lysias were composed to be spoken in court or at least on public occasions. We have no specimen of a discourse written by him purely as an example of his skill or for the delectation of his audience, nor do we know that he ever wrote such discourses. The discourse on love is certainly in the style of Lysias, that is to say, it approaches the style of his extant speeches as nearly as a discourse on such a subject can be expected to approach the style of a speech intended for delivery in a court of law; but Plato was a consummate literary artist, and there is surely every reason to believe that he could imitate the style of Lysias if he chose. Similarity to the style of Lysias is therefore no sufficient reason for the belief that

the discourse is not Plato's composition, especially as
the introduction of a genuine discourse by Lysias
would impair the unity, and, to a certain extent, the
dignity of the dialogue.

Toward the end of the *Phaedrus*, Plato inserts a
remarkable discussion of the relative value of the
spoken and the written word.   It is somewhat
startling to find so voluminous a writer maintaining
that the written word is only a plaything, or, at best,
a reminder; yet this must, apparently, be accepted
as his deliberate judgment.   In the Academy he
laid great stress upon oral instruction, and this
passage seems to indicate that he considered that
instruction more important than his writings.   It is
interesting to find this judgment of the written
word in a dialogue in which the playful element is
so strong.

Of Phaedrus, the only interlocutor and the sole
audience of Socrates in this dialogue, little or nothing
is known except what we learn from Plato.   He was
the son of Pythocles, of the Attic deme of Myrrhinus.
He appears in several dialogues of Plato as a follower
of Socrates, but no writings of his are extant, if any
ever existed.   Diogenes Laertius (iii., 29, 31), speaks
of him as Plato's favourite.   Some of the persons
mentioned in the dialogue are so well known that no
further account of them is necessary.   Such are the
great orator Lysias, the sophist and rhetorician
Gorgias of Leontini, the philosopher Zeno of Elea
(who masquerades under the name of Palamedes,
261 D), the distinguished sophist Protagoras of
Abdera, Hippocrates, the "father of medicine," and
the rhetorician, orator, and sage Isocrates. Acumenus
and his son, Eryximachus, were Athenian physicians,

INTRODUCTION TO THE *PHAEDRUS*

Herodicus was a physician of Megara, Morychus was an Athenian of some means, whose house had apparently been bought by Epicrates, who is described by a scholiast as an orator and demagogue. The other persons mentioned, Tisias of Sicily, Thrasymachus of Chalcedon, Theodorus of Byzantium, Evenus of Paros, Prodicus of Ceos, Hippias of Elis, Polus of Agrigentum, and his teacher, Licymnius, were all sophists and rhetoricians, whose inventiveness in the matter of rhetorical nomenclature is ridiculed.

Separate editions of the *Phaedrus* are few. The only one which appears to demand special mention is that of W. H. Thompson (1868).

ΦΑΙΔΡΟΣ

[Η ΠΕΡΙ ΚΑΛΟΥ· ΗΘΙΚΟΣ]

St.
III.
p. 227

ΤΑ ΤΟΥ ΔΙΑΛΟΓΟΥ ΠΡΟΣΩΠΑ

ΣΩΚΡΑΤΗΣ ΚΑΙ ΦΑΙΔΡΟΣ

A   1. ΣΩΚΡΑΤΗΣ. Ὦ φίλε Φαῖδρε, ποῖ δὴ καὶ πόθεν;

ΦΑΙΔΡΟΣ. Παρὰ Λυσίου, ὦ Σώκρατες, τοῦ Κεφάλου· πορεύομαι δὲ πρὸς περίπατον ἔξω τείχους. συχνὸν γὰρ ἐκεῖ διέτριψα χρόνον καθήμενος ἐξ ἑωθινοῦ· τῷ δὲ σῷ καὶ ἐμῷ ἑταίρῳ πειθόμενος Ἀκουμενῷ κατὰ τὰς ὁδοὺς ποιοῦμαι τοὺς περιπάτους· φησὶ γὰρ ἀκοπωτέρους εἶναι B τῶν ἐν τοῖς δρόμοις.

ΣΩΚΡΑΤΗΣ. Καλῶς γάρ, ὦ ἑταῖρε, λέγει. ἀτὰρ Λυσίας ἦν, ὡς ἔοικεν, ἐν ἄστει.

ΦΑΙΔΡΟΣ. Ναί, παρ' Ἐπικράτει, ἐν τῇδε τῇ πλησίον τοῦ Ὀλυμπίου οἰκίᾳ τῇ Μορυχίᾳ.

ΣΩΚΡΑΤΗΣ. Τίς οὖν δὴ ἦν ἡ διατριβή; ἢ δῆλον ὅτι τῶν λόγων ὑμᾶς Λυσίας εἰστία;

ΦΑΙΔΡΟΣ. Πεύσει, εἴ σοι σχολὴ προϊόντι ἀκούειν.

ΣΩΚΡΑΤΗΣ. Τί δέ; οὐκ ἂν οἴει με κατὰ Πίν-

412

PHAEDRUS

[or ON THE BEAUTIFUL, ethical]

CHARACTERS
Socrates, Phaedrus

socrates. Dear Phaedrus, whither away, and where do you come from?

phaedrus. From Lysias, Socrates, the son of Cephalus; and I am going for a walk outside the wall. For I spent a long time there with Lysias, sitting since early morning; and on the advice of your friend and mine, Acumenus, I am taking my walk on the roads; for he says they are less fatiguing than the streets.

socrates. He is right, my friend. Then Lysias, it seems, was in the city?

phaedrus. Yes, at Epicrates' house, the one that belonged to Morychus, near the Olympieum.

socrates. What was your conversation? But it is obvious that Lysias entertained you with his speeches.

phaedrus. You shall hear, if you have leisure to walk along and listen.

socrates. What? Don't you believe that I

δαρον καὶ ἀσχολίας ὑπέρτερον πρᾶγμα ποιήσα-
σθαι τὸ σήν τε καὶ Λυσίου διατριβὴν ἀκοῦσαι;

C   ΦΑΙΔΡΟΣ. Πρόαγε δή.

ΣΩΚΡΑΤΗΣ. Λέγοις ἄν.

ΦΑΙΔΡΟΣ. Καὶ μήν, ὦ Σώκρατες, προσήκουσά
γέ σοι ἡ ἀκοή. ὁ γάρ τοι λόγος ἦν, περὶ ὃν
διετρίβομεν, οὐκ οἶδ᾽ ὅντινα τρόπον ἐρωτικός.
γέγραφε γὰρ δὴ ὁ Λυσίας πειρώμενόν τινα τῶν
καλῶν, οὐχ ὑπ᾽ ἐραστοῦ δέ, ἀλλ᾽ αὐτὸ δὴ τοῦτο
καὶ κεκόμψευται· λέγει γὰρ ὡς χαριστέον μὴ
ἐρῶντι μᾶλλον ἢ ἐρῶντι.

ΣΩΚΡΑΤΗΣ. Ὦ γενναῖος, εἴθε γράψειεν ὡς χρὴ
πένητι μᾶλλον ἢ πλουσίῳ, καὶ πρεσβυτέρῳ ἢ
νεωτέρῳ, καὶ ὅσα ἄλλα ἐμοί τε πρόσεστι καὶ τοῖς
D πολλοῖς ἡμῶν· ἢ γὰρ ἂν ἀστεῖοι καὶ δημωφελεῖς
εἶεν οἱ λόγοι. ἔγωγ᾽ οὖν οὕτως ἐπιτεθύμηκα
ἀκοῦσαι, ὥστ᾽ ἐὰν βαδίζων ποιῇ τὸν περίπατον
Μέγαράδε, καὶ κατὰ Ἡρόδικον προσβὰς τῷ τείχει
πάλιν ἀπίῃς, οὐ μή σου ἀπολειφθῶ.

ΦΑΙΔΡΟΣ. Πῶς λέγεις, ὦ βέλτιστε Σώκρατες;
228 οἴει με, ἃ Λυσίας ἐν πολλῷ χρόνῳ κατὰ σχολὴν
συνέθηκε, δεινότατος ὢν τῶν νῦν γράφειν, ταῦτα
ἰδιώτην ὄντα ἀπομνημονεύσειν ἀξίως ἐκείνου;

---

[1] Pindar *Isthm.* i. 1. Μᾶτερ ἐμά, τὸ τεόν, χρύσασπι Θήβα,
πρᾶγμα καὶ ἀσχολίας ὑπέρτερον θήσομαι. "My mother, Thebes
of the golden shield, I will consider thy interest greater even
than business."

[2] Herodicus, Sch.: ἰατρὸς ἦν καὶ τὰ γυμνάσια ἔξω τείχους
ἐποιεῖτο, ἀρχόμενος ἀπό τινος διαστήματος οὐ μακροῦ ἀλλὰ συμμέ-
τρου, ἄχρι τοῦ τείχους, καὶ ἀναστρέφων. "He was a physician
and exercised outside the wall, beginning at some distance,
not great but moderate, going as far as the wall and turning
back."

consider hearing your conversation with Lysias " a greater thing even than business," as Pindar says ? [1]

PHAEDRUS.   Lead on, then.

SOCRATES.   Speak.

PHAEDRUS.   Indeed, Socrates, you are just the man to hear it.   For the discourse about which we conversed, was in a way, a love-speech.   For Lysias has represented one of the beauties being tempted, but not by a lover; this is just the clever thing about it ; for he says that favours should be granted rather to the one who is not in love than to the lover.

SOCRATES.   O noble Lysias !   I wish he would write that they should be granted to the poor rather than to the rich, to the old rather than to the young, and so of all the other qualities that I and most of us have ; for truly his discourse would be witty and of general utility.   I am so determined to hear you, that I will not leave you, even if you extend your walk to Megara, and, as Herodicus says, go to the wall and back again. [2]

PHAEDRUS.   What are you saying, my dear Socrates ? Do you suppose that I, who am a mere ordinary man, can tell from memory, in a way that is worthy of Lysias, what he, the cleverest writer of our day, composed at his leisure and took a long time for ?

πολλοῦ γε δέω· καί τοι ἐβουλόμην γ' ἂν μᾶλλον
ἤ μοι πολὺ χρυσίον γενέσθαι.

2. ΣΩΚΡΑΤΗΣ. Ὦ Φαῖδρε, εἰ ἐγὼ Φαῖδρον
ἀγνοῶ, καὶ ἐμαυτοῦ ἐπιλέλησμαι. ἀλλὰ γὰρ
οὐδέτερά ἐστι τούτων· εὖ οἶδα ὅτι Λυσίου λόγον
ἀκούων ἐκεῖνος οὐ μόνον ἅπαξ ἤκουσεν, ἀλλὰ
πολλάκις ἐπαναλαμβάνων ἐκέλευέν οἱ λέγειν· ὁ δὲ
B ἐπείθετο προθύμως. τῷ δὲ οὐδὲ ταῦτα ἦν ἱκανά,
ἀλλὰ τελευτῶν παραλαβὼν τὸ βιβλίον ἃ μάλιστα
ἐπεθύμει ἐπεσκόπει, καὶ τοῦτο δρῶν, ἐξ ἑωθινοῦ
καθήμενος, ἀπειπὼν εἰς περίπατον ᾔει, ὡς μὲν ἐγὼ
οἶμαι, νὴ τὸν κύνα, ἐξεπιστάμενος τὸν λόγον, εἰ
μὴ πάνυ τις[1] ἦν μακρός. ἐπορεύετο δ' ἐκτὸς
τείχους, ἵνα μελετῴη. ἀπαντήσας δὲ τῷ νοσοῦντι
περὶ λόγων ἀκοήν, ἰδὼν μὲν ἥσθη, ὅτι ἕξοι τὸν
C συγκορυβαντιῶντα, καὶ προάγειν ἐκέλευε· δεο-
μένου δὲ λέγειν τοῦ τῶν λόγων ἐραστοῦ, ἐθρύπτετο
ὡς δὴ οὐκ ἐπιθυμῶν λέγειν· τελευτῶν δὲ ἔμελλε,
καὶ εἰ μή τις ἑκὼν ἀκούοι, βίᾳ ἐρεῖν. σὺ οὖν, ὦ
Φαῖδρε, αὐτοῦ δεήθητι, ὅπερ τάχα πάντως ποιήσει,
νῦν ἤδη ποιεῖν.

ΦΑΙΔΡΟΣ. Ἐμοὶ ὡς ἀληθῶς πολὺ κράτιστόν
ἐστιν οὕτως ὅπως δύναμαι λέγειν. ὥς μοι δοκεῖς
σὺ οὐδαμῶς με ἀφήσειν, πρὶν ἂν εἴπω ἁμῶς
γέ πως.

ΣΩΚΡΑΤΗΣ. Πάνυ γάρ σοι ἀληθῆ δοκῶ.

D 3. ΦΑΙΔΡΟΣ. Οὑτωσὶ τοίνυν ποιήσω. τῷ ὄντι
γάρ, ὦ Σώκρατες, παντὸς μᾶλλον τά γε ῥήματα
οὐκ ἐξέμαθον· τὴν μέντοι διάνοιαν σχεδὸν ἁπάντων, οἷς ἔφη διαφέρειν τὰ τοῦ ἐρῶντος ἢ τὰ τοῦ
μή, ἐν κεφαλαίοις ἐφεξῆς δίειμι, ἀρξάμενος ἀπὸ
τοῦ πρώτου.

[1] τις B.T. τι Schanz.

Far from it; and yet I would rather have that ability than a good sum of money.

SOCRATES. O Phaedrus! If I don't know Phaedrus, I have forgotten myself. But since neither of these things is true, I know very well that when listening to Lysias he did not hear once only, but often urged him to repeat; and he gladly obeyed. Yet even that was not enough for Phaedrus, but at last he borrowed the book and read what he especially wished, and doing this he sat from early morning. Then, when he grew tired, he went for a walk, with the speech, as I believe, by the Dog, learned by heart, unless it was very long. And he was going outside the wall to practise it. And meeting the man who is sick with the love of discourse, he was glad when he saw him, because he would have someone to share his revel, and told him to lead on. But when the lover of discourse asked him to speak, he feigned coyness, as if he did not yearn to speak; at last, however, even if no one would listen willingly, he was bound to speak whether or no. So, Phaedrus, ask him to do now what he will presently do anyway.

PHAEDRUS. Truly it is best for me to speak as I may; since it is clear that you will not let me go until I speak somehow or other.

SOCRATES. You have a very correct idea about me.

PHAEDRUS. Then this is what I will do. Really, Socrates, I have not at all learned the words by heart; but I will repeat the general sense of the whole, the points in which he said the lover was superior to the non-lover, giving them in summary, one after the other, beginning with the first:

ΣΩΚΡΑΤΗΣ. Δείξας γε πρῶτον, ὦ φιλότης, τί ἄρα ἐν τῇ ἀριστερᾷ ἔχεις ὑπὸ τῷ ἱματίῳ. τοπάζω γάρ σε ἔχειν τὸν λόγον αὐτόν. εἰ δὲ τοῦτό ἐστιν, E οὑτωσὶ διανοοῦ περὶ ἐμοῦ, ὡς ἐγώ σε πάνυ μὲν φιλῶ, παρόντος δὲ Λυσίου ἐμαυτόν σοι ἐμμελετᾶν παρέχειν οὐ πάνυ δέδοκται. ἀλλ' ἴθι, δείκνυε.

ΦΑΙΔΡΟΣ. Παῦε. ἐκκέκρουκάς με ἐλπίδος, ὦ Σώκρατες, ἣν εἶχον ἐν σοὶ ὡς ἐγγυμνασόμενος. ἀλλὰ ποῦ δὴ βούλει καθιζόμενοι ἀναγνῶμεν;

229 ΣΩΚΡΑΤΗΣ. Δεῦρ' ἐκτραπόμενοι κατὰ τὸν Ἰλισσὸν ἴωμεν, εἶτα ὅπου ἂν δόξῃ ἐν ἡσυχίᾳ καθιζησόμεθα.

ΦΑΙΔΡΟΣ. Εἰς καιρόν, ὡς ἔοικεν, ἀνυπόδητος ὢν ἔτυχον· σὺ μὲν γὰρ δὴ ἀεί. ῥᾷστον οὖν ἡμῖν κατὰ τὸ ὑδάτιον βρέχουσι τοὺς πόδας ἰέναι, καὶ οὐκ ἀηδές, ἄλλως τε καὶ τήνδε τὴν ὥραν τοῦ ἔτους τε καὶ τῆς ἡμέρας.

ΣΩΚΡΑΤΗΣ. Πρόαγε δή, καὶ σκόπει ἅμα ὅπου καθιζησόμεθα.

ΦΑΙΔΡΟΣ. Ὁρᾷς οὖν ἐκείνην τὴν ὑψηλοτάτην πλάτανον;

ΣΩΚΡΑΤΗΣ Τί μήν;

B ΦΑΙΔΡΟΣ. Ἐκεῖ σκιά τ' ἐστὶ καὶ πνεῦμα μέτριον, καὶ πόα καθίζεσθαι ἢ ἂν βουλώμεθα κατακλιθῆναι.

ΣΩΚΡΑΤΗΣ. Προάγοις ἄν.

ΦΑΙΔΡΟΣ. Εἰπέ μοι, ὦ Σώκρατες, οὐκ ἐνθένδε μέντοι ποθὲν ἀπὸ τοῦ Ἰλισσοῦ λέγεται ὁ Βορέας τὴν Ὠρείθυιαν ἁρπάσαι;

ΣΩΚΡΑΤΗΣ. Λέγεται γάρ.

ΦΑΙΔΡΟΣ. Ἆρ' οὖν ἐνθένδε; χαρίεντα γοῦν καὶ

SOCRATES. Yes, my dear, when you have first shown me what you have in your left hand, under your cloak. For I suspect you have the actual discourse. And if that is the case, believe this of me, that I am very fond of you, but when Lysias is here I have not the slightest intention of lending you my ears to practise on. Come now, show it.

PHAEDRUS. Stop. You have robbed me of the hope I had of practising on you. But where shall we sit and read?

SOCRATES. Let us turn aside here and go along the Ilissus; then we can sit down quietly wherever we please.

PHAEDRUS. I am fortunate, it seems, in being barefoot; you are so always. It is easiest then for us to go along the brook with our feet in the water, and it is not unpleasant, especially at this time of the year and the day.

SOCRATES. Lead on then, and look out for a good place where we may sit.

PHAEDRUS. Do you see that very tall plane tree?

SOCRATES. What of it?

PHAEDRUS. There is shade there and a moderate breeze and grass to sit on, or, if we like, to lie down on.

SOCRATES. Lead the way.

PHAEDRUS. Tell me, Socrates, is it not from some place along here by the Ilissus that Boreas is said to have carried off Oreithyia?

SOCRATES. Yes, that is the story.

PHAEDRUS. Well, is it from here? The streamlet

καθαρὰ καὶ διαφανῆ τὰ ὑδάτια φαίνεται, καὶ
ἐπιτήδεια κόραις παίζειν παρ᾽ αὐτά.

C   ΣΩΚΡΑΤΗΣ. Οὔκ, ἀλλὰ κάτωθεν ὅσον δύ᾽ ἢ τρία
στάδια, ᾗ πρὸς τὸ τῆς Ἄγρας διαβαίνομεν· καὶ
πού τίς ἐστι βωμὸς αὐτόθι Βορέου.

ΦΑΙΔΡΟΣ. Οὐ πάνυ νενόηκα· ἀλλ᾽ εἰπὲ πρὸς
Διός, ὦ Σώκρατες· σὺ τοῦτο τὸ μυθολόγημα
πείθει ἀληθὲς εἶναι;

4. ΣΩΚΡΑΤΗΣ. Ἀλλ᾽ εἰ ἀπιστοίην, ὥσπερ οἱ
σοφοί, οὐκ ἂν ἄτοπος εἴην· εἶτα σοφιζόμενος
φαίην ἂν αὐτὴν πνεῦμα Βορέου κατὰ τῶν πλησίον
πετρῶν σὺν Φαρμακείᾳ παίζουσαν ὦσαι, καὶ
D οὕτω δὴ τελευτήσασαν λεχθῆναι ὑπὸ τοῦ Βορέου
ἀναρπαστὸν γεγονέναι. ἐγὼ δέ, ὦ Φαῖδρε, ἄλλως
μὲν τὰ τοιαῦτα χαρίεντα ἡγοῦμαι, λίαν δὲ δεινοῦ
καὶ ἐπιπόνου καὶ οὐ πάνυ εὐτυχοῦς ἀνδρός, κατ᾽
ἄλλο μὲν οὐδέν, ὅτι δ᾽ αὐτῷ ἀνάγκη μετὰ τοῦτο τὸ
τῶν Ἱπποκενταύρων εἶδος ἐπανορθοῦσθαι, καὶ
αὖθις τὸ τῆς Χιμαίρας, καὶ ἐπιρρεῖ δὲ ὄχλος
τοιούτων Γοργόνων καὶ Πηγάσων καὶ ἄλλων
E ἀμηχάνων πλήθη τε καὶ ἀτοπίαι τερατολόγων
τινῶν φύσεων· αἷς εἴ τις ἀπιστῶν προσβιβᾷ κατὰ
τὸ εἰκὸς ἕκαστον, ἅτε ἀγροίκῳ τινὶ σοφίᾳ χρώμενος, πολλῆς αὐτῷ σχολῆς δεήσει. ἐμοὶ δὲ πρὸς
αὐτὰ οὐδαμῶς ἐστι σχολή· τὸ δὲ αἴτιον, ὦ φίλε,
τούτου τόδε· οὐ δύναμαί πω κατὰ τὸ Δελφικὸν
γράμμα γνῶναι ἐμαυτόν· γελοῖον δή μοι φαίνεται,

looks very pretty and pure and clear and fit for girls
to play by.

SOCRATES. No, the place is about two or three
furlongs farther down, where you cross over to the
precinct of Agra; and there is an altar of Boreas
somewhere thereabouts.

PHAEDRUS. I have never noticed it. But, for
Heaven's sake, Socrates, tell me; do you believe this
tale is true?

SOCRATES. If I disbelieved, as the wise men do, I
should not be extraordinary; then I might give a
rational explanation, that a blast of Boreas, the north
wind, pushed her off the neighbouring rocks as she
was playing with Pharmacea, and that when she had
died in this manner she was said to have been carried
off by Boreas.[1] But I, Phaedrus, think such explanations are very pretty in general, but are the inventions
of a very clever and laborious and not altogether envi-
able man, for no other reason than because after this
he must explain the forms of the Centaurs, and then
that of the Chimaera, and there presses in upon him
a whole crowd of such creatures, Gorgons and Pegas,
and multitudes of strange, inconceivable, portentous
natures. If anyone disbelieves in these, and with a
rustic sort of wisdom, undertakes to explain each in
accordance with probability, he will need a great
deal of leisure. But I have no leisure for them at
all; and the reason, my friend, is this: I am not yet
able, as the Delphic inscription has it, to know myself; so it seems to me ridiculous, when I do not yet

---

[1] The MSS. insert here ἢ ἐξ Ἀρείου πάγου· λέγεται γὰρ αὖ
καὶ οὗτος ὁ λόγος, ὡς ἐκεῖθεν ἀλλ' οὐκ ἐνθένδε ἡρπάσθη, "or from
the Areopagus, for this story is also told, that she was
carried off from there and not from here." Schanz follows
Bast and many editors in rejecting this as a gloss.

230 τοῦτο ἔτι ἀγνοοῦντα τὰ ἀλλότρια σκοπεῖν. ὅθεν
δὴ χαίρειν ἐάσας ταῦτα, πειθόμενος δὲ τῷ νομιζο-
μένῳ περὶ αὐτῶν, ὃ νυνδὴ ἔλεγον, σκοπῶ οὐ
ταῦτα ἀλλὰ ἐμαυτόν, εἴτε τι θηρίον τυγχάνω
Τυφῶνος πολυπλοκώτερον καὶ μᾶλλον ἐπιτεθυμ-
μένον, εἴτε ἡμερώτερόν τε καὶ ἁπλούστερον ζῷον,
θείας τινὸς καὶ ἀτύφου μοίρας φύσει μετέχον.
ἀτάρ, ὦ ἑταῖρε, μεταξὺ τῶν λόγων, ἆρ' οὐ τόδε ἦν
τὸ δένδρον, ἐφ' ὅπερ ἦγες ἡμᾶς;

B   ΦΑΙΔΡΟΣ. Τοῦτο μὲν οὖν αὐτό.

5. ΣΩΚΡΑΤΗΣ. Νὴ τὴν "Ηραν, καλή γε ἡ κατα-
γωγή. ἥ τε γὰρ πλάτανος αὕτη μάλ' ἀμφιλαφής
τε καὶ ὑψηλή, τοῦ τε ἄγνου τὸ ὕψος καὶ τὸ
σύσκιον πάγκαλον, καὶ ὡς ἀκμὴν ἔχει τῆς ἄνθης,
ὡς ἂν εὐωδέστατον παρέχοι τὸν τόπον· ἥ τε αὖ
πηγὴ χαριεστάτη ὑπὸ τῆς πλατάνου ῥεῖ μάλα
ψυχροῦ ὕδατος, ὥστε γε τῷ ποδὶ τεκμήρασθαι·
Νυμφῶν τέ τινων καὶ Ἀχελῴου ἱερὸν ἀπὸ τῶν

C   κορῶν τε καὶ ἀγαλμάτων ἔοικεν εἶναι. εἰ δ' αὖ
βούλει, τὸ εὔπνουν τοῦ τόπου ὡς ἀγαπητὸν καὶ
σφόδρα ἡδύ· θερινόν τε καὶ λιγυρὸν ὑπηχεῖ τῷ
τῶν τεττίγων χορῷ. πάντων δὲ κομψότατον τὸ
τῆς πόας, ὅτι ἐν ἠρέμα προσάντει ἱκανὴ πέφυκε
κατακλινέντι τὴν κεφαλὴν παγκάλως ἔχειν. ὥστε
ἄριστά σοι ἐξενάγηται, ὦ φίλε Φαῖδρε.

ΦΑΙΔΡΟΣ. Σὺ δέ γε, ὦ θαυμάσιε, ἀτοπώτατός τις
φαίνει. ἀτεχνῶς γάρ, ὃ λέγεις, ξεναγουμένῳ τινὶ

D   καὶ οὐκ ἐπιχωρίῳ ἔοικας· οὕτως ἐκ τοῦ ἄστεος
οὔτ' εἰς τὴν ὑπερορίαν ἀποδημεῖς, οὔτ' ἔξω τείχους
ἔμοιγε δοκεῖς τὸ παράπαν ἐξιέναι.

ΣΩΚΡΑΤΗΣ. Συγγίγνωσκέ μοι, ὦ ἄριστε. φιλο-
μαθὴς γάρ εἰμι· τὰ μὲν οὖν χωρία καὶ τὰ δένδρα

know that, to investigate irrelevant things. And so
I dismiss these matters and accepting the customary
belief about them, as I was saying just now, I investigate not these things, but myself, to know whether
I am a monster more complicated and more furious
than Typhon or a gentler and simpler creature, to
whom a divine and quiet lot is given by nature.
But, my friend, while we were talking, is not this
the tree to which you were leading us?

PHAEDRUS. Yes, this is it.

SOCRATES. By Hera, it is a charming resting place.
For this plane tree is very spreading and lofty, and
the tall and shady willow is very beautiful, and it is
in full bloom, so as to make the place most fragrant;
then, too, the spring is very pretty as it flows under
the plane tree, and its water is very cool, to judge
by my foot. And it seems to be a sacred place
of some nymphs and of Achelous, judging by the
figurines and statues. Then again, if you please,
how lovely and perfectly charming the breeziness
of the place is! and it resounds with the shrill
summer music of the chorus of cicadas. But the
most delightful thing of all is the grass, as it grows
on the gentle slope, thick enough to be just right
when you lay your head on it. So you have guided
the stranger most excellently, dear Phaedrus.

PHAEDRUS. You are an amazing and most remarkable person. For you really do seem exactly
like a stranger who is being guided about, and not
like a native. You don't go away from the city out
over the border, and it seems to me you don't go
outside the walls at all.

SOCRATES. Forgive me, my dear friend. You see,
I am fond of learning. Now the country places and

οὐδέν μ' ἐθέλει διδάσκειν, οἱ δ' ἐν τῷ ἄστει
ἄνθρωποι. σὺ μέντοι δοκεῖς μοι τῆς ἐξόδου τὸ
φάρμακον εὑρηκέναι. ὥσπερ γὰρ οἱ τὰ πεινῶντα
θρέμματα θαλλὸν ἤ τινα καρπὸν προσείοντες
ἄγουσιν, σὺ ἐμοὶ λόγους οὕτω προτείνων ἐν βιβλίοις τήν τε Ἀττικὴν φαίνει περιάξειν ἄπασαν
καὶ ὅποι ἂν ἄλλοσε βούλῃ. νῦν οὖν ἐν τῷ παρόντι δεῦρ' ἀφικόμενος ἐγὼ μέν μοι δοκῶ κατακεί-
σεσθαι, σὺ δ' ἐν ὁποίῳ σχήματι οἴει ῥᾷστα ἀνα-
γνώσεσθαι, τοῦθ' ἑλόμενος ἀναγίγνωσκε.

ΦΑΙΔΡΟΣ. Ἄκουε δή.

6. Περὶ μὲν τῶν ἐμῶν πραγμάτων ἐπίστασαι,
καὶ ὡς νομίζω συμφέρειν ἡμῖν γενομένων τούτων
231 ἀκήκοας· ἀξιῶ δὲ μὴ διὰ τοῦτο ἀτυχῆσαι ὧν
δέομαι, ὅτι οὐκ ἐραστὴς ὤν σου τυγχάνω. ὡς
ἐκείνοις μὲν τότε μεταμέλει ὧν ἂν εὖ ποιήσωσιν,
ἐπειδὰν τῆς ἐπιθυμίας παύσωνται· τοῖς δὲ οὐκ
ἔστι χρόνος, ἐν ᾧ μεταγνῶναι προσήκει. οὐ γὰρ
ὑπ' ἀνάγκης ἀλλ' ἑκόντες, ὡς ἂν ἄριστα περὶ τῶν
οἰκείων βουλεύσαιντο, πρὸς τὴν δύναμιν τὴν
αὑτῶν εὖ ποιοῦσιν. ἔτι δὲ οἱ μὲν ἐρῶντες σκοποῦσιν ἅ τε κακῶς διέθεντο τῶν αὑτῶν διὰ τὸν
ἔρωτα καὶ ἃ πεποιήκασιν εὖ, καὶ ὃν εἶχον πόνον
Β προστιθέντες ἡγοῦνται πάλαι τὴν ἀξίαν ἀποδεδω-
κέναι χάριν τοῖς ἐρωμένοις· τοῖς δὲ μὴ ἐρῶσιν
οὔτε τὴν τῶν οἰκείων ἀμέλειαν διὰ τοῦτο ἔστι
προφασίζεσθαι, οὔτε τοὺς παρεληλυθότας πόνους
ὑπολογίζεσθαι, οὔτε τὰς πρὸς τοὺς προσήκοντας
διαφορὰς αἰτιάσασθαι· ὥστε περιῃρημένων τοσούτων κακῶν οὐδὲν ὑπολείπεται ἀλλ' ἢ ποιεῖν
προθύμως, ὅ τι ἂν αὑτοῖς οἴωνται πράξαντες
C χαριεῖσθαι. ἔτι δὲ εἰ διὰ τοῦτο ἄξιον τοὺς

the trees won't teach me anything, and the people in
the city do. But you seem to have found the charm
to bring me out. For as people lead hungry animals
by shaking in front of them a branch of leaves or
some fruit, just so, I think, you, by holding before
me discourses in books, will lead me all over Attica
and wherever else you please. So now that I have
come here, I intend to lie down, and do you choose
the position in which you think you can read most
easily, and read.

PHAEDRUS. Hear then.

You know what my condition is, and you have
heard how I think it is to our advantage to arrange
these matters. And I claim that I ought not to
be refused what I ask because I am not your lover.
For lovers repent of the kindnesses they have done
when their passion ceases; but there is no time when
non-lovers naturally repent. For they do kindnesses
to the best of their ability, not under compulsion,
but of their free will, according to their view of
their own best interest. And besides, lovers consider
the injury they have done to their own concerns on
account of their love, and the benefits they have
conferred, and they add the trouble they have had,
and so they think they have long ago made sufficient
return to the beloved; but non-lovers cannot aver
neglect of their own affairs because of their condition, nor can they take account of the pains they
have been at in the past, nor lay any blame for
quarrels with their relatives; and so, since all these
evils are removed, there is nothing left for them but
to do eagerly what they think will please the beloved.
And besides, if lovers ought to be highly esteemed

ἐρῶντας περὶ πολλοῦ ποιεῖσθαι, ὅτι τούτους
μάλιστά φασι φιλεῖν ὧν ἂν ἐρῶσιν καὶ ἕτοιμοί
εἰσι καὶ ἐκ τῶν λόγων καὶ ἐκ τῶν ἔργων τοῖς
ἄλλοις ἀπεχθανόμενοι τοῖς ἐρωμένοις χαρίζεσθαι, ῥᾴδιον γνῶναι, εἰ ἀληθῆ λέγουσιν, ὅτι
ὅσων ἂν ὕστερον ἐρασθῶσιν, ἐκείνους αὐτῶν περὶ
πλείονος ποιήσονται, καὶ δῆλον ὅτι, ἐὰν ἐκείνοις
δοκῇ, καὶ τούτους κακῶς ποιήσουσι. καί τοι πῶς
εἰκός ἐστι τοιοῦτον πρᾶγμα προέσθαι τοιαύτην
D ἔχοντι συμφοράν, ἣν οὐδ' ἂν ἐπιχειρήσειεν οὐδεὶς
ἔμπειρος ὢν ἀποτρέπειν; καὶ γὰρ αὐτοὶ ὁμολογοῦσιν νοσεῖν μᾶλλον ἢ σωφρονεῖν, καὶ εἰδέναι ὅτι
κακῶς φρονοῦσιν, ἀλλ' οὐ δύνασθαι αὑτῶν κρατεῖν·
ὥστε πῶς ἂν εὖ φρονήσαντες ταῦτα καλῶς ἔχειν
ἡγήσαιντο περὶ ὧν οὕτω διακείμενοι βεβούλευνται;
καὶ μὲν δὴ εἰ μὲν ἐκ τῶν ἐρώντων τὸν βέλτιστον
αἱροῖο, ἐξ ὀλίγων ἄν σοι ἡ ἔκλεξις εἴη· εἰ δ' ἐκ τῶν
ἄλλων τὸν σαυτῷ ἐπιτηδειότατον, ἐκ πολλῶν·
E ὥστε πολὺ πλείων ἐλπὶς ἐν τοῖς πολλοῖς ὄντα
τυχεῖν τὸν ἄξιον τῆς σῆς φιλίας.

7. Εἰ τοίνυν τὸν νόμον τὸν καθεστηκότα
δέδοικας, μὴ πυθομένων τῶν ἀνθρώπων ὄνειδός σοι
232 γένηται, εἰκός ἐστι τοὺς μὲν ἐρῶντας, οὕτως ἂν
οἰομένους καὶ ὑπὸ τῶν ἄλλων ζηλοῦσθαι ὥσπερ
αὐτοὺς ὑφ' αὑτῶν, ἐπαρθῆναι τῷ ἔχειν καὶ
φιλοτιμουμένους ἐπιδείκνυσθαι πρὸς ἅπαντας, ὅτι
οὐκ ἄλλως αὐτοῖς πεπόνηται· τοὺς δὲ μὴ ἐρῶντας, κρείττους αὑτῶν ὄντας, τὸ βέλτιστον ἀντὶ
τῆς δόξης τῆς παρὰ τῶν ἀνθρώπων αἱρεῖσθαι.
ἔτι δὲ τοὺς μὲν ἐρῶντας πολλοὺς ἀνάγκη πυθέσθαι
426

because they say they have the greatest love for the objects of their passion, since both by word and deed they are ready to make themselves hated by others to please the beloved, it is easy to see that, if what they say is true, whenever they fall in love afterwards, they will care for the new love more than for the old and will certainly injure the old love, if that pleases the new. And how can one reasonably entrust matters of such importance to one who is afflicted with a disease such that no one of any experience would even try to cure it? For they themselves confess that they are insane, rather than in their right mind, and that they know they are foolish, but cannot control themselves; and so, how could they, when they have come to their senses, think those acts were good which they determined upon when in such a condition? And if you were to choose the best from among your lovers, your choice would be limited to a few; whereas it would be made from a great number, if you chose the most congenial from non-lovers, so that you would have a better chance, in choosing among many, of finding the one most worthy of your affection.

Now if you are afraid of public opinion, and fear that if people find out your love affair you will be disgraced, consider that lovers, believing that others would be as envious of them as they are of others, are likely to be excited by possession and in their pride to show everybody that they have not toiled in vain; but the non-lovers, since they have control of their feelings, are likely to choose what is really best, rather than to court the opinion of mankind. Moreover, many are sure to notice and see the lovers going about with their beloved ones and making

καὶ ἰδεῖν, ἀκολουθοῦντας τοῖς ἐρωμένοις, καὶ ἔργον
B τοῦτο ποιουμένους, ὥστε ὅταν ὀφθῶσι διαλεγόμενοι
ἀλλήλοις, τότε αὐτοὺς οἴονται ἢ γεγενημένης ἢ
μελλούσης ἔσεσθαι τῆς ἐπιθυμίας συνεῖναι· τοὺς
δὲ μὴ ἐρῶντας οὐδ᾽ αἰτιᾶσθαι διὰ τὴν συνουσίαν
ἐπιχειροῦσιν, εἰδότες ὅτι ἀναγκαῖόν ἐστιν ἢ διὰ
φιλίαν τῳ διαλέγεσθαι ἢ δι᾽ ἄλλην τινὰ ἡδονήν.
καὶ μὲν δὴ εἴ σοι δέος παρέστηκεν ἡγουμένῳ
χαλεπὸν εἶναι φιλίαν συμμένειν, καὶ ἄλλῳ μὲν
τρόπῳ διαφορᾶς γενομένης κοινὴν ἂν¹ ἀμφοτέροις
καταστῆναι τὴν συμφοράν, προεμένου δέ σου ἃ
C περὶ πλείστου ποιεῖ μεγάλην δὴ² σοι βλάβην ἂν
γενέσθαι, εἰκότως δὴ τοὺς ἐρῶντας μᾶλλον ἂν
φοβοῖο· πολλὰ γὰρ αὐτούς ἐστι τὰ λυποῦντα, καὶ
πάντ᾽ ἐπὶ τῇ αὑτῶν βλάβῃ νομίζουσι γίγνεσθαι.
διόπερ καὶ τὰς πρὸς τοὺς ἄλλους τῶν ἐρωμένων
συνουσίας ἀποτρέπουσιν, φοβούμενοι τοὺς μὲν
οὐσίαν κεκτημένους, μὴ χρήμασιν αὐτοὺς ὑπερ-
βάλωνται, τοὺς δὲ πεπαιδευμένους, μὴ συνέσει
κρείττους γένωνται· τῶν δ᾽ ἄλλο τι κεκτημένων
D ἀγαθὸν τὴν δύναμιν ἑκάστου φυλάττονται. πείσαντες μὲν οὖν ἀπέχθεσθαί σε τούτοις εἰς ἐρημίαν
φίλων καθιστᾶσιν, ἐὰν δὲ τὸ σεαυτοῦ σκοπῶν
ἄμεινον ἐκείνων φρονῇς, ἥξεις αὐτοῖς εἰς διαφοράν·
ὅσοι δὲ μὴ ἐρῶντες ἔτυχον, ἀλλὰ δι᾽ ἀρετὴν
ἔπραξαν ὧν ἐδέοντο, οὐκ ἂν τοῖς συνοῦσι φθονοῖεν,
ἀλλὰ τοὺς μὴ ἐθέλοντας μισοῖεν, ἡγούμενοι σ᾽ ὑπ᾽
ἐκείνων μὲν ὑπερορᾶσθαι, ὑπὸ τῶν συνόντων δὲ

¹ ἂν inserted by Hirschig and Schanz.
² δὴ here and after εἰκότως is inserted by Schanz for ἂν
of BT.

that their chief business, and so, when they are seen
talking with each other, people think they are met
in connexion with some love-matter either past or
future; but no one ever thinks of finding fault with
non-lovers because they meet, since everyone knows
that one must converse with somebody, either because
of friendship or because it is pleasant for some other
reason. And then, too, if you are frightened by the
thought that it is hard for friendship to last, and that
under other circumstances any quarrel would be an
equal misfortune to both, but that when you have sur-
rendered what you prize most highly you would be
the chief sufferer, it would be reasonable for you to
be more afraid of the lovers; for they are pained by
many things and they think everything that happens
is done for the sake of hurting them. Therefore they
prevent their loves from associating with other men,
for they fear the wealthy, lest their money give them
an advantage, and the educated, lest they prove
superior in intellect; and they are on their guard
against the influence of everyone who possesses any
other good thing. If now they persuade you to
incur the dislike of all these, they involve you in
a dearth of friends, and if you consider your own
interest and are more sensible than they, you will
have to quarrel with them. But those who are not
in love, but who have gained the satisfaction of
their desires because of their merit, would not be
jealous of those who associated with you, but
would hate those who did not wish to do so,
thinking that you are slighted by these last and
benefited by the former, so that there is much more

PLATO

E ὠφελεῖσθαι, ὥστε πολὺ πλείων ἐλπὶς φιλίαν
αὐτοῖς ἐκ τοῦ πράγματος ἢ ἔχθραν γενήσεσθαι.

8. Καὶ μὲν δὴ τῶν μὲν ἐρώντων πολλοὶ
πρότερον τοῦ σώματος ἐπεθύμησαν ἢ τὸν τρόπον
ἔγνωσαν καὶ τῶν ἄλλων οἰκείων ἔμπειροι ἐγένοντο,
ὥστε ἄδηλον εἰ ἔτι βουλήσονται φίλοι εἶναι,
233 ἐπειδὰν τῆς ἐπιθυμίας παύσωνται· τοῖς δὲ μὴ
ἐρῶσιν, οἳ καὶ πρότερον ἀλλήλοις φίλοι ὄντες
ταῦτα ἔπραξαν, οὐκ ἐξ ὧν ἂν εὖ πάθωσι ταῦτα
εἰκός ἐλάττω τὴν φιλίαν αὐτοῖς ποιῆσαι, ἀλλὰ
ταῦτα μνημεῖα καταλειφθῆναι τῶν μελλόντων
ἔσεσθαι. καὶ μὲν δὴ βελτίονί σοι προσήκει
γενέσθαι ἐμοὶ πειθομένῳ ἢ ἐραστῇ. ἐκεῖνοι μὲν
γὰρ καὶ παρὰ τὸ βέλτιστον τά τε λεγόμενα καὶ
τὰ πραττόμενα ἐπαινοῦσι, τὰ μὲν δεδιότες μὴ
B ἀπέχθωνται, τὰ δὲ καὶ αὐτοὶ χεῖρον διὰ τὴν ἐπιθυ-
μίαν γιγνώσκοντες. τοιαῦτα γὰρ ὁ ἔρως ἐπιδεί-
κνυται· δυστυχοῦντας μέν, ἃ μὴ λύπην τοῖς
ἄλλοις παρέχει, ἀνιαρὰ ποιεῖ νομίζειν· εὐτυ-
χοῦντας δὲ καὶ τὰ μὴ ἡδονῆς ἄξια παρ᾽ ἐκείνων
ἐπαίνου ἀναγκάζει τυγχάνειν· ὥστε πολὺ μᾶλλον
ἐλεεῖν τοὺς ἐρωμένους ἢ ζηλοῦν αὐτοὺς προσήκει.
ἐὰν δ᾽ ἐμοὶ πείθῃ, πρῶτον μὲν οὐ τὴν παροῦσαν
ἡδονὴν θεραπεύων συνέσομαί σοι, ἀλλὰ καὶ τὴν
C μέλλουσαν ὠφελίαν ἔσεσθαι, οὐχ ὑπ᾽ ἔρωτος
ἡττώμενος, ἀλλ᾽ ἐμαυτοῦ κρατῶν, οὐδὲ διὰ σμικρὰ
ἰσχυρὰν ἔχθραν ἀναιρούμενος, ἀλλὰ διὰ μεγάλα
βραδέως ὀλίγην ὀργὴν ποιούμενος, τῶν μὲν ἀκουσίων συγγνώμην ἔχων, τὰ δὲ ἑκούσια πειρώμενος
ἀποτρέπειν· ταῦτα γάρ ἐστι φιλίας πολὺν χρόνον
ἐσομένης τεκμήρια. εἰ δ᾽ ἄρα σοι τοῦτο παρέστηκεν. ὡς οὐχ οἷόν τε ἰσχυρὰν φιλίαν γενέσθαι,

430

likelihood that they will gain friendship than enmity from their love-affair with you.

And then, too, many lovers are moved by physical passion before they know the character or have become acquainted with the connexions of the beloved, so that it is uncertain whether they will wish to be your friends after their passion has ceased. But in the case of those who are not in love, who were your friends before entering into the closer relation, the favours received are not likely to make the friendship less, but will remain as pledges of future joys. And then, too, it will be better for your character to yield to me than to a lover. For lovers praise your words and acts beyond due measure, partly through fear of incurring your displeasure, and partly because their own judgment is obscured by their passion. For such are the exhibitions of the power of Love : he makes the unsuccessful lovers think that things are grievous which cause no pain to others, and he compels the successful to praise what ought not to give pleasure ; therefore those whom they love are more to be pitied than envied. But if you yield to me, I shall consort with you, not with a view to present pleasure only, but to future advantage also, not being overcome by passion but in full control of myself, and not taking up violent enmity because of small matters, but slowly gathering little anger when the transgressions are great, forgiving involuntary wrongs and trying to prevent intentional ones; for these are the proofs of a friendship that will endure for a long time. But if you have a notion that friendship cannot be firm

D ἐὰν μή τις ἐρῶν τυγχάνῃ, ἐνθυμεῖσθαι χρή, ὅτι
οὔτ' ἂν τοὺς υἱεῖς περὶ πολλοῦ ἐποιούμεθα οὔτ'
ἂν τοὺς πατέρας καὶ τὰς μητέρας, οὔτ' ἂν πιστοὺς
φίλους ἐκεκτήμεθα, οἳ οὐκ ἐξ ἐπιθυμίας τοιαύτης
γεγόνασιν ἀλλ' ἐξ ἑτέρων ἐπιτηδευμάτων.

9. Ἔτι δὲ εἰ χρὴ τοῖς δεομένοις μάλιστα
χαρίζεσθαι, προσήκει καὶ τῶν ἄλλων μὴ τοὺς
βελτίστους ἀλλὰ τοὺς ἀπορωτάτους εὖ ποιεῖν·
μεγίστων γὰρ ἀπαλλαγέντες κακῶν πλείστην
χάριν αὐτοῖς εἴσονται. καὶ μὲν δὴ καὶ ἐν ταῖς
E ἰδίαις δαπάναις οὐ τοὺς φίλους ἄξιον παρακαλεῖν,
ἀλλὰ τοὺς προσαιτοῦντας καὶ τοὺς δεομένους
πλησμονῆς· ἐκεῖνοι γὰρ καὶ ἀγαπήσουσιν καὶ
ἀκολουθήσουσιν καὶ ἐπὶ τὰς θύρας ἥξουσιν καὶ
μάλιστα ἡσθήσονται καὶ οὐκ ἐλαχίστην χάριν
εἴσονται καὶ πολλὰ ἀγαθὰ αὐτοῖς εὔξονται. ἀλλ'
ἴσως προσήκει οὐ τοῖς σφόδρα δεομένοις χαρίζεσθαι, ἀλλὰ τοῖς μάλιστα ἀποδοῦναι χάριν
δυναμένοις· οὐδὲ τοῖς προσαιτοῦσι μόνον, ἀλλὰ
τοῖς τοῦ πράγματος ἀξίοις· οὐδὲ ὅσοι τῆς σῆς
234 ὥρας ἀπολαύσονται, ἀλλ' οἵ τινες πρεσβυτέρῳ
γενομένῳ τῶν σφετέρων ἀγαθῶν μεταδώσουσιν·
οὐδὲ οἳ διαπραξάμενοι πρὸς τοὺς ἄλλους φιλο-
τιμήσονται, ἀλλ' οἵ τινες αἰσχυνόμενοι πρὸς
ἅπαντας σιωπήσονται· οὐδὲ τοῖς ὀλίγον χρόνον
σπουδάζουσιν, ἀλλὰ τοῖς ὁμοίως διὰ παντὸς τοῦ
βίου φίλοις ἐσομένοις· οὐδὲ οἵ τινες παυόμενοι
τῆς ἐπιθυμίας ἔχθρας πρόφασιν ζητήσουσιν, ἀλλ'
B οἳ παυσαμένοις τῆς ὥρας τότε τὴν αὐτῶν ἀρετὴν
ἐπιδείξονται. σὺ οὖν τῶν τε εἰρημένων μέμνησο,
καὶ ἐκεῖνο ἐνθυμοῦ, ὅτι τοὺς μὲν ἐρῶντας οἱ φίλοι
νουθετοῦσιν ὡς ὄντος κακοῦ τοῦ ἐπιτηδεύματος,

unless one is in love, you should bear in mind that in
that case we should not have great affection for sons
or for fathers and mothers, nor should we possess
faithful friends who have been gained not through
passion but through associations of a different kind.

Besides, if you ought to grant favours to those who
ask for them most eagerly, you ought in other matters
also to confer benefits, not on the best, but on the
most needy; for they will be most grateful, since
they are relieved of the greatest ills. And then, too,
at private entertainments you ought not to invite
your friends, but beggars and those who need a
meal; for they will love you and attend you and
come to your doors and be most pleased and grateful,
and will call down many blessings upon your head.
Perhaps, however, you ought not to grant favours to
those who beg for them, but to those who are most
able to repay you; and not to those who ask
merely, but to the most deserving; and not to
those who will enjoy your youthful beauty, but
to those who will share their good things with
you when you are older; and not to those who, when
they have succeeded, will boast to others of their
success, but to those who will modestly keep it a
secret from all; and not to those who will be
enamoured for a little while, but to those who will
be your friends for life; and not to those who will
seek a pretext for a quarrel when their passion has
died out, but to those who will show their own merit
when your youth is passed. Do you, then, remember
what I have said, and bear this also in mind, that
lovers are admonished by their friends, who think

PLATO

τοῖς δὲ μὴ ἐρῶσιν οὐδεὶς πώποτε τῶν οἰκείων ἐμέμψατο ὡς διὰ τοῦτο κακῶς βουλευομένοις περὶ ἑαυτῶν.

Ἴσως μὲν οὖν ἂν ἔροιό με, εἰ ἅπασίν σοι παραινῶ τοῖς μὴ ἐρῶσι χαρίζεσθαι. ἐγὼ δὲ οἶμαι οὐδ' ἂν τὸν ἐρῶντα πρὸς ἅπαντάς σε κελεύειν τοὺς ἐρῶντας C ταύτην ἔχειν τὴν διάνοιαν. οὔτε γὰρ τῷ λόγῳ[1] λαμβάνοντι χάριτος ἴσης ἄξιον, οὔτε σοὶ βουλομένῳ τοὺς ἄλλους λανθάνειν ὁμοίως δυνατόν· δεῖ δὲ βλάβην μὲν ἀπ' αὐτοῦ μηδεμίαν, ὠφελίαν δὲ ἀμφοῖν γίγνεσθαι. ἐγὼ μὲν οὖν ἱκανά μοι νομίζω τὰ εἰρημένα. εἰ δέ τι[2] σὺ ποθεῖς, ἡγούμενος παραλελεῖφθαι, ἐρῶτα.

10. Τί σοι φαίνεται, ὦ Σώκρατες, ὁ λόγος; οὐχ D ὑπερφυῶς τά τε ἄλλα καὶ τοῖς ὀνόμασιν εἰρῆσθαι;

ΣΩΚΡΑΤΗΣ. Δαιμονίως μὲν οὖν, ὦ ἑταῖρε, ὥστε με ἐκπλαγῆναι. καὶ τοῦτο ἐγὼ ἔπαθον διὰ σέ, ὦ Φαῖδρε, πρὸς σὲ ἀποβλέπων, ὅτι ἐμοὶ ἐδόκεις γάνυσθαι ὑπὸ τοῦ λόγου μεταξὺ ἀναγιγνώσκων. ἡγούμενος γὰρ σὲ μᾶλλον ἢ ἐμὲ ἐπαΐειν περὶ τῶν τοιούτων σοὶ εἱπόμην, καὶ ἑπόμενος συνεβάκχευσα μετὰ σοῦ τῆς θείας κεφαλῆς.

ΦΑΙΔΡΟΣ. Εἶεν· οὕτω δὴ δοκεῖ[3] παίζειν;

ΣΩΚΡΑΤΗΣ. Δοκῶ γάρ σοι παίζειν καὶ οὐχὶ ἐσπουδακέναι;

E ΦΑΙΔΡΟΣ. Μηδαμῶς, ὦ Σώκρατες, ἀλλ' ὡς ἀληθῶς εἰπὲ πρὸς Διὸς φιλίου, οἴει ἄν τινα ἔχειν εἰπεῖν ἄλλον τῶν Ἑλλήνων ἕτερα τούτων μείζω καὶ πλείω περὶ τοῦ αὐτοῦ πράγματος;

---

[1] λόγῳ B. Omitted by Schanz.
[2] δέ τι BT. δ' ἔτι τι Schanz, following Heindorf.
[3] δὴ δοκεῖ T. δὴ B. δεῖ, Schanz.

434

their way of life is bad, but no relative ever blamed a non-lover for bad management of his own interests on account of that condition.

Perhaps you may ask me if I advise you to grant favours to all non-lovers. But I think the lover would not urge you to be so disposed toward all lovers either; for the favour, if scattered broadcast, is not so highly prized by the rational recipient, nor can you, if you wish, keep your relations with one hidden from the rest. But from love no harm ought to come, but benefit to both parties. Now I think I have said enough. But if you feel any lack, or think anything has been omitted, ask questions.

What do you think of the discourse, Socrates? Is it not wonderful, especially in diction?

SOCRATES. More than that, it is miraculous, my friend; I am quite overcome by it. And this is due to you, Phaedrus, because as I looked at you, I saw that you were delighted by the speech as you read. So, thinking that you know more than I about such matters, I followed in your train and joined you in the divine frenzy.

PHAEDRUS. Indeed! So you see fit to make fun of it?

SOCRATES. Do I seem to you to be joking and not to be in earnest?

PHAEDRUS. Do not jest, Socrates, but, in the name of Zeus, the god of friendship, tell me truly, do you think any other of the Greeks could speak better or more copiously than this on the same subject?

PLATO

ΣΩΚΡΑΤΗΣ. Τί δέ; καὶ ταύτῃ δεῖ ὑπ' ἐμοῦ τε καὶ σοῦ τὸν λόγον ἐπαινεθῆναι, ὡς τὰ δέοντα εἰρηκότος τοῦ ποιητοῦ, ἀλλ' οὐκ ἐκείνῃ μόνον, ὅτι σαφῆ καὶ στρογγύλα, καὶ ἀκριβῶς ἕκαστα τῶν ὀνομάτων ἀποτετόρνευται; εἰ γὰρ δεῖ, συγχωρη-τέον χάριν σήν, ἐπεὶ ἐμέ γε ἔλαθεν ὑπὸ τῆς ἐμῆς
235 οὐδενίας. τῷ γὰρ ῥητορικῷ αὐτοῦ μόνῳ τὸν νοῦν προσεῖχον, τοῦτο δὲ οὐδὲ αὐτὸν ᾤμην Λυσίαν οἴεσθαι ἱκανὸν εἶναι. καὶ οὖν μοι ἔδοξεν, ὦ Φαῖδρε, εἰ μή τι σὺ ἄλλο λέγεις, δὶς καὶ τρὶς τὰ αὐτὰ εἰρηκέναι, ὡς οὐ πάνυ εὐπορῶν τοῦ πολλὰ λέγειν περὶ τοῦ αὐτοῦ, ἢ ἴσως οὐδὲν αὐτῷ μέλον τοῦ τοιούτου· καὶ ἐφαίνετο δή μοι νεανιεύεσθαι ἐπιδεικνύμενος, ὡς οἷός τε ὢν ταὐτὰ ἑτέρως τε καὶ ἑτέρως λέγων ἀμφοτέρως εἰπεῖν ἄριστα.

B   ΦΑΙΔΡΟΣ. Οὐδὲν λέγεις, ὦ Σώκρατες· αὐτὸ γὰρ τοῦτο καὶ μάλιστα ὁ λόγος ἔχει. τῶν γὰρ ἐνόντων ἀξίως[1] ῥηθῆναι ἐν τῷ πράγματι οὐδὲν παραλέλοι-πεν, ὥστε παρὰ τὰ ἐκείνῳ εἰρημένα μηδέν' ἄν ποτε δύνασθαι εἰπεῖν ἄλλα πλείω καὶ πλείονος ἄξια.

ΣΩΚΡΑΤΗΣ. Τοῦτο ἐγώ σοι οὐκέτι οἷός τε ἔσομαι πιθέσθαι. παλαιοὶ γὰρ καὶ σοφοὶ ἄνδρες τε καὶ γυναῖκες περὶ αὐτῶν εἰρηκότες καὶ γεγραφότες ἐξελέγξουσί με, ἐάν σοι χαριζόμενος συγχωρῶ.

C   ΦΑΙΔΡΟΣ. Τίνες οὗτοι; καὶ ποῦ σὺ βελτίω τούτων ἀκήκοας;

11. ΣΩΚΡΑΤΗΣ. Νῦν μὲν οὕτως οὐκ ἔχω εἰπεῖν· δῆλον δὲ ὅτι τινῶν ἀκήκοα, ἤ που Σαπφοῦς τῆς καλῆς ἢ Ἀνακρέοντος τοῦ σοφοῦ ἢ καὶ συγγρα-φέων τινῶν. πόθεν δὴ τεκμαιρόμενος λέγω; πλῆρές πως, ὦ δαιμόνιε, τὸ στῆθος ἔχων αἰσθά-

---

[1] ἀξίως BT. ἀξίων Madvig, followed by Schanz.

SOCRATES. What? Are you and I to praise the discourse because the author has said what he ought, and not merely because all the expressions are clear and well rounded and finely turned? For if that is expected, I must grant it for your sake, since, because of my stupidity, I did not notice it. I was attending only to the rhetorical manner, and I thought even Lysias himself would not think that satisfactory. It seemed to me, Phaedrus, unless you disagree, that he said the same thing two or three times, as if he did not find it easy to say many things about one subject, or perhaps he did not care about such a detail; and he appeared to me in youthful fashion to be exhibiting his ability to say the same thing in two different ways and in both ways excellently.

PHAEDRUS. Nonsense, Socrates! Why that is the especial merit of the discourse. He has omitted none of the points that belong to the subject, so that nobody could ever speak about it more exhaustively or worthily than he has done.

SOCRATES. There I must cease to agree with you; for the wise men and women of old, who have spoken and written about these matters, will rise up to confute me, if, to please you, I assent.

PHAEDRUS. Who are they? and where have you heard anything better than this?

SOCRATES. I cannot say, just at this moment; but I certainly must have heard something, either from the lovely Sappho or the wise Anacreon, or perhaps from some prose writers. What ground have I for saying so? Why, my dear friend, I feel that my own

PLATO

νομαι παρὰ ταῦτα ἂν ἔχειν εἰπεῖν ἕτερα μὴ χείρω. ὅτι μὲν οὖν παρά γε ἐμαυτοῦ οὐδὲν αὐτῶν ἐννενόηκα, εὖ οἶδα, συνειδὼς ἐμαυτῷ ἀμαθίαν· λείπεται
D δή, οἶμαι, ἐξ ἀλλοτρίων ποθὲν ναμάτων διὰ τῆς ἀκοῆς πεπληρῶσθαί με δίκην ἀγγείου· ὑπὸ δὲ νωθείας αὖ καὶ αὐτὸ τοῦτο ἐπιλέλησμαι, ὅπως τε καὶ ὧν τινων ἤκουσα.

ΦΑΙΔΡΟΣ. Ἀλλ᾽, ὦ γενναιότατε, κάλλιστα εἴρηκας. σὺ γὰρ ἐμοὶ ὧν τινων μὲν καὶ ὅπως ἤκουσας, μηδ᾽ ἂν κελεύω εἴπῃς, τοῦτο δὲ αὐτὸ ὃ λέγεις ποίησον· τῶν ἐν τῷ βιβλίῳ βελτίω τε καὶ μὴ ἐλάττω ἕτερα ὑπόσχες[1] εἰπεῖν, τούτων ἀπεχόμενος. καί σοι ἐγώ, ὥσπερ οἱ ἐννέα ἄρχοντες, ὑπισχνοῦμαι χρυσῆν εἰκόνα ἰσομέτρητον εἰς Δελφοὺς ἀναθή-
E σειν, οὐ μόνον ἐμαυτοῦ ἀλλὰ καὶ σήν.

ΣΩΚΡΑΤΗΣ. Φίλτατος εἶ καὶ ὡς ἀληθῶς χρυσοῦς, ὦ Φαῖδρε, εἴ με οἴει λέγειν ὡς Λυσίας τοῦ παντὸς ἡμάρτηκε, καὶ οἷόν τε δὴ παρὰ πάντα ταῦτα ἄλλα εἰπεῖν· τοῦτο δὲ οἶμαι οὐδ᾽ ἂν τὸν φαυλότατον παθεῖν συγγραφέα. αὐτίκα περὶ οὗ ὁ λόγος, τίνα οἴει λέγοντα ὡς χρὴ μὴ ἐρῶντι μᾶλλον ἢ ἐρῶντι
236 χαρίζεσθαι, παρέντα τοῦ μὲν τὸ φρόνιμον ἐγκωμιάζειν, τοῦ δὲ τὸ ἄφρον ψέγειν, ἀναγκαῖα γοῦν ὄντα, εἶτ᾽ ἄλλ᾽ ἄττα ἕξειν λέγειν; ἀλλ᾽, οἶμαι, τὰ μὲν τοιαῦτα ἐατέα καὶ συγγνωστέα λέγοντι· καὶ τῶν μὲν τοιούτων οὐ τὴν εὕρεσιν ἀλλὰ τὴν διάθεσιν ἐπαινετέον, τῶν δὲ μὴ ἀναγκαίων τε καὶ χαλεπῶν εὑρεῖν πρὸς τῇ διαθέσει καὶ τὴν εὕρεσιν.

12. ΦΑΙΔΡΟΣ. Συγχωρῶ ὃ λέγεις· μετρίως γάρ μοι δοκεῖς εἰρηκέναι. ποιήσω οὖν καὶ ἐγὼ οὕτω·

[1] ὑποσχέσει BT, ἐπιχείρει Schanz. The reading in the text was first suggested by Wex.

bosom is full, and that I could make another speech,
different from this and quite as good. Now I am
conscious of my own ignorance, and I know very well
that I have never invented these things myself, so
the only alternative is that I have been filled through
the ears, like a pitcher, from the well springs of
another; but, again because of my stupidity, I have
forgotten how and from whom I heard it.

PHAEDRUS. Most noble Socrates, that is splendid!
Don't tell, even if I beg you, how or from whom
you heard it; only do as you say; promise to make
another speech better than that in the book and no
shorter and quite different. Then I promise, like the
nine archons, to set up at Delphi a statue as large as
life, not only of myself, but of you also.

SOCRATES. You are a darling and truly golden,
Phaedrus, if you think I mean that Lysias has failed
in every respect and that I can compose a discourse
containing nothing that he has said. That, I fancy,
could not happen even to the worst writer. For
example, to take the subject of his speech, who do
you suppose, in arguing that the non-lover ought to
be more favoured than the lover, could omit praise
of the non-lover's calm sense and blame of the
lover's unreason, which are inevitable arguments,
and then say something else instead? No, such
arguments, I think, must be allowed and excused;
and in these the arrangement, not the invention, is
to be praised; but in the case of arguments which are
not inevitable and are hard to discover, the invention
deserves praise as well as the arrangement.

PHAEDRUS. I concede your point, for I think what
you say is reasonable. So I will make this concession:

439

B τὸ μὲν τὸν ἐρῶντα τοῦ μὴ ἐρῶντος μᾶλλον νοσεῖν δώσω σοι ὑποτίθεσθαι, τῶν δὲ λοιπῶν ἕτερα πλείω καὶ πλείονος ἄξια εἰπὼν τῶν Λυσίου, παρὰ τὸ Κυψελιδῶν ἀνάθημα σφυρήλατος ἐν Ὀλυμπίᾳ στάθητι.[1]

ΣΩΚΡΑΤΗΣ. Ἐσπούδακας, ὦ Φαῖδρε, ὅτι σου τῶν παιδικῶν ἐπελαβόμην ἐρεσχηλῶν σε, καὶ οἴει δή με ὡς ἀληθῶς ἐπιχειρήσειν εἰπεῖν παρὰ τὴν ἐκείνου σοφίαν ἕτερόν τι ποικιλώτερον;

ΦΑΙΔΡΟΣ. Περὶ μὲν τούτου, ὦ φίλε, εἰς τὰς
C ὁμοίας λαβὰς ἐλήλυθας. ῥητέον μὲν γάρ σοι παντὸς μᾶλλον οὕτως ὅπως οἷός τε εἶ, ἵνα μὴ τὸ τῶν κωμῳδῶν φορτικὸν πρᾶγμα ἀναγκαζώμεθα ποιεῖν ἀνταποδιδόντες ἀλλήλοις, εὐλαβήθητι[2] καὶ μὴ βούλου με ἀναγκάσαι λέγειν ἐκεῖνο τὸ εἰ ἐγώ, ὦ Σώκρατες, Σωκράτην ἀγνοῶ, καὶ ἐμαυτοῦ ἐπιλέλησμαι, καὶ ὅτι ἐπεθύμει μὲν λέγειν, ἐθρύπτετο δέ· ἀλλὰ διανοήθητι ὅτι ἐντεῦθεν οὐκ ἄπιμεν, πρὶν ἂν σὺ εἴπῃς ἃ ἔφησθα ἐν τῷ στήθει ἔχειν. ἐσμὲν δὲ
D μόνω ἐν ἐρημίᾳ, ἰσχυρότερος δὲ ἐγὼ καὶ νεώτερος, ἐκ δ' ἁπάντων τούτων ξύνες ὅ σοι λέγω, καὶ μηδαμῶς πρὸς βίας βουληθῇς μᾶλλον ἢ ἑκὼν λέγειν.

ΣΩΚΡΑΤΗΣ. Ἀλλ', ὦ μακάριε Φαῖδρε, γελοῖος ἔσομαι παρ' ἀγαθὸν ποιητὴν ἰδιώτης αὐτοσχεδιάζων περὶ τῶν αὐτῶν.

ΦΑΙΔΡΟΣ. Οἶσθ' ὡς ἔχει; παῦσαι πρός με καλλωπιζόμενος· σχεδὸν γὰρ ἔχω ὃ εἰπὼν ἀναγκάσω σε λέγειν.

ΣΩΚΡΑΤΗΣ. Μηδαμῶς τοίνυν εἴπῃς.

ΦΑΙΔΡΟΣ. Οὔκ, ἀλλὰ καὶ δὴ λέγω· ὁ δέ μοι

---

[1] στάθητι BT, ἔσταθι Schanz following Cobet.
[2] Schanz, following Cobet, omits εὐλαβήθητι.

I will allow you to begin with the premise that the lover is more distraught than the non-lover; and if you speak on the remaining points more copiously and better than Lysias, without saying the same things, your statue of beaten metal shall stand at Olympia beside the offering of the Cypselids.

SOCRATES. Have you taken my jest in earnest, Phaedrus, because, to tease you, I laid hands on your beloved, and do you really suppose I am going to try to surpass the rhetoric of Lysias and make a speech more ingenious than his?

PHAEDRUS. Now, my friend, you have given me a fair hold; for you certainly must speak as best you can, lest we be compelled to resort to the comic " you're another "; be careful and do not force me to say " O Socrates, if I don't know Socrates, I have forgotten myself," and " he yearned to speak, but feigned coyness." Just make up your mind that we are not going away from here until you speak out what you said you had in your breast. We are alone in a solitary spot, and I am stronger and younger than you; so, under these circumstances, take my meaning, and speak voluntarily, rather than under compulsion.

SOCRATES. But, my dear Phaedrus, I shall make myself ridiculous if I, a mere amateur, try without preparation to speak on the same subject in competition with a master of his art.

PHAEDRUS. Now listen to me. Stop trying to fool me; for I can say something which will force you to speak.

SOCRATES. Then pray don't say it.

PHAEDRUS. Yes, but I will. And my saying shall

λόγος ὅρκος ἔσται· ὄμνυμι γάρ σοι—τίνα μέντοι,
E τίνα θεῶν; ἢ βούλει τὴν πλάτανον ταυτηνί; ἢ
μήν, ἐάν μοι μὴ εἴπῃς τὸν λόγον ἐναντίον αὐτῆς
ταύτης, μηδέποτέ σοι ἕτερον λόγον μηδένα μηδενὸς
ἐπιδείξειν μηδ' ἐξαγγελεῖν.

13. ΣΩΚΡΑΤΗΣ. Βαβαί, ὦ μιαρέ, ὡς εὖ ἀνεῦρες
τὴν ἀνάγκην ἀνδρὶ φιλολόγῳ ποιεῖν ὃ ἂν κελεύῃς.

ΦΑΙΔΡΟΣ. Τί δῆτα ἔχων στρέφει;

ΣΩΚΡΑΤΗΣ. Οὐδὲν ἔτι, ἐπειδὴ σύ γε ταῦτα
ὀμώμοκας. πῶς γὰρ ἂν οἷός τ' εἴην τοιαύτης
θοίνης ἀπέχεσθαι;

237 ΦΑΙΔΡΟΣ. Λέγε δή.

ΣΩΚΡΑΤΗΣ. Οἶσθ' οὖν ὡς ποιήσω;

ΦΑΙΔΡΟΣ. Τοῦ πέρι;

ΣΩΚΡΑΤΗΣ. Ἐγκαλυψάμενος ἐρῶ, ἵν' ὅ τι τάχιστα διαδράμω τὸν λόγον, καὶ μὴ βλέπων πρὸς σὲ
ὑπ' αἰσχύνης διαπορῶμαι.

ΦΑΙΔΡΟΣ. Λέγε μόνον, τὰ δ' ἄλλα ὅπως βούλει
ποίει.

ΣΩΚΡΑΤΗΣ. Ἄγετε δή, ὦ Μοῦσαι, εἴτε δι' ᾠδῆς
εἶδος λίγειαι, εἴτε διὰ γένος μουσικὸν τὸ Λιγύων
ταύτην ἔσχετε τὴν ἐπωνυμίαν, ξύμ μοι λάβεσθε
τοῦ μύθου, ὅν με ἀναγκάζει ὁ βέλτιστος οὑτοσὶ
B λέγειν, ἵν' ὁ ἑταῖρος αὐτοῦ, καὶ πρότερον δοκῶν
τούτῳ σοφὸς εἶναι, νῦν ἔτι μᾶλλον δόξῃ.

Ἦν οὕτω δὴ παῖς, μᾶλλον δὲ μειρακίσκος, μάλα
καλός· τούτῳ δὲ ἦσαν ἐρασταὶ πάνυ πολλοί. εἷς
δέ τις αὐτῶν αἱμύλος ἦν, ὃς οὐδενὸς ἧττον ἐρῶν
ἐπεπείκει τὸν παῖδα ὡς οὐκ ἐρῴη· καί ποτε αὐτὸν

be an oath. I swear to you by—by what god? By
this plane tree? I take my solemn oath that unless
you produce the discourse in the very presence of this
plane tree, I will never read you another or tell you
of another.

SOCRATES. Oh! Oh! You wretch! How well you
found out how to make a lover of discourse do your
will!

PHAEDRUS. Then why do you try to get out of it?

SOCRATES. I won't any more, since you have
taken this oath; for how could I give up such
pleasures?

PHAEDRUS. Speak then.

SOCRATES. Do you know what I'm going to do?

PHAEDRUS. About what?

SOCRATES. I'm going to keep my head wrapped up
while I talk, that I may get through my discourse as
quickly as possible and that I may not look at you
and become embarrassed.

PHAEDRUS. Only speak, and in other matters suit
yourself.

SOCRATES. Come then, O tuneful Muses, whether
ye receive this name from the quality of your song or
from the musical race of the Ligyans, grant me your
aid in the tale this most excellent man compels me
to relate, that his friend whom he has hitherto considered wise, may seem to him wiser still.

Now there was once upon a time a boy, or rather
a stripling, of great beauty : and he had many lovers.
And among these was one of peculiar craftiness, who
was as much in love with the boy as anyone, but had
made him believe that he was not in love ; and once
in wooing him, he tried to persuade him of this
very thing, that favours ought to be granted rather

αἰτῶν ἔπειθε τοῦτ' αὐτό, ὡς μὴ ἐρῶντι πρὸ τοῦ
ἐρῶντος δέοι χαρίζεσθαι, ἔλεγέν τε ὧδε·

14. Περὶ παντός, ὦ παῖ, μία ἀρχὴ τοῖς μέλ-
C λουσι καλῶς βουλεύεσθαι· εἰδέναι δεῖ περὶ οὗ ἂν
ᾖ ἡ βουλή, ἢ παντὸς ἁμαρτάνειν ἀνάγκη. τοὺς δὲ
πολλοὺς λέληθεν ὅτι οὐκ ἴσασι τὴν οὐσίαν
ἑκάστου. ὡς οὖν εἰδότες οὐ διομολογοῦνται ἐν
ἀρχῇ τῆς σκέψεως, προελθόντες δὲ τὸ εἰκὸς ἀπο-
διδόασιν· οὔτε γὰρ ἑαυτοῖς οὔτε ἀλλήλοις ὁμολογοῦσιν. ἐγὼ οὖν καὶ σὺ μὴ πάθωμεν ὃ ἄλλοις
ἐπιτιμῶμεν, ἀλλ' ἐπειδὴ σοὶ καὶ ἐμοὶ ὁ λόγος
πρόκειται, ἐρῶντι ἢ μὴ μᾶλλον εἰς φιλίαν ἰτέον,
περὶ ἔρωτος, οἷόν τ' ἔστι καὶ ἣν ἔχει δύναμιν,
D ὁμολογίᾳ θέμενοι ὅρον, εἰς τοῦτο ἀποβλέποντες
καὶ ἀναφέροντες τὴν σκέψιν ποιώμεθα, εἴτε ὠφελίαν εἴτε βλάβην παρέχει. ὅτι μὲν οὖν δὴ ἐπιθυμία τις ὁ ἔρως, ἅπαντι δῆλον· ὅτι δ' αὖ καὶ μὴ
ἐρῶντες ἐπιθυμοῦσι τῶν καλῶν, ἴσμεν. τῷ δὴ τὸν
ἐρῶντά τε καὶ μὴ κρινοῦμεν; δεῖ δὴ νοῆσαι, ὅτι
ἡμῶν ἐν ἑκάστῳ δύο τινέ ἐστον ἰδέα ἄρχοντε καὶ
ἄγοντε, οἷν ἑπόμεθα ᾗ ἂν ἄγητον, ἡ μὲν ἔμφυτος
οὖσα ἐπιθυμία ἡδονῶν, ἄλλη δὲ ἐπίκτητος δόξα,
E ἐφιεμένη τοῦ ἀρίστου. τούτω δὲ ἐν ἡμῖν τοτὲ μὲν
ὁμονοεῖτον, ἔστι δὲ ὅτε στασιάζετον· καὶ τοτὲ μὲν
ἡ ἑτέρα, ἄλλοτε δὲ ἡ ἑτέρα κρατεῖ. δόξης μὲν οὖν
ἐπὶ τὸ ἄριστον λόγῳ ἀγούσης καὶ κρατούσης τῷ
238 κράτει σωφροσύνη ὄνομα· ἐπιθυμίας δὲ ἀλόγως
ἑλκούσης ἐπὶ ἡδονὰς καὶ ἀρξάσης ἐν ἡμῖν τῇ ἀρχῇ
ὕβρις ἐπωνομάσθη. ὕβρις δὲ δὴ πολυώνυμον·
πολυμελὲς γὰρ καὶ πολυειδές. καὶ τούτων τῶν
ἰδεῶν ἐκπρεπὴς ἢ ἂν τύχῃ γενομένη, τὴν αὑτῆς
ἐπωνυμίαν ὀνομαζόμενον τὸν ἔχοντα παρέχεται,

to the non-lover than to the lover; and his words
were as follows:—

There is only one way, dear boy, for those to begin
who are to take counsel wisely about anything. One
must know what the counsel is about, or it is sure to
be utterly futile, but most people are ignorant of the
fact that they do not know the nature of things.
So, supposing that they do know it, they come to no
agreement in the beginning of their enquiry, and as
they go on they reach the natural result,—they agree
neither with themselves nor with each other. Now
you and I must not fall into the error which we condemn in others, but, since we are to discuss the question, whether the lover or the non-lover is to be
preferred let us first agree on a definition of love,
its nature and its power, and then, keeping this
definition in view and making constant reference to it,
let us enquire whether love brings advantage or harm.
Now everyone sees that love is a desire; and we know
too that non-lovers also desire the beautiful. How
then are we to distinguish the lover from the non-
lover? We must observe that in each one of us there
are two ruling and leading principles, which we follow
whithersoever they lead; one is the innate desire for
pleasures, the other an acquired opinion which strives
for the best. These two sometimes agree within us
and are sometimes in strife; and sometimes one, and
sometimes the other has the greater power. Now
when opinion leads through reason toward the best
and is more powerful, its power is called self-restraint,
but when desire irrationally drags us toward pleasures
and rules within us, its rule is called excess. Now excess
has many names, for it has many members and many
forms; and whichever of these forms is most marked

οὔτε τινὰ καλὴν οὔτε ἐπαξίαν κεκτῆσθαι.[1] περὶ
μὲν γὰρ ἐδωδὴν κρατοῦσα τοῦ λόγου τοῦ ἀρίστου
B καὶ τῶν ἄλλων ἐπιθυμιῶν ἐπιθυμία γαστριμαργία
τε καὶ τὸν ἔχοντα ταὐτὸν τοῦτο κεκλημένον παρέ-
ξεται· περὶ δ' αὖ μέθας τυραννεύσασα, τὸν κεκτη-
μένον ταύτῃ ἄγουσα, δῆλον οὗ τεύξεται προσ-
ρήματος· καὶ τἆλλα δὴ τὰ τούτων ἀδελφὰ καὶ
ἀδελφῶν ἐπιθυμιῶν ὀνόματα τῆς ἀεὶ δυνα-
στευούσης ᾗ προσήκει καλεῖσθαι πρόδηλον. ἧς δ'
ἕνεκα πάντα τὰ πρόσθεν εἴρηται, σχεδὸν μὲν
ἤδη φανερόν, λεχθὲν δὲ ἢ μὴ λεχθὲν πᾶν πως
σαφέστερον· ἡ γὰρ ἄνευ λόγου δόξης ἐπὶ τὸ
C ὀρθὸν ὁρμώσης κρατήσασα ἐπιθυμία πρὸς ἡδονὴν
ἀχθεῖσα κάλλους, καὶ ὑπὸ αὖ τῶν ἑαυτῆς
συγγενῶν ἐπιθυμιῶν ἐπὶ σωμάτων κάλλος ἐρρωμένως ῥωσθεῖσα νικήσασα ἀγωγῇ, ἀπ' αὐτῆς τῆς
ῥώμης ἐπωνυμίαν λαβοῦσα, ἔρως ἐκλήθη.

15. Ἀτάρ, ὦ φίλε Φαῖδρε, δοκῶ τι σοί, ὥσπερ
ἐμαυτῷ, θεῖον πάθος πεπονθέναι;

ΦΑΙΔΡΟΣ. Πάνυ μὲν οὖν, ὦ Σώκρατες, παρὰ τὸ
εἰωθὸς εὔροιά τίς σε εἴληφεν.

ΣΩΚΡΑΤΗΣ. Σιγῇ τοίνυν μου ἄκουε· τῷ ὄντι γὰρ
D θεῖος ἔοικεν ὁ τόπος εἶναι· ὥστε ἐὰν ἄρα πολλάκις
νυμφόληπτος προϊόντος τοῦ λόγου γένωμαι, μὴ
θαυμάσῃς· τὰ νῦν γὰρ οὐκέτι πόρρω διθυράμβων
φθέγγομαι.

ΦΑΙΔΡΟΣ. Ἀληθέστατα λέγεις.

ΣΩΚΡΑΤΗΣ. Τούτων μέντοι σὺ αἴτιος· ἀλλὰ τὰ
λοιπὰ ἄκουε· ἴσως γὰρ κἂν ἀποτράποιτο τὸ ἐπίον.

---

[1] Schanz reads ἐκτῆσθαι here and the corresponding forms
elsewhere.

gives its own name, neither beautiful nor honourable, to him who possesses it. For example, if the desire for food prevails over the higher reason and the other desires, it is called gluttony, and he who possesses it will be called by the corresponding name of glutton, and again, if the desire for drink becomes the tyrant and leads him who possesses it toward drink, we know what he is called; and it is quite clear what fitting names of the same sort will be given when any desire akin to these acquires the rule. The reason for what I have said hitherto is pretty clear by this time, but everything is plainer when spoken than when unspoken; so I say that the desire which overcomes the rational opinion that strives toward the right, and which is led away toward the enjoyment of beauty and again is strongly forced by the desires that are kindred to itself toward personal beauty, when it gains the victory, takes its name from that very force, and is called love.[1]

Well, my dear Phaedrus, does it seem to you, as it does to me, that I am inspired?

PHAEDRUS. Certainly, Socrates, you have an unusual fluency.

SOCRATES. Then listen to me in silence; for truly the place seems filled with a divine presence; so do not be surprised if I often seem to be in a frenzy as my discourse progresses, for I am already almost uttering dithyrambics.

PHAEDRUS. That is very true.

SOCRATES. You are responsible for that; but hear what follows; for perhaps the attack may be averted.

[1] This somewhat fanciful statement is based on a supposed etymological connexion between ἔρως and ῥώμη, ἐρρωμένως, ῥωσθεῖσα.

ταῦτα μὲν οὖν θεῷ μελήσει, ἡμῖν δὲ πρὸς τὸν παῖδα πάλιν τῷ λόγῳ ἰτέον.

Εἶεν, ὦ φέριστε· ὃ μὲν δὴ τυγχάνει ὂν περὶ οὗ βουλευτέον, εἴρηταί τε καὶ ὥρισται, βλέποντες δὲ

E δὴ πρὸς αὐτὸ τὰ λοιπὰ λέγωμεν, τίς ὠφελία ἢ βλάβη ἀπό τε ἐρῶντος καὶ μὴ τῷ χαριζομένῳ ἐξ εἰκότος συμβήσεται.

Τῷ δὴ ὑπὸ ἐπιθυμίας ἀρχομένῳ δουλεύοντί τε ἡδονῇ ἀνάγκη που τὸν ἐρώμενον ὡς ἥδιστον ἑαυτῷ παρασκευάζειν· νοσοῦντι δὲ πᾶν ἡδὺ τὸ μὴ ἀντιτεῖνον, κρεῖττον δὲ καὶ ἴσον ἐχθρόν. οὔτε

239 δὴ κρείττω οὔτε ἰσούμενον ἑκὼν ἐραστὴς παιδικὰ ἀνέξεται, ἥττω δὲ καὶ ὑποδεέστερον ἀεὶ ἀπεργάζεται· ἥττων δὲ ἀμαθὴς σοφοῦ, δειλὸς ἀνδρείου, ἀδύνατος εἰπεῖν ῥητορικοῦ, βραδὺς ἀγχίνου. τοσούτων κακῶν καὶ ἔτι πλειόνων κατὰ τὴν διάνοιαν ἐραστὴν ἐρωμένῳ ἀνάγκη γιγνομένων τε καὶ φύσει ἐνόντων, τῶν μὲν ἥδεσθαι, τὰ δὲ παρασκευάζειν, ἢ στέρεσθαι τοῦ παραυτίκα ἡδέος.

B φθονερὸν δὴ ἀνάγκη εἶναι, καὶ πολλῶν μὲν ἄλλων συνουσιῶν ἀπείργοντα καὶ ὠφελίμων, ὅθεν ἂν μάλιστ' ἀνὴρ γίγνοιτο, μεγάλης αἴτιον εἶναι βλάβης, μεγίστης δὲ τῆς ὅθεν ἂν φρονιμώτατος εἴη. τοῦτο δὲ ἡ θεία φιλοσοφία τυγχάνει ὄν, ἧς ἐραστὴν παιδικὰ ἀνάγκη πόρρωθεν εἴργειν, περίφοβον ὄντα τοῦ καταφρονηθῆναι· τά τε ἄλλα μηχανᾶσθαι, ὅπως ἂν ᾖ πάντα ἀγνοῶν καὶ πάντα ἀποβλέπων εἰς τὸν ἐραστήν, οἷος ὢν τῷ μὲν

C ἥδιστος, ἑαυτῷ[1] δὲ βλαβερώτατος ἂν εἴη. τὰ μὲν

---

[1] ἑαυτῷ T Stobaeus : τῷ ἑαυτῷ B Schanz.

That, however, is in the hands of God; we must return to our boy.

Well then, my dearest, what the subject is, about which we are to take counsel, has been said and defined, and now let us continue, keeping our attention fixed upon that definition, and tell what advantage or harm will naturally come from the lover or the non-lover to him who grants them his favours.

He who is ruled by desire and is a slave to pleasure will inevitably desire to make his beloved as pleasing to himself as possible. Now to one who is of unsound mind everything is pleasant which does not oppose him, but everything that is better or equal is hateful. So the lover will not, if he can help it, endure a beloved who is better than himself or his equal, but always makes him weaker and inferior; but the ignorant is inferior to the wise, the coward to the brave, the poor speaker to the eloquent, the slow of wit to the clever. Such mental defects, and still greater than these, in the beloved will necessarily please the lover, if they are implanted by Nature, and if they are not, he must implant them or be deprived of his immediate enjoyment. And he is of necessity jealous and will do him great harm by keeping him from many advantageous associations, which would most tend to make a man of him, especially from that which would do most to make him wise. This is divine philosophy, and from it the lover will certainly keep his beloved away, through fear of being despised; and he will contrive to keep him ignorant of everything else and make him look to his lover for everything, so that he will be most agreeable to him and most harmful to himself. In respect to

οὖν κατὰ διάνοιαν ἐπίτροπός τε καὶ κοινωνὸς
οὐδαμῇ λυσιτελὴς ἀνὴρ ἔχων ἔρωτα.

16. Τὴν δὲ τοῦ σώματος ἕξιν τε καὶ θεραπείαν
οἵαν τε καὶ ὡς θεραπεύσει οὗ ἂν γένηται κύριος,
ὃς ἡδὺ πρὸ ἀγαθοῦ ἠνάγκασται διώκειν, δεῖ μετὰ
ταῦτα ἰδεῖν. ὀφθήσεται δὲ[1] μαλθακόν τινα καὶ οὐ
στερεὸν διώκων, οὐδ' ἐν ἡλίῳ καθαρῷ τεθραμμένον
ἀλλ' ὑπὸ συμμιγεῖ σκιᾷ, πόνων μὲν ἀνδρείων καὶ
ἱδρώτων ξηρῶν ἄπειρον, ἔμπειρον δὲ ἁπαλῆς καὶ
D ἀνάνδρου διαίτης, ἀλλοτρίοις χρώμασι καὶ κόσμοις
χήτει οἰκείων κοσμούμενον, ὅσα τε ἄλλα τούτοις
ἕπεται πάντα ἐπιτηδεύοντα, ἃ δῆλα καὶ οὐκ ἄξιον
περαιτέρω προβαίνειν, ἀλλ' ἐν κεφάλαιον ὁρι-
σαμένους ἐπ' ἄλλο ἰέναι· τὸ γὰρ τοιοῦτον σῶμα
ἐν πολέμῳ τε καὶ ἄλλαις χρείαις ὅσαι μεγάλαι οἱ
μὲν ἐχθροὶ θαρροῦσιν, οἱ δὲ φίλοι καὶ αὐτοὶ οἱ
ἐρασταὶ φοβοῦνται.

Τοῦτο μὲν οὖν ὡς δῆλον ἐατέον, τὸ δ' ἐφεξῆς
E ῥητέον, τίνα ἡμῖν ὠφελίαν ἢ τίνα βλάβην περὶ
τὴν κτῆσιν ἡ τοῦ ἐρῶντος ὁμιλία τε καὶ ἐπιτρο-
πεία παρέξεται. σαφὲς δὴ τοῦτό γε παντὶ μέν,
μάλιστα δὲ τῷ ἐραστῇ, ὅτι τῶν φιλτάτων τε καὶ
εὐνουστάτων καὶ θειοτάτων κτημάτων ὀρφανὸν
πρὸ παντὸς εὔξαιτ' ἂν εἶναι τὸν ἐρώμενον· πατρὸς
γὰρ καὶ μητρὸς καὶ ξυγγενῶν καὶ φίλων στέρε-
240 σθαι ἂν αὐτὸν δέξαιτο, διακωλυτὰς καὶ ἐπιτι-
μητὰς ἡγούμενος τῆς ἡδίστης πρὸς αὐτὸν ὁμιλίας.
ἀλλὰ μὴν οὐσίαν γ' ἔχοντα χρυσοῦ ἤ τινος ἄλλης
κτήσεως οὔτ' εὐάλωτον ὁμοίως οὔτε ἁλόντα εὐ-
μεταχείριστον ἡγήσεται· ἐξ ὧν πᾶσα ἀνάγκη ἐραστὴν παιδικοῖς φθονεῖν μὲν οὐσίαν κεκτημένοις,

---

[1] δὲ BT, δὴ Schanz following Hirschig.

the intellect, then, a man in love is by no means a profitable guardian or associate.

We must next consider how he who is forced to follow pleasure and not good will keep the body of him whose master he is, and what care he will give to it. He will plainly court a beloved who is effeminate, not virile, not brought up in the pure sunshine, but in mingled shade, unused to manly toils and the sweat of exertion, but accustomed to a delicate and unmanly mode of life, adorned with a bright complexion of artificial origin, since he has none by nature, and in general living a life such as all this indicates, which it is certainly not worth while to describe further. We can sum it all up briefly and pass on. A person with such a body, in war and in all important crises, gives courage to his enemies, and fills his friends, and even his lovers themselves, with fear.

This may be passed over as self-evident, but the next question, what advantage or harm the intercourse and guardianship of the lover will bring to his beloved in the matter of his property, must be discussed. Now it is clear to everyone, and especially to the lover, that he would desire above all things to have his beloved bereft of the dearest and kindest and holiest possessions; for he would wish him to be deprived of father, mother, relatives and friends, thinking that they would hinder and censure his most sweet intercourse with him. But he will also think that one who has property in money or other possessions will be less easy to catch and when caught will be less manageable; wherefore the lover must necessarily begrudge his beloved the possession of

ἀπολλυμένης δὲ χαίρειν. ἔτι τοίνυν ἄγαμον,
ἄπαιδα, ἄοικον ὅ τι πλεῖστον χρόνον παιδικὰ
ἐραστὴς εὔξαιτ' ἂν γενέσθαι, τὸ αὑτοῦ γλυκὺ ὡς
πλεῖστον χρόνον καρποῦσθαι ἐπιθυμῶν.

17. Ἔστι μὲν δὴ καὶ ἄλλα κακά, ἀλλά τις
B δαίμων ἔμιξε τοῖς πλείστοις ἐν τῷ παραυτίκα
ἡδονήν, οἷον κόλακι, δεινῷ θηρίῳ καὶ βλάβῃ
μεγάλῃ, ὅμως ἐπέμιξεν ἡ φύσις ἡδονήν τινα οὐκ
ἄμουσον, καί τις ἑταίραν ὡς βλαβερὸν ψέξειεν ἄν,
καὶ ἄλλα πολλὰ τῶν τοιουτοτρόπων θρεμμάτων
τε καὶ ἐπιτηδευμάτων, οἷς τό γε καθ' ἡμέραν ἡδί-
στοισιν εἶναι ὑπάρχει· παιδικοῖς δὲ ἐραστὴς πρὸς
C τῷ βλαβερῷ καὶ εἰς τὸ συνημερεύειν πάντων
ἀηδέστατον. ἥλικα γὰρ καὶ ὁ παλαιὸς λόγος
τέρπειν τὸν ἥλικα· ἡ γάρ, οἶμαι, χρόνου ἰσότης
ἐπ' ἴσας ἡδονὰς ἄγουσα δι' ὁμοιότητα φιλίαν
παρέχεται· ἀλλ' ὅμως κόρον γε καὶ ἡ τούτων
συνουσία ἔχει. καὶ μὴν τό γε ἀναγκαῖον αὖ βαρὺ
παντὶ περὶ πᾶν λέγεται· ὃ δὴ πρὸς τῇ ἀνομοιότητι
μάλιστα ἐραστὴς πρὸς παιδικὰ ἔχει. νεωτέρῳ γὰρ
πρεσβύτερος συνὼν οὔθ' ἡμέρας οὔτε νυκτὸς ἑκὼν
D ἀπολείπεται, ἀλλ' ὑπ' ἀνάγκης τε καὶ οἴστρου
ἐλαύνεται, ὃς ἐκείνῳ μὲν ἡδονὰς ἀεὶ διδοὺς ἄγει
ὁρῶντι, ἀκούοντι, ἁπτομένῳ, καὶ πᾶσαν αἴσθησιν
αἰσθανομένῳ τοῦ ἐρωμένου, ὥστε μεθ' ἡδονῆς
ἀραρότως αὐτῷ ὑπηρετεῖν· τῷ δὲ δὴ ἐρωμένῳ
ποῖον παραμύθιον ἢ τίνας ἡδονὰς διδοὺς ποιήσει
τὸν ἴσον χρόνον συνόντα μὴ οὐχὶ ἐπ' ἔσχατον
ἐλθεῖν ἀηδίας; ὁρῶντι μὲν ὄψιν πρεσβυτέραν καὶ
οὐκ ἐν ὥρᾳ, ἑπομένων δὲ τῶν ἄλλων ταύτῃ, ἃ καὶ
E λόγῳ ἐστὶν ἀκούειν οὐκ ἐπιτερπές, μὴ ὅτι δὴ ἔργῳ
ἀνάγκης ἀεὶ προσκειμένης μεταχειρίζεσθαι· φυλα-

property and rejoice at its loss. Moreover the lover would wish his beloved to be as long as possible unmarried, childless, and homeless, since he wishes to enjoy as long as possible what is pleasant to himself.

Now there are also other evils, but God has mingled with most of them some temporary pleasure; so, for instance, a flatterer is a horrid creature and does great harm, yet Nature has combined with him a kind of pleasure that is not without charm, and one might find fault with a courtesan as an injurious thing, and there are many other such creatures and practices which are yet for the time being very pleasant; but a lover is not only harmful to his beloved but extremely disagreeable to live with as well. The old proverb says, " birds of a feather flock together " ; that is, I suppose, equality of age leads them to similar pleasures and through similarity begets friendship ; and yet even they grow tired of each other's society. Now compulsion of every kind is said to be oppressive to every one, and the lover not only is unlike his beloved, but he exercises the strongest compulsion. For he is old while his love is young, and he does not leave him day or night, if he can help it, but is driven by the sting of necessity, which urges him on, always giving him pleasure in seeing, hearing, touching, and by all his senses perceiving his beloved, so that he is glad to serve him constantly. But what consolation or what pleasure can he give the beloved ? Must not this protracted intercourse bring him to the uttermost disgust, as he looks at the old, unlovely face, and other things to match, which it is not pleasant even to hear about, to say nothing of being constantly compelled to come into contact with them ? And he

κάς τε δὴ καχυποτόπους φυλαττομένῳ διὰ παντὸς
καὶ πρὸς ἅπαντας, ἀκαίρους τε καὶ ἐπαίνους καὶ
ὑπερβάλλοντας ἀκούοντι, ὡς δ' αὕτως ψόγους
νήφοντος μὲν οὐκ ἀνεκτούς, εἰς δὲ μέθην ἰόντος
πρὸς τῷ μὴ ἀνεκτῷ ἐπαισχεῖς[1] παρρησίᾳ κατα-
κορεῖ καὶ ἀναπεπταμένῃ χρωμένου.

18. Καὶ ἐρῶν μὲν βλαβερός τε καὶ ἀηδής, λήξας
δὲ τοῦ ἔρωτος εἰς τὸν ἔπειτα χρόνον ἄπιστος, εἰς
241 ὃν πολλὰ καὶ μετὰ πολλῶν ὅρκων τε καὶ δεήσεων
ὑπισχνούμενος μόγις κατεῖχε τὴν ἐν τῷ τότε
ξυνουσίαν ἐπίπονον φέρειν δι' ἐλπίδα ἀγαθῶν.
τότε δὴ δέον ἐκτίνειν, μεταβαλὼν ἄλλον ἄρχοντα
ἐν αὑτῷ καὶ προστάτην, νοῦν καὶ σωφροσύνην ἀντ'
ἔρωτος καὶ μανίας, ἄλλος γεγονὼς λέληθεν τὰ
παιδικά. καὶ ὁ μὲν αὐτὸν χάριν ἀπαιτεῖ τῶν τότε,
ὑπομιμνήσκων τὰ πραχθέντα καὶ λεχθέντα, ὡς τῷ
αὐτῷ διαλεγόμενος· ὁ δὲ ὑπ' αἰσχύνης οὔτε εἰπεῖν
τολμᾷ ὅτι ἄλλος γέγονεν, οὔθ' ὅπως τὰ τῆς
προτέρας ἀνοήτου ἀρχῆς ὁρκωμόσιά τε καὶ
B ὑποσχέσεις ἐμπεδώσει ἔχει, νοῦν ἤδη ἐσχηκὼς καὶ
σεσωφρονηκώς, ἵνα μὴ πράττων ταὐτὰ τῷ πρόσθεν
ὅμοιός τε ἐκείνῳ καὶ ὁ αὐτὸς πάλιν γένηται. φυγὰς
δὴ γίγνεται ἐκ τούτων, καὶ ἀπεστερηκὼς ὑπ'
ἀνάγκης ὁ πρὶν ἐραστής, ὀστράκου μεταπεσόντος,
ἵεται φυγῇ μεταβαλών· ὁ δὲ ἀναγκάζεται διώκειν
ἀγανακτῶν καὶ ἐπιθεάζων, ἠγνοηκὼς τὸ ἅπαν ἐξ
ἀρχῆς, ὅτι οὐκ ἄρα ἔδει ποτὲ ἐρῶντι καὶ ὑπ'
C ἀνάγκης ἀνοήτῳ χαρίζεσθαι, ἀλλὰ πολὺ μᾶλλον

---

[1] ἐπαισχεῖς Schanz following Heindorf, ἐπ' αἴσχει BT.

is suspiciously guarded in all ways against everybody, and has to listen to untimely and exaggerated praises and to reproaches which are unendurable when the man is sober, and when he is in his cups and indulges in wearisome and unrestrained freedom of speech become not only unendurable but disgusting.

And while he is in love he is harmful and disagreeable, but when his love has ceased he is thereafter false to him whom he formerly hardly induced to endure his wearisome companionship through the hope of future benefits by making promises with many prayers and oaths. But now that the time of payment has come he has a new ruler and governor within him, sense and reason in place of love and madness, and has become a different person; but of this his beloved knows nothing. He asks of him a return for former favours, reminding him of past sayings and doings, as if he were speaking to the same man; but the lover is ashamed to say that he has changed, and yet he cannot keep the oaths and promises he made when he was ruled by his former folly, now that he has regained his reason and come to his senses, lest by doing what he formerly did he become again what he was. He runs away from these things, and the former lover is compelled to become a defaulter. The shell has fallen with the other side up;[1] and he changes his part and runs away; and the other is forced to run after him in anger and with imprecations, he who did not know at the start that he ought never to have accepted a lover who was necessarily without reason, but rather a reason-

[1] This refers to a game played with oyster shells, in which the players ran away or pursued as the shell fell with one or the other side uppermost.

455

μὴ ἐρῶντι καὶ νοῦν ἔχοντι· εἰ δὲ μή, ἀναγκαῖον
εἴη ἐνδοῦναι αὐτὸν ἀπίστῳ, δυσκόλῳ, φθονερῷ,[1]
ἀηδεῖ, βλαβερῷ μὲν πρὸς οὐσίαν, βλαβερῷ δὲ
πρὸς τὴν τοῦ σώματος ἕξιν, πολὺ δὲ βλαβερωτάτῳ
πρὸς τὴν τῆς ψυχῆς παίδευσιν, ἧς οὔτε ἀνθρώποις
οὔτε θεοῖς τῇ ἀληθείᾳ τιμιώτερον οὔτε ἔστιν οὔτε
ποτὲ ἔσται. ταῦτά τε οὖν χρή, ὦ παῖ, ξυννοεῖν,
καὶ εἰδέναι τὴν ἐραστοῦ φιλίαν, ὅτι οὐ μετ᾽
εὐνοίας γίγνεται, ἀλλὰ σιτίου τρόπον, χάριν
πλησμονῆς,

D   ὡς λύκοι ἄρν᾽ ἀγαπῶσ᾽, ὡς παῖδα φιλοῦσιν
ἐρασταί.

19. Τοῦτ᾽ ἐκεῖνο, ὦ Φαῖδρε. οὐκέτ᾽ ἂν τὸ πέρα
ἀκούσαις ἐμοῦ λέγοντος, ἀλλ᾽ ἤδη σοι τέλος ἐχέτω
ὁ λόγος.

ΦΑΙΔΡΟΣ. Καίτοι ᾤμην γε μεσοῦν αὐτόν, καὶ
ἐρεῖν τὰ ἴσα περὶ τοῦ μὴ ἐρῶντος, ὡς δεῖ ἐκείνῳ
χαρίζεσθαι μᾶλλον, λέγων[2] ὅσ᾽ αὖ ἔχει ἀγαθά·
νῦν δὲ δή, ὦ Σώκρατες, τί ἀποπαύει;

E   ΣΩΚΡΑΤΗΣ. Οὐκ ἤσθου, ὦ μακάριε, ὅτι ἤδη ἔπη
φθέγγομαι, ἀλλ᾽ οὐκέτι διθυράμβους, καὶ ταῦτα
ψέγων· ἐὰν δ᾽ ἐπαινεῖν τὸν ἕτερον ἄρξωμαι, τί με
οἴει ποιήσειν; ἆρ᾽ οἶσθ᾽ ὅτι ὑπὸ τῶν Νυμφῶν, αἷς
με σὺ προὔβαλες ἐκ προνοίας, σαφῶς ἐνθουσιάσω;
λέγω οὖν ἑνὶ λόγῳ, ὅτι ὅσα τὸν ἕτερον λελοιδορήκαμεν, τῷ ἑτέρῳ τἀναντία τούτων ἀγαθὰ πρόσεστι.
καὶ τί δεῖ μακροῦ λόγου; περὶ γὰρ ἀμφοῖν ἱκανῶς
εἴρηται. καὶ οὕτω δὴ ὁ μῦθος, ὅ τι πάσχειν
242 προσήκει αὐτῷ, τοῦτο πείσεται· κἀγὼ τὸν ποταμὸν

---

[1] δυσκόλῳ φθονερῷ omitted by Schanz, following Spengel.
[2] λέγων BT, λέγονθ᾽ Schanz.

able non-lover; for otherwise he would have to surrender himself to one who was faithless, irritable, jealous, and disagreeable, harmful to his property, harmful to his physical condition, and most harmful by far to the cultivation of his soul, than which there neither is nor ever will be anything of higher importance in truth either in heaven or on earth. These things, dear boy, you must bear in mind, and you must know that the fondness of the lover is not a matter of goodwill, but of appetite which he wishes to satisfy:

Just as the wolf loves the lamb, so the lover adores his beloved.

There it is, Phaedrus! Do not listen to me any longer; let my speech end here.

PHAEDRUS. But I thought you were in the middle of it, and would say as much about the non-lover as you have said about the lover, to set forth all his good points and show that he ought to be favoured. So now, Socrates, why do you stop?

SOCRATES. Did you not notice, my friend, that I am already speaking in hexameters, not mere dithyrambics, even though I am finding fault with the lover? But if I begin to praise the non-lover, what kind of hymn do you suppose I shall raise? I shall surely be possessed of the nymphs to whom you purposely exposed me. So, in a word, I say that the non-lover possesses all the advantages that are opposed to the disadvantages we found in the lover. Why make a long speech? I have said enough about both of them. And so my tale shall fare as

τοῦτον διαβὰς ἀπέρχομαι, πρὶν ὑπὸ σοῦ τι μεῖζον
ἀναγκασθῆναι.

ΦΑΙΔΡΟΣ. Μήπω γε, ὦ Σώκρατες, πρὶν ἂν τὸ
καῦμα παρέλθῃ· ἢ οὐχ ὁρᾷς ὡς σχεδὸν ἤδη
μεσημβρία ἵσταται;[1] ἀλλὰ περιμείναντες, καὶ ἅμα
περὶ τῶν εἰρημένων διαλεχθέντες, τάχα ἐπειδὰν
ἀποψυχῇ ἴμεν.

ΣΩΚΡΑΤΗΣ. Θεῖός γ᾽ εἶ περὶ τοὺς λόγους, ὦ
Φαῖδρε, καὶ ἀτεχνῶς θαυμάσιος. οἶμαι γὰρ ἐγὼ
B τῶν ἐπὶ τοῦ σοῦ βίου γεγονότων μηδένα πλείους ἢ
σὲ πεποιηκέναι γεγενῆσθαι ἤτοι αὐτὸν λέγοντα ἢ
ἄλλους ἑνί γέ τῳ τρόπῳ προσαναγκάζοντα.
Σιμμίαν Θηβαῖον ἐξαιρῶ λόγου· τῶν δὲ ἄλλων
πάμπολυ κρατεῖς· καὶ νῦν αὖ δοκεῖς αἴτιός μοι
γεγενῆσθαι λόγῳ τινὶ ῥηθῆναι.

ΦΑΙΔΡΟΣ. Οὐ πόλεμόν γε ἀγγέλλεις· ἀλλὰ πῶς
δὴ καὶ τίνι τούτῳ;

20. ΣΩΚΡΑΤΗΣ. Ἡνίκ᾽ ἔμελλον, ὦ ᾽γαθέ, τὸν
ποταμὸν διαβαίνειν, τὸ δαιμόνιόν τε καὶ τὸ εἰωθὸς
C σημεῖόν μοι γίγνεσθαι ἐγένετο—ἀεὶ δέ με ἐπίσχει,
ὃ ἂν μέλλω πράττειν[2]—καί τινα φωνὴν ἔδοξα
αὐτόθεν ἀκοῦσαι, ἥ με οὐκ ἐᾷ ἀπιέναι πρὶν ἂν
ἀφοσιώσωμαι, ὥς τι ἡμαρτηκότα εἰς τὸ θεῖον.
εἰμὶ δὴ οὖν μάντις μέν, οὐ πάνυ δὲ σπουδαῖος,
ἀλλ᾽ ὥσπερ οἱ τὰ γράμματα φαῦλοι, ὅσον μὲν
ἐμαυτῷ μόνον ἱκανός· σαφῶς οὖν ἤδη μανθάνω τὸ
ἁμάρτημα. ὡς δή τοι, ὦ ἑταῖρε, μαντικόν γέ τι
καὶ ἡ ψυχή· ἐμὲ γὰρ ἔθραξε μέν τι καὶ πάλαι
λέγοντα τὸν λόγον, καί πως ἐδυσωπούμην κατ᾽

---

[1] After ἵσταται BT have ἤδη (ἡ δὴ t, Stobaeus) καλουμένη
σταθερά, "which is called noontide," which Schanz brackets.

[2] Schanz follows Heindorf in bracketing ἀεὶ . . . πράττειν.

it may ; I shall cross this stream and go away before you put some further compulsion upon me.

PHAEDRUS. Not yet, Socrates, till the heat is past. Don't you see that it is already almost noon ? Let us stay and talk over what has been said, and then, when it is cooler, we will go away.

SOCRATES. Phaedrus, you are simply a superhuman wonder as regards discourses ! I believe no one of all those who have been born in your lifetime has produced more discourses than you, either by speaking them yourself or compelling others to do so. I except Simmias the Theban ; but you are far ahead of all the rest. And now I think you have become the cause of another, spoken by me.

PHAEDRUS. That is not exactly a declaration of war ! But how is this, and what is the discourse ?

SOCRATES. My good friend, when I was about to cross the stream, the spirit and the sign that usually comes to me came—it always holds me back from something I am about to do—and I thought I heard a voice from it which forbade my going away before clearing my conscience, as if I had committed some sin against deity. Now I am a seer, not a very good one, but, as the bad writers say, good enough for my own purposes ; so now I understand my error. How prophetic the soul is, my friend ! For all along, while I was speaking my discourse, something troubled

459

D Ἴβυκον, μή τι παρὰ θεοῖς ἀμβλακὼν τιμὰν πρὸς
ἀνθρώπων ἀμείψω· νῦν δ' ᾔσθημαι τὸ ἁμάρτημα.

ΦΑΙΔΡΟΣ. Λέγεις δὲ δὴ τί;

ΣΩΚΡΑΤΗΣ. Δεινόν, ὦ Φαῖδρε, δεινὸν λόγον αὐτός
τε ἐκόμισας ἐμέ τε ἠνάγκασας εἰπεῖν.

ΦΑΙΔΡΟΣ. Πῶς δή;

ΣΩΚΡΑΤΗΣ. Εὐήθη καὶ ὑπό τι ἀσεβῆ· οὗ τίς ἂν
εἴη δεινότερος;

ΦΑΙΔΡΟΣ. Οὐδείς, εἴ γε σὺ ἀληθῆ λέγεις.

ΣΩΚΡΑΤΗΣ. Τί οὖν; τὸν Ἔρωτα οὐκ Ἀφροδίτης
καὶ θεόν τινα ἡγεῖ;

ΦΑΙΔΡΟΣ. Λέγεταί γε δή.

ΣΩΚΡΑΤΗΣ. Οὔ τι ὑπό γε Λυσίου, οὐδὲ ὑπὸ τοῦ
E σοῦ λόγου, ὃς διὰ τοῦ ἐμοῦ στόματος καταφαρ-
μακευθέντος ὑπὸ σοῦ ἐλέχθη. εἰ δ' ἔστιν, ὥσπερ
οὖν ἔστι, θεὸς ἤ τι θεῖον ὁ Ἔρως, οὐδὲν ἂν κακὸν
εἴη· τὼ δὲ λόγω τὼ νῦν δὴ περὶ αὐτοῦ εἰπέτην
ὡς τοιούτου ὄντος. ταύτῃ τε οὖν ἡμαρτανέτην
περὶ τὸν Ἔρωτα, ἔτι τε ἡ εὐήθεια αὐτοῖν πάνυ
ἀστεία, τὸ μηδὲν ὑγιὲς λέγοντε μηδὲ ἀληθὲς
243 σεμνύνεσθαι ὡς τὶ ὄντε, εἰ ἄρα ἀνθρωπίσκους
τινὰς ἐξαπατήσαντε εὐδοκιμήσετον ἐν αὐτοῖς.
ἐμοὶ μὲν οὖν, ὦ φίλε, καθήρασθαι ἀνάγκη· ἔστι δὲ
τοῖς ἁμαρτάνουσι περὶ μυθολογίαν καθαρμὸς
ἀρχαῖος, ὃν Ὅμηρος μὲν οὐκ ᾔσθετο, Στησίχορος
δέ. τῶν γὰρ ὀμμάτων στερηθεὶς διὰ τὴν Ἑλένης
κακηγορίαν οὐκ ἠγνόησεν ὥσπερ Ὅμηρος, ἀλλ'

me, and " I was distressed," as Ibycus says, " lest I
be buying honour among men by sinning against the
gods." [1]   But now I have seen my error.

PHAEDRUS.   What do you mean?

SOCRATES.   Phaedrus, a dreadful speech it was, a
dreadful speech, the one you brought with you, and
the one you made me speak.

PHAEDRUS.   How so?

SOCRATES.   It was foolish, and somewhat impious.
What could be more dreadful than that?

PHAEDRUS.   Nothing, if you are right about it.

SOCRATES.   Well, do you not believe that Love is
the son of Aphrodite and is a god?

PHAEDRUS.   So it is said.

SOCRATES.   Yes, but not by Lysias, nor by your
speech which was spoken by you through my mouth
that you bewitched. If Love is, as indeed he is, a
god or something divine, he can be nothing evil; but
the two speeches just now said that he was evil. So
then they sinned against Love; but their foolishness
was really very funny besides, for while they
were saying nothing sound or true, they put on airs
as though they amounted to something, if they
could cheat some mere manikins and gain honour
among them. Now I, my friend, must purify myself;
and for those who have sinned in matters of mytho-
logy there is an ancient purification, unknown to
Homer, but known to Stesichorus. For when he
was stricken with blindness for speaking ill of Helen,
he was not, like Homer, ignorant of the reason, but

[1] Fragment 24, Bergk.

ἅτε μουσικὸς ὢν ἔγνω τὴν αἰτίαν, καὶ ποιεῖ
εὐθὺς

οὐκ ἔστ᾽ ἔτυμος λόγος οὗτος,
οὐδ᾽ ἔβας ἐν νηυσὶν εὐσέλμοις, οὐδ᾽ ἵκεο·
B   Πέργαμα Τροίας·

καὶ ποιήσας δὴ πᾶσαν τὴν καλουμένην παλινῳδίαν
παραχρῆμα ἀνέβλεψεν. ἐγὼ οὖν σοφώτερος
ἐκείνων γενήσομαι κατ᾽ αὐτό γε τοῦτο· πρὶν γάρ
τι παθεῖν διὰ τὴν τοῦ Ἔρωτος κακηγορίαν πειράσομαι αὐτῷ ἀποδοῦναι τὴν παλινῳδίαν, γυμνῇ τῇ
κεφαλῇ, καὶ οὐχ ὥσπερ τότε ὑπ᾽ αἰσχύνης
ἐγκεκαλυμμένος.

ΦΑΙΔΡΟΣ. Τουτωνί, ὦ Σώκρατες, οὐκ ἔστιν ἅττ᾽
ἂν ἐμοὶ εἶπες ἥδίω.

21. ΣΩΚΡΑΤΗΣ. Καὶ γάρ, ὦ 'γαθὲ Φαῖδρε, ἐννοεῖς
C ὡς ἀναιδῶς εἴρησθον τὼ λόγω, οὗτός τε καὶ ὁ ἐκ
τοῦ βιβλίου ῥηθείς. εἰ γὰρ ἀκούων τις τύχοι
ἡμῶν γεννάδας καὶ πρᾷος τὸ ἦθος, ἑτέρου δὲ
τοιούτου ἐρῶν ἢ καὶ πρότερόν ποτε ἐρασθείς,
λεγόντων ὡς διὰ σμικρὰ μεγάλας ἔχθρας οἱ
ἐρασταὶ ἀναιροῦνται καὶ ἔχουσι πρὸς τὰ παιδικὰ
φθονερῶς τε καὶ βλαβερῶς, πῶς οὐκ ἂν οἴει αὐτὸν
ἡγεῖσθαι ἀκούειν ἐν ναύταις που τεθραμμένων καὶ
οὐδένα ἐλεύθερον ἔρωτα ἑωρακότων, πολλοῦ δ᾽ ἂν
D δεῖν ἡμῖν ὁμολογεῖν ἃ ψέγομεν τὸν Ἔρωτα;

ΦΑΙΔΡΟΣ. Ἴσως νὴ Δί᾽, ὦ Σώκρατες.

ΣΩΚΡΑΤΗΣ. Τοῦτόν γε τοίνυν ἔγωγε αἰσχυνόμενος, καὶ αὐτὸν τὸν Ἔρωτα δεδιώς, ἐπιθυμῶ
ποτίμῳ λόγῳ οἷον ἁλμυρὰν ἀκοὴν ἀποκλύσασθαι·
συμβουλεύω δὲ καὶ Λυσίᾳ ὅ τι τάχιστα γράψαι,

since he was educated, he knew it and straightway he writes the poem:

" That saying is not true; thou didst not go within the well-oared ships, nor didst thou come to the walls of Troy " ; [1]

and when he had written all the poem, which is called the recantation, he saw again at once. Now I will be wiser than they in just this point : before suffering any punishment for speaking ill of Love, I will try to atone by my recantation, with my head bare this time, not, as before, covered through shame.

PHAEDRUS. This indeed, Socrates, is the most delightful thing you could say.

SOCRATES. Just consider, my good Phaedrus, how shameless the two speeches were, both this of mine and the one you read out of the book. For if any man of noble and gentle nature, one who was himself in love with another of the same sort, or who had ever been loved by such a one, had happened to hear us saying that lovers take up violent enmity because of small matters and are jealously disposed and harmful to the beloved, don't you think he would imagine he was listening to people brought up among low sailors, who had never seen a generous love? Would he not refuse utterly to assent to our censure of Love ?

PHAEDRUS. I declare, Socrates, perhaps he would.

SOCRATES. I therefore, because I am ashamed at the thought of this man and am afraid of Love himself, wish to wash out the brine from my ears with the water of a sweet discourse. And I advise Lysias

[1] Fragment 32, Bergk.

ὡς χρὴ ἐραστῇ μᾶλλον ἢ μὴ ἐρῶντι ἐκ τῶν ὁμοίων χαρίζεσθαι.

ΦΑΙΔΡΟΣ. Ἀλλ' εὖ ἴσθι ὅτι ἕξει τοῦθ' οὕτω· σοῦ γὰρ εἰπόντος τὸν τοῦ ἐραστοῦ ἔπαινον, πᾶσα Ε ἀνάγκη Λυσίαν ὑπ' ἐμοῦ ἀναγκασθῆναι γράψαι αὖ περὶ τοῦ αὐτοῦ λόγον.

ΣΩΚΡΑΤΗΣ. Τοῦτο μὲν πιστεύω, ἕωσπερ ἂν ᾖς ὃς εἶ.

ΦΑΙΔΡΟΣ. Λέγε τοίνυν θαρρῶν.

ΣΩΚΡΑΤΗΣ. Ποῦ δή μοι ὁ παῖς πρὸς ὃν ἔλεγον; ἵνα καὶ τοῦτο ἀκούσῃ, καὶ μὴ ἀνήκοος ὢν φθάσῃ χαρισάμενος τῷ μὴ ἐρῶντι.

ΦΑΙΔΡΟΣ. Οὗτος παρά σοι μάλα πλησίον ἀεὶ πάρεστιν, ὅταν σὺ βούλῃ.

22. ΣΩΚΡΑΤΗΣ. Οὑτωσὶ τοίνυν, ὦ παῖ καλέ, 244 ἐννόησον, ὡς ὁ μὲν πρότερος ἦν λόγος Φαίδρου τοῦ Πυθοκλέους, Μυρρινουσίου ἀνδρός· ὃν δὲ μέλλω λέγειν, Στησιχόρου τοῦ Εὐφήμου, Ἱμεραίου. λεκτέος δὲ ὧδε, ὅτι οὐκ ἔστ' ἔτυμος λόγος, ὃς ἂν παρόντος ἐραστοῦ τῷ μὴ ἐρῶντι μᾶλλον φῇ δεῖν χαρίζεσθαι, διότι δὴ ὁ μὲν μαίνεται, ὁ δὲ σωφρονεῖ. εἰ μὲν γὰρ ἦν ἁπλοῦν τὸ μανίαν κακὸν εἶναι, καλῶς ἂν ἐλέγετο· νῦν δὲ τὰ μέγιστα τῶν ἀγαθῶν ἡμῖν γίγνεται διὰ μανίας, θείᾳ μέντοι δόσει διδομένης. ἥ τε γὰρ δὴ ἐν Δελφοῖς προΒ φῆτις αἵ τ' ἐν Δωδώνῃ ἱέρειαι μανεῖσαι μὲν πολλὰ δὴ καὶ καλὰ ἰδίᾳ τε καὶ δημοσίᾳ τὴν Ἑλλάδα εἰργάσαντο, σωφρονοῦσαι δὲ βραχέα ἢ οὐδέν· καὶ ἐὰν δὴ λέγωμεν Σίβυλλάν τε καὶ ἄλλους, ὅσοι

also to write as soon as he can, that other things being equal, the lover should be favoured rather than the non-lover.

PHAEDRUS. Be assured that he will do so : for when you have spoken the praise of the lover, Lysias must of course be compelled by me to write another discourse on the same subject.

SOCRATES. I believe you, so long as you are what you are.

PHAEDRUS. Speak then without fear.

SOCRATES. Where is the youth to whom I was speaking ? He must hear this also, lest if he do not hear it, he accept a non-lover before we can stop him.

PHAEDRUS. Here he is, always close at hand whenever you want him.

SOCRATES. Understand then, fair youth, that the former discourse was by Phaedrus, the son of Pythocles (Eager for Fame) of Myrrhinus (Myrrhtown); but this which I shall speak is by Stesichorus, son of Euphemus (Man of pious Speech) of Himera (Town of Desire). And I must say that this saying is not true, which teaches that when a lover is at hand the non-lover should be more favoured, because the lover is insane, and the other sane. For if it were a simple fact that insanity is an evil, the saying would be true ; but in reality the greatest of blessings come to us through madness, when it is sent as a gift of the gods. For the prophetess at Delphi and the priestesses at Dodona when they have been mad have conferred many splendid benefits upon Greece both in private and in public affairs, but few or none when they have been in their right minds ; and if we should speak of the Sibyl and all the others who by pro-

μαντικῇ χρώμενοι ἐνθέῳ πολλὰ δὴ πολλοῖς προ-
λέγοντες εἰς τὸ μέλλον ὤρθωσαν, μηκύνοιμεν ἂν
δῆλα παντὶ λέγοντες· τόδε μὴν ἄξιον ἐπιμαρτύ-
ρασθαι, ὅτι καὶ τῶν παλαιῶν οἱ τὰ ὀνόματα
τιθέμενοι οὐκ αἰσχρὸν ἡγοῦντο οὐδὲ ὄνειδος μανίαν.
C οὐ γὰρ ἂν τῇ καλλίστῃ τέχνῃ, ᾗ τὸ μέλλον κρίνε-
ται, αὐτὸ τοῦτο τοὔνομα ἐμπλέκοντες μανικὴν
ἐκάλεσαν· ἀλλ' ὡς καλοῦ ὄντος, ὅταν θείᾳ μοίρᾳ
γίγνηται, οὕτω νομίσαντες ἔθεντο, οἱ δὲ νῦν
ἀπειροκάλως τὸ ταῦ ἐπεμβάλλοντες μαντικὴν
ἐκάλεσαν. ἐπεὶ καὶ τήν γε τῶν ἐμφρόνων ζήτησιν
τοῦ μέλλοντος διά τε ὀρνίθων ποιουμένων [1] καὶ τῶν
ἄλλων σημείων, ἅτ' ἐκ διανοίας ποριζομένων ἀνθρω-
D πίνῃ οἰήσει νοῦν τε καὶ ἱστορίαν, οἰονοϊστικὴν
ἐπωνόμασαν, ἣν νῦν οἰωνιστικὴν τῷ ω σεμνύνοντες
οἱ νέοι καλοῦσιν· ὅσῳ δὴ οὖν τελεώτερον καὶ ἐντιμότερον μαντικὴ οἰωνιστικῆς, τό τε ὄνομα τοῦ
ὀνόματος ἔργον τ' ἔργου, τόσῳ κάλλιον μαρτυ-
ροῦσιν οἱ παλαιοὶ μανίαν σωφροσύνης τὴν ἐκ θεοῦ
τῆς παρ' ἀνθρώπων γιγνομένης. ἀλλὰ μὴν νόσων
γε καὶ πόνων τῶν μεγίστων, ἃ δὴ παλαιῶν ἐκ
μηνιμάτων ποθὲν ἔν τισι τῶν γενῶν, ἡ μανία
E ἐγγενομένη καὶ προφητεύσασα οἷς ἔδει ἀπαλλαγὴν
εὕρετο, καταφυγοῦσα πρὸς θεῶν εὐχάς τε καὶ
λατρείας, ὅθεν δὴ καθαρμῶν τε καὶ τελετῶν
τυχοῦσα ἐξάντη ἐποίησε τὸν ἑαυτῆς ἔχοντα πρός

---

[1] Schanz brackets ποιουμένων.

phetic inspiration have foretold many things to many
persons and thereby made them fortunate afterwards,
anyone can see that we should speak a long time.
And it is worth while to adduce also the fact that
those men of old who invented names thought that
madness was neither shameful nor disgraceful ; otherwise they would not have connected the very word
mania with the noblest of arts, that which foretells
the future, by calling it the manic art. No, they
gave this name thinking that mania, when it comes
by gift of the gods, is a noble thing, but nowadays
people call prophecy the mantic art, tastelessly
inserting a T in the word. So also, when they gave
a name to the investigation of the future which
rational persons conduct through observation of birds
and by other signs, since they furnish mind (nous)
and information (historia) to human thought (oiesis)
from the intellect (dianoia) they called it the oiono-
ïstic (oionoistike) art, which modern folk now call
oiōnistic, making it more high-sounding by introducing the long O. The ancients, then testify that
in proportion as prophecy (mantike) is superior
to augury, both in name and in fact, in the same
proportion madness, which comes from god, is superior
to sanity, which is of human origin. Moreover, when
diseases and the greatest troubles have been visited
upon certain families through some ancient guilt,
madness has entered in and by oracular power has
found a way of release for those in need, taking
refuge in prayers and the service of the gods, and so,
by purifications and sacred rites, he who has this
madness is made safe for the present and the after
time, and for him who is rightly possessed of

τε τὸν παρόντα καὶ τὸν ἔπειτα χρόνον, λύσιν τῷ
ὀρθῶς μανέντι τε καὶ κατασχομένῳ τῶν παρόντων
245 κακῶν εὑρομένη. τρίτη δὲ ἀπὸ Μουσῶν κατοκωχή
τε καὶ μανία, λαβοῦσα ἁπαλὴν καὶ ἄβατον ψυχήν,
ἐγείρουσα καὶ ἐκβακχεύουσα κατά τε ᾠδὰς καὶ
κατὰ τὴν ἄλλην ποίησιν, μυρία τῶν παλαιῶν ἔργα
κοσμοῦσα τοὺς ἐπιγιγνομένους παιδεύει· ὃς δ᾽ ἂν
ἄνευ μανίας Μουσῶν ἐπὶ ποιητικὰς θύρας ἀφίκηται, πεισθεὶς ὡς ἄρα ἐκ τέχνης ἱκανὸς ποιητὴς
ἐσόμενος, ἀτελὴς αὐτός τε καὶ ἡ ποίησις ὑπὸ τῆς
τῶν μαινομένων ἡ τοῦ σωφρονοῦντος ἠφανίσθη.

B   23. Τοσαῦτα μέντοι καὶ ἔτι πλείω ἔχω μανίας
γιγνομένης ἀπὸ θεῶν λέγειν καλὰ ἔργα· ὥστε
τοῦτό γε αὐτὸ μὴ φοβώμεθα, μηδέ τις ἡμᾶς λόγος
θορυβείτω δεδιττόμενος, ὡς πρὸ τοῦ κεκινημένου
τὸν σώφρονα δεῖ προαιρεῖσθαι φίλον· ἀλλὰ τόδε
πρὸς ἐκείνῳ δείξας φερέσθω τὰ νικητήρια, ὡς οὐκ
ἐπ᾽ ὠφελίᾳ ὁ ἔρως τῷ ἐρῶντι καὶ τῷ ἐρωμένῳ ἐκ
θεῶν ἐπιπέμπεται. ἡμῖν δὲ ἀποδεικτέον αὖ τοὐναντίον, ὡς ἐπ᾽ εὐτυχίᾳ τῇ μεγίστῃ παρὰ θεῶν ἡ
C   τοιαύτη μανία δίδοται· ἡ δὲ δὴ ἀπόδειξις ἔσται
δεινοῖς μὲν ἄπιστος, σοφοῖς δὲ πιστή. δεῖ οὖν
πρῶτον ψυχῆς φύσεως πέρι θείας τε καὶ ἀνθρωπίνης ἰδόντα πάθη τε καὶ ἔργα τἀληθὲς νοῆσαι·
ἀρχὴ δὲ ἀποδείξεως ἥδε.

24. Ψυχὴ πᾶσα ἀθάνατος. τὸ γὰρ ἀεικίνητον
ἀθάνατον· τὸ δ᾽ ἄλλο κινοῦν καὶ ὑπ᾽ ἄλλου κινούμενον, παῦλαν ἔχον κινήσεως, παῦλαν ἔχει ζωῆς·
μόνον δὴ τὸ αὑτὸ κινοῦν, ἅτε οὐκ ἀπολεῖπον ἑαυτό,
οὔ ποτε λήγει κινούμενον, ἀλλὰ καὶ τοῖς ἄλλοις
D   ὅσα κινεῖται τοῦτο πηγὴ καὶ ἀρχὴ κινήσεως.
ἀρχὴ δὲ ἀγένητον. ἐξ ἀρχῆς γὰρ ἀνάγκη πᾶν τὸ

madness a release from present ills is found. And a third kind of possession and madness comes from the Muses. This takes hold upon a gentle and pure soul, arouses it and inspires it to songs and other poetry, and thus by adorning countless deeds of the ancients educates later generations. But he who without the divine madness comes to the doors of the Muses, confident that he will be a good poet by art, meets with no success, and the poetry of the sane man vanishes into nothingness before that of the inspired madmen.

All these noble results of inspired madness I can mention, and many more. Therefore let us not be afraid on that point, and let no one disturb and frighten us by saying that the reasonable friend should be preferred to him who is in a frenzy. Let him show in addition that love is not sent from heaven for the advantage of lover and beloved alike, and we will grant him the prize of victory. We, on our part, must prove that such madness is given by the gods for our greatest happiness; and our proof will not be believed by the merely clever, but will be accepted by the truly wise. First, then, we must learn the truth about the soul divine and human by observing how it acts and is acted upon. And the beginning of our proof is as follows:

Every soul is immortal. For that which is ever moving is immortal; but that which moves something else or is moved by something else, when it ceases to move, ceases to live. Only that which moves itself, since it does not leave itself, never ceases to move, and this is also the source and beginning of motion for all other things which have motion. But the

γιγνόμενον γίγνεσθαι, αὐτὴν δὲ μηδ' ἐξ ἑνός· εἰ
γὰρ ἔκ του ἀρχὴ γίγνοιτο,[1] οὐκ ἂν ἐξ ἀρχῆς
γίγνοιτο. ἐπειδὴ δὲ ἀγένητόν ἐστι, καὶ ἀδιάφθορον αὐτὸ ἀνάγκη εἶναι. ἀρχῆς γὰρ δὴ ἀπολομένης οὔτε αὐτή ποτε ἔκ του οὔτε ἄλλο ἐξ ἐκείνης
γενήσεται, εἴπερ ἐξ ἀρχῆς δεῖ τὰ πάντα γίγνεσθαι.
οὕτω δὴ κινήσεως μὲν ἀρχὴ τὸ αὐτὸ αὑτὸ κινοῦν.
τοῦτο δὲ οὔτ' ἀπόλλυσθαι οὔτε γίγνεσθαι δυνατόν,

E ἢ πάντα τε οὐρανὸν πᾶσάν τε γένεσιν συμπε-
σοῦσαν στῆναι καὶ μήποτε αὖθις ἔχειν ὅθεν κινη-
θέντα γενήσεται. ἀθανάτου δὲ πεφασμένου τοῦ
ὑφ' ἑαυτοῦ κινουμένου, ψυχῆς οὐσίαν τε καὶ λόγον
τοῦτον αὐτόν τις λέγων οὐκ αἰσχυνεῖται. πᾶν
γὰρ σῶμα, ᾧ μὲν ἔξωθεν τὸ κινεῖσθαι, ἄψυχον, ᾧ
δὲ ἔνδοθεν αὐτῷ ἐξ αὑτοῦ, ἔμψυχον, ὡς ταύτης
οὔσης φύσεως ψυχῆς· εἰ δ' ἔστιν τοῦτο οὕτως

246 ἔχον, μὴ ἄλλο τι εἶναι τὸ αὐτὸ ἑαυτὸ κινοῦν ἢ
ψυχήν, ἐξ ἀνάγκης ἀγένητόν τε καὶ ἀθάνατον
ψυχὴ ἂν εἴη.

25. Περὶ μὲν οὖν ἀθανασίας αὐτῆς ἱκανῶς· περὶ
δὲ τῆς ἰδέας αὐτῆς ὧδε λεκτέον· οἷον μέν ἐστι,
πάντῃ πάντως θείας εἶναι καὶ μακρᾶς διηγήσεως,
ᾧ δὲ ἔοικεν, ἀνθρωπίνης τε καὶ ἐλάττονος· ταύτῃ
οὖν λέγωμεν. ἐοικέτω δὴ ξυμφύτῳ δυνάμει ὑπο-
πτέρου ζεύγους τε καὶ ἡνιόχου. θεῶν μὲν οὖν
ἵπποι τε καὶ ἡνίοχοι πάντες αὐτοί τε ἀγαθοὶ καὶ

B ἐξ ἀγαθῶν, τὸ δὲ τῶν ἄλλων μέμικται· καὶ πρῶτον

---

[1] Schanz adds τοῦτο before οὐκ.

beginning is ungenerated. For everything that is generated must be generated from a beginning, but the beginning is not generated from anything; for if the beginning were generated from anything, it would not be generated from a beginning. And since it is ungenerated, it must be also indestructible; for if the beginning were destroyed, it could never be generated from anything nor anything else from it, since all things must be generated from a beginning. Thus that which moves itself must be the beginning of motion. And this can be neither destroyed nor generated, otherwise all the heavens and all generation must fall in ruin and stop and never again have any source of motion or origin. But since that which is moved by itself has been seen to be immortal, one who says that this self-motion is the essence and the very idea of the soul, will not be disgraced. For every body which derives motion from without is soulless, but that which has its motion within itself has a soul, since that is the nature of the soul; but if this is true,—that that which moves itself is nothing else than the soul,—then the soul would necessarily be ungenerated and immortal.

Concerning the immortality of the soul this is enough; but about its form we must speak in the following manner. To tell what it really is would be a matter for utterly superhuman and long discourse, but it is within human power to describe it briefly in a figure; let us therefore speak in that way. We will liken the soul to the composite nature of a pair of winged horses and a charioteer. Now the horses and charioteers of the gods are all good and of good descent, but those of other races are mixed; and first

μὲν ἡμῶν ὁ ἄρχων ξυνωρίδος ἡνιοχεῖ, εἶτα τῶν
ἵππων ὁ μὲν αὐτῷ καλός τε καὶ ἀγαθὸς καὶ ἐκ
τοιούτων, ὁ δὲ ἐξ ἐναντίων τε καὶ ἐναντίος· χαλεπὴ
δὴ καὶ δύσκολος ἐξ ἀνάγκης ἡ περὶ ἡμᾶς ἡνιό-
χησις. πῇ δὴ οὖν θνητὸν καὶ ἀθάνατον ζῷον
ἐκλήθη, πειρατέον εἰπεῖν. πᾶσα ἡ ψυχὴ παντὸς
ἐπιμελεῖται τοῦ ἀψύχου, πάντα δὲ οὐρανὸν περι-
πολεῖ, ἄλλοτ' ἐν ἄλλοις εἴδεσι γιγνομένη· τελέα
C μὲν οὖν οὖσα καὶ ἐπτερωμένη μετεωροπορεῖ τε καὶ
πάντα τὸν κόσμον διοικεῖ· ἡ δὲ πτερορρυήσασα
φέρεται, ἕως ἂν στερεοῦ τινος ἀντιλάβηται, οὗ
κατοικισθεῖσα, σῶμα γήϊνον λαβοῦσα, αὐτὸ αὑτὸ
δοκοῦν κινεῖν διὰ τὴν ἐκείνης δύναμιν, ζῷον τὸ
ξύμπαν ἐκλήθη, ψυχὴ καὶ σῶμα παγέν, θνητόν
τ' ἔσχεν ἐπωνυμίαν· ἀθάνατον δὲ οὐδ' ἐξ ἑνὸς
λόγου λελογισμένου, ἀλλὰ πλάττομεν οὔτε ἰδόντες
D οὔτε ἱκανῶς νοήσαντες θεόν, ἀθάνατόν τι ζῷον,
ἔχον μὲν ψυχήν, ἔχον δὲ σῶμα, τὸν ἀεὶ δὲ χρόνον
ταῦτα ξυμπεφυκότα. ἀλλὰ ταῦτα μὲν δή, ὅπῃ
τῷ θεῷ φίλον, ταύτῃ ἐχέτω τε καὶ λεγέσθω· τὴν
δ' αἰτίαν τῆς τῶν πτερῶν ἀποβολῆς, δι' ἣν ψυχῆς
ἀπορρεῖ, λάβωμεν. ἔστι δέ τις τοιάδε.

26. Πέφυκεν ἡ πτεροῦ δύναμις τὸ ἐμβριθὲς
ἄγειν ἄνω μετεωρίζουσα, ᾗ τὸ τῶν θεῶν γένος
οἰκεῖ· κεκοινώνηκε δέ πῃ μάλιστα τῶν περὶ τὸ
E σῶμα τοῦ θείου.[1] τὸ δὲ θεῖον καλόν, σοφόν,
ἀγαθόν, καὶ πᾶν ὅ τι τοιοῦτον· τούτοις δὴ τρέ-
φεταί τε καὶ αὔξεται μάλιστά γε τὸ τῆς ψυχῆς
πτέρωμα, αἰσχρῷ δὲ καὶ κακῷ καὶ τοῖς ἐναντίοις[2]

---

[1] The word ψυχή, given in the MSS. after θείου, is omitted
by Plutarch and most modern editors, including Schanz.
[2] Schanz omits καὶ τοῖς ἐναντίοις.

the charioteer of the human soul drives a pair, and
secondly one of the horses is noble and of noble breed,
but the other quite the opposite in breed and character.
Therefore in our case the driving is necessarily difficult and troublesome. Now we must try to tell why
a living being is called mortal or immortal. Soul,
considered collectively, has the care of all that which
is soulless, and it traverses the whole heaven,
appearing sometimes in one form and sometimes in
another ; now when it is perfect and fully winged, it
mounts upward and governs the whole world ; but
the soul which has lost its wings is borne along
until it gets hold of something solid, when it settles
down, taking upon itself an earthly body, which
seems to be self-moving, because of the power of the
soul within it ; and the whole, compounded of soul
and body, is called a living being, and is further
designated as mortal. It is not immortal by any
reasonable supposition, but we, though we have never
seen or rightly conceived a god, imagine an immortal
being which has both a soul and a body which are
united for all time. Let that, however, and our
words concerning it, be as is pleasing to God ; we will
now consider the reason why the soul loses its wings.
It is something like this.

The natural function of the wing is to soar upwards and carry that which is heavy up to the place
where dwells the race of the gods. More than any
other thing that pertains to the body it partakes of
the nature of the divine. But the divine is beauty,
wisdom, goodness, and all such qualities ; by these
then the wings of the soul are nourished and grow,
but by the opposite qualities, such as vileness and

φθίνει τε καὶ διόλλυται. ὁ μὲν δὴ μέγας ἡγεμὼν
ἐν οὐρανῷ Ζεύς, ἐλαύνων πτηνὸν ἅρμα, πρῶτος
πορεύεται, διακοσμῶν πάντα καὶ ἐπιμελούμενος·
247 τῷ δ' ἕπεται στρατιὰ θεῶν τε καὶ δαιμόνων, κατὰ
ἕνδεκα μέρη κεκοσμημένη· μένει γὰρ Ἑστία ἐν
θεῶν οἴκῳ μόνη· τῶν δὲ ἄλλων ὅσοι ἐν τῷ τῶν
δώδεκα ἀριθμῷ τεταγμένοι θεοὶ ἄρχοντες ἡγοῦνται
κατὰ τάξιν ἣν ἕκαστος ἐτάχθη. πολλαὶ μὲν οὖν
καὶ μακάριαι θέαι τε καὶ διέξοδοι ἐντὸς οὐρανοῦ,
ἃς θεῶν γένος εὐδαιμόνων[1] ἐπιστρέφεται, πράττων
ἕκαστος αὐτῶν τὸ αὑτοῦ, ἕπεται δὲ ὁ ἀεὶ ἐθέλων
τε καὶ δυνάμενος· φθόνος γὰρ ἔξω θείου χοροῦ
ἵσταται· ὅταν δὲ δὴ πρὸς δαῖτα καὶ ἐπὶ θοίνην
B ἴωσιν, ἄκραν ὑπὸ τὴν ὑπουράνιον ἁψῖδα πορεύονται[2] πρὸς ἄναντες· ᾗ δὴ[3] τὰ μὲν θεῶν ὀχήματα
ἰσορρόπως εὐήνια ὄντα ῥᾳδίως πορεύεται, τὰ δὲ
ἄλλα μόγις· βρίθει γὰρ ὁ τῆς κάκης ἵππος
μετέχων, ἐπὶ τὴν γῆν ῥέπων τε καὶ βαρύνων, ᾧ μὴ
καλῶς ᾖ τεθραμμένος τῶν ἡνιόχων· ἔνθα δὴ πόνος
τε καὶ ἀγὼν ἔσχατος ψυχῇ πρόκειται. αἱ μὲν
γὰρ ἀθάνατοι καλούμεναι, ἡνίκ' ἂν πρὸς ἄκρῳ
C γένωνται, ἔξω πορευθεῖσαι ἔστησαν ἐπὶ τῷ τοῦ
οὐρανοῦ νώτῳ, στάσας δὲ αὐτὰς περιάγει ἡ περι-
φορά, αἱ δὲ θεωροῦσι τὰ ἔξω τοῦ οὐρανοῦ.
27. Τὸν δὲ ὑπερουράνιον τόπον οὔτε τις ὕμνησέ
πω τῶν τῇδε ποιητὴς οὔτε ποτὲ ὑμνήσει κατ'
ἀξίαν, ἔχει δὲ ὧδε. τολμητέον γὰρ οὖν τό γε
ἀληθὲς εἰπεῖν, ἄλλως τε καὶ περὶ ἀληθείας
λέγοντα. ἡ γὰρ ἀχρώματός τε καὶ ἀσχημάτιστος

---

[1] Schanz reads εὐδαιμόνως.
[2] Schanz brackets πορεύονται.
[3] ᾗ δὴ Proclus, followed by Burnet. ἤδη BT Schanz et al.

evil, they are wasted away and destroyed. Now the great leader in heaven, Zeus, driving a winged chariot, goes first, arranging all things and caring for all things. He is followed by an army of gods and spirits, arrayed in eleven squadrons; Hestia alone remains in the house of the gods. Of the rest, those who are included among the twelve great gods and are accounted leaders, are assigned each to his place in the army. There are many blessed sights and many ways hither and thither within the heaven, along which the blessed gods go to and fro attending each to his own duties; and whoever wishes, and is able, follows, for jealousy is excluded from the celestial band. But when they go to a feast and a banquet, they proceed steeply upward to the top of the vault of heaven, where the chariots of the gods, whose well matched horses obey the rein, advance easily, but the others with difficulty; for the horse of evil nature weighs the chariot down, making it heavy and pulling toward the earth the charioteer whose horse is not well trained. There the utmost toil and struggle await the soul. For those that are called immortal, when they reach the top, pass outside and take their place on the outer surface of the heaven, and when they have taken their stand, the revolution carries them round and they behold the things outside of the heaven.

But the region above the heaven was never worthily sung by any earthly poet, nor will it ever be. It is, however, as I shall tell; for I must dare to speak the truth, especially as truth is my theme. For the colourless, formless, and intangible truly

PLATO

καὶ ἀναφὴς οὐσία ὄντως οὖσα ψυχῆς[1] κυβερνήτῃ
μόνῳ θεατὴ νῷ, περὶ ἣν τὸ τῆς ἀληθοῦς
D ἐπιστήμης γένος τοῦτον ἔχει τὴν τόπον. ἅτ᾽[2] οὖν
θεοῦ διάνοια νῷ τε καὶ ἐπιστήμῃ ἀκηράτῳ τρεφομένη καὶ ἁπάσης ψυχῆς, ὅση ἂν μέλλῃ τὸ προσῆκον δέξεσθαι,[3] ἰδοῦσα διὰ χρόνου τὸ ὂν ἀγαπᾷ
τε καὶ θεωροῦσα τἀληθῆ τρέφεται καὶ εὐπαθεῖ,
ἕως ἂν κύκλῳ ἡ περιφορὰ εἰς ταὐτὸν περιενέγκῃ·
ἐν δὲ τῇ περιόδῳ καθορᾷ μὲν αὐτὴν δικαιοσύνην,
καθορᾷ δὲ σωφροσύνην, καθορᾷ δὲ ἐπιστήμην, οὐχ
ᾗ γένεσις πρόσεστιν, οὐδ᾽ ἥ ἐστίν που ἑτέρα ἐν
E ἑτέρῳ οὖσα ὧν ἡμεῖς νῦν ὄντων καλοῦμεν, ἀλλὰ
τὴν ἐν τῷ ὅ ἐστιν ὂν ὄντως ἐπιστήμην οὖσαν· καὶ
τἆλλα ὡσαύτως τὰ ὄντα ὄντως θεασαμένη καὶ
ἑστιαθεῖσα, δῦσα πάλιν εἰς τὸ εἴσω τοῦ οὐρανοῦ,
οἴκαδε ἦλθεν, ἐλθούσης δὲ αὐτῆς ὁ ἡνίοχος πρὸς
τὴν φάτνην τοὺς ἵππους στήσας παρέβαλεν ἀμ-
βροσίαν τε καὶ ἐπ᾽ αὐτῇ νέκταρ ἐπότισεν.

28. Καὶ οὗτος μὲν θεῶν βίος· αἱ δὲ ἄλλαι ψυ-
248 χαί, ἡ μὲν ἄριστα θεῷ ἑπομένη καὶ εἰκασμένη
ὑπερῆρεν εἰς τὸν ἔξω τόπον τὴν τοῦ ἡνιόχου
κεφαλήν, καὶ συμπεριηνέχθη τὴν περιφοράν, θορυ-
βουμένη ὑπὸ τῶν ἵππων καὶ μόγις καθορῶσα τὰ
ὄντα· ἡ δὲ τοτὲ μὲν ἦρε, τοτὲ δ᾽ ἔδυ, βιαζομένων
δὲ τῶν ἵππων τὰ μὲν εἶδεν, τὰ δ᾽ οὔ· αἱ δὲ δὴ ἄλλαι
γλιχόμεναι μὲν ἅπασαι τοῦ ἄνω ἕπονται, ἀδυ-
νατοῦσαι δὲ ὑποβρύχιαι ξυμπεριφέρονται, πα-
B τοῦσαι ἀλλήλας καὶ ἐπιβάλλουσαι, ἑτέρα πρὸ τῆς

[1] ψυχῇ οὖσα B οὖσα ψυχῆς T.   οὖσα Madvig, Schanz.
[2] ἅτ᾽ BT ἥ τ᾽ Heindorf, Schanz.
[3] καὶ ἁπάσης . . . δέξεσθαι bracketed by Schanz, following Suckow.

476

existing essence, with which all true knowledge is concerned, holds this region and is visible only to the mind, the pilot of the soul. Now the divine intelligence, since it is nurtured on mind and pure knowledge, and the intelligence of every soul which is capable of receiving that which befits it, rejoices in seeing reality for a space of time and by gazing upon truth is nourished and made happy until the revolution brings it again to the same place. In the revolution it beholds absolute justice, temperance, and knowledge, not such knowledge as has a beginning and varies as it is associated with one or another of the things we call realities, but that which abides in the real eternal absolute; and in the same way it beholds and feeds upon the other eternal verities, after which, passing down again within the heaven, it goes home, and there the charioteer puts up the horses at the manger and feeds them with ambrosia and then gives them nectar to drink.

Such is the life of the gods; but of the other souls, that which best follows after God and is most like him, raises the head of the charioteer up into the outer region and is carried round in the revolution, troubled by the horses and hardly beholding the realities; and another sometimes rises and sometimes sinks, and, because its horses are unruly, it sees some things and fails to see others. The other souls follow after, all yearning for the upper region but unable to reach it, and are carried round beneath, trampling upon and colliding with one another, each

ἑτέρας πειρωμένη γενέσθαι. θόρυβος οὖν καὶ
ἄμιλλα καὶ ἱδρὼς ἔσχατος γίγνεται, οὗ δὴ κακίᾳ
ἡνιόχων πολλαὶ μὲν χωλεύονται, πολλαὶ δὲ
πολλὰ πτερὰ θραύονται· πᾶσαι δὲ πολὺν ἔχουσαι
πόνον ἀτελεῖς τῆς τοῦ ὄντος θέας ἀπέρχονται,
καὶ ἀπελθοῦσαι τροφῇ δοξαστῇ χρῶνται. οὗ
δ' ἕνεχ' ἡ πολλὴ σπουδὴ τὸ ἀληθείας ἰδεῖν πεδίον
οὗ¹ ἐστίν, ἥ τε δὴ προσήκουσα ψυχῆς τῷ ἀρίστῳ
νομὴ ἐκ τοῦ ἐκεῖ λειμῶνος τυγχάνει οὖσα, ἥ τε τοῦ
C πτεροῦ φύσις, ᾧ ψυχὴ κουφίζεται, τούτῳ τρέ-
φεται· θεσμός τε Ἀδραστείας ὅδε, ἥτις ἂν ψυχὴ
θεῷ ξυνοπαδὸς γενομένη κατίδῃ τι τῶν ἀληθῶν,
μέχρι τε τῆς ἑτέρας περιόδου εἶναι ἀπήμονα, κἂν
ἀεὶ τοῦτο δύνηται ποιεῖν, ἀεὶ ἀβλαβῆ εἶναι. ὅταν
δὲ ἀδυνατήσασα ἐπισπέσθαι μὴ ἴδῃ, καί τινι
συντυχίᾳ χρησαμένη λήθης τε καὶ κακίας πλη-
σθεῖσα βαρυνθῇ, βαρυνθεῖσα δὲ πτερορρυήσῃ τε
καὶ ἐπὶ τὴν γῆν πέσῃ, τότε νόμος ταύτην μὴ
D φυτεῦσαι εἰς μηδεμίαν θήρειον φύσιν ἐν τῇ πρώτῃ
γενέσει, ἀλλὰ τὴν μὲν πλεῖστα ἰδοῦσαν εἰς γονὴν
ἀνδρὸς γενησομένου φιλοσόφου ἢ φιλοκάλου ἢ
μουσικοῦ τινος καὶ ἐρωτικοῦ, τὴν δὲ δευτέραν εἰς
βασιλέως ἐννόμου ἢ πολεμικοῦ καὶ ἀρχικοῦ,
τρίτην εἰς πολιτικοῦ ἤ τινος οἰκονομικοῦ ἢ χρη-
ματιστικοῦ, τετάρτην εἰς φιλοπόνου γυμναστικοῦ
ἢ περὶ σώματος ἴασίν τινος ἐσομένου, πέμπτην
E μαντικὸν βίον ἤ τινα τελεστικὸν ἕξουσαν· ἕκτῃ
ποιητικὸς ἢ τῶν περὶ μίμησίν τις ἄλλος ἁρμόσει,
ἑβδόμῃ δημιουργικὸς ἢ γεωργικός, ὀγδόῃ σοφι-
στικὸς ἢ δημοτικός, ἐννάτη τυραννικός.

¹ οὗ is omitted by Schanz, following Madvig.

striving to pass its neighbour. So there is the greatest confusion and sweat of rivalry, wherein many are lamed, and many wings are broken through the incompetence of the drivers; and after much toil they all go away without gaining a view of reality, and when they have gone away they feed upon opinion. But the reason of the great eagerness to see where the plain of truth is, lies in the fact that the fitting pasturage for the best part of the soul is in the meadow there, and the wing on which the soul is raised up is nourished by this. And this is a law of Destiny, that the soul which follows after God and obtains a view of any of the truths is free from harm until the next period, and if it can always attain this, is always unharmed; but when, through inability to follow, it fails to see, and through some mischance is filled with forgetfulness and evil and grows heavy, and when it has grown heavy, loses its wings and falls to the earth, then it is the law that this soul shall never pass into any beast at its first birth, but the soul that has seen the most shall enter into the birth of a man who is to be a philosopher or a lover of beauty, or one of a musical or loving nature, and the second soul into that of a lawful king or a warlike ruler, and the third into that of a politician or a man of business or a financier, the fourth into that of a hard-working gymnast or one who will be concerned with the cure of the body, and the fifth will lead the life of a prophet or someone who conducts mystic rites; to the sixth, a poet or some other imitative artist will be united, to the seventh, a craftsman or a husbandman, to the eighth, a sophist or a demagogue, to the ninth, a tyrant.

29. Ἐν δὴ τούτοις ἅπασιν ὃς μὲν ἂν δικαίως διαγάγῃ, ἀμείνονος μοίρας μεταλαμβάνει, ὃς δ' ἂν ἀδίκως, χείρονος. εἰς μὲν γὰρ τὸ αὐτὸ ὅθεν ἥκει ἡ ψυχὴ ἑκάστη οὐκ ἀφικνεῖται ἐτῶν μυρίων· οὐ

249 γὰρ πτεροῦται πρὸ τοσούτου χρόνου, πλὴν ἡ τοῦ φιλοσοφήσαντος ἀδόλως ἢ παιδεραστήσαντος μετὰ φιλοσοφίας· αὗται δὲ τρίτῃ περιόδῳ τῇ χιλιετεῖ, ἐὰν ἕλωνται τρὶς ἐφεξῆς τὸν βίον τοῦτον, οὕτω πτερωθεῖσαι τρισχιλιοστῷ ἔτει ἀπέρχονται· αἱ δὲ ἄλλαι, ὅταν τὸν πρῶτον βίον τελευτήσωσι, κρίσεως ἔτυχον, κριθεῖσαι δὲ αἱ μὲν εἰς τὰ ὑπὸ γῆς δικαιωτήρια ἐλθοῦσαι δίκην ἐκτίνουσιν, αἱ δ' εἰς

B τοὐρανοῦ τινὰ τόπον ὑπὸ τῆς δίκης κουφισθεῖσαι διάγουσιν ἀξίως οὗ ἐν ἀνθρώπου εἴδει ἐβίωσαν βίου. τῷ δὲ χιλιοστῷ ἀμφότεραι ἀφικνούμεναι ἐπὶ κλήρωσίν τε καὶ αἵρεσιν τοῦ δευτέρου βίου αἱροῦνται ὃν ἂν ἐθέλῃ ἑκάστη· ἔνθα καὶ εἰς θηρίου βίον ἀνθρωπίνη ψυχὴ ἀφικνεῖται, καὶ ἐκ θηρίου, ὅς ποτε ἄνθρωπος ἦν, πάλιν εἰς ἄνθρωπον. οὐ γὰρ ἥ γε μή ποτε ἰδοῦσα τὴν ἀλήθειαν εἰς τόδε ἥξει τὸ σχῆμα. δεῖ γὰρ ἄνθρωπον ξυνιέναι κατ'[1] εἶδος λεγόμενον, ἐκ πολλῶν ἰὸν αἰσθήσεων εἰς ἓν

C λογισμῷ ξυναιρούμενον·[2] τοῦτο δ' ἐστὶν ἀνάμνησις ἐκείνων, ἅ ποτ' εἶδεν ἡμῶν ἡ ψυχὴ συμπορευθεῖσα θεῷ καὶ ὑπεριδοῦσα ἃ νῦν εἶναί φαμεν, καὶ ἀνακύψασα εἰς τὸ ὂν ὄντως. διὸ δὴ δικαίως μόνη πτεροῦται ἡ τοῦ φιλοσόφου διάνοια· πρὸς γὰρ ἐκείνοις ἀεί ἐστιν μνήμῃ κατὰ δύναμιν, πρὸς

---

[1] Schanz inserts τὸ after κατ'.
[2] Schanz, following Heindorf, reads ξυναιρουμένων.

Now in all these states, whoever lives justly obtains a better lot, and whoever lives unjustly, a worse. For each soul returns to the place whence it came in ten thousand years; for it does not regain its wings before that time has elapsed, except the soul of him who has been a guileless philosopher or a philosophical lover; these, when for three successive periods of a thousand years they have chosen such a life, after the third period of a thousand years become winged in the three thousandth year and go their way; but the rest, when they have finished their first life, receive judgment, and after the judgment some go to the places of correction under the earth and pay their penalty, while the others, made light and raised up into a heavenly place by justice, live in a manner worthy of the life they led in human form. But in the thousandth year both come to draw lots and choose their second life, each choosing whatever it wishes. Then a human soul may pass into the life of a beast, and a soul which was once human, may pass again from a beast into a man. For the soul which has never seen the truth can never pass into human form. For a human being must understand a general conception formed by collecting into a unity by means of reason the many perceptions of the senses; and this is a recollection of those things which our soul once beheld, when it journeyed with God and, lifting its vision above the things which we now say exist, rose up into real being. And therefore it is just that the mind of the philosopher only has wings, for he is always, so far as he is able, in communion through memory with those things

οἷσπερ θεὸς ὢν θεῖός ἐστιν. τοῖς δὲ δὴ τοιούτοις ἀνὴρ ὑπομνήμασιν ὀρθῶς χρώμενος, τελέους ἀεὶ τελετὰς τελούμενος, τέλεος ὄντως μόνος γίγνεται· D ἐξιστάμενος δὲ τῶν ἀνθρωπίνων σπουδασμάτων καὶ πρὸς τῷ θείῳ γιγνόμενος νουθετεῖται μὲν ὑπὸ τῶν πολλῶν ὡς παρακινῶν, ἐνθουσιάζων δὲ λέληθε τοὺς πολλούς.

30. Ἔστιν δὴ οὖν δεῦρο ὁ πᾶς ἥκων λόγος περὶ τῆς τετάρτης μανίας, ἣν ὅταν τὸ τῇδέ τις ὁρῶν κάλλος, τοῦ ἀληθοῦς ἀναμιμνησκόμενος, πτερῶταί τε καὶ[1] ἀναπτερούμενος προθυμούμενος ἀναπτέσθαι, ἀδυνατῶν δέ, ὄρνιθος δίκην βλέπων ἄνω, τῶν κάτω δὲ ἀμελῶν, αἰτίαν ἔχει ὡς μανικῶς E διακείμενος· ὡς ἄρα αὕτη πασῶν τῶν ἐνθουσιάσεων ἀρίστη τε καὶ ἐξ ἀρίστων τῷ τε ἔχοντι καὶ τῷ κοινωνοῦντι αὐτῆς γίγνεται, καὶ ὅτι ταύτης μετέχων τῆς μανίας ὁ ἐρῶν τῶν καλῶν ἐραστὴς καλεῖται. καθάπερ γὰρ εἴρηται, πᾶσα μὲν ἀνθρώπου ψυχὴ φύσει τεθέαται τὰ ὄντα, ἢ οὐκ ἂν 250 ἦλθεν εἰς τόδε τὸ ζῷον, ἀναμιμνήσκεσθαι δ᾽ ἐκ τῶνδε ἐκεῖνα οὐ ῥάδιον ἁπάσῃ, οὔτε ὅσαι βραχέως εἶδον τότε τἀκεῖ, οὔτε αἳ δεῦρο πεσοῦσαι ἐδυστύχησαν, ὥστε ὑπό τινων ὁμιλιῶν ἐπὶ τὸ ἄδικον τραπόμεναι λήθην ὧν τότε εἶδον ἱερῶν ἔχειν. ὀλίγαι δὴ λείπονται, αἷς τὸ τῆς μνήμης ἱκανῶς πάρεστιν· αὗται δέ, ὅταν τι τῶν ἐκεῖ ὁμοίωμα ἴδωσιν, ἐκπλήττονται καὶ οὐκέθ᾽ αὑτῶν γίγνον-

---

[1] Schanz omits τε καὶ.

the communion with which causes God to be divine. Now a man who employs such memories rightly is always being initiated into perfect mysteries and he alone becomes truly perfect; but since he separates himself from human interests and turns his attention toward the divine, he is rebuked by the vulgar, who consider him mad and do not know that he is inspired.

All my discourse so far has been about the fourth kind of madness, which causes him to be regarded as mad, who, when he sees the beauty on earth, remembering the true beauty, feels his wings growing and longs to stretch them for an upward flight, but cannot do so, and, like a bird, gazes upward and neglects the things below. My discourse has shown that this is, of all inspirations, the best and of the highest origin to him who has it or who shares in it, and that he who loves the beautiful, partaking in this madness, is called a lover. For, as has been said, every soul of man has by the law of nature beheld the realities, otherwise it would not have entered into a human being, but it is not easy for all souls to gain from earthly things a recollection of those realities, either for those which had but a brief view of them at that earlier time, or for those which, after falling to earth, were so unfortunate as to be turned toward unrighteousness through some evil communications and to have forgotten the holy sights they once saw. Few then are left which retain an adequate recollection of them; but these when they see here any likeness of the things of that other world, are stricken with amazement and can no longer control themselves; but they do not

PLATO

ται, ὃ δ' ἔστι τὸ πάθος ἀγνοοῦσιν διὰ τὸ μὴ ἱκανῶς
B διαισθάνεσθαι. δικαιοσύνης μὲν οὖν καὶ σωφροσύνης, καὶ ὅσα ἄλλα τίμια ψυχαῖς, οὐκ ἔνεστι
φέγγος οὐδὲν ἐν τοῖς τῇδε ὁμοιώμασιν, ἀλλὰ δι'
ἀμυδρῶν ὀργάνων μόγις αὐτῶν καὶ ὀλίγοι ἐπὶ τὰς
εἰκόνας ἰόντες θεῶνται τὸ τοῦ εἰκασθέντος γένος·
κάλλος δὲ τότ' ἦν ἰδεῖν λαμπρόν, ὅτε σὺν εὐδαίμονι χορῷ μακαρίαν ὄψιν τε καὶ θέαν, ἑπόμενοι
μετὰ μὲν Διὸς ἡμεῖς, ἄλλοι δὲ μετ' ἄλλου θεῶν,
εἶδόν τε καὶ ἐτελοῦντο τῶν τελετῶν ἣν θέμις
C λέγειν μακαριωτάτην, ἣν ὠργιάζομεν ὁλόκληροι
μὲν αὐτοὶ ὄντες καὶ ἀπαθεῖς κακῶν, ὅσα ἡμᾶς ἐν
ὑστέρῳ χρόνῳ ὑπέμενεν, ὁλόκληρα δὲ καὶ ἁπλᾶ
καὶ ἀτρεμῆ καὶ εὐδαίμονα φάσματα μυούμενοί τε
καὶ ἐποπτεύοντες ἐν αὐγῇ καθαρᾷ, καθαροὶ ὄντες
καὶ ἀσήμαντοι τούτου, ὃ νῦν σῶμα περιφέροντες
ὀνομάζομεν, ὀστρέου τρόπον δεδεσμευμένοι.

31. Ταῦτα μὲν οὖν μνήμῃ κεχαρίσθω, δι' ἣν
πόθῳ τῶν τότε νῦν μακρότερα εἴρηται· περὶ δὲ
D κάλλους, ὥσπερ εἴπομεν, μετ' ἐκείνων τε ἔλαμπεν
ὄν, δεῦρό τ' ἐλθόντες κατειλήφαμεν αὐτὸ διὰ τῆς
ἐναργεστάτης αἰσθήσεως τῶν ἡμετέρων στίλβον
ἐναργέστατα. ὄψις γὰρ ἡμῖν ὀξυτάτη τῶν διὰ τοῦ
σώματος ἔρχεται αἰσθήσεων, ᾗ φρόνησις οὐχ
ὁρᾶται—δεινοὺς γὰρ ἂν παρεῖχεν ἔρωτας, εἴ τι
τοιοῦτον ἑαυτῆς ἐναργὲς εἴδωλον παρείχετο εἰς
ὄψιν ἰόν—καὶ τἆλλα ὅσα ἐραστά· νῦν δὲ κάλλος
μόνον ταύτην ἔσχε μοῖραν, ὥστ' ἐκφανέστατον
E εἶναι καὶ ἐρασμιώτατον. ὁ μὲν οὖν μὴ νεοτελὴς ἢ
484

understand their condition, because they do not
clearly perceive. Now in the earthly copies of
justice and temperance and the other ideas which
are precious to souls there is no light, but only a few,
approaching the images through the darkling organs
of sense, behold in them the nature of that which
they imitate, and these few do this with difficulty.
But at that former time they saw beauty shining in
brightness, when, with a blessed company—we following in the train of Zeus, and others in that of some
other god—they saw the blessed sight and vision
and were initiated into that which is rightly called
the most blessed of mysteries, which we celebrated
in a state of perfection, when we were without
experience of the evils which awaited us in the time
to come, being permitted as initiates to the sight of
perfect and simple and calm and happy apparitions,
which we saw in the pure light, being ourselves pure
and not entombed in this which we carry about with
us and call the body, in which we are imprisoned
like an oyster in its shell.

So much, then, in honour of memory, on account of which I have now spoken at some length,
through yearning for the joys of that other time.
But beauty, as I said before, shone in brilliance
among those visions; and since we came to earth
we have found it shining most clearly through
the clearest of our senses; for sight is the sharpest
of the physical senses, though wisdom is not seen
by it, for wisdom would arouse terrible love, if such
a clear image of it were granted as would come
through sight, and the same is true of the other
lovely realities; but beauty alone has this privilege,
and therefore it is most clearly seen and loveliest.

485

PLATO

διεφθαρμένος οὐκ ὀξέως ἐνθένδε ἐκεῖσε φέρεται
πρὸς αὐτὸ τὸ κάλλος, θεώμενος αὐτοῦ τὴν τῇδε
ἐπωνυμίαν, ὥστ᾽ οὐ σέβεται προσορῶν, ἀλλ᾽ ἡδονῇ
παραδοὺς τετράποδος νόμον βαίνειν ἐπιχειρεῖ καὶ
251 παιδοσπορεῖν, καὶ ὕβρει προσομιλῶν οὐ δέδοικεν
οὐδ᾽ αἰσχύνεται παρὰ φύσιν ἡδονὴν διώκων· ὁ δὲ
ἀρτιτελής, ὁ τῶν τότε πολυθεάμων, ὅταν θεοειδὲς
πρόσωπον ἴδῃ κάλλος εὖ μεμιμημένον ἤ τινα
σώματος ἰδέαν, πρῶτον μὲν ἔφριξεν καί τι τῶν
τότε ὑπῆλθεν αὐτὸν δειμάτων, εἶτα προσορῶν ὡς
θεὸν σέβεται, καὶ εἰ μὴ ᾽δεδίει τὴν τῆς σφόδρα
μανίας δόξαν, θύοι ἂν ὡς ἀγάλματι καὶ θεῷ τοῖς
παιδικοῖς. ἰδόντα δ᾽ αὐτὸν οἷον ἐκ τῆς φρίκης
μεταβολή τε καὶ ἱδρὼς καὶ θερμότης ἀήθης
B λαμβάνει· δεξάμενος γὰρ τοῦ κάλλους τὴν
ἀπορροὴν διὰ τῶν ὀμμάτων ἐθερμάνθη, ᾗ ἡ τοῦ
πτεροῦ φύσις ἄρδεται,[1] θερμανθέντος δὲ ἐτάκη
τὰ περὶ τὴν ἔκφυσιν, ἃ πάλαι ὑπὸ σκληρότητος
συμμεμυκότα εἶργε μὴ βλαστάνειν, ἐπιρρυείσης
δὲ τῆς τροφῆς ᾤδησέ τε καὶ ὥρμησε φύεσθαι ἀπὸ
τῆς ῥίζης ὁ τοῦ πτεροῦ καυλὸς ὑπὸ πᾶν τὸ τῆς
ψυχῆς εἶδος· πᾶσα γὰρ ἦν τὸ πάλαι πτερωτή.
32. Ζεῖ οὖν ἐν τούτῳ ὅλη καὶ ἀνακηκίει, καὶ
C ὅπερ τὸ τῶν ὀδοντοφυούντων πάθος περὶ τοὺς
ὀδόντας γίγνεται, ὅταν ἄρτι φύωσιν, κνῆσίς τε καὶ
ἀγανάκτησις περὶ τὰ οὖλα, ταὐτὸν δὴ πέπονθεν ἡ
τοῦ πτεροφυεῖν ἀρχομένου ψυχή· ζεῖ τε καὶ
ἀγανακτεῖ καὶ γαργαλίζεται φύουσα τὰ πτερά.
ὅταν μὲν οὖν βλέπουσα πρὸς τὸ τοῦ παιδὸς

[1] Schanz brackets ᾗ . . . ἄρδεται.

Now he who is not newly initiated, or has been corrupted, does not quickly rise from this world to that other world and to absolute beauty when he sees its namesake here, and so he does not revere it when he looks upon it, but gives himself up to pleasure and like a beast proceeds to lust and begetting; he makes licence his companion and is not afraid or ashamed to pursue pleasure in violation of nature. But he who is newly initiated, who beheld many of those realities, when he sees a god-like face or form which is a good image of beauty, shudders at first, and something of the old awe comes over him, then, as he gazes, he reveres the beautiful one as a god, and if he did not fear to be thought stark mad, he would offer sacrifice to his beloved as to an idol or a god. And as he looks upon him, a reaction from his shuddering comes over him, with sweat and unwonted heat; for as the effluence of beauty enters him through the eyes, he is warmed; the effluence moistens the germ of the feathers, and as he grows warm, the parts from which the feathers grow, which were before hard and choked, and prevented the feathers from sprouting, become soft, and as the nourishment streams upon him, the quills of the feathers swell and begin to grow from the roots over all the form of the soul; for it was once all feathered.

Now in this process the whole soul throbs and palpitates, and as in those who are cutting teeth there is an irritation and discomfort in the gums, when the teeth begin to grow, just so the soul suffers when the growth of the feathers begins; it is feverish and is uncomfortable and itches when they begin to grow. Then when it gazes upon the beauty of the boy and

κάλλος ἐκεῖθεν μέρη ἐπιόντα καὶ ῥέοντ', ἃ δὴ διὰ
ταῦτα ἵμερος καλεῖται, δεχομένη[1] ἄρδηταί τε καὶ
D θερμαίνηται, λωφᾷ τε τῆς ὀδύνης καὶ γέγηθεν·
ὅταν δὲ χωρὶς γένηται καὶ αὐχμήσῃ, τὰ τῶν
διεξόδων στόματα, ᾗ τὸ πτερὸν ὁρμᾷ, συναυαινό-
μενα μύσαντα ἀποκλῄει τὴν βλάστην τοῦ πτεροῦ,
ἡ δ' ἐντὸς μετὰ τοῦ ἱμέρου ἀποκεκλημένη, πηδῶσα
οἷον τὰ σφύζοντα, τῇ διεξόδῳ ἐγχρίει ἑκάστη τῇ
καθ' αὑτήν, ὥστε πᾶσα κεντουμένη κύκλῳ ἡ
ψυχὴ οἰστρᾷ καὶ ὀδυνᾶται· μνήμην δ' αὖ ἔχουσα
τοῦ καλοῦ γέγηθεν. ἐκ δ' ἀμφοτέρων μεμιγμένων
E ἀδημονεῖ τε τῇ ἀτοπίᾳ τοῦ πάθους καὶ ἀποροῦσα
λυττᾷ, καὶ ἐμμανὴς οὖσα οὔτε νυκτὸς δύναται
καθεύδειν οὔτε μεθ' ἡμέραν οὗ ἂν ᾖ μένειν, θεῖ δὲ
ποθοῦσα, ὅπου ἂν οἴηται ὄψεσθαι τὸν ἔχοντα τὸ
κάλλος· ἰδοῦσα δὲ καὶ ἐποχετευσαμένη ἵμερον
ἔλυσε μὲν τὰ τότε συμπεφραγμένα, ἀναπνοὴν δὲ
λαβοῦσα κέντρων τε καὶ ὠδίνων ἔληξεν, ἡδονὴν δ'
252 αὖ ταύτην γλυκυτάτην ἐν τῷ παρόντι καρποῦται.
ὅθεν δὴ ἑκοῦσα εἶναι οὐκ ἀπολείπεται, οὐδέ τινα
τοῦ καλοῦ περὶ πλείονος ποιεῖται, ἀλλὰ μητέρων
τε καὶ ἀδελφῶν καὶ ἑταίρων πάντων λέλησται,
καὶ οὐσίας δι' ἀμέλειαν ἀπολλυμένης παρ' οὐδὲν
τίθεται, νομίμων δὲ καὶ εὐσχημόνων, οἷς πρὸ τοῦ
ἐκαλλωπίζετο, πάντων καταφρονήσασα δουλεύειν
ἑτοίμη καὶ κοιμᾶσθαι ὅπου ἂν ἐᾷ τις ἐγγυτάτω
τοῦ πόθου· πρὸς γὰρ τῷ σέβεσθαι τὸν τὸ κάλλος
B ἔχοντα ἰατρὸν ηὕρηκε μόνον τῶν μεγίστων πόνων.

[1] After δεχομένη the best MSS. read τὸν ἵμερον. Schanz
follows Stallbaum in omitting it.

receives the particles which flow thence to it (for which reason they are called yearning),[1] it is moistened and warmed, ceases from its pain and is filled with joy ; but when it is alone and grows dry, the mouths of the passages in which the feathers begin to grow become dry and close up, shutting in the sprouting feathers, and the sprouts within, shut in with the yearning, throb like pulsing arteries, and each sprout pricks the passage in which it is, so that the whole soul, stung in every part, rages with pain ; and then again, remembering the beautiful one, it rejoices. So, because of these two mingled sensations, it is greatly troubled by its strange condition ; it is perplexed and maddened, and in its madness it cannot sleep at night or stay in any one place by day, but it is filled with longing and hastens wherever it hopes to see the beautiful one. And when it sees him and is bathed with the waters of yearning, the passages that were sealed are opened, the soul has respite from the stings and is eased of its pain, and this pleasure which it enjoys is the sweetest of pleasures at the time. Therefore the soul will not, if it can help it, be left alone by the beautiful one, but esteems him above all others, forgets for him mother and brothers and all friends, neglects property and cares not for its loss, and despising all the customs and proprieties in which it formerly took pride, it is ready to be a slave and to sleep wherever it is allowed, as near as possible to the beloved ; for it not only reveres him who possesses beauty, but finds in him the only healer of its greatest woes. Now this

[1] The play on the words μέρη and ἵμερος cannot be rendered accurately in English. Jowett approaches a rendering by the use of the words motion and emotion, but emotion is too weak a word for ἵμερος.

τοῦτο δὲ τὸ πάθος, ὦ παῖ καλέ, πρὸς ὃν δή μοι ὁ
λόγος, ἄνθρωποι μὲν Ἔρωτα ὀνομάζουσιν, θεοὶ δὲ
ὃ καλοῦσιν ἀκούσας εἰκότως διὰ νεότητα γελάσει.
λέγουσι δέ, οἶμαι, τινὲς Ὁμηριδῶν ἐκ τῶν ἀπο-
θέτων ἐπῶν δύο ἔπη εἰς τὸν Ἔρωτα, ὧν τὸ ἕτερον
ὑβριστικὸν πάνυ καὶ οὐ σφόδρα τι ἔμμετρον·
ὑμνοῦσι δὲ ὧδε·

C   τὸν δ' ἤτοι θνητοὶ μὲν Ἔρωτα καλοῦσι ποτηνόν,
       ἀθάνατοι δὲ Πτέρωτα, διὰ πτεροφύτορ' ἀνάγκην.

τούτοις δὴ ἔξεστι μὲν πείθεσθαι, ἔξεστιν δὲ μή·
ὅμως δὲ ἥ γε αἰτία καὶ τὸ πάθος τῶν ἐρώντων
τοῦτο ἐκεῖνο τυγχάνει ὄν.
       33. Τῶν μὲν οὖν Διὸς ὀπαδῶν ὁ ληφθεὶς ἐμβρι-
θέστερον δύναται φέρειν τὸ τοῦ πτερωνύμου
ἄχθος· ὅσοι δὲ Ἄρεώς τε θεραπευταὶ καὶ μετ'
ἐκείνου περιεπόλουν, ὅταν ὑπ' Ἔρωτος ἁλῶσιν καὶ
τι οἰηθῶσιν ἀδικεῖσθαι ὑπὸ τοῦ ἐρωμένου, φονικοὶ
καὶ ἕτοιμοι καθιερεύειν αὑτούς τε καὶ τὰ παιδικά·
D   καὶ οὕτω καθ' ἕκαστον θεόν, οὗ ἕκαστος ἦν
χορευτής, ἐκεῖνον τιμῶν τε καὶ μιμούμενος εἰς τὸ
δυνατὸν ζῇ, ἕως ἂν ᾖ ἀδιάφθορος, καὶ τὴν τῇδε πρώτην γένεσιν βιοτεύῃ, καὶ τούτῳ τῷ τρόπῳ πρός τε
τοὺς ἐρωμένους καὶ πρὸς τοὺς ἄλλους ὁμιλεῖ τε καὶ
προσφέρεται.   τόν τε οὖν ἔρωτα τῶν καλῶν πρὸς
τρόπου ἐκλέγεται ἕκαστος, καὶ ὡς θεὸν αὐτὸν
ἐκεῖνον ὄντα ἑαυτῷ οἷον ἄγαλμα τεκταίνεταί τε
E   καὶ κατακοσμεῖ, ὡς τιμήσων τε καὶ ὀργιάσων. οἱ
μὲν δὴ οὖν Διὸς δῖόν τινα εἶναι ζητοῦσι τὴν
ψυχὴν τὸν ὑφ' αὑτῶν ἐρώμενον· σκοποῦσιν οὖν,
εἰ φιλόσοφός τε καὶ ἡγεμονικὸς τὴν φύσιν, καὶ
ὅταν αὐτὸν εὑρόντες ἐρασθῶσι, πᾶν ποιοῦσιν ὅπως

condition, fair boy, about which I am speaking, is called Love by men, but when you hear what the gods call it, perhaps because of your youth you will laugh. But some of the Homeridae, I believe, repeat two verses on Love from the spurious poems of Homer, one of which is very outrageous and not perfectly metrical. They sing them as follows :

" Mortals call him winged Love, but the immortals call him The Winged One, because he must needs grow wings."

You may believe this, or not ; but the condition of lovers and the cause of it are just as I have said.

Now he who is a follower of Zeus, when seized by Love can bear a heavier burden of the winged god ; but those who are servants of Ares and followed in his train, when they have been seized by Love and think they have been wronged in any way by the beloved, become murderous and are ready to sacrifice themselves and the beloved. And so it is with the follower of each of the other gods ; he lives, so far as he is able, honouring and imitating that god, so long as he is uncorrupted, and is living his first life on earth, and in that way he behaves and conducts himself toward his beloved and toward all others. Now each one chooses his love from the ranks of the beautiful according to his character, and he fashions him and adorns him like a statue, as though he were his god, to honour and worship him. The followers of Zeus desire that the soul of him whom they love be like Zeus; so they seek for one of philosophical and lordly nature, and when they find him and love him, they do all they can to give him such a character.

τοιοῦτος ἔσται. ἐὰν οὖν μὴ πρότερον ἐμβεβῶσι
τῷ ἐπιτηδεύματι, τότε ἐπιχειρήσαντες μανθάνουσί
τε ὅθεν ἄν τι δύνωνται καὶ αὐτοὶ μετέρχονται,
253 ἰχνεύοντες δὲ παρ' ἑαυτῶν ἀνευρίσκειν τὴν τοῦ
σφετέρου θεοῦ φύσιν εὐποροῦσι διὰ τὸ συντόνως
ἠναγκάσθαι πρὸς τὸν θεὸν βλέπειν, καὶ ἐφαπτόμενοι αὐτοῦ τῇ μνήμῃ ἐνθουσιῶντες ἐξ ἐκείνου
λαμβάνουσι τὰ ἔθη καὶ τὰ ἐπιτηδεύματα, καθ'
ὅσον δυνατὸν θεοῦ ἀνθρώπῳ μετασχεῖν· καὶ
τούτων δὴ τὸν ἐρώμενον αἰτιώμενοι ἔτι τε μᾶλλον
ἀγαπῶσι, κἂν[1] ἐκ Διὸς ἀρύτωσιν, ὥσπερ αἱ
βάκχαι, ἐπὶ τὴν τοῦ ἐρωμένου ψυχὴν ἐπαντλοῦντες
ποιοῦσιν ὡς δυνατὸν ὁμοιότατον τῷ σφετέρῳ θεῷ.
B ὅσοι δ' αὖ μεθ' Ἥρας εἵποντο, βασιλικὸν ζητοῦσι,
καὶ εὑρόντες περὶ τοῦτον πάντα δρῶσιν τὰ αὐτά.
οἱ δὲ Ἀπόλλωνός τε καὶ ἑκάστου τῶν θεῶν οὕτω
κατὰ τὸν θεὸν ἰόντες ζητοῦσι τὸν σφέτερον παῖδα
πεφυκέναι, καὶ ὅταν κτήσωνται, μιμούμενοι αὐτοί
τε καὶ τὰ παιδικὰ πείθοντες καὶ ῥυθμίζοντες εἰς
τὸ ἐκείνου ἐπιτήδευμα καὶ ἰδέαν ἄγουσιν, ὅση
ἑκάστῳ δύναμις, οὐ φθόνῳ οὐδ' ἀνελευθέρῳ δυσμε-
νείᾳ χρώμενοι πρὸς τὰ παιδικά, ἀλλ' εἰς ὁμοιότητα
C αὑτοῖς τῷ θεῷ, ὃν ἂν τιμῶσι, πᾶσαν πάντως ὅ τι
μάλιστα πειρώμενοι ἄγειν οὕτω ποιοῦσι. προθυμία
μὲν οὖν τῶν ὡς ἀληθῶς ἐρώντων καὶ τελετή, ἐάν
γε διαπράξωνται ὃ προθυμοῦνται ᾗ λέγω, οὕτω
καλή τε καὶ εὐδαιμονικὴ ὑπὸ τοῦ δι' ἔρωτα

---

[1] Schanz, following Madvig, reads χἂν.

If they have not previously had experience, they learn then from all who can teach them anything; they seek after information themselves, and when they search eagerly within themselves to find the nature of their god, they are successful, because they have been compelled to keep their eyes fixed upon the god, and as they reach and grasp him by memory they are inspired and receive from him character and habits, so far as it is possible for a man to have part in God. Now they consider the beloved the cause of all this, so they love him more than before, and if they draw the waters of their inspiration from Zeus, like the bacchantes, they pour it out upon the beloved and make him, so far as possible, like their god. And those who followed after Hera seek a kingly nature, and when they have found such an one, they act in a corresponding manner toward him in all respects; and likewise the followers of Apollo, and of each of the gods, go out and seek for their beloved a youth whose nature accords with that of the god, and when they have gained his affection, by imitating the god themselves and by persuasion and education they lead the beloved to the conduct and nature of the god, so far as each of them can do so; they exhibit no jealousy or meanness toward the loved one, but endeavour by every means in their power to lead him to the likeness of the god whom they honour. Thus the desire of the true lovers, and the initiation into the mysteries of love, which they teach, if they accomplish what they desire in the way I describe, is beautiful and brings happiness from the inspired lover to the loved one, if he be captured; and the

μανέντος φίλου τῷ φιληθέντι γίγνεται, ἐὰν αἱρεθῇ·
ἁλίσκεται δὲ δὴ ὁ αἱρεθεὶς[1] τοιῷδε τρόπῳ.

34. Καθάπερ ἐν ἀρχῇ τοῦδε τοῦ μύθου τριχῇ
διειλόμην ψυχὴν ἑκάστην, ἱππομόρφω μὲν δύο
D τινὲ εἴδη, ἡνιοχικὸν δὲ εἶδος τρίτον, καὶ νῦν ἔτι
ἡμῖν ταῦτα μενέτω. τῶν δὲ δὴ ἵππων ὁ μέν, φαμέν,
ἀγαθός, ὁ δ' οὔ· ἀρετὴ δὲ τίς τοῦ ἀγαθοῦ ἢ κακοῦ
κακία, οὐ διείπομεν, νῦν δὲ λεκτέον. ὁ μὲν τοίνυν
αὐτοῖν ἐν τῇ καλλίονι στάσει ὢν τό τε εἶδος ὀρθὸς
καὶ διηρθρωμένος, ὑψαύχην, ἐπίγρυπος, λευκὸς
ἰδεῖν, μελανόμματος, τιμῆς ἐραστὴς μετὰ σωφροσύνης τε καὶ αἰδοῦς, καὶ ἀληθινῆς δόξης ἑταῖρος,
ἄπληκτος, κελεύματι μόνον καὶ λόγῳ ἡνιοχεῖται·
E ὁ δ' αὖ σκολιός, πολύς, εἰκῇ συμπεφορημένος,
κρατεραύχην, βραχυτράχηλος, σιμοπρόσωπος,
μελάγχρως, γλαυκόμματος, ὕφαιμος, ὕβρεως καὶ
ἀλαζονείας ἑταῖρος, περὶ ὦτα λάσιος, κωφός,
μάστιγι μετὰ κέντρων μόγις ὑπείκων. ὅταν δ' οὖν
ὁ ἡνίοχος ἰδὼν τὸ ἐρωτικὸν ὄμμα, πᾶσαν αἰσθήσει
διαθερμήνας τὴν ψυχήν, γαργαλισμοῦ τε καὶ
254 πόθου κέντρων ὑποπλησθῇ, ὁ μὲν εὐπειθὴς τῷ
ἡνιόχῳ τῶν ἵππων, ἀεί τε καὶ τότε αἰδοῖ βιαζόμενος, ἑαυτὸν κατέχει μὴ ἐπιπηδᾶν τῷ ἐρωμένῳ·
ὁ δὲ οὔτε κέντρων ἡνιοχικῶν οὔτε μάστιγος ἔτι
ἐντρέπεται, σκιρτῶν δὲ βίᾳ φέρεται, καὶ πάντα
πράγματα παρέχων τῷ σύζυγί τε καὶ ἡνιόχῳ
ἀναγκάζει ἰέναι τε πρὸς τὰ παιδικὰ καὶ μνείαν
ποιεῖσθαι τῆς τῶν ἀφροδισίων χάριτος. τὼ δὲ
κατ' ἀρχὰς μὲν ἀντιτείνετον ἀγανακτοῦντε, ὡς
B δεινὰ καὶ παράνομα ἀναγκαζομένω· τελευτῶντες
δέ, ὅταν μηδὲν ᾖ πέρας κακοῦ, πορεύεσθον

_____
[1] Schanz brackets ὁ αἱρεθείς, following Badham.

fair one who is captured is caught in the following manner :—

In the beginning of this tale I divided each soul into three parts, two of which had the form of horses, the third that of a charioteer. Let us retain this division. Now of the horses we say one is good and the other bad ; but we did not define what the goodness of the one and the badness of the other was. That we must now do. The horse that stands at the right hand is upright and has clean limbs ; he carries his neck high, has an aquiline nose, is white in colour, and has dark eyes ; he is a friend of honour joined with temperance and modesty, and a follower of true glory ; he needs no whip, but is guided only by the word of command and by reason. The other, however, is crooked, heavy, ill put together, his neck is short and thick, his nose flat, his colour dark, his eyes grey and bloodshot ; he is the friend of insolence and pride, is shaggy-eared and deaf, hardly obedient to whip and spurs. Now when the charioteer beholds the love-inspiring vision, and his whole soul is warmed by the sight, and is full of the tickling and prickings of yearning, the horse that is obedient to the charioteer, constrained then as always by modesty, controls himself and does not leap upon the beloved ; but the other no longer heeds the pricks or the whip of the charioteer, but springs wildly forward, causing all possible trouble to his mate and to the charioteer, and forcing them to approach the beloved and propose the joys of love. And they at first pull back indignantly and will not be forced to do terrible and unlawful deeds; but finally, as the trouble has no

ἀγομένω, εἴξαντε καὶ ὁμολογήσαντε ποιήσειν τὸ
κελευόμενον. καὶ πρὸς αὐτῷ τ' ἐγένοντο καὶ εἶδον
τὴν ὄψιν τὴν τῶν παιδικῶν ἀστράπτουσαν.

35. Ἰδόντος δὲ τοῦ ἡνιόχου ἡ μνήμη πρὸς τὴν
τοῦ κάλλους φύσιν ἠνέχθη, καὶ πάλιν εἶδεν αὐτὴν
μετὰ σωφροσύνης ἐν ἁγνῷ βάθρῳ βεβῶσαν·
ἰδοῦσα δὲ ἔδεισέ τε καὶ σεφθεῖσα ἀνέπεσεν ὑπτία,
καὶ ἅμα ἠναγκάσθη εἰς τοὐπίσω ἑλκύσαι τὰς
C ἡνίας οὕτω σφόδρα, ὥστ' ἐπὶ τὰ ἰσχία ἄμφω
καθίσαι τὼ ἵππω, τὸν μὲν ἑκόντα διὰ τὸ μὴ
ἀντιτείνειν, τὸν δὲ ὑβριστὴν μάλ' ἄκοντα. ἀπελ-
θόντε δὲ ἀπωτέρω, ὁ μὲν ὑπ' αἰσχύνης τε καὶ
θάμβους ἱδρῶτι πᾶσαν ἔβρεξε τὴν ψυχήν, ὁ δὲ
λήξας τῆς ὀδύνης, ἣν ὑπὸ τοῦ χαλινοῦ τε ἔσχεν
καὶ τοῦ πτώματος, μόγις ἐξαναπνεύσας ἐλοιδόρη-
σεν ὀργῇ, πολλὰ κακίζων τόν τε ἡνίοχον καὶ
D τὸν ὁμόζυγα ὡς δειλίᾳ τε καὶ ἀνανδρίᾳ λιπόντε
τὴν τάξιν καὶ ὁμολογίαν· καὶ πάλιν οὐκ ἐθέλοντας
προσιέναι ἀναγκάζων μόγις συνεχώρησε δεομένων
εἰσαῦθις ὑπερβαλέσθαι. ἐλθόντος δὲ τοῦ συντε-
θέντος χρόνου, ἀμνημονεῖν προσποιουμένω ἀνα-
μιμνήσκων, βιαζόμενος, χρεμετίζων, ἕλκων ἠνάγκασεν αὖ προσελθεῖν τοῖς παιδικοῖς ἐπὶ τοὺς
αὐτοὺς λόγους, καὶ ἐπειδὴ ἐγγὺς ἦσαν, ἐγκύψας
καὶ ἐκτείνας τὴν κέρκον, ἐνδακὼν τὸν χαλινόν,
E μετ' ἀναιδείας ἕλκει· ὁ δ' ἡνίοχος ἔτι μᾶλλον
ταὐτὸν πάθος παθών, ὥσπερ ἀπὸ ὕσπληγος
ἀναπεσών, ἔτι μᾶλλον τοῦ ὑβριστοῦ ἵππου ἐκ
τῶν ὀδόντων βίᾳ ὀπίσω σπάσας τὸν χαλινόν, τήν
τε κακήγορον γλῶτταν καὶ τὰς γνάθους καθήμαξεν
καὶ τὰ σκέλη τε καὶ τὰ ἰσχία πρὸς τὴν γῆν

end, they go forward with him, yielding and agreeing
to do his bidding. And they come to the beloved
and behold his radiant face.

And as the charioteer looks upon him, his memory
is borne back to the true nature of beauty, and he
sees it standing with modesty upon a pedestal of
chastity, and when he sees this he is afraid and falls
backward in reverence, and in falling he is forced to
pull the reins so violently backward as to bring both
horses upon their haunches, the one quite willing,
since he does not oppose him, but the unruly beast
very unwilling. And as they go away, one horse
in his shame and wonder wets all the soul with
sweat, but the other, as soon as he is recovered
from the pain of the bit and the fall, before he has
fairly taken breath, breaks forth into angry reproaches,
bitterly reviling his mate and the charioteer for their
cowardice and lack of manhood in deserting their
post and breaking their agreement; and again, in
spite of their unwillingness, he urges them forward
and hardly yields to their prayer that he postpone
the matter to another time. Then when the time
comes which they have agreed upon, they pretend
that they have forgotten it, but he reminds them;
struggling, and neighing, and pulling he forces them
again with the same purpose to approach the beloved
one, and when they are near him, he lowers his head,
raises his tail, takes the bit in his teeth, and pulls
shamelessly. The effect upon the charioteer is the
same as before, but more pronounced; he falls back
like a racer from the starting-rope, pulls the bit
backward even more violently than before from the
teeth of the unruly horse, covers his scurrilous tongue
and jaws with blood, and forces his legs and haunches

ἐρείσας ὀδύναις ἔδωκεν. ὅταν δὲ ταὐτὸν πολλάκις
πάσχων ὁ πονηρὸς τῆς ὕβρεως λήξῃ, ταπεινωθεὶς
ἕπεται ἤδη τῇ τοῦ ἡνιόχου προνοίᾳ, καὶ ὅταν ἴδῃ
τὸν καλόν, φόβῳ διόλλυται· ὥστε ξυμβαίνει τότ'
ἤδη τὴν τοῦ ἐραστοῦ ψυχὴν τοῖς παιδικοῖς αἰδου-
μένην τε καὶ δεδιυῖαν ἕπεσθαι.

255   36. Ἅτε οὖν πᾶσαν θεραπείαν ὡς ἰσόθεος
θεραπευόμενος οὐχ ὑπὸ σχηματιζομένου τοῦ
ἐρῶντος, ἀλλ' ἀληθῶς τοῦτο πεπονθότος, καὶ
αὐτὸς ὢν φύσει φίλος τῷ θεραπεύοντι, ἐὰν ἄρα
καὶ ἐν τῷ πρόσθεν ὑπὸ ξυμφοιτητῶν ἤ τινων
ἄλλων διαβεβλημένος ᾖ, λεγόντων ὡς αἰσχρὸν
ἐρῶντι πλησιάζειν, καὶ διὰ τοῦτο ἀπωθῇ τὸν
ἐρῶντα· προϊόντος δὲ ἤδη τοῦ χρόνου ἥ τε ἡλικία
B καὶ τὸ χρεὼν ἤγαγεν εἰς τὸ προσέσθαι αὐτὸν εἰς
ὁμιλίαν. οὐ γὰρ δή ποτε εἵμαρται κακὸν κακῷ
φίλον οὐδ' ἀγαθὸν μὴ φίλον ἀγαθῷ εἶναι. προσε-
μένου δὲ καὶ λόγον καὶ ὁμιλίαν δεξαμένου, ἐγγύθεν
ἡ εὔνοια γιγνομένη τοῦ ἐρῶντος ἐκπλήττει τὸν
ἐρώμενον διαισθανόμενον, ὅτι οὐδ' οἱ ξύμπαντες
ἄλλοι φίλοι τε καὶ οἰκεῖοι μοῖραν φιλίας οὐδεμίαν
παρέχονται πρὸς τὸν ἔνθεον φίλον. ὅταν δὲ
χρονίζῃ τοῦτο δρῶν καὶ πλησιάζῃ μετὰ τοῦ
ἅπτεσθαι ἔν τε γυμνασίοις καὶ ἐν ταῖς ἄλλαις
C ὁμιλίαις, τότ' ἤδη ἡ τοῦ ῥεύματος ἐκείνου πηγή,
ὃν ἵμερον Ζεὺς Γανυμήδους ἐρῶν ὠνόμασεν, πολλὴ
φερομένη πρὸς τὸν ἐραστήν, ἡ μὲν εἰς αὐτὸν ἔδυ,
ἡ δ' ἀπομεστουμένου ἔξω ἀπορρεῖ· καὶ οἷον πνεῦμα
ἤ τις ἠχὼ ἀπὸ λείων τε καὶ στερεῶν ἁλλομένη

to the ground, causing him much pain. Now when the bad horse has gone through the same experience many times and has ceased from his unruliness, he is humbled and follows henceforth the wisdom of the charioteer, and when he sees the beautiful one, he is overwhelmed with fear ; and so from that time on the soul of the lover follows the beloved in reverence and.awe.

Now the beloved, since he receives all service from his lover, as if he were a god, and since the lover is not feigning, but is really in love, and since the beloved himself is by nature friendly to him who serves him, although he may at some earlier time have been prejudiced by his schoolfellows or others, who said that it was a disgrace to yield to a lover, and may for that reason have repulsed his lover, yet, as time goes on, his youth and destiny cause him to admit him to his society. For it is the law of fate that evil can never be a friend to evil and that good must always be friend to good. And when the lover is thus admitted, and the privilege of conversation and intimacy has been granted him, his good will, as it shows itself in close intimacy, astonishes the beloved, who discovers that the friendship of all his other friends and relatives is as nothing when compared with that of his inspired lover. And as this intimacy continues and the lover comes near and touches the beloved in the gymnasia and in their general intercourse, then the fountain of that stream which Zeus, when he was in love with Ganymede, called " desire " flows copiously upon the lover ; and some of it flows into him, and some, when he is filled, overflows outside ; and just as the wind or an echo rebounds from smooth, hard surfaces and

499

πάλιν ὅθεν ὡρμήθη φέρεται, οὕτω τὸ τοῦ κάλλους
ῥεῦμα πάλιν εἰς τὸν καλὸν διὰ τῶν ὀμμάτων ἰόν,
ᾗ πέφυκεν ἐπὶ τὴν ψυχὴν ἰέναι ἀφικόμενον, καὶ
D ἀναπτερῶσαν τὰς διόδους τῶν πτερῶν, ἄρδει τε
καὶ ὥρμησε πτεροφυεῖν τε καὶ τὴν τοῦ ἐρωμένου
αὖ ψυχὴν ἔρωτος ἐνέπλησεν. ἐρᾷ μὲν οὖν, ὅτου
δέ, ἀπορεῖ· καὶ οὐδ᾽ ὅ τι πέπονθεν οἶδεν οὐδ᾽ ἔχει
φράσαι, ἀλλ᾽ οἷον ἀπ᾽ ἄλλου ὀφθαλμίας ἀπολε-
λαυκὼς πρόφασιν εἰπεῖν οὐκ ἔχει, ὥσπερ δ᾽ ἐν
κατόπτρῳ ἐν τῷ ἐρῶντι ἑαυτὸν ὁρῶν λέληθεν. καὶ
ὅταν μὲν ἐκεῖνος παρῇ, λήγει κατὰ ταὐτὰ ἐκείνῳ
τῆς ὀδύνης· ὅταν δὲ ἀπῇ, κατὰ ταὐτὰ αὖ ποθεῖ
καὶ ποθεῖται, εἴδωλον ἔρωτος ἀντέρωτα ἔχων·
E καλεῖ δὲ αὐτὸν καὶ οἴεται οὐκ ἔρωτα ἀλλὰ φιλίαν
εἶναι. ἐπιθυμεῖ δὲ ἐκείνῳ παραπλησίως μέν,
ἀσθενεστέρως δέ, ὁρᾶν, ἅπτεσθαι, φιλεῖν, συγκατα-
κεῖσθαι· καὶ δή, οἷον εἰκός, ποιεῖ τὸ μετὰ τοῦτο
ταχὺ ταῦτα. ἐν οὖν τῇ συγκοιμήσει τοῦ μὲν
ἐραστοῦ ὁ ἀκόλαστος ἵππος ἔχει ὅ τι λέγῃ πρὸς
τὸν ἡνίοχον, καὶ ἀξιοῖ ἀντὶ πολλῶν πόνων σμικρὰ
256 ἀπολαῦσαι· ὁ δὲ τῶν παιδικῶν ἔχει μὲν οὐδὲν
εἰπεῖν, σπαργῶν δὲ καὶ ἀπορῶν περιβάλλει τὸν
ἐραστὴν καὶ φιλεῖ, ὡς σφόδρ᾽ εὔνουν ἀσπαζόμενος·
ὅταν τε συγκατακέωνται, οἷός ἐστι μὴ ἀπαρνη-
θῆναι τὸ αὑτοῦ μέρος χαρίσασθαι τῷ ἐρῶντι, εἰ
δεηθείη τυχεῖν· ὁ δὲ ὁμόζυξ αὖ μετὰ τοῦ ἡνιόχου
πρὸς ταῦτα μετ᾽ αἰδοῦς καὶ λόγου ἀντιτείνει.

37. Ἐὰν μὲν δὴ οὖν εἰς τεταγμένην τε δίαιταν
καὶ φιλοσοφίαν νικήσῃ τὰ βελτίω τῆς διανοίας
B ἀγαγόντα, μακάριον μὲν καὶ ὁμονοητικὸν τὸν
ἐνθάδε βίον διάγουσιν, ἐγκρατεῖς αὑτῶν καὶ
κόσμιοι ὄντες, δουλωσάμενοι μὲν ᾧ κακία ψυχῆς

returns whence it came, so the stream of beauty passes back into the beautiful one through the eyes, the natural inlet to the soul, where it reanimates the passages of the feathers, waters them and makes the feathers begin to grow, filling the soul of the loved one with love. So he is in love, but he knows not with whom; he does not understand his own condition and cannot explain it; like one who has caught a disease of the eyes from another, he can give no reason for it; he sees himself in his lover as in a mirror, but is not conscious of the fact. And in the lover's presence, like him he ceases from his pain, and in his absence, like him he is filled with yearning such as he inspires, and love's image, requited love, dwells within him; but he calls it, and believes it to be, not love, but friendship. Like the lover, though less strongly, he desires to see his friend, to touch him, kiss him, and lie down by him; and naturally these things are soon brought about. Now as they lie together, the unruly horse of the lover has something to say to the charioteer, and demands a little enjoyment in return for his many troubles; and the unruly horse of the beloved says nothing, but teeming with passion and confused emotions he embraces and kisses his lover, caressing him as his best friend; and when they lie together, he would not refuse his lover any favour, if he asked it; but the other horse and the charioteer oppose all this with modesty and reason.

If now the better elements of the mind, which lead to a well ordered life and to philosophy, prevail, they live a life of happiness and harmony here on earth, self controlled and orderly, holding in subjection that which causes evil in the soul and giving

ἐνεγίγνετο, ἐλευθερώσαντες δὲ ᾧ ἀρετή· τελευτήσαντες δὲ δὴ ὑπόπτεροι καὶ ἐλαφροὶ γεγονότες
τῶν τριῶν παλαισμάτων τῶν ὡς ἀληθῶς Ὀλυμ-
πιακῶν ἓν νενικήκασιν, οὗ μεῖζον ἀγαθὸν οὔτε
σωφροσύνη ἀνθρωπίνη οὔτε θεία μανία δυνατὴ
πορίσαι ἀνθρώπῳ. ἐὰν δὲ δὴ διαίτῃ φορτικωτέρᾳ
τε καὶ ἀφιλοσόφῳ, φιλοτίμῳ δὲ χρήσωνται, τάχ᾽
C ἄν που ἐν μέθαις ἤ τινι ἄλλῃ ἀμελείᾳ τὼ ἀκο-
λάστω αὐτοῖν ὑποζυγίω λαβόντε τὰς ψυχὰς
ἀφρούρους, ξυναγαγόντε εἰς ταὐτόν, τὴν ὑπὸ τῶν
πολλῶν μακαριστὴν αἵρεσιν εἱλέσθην τε καὶ
διεπράξαντο· καὶ διαπραξαμένω τὸ λοιπὸν ἤδη
χρῶνται μὲν αὐτῇ, σπανίᾳ δέ, ἅτε οὐ πάσῃ
δεδογμένα τῇ διανοίᾳ πράττοντες. φίλω μὲν
οὖν καὶ τούτω, ἧττον δὲ ἐκείνων, ἀλλήλοιν διά τε
D τοῦ ἔρωτος καὶ ἔξω γενομένω διάγουσι, πίστεις
τὰς μεγίστας ἡγουμένω ἀλλήλοιν δεδωκέναι τε
καὶ δεδέχθαι, ἃς οὐ θεμιτὸν εἶναι λύσαντας εἰς
ἔχθραν ποτὲ ἐλθεῖν. ἐν δὲ τῇ τελευτῇ ἄπτεροι
μέν, ὡρμηκότες δὲ πτεροῦσθαι ἐκβαίνουσι τοῦ
σώματος, ὥστε οὐ σμικρὸν ἆθλον τῆς ἐρωτικῆς
μανίας φέρονται· εἰς γὰρ σκότον καὶ τὴν ὑπὸ γῆς
πορείαν οὐ νόμος ἐστὶν ἔτι ἐλθεῖν τοῖς κατηργ-
μένοις ἤδη τῆς ἐπουρανίου πορείας, ἀλλὰ φανὸν
βίον διάγοντας εὐδαιμονεῖν μετ᾽ ἀλλήλων πορευο-
μένους, καὶ ὁμοπτέρους ἔρωτος χάριν, ὅταν γένωνται, γενέσθαι.

E 38. Ταῦτα τοσαῦτα, ὦ παῖ, καὶ θεῖα οὕτω
σοι δωρήσεται ἡ παρ᾽ ἐραστοῦ φιλία· ἡ δὲ ἀπὸ
τοῦ μὴ ἐρῶντος οἰκειότης, σωφροσύνῃ θνητῇ
κεκραμένη, θνητά τε καὶ φειδωλὰ οἰκονομοῦσα,
ἀνελευθερίαν ὑπὸ πλήθους ἐπαινουμένην ὡς

freedom to that which makes for virtue; and when this
life is ended they are light and winged, for they have
conquered in one of the three truly Olympic contests.
Neither human wisdom nor divine inspiration can
confer upon man any greater blessing than this. If
however they live a life less noble and without
philosophy, but yet ruled by the love of honour,
probably, when they have been drinking, or in some
other moment of carelessness, the two unruly horses,
taking the souls off their guard, will bring them
together and seize upon and accomplish that which
is by the many accounted blissful; and when this
has once been done, they continue the practice, but
infrequently, since what they are doing is not
approved by the whole mind. So these two pass
through life as friends, though not such friends as
the others, both at the time of their love and
afterwards, believing that they have exchanged the
most binding pledges of love, and that they can
never break them and fall into enmity. And at last,
when they depart from the body, they are not winged,
to be sure, but their wings have begun to grow, so
that the madness of love brings them no small
reward; for it is the law that those who have once
begun their upward progress shall never again pass
into darkness and the journey under the earth, but
shall live a happy life in the light as they journey
together, and because of their love shall be alike in
their plumage when they receive their wings.

These blessings, so great and so divine, the friendship of a lover will confer upon you, dear boy; but
the affection of the non-lover, which is alloyed with
mortal prudence and follows mortal and parsimonious
rules of conduct, will beget in the beloved soul the

ἀρετὴν τῇ φίλῃ ψυχῇ ἐντεκοῦσα, ἐννέα χιλιάδας
257 ἐτῶν περὶ γῆν κυλινδουμένην αὐτὴν καὶ ὑπὸ γῆς
ἄνουν παρέξει. αὕτη σοι, ὦ φίλε Ἔρως, εἰς
ἡμετέραν δύναμιν ὅ τι καλλίστη καὶ ἀρίστη
δέδοταί τε καὶ ἐκτέτισται παλινῳδία, τά τε
ἄλλα καὶ τοῖς ὀνόμασιν ἠναγκασμένη ποιη-
τικοῖς τισιν διὰ Φαῖδρον εἰρῆσθαι. ἀλλὰ τῶν
προτέρων τε συγγνώμην καὶ τῶνδε χάριν ἔχων,
εὐμενὴς καὶ ἵλεως τὴν ἐρωτικήν μοι τέχνην, ἣν
ἔδωκας, μήτε ἀφέλῃ μήτε πηρώσῃς δι' ὀργήν,
δίδου δ' ἔτι μᾶλλον ἢ νῦν παρὰ τοῖς καλοῖς τίμιον
B εἶναι. τῷ πρόσθεν δ' εἴ τι λόγῳ σοι ἀπηνὲς
εἴπομεν Φαῖδρός τε καὶ ἐγώ, Λυσίαν τὸν τοῦ
λόγου πατέρα αἰτιώμενος παῦε τῶν τοιούτων
λόγων, ἐπὶ φιλοσοφίαν δέ, ὥσπερ ὁ ἀδελφὸς
αὐτοῦ Πολέμαρχος τέτραπται, τρέψον, ἵνα καὶ ὁ
ἐραστὴς ὅδε αὐτοῦ μηκέτι ἐπαμφοτερίζῃ καθάπερ
νῦν, ἀλλ' ἁπλῶς πρὸς Ἔρωτα μετὰ φιλοσόφων
λόγων τὸν βίον ποιῆται.

39. ΦΑΙΔΡΟΣ. Συνεύχομαί σοι, ὦ Σώκρατες,
C εἴπερ ἄμεινον ταῦθ' ἡμῖν εἶναι, ταῦτα γίγνεσθαι.
τὸν λόγον δέ σου πάλαι θαυμάσας ἔχω, ὅσῳ
καλλίω τοῦ προτέρου ἀπειργάσω· ὥστε ὀκνῶ μή
μοι ὁ Λυσίας ταπεινὸς φανῇ, ἐὰν ἄρα καὶ ἐθελήσῃ
πρὸς αὐτὸν ἄλλον ἀντιπαρατεῖναι. καὶ γάρ τις
αὐτόν, ὦ θαυμάσιε, ἔναγχος τῶν πολιτικῶν τοῦτ'
αὐτὸ λοιδορῶν ὠνείδιζε, καὶ διὰ πάσης τῆς λοι-
δορίας ἐκάλει λογογράφον· τάχ' οὖν ἂν ὑπὸ
φιλοτιμίας ἐπίσχοι ἡμῖν ἂν τοῦ γράφειν.

D ΣΩΚΡΑΤΗΣ. Γελοῖόν γ', ὦ νεανία, τὸ δόγμα
λέγεις, καὶ τοῦ ἑταίρου συχνὸν διαμαρτάνεις, εἰ
αὐτὸν οὕτως ἡγεῖ τινα ψοφοδεᾶ. ἴσως δὲ καὶ

narrowness which the common folk praise as virtue; it will cause the soul to be a wanderer upon the earth for nine thousand years and a fool below the earth at last. There, dear Love, thou hast my recantation, which I have offered and paid as beautifully and as well as I could, especially in the poetical expressions which I was forced to employ on account of Phaedrus. Pardon, I pray, my former words and accept these words with favour; be kind and gracious to me; do not in anger take from me the art of love which thou didst give me, and deprive me not of sight, but grant unto me to be even more than now esteemed by the beautiful. And if in our former discourse Phaedrus and I said anything harsh against thee, blame Lysias, the father of that discourse, make him to cease from such speeches, and turn him, as his brother Polemarchus is turned, toward philosophy, that his lover Phaedrus may no longer hesitate, as he does now, between two ways, but may direct his life with all singleness of purpose toward love and philosophical discourses.

PHAEDRUS. I join in your prayer, Socrates, and pray that this may come to pass, if this is best for us. But all along I have been wondering at your discourse, you made it so much more beautiful than the first; so that I am afraid Lysias will make a poor showing, if he consents to compete with it. Indeed, lately one of the politicians was abusing him for this very thing, and through all his abusive speech kept calling him a speech-writer; so perhaps out of pride he may refrain from writing.

SOCRATES. That is an absurd idea, young man, and you are greatly mistaken in your friend if you think he is so much afraid of noise. Perhaps, too, you·think

τὸν λοιδορούμενον αὐτῷ οἴει νομίζοντα λέγειν ἃ ἔλεγεν.

ΦΑΙΔΡΟΣ. Ἐφαίνετο γάρ, ὦ Σώκρατες· καὶ σύνοισθά που καὶ αὐτὸς ὅτι οἱ μέγιστον δυνάμενοί τε καὶ σεμνότατοι ἐν ταῖς πόλεσιν αἰσχύνονται λόγους τε γράφειν καὶ καταλείπειν συγγράμματα ἑαυτῶν, δόξαν φοβούμενοι τοῦ ἔπειτα χρόνου, μὴ σοφισταὶ καλῶνται.

ΣΩΚΡΑΤΗΣ. Γλυκὺς ἀγκών, ὦ Φαῖδρε, λέληθέν
E σε·[1] καὶ πρὸς τῷ ἀγκῶνι λανθάνει σε, ὅτι οἱ μέγιστον φρονοῦντες τῶν πολιτικῶν μάλιστα ἐρῶσι λογογραφίας τε καὶ καταλείψεως συγγραμμάτων, οἵ γε καὶ ἐπειδάν τινα γράφωσι λόγον, οὕτως ἀγαπῶσι τοὺς ἐπαινέτας, ὥστε προσπαραγράφουσι πρώτους, οἳ ἂν ἑκασταχοῦ ἐπαινῶσιν αὐτούς.

258   ΦΑΙΔΡΟΣ. Πῶς λέγεις τοῦτο; οὐ γὰρ μανθάνω.

ΣΩΚΡΑΤΗΣ. Οὐ μανθάνεις ὅτι ἐν ἀρχῇ[2] ἀνδρὸς πολιτικοῦ συγγράμματι πρῶτος ὁ ἐπαινέτης γέγραπται.

ΦΑΙΔΡΟΣ. Πῶς;

ΣΩΚΡΑΤΗΣ. Ἔδοξέν πού φησι τῇ βουλῇ ἢ τῷ δήμῳ ἢ ἀμφοτέροις, καὶ ὃς εἶπε, τὸν αὐτὸν δὴ λέγων μάλα σεμνῶς καὶ ἐγκωμιάζων ὁ συγγραφεύς, ἔπειτα λέγει δὴ[3] μετὰ τοῦτο, ἐπιδεικνύμενος τοῖς ἐπαινέταις τὴν ἑαυτοῦ σοφίαν, ἐνίοτε πάνυ μακρὸν

---

[1] After λέληθέν σε the MSS. read ὅτι ἀπὸ τοῦ μακροῦ ἀγκῶνος τοῦ κατὰ Νεῖλον ἐκλήθη. Schanz and Burnet bracket these words, following Heindorf.

[2] Schanz, following Madvig, brackets ἀρχῇ. Burnet brackets συγγράμματι below.

[3] Schanz, following Krische, inserts τὸ after δὴ.

the man who abused him believed what he was saying.

PHAEDRUS. He seemed to believe, Socrates; and you know yourself that the most influential and important men in our cities are ashamed to write speeches and leave writings behind them, through fear of being called sophists by posterity.

SOCRATES. You seem to be unacquainted with the "sweet elbow,"[1] Phaedrus, and besides the elbow, you seem not to know that the proudest of the statesmen are most fond of writing and of leaving writings behind them, since they care so much for praise that when they write a speech they add at the beginning the names of those who praise them in each instance.

PHAEDRUS. What do you mean? I don't understand.

SOCRATES. You don't understand that the name of the approver is written first in the writings of statesmen.

PHAEDRUS. How so?

SOCRATES. The writer says, "It was voted by the senate (or the people, or both), and so-and-so moved," mentioning his own name with great dignity and praise, then after that he goes on, displaying his own wisdom to his approvers, and sometimes making a very long document. Does it seem to you that a

---

[1] This is a proverbial expression, similar in meaning to our "sour grapes." The explanation given in the MSS., that the sweet elbow gets its name from the long bend, or elbow, in the Nile may be an addition by some commentator; at any rate, it hardly fits our passage.

B ποιησάμενος σύγγραμμα· ἢ σοι ἄλλο τι φαίνεται
τὸ τοιοῦτον ἢ λόγος συγγεγραμμένος;

ΦΑΙΔΡΟΣ. Οὐκ ἔμοιγε.

ΣΩΚΡΑΤΗΣ. Οὐκοῦν ἐὰν μὲν οὗτος ἐμμένῃ, γε-
γηθὼς ἀπέρχεται ἐκ τοῦ θεάτρου ὁ ποιητής· ἐὰν
δὲ ἐξαλιφῇ καὶ ἄμοιρος γένηται λογογραφίας τε
καὶ τοῦ ἄξιος εἶναι συγγράφειν, πενθεῖ αὐτός τε
καὶ οἱ ἑταῖροι.

ΦΑΙΔΡΟΣ. Καὶ μάλα.

ΣΩΚΡΑΤΗΣ. Δῆλόν γε ὅτι οὐχ ὡς ὑπερφρονοῦντες
τοῦ ἐπιτηδεύματος, ἀλλ᾽ ὡς τεθαυμακότες.

ΦΑΙΔΡΟΣ. Πάνυ μὲν οὖν.

C ΣΩΚΡΑΤΗΣ. Τί δέ; ὅταν ἱκανὸς γένηται ῥήτωρ
ἢ βασιλεὺς ὥστε λαβὼν τὴν Λυκούργου ἢ Σό-
λωνος ἢ Δαρείου δύναμιν ἀθάνατος γενέσθαι
λογογράφος ἐν πόλει, ἆρ᾽ οὐκ ἰσόθεον ἡγεῖται
αὐτός τε αὑτὸν ἔτι ζῶν, καὶ οἱ ἔπειτα γιγνόμενοι
ταὐτὰ ταῦτα περὶ αὐτοῦ νομίζουσι, θεώμενοι
αὐτοῦ τὰ συγγράμματα;

ΦΑΙΔΡΟΣ. Καὶ μάλα.

ΣΩΚΡΑΤΗΣ. Οἴει τινὰ οὖν τῶν τοιούτων, ὅστις
καὶ ὁπωστιοῦν δύσνους Λυσίᾳ, ὀνειδίζειν αὐτὸ
τοῦτο ὅτι συγγράφει;

ΦΑΙΔΡΟΣ. Οὔκουν εἰκός γε ἐξ ὧν σὺ λέγεις· καὶ
γὰρ ἂν τῇ ἑαυτοῦ ἐπιθυμίᾳ, ὡς ἔοικεν, ὀνειδίζοι.

D 40. ΣΩΚΡΑΤΗΣ. Τοῦτο μὲν ἄρα παντὶ δῆλον,
ὅτι οὐκ αἰσχρὸν αὐτό γε τὸ γράφειν λόγους.

ΦΑΙΔΡΟΣ. Τί γάρ;

ΣΩΚΡΑΤΗΣ. Ἀλλ᾽ ἐκεῖνο οἶμαι αἰσχρὸν ἤδη,
τὸ μὴ καλῶς λέγειν τε καὶ γράφειν, ἀλλ᾽ αἰσχρῶς
τε καὶ κακῶς.

ΦΑΙΔΡΟΣ. Δῆλον δή.

thing of that sort is anything else than a written speech?

PHAEDRUS. No, certainly not.

SOCRATES. Then if this speech is approved, the writer leaves the theatre in great delight; but if it is not recorded and he is not granted the privilege of speech-writing and is not considered worthy to be an author, he is grieved, and his friends with him.

PHAEDRUS. Decidedly.

SOCRATES. Evidently not because they despise the profession, but because they admire it.

PHAEDRUS. To be sure.

SOCRATES. Well then, when an orator or a king is able to rival the greatness of Lycurgus or Solon or Darius and attain immortality as a writer in the state, does he not while living think himself equal to the gods, and has not posterity the same opinion of him, when they see his writings?

PHAEDRUS. Very true.

SOCRATES. Do you think, then, that any of the statesmen, no matter how ill-disposed toward Lysias, reproaches him for being a writer?

PHAEDRUS. It is not likely, according to what you say; for he would be casting reproach upon that which he himself desires to be.

SOCRATES. Then that is clear to all, that writing speeches is not in itself a disgrace.

PHAEDRUS. How can it be?

SOCRATES. But the disgrace, I fancy, consists in speaking or writing not well, but disgracefully and badly.

PHAEDRUS. Evidently.

PLATO

ΣΩΚΡΑΤΗΣ. Τίς οὖν ὁ τρόπος τοῦ καλῶς τε καὶ μὴ γράφειν; δεόμεθά τι, ὦ Φαῖδρε, Λυσίαν τε περὶ τούτων ἐξετάσαι καὶ ἄλλον, ὅστις πώποτέ τι γέγραφεν ἢ γράψει, εἴτε πολιτικὸν σύγγραμμα εἴτε ἰδιωτικόν, ἐν μέτρῳ ὡς ποιητής, ἢ ἄνευ μέτρου ὡς ἰδιώτης;

E ΦΑΙΔΡΟΣ. Ἐρωτᾷς εἰ δεόμεθα; τίνος μὲν οὖν ἕνεκα κἄν τις ὡς εἰπεῖν ζῴη, ἀλλ' ἢ τῶν τοιούτων ἡδονῶν ἕνεκα; οὐ γάρ που ἐκείνων γε ὧν προλυπηθῆναι δεῖ ἢ μηδὲ ἡσθῆναι, ὃ δὴ ὀλίγου πᾶσαι αἱ περὶ τὸ σῶμα ἡδοναὶ ἔχουσι· διὸ καὶ δικαίως ἀνδραποδώδεις κέκληνται.

ΣΩΚΡΑΤΗΣ. Σχολὴ μὲν δή, ὡς ἔοικε· καὶ ἅμα μοι δοκοῦσιν ὡς ἐν τῷ πνίγει ὑπὲρ κεφαλῆς ἡμῶν οἱ τέττιγες ᾄδοντες καὶ ἀλλήλοις διαλεγόμενοι

259 καθορᾶν. εἰ οὖν ἴδοιεν καὶ νὼ καθάπερ τοὺς πολλοὺς ἐν μεσημβρίᾳ μὴ διαλεγομένους, ἀλλὰ νυστάζοντας καὶ κηλουμένους ὑφ' αὑτῶν δι' ἀργίαν τῆς διανοίας, δικαίως ἂν καταγελῷεν, ἡγούμενοι ἀνδράποδα ἄττα σφίσιν ἐλθόντα εἰς τὸ καταγώγιον ὥσπερ προβάτια μεσημβριάζοντα περὶ τὴν κρήνην εὕδειν· ἐὰν δὲ ὁρῶσι διαλεγομένους καὶ παραπλέοντάς σφας ὥσπερ Σειρῆνας ἀκηλή-

B τους, ὃ γέρας παρὰ θεῶν ἔχουσιν ἀνθρώποις διδόναι, τάχ' ἂν δοῖεν ἀγασθέντες.

41. ΦΑΙΔΡΟΣ. Ἔχουσι δὲ δὴ τί τοῦτο; ἀνήκοος γάρ, ὡς ἔοικε, τυγχάνω ὤν.

ΣΩΚΡΑΤΗΣ. Οὐ μὲν δὴ πρέπει γε φιλόμουσον ἄνδρα τῶν τοιούτων ἀνήκοον εἶναι· λέγεται δ' ὥς ποτ' ἦσαν οὗτοι ἄνθρωποι τῶν πρὶν Μούσας γεγονέναι, γενομένων δὲ Μουσῶν καὶ φανείσης ᾠδῆς οὕτως ἄρα τινὲς τῶν τότε ἐξεπλάγησαν ὑφ'

510

PHAEDRUS

socrates. What, then, is the method of writing well or badly? Do we want to question Lysias about this, and anyone else who ever has written or will write anything, whether a public or private document, in verse or in prose, be he poet or ordinary man?

phaedrus. You ask if we want to question them? What else should one live for, so to speak, but for such pleasures? Certainly not for those which cannot be enjoyed without previous pain, which is the case with nearly all bodily pleasures and causes them to be justly called slavish.

socrates. We have plenty of time, apparently; and besides, the locusts seem to be looking down upon us as they sing and talk with each other in the heat. Now if they should see us not conversing at mid-day, but, like most people, dozing, lulled to sleep by their song because of our mental indolence, they would quite justly laugh at us, thinking that some slaves had come to their resort and were slumbering about the fountain at noon like sheep. But if they see us conversing and sailing past them unmoved by the charm of their Siren voices, perhaps they will be pleased and give us the gift which the gods bestowed on them to give to men.

phaedrus. What is this gift? I don't seem to have heard of it.

socrates. It is quite improper for a lover of the Muses never to have heard of such things. The story goes that these locusts were once men, before the birth of the Muses, and when the Muses were born and song appeared, some of the men were so

ⅴ ἡδονῆς, ὥστε ᾄδοντες ἠμέλησαν σίτων τε καὶ
ποτῶν, καὶ ἔλαθον τελευτήσαντες αὑτούς· ἐξ ὧν
τὸ τεττίγων γένος μετ' ἐκεῖνο φύεται, γέρας τοῦτο
παρὰ Μουσῶν λαβόν, μηδὲν τροφῆς δεῖσθαι
γενόμενον,[1] ἀλλ' ἄσιτόν τε καὶ ἄποτον εὐθὺς ᾄδειν,
ἕως ἂν τελευτήσῃ, καὶ μετὰ ταῦτα ἐλθὸν παρὰ
Μούσας ἀπαγγέλλειν, τίς τίνα αὐτῶν τιμᾷ τῶν
ἐνθάδε. Τερψιχόρᾳ μὲν οὖν τοὺς ἐν τοῖς χοροῖς
τετιμηκότας αὐτὴν ἀπαγγέλλοντες ποιοῦσι προσ-
ⅾ φιλεστέρους, τῇ δὲ Ἐρατοῖ τοὺς ἐν τοῖς ἐρωτικοῖς,
καὶ ταῖς ἄλλαις οὕτω, κατὰ τὸ εἶδος ἑκάστης
τιμῆς· τῇ δὲ πρεσβυτάτῃ Καλλιόπῃ καὶ τῇ μετ'
αὐτὴν Οὐρανίᾳ τοὺς ἐν φιλοσοφίᾳ διάγοντάς τε
καὶ τιμῶντας τὴν ἐκείνων μουσικὴν ἀγγέλλουσιν,
αἳ δὴ μάλιστα τῶν Μουσῶν περί τε οὐρανὸν καὶ
λόγους οὖσαι θείους τε καὶ ἀνθρωπίνους ἱᾶσι
καλλίστην φωνήν. πολλῶν δὴ οὖν ἕνεκα λεκτέον
τι καὶ οὐ καθευδητέον ἐν τῇ μεσημβρίᾳ.

ΦΑΙΔΡΟΣ. Λεκτέον γὰρ οὖν.

ⅇ 42. ΣΩΚΡΑΤΗΣ. Οὐκοῦν, ὅπερ νῦν προὐθέμεθα
σκέψασθαι, τὸν λόγον ὅπῃ καλῶς ἔχει λέγειν τε
καὶ γράφειν καὶ ὅπῃ μή, σκεπτέον.

ΦΑΙΔΡΟΣ. Δῆλον.

ΣΩΚΡΑΤΗΣ. Ἆρ' οὖν οὐχ ὑπάρχειν δεῖ τοῖς εὖ
γε καὶ καλῶς ῥηθησομένοις τὴν τοῦ λέγοντος διάνοιαν εἰδυῖαν τ' ἀληθὲς ὧν ἂν ἐρεῖν πέρι μέλλῃ;

260 ΦΑΙΔΡΟΣ. Οὑτωσὶ περὶ τούτου ἀκήκοα, ὦ φίλε
Σώκρατες, οὐκ εἶναι ἀνάγκην τῷ μέλλοντι ῥήτορι
ἔσεσθαι τὰ τῷ ὄντι δίκαια μανθάνειν, ἀλλὰ τὰ
δόξαντ' ἂν πλήθει, οἵπερ δικάσουσιν, οὐδὲ τὰ
ὄντως ἀγαθὰ ἢ καλά, ἀλλ' ὅσα δόξει· ἐκ γὰρ

---

[1] Schanz, following Badham, puts γενόμενον after εὐθύς.

overcome with delight that they sang and sang, forgetting food and drink, until at last unconsciously they died. From them the locust tribe afterwards arose, and they have this gift from the Muses, that from the time of their birth they need no sustenance, but sing continually, without food or drink, until they die, when they go to the Muses and report who honours each of them on earth. They tell Terpsichore of those who have honoured her in dances, and make them dearer to her; they gain the favour of Erato for the poets of love, and that of the other Muses for their votaries, according to their various ways of honouring them; and to Calliope, the eldest of the Muses, and to Urania who is next to her, they make report of those who pass their lives in philosophy and who worship these Muses who are most concerned with heaven and with thought divine and human and whose music is the sweetest. So for many reasons we ought to talk and not sleep in the noontime.

PHAEDRUS. Yes, we ought to talk.

SOCRATES. We should, then, as we were proposing just now, discuss the theory of good (or bad) speaking and writing.

PHAEDRUS. Clearly.

SOCRATES. If a speech is to be good, must not the mind of the speaker know the truth about the matters of which he is to speak?

PHAEDRUS. On that point, Socrates, I have heard that one who is to be an orator does not need to know what is really just, but what would seem just to the multitude who are to pass judgment, and not what is really good or noble, but what will seem to be so;

513

τούτων εἶναι τὸ πείθειν, ἀλλ' οὐκ ἐκ τῆς ἀληθείας.

ΣΩΚΡΑΤΗΣ. Οὗτοι ἀπόβλητον ἔπος εἶναι δεῖ, ὦ
Φαῖδρε, ὃ ἂν εἴπωσι σοφοί, ἀλλὰ σκοπεῖν μὴ τὶ
λέγωσι·[1] καὶ δὴ καὶ τὸ νῦν λεχθὲν οὐκ ἀφετέον.

ΦΑΙΔΡΟΣ. Ὀρθῶς λέγεις.

ΣΩΚΡΑΤΗΣ. Ὧδε δὴ σκοπῶμεν αὐτό.

ΦΑΙΔΡΟΣ. Πῶς;

B   ΣΩΚΡΑΤΗΣ. Εἴ σε πείθοιμι ἐγὼ πολεμίους ἀμύνειν
κτησάμενον ἵππον, ἄμφω δὲ ἵππον ἀγνοοῖμεν,
τοσόνδε μέντοι τυγχάνοιμι εἰδὼς περὶ σοῦ, ὅτι
Φαῖδρος ἵππον ἡγεῖται τὸ τῶν ἡμέρων ζῴων
μέγιστα ἔχον ὦτα—

ΦΑΙΔΡΟΣ. Γελοῖόν γ' ἄν, ὦ Σώκρατες, εἴη.

ΣΩΚΡΑΤΗΣ. Οὔπω γε· ἀλλ' ὅτε σπουδῇ σε
πείθοιμι, συντιθεὶς λόγον ἔπαινον κατὰ τοῦ ὄνου,
ἵππον ἐπονομάζων καὶ λέγων ὡς παντὸς ἄξιον τὸ
θρέμμα οἴκοι τε κεκτῆσθαι καὶ ἐπὶ στρατείας,
ἀποπολεμεῖν τε χρήσιμον, καὶ προσενεγκεῖν δυνα-
C   τὸν σκεύη καὶ ἄλλα πολλὰ ὠφέλιμον.

ΦΑΙΔΡΟΣ. Παγγέλοιόν γ' ἂν ἤδη εἴη.

ΣΩΚΡΑΤΗΣ. Ἆρ' οὖν οὐ κρεῖττον γελοῖον ἢ δεινόν
τε καὶ ἐχθρὸν εἶναι;[2]

ΦΑΙΔΡΟΣ. Φαίνεται.

ΣΩΚΡΑΤΗΣ. Ὅταν οὖν ὁ ῥητορικὸς ἀγνοῶν ἀγαθὸν
καὶ κακόν, λαβὼν πόλιν ὡσαύτως ἔχουσαν πείθῃ,
μὴ περὶ ὄνου σκιᾶς[3] ὡς ἵππου τὸν ἔπαινον ποιούμενος, ἀλλὰ περὶ κακοῦ ὡς ἀγαθοῦ, δόξας δὲ

---

[1] Schanz, following Schaefer, reads λέγουσι.
[2] εἶναι ἢ φίλον BT. Schanz follows Bekker in omitting
ἢ φίλον.
[3] Schanz follows Spalding in omitting σκιᾶς.

for they say that persuasion comes from what seems to be true, not from the truth.

SOCRATES. "The word," Phaedrus, which the wise "speak must not be rejected," [1] but we must see if they are right; so we must not pass by this which you just said.

PHAEDRUS. You are right.

SOCRATES. Let us then examine it in this way.

PHAEDRUS. How?

SOCRATES. If I should urge you to buy a horse and fight against the invaders, and neither of us knew what a horse was, but I merely knew this about you, that Phaedrus thinks a horse is the one of the tame animals which has the longest ears—

PHAEDRUS. It would be ridiculous, Socrates.

SOCRATES. No, not yet; but if I tried to persuade you in all seriousness, composing a speech in praise of the ass, which I called a horse, and saying that the beast was a most valuable possession at home and in war, that you could use him as a mount in battle, and that he was able to carry baggage and was useful for many other purposes—

PHAEDRUS. Then it would be supremely ridiculous.

SOCRATES. But is it not better to be ridiculous than to be clever and an enemy?

PHAEDRUS. To be sure.

SOCRATES. Then when the orator who does not know what good and evil are undertakes to persuade a state which is equally ignorant, not by praising the "shadow of an ass" [2] under the name of a horse, but by praising evil under the name of good, and having studied the opinions of the multitude persuades them

---

[1] Homer, *Iliad* ii. 361. [2] A proverbial expression.

πλήθους μεμελετηκὼς πείσῃ κακὰ πράττειν ἀντ'
ἀγαθῶν, ποῖόν τινα οἴει μετὰ ταῦτα τὴν ῥητορικὴν
D καρπὸν ὧν ἔσπειρε θερίζειν;

ΦΑΙΔΡΟΣ. Οὐ πάνυ γε ἐπιεικῆ.

43. ΣΩΚΡΑΤΗΣ. Ἆρ' οὖν, ὦ 'γαθέ, ἀγροικότερον
τοῦ δέοντος λελοιδορήκαμεν τὴν τῶν λόγων
τέχνην; ἡ δ' ἴσως ἂν εἴποι· τί ποτ', ὦ θαυμάσιοι,
ληρεῖτε; ἐγὼ γὰρ οὐδέν' ἀγνοοῦντα τἀληθὲς
ἀναγκάζω μανθάνειν λέγειν, ἀλλ', εἴ τις ἐμὴ
ξυμβουλή,[1] κτησάμενος ἐκεῖνο οὕτως ἐμὲ λαμβάνει·
τόδε δ' οὖν μέγα λέγω, ὡς ἄνευ ἐμοῦ τῷ τὰ ὄντα
εἰδότι οὐδέν τι μᾶλλον ἔσται πείθειν τέχνῃ.

ΦΑΙΔΡΟΣ. Οὐκοῦν δίκαια ἐρεῖ, λέγουσα ταῦτα;

E ΣΩΚΡΑΤΗΣ. Φημί, ἐὰν οἵ γε ἐπιόντες αὐτῇ λόγοι
μαρτυρῶσιν εἶναι τέχνη. ὥσπερ γὰρ ἀκούειν
δοκῶ τινῶν προσιόντων καὶ διαμαρτυρομένων
λόγων, ὅτι ψεύδεται καὶ οὐκ ἔστι τέχνη ἀλλ'
ἄτεχνος τριβή· τοῦ δὲ λέγειν, φησὶν ὁ Λάκων,
ἔτυμος τέχνη ἄνευ τοῦ ἀληθείας ἧφθαι οὔτ' ἔστιν
οὔτε μή ποτε ὕστερον γένηται.[2]

261 ΦΑΙΔΡΟΣ. Τούτων δεῖ τῶν λόγων, ὦ Σώκρατες·
ἀλλὰ δεῦρο αὐτοὺς παράγων ἐξέταζε, τί καὶ πῶς
λέγουσι.

ΣΩΚΡΑΤΗΣ. Πάριτε δή, θρέμματα γενναῖα, καλλί-
παιδά τε Φαῖδρον πείθετε, ὡς ἐὰν μὴ ἱκανῶς
φιλοσοφήσῃ, οὐδὲ ἱκανός ποτε λέγειν ἔσται περὶ
οὐδενός. ἀποκρινέσθω δὴ ὁ Φαῖδρος.

ΦΑΙΔΡΟΣ. Ἐρωτᾶτε.

ΣΩΚΡΑΤΗΣ. Ἆρ' οὖν οὐ τὸ μὲν ὅλον ἡ ῥητορικὴ

---

[1] εἴ τις ἐμῇ ξυμβουλῇ χρῆται Schanz, following Stephanus.
εἴ τι ἐμῇ ξυμβουλῇ B. εἴ τις ἐμῇ ξυμβουλῇ T.
[2] Schanz brackets τοῦ . . . γένηται.

to do evil instead of good, what harvest do you suppose his oratory will reap thereafter from the seed he has sown ?

PHAEDRUS. No very good harvest.

SOCRATES. Well, do you think we have reproached the art of speaking too harshly ? Perhaps she might say : " Why do you talk such nonsense, you strange men ? I do not compel anyone to learn to speak without knowing the truth, but if my advice is of any value, he learns that first and then acquires me. So what I claim is this, that without my help the knowledge of the truth does not give the art of persuasion."

PHAEDRUS. And will she be right in saying this ?

SOCRATES. Yes, if the arguments that are coming against her testify that she is an art. For I seem, as it were, to hear some arguments approaching and protesting that she is lying and is not an art, but a craft devoid of art. A real art of speaking, says the Laconian, which does not seize hold of truth, does not exist and never will.

PHAEDRUS. We have need of these arguments, Socrates. Bring them here and examine their words and their meaning.

SOCRATES. Come here, then, noble creatures, and persuade the fair young Phaedrus that unless he pay proper attention to philosophy he will never be able to speak properly about anything. And let Phaedrus answer.

PHAEDRUS. Ask your questions.

SOCRATES. Is not rhetoric in its entire nature an

PLATO

ἂν εἴη τέχνη ψυχαγωγία τις διὰ λόγων, οὐ μόνον
ἐν δικαστηρίοις καὶ ὅσοι ἄλλοι δημόσιοι σύλλογοι,
B ἀλλὰ καὶ ἐν ἰδίοις, ἡ αὐτὴ σμικρῶν τε καὶ μεγάλων
πέρι, καὶ οὐδὲν ἐντιμότερον τό γε ὀρθὸν περὶ
σπουδαῖα ἢ περὶ φαῦλα γιγνόμενον; ἢ πῶς σὺ
ταῦτ᾽ ἀκήκοας;

ΦΑΙΔΡΟΣ. Οὐ μὰ τὸν Δία οὐ παντάπασιν οὕτως,
ἀλλὰ μάλιστα μέν πως περὶ τὰς δίκας λέγεταί τε
καὶ γράφεται τέχνη, λέγεται δὲ καὶ περὶ δημη-
γορίας· ἐπὶ πλέον δὲ οὐκ ἀκήκοα.

ΣΩΚΡΑΤΗΣ. Ἀλλ᾽ ἦ τὰς Νέστορος καὶ Ὀδυσσέως
τέχνας μόνον περὶ λόγων ἀκήκοας, ἃς ἐν Ἰλίῳ
C σχολάζοντες συνεγραψάτην, τῶν δὲ Παλαμήδους
ἀνήκοος γέγονας;

ΦΑΙΔΡΟΣ. Καὶ ναὶ μὰ Δία ἔγωγε τῶν Νέστορος,
εἰ μὴ Γοργίαν Νέστορά τινα κατασκευάζεις, ἤ
τινα Θρασύμαχόν τε καὶ Θεόδωρον Ὀδυσσέα.

44. ΣΩΚΡΑΤΗΣ. Ἴσως. ἀλλὰ γὰρ τούτους ἐῶμεν·
σὺ δ᾽ εἰπέ, ἐν δικαστηρίοις οἱ ἀντίδικοι τί δρῶσιν;
οὐκ ἀντιλέγουσιν μέντοι, ἢ τί φήσομεν;

ΦΑΙΔΡΟΣ. Τοῦτ᾽ αὐτό.

ΣΩΚΡΑΤΗΣ. Περὶ τοῦ δικαίου τε καὶ ἀδίκου;

ΦΑΙΔΡΟΣ. Ναί.

ΣΩΚΡΑΤΗΣ. Οὐκοῦν ὁ τέχνῃ τοῦτο δρῶν ποιήσει
D φανῆναι τὸ αὐτὸ τοῖς αὐτοῖς τοτὲ μὲν δίκαιον, ὅταν
δὲ βούληται, ἄδικον;

ΦΑΙΔΡΟΣ. Τί μήν;

ΣΩΚΡΑΤΗΣ. Καὶ ἐν δημηγορίᾳ δὴ τῇ πόλει δοκεῖν
τὰ αὐτὰ τοτὲ μὲν ἀγαθά, τοτὲ δ᾽ αὖ τἀναντία;

ΦΑΙΔΡΟΣ. Οὕτως.

ΣΩΚΡΑΤΗΣ. Τὸν οὖν Ἐλεατικὸν Παλαμήδην

art which leads the soul by means of words, not only in law courts and the various other public assemblages, but in private companies as well? And is it not the same when concerned with small things as with great, and, properly speaking, no more to be esteemed in important than in trifling matters? Is this what you have heard?

PHAEDRUS. No, by Zeus, not that exactly; but the art of speaking and writing is exercised chiefly in lawsuits, and that of speaking also in public assemblies; and I never heard of any further uses.

SOCRATES. Then you have heard only of the treatises on rhetoric by Nestor and Odysseus, which they wrote when they had nothing to do at Troy, and you have not heard of that by Palamedes?

PHAEDRUS. Nor of Nestor's either, unless you are disguising Gorgias under the name of Nestor and Thrasymachus or Theodorus under that of Odysseus.

SOCRATES. Perhaps I am. However, never mind them; but tell me, what do the parties in a lawsuit do in court? Do they not contend in speech, or what shall we say they do?

PHAEDRUS. Exactly that.

SOCRATES. About the just and the unjust?

PHAEDRUS. Yes.

SOCRATES. Then he whose speaking is an art will make the same thing appear to the same persons at one time just and at another, if he wishes, unjust?

PHAEDRUS. Certainly.

SOCRATES. And in political speaking he will make the same things seem to the State at one time good and at another the opposite?

PHAEDRUS. Just so.

SOCRATES. Do we not know that the Eleatic

λέγοντα οὐκ ἴσμεν τέχνῃ, ὥστε φαίνεσθαι τοῖς ἀκούουσι τὰ αὐτὰ ὅμοια καὶ ἀνόμοια, καὶ ἓν καὶ πολλά, μένοντά τε αὖ καὶ φερόμενα;

ΦΑΙΔΡΟΣ. Μάλα γε.

ΣΩΚΡΑΤΗΣ. Οὐκ ἄρα μόνον περὶ δικαστήριά τέ Ε ἐστιν ἡ ἀντιλογικὴ καὶ περὶ δημηγορίαν, ἀλλ᾽, ὡς ἔοικε, περὶ πάντα τὰ λεγόμενα μία τις τέχνη, εἴπερ ἔστιν, αὕτη ἂν εἴη, ᾗ τις οἷός τ᾽ ἔσται πᾶν παντὶ ὁμοιοῦν τῶν δυνατῶν καὶ οἷς δυνατόν, καὶ ἄλλου ὁμοιοῦντος καὶ ἀποκρυπτομένου εἰς φῶς ἄγειν.

ΦΑΙΔΡΟΣ. Πῶς δὴ τὸ τοιοῦτον λέγεις;

ΣΩΚΡΑΤΗΣ. Τῇδε δοκῶ ζητοῦσιν φανεῖσθαι. ἀπάτη πότερον ἐν πολὺ διαφέρουσι γίγνεται μᾶλλον ἢ ὀλίγον;

262 ΦΑΙΔΡΟΣ. Ἐν τοῖς ὀλίγον.

ΣΩΚΡΑΤΗΣ. Ἀλλά γε δὴ κατὰ σμικρὸν μεταβαίνων μᾶλλον λήσεις ἐλθὼν ἐπὶ τὸ ἐναντίον ἢ κατὰ μέγα.

ΦΑΙΔΡΟΣ. Πῶς δ᾽ οὔ;

ΣΩΚΡΑΤΗΣ. Δεῖ ἄρα τὸν μέλλοντα ἀπατήσειν μὲν ἄλλον, αὐτὸν δὲ μὴ ἀπατήσεσθαι, τὴν ὁμοιότητα τῶν ὄντων καὶ ἀνομοιότητα ἀκριβῶς διειδέναι.

ΦΑΙΔΡΟΣ. Ἀνάγκη μὲν οὖν.

ΣΩΚΡΑΤΗΣ. Ἦ οὖν οἷός τε ἔσται, ἀλήθειαν ἀγνοῶν ἑκάστου, τὴν τοῦ ἀγνοουμένου ὁμοιότητα σμικράν Β τε καὶ μεγάλην ἐν τοῖς ἄλλοις διαγιγνώσκειν;

ΦΑΙΔΡΟΣ. Ἀδύνατον.

ΣΩΚΡΑΤΗΣ. Οὐκοῦν τοῖς παρὰ τὰ ὄντα δοξάζουσιν

Palamedes (Zeno) has such an art of speaking that
the same things appear to his hearers to be alike and
unlike, one and many, stationary and in motion?

PHAEDRUS. Certainly.

SOCRATES. Then the art of contention in speech is
not confined to courts and political gatherings, but
apparently, if it is an art at all, it would be one and
the same in all kinds of speaking, the art by which a
man will be able to produce a resemblance between
all things between which it can be produced, and to
bring to the light the resemblances produced and
disguised by anyone else.

PHAEDRUS. What do you mean by that?

SOCRATES. I think it will be plain if we examine
the matter in this way. Is deception easier when
there is much difference between things or when
there is little?

PHAEDRUS. When there is little.

SOCRATES. And if you make a transition by small
steps from anything to its opposite you will be more
likely to escape detection than if you proceed by
leaps and bounds.

PHAEDRUS. Of course.

SOCRATES. Then he who is to deceive another, and
is not to be deceived himself, must know accurately
the similarity and dissimilarity of things.

PHAEDRUS. Yes, he must.

SOCRATES. Now will he be able, not knowing the
truth about a given thing, to recognise in other
things the great or small degree of likeness to that
which he does not know?

PHAEDRUS. It is impossible.

SOCRATES. In .the case, then, of those whose
opinions are at variance with facts and who are

καὶ ἀπατωμένοις δῆλον ὡς τὸ πάθος τοῦτο δι'
ὁμοιοτήτων τινῶν εἰσερρύη.

ΦΑΙΔΡΟΣ. Γίγνεται γοῦν οὕτως.

ΣΩΚΡΑΤΗΣ. Ἔστιν οὖν ὅπως τεχνικὸς ἔσται μετα-
βιβάζειν κατὰ σμικρὸν διὰ τῶν ὁμοιοτήτων ἀπὸ
τοῦ ὄντος ἑκάστοτε ἐπὶ τοὐναντίον ἀπάγων, ἢ
αὐτὸς τοῦτο διαφεύγειν, ὁ μὴ ἐγνωρικὼς ὃ ἔστιν
ἕκαστον τῶν ὄντων;

ΦΑΙΔΡΟΣ. Οὐ μή ποτε.

C   ΣΩΚΡΑΤΗΣ. Λόγων ἄρα τέχνην, ὦ ἑταῖρε, ὁ τὴν
ἀλήθειαν μὴ εἰδώς, δόξας δὲ τεθηρευκώς, γελοίαν
τινά, ὡς ἔοικε, καὶ ἄτεχνον παρέξεται.

ΦΑΙΔΡΟΣ. Κινδυνεύει.

45. ΣΩΚΡΑΤΗΣ. Βούλει οὖν ἐν τῷ Λυσίου λόγῳ,
ὃν φέρεις, καὶ ἐν οἷς ἡμεῖς εἴπομεν ἰδεῖν τι ὧν
φαμὲν ἀτέχνων τε καὶ ἐντέχνων εἶναι;

ΦΑΙΔΡΟΣ. Πάντων γέ που μάλιστα, ὡς νῦν γε
ψιλῶς πως λέγομεν, οὐκ ἔχοντες ἱκανὰ παραδείγματα.

ΣΩΚΡΑΤΗΣ. Καὶ μὴν κατὰ τύχην γέ τινα, ὡς
D ἔοικεν, ἐρρηθήτην τὼ λόγω ἔχοντέ τι παράδειγμα,
ὡς ἂν ὁ εἰδὼς τὸ ἀληθὲς προσπαίζων ἐν λόγοις
παράγοι τοὺς ἀκούοντας. καὶ ἔγωγε, ὦ Φαῖδρε,
αἰτιῶμαι τοὺς ἐντοπίους θεούς· ἴσως δὲ καὶ οἱ τῶν
Μουσῶν προφῆται οἱ ὑπὲρ κεφαλῆς ᾠδοὶ ἐπιπε-
πνευκότες ἂν ἡμῖν εἶεν τοῦτο τὸ γέρας· οὐ γάρ που
ἔγωγε τέχνης τινὸς τοῦ λέγειν μέτοχος.

ΦΑΙΔΡΟΣ. Ἔστω ὡς λέγεις· μόνον δήλωσον
ὃ φής.

ΣΩΚΡΑΤΗΣ. Ἴθι δή μοι ἀνάγνωθι τὴν τοῦ Λυσίου
λόγου ἀρχήν.

E   ΦΑΙΔΡΟΣ. Περὶ μὲν τῶν ἐμῶν πραγμάτων ἐπί-

deceived, this error evidently slips in through some resemblances.

PHAEDRUS. It does happen in that way.

SOCRATES. Then he who does not understand the real nature of things will not possess the art of making his hearers pass from one thing to its opposite by leading them through the intervening resemblances, or of avoiding such deception himself?

PHAEDRUS. Never in the world.

SOCRATES. Then, my friend, he who knows not the truth, but pursues opinions, will, it seems, attain an art of speech which is ridiculous, and not an art at all.

PHAEDRUS. Probably.

SOCRATES. Shall we look in the speech of Lysias, which you have with you, and in what I said, for something which we think shows art and the lack of art?

PHAEDRUS. By all means, for now our talk is too abstract, since we lack sufficient examples.

SOCRATES. And by some special good fortune, as it seems, the two discourses contain an example of the way in which one who knows the truth may lead his hearers on with sportive words; and I, Phaedrus, think the divinities of the place are the cause thereof; and perhaps, too, the prophets of the Muses, who are singing above our heads, may have granted this boon to us by inspiration; at any rate, I possess no art of speaking.

PHAEDRUS. So be it; only make your meaning clear.

SOCRATES. Read me the beginning of Lysias' discourse.

PHAEDRUS. You know what my condition is, and

στᾶσαι, καὶ ὡς νομίζω συμφέρειν ἡμῖν τούτων
γενομένων, ἀκήκοας. ἀξιῶ δὲ μὴ διὰ τοῦτο
ἀτυχῆσαι ὧν δέομαι, ὅτι οὐκ ἐραστὴς ὢν σοῦ
τυγχάνω. ὡς ἐκείνοις μὲν τότε μεταμέλει—

263 ΣΩΚΡΑΤΗΣ. Παῦσαι. τί δὴ οὖν οὗτος ἁμαρτάνει
καὶ ἄτεχνον ποιεῖ, λεκτέον. ἦ γάρ;

ΦΑΙΔΡΟΣ. Ναί.

46. ΣΩΚΡΑΤΗΣ. Ἆρ' οὖν οὐ παντὶ δῆλον τό γε
τοιόνδε, ὡς περὶ μὲν ἔνια τῶν τοιούτων ὁμονοητι-
κῶς ἔχομεν, περὶ δ' ἔνια στασιωτικῶς;

ΦΑΙΔΡΟΣ. Δοκῶ μὲν ὃ λέγεις μανθάνειν, ἔτι δ'
εἰπὲ σαφέστερον.

ΣΩΚΡΑΤΗΣ. Ὅταν τις ὄνομα εἴπῃ σιδήρου ἢ
ἀργύρου, ἆρ' οὐ τὸ αὐτὸ πάντες διενοήθημεν;

ΦΑΙΔΡΟΣ. Καὶ μάλα.

ΣΩΚΡΑΤΗΣ. Τί δ' ὅταν δικαίου ἢ ἀγαθοῦ; οὐκ
ἄλλος ἄλλῃ φέρεται, καὶ ἀμφισβητοῦμεν ἀλλήλοις
τε καὶ ἡμῖν αὐτοῖς;

ΦΑΙΔΡΟΣ. Πάνυ μὲν οὖν.

B ΣΩΚΡΑΤΗΣ. Ἐν μὲν ἄρα τοῖς συμφωνοῦμεν, ἐν
δὲ τοῖς οὔ.

ΦΑΙΔΡΟΣ. Οὕτω.

ΣΩΚΡΑΤΗΣ. Ποτέρωθι οὖν εὐαπατητότεροί ἐσμεν,
καὶ ἡ ῥητορικὴ ἐν ποτέροις μεῖζον δύναται;

ΦΑΙΔΡΟΣ. Δῆλον ὅτι ἐν οἷς πλανώμεθα.

ΣΩΚΡΑΤΗΣ. Οὐκοῦν τὸν μέλλοντα τέχνην ῥητορικὴν μετιέναι πρῶτον μὲν δεῖ ταῦτα ὁδῷ διῃρῆ-
σθαι, καὶ εἰληφέναι τινὰ χαρακτῆρα ἑκατέρου
τοῦ εἴδους, ἐν ᾧ τε ἀνάγκη τὸ πλῆθος πλανᾶσθαι
καὶ ἐν ᾧ μή.

C ΦΑΙΔΡΟΣ. Καλὸν γοῦν ἄν, ὦ Σώκρατες, εἶδος
εἴη κατανενοηκὼς ὁ τοῦτο λαβών.

you have heard how I think it is to our advantage to arrange these matters. And I claim that I ought not to be refused what I ask because I am not your lover. For lovers repent of—

SOCRATES. Stop. Now we must tell what there is in this that is faulty and lacks art, must we not?

PHAEDRUS. Yes.

SOCRATES. It is clear to everyone that we are in accord about some matters of this kind and at variance about others, is it not?

PHAEDRUS. I think I understand your meaning, but express it still more clearly.

SOCRATES. When one says "iron" or "silver," we all understand the same thing, do we not?

PHAEDRUS. Surely.

SOCRATES. What if he says "justice" or "goodness"? Do we not part company, and disagree with each other and with ourselves?

PHAEDRUS. Certainly.

SOCRATES. Then in some things we agree and in others we do not.

PHAEDRUS. True.

SOCRATES. Then in which of the two are we more easy to deceive, and in which has rhetoric the greater power?

PHAEDRUS. Evidently in the class of doubtful things.

SOCRATES. Then he who is to develop an art of rhetoric must first make a methodical division and acquire a clear impression of each class, that in which people must be in doubt and that in which they are not.

PHAEDRUS. He who has acquired that would have conceived an excellent principle.

PLATO

ΣΩΚΡΑΤΗΣ. Ἔπειτά γε οἶμαι πρὸς ἑκάστῳ γιγνόμενον μὴ λανθάνειν, ἀλλ' ὀξέως αἰσθάνεσθαι, περὶ οὗ ἂν μέλλῃ ἐρεῖν, ποτέρου ὂν τυγχάνει τοῦ γένους.

ΦΑΙΔΡΟΣ. Τί μήν;

ΣΩΚΡΑΤΗΣ. Τί οὖν; τὸν Ἔρωτα πότερον φῶμεν εἶναι τῶν ἀμφισβητησίμων ἢ τῶν μή;

ΦΑΙΔΡΟΣ. Τῶν ἀμφισβητησίμων δή που· ἢ οἴει ἄν σοι συγχωρῆσαι εἰπεῖν ἃ νῦν δὴ εἶπες περὶ αὐτοῦ, ὡς βλάβη τέ ἐστι τῷ ἐρωμένῳ καὶ ἐρῶντι, D καὶ αὖθις ὡς μέγιστον τῶν ἀγαθῶν τυγχάνει;

ΣΩΚΡΑΤΗΣ. Ἄριστα λέγεις· ἀλλ' εἰπὲ καὶ τόδε—ἐγὼ γάρ τοι διὰ τὸ ἐνθουσιαστικὸν οὐ πάνυ μέμνημαι—εἰ ὡρισάμην ἔρωτα ἀρχόμενος τοῦ λόγου.

ΦΑΙΔΡΟΣ. Νὴ Δία ἀμηχάνως γε ὡς σφόδρα.

ΣΩΚΡΑΤΗΣ. Φεῦ, ὅσῳ λέγεις τεχνικωτέρας Νύμφας τὰς Ἀχελώου καὶ Πᾶνα τὸν Ἑρμοῦ Λυσίου τοῦ Κεφάλου πρὸς λόγους εἶναι. ἢ οὐδὲν λέγω, ἀλλὰ καὶ ὁ Λυσίας ἀρχόμενος τοῦ ἐρωτικοῦ ἠνάγκασεν ἡμᾶς ὑπολαβεῖν τὸν Ἔρωτα ἕν τι τῶν E ὄντων, ὃ αὐτὸς ἐβουλήθη, καὶ πρὸς τοῦτο ἤδη συνταξάμενος πάντα τὸν ὕστερον λόγον διεπεράνατο; βούλει πάλιν ἀναγνῶμεν τὴν ἀρχὴν αὐτοῦ;

ΦΑΙΔΡΟΣ. Εἰ σοί γε δοκεῖ· ὃ μέντοι ζητεῖς, οὐκ ἔστ' αὐτόθι.

ΣΩΚΡΑΤΗΣ. Λέγε, ἵνα ἀκούσω αὐτοῦ ἐκείνου.

47. ΦΑΙΔΡΟΣ. Περὶ μὲν τῶν ἐμῶν πραγμάτων ἐπίστασαι, καὶ ὡς νομίζω συμφέρειν ἡμῖν τούτων 264 γενομένων, ἀκήκοας. ἀξιῶ δὲ μὴ διὰ τοῦτο ἀτυχῆσαι ὧν δέομαι, ὅτι οὐκ ἐραστὴς ὢν σου

SOCRATES. Then I think when he has to do with a particular case, he will not be ignorant, but will know clearly to which of the two classes the thing belongs about which he is to speak.

PHAEDRUS. Of course.

SOCRATES. Well then, to which does Love belong? To the doubtful things or the others?

PHAEDRUS. To the doubtful, surely; if he did not, do you think he would have let you say what you said just now about him, that he is an injury to the beloved and to the lover, and again that he is the greatest of blessings?

SOCRATES. Excellent. But tell me this—for I was in such an ecstasy that I have quite forgotten—whether I defined love in the beginning of my discourse.

PHAEDRUS. Yes, by Zeus, and wonderfully well.

SOCRATES. Oh, how much more versed the nymphs, daughters of Achelous, and Pan, son of Hermes, are in the art of speech than Lysias, son of Cephalus! Or am I wrong, and did Lysias also, in the beginning of his discourse on Love, compel us to suppose Love to be some one thing which he chose to consider it, and did he then compose and finish his discourse with that in view? Shall we read the beginning of it again?

PHAEDRUS. If you like; but what you seek is not in it.

SOCRATES. Read, that I may hear Lysias himself.

PHAEDRUS. You know what my condition is, and you have heard how I think it is to our advantage to arrange these matters. And I claim that I ought not to be refused what I ask because I am not your

τυγχάνω. ὡς ἐκείνοις μὲν τότε μεταμέλει ὧν ἂν
εὖ ποιήσωσιν, ἐπειδὰν τῆς ἐπιθυμίας παύσωνται.

ΣΩΚΡΑΤΗΣ. Ἦ πολλοῦ δεῖν ἔοικε ποιεῖν ὅδε γε
ὃ ζητοῦμεν, ὃς οὐδὲ ἀπ' ἀρχῆς ἀλλ' ἀπὸ τελευτῆς
ἐξ ὑπτίας ἀνάπαλιν διανεῖν ἐπιχειρεῖ τὸν λόγον,
καὶ ἄρχεται ἀφ' ὧν πεπαυμένος ἂν ἤδη ὁ ἐραστὴς
λέγοι πρὸς τὰ παιδικά. ἢ οὐδὲν εἶπον, Φαῖδρε,
φίλη κεφαλή;

B   ΦΑΙΔΡΟΣ. Ἔστιν γέ τοι δή, ὦ Σώκρατες, τελευτή,
περὶ οὗ τὸν λόγον ποιεῖται.

ΣΩΚΡΑΤΗΣ. Τί δὲ τἆλλα; οὐ χύδην δοκεῖ βεβλῆ-
σθαι τὰ τοῦ λόγου; ἢ φαίνεται τὸ δεύτερον εἰρη-
μένον ἔκ τινος ἀνάγκης δεύτερον δεῖν τεθῆναι, ἤ
τι ἄλλο τῶν ῥηθέντων; ἐμοὶ μὲν γὰρ ἔδοξεν, ὡς
μηδὲν εἰδότι, οὐκ ἀγεννῶς τὸ ἐπιὸν εἰρῆσθαι τῷ
γράφοντι· σὺ δ' ἔχεις τινὰ ἀνάγκην λογογραφικήν,
ᾗ ταῦτα ἐκεῖνος οὕτως ἐφεξῆς παρ' ἄλληλα
ἔθηκεν;

C   ΦΑΙΔΡΟΣ. Χρηστὸς εἶ, ὅτι με ἡγεῖ ἱκανὸν εἶναι
τὰ ἐκείνου οὕτως ἀκριβῶς διιδεῖν.

ΣΩΚΡΑΤΗΣ. Ἀλλὰ τόδε γε οἶμαί σε φάναι ἄν,
δεῖν πάντα λόγον ὥσπερ ζῷον συνεστάναι σῶμά τι
ἔχοντα αὐτὸν αὑτοῦ, ὥστε μήτε ἀκέφαλον εἶναι
μήτε ἄπουν, ἀλλὰ μέσα τε ἔχειν καὶ ἄκρα,
πρέποντ' ἀλλήλοις καὶ τῷ ὅλῳ γεγραμμένα.

ΦΑΙΔΡΟΣ. Πῶς γὰρ οὔ;

ΣΩΚΡΑΤΗΣ. Σκέψαι τοίνυν τὸν τοῦ ἑταίρου σου
λόγον, εἴτε οὕτως εἴτε ἄλλως ἔχει· καὶ εὑρήσεις
D   τοῦ ἐπιγράμματος οὐδὲν διαφέροντα, ὃ Μίδᾳ τῷ
Φρυγί φασί τινες ἐπιγεγράφθαι.

ΦΑΙΔΡΟΣ. Ποῖον τοῦτο, καὶ τί πεπονθός;

lover. For lovers repent of the kindnesses they
have done when their passion ceases.

SOCRATES. He certainly does not at all seem to do
what we demand, for he does not even begin at the
beginning, but undertakes to swim on his back up
the current of his discourse from its end, and begins
with what the lover would say at the end to his
beloved. Am I not right, Phaedrus my dear?

PHAEDRUS. Certainly that of which he speaks is
an ending.

SOCRATES. And how about the rest? Don't you
think the parts of the discourse are thrown out
helter-skelter? Or does it seem to you that the
second topic had to be put second for any cogent
reason, or that any of the other things he says are so
placed? It seemed to me, who am wholly ignorant,
that the writer uttered boldly whatever occurred to
him. Do you know any rhetorical reason why he
arranged his topics in this order?

PHAEDRUS. You flatter me in thinking that I can
discern his motives so accurately.

SOCRATES. But I do think you will agree to this,
that every discourse must be organised, like a living
being, with a body of its own, as it were, so as not
to be headless or footless, but to have a middle and
members, composed in fitting relation to each other
and to the whole.

PHAEDRUS. Certainly.

SOCRATES. See then whether this is the case with
your friend's discourse, or not. You will find that it
is very like the inscription that some say is inscribed
on the tomb of Midas the Phrygian.

PHAEDRUS. What sort of inscription is that, and
what is the matter with it?

PLATO

ΣΩΚΡΑΤΗΣ. Ἔστι μὲν τοῦτο τόδε·

χαλκῆ παρθένος εἰμί, Μίδα δ' ἐπὶ σήματι
κεῖμαι.
ὄφρ' ἂν ὕδωρ τε νάῃ καὶ δένδρεα μακρὰ
τεθήλῃ,
αὐτοῦ τῇδε μένουσα πολυκλαύτου ἐπὶ
τύμβου,
ἀγγελέω παριοῦσι Μίδας ὅτι τῇδε τέθαπται.

E ὅτι δὲ οὐδὲν διαφέρει αὐτοῦ πρῶτον ἢ ὕστατόν τι
λέγεσθαι, ἐννοεῖς που, ὡς ἐγῷμαι.

ΦΑΙΔΡΟΣ. Σκώπτεις τὸν λόγον ἡμῶν, ὦ Σώκρατες.

48. ΣΩΚΡΑΤΗΣ. Τοῦτον μὲν τοίνυν, ἵνα μὴ σὺ
ἄχθῃ, ἐάσωμεν· καί τοι συχνά γε ἔχειν μοι δοκεῖ
παραδείγματα, πρὸς ἅ τις βλέπων ὀνίναιτ' ἄν,
μιμεῖσθαι αὐτὰ ἐπιχειρῶν μὴ πάνυ τι· εἰς δὲ τοὺς
ἑτέρους λόγους ἴωμεν. ἦν γάρ τι ἐν αὐτοῖς, ὡς
265 δοκῶ, προσῆκον ἰδεῖν τοῖς βουλομένοις περὶ λόγων
σκοπεῖν.

ΦΑΙΔΡΟΣ. Τὸ ποῖον δὴ λέγεις;

ΣΩΚΡΑΤΗΣ. Ἐναντίω που ἤστην· ὁ μὲν γάρ,
ὡς τῷ ἐρῶντι, ὁ δ' ὡς τῷ μὴ δεῖ χαρίζεσθαι,
ἐλεγέτην.

ΦΑΙΔΡΟΣ. Καὶ μάλ' ἀνδρικῶς.

ΣΩΚΡΑΤΗΣ. Ὤιμην σε τἀληθὲς ἐρεῖν, ὅτι μανι-
κῶς· ὃ μέντοι ἐζήτουν, ἐστὶν αὐτὸ τοῦτο. μανίαν
γάρ τινα ἐφήσαμεν εἶναι τὸν ἔρωτα, ἢ γάρ;

ΦΑΙΔΡΟΣ. Ναί.

ΣΩΚΡΑΤΗΣ. Μανίας δέ γε εἴδη δύο, τὴν μὲν ὑπὸ
νοσημάτων ἀνθρωπίνων, τὴν δὲ ὑπὸ θείας ἐξαλ-
λαγῆς τῶν εἰωθότων νομίμων γιγνομένην.

530

SOCRATES.　This is it:

> A bronze maiden am I; and I am placed upon
> the tomb of Midas.
> So long as water runs and tall trees put forth
> leaves,
> Remaining in this very spot upon a much
> lamented tomb,
> I shall declare to passers by that Midas is
> buried here;

and you perceive, I fancy, that it makes no difference
whether any line of it is put first or last.

PHAEDRUS.　You are making fun of our discourse,
Socrates.

SOCRATES.　Then, to spare your feelings, let us say
no more of this discourse—and yet I think there
were many things in it which would be useful
examples to consider, though not exactly to imitate—
and let us turn to the other discourses; for there
was in them, I think, something which those who
wish to investigate rhetoric might well examine.

PHAEDRUS.　What do you mean?

SOCRATES.　The two discourses were opposites; for
one maintained that the lover, and the other that the
non-lover, should be favoured.

PHAEDRUS.　And they did it right manfully.

SOCRATES.　I thought you were going to speak the
truth and say "madly"; however, that is just what
I had in mind. We said that love was a kind of
madness, did we not?

PHAEDRUS.　Yes.

SOCRATES.　And that there are two kinds of madness, one arising from human diseases, and the other
from a divine release from the customary habits.

B ΦΑΙΔΡΟΣ. Πάνυ γε.

ΣΩΚΡΑΤΗΣ. Τῆς δὲ θείας τεττάρων θεῶν[1] τέτταρα μέρη διελόμενοι, μαντικὴν μὲν ἐπίπνοιαν Ἀπόλλωνος θέντες, Διονύσου δὲ τελεστικήν, Μουσῶν δ᾽ αὖ ποιητικήν, τετάρτην δὲ Ἀφροδίτης καὶ Ἔρωτος ἐρωτικὴν μανίαν ἐφήσαμέν τε ἀρίστην εἶναι, καὶ οὐκ οἶδ᾽ ὅπῃ τὸ ἐρωτικὸν πάθος ἀπεικάζοντες, ἴσως μὲν ἀληθοῦς τινος ἐφαπτόμενοι, τάχα δ᾽ ἂν καὶ ἄλλοσε παραφερόμενοι, κεράσαντες οὐ

C παντάπασιν ἀπίθανον λόγον, μυθικόν τινα ὕμνον προσεπαίσαμεν μετρίως τε καὶ εὐφήμως τὸν ἐμόν τε καὶ σὸν δεσπότην Ἔρωτα, ὦ Φαῖδρε, καλῶν παίδων ἔφορον.

ΦΑΙΔΡΟΣ. Καὶ μάλα ἔμοιγε οὐκ ἀηδῶς ἀκοῦσαι.

49. ΣΩΚΡΑΤΗΣ. Τόδε τοίνυν αὐτόθεν λάβωμεν, ὡς ἀπὸ τοῦ ψέγειν πρὸς τὸ ἐπαινεῖν ἔσχεν ὁ λόγος μεταβῆναι.

ΦΑΙΔΡΟΣ. Πῶς δὴ οὖν αὐτὸ λέγεις;

ΣΩΚΡΑΤΗΣ. Ἐμοὶ μὲν φαίνεται τὰ μὲν ἄλλα τῷ

D ὄντι παιδιᾷ πεπαῖσθαι· τούτων δέ τινων ἐκ τύχης ῥηθέντων δυοῖν εἰδοῖν, εἰ αὐτοῖν τὴν δύναμιν τέχνῃ λαβεῖν δύναιτό τις, οὐκ ἄχαρι.

ΦΑΙΔΡΟΣ. Τίνων δή;

ΣΩΚΡΑΤΗΣ. Εἰς μίαν τε ἰδέαν συνορῶντα ἄγειν τὰ πολλαχῇ διεσπαρμένα, ἵν᾽ ἕκαστον ὁριζόμενος δῆλον ποιῇ, περὶ οὗ ἂν ἀεὶ διδάσκειν ἐθέλῃ, ὥσπερ τὸ νυνδὴ περὶ Ἔρωτος ὃ ἔστιν ὁρισθέν, εἴτ᾽ εὖ εἴτε κακῶς ἐλέχθη· τὸ γοῦν σαφὲς καὶ τὸ αὐτὸ αὑτῷ ὁμολογούμενον διὰ ταῦτ᾽ ἔσχεν εἰπεῖν ὁ λόγος.

[1] Schanz brackets τεττάρων θεῶν.

PHAEDRUS

PHAEDRUS. Certainly.

SOCRATES. And we made four divisions of the divine madness, ascribing them to four gods, saying that prophecy was inspired by Apollo, the mystic madness by Dionysus, the poetic by the Muses, and the madness of love, inspired by Aphrodite and Eros, we said was the best. We described the passion of love in some sort of figurative manner, expressing some truth, perhaps, and perhaps being led away in another direction, and after composing a somewhat plausible discourse, we chanted a sportive and mythic hymn in meet and pious strain to the honour of your lord and mine, Phaedrus, Love, the guardian of beautiful boys.

PHAEDRUS. Yes, and I found it very pleasant to hear.

SOCRATES. Here let us take up this point and see how the discourse succeeded in passing from blame to praise.

PHAEDRUS. What do you mean?

SOCRATES. It seems to me that the discourse was, as a whole, really sportive jest; but in these chance utterances were involved two principles, the essence of which it would be gratifying to learn, if art could teach it.

PHAEDRUS. What principles?

SOCRATES. That of perceiving and bringing together in one idea the scattered particulars, that one may make clear by definition the particular thing which he wishes to explain; just as now, in speaking of Love, we said what he is and defined it, whether well or ill. Certainly by this means the discourse acquired clearness and consistency.

PLATO

ΦΑΙΔΡΟΣ. Τὸ δ' ἕτερον δὴ εἶδος τί λέγεις, ὦ Σώκρατες;

E ΣΩΚΡΑΤΗΣ. Τὸ πάλιν κατ' εἴδη δύνασθαι τέμνειν, κατ' ἄρθρα, ᾗ πέφυκε, καὶ μὴ ἐπιχειρεῖν καταγνύναι μέρος μηδέν, κακοῦ μαγείρου τρόπῳ χρώμενον· ἀλλ' ὥσπερ ἄρτι τὼ λόγω τὸ μὲν ἄφρον τῆς διανοίας ἕν τι κοινῇ εἶδος ἐλαβέτην, 266 ὥσπερ δὲ σώματος ἐξ ἑνὸς διπλᾶ καὶ ὁμώνυμα πέφυκε, σκαιά, τὰ δὲ δεξιὰ κληθέντα, οὕτω καὶ τὸ τῆς παρανοίας ὡς ἓν ἐν ἡμῖν πεφυκὸς εἶδος ἡγησαμένω τὼ λόγω, ὁ μὲν τὸ ἐπ' ἀριστερὰ τεμνόμενος μέρος, πάλιν τοῦτο τέμνων οὐκ ἐπανῆκεν, πρὶν ἐν αὐτοῖς ἐφευρὼν ὀνομαζόμενον σκαιόν τινα ἔρωτα ἐλοιδόρησε μάλ' ἐν δίκῃ, ὁ δ' εἰς τὰ ἐν δεξιᾷ τῆς μανίας ἀγαγὼν ἡμᾶς, ὁμώνυμον μὲν B ἐκείνῳ, θεῖον δ' αὖ τιν' ἔρωτα ἐφευρὼν καὶ προτεινάμενος ἐπῄνεσεν ὡς μεγίστων αἴτιον ἡμῖν ἀγαθῶν.

ΦΑΙΔΡΟΣ. Ἀληθέστατα λέγεις.

50. ΣΩΚΡΑΤΗΣ. Τούτων δὴ ἔγωγε αὐτός τε ἐραστής, ὦ Φαῖδρε, τῶν διαιρέσεων καὶ συναγωγῶν, ἵν' οἷός τε ὦ λέγειν τε καὶ φρονεῖν· ἐάν τέ τιν' ἄλλον ἡγήσωμαι δυνατὸν εἰς ἓν καὶ ἐπὶ πολλὰ πεφυκόθ' ὁρᾶν, τοῦτον διώκω κατόπισθε μετ' ἴχνιον ὥστε θεοῖο. καὶ μέντοι καὶ τοὺς δυναμένους αὐτὸ δρᾶν εἰ μὲν ὀρθῶς ἢ μὴ προσαγορεύω, θεὸς C οἶδεν, καλῶ δὲ οὖν μέχρι τοῦδε διαλεκτικούς. τὰ δὲ νῦν παρὰ σοῦ τε καὶ Λυσίου μαθόντας εἰπὲ τί χρὴ καλεῖν· ἢ τοῦτο ἐκεῖνό ἐστιν ἡ λόγων τέχνη, ᾗ Θρασύμαχός τε καὶ οἱ ἄλλοι χρώμενοι σοφοὶ

PHAEDRUS. And what is the other principle, Socrates?

SOCRATES. That of dividing things again by classes, where the natural joints are, and not trying to break any part, after the manner of a bad carver. As our two discourses just now assumed one common principle, unreason, and then, just as the body, which is one, is naturally divisible into two, right and left, with parts called by the same names, so our two discourses conceived of madness as naturally one principle within us, and one discourse, cutting off the left-hand part, continued to divide this until it found among its parts a sort of left-handed love, which it very justly reviled, but the other discourse, leading us to the right-hand part of madness, found a love having the same name as the first, but divine, which it held up to view and praised as the author of our greatest blessings.

PHAEDRUS. Very true.

SOCRATES. Now I myself, Phaedrus, am a lover of these processes of division and bringing together, as aids to speech and thought; and if I think any other man is able to see things that can naturally be collected into one and divided into many, him I follow after and "walk in his footsteps as if he were a god." [1] And whether the name I give to those who can do this is right or wrong, God knows, but I have called them hitherto dialecticians. But tell me now what name to give to those who are taught by you and Lysias, or is this that art of speech by means of which Thrasymachus and the rest have

[1] Homer, *Odyssey* v, 193. ὃ δ' ἔπειτα μετ' ἴχνια βαῖνε θεοῖο (and he walked in the footsteps of the god).

535

μὲν αὐτοὶ λέγειν γεγόνασιν, ἄλλους τε ποιοῦσιν, οἳ ἂν δωροφορεῖν αὐτοῖς ὡς βασιλεῦσιν ἐθέλωσιν;

ΦΑΙΔΡΟΣ. Βασιλικοὶ μὲν ἄνδρες, οὐ μὲν δὴ ἐπιστήμονές γε ὧν ἐρωτᾷς. ἀλλὰ τοῦτο μὲν τὸ εἶδος ὀρθῶς ἔμοιγε δοκεῖς καλεῖν, διαλεκτικὸν

D καλῶν· τὸ δὲ ῥητορικὸν δοκεῖ μοι διαφεύγειν ἔθ' ἡμᾶς.

ΣΩΚΡΑΤΗΣ. Πῶς φῄς; καλόν πού τι ἂν εἴη, ὃ τούτων ἀπολειφθὲν ὅμως τέχνῃ λαμβάνεται; πάντως δ' οὐκ ἀτιμαστέον αὐτὸ σοί τε καὶ ἐμοί, λεκτέον δὲ τί μέντοι καὶ ἔστι τὸ λειπόμενον τῆς ῥητορικῆς.

ΦΑΙΔΡΟΣ. Καὶ μάλα που συχνά, ὦ Σώκρατες, τά γ' ἐν τοῖς βιβλίοις τοῖς περὶ λόγων τέχνης γεγραμμένοις.

51. ΣΩΚΡΑΤΗΣ. Καλῶς γε ὑπέμνησας. προοίμιον μὲν οἶμαι πρῶτον ὡς δεῖ τοῦ λόγου λέγεσθαι ἐν ἀρχῇ· ταῦτα λέγεις—ἢ γάρ; τὰ κομψὰ τῆς τέχνης;

E ΦΑΙΔΡΟΣ. Ναί.

ΣΩΚΡΑΤΗΣ. Δεύτερον δὲ δὴ διήγησίν τινα μαρτυρίας τ' ἐπ' αὐτῇ, τρίτον τεκμήρια, τέταρτον εἰκότα· καὶ πίστωσιν οἶμαι καὶ ἐπιπίστωσιν λέγειν τόν γε βέλτιστον λογοδαίδαλον Βυζάντιον ἄνδρα.

ΦΑΙΔΡΟΣ. Τὸν χρηστὸν λέγεις Θεόδωρον;

267 ΣΩΚΡΑΤΗΣ. Τί μήν; καὶ ἔλεγχόν γε καὶ ἐπεξέλεγχον ὡς ποιητέον ἐν κατηγορίᾳ τε καὶ ἀπολογίᾳ. τὸν δὲ κάλλιστον Πάριον Εὐηνὸν εἰς μέσον οὐκ ἄγομεν, ὃς ὑποδήλωσίν τε πρῶτος εὗρε καὶ παρεπαίνους; οἱ δ' αὐτὸν καὶ παραψόγους φασὶν ἐν μέτρῳ λέγειν μνήμης χάριν· σοφὸς γὰρ ἀνήρ. Τισίαν δὲ Γοργίαν τε ἐάσομεν εὕδειν, οἳ πρὸ τῶν

become able speakers themselves, and make others so, if they are willing to pay them royal tribute?

PHAEDRUS. They are royal men, but not trained in the matters about which you ask. I think you give this method the right name when you call it dialectic; but it seems to me that rhetoric still escapes us.

SOCRATES. What do you mean? Can there be anything of importance, which is not included in these processes and yet comes under the head of art? Certainly you and I must not neglect it, but must say what it is that remains of rhetoric.

PHAEDRUS. A great many things remain, Socrates, the things that are written in the books on rhetoric.

SOCRATES. Thank you for reminding me. You mean that there must be an introduction first, at the beginning of the discourse; these are the things you mean, are they not?—the niceties of the art.

PHAEDRUS. Yes.

SOCRATES. And the narrative must come second with the testimony after it, and third the proofs, and fourth the probabilities; and confirmation and further confirmation are mentioned, I believe, by the man from Byzantium, that most excellent artist in words.

PHAEDRUS. You mean the worthy Theodorus?

SOCRATES. Of course. And he tells how refutation and further refutation must be accomplished, both in accusation and in defence. Shall we not bring the illustrious Parian, Evenus, into our discussion, who invented covert allusion and indirect praises? And some say that he also wrote indirect censures, composing them in verse as an aid to memory; for he is a clever man. And shall we leave Gorgias and

ἀληθῶν τὰ εἰκότα εἶδον ὡς τιμητέα μᾶλλον, τά τε
αὖ σμικρὰ μεγάλα καὶ τὰ μεγάλα σμικρὰ φαί-
Β νεσθαι ποιοῦσιν διὰ ῥώμην λόγου, καινά τε ἀρχαίως
τά τ᾽ ἐναντία καινῶς, συντομίαν τε λόγων καὶ
ἄπειρα μήκη περὶ πάντων ἀνηῦρον· ταῦτα δὲ
ἀκούων ποτέ μου Πρόδικος ἐγέλασεν, καὶ μόνος
αὐτὸς ηὑρηκέναι ἔφη ὧν δεῖ λόγων τέχνην· δεῖν δὲ
οὔτε μακρῶν οὔτε βραχέων, ἀλλὰ μετρίων.

ΦΑΙΔΡΟΣ. Σοφώτατά γε, ὦ Πρόδικε.

ΣΩΚΡΑΤΗΣ. Ἱππίαν δὲ οὐ λέγομεν; οἶμαι γὰρ ἂν
σύμψηφον αὐτῷ καὶ τὸν Ἠλεῖον ξένον γενέσθαι.

ΦΑΙΔΡΟΣ. Τί δ᾽ οὔ;

C ΣΩΚΡΑΤΗΣ. Τὰ δὲ Πώλου πῶς φράσωμεν[1] αὖ
μουσεῖα λόγων, ὡς[2] διπλασιολογίαν καὶ γνωμο-
λογίαν καὶ εἰκονολογίαν, ὀνομάτων τε Λικυμνείων
ἃ ἐκείνῳ ἐδωρήσατο[3] πρὸς ποίησιν εὐεπείας;[4]

ΦΑΙΔΡΟΣ. Πρωταγόρεια δέ, ὦ Σώκρατες, οὐκ ἦν
μέντοι τοιαῦτ᾽ ἄττα;

ΣΩΚΡΑΤΗΣ. Ὀρθοέπειά γέ τις, ὦ παῖ, καὶ ἄλλα
πολλὰ καὶ καλά. τῶν γε μὴν οἰκτρογόων ἐπὶ
γῆρας καὶ πενίαν ἑλκομένων λόγων κεκρατηκέναι
τέχνῃ μοι φαίνεται τὸ τοῦ Χαλκηδονίου σθένος,
ὀργίσαι τε αὖ πολλοὺς ἅμα δεινὸς ἀνὴρ γέγονεν,
D καὶ πάλιν ὠργισμένοις ἐπᾴδων κηλεῖν, ὡς ἔφη·
διαβάλλειν τε καὶ ἀπολύσασθαι διαβολὰς ὁθενδὴ
κράτιστος. τὸ δὲ δὴ τέλος τῶν λόγων κοινῇ πᾶσιν
ἔοικεν συνδεδογμένον εἶναι, ᾧ τινες μὲν ἐπάνοδον,
ἄλλοι δὲ ἄλλο τίθενται ὄνομα.

[1] πῶς φράσωμεν B. πῶς φράσομεν T. πῶς οὐ φράσομεν
Schanz. [2] ὡς B. ὃς T, Schanz.
[3] Schanz, following Ast, brackets ἃ ἐκείνῳ ἐδωρήσατο.
[4] Schanz reads προσεποίησεν εὐέπειαν (προσεποίησεν after
Cornerius).

Tisias undisturbed, who saw that probabilities are
more to be esteemed than truths, who make small
things seem great and great things small by the
power of their words, and new things old and old
things the reverse, and who invented conciseness of
speech and measureless length on all subjects? And
once when Prodicus heard these inventions, he
laughed, and said that he alone had discovered the
art of proper speech, that discourses should be
neither long nor short, but of reasonable length.

PHAEDRUS. O Prodicus! How clever!

SOCRATES. And shall we not mention Hippias, our
friend from Elis? I think he would agree with him.

PHAEDRUS. Oh yes.

SOCRATES. And what shall we say of Polus and
his shrines of learned speech, such as duplication and
sententiousness and figurativeness, and what of the
names with which Licymnius presented him to effect
beautiful diction?

PHAEDRUS. Were there not some similar inventions
of Protagoras, Socrates?

SOCRATES. Yes, my boy, correctness of diction,
and many other fine things. For tearful speeches,
to arouse pity for old age and poverty, I think the
precepts of the mighty Chalcedonian hold the palm,
and he is also a genius, as he said, at rousing large
companies to wrath, and soothing them again by his
charms when they are angry, and most powerful in
devising and abolishing calumnies on any grounds
whatsoever. But all seem to be in agreement
concerning the conclusion of discourses, which some
call recapitulation, while others give it some other
name.

E   ΦΑΙΔΡΟΣ. Τὸ ἐν κεφαλαίῳ ἕκαστα λέγεις ὑπομνῆσαι ἐπὶ τελευτῆς τοὺς ἀκούοντας περὶ τῶν
εἰρημένων;

ΣΩΚΡΑΤΗΣ. Ταῦτα λέγω, καὶ εἴ τι σὺ ἄλλο ἔχεις
εἰπεῖν λόγων τέχνης πέρι.

ΦΑΙΔΡΟΣ. Σμικρά γε καὶ οὐκ ἄξια λέγειν.

268   ΣΩΚΡΑΤΗΣ. Ἐῶμεν δὴ τά γε σμικρά· ταῦτα δὲ
ὑπ' αὐγὰς μᾶλλον ἴδωμεν, τίνα καὶ πότ' ἔχει τὴν
τῆς τέχνης δύναμιν.

ΦΑΙΔΡΟΣ. Καὶ μάλα ἐρρωμένην, ὦ Σώκρατες, ἔν
γε δὴ πλήθους συνόδοις.

ΣΩΚΡΑΤΗΣ. Ἔχει γάρ· ἀλλ', ὦ δαιμόνιε, ἰδὲ καὶ
σύ, εἰ ἄρα καὶ σοὶ φαίνεται διεστηκὸς αὐτῶν τὸ
ἠτρίον ὥσπερ ἐμοί.

ΦΑΙΔΡΟΣ. Δείκνυε μόνον.

52. ΣΩΚΡΑΤΗΣ. Εἰπὲ δή μοι· εἴ τις προσελθὼν
τῷ ἑταίρῳ σου Ἐρυξιμάχῳ ἢ τῷ πατρὶ αὐτοῦ
Ἀκουμενῷ εἴποι ὅτι Ἐγὼ ἐπίσταμαι τοιαῦτ' ἄττα
B σώμασι προσφέρειν, ὥστε θερμαίνειν τ' ἐὰν
βούλωμαι καὶ ψύχειν, καὶ ἐὰν μὲν δόξῃ μοι, ἐμεῖν
ποιεῖν, ἐὰν δ' αὖ, κάτω διαχωρεῖν, καὶ ἄλλα
πάμπολλα τοιαῦτα· καὶ ἐπιστάμενος αὐτὰ ἀξιῶ
ἰατρικὸς εἶναι καὶ ἄλλον ποιεῖν, ᾧ ἂν τὴν τούτων
ἐπιστήμην παραδῶ· τί ἂν οἴει ἀκούσαντας εἰπεῖν;

ΦΑΙΔΡΟΣ. Τί γε ἄλλο ἢ ἐρέσθαι, εἰ προσεπί-
σταται καὶ οὕστινας δεῖ καὶ ὁπότε ἕκαστα τούτων
ποιεῖν, καὶ μέχρι ὁπόσου;

ΣΩΚΡΑΤΗΣ. Εἰ οὖν εἴποι ὅτι οὐδαμῶς· ἀλλ' ἀξιῶ
τὸν ταῦτα παρ' ἐμοῦ μαθόντα αὐτὸν οἷόν τ' εἶναι
ποιεῖν ἃ ἐρωτᾷς;

PHAEDRUS. You mean making a summary of the points of the speech at the end of it, so as to remind the hearers of what has been said?

SOCRATES. These are the things I mean, these and anything else you can mention concerned with the art of rhetoric.

PHAEDRUS. There are only little things, not worth mentioning.

SOCRATES. Never mind the little things; let us bring these other things more under the light and see what force of art they have and when.

PHAEDRUS. They have a very powerful force, at least in large assemblies.

SOCRATES. They have; but my friend, see if you agree with me in thinking that their warp has gaps in it.

PHAEDRUS. Go on and show them.

SOCRATES. Tell me; if anyone should go to your friend Eryximachus or to his father Acumenus and should say "I know how to apply various drugs to people, so as to make them warm or, if I wish, cold, and I can make them vomit, if I like, or can make their bowels move, and all that sort of thing; and because of this knowledge I claim that I am a physician and can make any other man a physician, to whom I impart the knowledge of these things"; what do you think they would say?

PHAEDRUS. They would ask him, of course, whether he knew also whom he ought to cause to do these things, and when, and how much.

SOCRATES. If then he should say: "No, not at all; but I think that he who has learned these things from me will be able to do by himself the things you ask about?"

C ΦΑΙΔΡΟΣ. Εἴποιεν ἄν, οἶμαι, ὅτι μαίνεται ἄνθρωπος, καὶ ἐκ βιβλίου ποθὲν ἀκούσας ἢ περιτυχὼν φαρμακίοις ἰατρὸς οἴεται γεγονέναι, οὐδὲν ἐπαΐων τῆς τέχνης.

ΣΩΚΡΑΤΗΣ. Τί δ' εἰ Σοφοκλεῖ αὖ προσελθὼν καὶ Εὐριπίδῃ τις λέγοι, ὡς ἐπίσταται περὶ σμικροῦ πράγματος ῥήσεις παμμήκεις ποιεῖν καὶ περὶ μεγάλου πάνυ σμικράς, ὅταν τε βούληται οἰκτράς, καὶ τοὐναντίον αὖ φοβερὰς καὶ ἀπειλητικάς, ὅσα
D τ' ἄλλα τοιαῦτα, καὶ διδάσκων αὐτὰ τραγῳδίας ποίησιν οἴεται παραδιδόναι;

ΦΑΙΔΡΟΣ. Καὶ οὗτοι ἄν, ὦ Σώκρατες, οἶμαι, καταγελῷεν, εἴ τις οἴεται τραγῳδίαν ἄλλο τι εἶναι ἢ τὴν τούτων σύστασιν πρέπουσαν, ἀλλήλοις τε καὶ τῷ ὅλῳ συνισταμένην.

ΣΩΚΡΑΤΗΣ. Ἀλλ' οὐκ ἂν ἀγροίκως γε, οἶμαι, λοιδορήσειαν, ἀλλ' ὥσπερ ἂν μουσικὸς ἐντυχὼν ἀνδρὶ οἰομένῳ ἁρμονικῷ εἶναι, ὅτι δὴ τυγχάνει ἐπιστάμενος ὡς οἷόν τε ὀξυτάτην καὶ βαρυτάτην
E χορδὴν ποιεῖν, οὐκ ἀγρίως εἴποι ἄν· ὦ μοχθηρέ, μελαγχολᾷς, ἀλλ' ἅτε μουσικὸς ὢν πρᾳότερον ὅτι, ὦ ἄριστε, ἀνάγκη μὲν καὶ ταῦτ' ἐπίστασθαι τὸν μέλλοντα ἁρμονικὸν ἔσεσθαι, οὐδὲν μὴν κωλύει μηδὲ σμικρὸν ἁρμονίας ἐπαΐειν τὸν τὴν σὴν ἕξιν ἔχοντα· τὰ γὰρ πρὸ ἁρμονίας ἀναγκαῖα μαθήματα ἐπίστασαι, ἀλλ' οὐ τὰ ἁρμονικά.

ΦΑΙΔΡΟΣ. Ὀρθότατά γε.

269 ΣΩΚΡΑΤΗΣ. Οὐκοῦν καὶ ὁ Σοφοκλῆς τὸν σφίσιν ἐπιδεικνύμενον τὰ πρὸ τραγῳδίας ἂν φαίη ἀλλ' οὐ

PHAEDRUS

PHAEDRUS. They would say, I fancy, that the man was crazy and, because he had read something in a book or had stumbled upon some medicines, imagined that he was a physician when he really had no knowledge of the art.

SOCRATES. And what if someone should go to Sophocles or Euripides and should say that he knew how to make very long speeches about a small matter, and very short ones about a great affair, and pitiful utterances, if he wished, and again terrible and threatening ones, and all that sort of thing, and that he thought by imparting those things he could teach the art of writing tragedies?

PHAEDRUS. They also, I fancy, Socrates, would laugh at him, if he imagined that tragedy was anything else than the proper combination of these details in such a way that they harmonize with each other and with the whole composition.

SOCRATES. But they would not, I suppose, rebuke him harshly, but they would behave as a musician would, if he met a man who thought he understood harmony because he could strike the highest and lowest notes. He would not say roughly, " You wretch, you are mad," but being a musician, he would say in gentler tones, " My friend, he who is to be a harmonist must know these things you mention, but nothing prevents one who is at your stage of knowledge from being quite ignorant of harmony. You know the necessary preliminaries of harmony, but not harmony itself."

PHAEDRUS. Quite correct.

SOCRATES. So Sophocles would say that the man exhibited the preliminaries of tragedy, not tragedy

543

τὰ τραγικά, καὶ ὁ Ἀκουμενὸς τὰ πρὸ ἰατρικῆς
ἀλλ' οὐ τὰ ἰατρικά.

ΦΑΙΔΡΟΣ. Παντάπασι μὲν οὖν.

53. ΣΩΚΡΑΤΗΣ. Τί δέ; τὸν μελίγηρυν Ἄδραστον
οἰόμεθα ἢ καὶ Περικλέα, εἰ ἀκούσειαν ὧν νῦν δὴ
ἡμεῖς διῇμεν τῶν παγκάλων τεχνημάτων, βραχυ-
λογιῶν τε καὶ εἰκονολογιῶν καὶ ὅσα ἄλλα
διελθόντες ὑπ' αὐγὰς ἔφαμεν εἶναι σκεπτέα,
B πότερον χαλεπῶς ἂν αὐτούς, ὥσπερ ἐγώ τε καὶ
σύ, ὑπ' ἀγροικίας ῥῆμά τι εἰπεῖν ἀπαίδευτον εἰς
τοὺς ταῦτα γεγραφότας τε καὶ διδάσκοντας ὡς
ῥητορικὴν τέχνην, ἢ ἅτε ἡμῶν ὄντας σοφωτέρους
κἂν νῷν ἐπιπλῆξαι εἰπόντας· ὦ Φαῖδρέ τε καὶ
Σώκρατες, οὐ χρὴ χαλεπαίνειν ἀλλὰ συγγιγνώ-
σκειν, εἴ τινες μὴ ἐπιστάμενοι διαλέγεσθαι
ἀδύνατοι ἐγένοντο ὁρίσασθαι, τί ποτ' ἔστιν
ῥητορική, ἐκ δὲ τούτου τοῦ πάθους τὰ πρὸ τῆς
τέχνης ἀναγκαῖα μαθήματα ἔχοντες ῥητορικὴν
C ᾠήθησαν ηὑρηκέναι, καὶ ταῦτα δὴ διδάσκοντες
ἄλλους ἡγοῦνται σφίσιν τελέως ῥητορικὴν δεδι-
δάχθαι, τὸ δὲ ἕκαστα τούτων πιθανῶς λέγειν τε
καὶ τὸ ὅλον συνίστασθαι, οὐδὲν ἔργον, αὐτοὺς δεῖν
παρ' ἑαυτῶν τοὺς μαθητὰς σφῶν πορίζεσθαι ἐν
τοῖς λόγοις.

ΦΑΙΔΡΟΣ. Ἀλλὰ μήν, ὦ Σώκρατες, κινδυνεύει
τοιοῦτόν τι εἶναι τὸ τῆς τέχνης, ἣν οὗτοι οἱ ἄνδρες
ὡς ῥητορικὴν διδάσκουσίν τε καὶ γράφουσιν· καὶ
D ἔμοιγε δοκεῖς ἀληθῆ εἰρηκέναι· ἀλλὰ δὴ τὴν τοῦ

itself, and Acumenus that he knew the preliminaries of medicine, not medicine itself.

PHAEDRUS. Exactly so.

SOCRATES. Well then, if the mellifluous Adrastus [1] or Pericles heard of the excellent accomplishments which we just enumerated, brachylogies and figurative speech and all the other things we said we must bring to the light and examine, do we suppose they would, like you and me, be so illbred as to speak discourteously of those who have written and taught these things as the art of rhetoric? Would they not, since they are wiser than we, censure us also and say, "Phaedrus and Socrates, we ought not to be angry, but lenient, if certain persons who are ignorant of dialectics have been unable to define the nature of rhetoric and on this account have thought, when they possessed the knowledge that is a necessary preliminary to rhetoric, that they had discovered rhetoric, and believe that by teaching these preliminaries to others they have taught them rhetoric completely, and that the persuasive use of these details and the composition of the whole discourse is a small matter which their pupils must supply of themselves in their writings or speeches."

PHAEDRUS. Well, Socrates, it does seem as if that which those men teach and write about as the art of rhetoric were such as you describe. I think you are

---

[1] Tyrtaeus, ed. Bergk, first ed. frg. 9, 7, οὐδ' εἰ Ταντα λ.δεω Πέλοπος βασιλεύτερος εἴη γλῶσσαν δ' Ἀδρήστου μειλιχόγηρυν ἔχοι, "not even if he were more kingly than Pelops and had the mellifluous tongue of Adrastus." Perhaps the orator Antiphon is referred to under the name of Adrastus, cf. chapter xliii. above.

τῷ ὄντι ῥητορικοῦ τε καὶ πιθανοῦ τέχνην πῶς
καὶ πόθεν ἄν τις δύναιτο πορίσασθαι;

ΣΩΚΡΑΤΗΣ. Τὸ μὲν δύνασθαι, ὦ Φαῖδρε, ὥστε
ἀγωνιστὴν τέλεον γενέσθαι, εἰκός, ἴσως δὲ καὶ
ἀναγκαῖον, ἔχειν ὥσπερ τἆλλα. εἰ μέν σοι
ὑπάρχει φύσει ῥητορικῷ εἶναι, ἔσει ῥήτωρ
ἐλλόγιμος, προσλαβὼν ἐπιστήμην τε καὶ μελέτην·
ὅτου δ' ἂν ἐλλίπῃς τούτων, ταύτῃ ἀτελὴς ἔσει.
ὅσον δὲ αὐτοῦ τέχνη, οὐχ ᾗ Λυσίας τε καὶ Θρασύ-
μαχος πορεύεται, δοκεῖ μοι φαίνεσθαι ἡ μέθοδος.

E   ΦΑΙΔΡΟΣ. Ἀλλὰ πῇ δή;

ΣΩΚΡΑΤΗΣ. Κινδυνεύει, ὦ ἄριστε, εἰκότως ὁ
Περικλῆς πάντων τελεώτατος εἰς τὴν ῥητορικὴν
γενέσθαι.

ΦΑΙΔΡΟΣ. Τί δή;

54. ΣΩΚΡΑΤΗΣ. Πᾶσαι ὅσαι μεγάλαι τῶν τεχνῶν,
προσδέονται ἀδολεσχίας καὶ μετεωρολογίας
φύσεως πέρι· τὸ γὰρ ὑψηλόνουν τοῦτο καὶ πάντῃ
270 τελεσιουργὸν ἔοικεν ἐντεῦθέν ποθεν εἰσιέναι.
ὃ καὶ Περικλῆς πρὸς τῷ εὐφυὴς εἶναι ἐκτήσατο·
προσπεσὼν γάρ, οἶμαι, τοιούτῳ ὄντι Ἀναξαγόρᾳ,
μετεωρολογίας ἐμπλησθεὶς καὶ ἐπὶ φύσιν νοῦ τε
καὶ ἀνοίας ἀφικόμενος, ὧν δὴ πέρι τὸν πολὺν
λόγον ἐποιεῖτο Ἀναξαγόρας, ἐντεῦθεν εἵλκυσεν
ἐπὶ τὴν τῶν λόγων τέχνην τὸ πρόσφορον αὐτῇ.

ΦΑΙΔΡΟΣ. Πῶς τοῦτο λέγεις;

B   ΣΩΚΡΑΤΗΣ. Ὁ αὐτός που τρόπος τέχνης ἰατρικῆς,
ὅσπερ καὶ ῥητορικῆς.

ΦΑΙΔΡΟΣ. Πῶς δή;

ΣΩΚΡΑΤΗΣ. Ἐν ἀμφοτέραις δεῖ διελέσθαι φύσιν,
σώματος μὲν ἐν τῇ ἑτέρᾳ, ψυχῆς δὲ ἐν τῇ ἑτέρᾳ, εἰ

right. But how and from whom is the truly rhetorical and persuasive art to be acquired?

SOCRATES. Whether one can acquire it, so as to become a perfect orator, Phaedrus, is probably, and perhaps must be, dependent on conditions, like everything else. If you are naturally rhetorical, you will become a notable orator, when to your natural endowments you have added knowledge and practice; at whatever point you are deficient in these, you will be incomplete. But so far as the art is concerned, I do not think the quest of it lies along the path of Lysias and Thrasymachus.

PHAEDRUS. Where then?

SOCRATES. I suppose, my friend, Pericles is the most perfect orator in existence.

PHAEDRUS. Well?

SOCRATES. All great arts demand discussion and high speculation about nature; for this loftiness of mind and effectiveness in all directions seem somehow to come from such pursuits. This was in Pericles added to his great natural abilities; for it was, I think, his falling in with Anaxagoras, who was just such a man, that filled him with high thoughts and taught him the nature of mind and of lack of mind, subjects about which Anaxagoras used chiefly to discourse, and from these speculations he drew and applied to the art of speaking what is of use to it.

PHAEDRUS. What do you mean by that?

SOCRATES. The method of the art of healing is much the same as that of rhetoric.

PHAEDRUS. How so?

SOCRATES. In both cases you must analyse a nature, in one that of the body and in the other that of the

μέλλεις μὴ τριβῇ μόνον καὶ ἐμπειρίᾳ, ἀλλὰ τέχνῃ,
τῷ μὲν φάρμακα καὶ τροφὴν προσφέρων ὑγίειαν
καὶ ῥώμην ἐμποιήσειν, τῇ δὲ λόγους τε καὶ ἐπιτη-
δεύσεις νομίμους πειθὼ ἣν ἂν βούλῃ καὶ ἀρετὴν
παραδώσειν.

ΦΑΙΔΡΟΣ. Τὸ γοῦν εἰκός, ὦ Σώκρατες, οὕτως.

C   ΣΩΚΡΑΤΗΣ. Ψυχῆς οὖν φύσιν ἀξίως λόγου κατανοῆσαι οἴει δυνατὸν εἶναι ἄνευ τῆς τοῦ ὅλου
φύσεως;

ΦΑΙΔΡΟΣ. Εἰ μὲν Ἱπποκράτει γε τῷ τῶν Ἀσκλη-
πιαδῶν δεῖ τι πιθέσθαι, οὐδὲ περὶ σώματος ἄνευ
τῆς μεθόδου ταύτης.

ΣΩΚΡΑΤΗΣ. Καλῶς γάρ, ὦ ἑταῖρε, λέγει· χρὴ
μέντοι πρὸς τῷ Ἱπποκράτει τὸν λόγον ἐξετάζοντα
σκοπεῖν, εἰ συμφωνεῖ.

ΦΑΙΔΡΟΣ. Φημί.

55. ΣΩΚΡΑΤΗΣ. Τὸ τοίνυν περὶ φύσεως σκόπει τί
D   ποτε λέγει Ἱπποκράτης τε καὶ ὁ ἀληθὴς λόγος.
ἆρ᾽ οὐχ ὧδε δεῖ διανοεῖσθαι περὶ ὁτουοῦν φύσεως·
πρῶτον μέν, ἁπλοῦν ἢ πολυειδές ἐστιν, οὗ πέρι
βουλησόμεθα εἶναι αὐτοὶ τεχνικοὶ καὶ ἄλλον
δυνατοὶ ποιεῖν, ἔπειτα δέ, ἂν μὲν ἁπλοῦν ᾖ,
σκοπεῖν τὴν δύναμιν αὐτοῦ, τίνα πρὸς τί πέφυκεν
εἰς τὸ δρᾶν ἔχον ἢ τίνα εἰς τὸ παθεῖν ὑπὸ τοῦ, ἐὰν
δὲ πλείω εἴδη ἔχῃ, ταῦτα ἀριθμησάμενον, ὅπερ
ἐφ᾽ ἑνός, τοῦτ᾽ ἰδεῖν ἐφ᾽ ἑκάστου, τῷ τί ποιεῖν
αὐτὸ πέφυκεν ἢ τῷ τί παθεῖν ὑπὸ τοῦ;

ΦΑΙΔΡΟΣ. Κινδυνεύει, ὦ Σώκρατες.

ΣΩΚΡΑΤΗΣ. Ἡ γοῦν ἄνευ τούτων μέθοδος ἐοίκοι
E   ἂν ὥσπερ τυφλοῦ πορείᾳ· ἀλλ᾽ οὐ μὴν ἀπεικα-
στέον τόν γε τέχνῃ μετιόντα ὁτιοῦν τυφλῷ οὐδὲ
κωφῷ, ἀλλὰ δῆλον ὡς, ἄν τῷ τις τέχνῃ λόγους

soul, if you are to proceed in a scientific manner, not merely by practice and routine, to impart health and strength to the body by prescribing medicine and diet, or by proper discourses and training to give to the soul the desired belief and virtue.

PHAEDRUS. That, Socrates, is probably true.

SOCRATES. Now do you think one can acquire any appreciable knowledge of the nature of the soul without knowing the nature of the whole man?

PHAEDRUS. If Hippocrates the Asclepiad is to be trusted, one cannot know the nature of the body, either, except in that way.

SOCRATES. He is right, my friend; however, we ought not to be content with the authority of Hippocrates, but to see also if our reason agrees with him on examination.

PHAEDRUS. I assent.

SOCRATES. Then see what Hippocrates and true reason say about nature. In considering the nature of anything, must we not consider first, whether that in respect to which we wish to be learned ourselves and to make others learned is simple or multiform, and then, if it is simple, enquire what power of acting it possesses, or of being acted upon, and by what, and if it has many forms, number them, and then see in the case of each form, as we did in the case of the simple nature, what its action is and how it is acted upon and by what?

PHAEDRUS. Very likely, Socrates.

SOCRATES. At any rate, any other mode of procedure would be like the progress of a blind man. Yet surely he who pursues any study scientifically ought not to be comparable to a blind or a deaf man, but evidently the man whose rhetorical teaching

διδῷ, τὴν οὐσίαν δείξει ἀκριβῶς τῆς φύσεως
τούτου, πρὸς ὃ τοὺς λόγους προσοίσει· ἔσται δέ
που ψυχὴ τοῦτο.

ΦΑΙΔΡΟΣ. Τί μήν;

271 ΣΩΚΡΑΤΗΣ. Οὐκοῦν ἡ ἅμιλλα αὐτῷ τέταται πρὸς
τοῦτο πᾶσα· πειθὼ γὰρ ἐν τούτῳ ποιεῖν ἐπιχειρεῖ.
ἢ γάρ;

ΦΑΙΔΡΟΣ. Ναί.

ΣΩΚΡΑΤΗΣ. Δῆλον ἄρα ὅτι ὁ Θρασύμαχός τε καὶ
ὃς ἂν ἄλλος σπουδῇ τέχνην· ῥητορικὴν διδῷ,
πρῶτον πάσῃ ἀκριβείᾳ γράψει τε καὶ ποιήσει
ψυχὴν ἰδεῖν, πότερον ἓν καὶ ὅμοιον πέφυκεν ἢ
κατὰ σώματος μορφὴν πολυειδές· τοῦτο γάρ φαμεν
φύσιν εἶναι δεικνύναι.

ΦΑΙΔΡΟΣ. Παντάπασι μὲν οὖν.

ΣΩΚΡΑΤΗΣ. Δεύτερον δέ γε, ὅτῳ τί ποιεῖν ἢ
παθεῖν ὑπὸ τοῦ πέφυκεν.

ΦΑΙΔΡΟΣ. Τί μήν;

B ΣΩΚΡΑΤΗΣ. Τρίτον δὲ δὴ διαταξάμενος τὰ λόγων
τε καὶ ψυχῆς γένη καὶ τὰ τούτων παθήματα
δίεισι τὰς αἰτίας, προσαρμόττων ἕκαστον ἑκάστῳ
καὶ διδάσκων, οἷα οὖσα ὑφ' οἵων λόγων δι' ἣν
αἰτίαν ἐξ ἀνάγκης ἡ μὲν πείθεται, ἡ δὲ ἀπειθεῖ.

ΦΑΙΔΡΟΣ. Κάλλιστα γοῦν ἄν, ὡς ἔοικ', ἔχοι οὕτως.

ΣΩΚΡΑΤΗΣ. Οὗτοι μὲν οὖν, ὦ φίλε, ἄλλως ἐνδεικ-
νύμενον ἢ λεγόμενον τέχνῃ ποτὲ λεχθήσεται ἢ
C γραφήσεται οὔτε τι ἄλλο οὔτε τοῦτο· ἀλλ' οἱ νῦν
γράφοντες, ὧν σὺ ἀκήκοας, τέχνας λόγων
πανοῦργοί εἰσι καὶ ἀποκρύπτονται, εἰδότες ψυχῆς
πέρι παγκάλως· πρὶν ἂν οὖν τὸν τρόπον τοῦτον
λέγωσί τε καὶ γράφωσι, μὴ πειθώμεθα αὐτοῖς
τέχνῃ γράφειν.

is a real art will explain accurately the nature of that
to which his words are to be addressed, and that is
the soul, is it not?

PHAEDRUS. Of course.

SOCRATES. Then this is the goal of all his effort;
he tries to produce conviction in the soul. Is not
that so?

PHAEDRUS. Yes.

SOCRATES. So it is clear that Thrasymachus, or
anyone else who seriously teaches the art of rhetoric,
will first describe the soul with perfect accuracy
and make us see whether it is one and all alike, or,
like the body, of multiform aspect; for this is what
we call explaining its nature.

PHAEDRUS. Certainly.

SOCRATES. And secondly he will say what its
action is and toward what it is directed, or how it is
acted upon and by what.

PHAEDRUS. To be sure.

SOCRATES. Thirdly, he will classify the speeches
and the souls and will adapt each to the other,
showing the causes of the effects produced and why
one kind of soul is necessarily persuaded by certain
classes of speeches, and another is not.

PHAEDRUS. That would, I think, be excellent.

SOCRATES. By no other method of exposition or
speech will this, or anything else, ever be written or
spoken with real art. But those whom you have
heard, who write treatises on the art of speech
nowadays, are deceivers and conceal the nature of
the soul, though they know it very well. Until they
write and speak by this method we cannot believe
that they write by the rules of art.

ΦΑΙΔΡΟΣ. Τίνα τοῦτον;

ΣΩΚΡΑΤΗΣ. Αὐτὰ μὲν τὰ ῥήματα εἰπεῖν οὐκ εὐπετές· ὡς δὲ δεῖ γράφειν, εἰ μέλλει τεχνικῶς ἔχειν καθ' ὅσον ἐνδέχεται, λέγειν ἐθέλω.

ΦΑΙΔΡΟΣ. Λέγε δή.

56. ΣΩΚΡΑΤΗΣ. Ἐπειδὴ λόγου δύναμις τυγ-
D χάνει ψυχαγωγία οὖσα, τὸν μέλλοντα ῥητορικὸν ἔσεσθαι ἀνάγκη εἰδέναι ψυχὴ ὅσα εἴδη ἔχει. ἔστιν οὖν τόσα καὶ τόσα, καὶ τοῖα καὶ τοῖα· ὅθεν οἱ μὲν τοιοίδε, οἱ δὲ τοιοίδε γίγνονται· τούτων δὲ δὴ διῃρημένων, λόγων αὖ τόσα καὶ τόσα ἔστιν εἴδη, τοιόνδε ἕκαστον. οἱ μὲν οὖν τοιοίδε ὑπὸ τῶν τοιῶνδε λόγων διὰ τήνδε τὴν αἰτίαν εἰς τὰ τοιάδε εὐπειθεῖς, οἱ δὲ τοιοίδε διὰ τάδε δυσπειθεῖς· δεῖ δὴ ταῦτα ἱκανῶς νοήσαντα, μετὰ ταῦτα θεώμενον
E αὐτὰ ἐν ταῖς πράξεσιν ὄντα τε καὶ πραττόμενα, ὀξέως τῇ αἰσθήσει δύνασθαι ἐπακολουθεῖν, ἢ μηδὲν εἶναί πω πλέον αὐτῷ ὧν τότε ἤκουεν λόγων ξυνών. ὅταν δὲ εἰπεῖν τε ἱκανῶς ἔχῃ, οἷος ὑφ' οἵων πείθεται, παραγιγνόμενόν τε δυνατὸς ᾖ δι-
272 αισθανόμενος ἑαυτῷ ἐνδείκνυσθαι, ὅτι οὗτός ἐστιν καὶ αὕτη ἡ φύσις, περὶ ἧς τότε ἦσαν οἱ λόγοι, νῦν ἔργῳ παροῦσά οἱ, ᾗ προσοιστέον τούσδε ὧδε τοὺς λόγους ἐπὶ τὴν τῶνδε πειθώ, ταῦτα δ' ἤδη πάντα ἔχοντι, προσλαβόντι καιροὺς τοῦ πότε λεκτέον καὶ ἐπισχετέον, βραχυλογίας τε αὖ καὶ ἐλεεινολογίας καὶ δεινώσεως ἑκάστων τε ὅσ' ἂν

PHAEDRUS. What is this method?

SOCRATES. It is not easy to tell the exact expressions to be used ; but I will tell how one must write, if one is to do it, so far as possible, in a truly artistic way.

PHAEDRUS. Speak then.

SOCRATES. Since it is the function of speech to lead souls by persuasion, he who is to be a rhetorician must know the various forms of soul. Now they are so and so many and of such and such kinds, wherefore men also are of different kinds : these we must classify. Then there are also various classes of speeches, to one of which every speech belongs. So men of a certain sort are easily persuaded by speeches of a certain sort for a certain reason to actions or beliefs of a certain sort, and men of another sort cannot be so persuaded. The student of rhetoric must, accordingly, acquire a proper knowledge of these classes and then be able to follow them accurately with his senses when he sees them in the practical affairs of life ; otherwise he can never have any profit from the lectures he may have heard. But when he has learned to tell what sort of man is influenced by what sort of speech, and is able, if he comes upon such a man, to recognize him and to convince himself that this is the man and this now actually before him is the nature spoken of in a certain lecture, to which he must now make a practical application of a certain kind of speech in a certain way to persuade his hearer to a certain action or belief—when he has acquired all this, and has added thereto a knowledge of the times for speaking and for keeping silence, and has also distinguished the favourable occasions for brief speech or pitiful speech or intensity and all the classes

εἴδη μάθῃ λόγων, τούτων τὴν εὐκαιρίαν τε καὶ
ἀκαιρίαν διαγνόντι, καλῶς τε καὶ τελέως ἐστὶν ἡ
B τέχνη ἀπειργασμένη, πρότερον δ' οὔ· ἀλλ' ὅ τι
ἂν αὐτῶν τις ἐλλείπῃ λέγων ἢ διδάσκων ἢ γράφων, φῇ δὲ τέχνῃ λέγειν, ὁ μὴ πειθόμενος κρατεῖ.
τί δὴ οὖν; φήσει ἴσως ὁ συγγραφεύς, ὦ Φαῖδρέ τε
καὶ Σώκρατες, δοκεῖ οὕτως; ἢ ἄλλως πως ἀπο-
δεκτέον λεγομένης λόγων τέχνης;

ΦΑΙΔΡΟΣ. Ἀδύνατόν που, ὦ Σώκρατες, ἄλλως·
καίτοι οὐ σμικρόν γε φαίνεται ἔργον.

ΣΩΚΡΑΤΗΣ. Ἀληθῆ λέγεις. τούτου τοι ἕνεκα
C χρὴ πάντας τοὺς λόγους ἄνω καὶ κάτω μετα-
στρέφοντα ἐπισκοπεῖν, εἴ τίς πῃ ῥᾴων καὶ βραχυ-
τέρα φαίνεται ἐπ' αὐτὴν ὁδός, ἵνα μὴ μάτην
πολλὴν ἴῃ καὶ τραχεῖαν, ἐξὸν ὀλίγην τε καὶ λείαν.
ἀλλ' εἴ τινά πῃ βοήθειαν ἔχεις ἐπακηκοὼς Λυσίου
ἤ τινος ἄλλου, πειρῶ λέγειν ἀναμιμνῃσκόμενος.

ΦΑΙΔΡΟΣ. Ἕνεκα μὲν πείρας ἔχοιμ' ἄν,[1] ἀλλ'
οὔτι νῦν γ' οὕτως ἔχω.

ΣΩΚΡΑΤΗΣ. Βούλει οὖν ἐγώ τιν' εἴπω λόγον, ὃν
τῶν περὶ ταῦτά τινων ἀκήκοα;

ΦΑΙΔΡΟΣ. Τί μήν;

ΣΩΚΡΑΤΗΣ. Λέγεται γοῦν, ὦ Φαῖδρε, δίκαιον
εἶναι καὶ τὸ τοῦ λύκου εἰπεῖν.

D ΦΑΙΔΡΟΣ. Καὶ σύ γε οὕτω ποίει.

57. ΣΩΚΡΑΤΗΣ. Φασὶ τοίνυν οὐδὲν οὕτω ταῦτα
δεῖν σεμνύνειν οὐδ' ἀνάγειν ἄνω μακρὰν περι-
βαλλομένους· παντάπασι γάρ, ὃ καὶ κατ' ἀρχὰς
εἴπομεν τοῦδε τοῦ λόγου, ὅτι οὐδὲν ἀληθείας
μετέχειν δέοι δικαίων ἢ ἀγαθῶν πέρι πραγμάτων,

---

[1] Schanz reads λέγοιμ' ἄν.

of speech which he has learned, then, and not till then, will his art be fully and completely finished; and if anyone who omits any of these points in his speaking or writing claims to speak by the rules of art, the one who disbelieves him is the better man. "Now then," perhaps the writer of our treatise will say, "Phaedrus and Socrates, do you agree to all this? Or must the art of speech be described in some other way?"

PHAEDRUS. No other way is possible, Socrates. But it seems a great task to attain to it.

SOCRATES. Very true. Therefore you must examine all that has been said from every point of view, to see if no shorter and easier road to the art appears, that one may not take a long and rough road, when there is a short and smooth one. If you have heard from Lysias or anyone else anything that can help us, try to remember it and tell it.

PHAEDRUS. If it depended on trying, I might, but just now I have nothing to say.

SOCRATES. Then shall I tell something that I have heard some of those say who make these matters their business?

PHAEDRUS. Pray do.

SOCRATES. Even the wolf, you know, Phaedrus, has a right to an advocate, as they say.

PHAEDRUS. Do you be his advocate.

SOCRATES. Very well. They say that there is no need of treating these matters with such gravity and carrying them back so far to first principles with many words; for, as we said in the beginning of this discussion, he who is to be a competent rhetorician need have nothing at all to do, they say, with truth

ἢ καὶ ἀνθρώπων γε τοιούτων φύσει ὄντων ἢ τροφῇ,
τὸν μέλλοντα ἱκανῶς ῥητορικὸν ἔσεσθαι. τὸ
παράπαν γὰρ οὐδὲν ἐν τοῖς δικαστηρίοις τούτων
E ἀληθείας μέλειν οὐδενί, ἀλλὰ τοῦ πιθανοῦ· τοῦτο
δ᾽ εἶναι τὸ εἰκός, ᾧ δεῖν προσέχειν τὸν μέλλοντα
τέχνῃ ἐρεῖν. οὐδὲ γὰρ αὐτὰ τὰ πραχθέντα δεῖν
λέγειν ἐνίοτε, ἐὰν μὴ εἰκότως ᾖ πεπραγμένα, ἀλλὰ
τὰ εἰκότα, ἔν τε κατηγορίᾳ καὶ ἀπολογίᾳ· καὶ
πάντως λέγοντα τὸ δὴ εἰκὸς διωκτέον εἶναι, πολλὰ
273 εἰπόντα χαίρειν τῷ ἀληθεῖ· τοῦτο γὰρ διὰ παντὸς
τοῦ λόγου γιγνόμενον τὴν ἅπασαν τέχνην πορί-
ζειν.

ΦΑΙΔΡΟΣ. Αὐτά γε, ὦ Σώκρατες, διελήλυθας
ἃ λέγουσιν οἱ περὶ τοὺς λόγους τεχνικοὶ προσποιούμενοι εἶναι. ἀνεμνήσθην γὰρ ὅτι ἐν τῷ
πρόσθεν βραχέως τοῦ τοιούτου ἐφηψάμεθα, δοκεῖ
δὲ τοῦτο πάμμεγα εἶναι τοῖς περὶ ταῦτα.

ΣΩΚΡΑΤΗΣ. Ἀλλὰ μὴν τόν γε Τισίαν αὐτὸν
πεπάτηκας ἀκριβῶς· εἰπέτω τοίνυν καὶ τόδε ἡμῖν
B ὁ Τισίας, μή τι ἄλλο λέγει τὸ εἰκὸς ἢ τὸ τῷ
πλήθει δοκοῦν.

ΦΑΙΔΡΟΣ. Τί γὰρ ἄλλο;

ΣΩΚΡΑΤΗΣ. Τοῦτο δή, ὡς ἔοικε, σοφὸν εὑρὼν
ἅμα καὶ τεχνικὸν ἔγραψεν, ὡς ἐάν τις ἀσθενὴς
καὶ ἀνδρικὸς ἰσχυρὸν καὶ δειλὸν συγκόψας, ἱμάτιον
ἤ τι ἄλλο ἀφελόμενος, εἰς δικαστήριον ἄγηται,
δεῖ δὴ τἀληθὲς μηδέτερον λέγειν, ἀλλὰ τὸν μὲν
δειλὸν μὴ ὑπὸ μόνου φάναι τοῦ ἀνδρικοῦ συγ-
κεκόφθαι, τὸν δὲ τοῦτο μὲν ἐλέγχειν ὡς μόνω
C ἤστην, ἐκείνῳ δὲ καταχρήσασθαι τῷ πῶς δ᾽ ἂν
ἐγὼ τοιόσδε τοιῷδε ἐπεχείρησα; ὁ δ᾽ οὐκ ἐρεῖ δὴ

in considering things which are just or good, or men who are so, whether by nature or by education. For in the courts, they say, nobody cares for truth about these matters, but for that which is convincing; and that is probability, so that he who is to be an artist in speech must fix his attention upon probability. For sometimes one must not even tell what was actually done, if it was not likely to be done, but what was probable, whether in accusation or defence; and in brief, a speaker must always aim at probability, paying no attention to truth; for this method, if pursued throughout the whole speech, provides us with the entire art.

PHAEDRUS. You have stated just what those say who pretend to possess the art of speech, Socrates. I remember that we touched upon this matter briefly before,[1] but the professional rhetoricians think it is of great importance.

SOCRATES. Well, there is Tisias whom you have studied carefully; now let Tisias himself tell us if he does not say that probability is that which most people think.

PHAEDRUS. That is just what he says.

SOCRATES. Apparently after he had invented this clever scientific definition, he wrote that if a feeble and brave man assaulted a strong coward, robbed him of his cloak or something, and was brought to trial for it, neither party ought to speak the truth; the coward should say that he had not been assaulted by the brave man alone, whereas the other should prove that only they two were present and should use the well-known argument, "How could a little man like me assault such a man as he is?" The coward will

[1] See 259 E.

557

τὴν ἑαυτοῦ κάκην, ἀλλά τι ἄλλο ψεύδεσθαι
ἐπιχειρῶν τάχ᾽ ἂν ἔλεγχόν πη παραδοίη τῷ
ἀντιδίκῳ. καὶ περὶ τἆλλα δὴ τοιαῦτ᾽ ἄττα ἐστὶν
τὰ τέχνη λεγόμενα. οὐ γάρ, ὦ Φαῖδρε;

ΦΑΙΔΡΟΣ. Τί μήν;

ΣΩΚΡΑΤΗΣ. Φεῦ, δεινῶς γ᾽ ἔοικεν ἀποκεκρυμ-
μένην τέχνην ἀνευρεῖν ὁ Τισίας ἢ ἄλλος ὅστις δή
ποτ᾽ ὢν τυγχάνει καὶ ὁπόθεν χαίρει ὀνομαζόμενος.
D ἀτάρ, ὦ ἑταῖρε, τούτῳ ἡμεῖς πότερον λέγωμεν
ἢ μή—

ΦΑΙΔΡΟΣ. Τὸ ποῖον;

58. ΣΩΚΡΑΤΗΣ. Ὅτι, ὦ Τισία, πάλαι ἡμεῖς,
πρὶν καὶ σὲ παρελθεῖν, τυγχάνομεν λέγοντες, ὡς
ἄρα τοῦτο τὸ εἰκὸς τοῖς πολλοῖς δι᾽ ὁμοιότητα τοῦ
ἀληθοῦς τυγχάνει ἐγγιγνόμενον· τὰς δὲ ὁμοιότητας
ἄρτι διήλθομεν ὅτι πανταχοῦ ὁ τὴν ἀλήθειαν
εἰδὼς κάλλιστα ἐπίσταται εὑρίσκειν. ὥστ᾽ εἰ
μὲν ἄλλο τι περὶ τέχνης λόγων λέγεις, ἀκούοιμεν
ἄν· εἰ δὲ μή, οἷς νυνδὴ διήλθομεν πεισόμεθα, ὡς
ἐὰν μή τις τῶν τε ἀκουσομένων τὰς φύσεις διαριθ-
E μήσηται, καὶ κατ᾽ εἴδη τε διαιρεῖσθαι τὰ ὄντα καὶ
μιᾷ ἰδέᾳ δυνατὸς ᾖ καθ᾽ ἓν ἕκαστον περιλαμβά-
νειν, οὔ ποτ᾽ ἔσται τεχνικὸς λόγων πέρι καθ᾽ ὅσον
δυνατὸν ἀνθρώπῳ. ταῦτα δὲ οὐ μή ποτε κτήσηται
ἄνευ πολλῆς πραγματείας· ἣν οὐχ ἕνεκα τοῦ
λέγειν καὶ πράττειν πρὸς ἀνθρώπους δεῖ διαπο-
νεῖσθαι τὸν σώφρονα, ἀλλὰ τοῦ θεοῖς κεχαρισμένα
μὲν λέγειν δύνασθαι, κεχαρισμένως δὲ πράττειν
274 τὸ πᾶν εἰς δύναμιν. οὐ γὰρ δὴ ἄρα, ὦ Τισία,
φασὶν οἱ σοφώτεροι ἡμῶν, ὁμοδούλοις δεῖ χαρίζεσθαι μελετᾶν τὸν νοῦν ἔχοντα, ὅ τι μὴ πάρεργον,
ἀλλὰ δεσπόταις ἀγαθοῖς τε καὶ ἐξ ἀγαθῶν· ὥστ᾽

558

not acknowledge his cowardice, but will perhaps try
to invent some other lie, and thus give his oppo-
nent a chance to confute him. And in other cases
there are other similar rules of art. Is that not so,
Phaedrus?

PHAEDRUS. Certainly.

SOCRATES. Oh, a wonderfully hidden art it seems
to be which Tisias has brought to light, or some
other, whoever he may be and whatever country he
is proud to call his own! But, my friend, shall we
say in reply to this, or shall we not—

PHAEDRUS. What?

SOCRATES. "Tisias, some time ago, before you
came along, we were saying that this probability of
yours was accepted by the people because of its
likeness to truth; and we just stated that he who
knows the truth is always best able to discover likenesses. And so, if you have anything else to say about
the art of speech, we will listen to you; but if not,
we will put our trust in what we said just now, that
unless a man take account of the characters of his
hearers and is able to divide things by classes and to
comprehend particulars under a general idea, he will
never attain the highest human perfection in the art of
speech. But this ability he will not gain without
much diligent toil, which a wise man ought not to
undergo for the sake of speaking and acting before
men, but that he may be able to speak and to do
everything, so far as possible, in a manner pleasing
to the gods. For those who are wiser than we,
Tisias, say that a man of sense should surely practise
to please not his fellow slaves, except as a secondary
consideration, but his good and noble masters.
Therefore, if the path is long, be not astonished;

εἰ μακρὰ ἡ περίοδος, μὴ θαυμάσῃς· μεγάλων γὰρ
ἕνεκα περιτέον, οὐχ ὡς σὺ δοκεῖς. ἔσται μήν,
ὡς ὁ λόγος φησίν, ἐάν τις ἐθέλῃ, καὶ ταῦτα
κάλλιστα ἐξ ἐκείνων γιγνόμενα.

ΦΑΙΔΡΟΣ. Παγκάλως ἔμοιγε δοκεῖ λέγεσθαι, ὦ
Σώκρατες, εἴπερ οἷός τέ τις εἴη.

ΣΩΚΡΑΤΗΣ. Ἀλλὰ καὶ ἐπιχειροῦντί τοι τοῖς
B καλοῖς καλὸν καὶ πάσχειν ὅ τι ἄν τῳ ξυμβῇ
παθεῖν.

ΦΑΙΔΡΟΣ. Καὶ μάλα.

ΣΩΚΡΑΤΗΣ. Οὐκοῦν τὸ μὲν τέχνης τε καὶ ἀτε-
χνίας λόγων πέρι ἱκανῶς ἐχέτω.

ΦΑΙΔΡΟΣ. Τί μήν;

ΣΩΚΡΑΤΗΣ. Τὸ δ' εὐπρεπείας δὴ γραφῆς πέρι
καὶ ἀπρεπείας, πῇ γιγνόμενον καλῶς ἄν ἔχοι καὶ
ὅπῃ ἀπρεπῶς, λοιπόν. ἤ γάρ;

ΦΑΙΔΡΟΣ. Ναί.

59. ΣΩΚΡΑΤΗΣ. Οἶσθ' οὖν ὅπῃ μάλιστα θεῷ
χαριεῖ λόγων πέρι πράττων ἤ λέγων;

ΦΑΙΔΡΟΣ. Οὐδαμῶς· σὺ δέ;

C ΣΩΚΡΑΤΗΣ. Ἀκοήν γ' ἔχω λέγειν τῶν προτέρων,
τὸ δ' ἀληθὲς αὐτοὶ ἴσασιν. εἰ δὲ τοῦτο εὕροιμεν
αὐτοί, ἆρά γ' ἄν ἔθ' ἡμῖν μέλοι τι τῶν ἀνθρωπίνων δοξασμάτων;

ΦΑΙΔΡΟΣ. Γελοῖον ἤρου· ἀλλ' ἃ φῂς ἀκηκοέναι,
λέγε.

ΣΩΚΡΑΤΗΣ. Ἤκουσα τοίνυν περὶ Ναύκρατιν τῆς
Αἰγύπτου γενέσθαι τῶν ἐκεῖ παλαιῶν τινὰ θεῶν,
οὗ καὶ τὸ ὄρνεον τὸ ἱερόν, ὃ δὴ καλοῦσιν ἴβιν·
αὐτῷ δὲ ὄνομα τῷ δαίμονι εἶναι Θεύθ. τοῦτον δὲ
D πρῶτον ἀριθμόν τε καὶ λογισμὸν εὑρεῖν καὶ
γεωμετρίαν καὶ ἀστρονομίαν, ἔτι δὲ πεττείας τε

for it must be trodden for great ends, not for those you have in mind. Yet your ends also, as our argument says, will be best gained in this way, if one so desires."

PHAEDRUS. I think what you have said is admirable, if one could only do it.

SOCRATES. But it is noble to strive after noble objects, no matter what happens to us.

PHAEDRUS. Certainly.

SOCRATES. We have, then, said enough about the art of speaking and that which is no art.

PHAEDRUS. Assuredly.

SOCRATES. But we have still to speak of propriety and impropriety in writing, how it should be done and how it is improper, have we not?

PHAEDRUS. Yes.

SOCRATES. Do you know how you can act or speak about rhetoric so as to please God best?

PHAEDRUS. Not at all; do you?

SOCRATES. I can tell something I have heard of the ancients; but whether it is true, they only know. But if we ourselves should find it out, should we care any longer for human opinions?

PHAEDRUS. A ridiculous question! But tell me what you say you have heard.

SOCRATES. I heard, then, that at Naucratis, in Egypt, was one of the ancient gods of that country, the one whose sacred bird is called the ibis, and the name of the god himself was Theuth. He it was who invented numbers and arithmetic and geometry and astronomy, also draughts and dice, and, most

καὶ κυβείας, καὶ δὴ καὶ γράμματα· βασιλέως δ'
αὖ τότε ὄντος Αἰγύπτου ὅλης Θαμοῦ περὶ τὴν
μεγάλην πόλιν τοῦ ἄνω τόπου, ἣν οἱ Ἕλληνες
Αἰγυπτίας Θήβας καλοῦσι, καὶ τὸν θεὸν Ἄμμωνα,
παρὰ τοῦτον ἐλθὼν ὁ Θεὺθ τὰς τέχνας ἐπέδειξεν,
καὶ ἔφη δεῖν διαδοθῆναι τοῖς ἄλλοις Αἰγυπτίοις.
ὁ δὲ ἤρετο, ἥντινα ἑκάστη ἔχοι ὠφελίαν, διεξιόντος
δέ, ὅ τι καλῶς ἢ μὴ καλῶς δοκοῖ λέγειν, τὸ μὲν
E ἔψεγε, τὸ δ' ἐπήνει. πολλὰ μὲν δὴ περὶ ἑκάστης
τῆς τέχνης ἐπ' ἀμφότερα Θαμοῦν τῷ Θεὺθ
λέγεται ἀποφήνασθαι, ἃ λόγος πολὺς ἂν εἴη
διελθεῖν· ἐπειδὴ δὲ ἐπὶ τοῖς γράμμασιν ἦν, τοῦτο
δέ, ὦ βασιλεῦ, τὸ μάθημα, ἔφη ὁ Θεύθ, σοφωτέρους Αἰγυπτίους καὶ μνημονικωτέρους παρέξει·
μνήμης τε γὰρ καὶ σοφίας φάρμακον ηὑρέθη. ὁ δ'
εἶπεν· ὦ τεχνικώτατε Θεύθ, ἄλλος μὲν τεκεῖν
δυνατὸς τὰ τῆς τέχνης, ἄλλος δὲ κρῖναι, τίν' ἔχει
μοῖραν βλάβης τε καὶ ὠφελίας τοῖς μέλλουσι
275 χρῆσθαι· καὶ νῦν σύ, πατὴρ ὢν γραμμάτων, δι'
εὔνοιαν τοὐναντίον εἶπες ἢ δύναται. τοῦτο γὰρ
τῶν μαθόντων λήθην μὲν ἐν ψυχαῖς παρέξει
μνήμης ἀμελετησίᾳ, ἅτε διὰ πίστιν γραφῆς ἔξωθεν
ὑπ' ἀλλοτρίων τύπων, οὐκ ἔνδοθεν αὐτοὺς ὑφ'
αὑτῶν ἀναμιμνῃσκομένους· οὔκουν μνήμης ἀλλ'
ὑπομνήσεως φάρμακον ηὗρες. σοφίας δὲ τοῖς
μαθηταῖς δόξαν, οὐκ ἀλήθειαν πορίζεις· πολυή-
κοοι γάρ σοι γενόμενοι ἄνευ διδαχῆς πολυγνώμονες
B εἶναι δόξουσιν, ἀγνώμονες ὡς ἐπὶ τὸ πλῆθος ὄντες

important of all, letters. Now the king of all Egypt at that time was the god Thamus, who lived in the great city of the upper region, which the Greeks call the Egyptian Thebes, and they call the god himself Ammon. To him came Theuth to show his inventions, saying that they ought to be imparted to the other Egyptians. But Thamus asked what use there was in each, and as Theuth enumerated their uses, expressed praise or blame, according as he approved or disapproved. The story goes that Thamus said many things to Theuth in praise or blame of the various arts, which it would take too long to repeat; but when they came to the letters, "This invention, O king," said Theuth, "will make the Egyptians wiser and will improve their memories; for it is an elixir of memory and wisdom that I have discovered." But Thamus replied, "Most ingenious Theuth, one man has the ability to beget arts, but the ability to judge of their usefulness or harmfulness to their users belongs to another; and now you, who are the father of letters, have been led by your affection to ascribe to them a power the opposite of that which they really possess. For this invention will produce forgetfulness in the minds of those who learn to use it, because they will not practise their memory. Their trust in writing, produced by external characters which are no part of themselves, will discourage the use of their own memory within them. You have invented an elixir not of memory, but of reminding; and you offer your pupils the appearance of wisdom, not true wisdom, for they will read many things without instruction and will therefore seem to know many things, when they are for the most part ignorant

PLATO

καὶ χαλεποὶ ξυνεῖναι, δοξόσοφοι γεγονότες ἀντὶ σοφῶν.

ΦΑΙΔΡΟΣ. Ὦ Σώκρατες, ῥᾳδίως σὺ Αἰγυπτίους καὶ ὁποδαποὺς ἂν ἐθέλῃς λόγους ποιεῖς.

ΣΩΚΡΑΤΗΣ. Οἱ δέ γ', ὦ φίλε, ἐν τῷ τοῦ Διὸς τοῦ Δωδωναίου ἱερῷ δρυὸς λόγους ἔφησαν μαντικοὺς πρώτους γενέσθαι. τοῖς μὲν οὖν τότε, ἅτε οὐκ οὖσι σοφοῖς ὥσπερ ὑμεῖς οἱ νέοι, ἀπέχρη δρυὸς C καὶ πέτρας ἀκούειν ὑπ' εὐηθείας, εἰ μόνον ἀληθῆ λέγοιεν· σοὶ δ' ἴσως διαφέρει τίς ὁ λέγων καὶ ποδαπός. οὐ γὰρ ἐκεῖνο μόνον σκοπεῖς, εἴτε οὕτως εἴτε ἄλλως ἔχει;

ΦΑΙΔΡΟΣ. Ὀρθῶς ἐπέπληξας, καί μοι δοκεῖ περὶ γραμμάτων ἔχειν ᾗπερ ὁ Θηβαῖος λέγει.

60. ΣΩΚΡΑΤΗΣ. Οὐκοῦν ὁ τέχνην οἰόμενος ἐν γράμμασι καταλιπεῖν, καὶ αὖ ὁ παραδεχόμενος ὥς τι σαφὲς καὶ βέβαιον ἐκ γραμμάτων ἐσόμενον, πολλῆς ἂν εὐηθείας γέμοι καὶ τῷ ὄντι τὴν Ἄμμωνος μαντείαν ἀγνοοῖ, πλέον τι οἰόμενος D εἶναι λόγους γεγραμμένους τοῦ τὸν εἰδότα ὑπομνῆσαι περὶ ὧν ἂν ᾖ τὰ γεγραμμένα.

ΦΑΙΔΡΟΣ. Ὀρθότατα.

ΣΩΚΡΑΤΗΣ. Δεινὸν γάρ που, ὦ Φαῖδρε, τοῦτ' ἔχει γραφή, καὶ ὡς ἀληθῶς ὅμοιον ζωγραφίᾳ. καὶ γὰρ τὰ ἐκείνης ἔκγονα ἕστηκε μὲν ὡς ζῶντα, ἐὰν δ' ἀνέρῃ τι, σεμνῶς πάνυ σιγᾷ. ταὐτὸν δὲ καὶ οἱ λόγοι· δόξαις μὲν ἂν ὥς τι φρονοῦντας αὐτοὺς λέγειν, ἐὰν δέ τι ἔρῃ τῶν λεγομένων βουλόμενος μαθεῖν, ἕν τι σημαίνει μόνον ταὐτὸν ἀεί. ὅταν δὲ E ἅπαξ γραφῇ, κυλινδεῖται μὲν πανταχοῦ πᾶς λόγος ὁμοίως παρὰ τοῖς ἐπαΐουσιν, ὡς δ' αὕτως παρ'

564

and hard to get along with, since they are not wise, but only appear wise."

PHAEDRUS. Socrates, you easily make up stories of Egypt or any country you please.

SOCRATES. They used to say, my friend, that the words of the oak in the holy place of Zeus at Dodona were the first prophetic utterances. The people of that time, not being so wise as you young folks, were content in their simplicity to hear an oak or a rock, provided only it spoke the truth; but to you, perhaps, it makes a difference who the speaker is and where he comes from, for you do not consider only whether his words are true or not.

PHAEDRUS. Your rebuke is just; and I think the Theban is right in what he says about letters.

SOCRATES. He who thinks, then, that he has left behind him any art in writing, and he who receives it in the belief that anything in writing will be clear and certain, would be an utterly simple person, and in truth ignorant of the prophecy of Ammon, if he thinks written words are of any use except to remind him who knows the matter about which they are written.

PHAEDRUS. Very true.

SOCRATES. Writing, Phaedrus, has this strange quality, and is very like painting; for the creatures of painting stand like living beings, but if one asks them a question, they preserve a solemn silence. And so it is with written words; you might think they spoke as if they had intelligence, but if you question them, wishing to know about their sayings, they always say only one and the same thing. And every word, when once it is written, is bandied about, alike among those who understand and those who

οἷς οὐδὲν προσήκει, καὶ οὐκ ἐπίσταται λέγειν οἷς
δεῖ γε καὶ μή· πλημμελούμενος δὲ καὶ οὐκ ἐν δίκῃ
λοιδορηθεὶς τοῦ πατρὸς ἀεὶ δεῖται βοηθοῦ· αὐτὸς
γὰρ οὔτ' ἀμύνασθαι οὔτε βοηθῆσαι δυνατὸς αὑτῷ.

ΦΑΙΔΡΟΣ. Καὶ ταῦτά σοι ὀρθότατα εἴρηται.

276   ΣΩΚΡΑΤΗΣ. Τί δ'; ἄλλον ὁρῶμεν λόγον τούτου
ἀδελφὸν γνήσιον, τῷ τρόπῳ τε γίγνεται, καὶ ὅσῳ
ἀμείνων καὶ δυνατώτερος τούτου φύεται;

ΦΑΙΔΡΟΣ. Τίνα τοῦτον καὶ πῶς λέγεις γιγνόμενον;

ΣΩΚΡΑΤΗΣ. Ὃς μετ' ἐπιστήμης γράφεται ἐν τῇ
τοῦ μανθάνοντος ψυχῇ, δυνατὸς μὲν ἀμῦναι ἑαυτῷ,
ἐπιστήμων δὲ λέγειν τε καὶ σιγᾶν πρὸς οὓς δεῖ.

ΦΑΙΔΡΟΣ. Τὸν τοῦ εἰδότος λόγον λέγεις ζῶντα
καὶ ἔμψυχον, οὗ ὁ γεγραμμένος εἴδωλον ἄν τι
λέγοιτο δικαίως.

B   61. ΣΩΚΡΑΤΗΣ. Παντάπασι μὲν οὖν. τόδε δή μοι
εἰπέ· ὁ νοῦν ἔχων γεωργός, ὧν σπερμάτων κήδοιτο
καὶ ἔγκαρπα βούλοιτο γενέσθαι, πότερα σπουδῇ
ἂν θέρους εἰς Ἀδώνιδος κήπους ἀρῶν χαίροι
θεωρῶν καλοὺς ἐν ἡμέραισιν ὀκτὼ γιγνομένους, ἢ
ταῦτα μὲν δὴ παιδιᾶς τε καὶ ἑορτῆς χάριν δρῴη ἄν,
ὅτε καὶ ποιοῖ· ἐφ' οἷς δὲ ἐσπούδακε, τῇ γεωργικῇ
χρώμενος ἂν τέχνῃ, σπείρας εἰς τὸ προσῆκον,
ἀγαπῴη ἂν ἐν ὀγδόῳ μηνὶ ὅσα ἔσπειρεν τέλος
λαβόντα;

C   ΦΑΙΔΡΟΣ. Οὕτω που, ὦ Σώκρατες, τὰ μὲν
σπουδῇ, τὰ δὲ ὡς ἑτέρως ἄν, ᾗ λέγεις, ποιοῖ.

have no interest in it, and it knows not to whom to speak or not to speak; when ill-treated or unjustly reviled it always needs its father to help it; for it has no power to protect or help itself.

PHAEDRUS. You are quite right about that, too.

SOCRATES. Now tell me; is there not another kind of speech, or word, which shows itself to be the legitimate brother of this bastard one, both in the manner of its begetting and in its better and more powerful nature?

PHAEDRUS. What is this word and how is it begotten, as you say?

SOCRATES. The word which is written with intelligence in the mind of the learner, which is able to defend itself and knows to whom it should speak, and before whom to be silent.

PHAEDRUS. You mean the living and breathing word of him who knows, of which the written word may justly be called the image.

SOCRATES. Exactly. Now tell me this. Would a sensible husbandman, who has seeds which he cares for and which he wishes to bear fruit, plant them with serious purpose in the heat of summer in some garden of Adonis, and delight in seeing them appear in beauty in eight days, or would he do that sort of thing, when he did it at all, only in play and for amusement? Would he not, when he was in earnest, follow the rules of husbandry, plant his seeds in fitting ground, and be pleased when those which he had sowed reached their perfection in the eighth month?

PHAEDRUS. Yes, Socrates, he would, as you say, act in that way when in earnest and in the other way only for amusement.

ΣΩΚΡΑΤΗΣ. Τὸν δὲ δικαίων τε καὶ καλῶν καὶ ἀγαθῶν ἐπιστήμας ἔχοντα τοῦ γεωργοῦ φῶμεν ἧττον νοῦν ἔχειν εἰς τὰ ἑαυτοῦ σπέρματα;

ΦΑΙΔΡΟΣ. Ἥκιστά γε.

ΣΩΚΡΑΤΗΣ. Οὐκ ἄρα σπουδῇ αὐτὰ ἐν ὕδατι γράψει μέλανι σπείρων διὰ καλάμου μετὰ λόγων ἀδυνάτων μὲν αὑτοῖς λόγῳ βοηθεῖν, ἀδυνάτων δὲ ἱκανῶς τἀληθῆ διδάξαι.

ΦΑΙΔΡΟΣ. Οὔκουν δὴ τό γ᾽ εἰκός.

D ΣΩΚΡΑΤΗΣ. Οὐ γάρ· ἀλλὰ τοὺς μὲν ἐν γράμμασι κήπους, ὡς ἔοικε, παιδιᾶς χάριν σπερεῖ τε καὶ γράψει, ὅταν γράφῃ, ἑαυτῷ τε ὑπομνήματα θησαυριζόμενος, εἰς τὸ λήθης γῆρας ἐὰν ἵκηται, καὶ παντὶ τῷ ταὐτὸν ἴχνος μετιόντι, ἡσθήσεταί τε αὐτοὺς θεωρῶν φυομένους ἁπαλούς· ὅταν δὲ ἄλλοι παιδιαῖς ἄλλαις χρῶνται, συμποσίοις τε ἄρδοντες αὑτοὺς ἑτέροις τε ὅσα τούτων ἀδελφά, τότ᾽ ἐκεῖνος, ὡς ἔοικεν, ἀντὶ τούτων οἷς[1] λέγω παίζων διάξει.

E ΦΑΙΔΡΟΣ. Παγκάλην λέγεις παρὰ φαύλην παιδιάν, ὦ Σώκρατες, τοῦ ἐν λόγοις δυναμένου παίζειν, δικαιοσύνης τε καὶ ἄλλων ὧν λέγεις πέρι μυθολογοῦντα.

ΣΩΚΡΑΤΗΣ. Ἔστι γάρ, ὦ φίλε Φαῖδρε, οὕτω· πολὺ δ᾽, οἶμαι, καλλίων σπουδὴ περὶ αὐτὰ γίγνεται, ὅταν τις τῇ διαλεκτικῇ τέχνῃ χρώμενος, λαβὼν ψυχὴν προσήκουσαν, φυτεύῃ τε καὶ σπείρῃ μετ᾽ ἐπιστήμης λόγους, οἳ ἑαυτοῖς τῷ τε 277 φυτεύσαντι βοηθεῖν ἱκανοὶ καὶ οὐχὶ ἄκαρποι ἀλλὰ ἔχοντες σπέρμα, ὅθεν ἄλλοι ἐν ἄλλοις ἤθεσι

[1] οἷς BT.   οὗ Schanz.

SOCRATES. And shall we suppose that he who has knowledge of the just and the good and beautiful has less sense about his seeds than the husbandman?

PHAEDRUS. By no means.

SOCRATES. Then he will not, when in earnest, write them in ink, sowing them through a pen with words which cannot defend themselves by argument and cannot teach the truth effectually.

PHAEDRUS. No, at least, probably not.

SOCRATES. No. The gardens of letters he will, it seems, plant for amusement, and will write, when he writes, to treasure up reminders for himself, when he comes to the forgetfulness of old age, and for others who follow the same path, and he will be pleased when he sees them putting forth tender leaves. When others engage in other amusements, refreshing themselves with banquets and kindred entertainments, he will pass the time in such pleasures as I have suggested.

PHAEDRUS. A noble pastime, Socrates, and a contrast to those base pleasures, the pastime of the man who can find amusement in discourse, telling stories about justice, and the other subjects of which you speak.

SOCRATES. Yes, Phaedrus, so it is; but, in my opinion, serious discourse about them is far nobler, when one employs the dialectic method and plants and sows in a fitting soul intelligent words which are able to help themselves and him who planted them, which are not fruitless, but yield seed from which there spring up in other minds other words capable

φυόμενοι τοῦτ' ἀεὶ ἀθάνατον παρέχειν ἱκανοί, καὶ[1]
τὸν ἔχοντα εὐδαιμονεῖν ποιοῦντες εἰς ὅσον
ἀνθρώπῳ δυνατὸν μάλιστα.

ΦΑΙΔΡΟΣ. Πολὺ γὰρ τοῦτ' ἔτι κάλλιον λέγεις.

62. ΣΩΚΡΑΤΗΣ. Νῦν δὴ ἐκεῖνα ἤδη, ὦ Φαῖδρε,
δυνάμεθα κρίνειν, τούτων ὡμολογημένων.

ΦΑΙΔΡΟΣ. Τὰ ποῖα;

ΣΩΚΡΑΤΗΣ. Ὧν δὴ πέρι βουληθέντες ἰδεῖν
B ἀφικόμεθα εἰς τόδε, ὅπως τὸ Λυσίου τε ὄνειδος
ἐξετάσαιμεν τῆς τῶν λόγων γραφῆς πέρι, καὶ
αὐτοὺς τοὺς λόγους οἳ τέχνῃ καὶ ἄνευ τέχνης
γράφοιντο. τὸ μὲν οὖν ἔντεχνον καὶ μὴ δοκεῖ μοι
δεδηλῶσθαι μετρίως.

ΦΑΙΔΡΟΣ. Ἔδοξέ γε δή· πάλιν δὲ ὑπόμνησόν με
πῶς.

ΣΩΚΡΑΤΗΣ. Πρὶν ἄν τις τό τε ἀληθὲς ἑκάστων
εἰδῇ πέρι ὧν λέγει ἢ γράφει, κατ' αὐτό τε πᾶν
ὁρίζεσθαι δυνατὸς γένηται, ὁρισάμενός τε πάλιν
κατ' εἴδη μέχρι τοῦ ἀτμήτου τέμνειν ἐπιστηθῇ·
περί τε ψυχῆς φύσεως διιδὼν κατὰ ταὐτά, τὸ
C προσαρμόττον ἑκάστῃ φύσει εἶδος ἀνευρίσκων,
οὕτω τιθῇ καὶ διακοσμῇ τὸν λόγον, ποικίλῃ μὲν
ποικίλους ψυχῇ καὶ παναρμονίους διδοὺς λόγους,
ἁπλοῦς δὲ ἁπλῇ· οὐ πρότερον δυνατὸν τέχνῃ
ἔσεσθαι καθ' ὅσον πέφυκε μεταχειρισθῆναι τὸ
λόγων γένος, οὔτε τι πρὸς τὸ διδάξαι οὔτε τι πρὸς
τὸ πεῖσαι, ὡς ὁ ἔμπροσθεν πᾶς μεμήνυκεν ἡμῖν
λόγος.

[1] Schanz omits καί.

of continuing the process for ever, and which make their possessor happy, to the farthest possible limit of human happiness.

PHAEDRUS. Yes, that is far nobler.

SOCRATES. And now, Phaedrus, since we have agreed about these matters, we can decide the others.

PHAEDRUS. What others?

SOCRATES. Those which brought us to this point through our desire to investigate them, for we wished to examine into the reproach against Lysias as a speech-writer,[1] and also to discuss the speeches themselves and see which were the products of art and which were not. I think we have shown pretty clearly what is and what is not a work of art.

PHAEDRUS. Yes, I thought so, too; but please recall to my mind what was said.

SOCRATES. A man must know the truth about all the particular things of which he speaks or writes, and must be able to define everything separately; then when he has defined them, he must know how to divide them by classes until further division is impossible; and in the same way he must understand the nature of the soul, must find out the class of speech adapted to each nature, and must arrange and adorn his discourse accordingly, offering to the complex soul elaborate and harmonious discourses, and simple talks to the simple soul. Until he has attained to all this, he will not be able to speak by the method of art, so far as speech can be controlled by method, either for purposes of instruction or of persuasion. This has been taught by our whole preceding discussion.

[1] See 257 c.

ΦΑΙΔΡΟΣ. Παντάπασι μὲν οὖν τοῦτό γε οὕτω πως ἐφάνη.

63. ΣΩΚΡΑΤΗΣ. Τί δ' αὖ περὶ τοῦ καλὸν ἢ αἰσχρὸν εἶναι τὸ λόγους λέγειν τε καὶ γράφειν,

D καὶ ὅπῃ γιγνόμενον ἐν δίκῃ λέγοιτ' ἂν ὄνειδος ἢ μή, ἆρα οὐ δεδήλωκεν τὰ λεχθέντα ὀλίγον ἔμπροσθεν —

ΦΑΙΔΡΟΣ. Τὰ ποῖα;

ΣΩΚΡΑΤΗΣ. Ὡς εἴτε Λυσίας ἤ τις ἄλλος πώποτε ἔγραψεν ἢ γράψει ἰδίᾳ ἢ δημοσίᾳ νόμους τιθείς,[1] σύγγραμμα πολιτικὸν γράφων καὶ μεγάλην τινὰ ἐν αὐτῷ βεβαιότητα ἡγούμενος καὶ σαφήνειαν, οὕτω μὲν ὄνειδος τῷ γράφοντι, εἴτε τίς φησιν εἴτε μή· τὸ γὰρ ἀγνοεῖν ὕπαρ τε καὶ ὄναρ δικαίων τε καὶ ἀδίκων πέρι καὶ κακῶν καὶ ἀγαθῶν οὐκ ἐκφεύ-

E γει τῇ ἀληθείᾳ μὴ οὐκ ἐπονείδιστον εἶναι, οὐδὲ ἂν ὁ πᾶς ὄχλος αὐτὸ ἐπαινέσῃ.

ΦΑΙΔΡΟΣ. Οὐ γὰρ οὖν.

ΣΩΚΡΑΤΗΣ. Ὁ δέ γε ἐν μὲν τῷ γεγραμμένῳ λόγῳ περὶ ἑκάστου παιδιάν τε ἡγούμενος πολλὴν ἀναγκαῖον εἶναι, καὶ οὐδένα πώποτε λόγον ἐν μέτρῳ οὐδ' ἄνευ μέτρου μεγάλης ἄξιον σπουδῆς γραφῆναι, οὐδὲ λεχθῆναι ὡς οἱ ῥαψῳδούμενοι ἄνευ ἀνακρίσεως καὶ διδαχῆς πειθοῦς ἕνεκα ἐλέ-

278 χθησαν,[2] ἀλλὰ τῷ ὄντι αὐτῶν τοὺς βελτίστους εἰδότων ὑπόμνησιν γεγονέναι, ἐν δὲ τοῖς διδασκομένοις καὶ μαθήσεως χάριν λεγομένοις καὶ τῷ ὄντι γραφομένοις ἐν ψυχῇ περὶ δικαίων τε καὶ καλῶν καὶ ἀγαθῶν μόνοις τό τε ἐναργὲς εἶναι καὶ τέλεον καὶ ἄξιον σπουδῆς· δεῖν δὲ τοὺς τοιούτους

---

[1] Schanz, following Schleiermacher, brackets νόμους τιθείς.
[2] Schanz brackets οὐδὲ . . . ἐλέχθησαν.

PHAEDRUS. Yes, certainly, that is just about our result.

SOCRATES. How about the question whether it is a fine or a disgraceful thing to be a speaker or writer and under what circumstances the profession might properly be called a disgrace or not? Was that made clear a little while ago when we said—

PHAEDRUS. What?

SOCRATES. That if Lysias or anyone else ever wrote or ever shall write, in private, or in public as lawgiver, a political document, and in writing it believes that it possesses great certainty and clearness, then it is a disgrace to the writer, whether anyone says so, or not. For whether one be awake or asleep, ignorance of right and wrong and good and bad is in truth inevitably a disgrace, even if the whole mob applaud it.

PHAEDRUS. That is true.

SOCRATES. But the man who thinks that in the written word there is necessarily much that is playful, and that no written discourse, whether in metre or in prose, deserves to be treated very seriously (and this applies also to the recitations of the rhapsodes, delivered to sway people's minds, without opportunity for questioning and teaching), but that the best of them really serve only to remind us of what we know; and who thinks that only in words about justice and beauty and goodness spoken by teachers for the sake of instruction and really written in a soul is clearness and perfection and serious value, that such words should be considered

λόγους αὑτοῦ λέγεσθαι οἷον υἱεῖς γνησίους εἶναι,
πρῶτον μὲν τὸν ἐν αὐτῷ, ἐὰν εὑρεθεὶς ἐνῇ, ἔπειτα
B εἴ τινες τούτου ἔκγονοί τε καὶ ἀδελφοὶ ἅμα ἐν
ἄλλαισιν ἄλλων ψυχαῖς κατ' ἀξίαν ἐνέφυσαν·
τοὺς δὲ ἄλλους χαίρειν ἐῶν — οὗτος δὲ ὁ τοιοῦτος
ἀνὴρ κινδυνεύει, ὦ Φαῖδρε, εἶναι οἷον ἐγώ τε καὶ
σὺ εὐξαίμεθ' ἂν σέ τε καὶ ἐμὲ γενέσθαι.

ΦΑΙΔΡΟΣ. Παντάπασι μὲν οὖν ἔγωγε βούλομαί
τε καὶ εὔχομαι ἃ λέγεις.

64. ΣΩΚΡΑΤΗΣ. Οὐκοῦν ἤδη πεπαίσθω μετρίως
ἡμῖν τὰ περὶ λόγων· καὶ σύ τε ἐλθὼν φράζε
Λυσίᾳ, ὅτι νὼ καταβάντε εἰς τὸ Νυμφῶν νᾶμά τε
C καὶ μουσεῖον ἠκούσαμεν λόγων, οἳ ἐπέστελλον
λέγειν Λυσίᾳ τε καὶ εἴ τις ἄλλος συντίθησι
λόγους, καὶ Ὁμήρῳ καὶ εἴ τις ἄλλος αὖ ποίησιν
ψιλὴν ἢ ἐν ᾠδῇ συντέθεικε, τρίτον δὲ Σόλωνι καὶ
ὅστις ἐν πολιτικοῖς λόγοις νόμους ὀνομάζων συγγράμματα ἔγραψεν· εἰ μὲν εἰδὼς ᾗ τὸ ἀληθὲς ἔχει
συνέθηκε ταῦτα, καὶ ἔχων βοηθεῖν εἰς ἔλεγχον
ἰὼν περὶ ὧν ἔγραψε, καὶ λέγων αὐτὸς δυνατὸς τὰ
γεγραμμένα φαῦλα ἀποδεῖξαι, οὔ τι τῶνδε ἐπωνυ-
D μίαν ἔχοντα δεῖ λέγεσθαι τὸν τοιοῦτον, ἀλλ' ἐφ'
οἷς ἐσπούδακεν ἐκείνων.

ΦΑΙΔΡΟΣ. Τίνας οὖν τὰς ἐπωνυμίας αὐτῷ νέμεις;

ΣΩΚΡΑΤΗΣ. Τὸ μὲν σοφόν, ὦ Φαῖδρε, καλεῖν
ἔμοιγε μέγα εἶναι δοκεῖ καὶ θεῷ μόνῳ πρέπειν· τὸ
δὲ ἢ φιλόσοφον ἢ τοιοῦτόν τι μᾶλλόν τε ἂν αὐτῷ
ἁρμόττοι καὶ ἐμμελεστέρως ἔχοι.

ΦΑΙΔΡΟΣ. Καὶ οὐδέν γε ἄπο τρόπου.

ΣΩΚΡΑΤΗΣ. Οὐκοῦν αὖ τὸν μὴ ἔχοντα τιμιώτερα
ὧν συνέθηκεν ἢ ἔγραψεν ἄνω κάτω στρέφων ἐν

the speaker's own legitimate offspring, first the word
within himself, if it be found there, and secondly its
descendants or brothers which may have sprung up in
worthy manner in the souls of others, and who pays
no attention to the other words,—that man,
Phaedrus, is likely to be such as you and I might
pray that we ourselves may become.

PHAEDRUS. By all means that is what I wish and
pray for.

SOCRATES. We have amused ourselves with talk
about words long enough. Go and tell Lysias that
you and I came down to the fountain and sacred
place of the nymphs, and heard words which they
told us to repeat to Lysias and anyone else who
composed speeches, and to Homer or any other who
has composed poetry with or without musical
accompaniment, and third to Solon and whoever has
written political compositions which he calls laws :—
If he has composed his writings with knowledge of
the truth, and is able to support them by discussion
of that which he has written, and has the power to
show by his own speech that the written words are
of little worth, such a man ought not to derive his
title from such writings, but from the serious
pursuit which underlies them.

PHAEDRUS. What titles do you grant them then ?

SOCRATES. I think, Phaedrus, that the epithet
"wise" is too great and befits God alone ; but the
name "philosopher," that is, "lover of wisdom," or
something of the sort would be more fitting and
modest for such a man.

PHAEDRUS. And quite appropriate.

SOCRATES. On the other hand, he who has nothing
more valuable than the things he has composed or

PLATO

E χρόνῳ, πρὸς ἄλληλα κολλῶν τε καὶ ἀφαιρῶν, ἐν
δίκῃ που ποιητὴν ἢ λόγων συγγραφέα ἢ νομο-
γράφον προσερεῖς;

ΦΑΙΔΡΟΣ. Τί μήν;

ΣΩΚΡΑΤΗΣ. Ταῦτα τοίνυν τῷ ἑταίρῳ φράζε.

ΦΑΙΔΡΟΣ. Τί δέ; σὺ πῶς ποιήσεις; οὐδὲ γὰρ
οὐδὲ τὸν σὸν ἑταῖρον δεῖ παρελθεῖν.

ΣΩΚΡΑΤΗΣ. Τίνα τοῦτον;

ΦΑΙΔΡΟΣ. Ἰσοκράτη τὸν καλόν· ᾧ τί ἀπαγγελεῖς,
ὦ Σώκρατες; τίν᾽ αὐτὸν φήσομεν εἶναι;

ΣΩΚΡΑΤΗΣ. Νέος ἔτι, ὦ Φαῖδρε, Ἰσοκράτης· ὃ
279 μέντοι μαντεύομαι κατ᾽ αὐτοῦ, λέγειν ἐθέλω.

ΦΑΙΔΡΟΣ. Τὸ ποῖον δή;

ΣΩΚΡΑΤΗΣ. Δοκεῖ μοι ἀμείνων ἢ κατὰ τοὺς περὶ
Λυσίαν εἶναι λόγους τὰ τῆς φύσεως, ἔτι τε ἤθει
γεννικωτέρῳ κεκρᾶσθαι· ὥστε οὐδὲν ἂν γένοιτο
θαυμαστὸν προϊούσης τῆς ἡλικίας εἰ περὶ αὐτούς
τε τοὺς λόγους, οἷς νῦν ἐπιχειρεῖ, πλέον ἢ παίδων
διενέγκοι τῶν πώποτε ἁψαμένων λόγων, ἔτι τε εἰ
αὐτῷ μὴ ἀποχρήσαι ταῦτα, ἐπὶ μείζω τις αὐτὸν
B ἄγοι ὁρμὴ θειοτέρα· φύσει γάρ, ὦ φίλε, ἔνεστί τις
φιλοσοφία τῇ τοῦ ἀνδρὸς διανοίᾳ. ταῦτα δὴ οὖν
ἐγὼ μὲν παρὰ τῶνδε τῶν θεῶν ὡς ἐμοῖς παιδικοῖς
Ἰσοκράτει ἐξαγγέλλω, σὺ δ᾽ ἐκεῖνα ὡς σοῖς Λυσίᾳ.

ΦΑΙΔΡΟΣ. Ταῦτα ἔσται· ἀλλὰ ἴωμεν, ἐπειδὴ καὶ
τὸ πνῖγος ἠπιώτερον γέγονεν.

ΣΩΚΡΑΤΗΣ. Οὐκοῦν εὐξαμένῳ πρέπει τοῖσδε
πορεύεσθαι;

ΦΑΙΔΡΟΣ. Τί μήν;

ΣΩΚΡΑΤΗΣ. Ὦ φίλε Πάν τε καὶ ἄλλοι ὅσοι τῇδε
θεοί, δοίητέ[1] μοι καλῷ γενέσθαι τἄνδοθεν· ἔξωθεν

[1] Schanz reads δοῖτέ.

written, turning his words up and down at his leisure, adding this phrase and taking that away, will you not properly address him as poet or writer of speeches or of laws?

PHAEDRUS. Certainly.

SOCRATES. Tell this then to your friend.

PHAEDRUS. But what will you do? For your friend ought not to be passed by.

SOCRATES. What friend?

PHAEDRUS. The fair Isocrates. What message will you give him? What shall we say that he is?

SOCRATES. Isocrates is young yet, Phaedrus; however, I am willing to say what I prophesy for him.

PHAEDRUS. What is it?

SOCRATES. I think he has a nature above the speeches of Lysias and possesses a nobler character; so that I should not be surprised if, as he grows older, he should so excel in his present studies that all who have ever treated of rhetoric shall seem less than children; and I suspect that these studies will not satisfy him, but a more divine impulse will lead him to greater things; for my friend, something of philosophy is inborn in his mind. This is the message that I carry from these deities to my favourite Isocrates, and do you carry the other to Lysias, your favourite.

PHAEDRUS. It shall be done; but now let us go, since the heat has grown gentler.

SOCRATES. Is it not well to pray to the deities here before we go?

PHAEDRUS. Of course.

SOCRATES. O beloved Pan and all ye other gods of this place, grant to me that I be made beautiful

δὲ ὅσα ἔχω, τοῖς ἐντὸς εἶναί μοι φίλια. πλούσιον
C δὲ νομίζοιμι τὸν σοφόν· τὸ δὲ χρυσοῦ πλῆθος εἴη
μοι ὅσον μήτε φέρειν μήτε ἄγειν δύναιτ' ἄλλος ἢ ὁ
σώφρων.—Ἔτ' ἄλλου του δεόμεθα, ὦ Φαῖδρε;
ἐμοὶ μὲν γὰρ μετρίως ηὖκται.

ΦΑΙΔΡΟΣ. Καὶ ἐμοὶ ταῦτα συνεύχου· κοινὰ γὰρ
τὰ τῶν φίλων.

ΣΩΚΡΑΤΗΣ. Ἴωμεν.

in my soul within, and that all external possessions be in harmony with my inner man. May I consider the wise man rich ; and may I have such wealth as only the self-restrained man can bear or endure.—Do we need anything more, Phaedrus? For me that prayer is enough.

PHAEDRUS. Let me also share in this prayer; for friends have all things in common.

SOCRATES. Let us go.

INDEX

INDEX

INDEX